PHILOSOPHY OF EDUCATION

Major Themes in the Analytic Tradition

In the last forty years philosophy of education has become established as a distinct area of philosophical study concerned with educational thought and practice. Twentieth-century analytic philosophy prompted its emergence as a separate subject and remains central to its contemporary flourishing.

The work collected here represents the major ideas and arguments which have come to characterize philosophy of education and in relation to which current work is now developing. As well as work more exclusively in the analytic tradition, it also includes papers influenced by Marxism, phenomenology, feminist theory and critical theory. For those engaged in research in philosophy of education, as well as those in the broader field of educational studies and educationally-oriented policy studies, it offers a gateway to an influential body of work, providing an essential map of seminal writing within the analytic and intersecting traditions.

PHILOSOPHY OF EDUCATION

Major Themes in the Analytic Tradition

VOLUME IV
Problems of Educational Content and Practices

Edited by

Paul H. Hirst and Patricia White

London and New York

First published 1998
by Routledge
11 New Fetter Lane, London EC4P 4EE

Simultaneously published in the USA and Canada
by Routledge
29 West 35th Street, New York, NY 10001

Typeset in Baskerville by
J&L Composition Ltd, Filey, North Yorkshire

Printed and bound in Great Britain by
TJ International Ltd, Padstow, Cornwall

British Library Cataloguing in Publication Data
A catalogue record for this book is available
from the British Library

Library of Congress Cataloguing in Publication Data
The philosophy of education: [edited by]
Paul H. Hirst and Patricia White.
p. cm.
Includes bibliographical references.
Contents: v. 1. Philosophy and education – v. 2. Education and
human being – v. 3. Society and education – v. 4. Problems of
educational content and practice.
1. Education–Philosophy. 2. Critical pedagogy–Philosophy.
3. Educational sociology. I. Hirst, Paul Heywood. II. White,
Patricia.
LB7.P5432 1998
370′.1–dc21
97–30748
CIP

ISBN 0–415–12944–3 (Set)
0–415–12945–1 (Volume I)
0–415–12946–X (Volume II)
0–415–12947–8 (Volume III)
0–415–12948–6 (Volume IV)

CONTENTS

Volume IV
Problems of educational content and practices

CONTENTS

CONTENTS

INDEX OF AUTHORS

INTRODUCTION

Volume I in this collection focuses on the scope of philosophy of education, its relationship to other areas of philosophy, educational theory and practice and conceptions of education. Volumes II and III centre on the nature of the human being to be educated, and the character of the social values and society in which this is to occur, respectively. They draw on work in philosophy of mind and political philosophy and apply it to illuminate problems in educational theory and practice. Volume IV is directly about the content and procedures of education. Given the structural backdrop offered by the previous volumes, it is tempting to see it as exemplifying the core of philosophy of education. For here the impetus for the work comes directly from problems posed by particular controversial curriculum areas, processes of teaching and learning and more general matters of curriculum design. Such a core and periphery view, however, fails to do justice to the manifold and complex interrelationship of the different aspects of philosophy of education. To be sure, education involves learning and subject matter to be learned and without these elements there would be no subject of philosophy of education. These concerns, however, are necessarily and closely linked to others about the nature of the human being to be educated, the aims of upbringing and their connection to conceptions of the good life for human beings and the kind of community in which that life and education for it should take place, issues which fill the other three volumes in this collection. The great classical theorists of education, Plato, Rousseau and Dewey, demonstrate these diverse interrelations in their integrated complexity in their writings on education. Their substantive views show sharp differences but each of their bodies of work demonstrates the pivotal position of education in human life and the way in which questions of its aims, content and the manner in which it should be conducted demand answers for which we need to draw on the whole resources of philosophy.

For the purposes of this collection topics have had to be grouped into volumes and divided into parts but, as we have sought to show in the introductions to the other volumes, the linkages between discussions in different parts and volumes are important and multifold. And so it is with this volume too. The papers collected here exemplify the integrated nature of this area, in many cases, for instance, presupposing major discussions elsewhere in these volumes or even whole areas of philosophical work not represented here.

Overview of the sections

With Volume IV we were faced with a vast number of papers with strong claims to be included, as its size relative to that of the other volumes indicates.

Despite this wealth of material, however, in Part I our selection was constrained in two ways. On the one hand work on different areas of curriculum content has not developed evenly across the whole range of the major curriculum areas and so, to take two extremes, whereas there is an abundance of material on moral education, we found little material on the philosophical issues raised in the teaching of languages. Thus, as elsewhere in this collection, our choice was very much determined by the material available. The second constraint was self-imposed. We decided that in making our selection from the existing material we would resist the magpie principle of assembling bright gems in comparative isolation from other considerations, so withstanding the temptation to offer an array of single, self-standing papers. As a result, not included here is significant work on sport, physical education, movement and dance (Arnold 1988, 1997) and science education (Matthews 1992, 1996). Instead, this large, subdivided section is devoted to clusters of papers in areas of educational content which have proved to be controversial, perhaps, for instance, because they have their roots in contested areas in philosophy or perhaps because there is disagreement over their possible aims and there has been, and continues to be, considerable debate over these. In all cases our selection aims to give readers at least an initial understanding of the issues.

The writers in the second major section examine educational practices and malpractices, in some cases disagreeing fundamentally about the category to which some procedures or processes should be assigned. In this area, too, there is not, as yet, anything like a comprehensive coverage of relevant topics. Research to date has been influenced, rather, by response to political initiatives and personal interests. Many other issues still await philosophical attention.

The final section is devoted to broader concerns affecting curriculum design and development.

Here, as elsewhere in this collection, work referred to which is *not* in other volumes is in a bibliography following this introduction.

Part I: Controversial areas of educational content

1 Moral education

The papers in this section concentrate on particular issues affecting moral education rather than offering broad overviews of the area. For such an overview two excellent conspectus papers can be recommended, offering between them an extremely broad picture of the field: Kenneth Strike's (1991) paper discussing policy issues in moral education in a democratic society and Brian Crittenden's (1981) examination of school curriculum issues, which includes extended discussions of moral education projects.

One of the concerns of Anthony O'Hear's paper is that a focus on the development of a particularly narrow conception of moral autonomy should not dominate in moral education. Thus his paper links with the topic of Volume II Part I and even more closely with Richard Peters' paper, discussed by O'Hear, which follows. His view of the importance of art and literature for moral education also connects his paper with that of Hepburn in sub-section (3) of this part.

Richard Peters' paper, in the use it makes of psychological work and the call in its final paragraph for further empirical research, displays his concern, commented on in the general introduction to this collection, that to make headway with the practical concerns of education philosophers need to work in collaboration with psychologists. (An interesting attempt to do just that was made by John Wilson (1967), who worked on a highly influential mapping of the area of moral education in collaboration with a psychologist and a sociologist.)

Nel Noddings, influenced, like O'Hear, by the work of Iris Murdoch as well as by Martin Heidegger and Simone Weil, focusses on the central importance of a caring attitude and the way in which it can be fostered in schools. She considers the empirical work of Carol Gilligan which suggests that there may be two orientations in morality, justice and caring, the former characteristic of a masculine approach to moral issues, though not exclusively or universally employed by men, and the latter associated especially, but again not universally, with women. Eamonn Callan's paper argues challengingly that a bifurcation of morality into independent ideals of caring and justice is a bad mistake and argues for a sense of justice aligned with an unselfish caring.

In the next paper Betty Sichel takes up the idea of the moral community and its significance – the importance of which for moral development O'Hear touches on – and discusses its implications for school organisation and moral education.

Several papers in this section have brought out the importance of seeing moral education not as a matter of instilling rules but as the development of persons with the appropriate virtuous dispositions. David Carr's book-length discussion of this and related issues in *Educating the Virtues* (1991) is a useful background text here. In the last paper in this section Patricia White discusses friendship as an example of one such disposition. The treatment of it in the context of a democratic society connects it with discussions in Volume III Part I.

Several writers (see O'Hear and Sichel) raise the issue of indoctrination, which is then discussed in Part II of this volume.

2 Religious education

The wealth of discussion on philosophical issues raised by religious education is represented in this volume by a sprightly and closely argued exchange between

Peter Gardner and T.H. McLaughlin on whether a religious upbringing need endanger a child's autonomy. It is an exchange which forms part of a debate begun in the mid-eighties between T.H. McLaughlin, Eamonn Callan and Peter Gardner in the *Journal of Philosophy of Education*, for which exact references are given in the footnotes to both papers. The central issues in the exchange have far-reaching links to other major discussions in these volumes and elsewhere. On autonomy there are links to the papers in Volume II Part I, and to other seminal work, like that of R.F. Dearden, Gerald Dworkin and Richard Lindley, bibliographic details of which are given in the footnotes to the two papers. The issues raised about indoctrination also connect with papers in the next section of this volume on that topic and those about the rights of parents over their children's upbringing with Volume III Part III. Also McLaughlin's 'Wittgenstein, Education and Religion' (1995) will be of interest to readers seeking a wide-ranging consideration of analytic work in philosophy of religion in relation to questions about the form religious education should take.

3 The arts and education

The three papers here complement each other. Bennett Reimer's is concerned with the kinds of aesthetic knowledge and how these might be acquired through an education in the arts. R.W. Hepburn's paper, 'The Arts and the Education of Feeling and Emotion', as its title suggests, can also be seen as a contribution to the symposium on the education of the emotions in Volume II Part III. John White's paper, looking at the place of the arts in human life and education, agrees with Paul Hirst on the importance of the arts in a flourishing human life but for different reasons from those advanced in Hirst's paper 'Liberal Education and the Nature of Knowledge' in Volume I Part III of this collection. There are connections too between the papers of this sub-section and Elliott's 'Versions of Creativity' and Passmore's 'Cultivating Imagination' in Volume II Part III. *The Companion to Aesthetics*, edited by David Cooper (1992), and John Hospers' (1969) *Introductory Readings in Aesthetics* provide a background to topics in aesthetics raised in these papers, and David Best (1992) offers further discussion of the place of the arts in education.

4 Critical thinking

As with religious education in section (2) above, this lively exchange between Harvey Siegel and John McPeck must serve as a sample of the considerable amount of debate in the area. Nel Noddings (1995) provides a succinct and even-handed review of work on the nature of critical thinking and its place in the curriculum, and Frances Schrag (1988) a book-length treatment which has the merit of considering relevant empirical research.

5 *Gender and education*

One important thing to be said about this section is that it does not exhaust the treatment of gender issues in this collection. Discussions of other aspects of gender occur in Volume I Part III, and Volume III Part IV. These two papers focus specifically on curriculum issues and both draw on other work in these volumes, Lyn Yates's paper on Hirst's 'Liberal Education and the Nature of Knowledge' in Volume I Part III and Ann Diller's and Barbara Houston's on Jane Martin's papers 'The Ideal of the Educated Person' in Volume I Part III and 'What Should We Do with a Hidden Curriculum When We Find One?' in the last part of this volume.

Part II: Educational practices

The first three papers in this section all focus on the nature of teaching and the different forms it may take. The first is an extract from Israel Scheffler's classic work on the concept of teaching in *The Language of Education* (1960), mentioned in the historical introduction to these volumes. The second paper, by Robert Dearden, looks at several conceptions of 'learning by discovery' and argues that only one constitutes a defensible form of teaching. David Bridges' treatment of the use of discussion in education, which takes into consideration a range of empirical research into teachers' use of discussion, demonstrates that consideration of teaching techniques, like this one, cannot be divorced from the broader ends of education. From this point of view it can be read in conjunction with Kenneth Strike's paper on the importance of certain kinds of dialogue in a pluralist society in Volume III Part I.

The papers on teaching have implicit references to learning, but for those seeking to focus on learning, John Wilson, in *Preface to the Philosophy of Education* (1979), offers a detailed discussion of the concept and its implications for education. Further discussion of teaching and learning can be found in Passmore's *Philosophy of Teaching* (1980) and in the Teachers College Press series, *Foundations of Education*, see, e.g., Fenstermacher and Soltis (1992) and Phillips and Soltis (1985).

The following two papers, by Ivan Snook and Henry Rosemont Jr, are in contention on the nature of indoctrination. The target of Rosemont's criticism is actually a lengthy journal paper by Snook, not the chapter from Snook's book *Indoctrination and Education*, which is reproduced here with minor changes. However, the exchange loses nothing of significance by the inclusion of the chapter rather than the paper, for Rosemont, in agreement with much of the paper, is particularly concerned to contest those ideas in it which constitute the subject of the chapter. This topic, dealing as it does with obstacles to understanding, is of the broadest relevance to liberal education and particularly to discussions in the previous section.

There is strong disagreement over the place of competition in education in the next two papers. Michael Fielding holds that it should be totally eradicated, whilst Robert Dearden argues for it, given certain safeguards and constraints. This exchange has a further interest in that Fielding raises questions about the nature of philosophical analysis which might be read in the light of the debate in Volume I Part I.

In the following two linked extracts, Richard Smith examines the place of punishment and discipline in the context of the moral life of the school. By a deft use of the work of classical writers, like Kant, as well as contemporaries, like Hart and Rawls, Smith illuminates with telling insight problems teachers face in everyday classroom practice.

Philosophical critiques of grading and testing are the subject of the last two papers in this section. Randall Curren examines in some detail the libertarian view that compulsory systems of grading and testing of students are intrinsically coercive and argues that they are necessary to the development of good practical judgement and intellectual self-determination. This conclusion offers selective support to some ways of grading and testing rather than others. Curren's paper connects with those concerned with autonomy in Volume II Part I. Paul Hager, after reviewing notions of professional competence which prevailed in the 1970s and the often constructive arguments of their philosophical critics (like Kerr, Soltis, Noddings), concludes that it is possible to defend a richer conception of professional competence. A monograph which looks at philosophical issues raised by practices of accountability and the reviewing of educational standards in the UK is Christopher Winch's *Quality and Education* (1996).

Part III: Controversial issues of curriculum development

In two trenchant extracts, Robin Barrow first questions the status of curriculum theory as an applied science and then suggests that there is very little of importance that educators can learn from the study of learning theory, child development and personality which is of use in planning a curriculum.

Jane Roland Martin brings philosophical precision to the idea of a 'hidden curriculum', exploring what it is, from whom it might be hidden and how it might be revealed.

Finally, Cleo Cherryholmes aptly brings this combative section to a close by arguing from a poststructuralist perspective that the study of curriculum cannot be a matter of consensus, stability and agreement, but must be characterised by conflict and turbulence.

Bibliography

Arnold, P. (1988) *Education, Movement and the Curriculum*, London, The Falmer Press.
Arnold, P. (1997) *Sport, Ethics and Education*, London, Cassell.

Best, D. (1992) *The Rationality of Feeling: Understanding the Arts in Education*, London, The Falmer Press.

Carr, D. (1991) *Educating the Virtues*, London, Routledge.

Crittenden, B. (1981) 'The Place of Moral Education in the School Curriculum', in his *Education for Rational Understanding*, Melbourne, Australian Council for Educational Research.

Cooper, David E. (1992) *A Companion to Aesthetics*, Oxford, Blackwell.

Fenstermacher, Gary D. and Soltis, Jonas F. (1992) *Approaches to Teaching* (second edition), New York, Teachers College Press.

Hospers, John (1969) *Introductory Readings in Aesthetics*, Free Press Macmillan.

McLaughlin, T.H. (1995) 'Wittgenstein, Education and Religion', *Studies in Philosophy and Education*, 14, 295–311.

Matthews, Michael R. (1992) 'History, Philosophy and Science Teaching: The Present Rapprochement', *Science and Education*, 1, 11–47.

Matthews, Michael R. (1996) 'The Nature of Science and Science Education', in K. Tobin and B. Fraser (eds) *Handbook of Research: Science Education*, Dordrecht, Kluwer Academic Publishers, 1996.

Noddings, N. (1995) 'Logic and Critical Thinking', in *Philosophy of Education*, Oxford, Westview Press.

Passmore, John (1980) *Philosophy of Teaching*, London, Duckworth.

Phillips, D.C. and Soltis, Jonas F. (1985) *Perspectives on Learning*, New York, Teachers College Press.

Scheffler, I. (1960), *The Language of Education*, Illinois, Charles C. Thomas.

Schrag, F. (1988) *Thinking in School and Society*, London, Routledge.

Strike, K. (1991) 'The Moral Role of Schooling in a Liberal Democratic Society', in Gerald Grant (ed.) *Review of Research in Teaching*, 17.

Wilson, J. (1967) *Introduction to Moral Education*, Harmondsworth, Penguin Books.

Wilson, J. (1979) *Preface to the Philosophy of Education*, London, Routledge & Kegan Paul.

Winch, Christopher (1996) *Quality and Education*, Oxford, Blackwell.

Part I

CONTROVERSIAL AREAS OF EDUCATIONAL CONTENT

(1) Moral education

1

MORAL EDUCATION

Anthony O'Hear

One of the tasks of education is to impart an understanding of morality. There are obvious reasons why this is desirable. What we want to do in schooling is to prepare pupils for adult life. Therefore it is necessary to give them a good basis for self-sufficiency, both economic and intellectual. Equally, though, as life is not purely economic and intellectual but also emotional and personal, some insight is needed into the way in which one ought to conduct one's personal and social life. This is the place of moral education.

   Now, it might be argued that school is not the right place for moral education, on at least two grounds. First, that whatever values are considered desirable and worth teaching, such as honesty or respect for others, are best and most effectively learned in more informal circumstances than in school, above all in the home, where the child will have his or her original and closest experiences of being treated as a moral being and of seeing moral attitudes in practice. Undoubtedly, this last point is true; indeed, it is hard to see how, in the absence of love and respect and honesty from parents and relatives or substitutes for them, a child could even begin to learn what it is to be a person or to see others as persons at all. For to see oneself or another as a person is to see or be seen as a centre of feeling and consciousness, entitled to care and respect. Without some experience of being treated oneself in this way, and without seeing others being treated like this by those close to one, it is unlikely that one could ever come to know what it is for oneself to be a person, or for others to be any more than objects capable either of furthering or frustrating one's own aims. But the importance of the immediate family in moral education does not mean that the school does not have a genuine role to play. For even if the basic experience necessary for an understanding of what it is to be a moral being (or a person) and the basic moral attitudes themselves cannot be transmitted in school, a more systematic treatment of morality can certainly be undertaken there. Moreover, new applications of morality and further discussion of moral questions will arise necessarily both in school life and in subjects studied at school. This last point means that moral matters cannot be avoided in school, even if it was thought

Source: Anthony O'Hear, *Education, Society and Human Nature*, Routledge, 1981, ch. 5.

desirable that they should be. Morality is intrinsic both to the conduct of teachers and teaching, and, in various ways, to the content of the various subjects being taught.

This, however, brings us to a second line of doubt about the place of morality in school. In speaking of the teaching of morality is one speaking of teaching a specific subject, like history or physics? To suggest that this was the case would be to imply that there could be experts in morality and that there could be research and discovery in it. Against this idea, it will be said that being moral does not involve cleverness, intellectual expertise or education, and that the prime aim of moral education is to produce habitual moral behaviour. So a good man does not need lessons in morality, any more than a runner needs lessons in physiology. This is not a conclusive reply, however, for two reasons. First, even though cleverness is neither necessary nor sufficient for goodness, a study of moral principles and argument might help people to realize that they would be inconsistent if they did not apply their principles, such as those of justice or fairness, to cases they had not previously thought of as falling under them. Also, there surely is some virtue in getting people to reflect on just what principles they hold and how they might be justified. This brings us on to the second way in which morality might be regarded as a specific study in its own right; for there is room for a systematic analysis of the basis of moral argument. However, moral philosophy – for this is what such an analysis would be – would hardly be in place in school except at the higest level, while what I have been calling the moral aspect of teaching and the various subjects is pervasive throughout schooling. So it is perhaps better not to think of moral education in terms of the teaching of a specific subject, but rather in terms of its implications for schooling as a whole.

It is clear that a teacher dealing with a class of pupils is in an exposed personal position. What he or she does on a personal level will be scrutinized by the pupils, who will obviously pick on such traits as impartiality, fairness, lateness, tidiness, impatience, sobriety, consistency and so on. All this is too obvious to need any further comment, beyond underlining the fact that, whether the teacher likes it or not, he or she is being judged on a moral and personal level by the pupils all the time. Clearly one important part of moral education in the school consists in the training by example given by the teachers.

But there is something else of great moral significance which the teacher can communicate to pupils through his classroom behaviour which is not, perhaps, so obvious, and this is the attitude manifested to the subject in the teaching itself. All subjects have standards internal to them, but what should be emphasized here is that these standards have a moral side to them. Clearly, in any field of study respect for truth and accuracy is of paramount importance, and this should become apparent in teaching. In practice this means that such moral qualities as impartiality, objectivity, willingness to listen to others and to submit to evidence and reason are central to the pursuit and teaching of any subject. That these are moral qualities becomes clear when one reflects that a large part of moral behaviour consists in the readiness to consider one's own desires and opinions in the light of the desires and opinions of others, and to see oneself as only one person among others, who may have equally valid rights and points of view. In the study of science, particularly, the virtues of impartiality and submission to evidence ought to be cultivated, while the study of literature should help to develop a sense of the feelings and humanity of others, without which (as I shall explain further later) the attempt to apply moral principles in one's dealings with others is likely to be ineffectual.

So, both in his attitude to his subject and in his behaviour generally, the teacher will necessarily be communicating certain moral qualities (good or bad) to the pupils. This is one reason why it would be wrong to think of moral education in terms of a special class in 'morality' or moral philosophy. Morality is not, in fact, a body of knowledge in the way physics (for example) is. This is what is right in the claim that there is no special subject here. To speak of a man's moral beliefs or his immoral behaviour is to speak of his attitudes and behaviour in his life as a whole, to those around him and to his work, in so far as those attitudes and the resulting actions can be seen as good or bad, right or wrong, humanly speaking. This involves an assessment of his attitudes and behaviour in the light of the respect he shows or fails to show to others, his concern for their rights, for justice, for truth, for not causing unnecessary pain, for fulfilling the duties he has and so on. Although different people may have different attitudes on these matters, it is the stand that is taken on them that characterizes a man's morality. Hence, as has been said, morality and questions of morality inevitably arise in the very activity of teaching, even if the content of what was being taught was completely abstract and appeared to have no moral implications in itself.

But a great deal of what is taught has a substantive bearing on morality, both in raising moral questions and in providing material relevant to them. This shows again that morality is not something over and above other activities and on a par with them, but rather arises from the human concerns and implications of these other activities, and points to another way in which moral issues inevitably arise throughout schooling. It is obvious that this is the case with literary and historical studies, where a large part of one's attention will constantly be directed to questions of the rightness or wrongness of the behaviour of individuals. Indeed, I shall suggest later that literary studies are an indispensable part of moral education. But even in studying the 'pure' sciences, moral questions can arise, on, for example, the acceptability of certain lines of research, or perhaps, very generally, on the human implications of a scientific or technological attitude to nature and life. Also, scientific knowledge is often necessary for an informed attitude to moral issues, particularly those raised by technology itself, such as the ethics of genetic or nuclear engineering. One of the ethical values of science teaching could well be to show pupils how ethical questions are often very complex and require knowledge and judgment over and above emotion, how ever deep and well intentioned. As teachers are not just subject experts or teaching machines, but also human beings in a human relationship with their pupils, it would be quite wrong for them not to spend some time exploring the ethical implications of what they are teaching. Some of the left-wing strictures on curricular divisions and the examination system will be justified if scholastic divisions and syllabuses lead teachers to approach and present their subjects in a moral and human vacuum, though even to do this will be for teachers to evince a moral attitude by default, so to speak.

What has emerged so far is that teaching is an activity in which moral issues arise inevitably, and in which teachers necessarily manifest some of their moral attitudes and qualities (or lack of them). Given this, the question arises as to the type of attitude to moral issues a teacher should adopt when dealing with them explicitly, as I have argued that he should. There would appear to be a double danger here, arising from the fact that the teacher is in a position of authority over his pupils. This authority itself has two aspects. First, the teacher knows more than the pupils about particular subjects. Second, he has to keep some sort of control within the class, and this will involve, among other things, protecting individual pupils from being bullied, stamping out thieving and so on. In the performance of these duties, teachers cannot necessarily wait for acquiescence and reason from all members of a class. Sometimes moral rules will have to be enforced in much the same way as school rules, which may have little or no intrinsic validity outside the school (such as silence at assembly). In other words, pupils may, on occasion, just have to be forced to restrain aggressive or acquisitive impulses. There is the further complicaiton that with young children, at least, moral reasoning may be impossible, in that they are psychologically unable to see or understand appeals to general moral principles such as those of fairness, sympathy and so on. The dangers arising from all this are, first, that pupils may come to see and obey moral rules as stemming largely from the personal authority of educators, and second, that they may fail to distinguish rules of moral importance from those which simply have to do with the good running of a particular institution. If this is what results from schooling, then it is quite likely that the moral rules which have been enforced there will be given up after school, along with the authority of the teacher and the demands of the institution.

The problem of the authoritarian aspects of moral education is exacerbated when we remember that what we want from moral education is not any sort of adherence to moral principles, but an adherence that is fully internalized and does not require policing. Now it may be psychologically possible to internalize external authorities and their edicts (according to Freud we all do this to a greater or lesser extent). But a mere internalization of an authority is not, it will be said, what truly moral behaviour is based on. Since Kant, it has been customary for moral philosophers to distinguish between autonomous and het-eronomous moralities, the former accepted because the agent himself thinks on the basis of rational reflection that it is good, and the latter because he feels forced to obey some authority, human or divine. Only the former – a morality freely chosen in the light of reason – is a morality worthy of the name when we are dealing with free, rational agents. According to Kant, if we follow the words of Christ, believing him to be the Blessed One of God, we are implicitly judging for ourselves that his words are good, and we should ideally make and defend this choice in the light of reason. Autonomy in morals, free rational choice of principles, is then taken to be the ideal outcome of moral education. For Peters (1966: p. 197), as for many others who have written on moral education, being morally autonomous involves regulating one's life by rules or principles 'which one has accepted for oneself', and which can be given justification through appeal to higher-order principles, such as 'impartiality, liberty, truth-telling, and the consideration of interests', which are themselves rationally justifiable (1963: p. 30). Downie, Loudfoot and Telfer (1974: p. 58) rather grandly follow Kant in seeing the possession of a rational will as the ability to govern one's conduct by rules which one sees as binding on oneself and on all rational beings. Hare (1964: pp. 77-8) sees moral maturity in learning to make decisions of principle, which we realize can 'only be verified by reference to a standard or set of principles which we have by our own decision accepted and made our own.' Anything else will be objectionably heteronomous, and in any case, it might be added, who is in a position to tell other people what is really good? Is this not pre-eminently a matter which each man has a duty to consider for himself? So a problem necessarily involved in moral education is to see how a moral educator can avoid being an authoritarian indoctrinator, trying to enforce a morality on an agent who should ideally be freely and rationally deciding for himself.

As the problem has so far been put, it amounts to this. The child's initiation into morality consists in his being ordered to obey rules. He obeys only because he sees the rules as upheld by an authority whom he knows he has to obey and who, in any case, is giving him other non-moral orders too. Yet moral behaviour is behaviour governed by principles rationally accepted by a self-determining agent. How can what is originally obeyed as a heteronomous rule become something genuinely chosen, freely and rationally? This picture of moral development and the moral philosophy behind it will be widely familiar from psychological as well as philosophical sources. On reflection, though, it is difficult to see what special problem this picture presents for moral education. For surely, in all subjects, we begin by simply telling children things. Only later do they come to understand the reasons for what they are told, and to accept or reject things for themselves on their own merits. In morality, as in other areas, there is nothing inconsistent or paradoxical in first laying down things that have to be accepted and later leading pupils to see and evaluate the reasons for what they have been told. Indeed, it is hard to see how reasons could be appreciated for what they are unless they were seen as supporting or justifying propositions that were already understood and (provisionally) accepted. A teacher or a school would be going against the ideal of moral autonomy only if he or they laid down moral commands that were in their eyes unreasonable, or else at a later stage there were no provision for introducing pupils to the elements involved in moral reasoning and moral choice. If there is provision for a later introduction to moral reasoning, there is nothing necessarily objectionable in a teacher or a school initially simply telling pupils what they thought was right and making them conform to these principles, providing the means of enforcement respect the fact that the subjects involved are children with individual needs and personalities and capable of feeling, if not mature reasoning. People have to do the best they can, and in the moral case this means passing on those principles one sincerely and reasonably holds. To fail to do this where it is appropriate is to be less than fully human in one's attitude to others, and, as we have seen, there are occasions where it is appropriate for a teacher to do this. The fact that an individual teacher's principles may be misguided or open to criticism does not mean that he is indoctrinating his pupils in an objectionable way, so long as they are later given the materials necessary for them to evaluate for themselves what in the first instance they had simply been told.

So the necessarily authoritarian nature of moral education in the early years need not conflict with ideals of moral autonomy, providing scope is later given for more mature moral reasoning. So far, I have been speaking of morality in terms of the acceptance and justification of rules, and the 'paradox' of moral education, as it is sometimes called, is that to start with the child is simply forced to obey the rules. What has been so far left out of this picture is the fact, stressed by Aristotle (*Nicomachean Ethics*, bk 2, ch. 4) that being virtuous is not simply a matter of doing good things on isolated occasions, it is also a matter of the habitual exercise of the virtues, and that the acquisition of a virtue depends on the formation of a virtuous habit. The question that now arises is whether seeing moral education is involving the inculcation and formation of habits, at a time when the child is unable to reason morally in any way, intensifies the paradox of moral education. Peters, whose analysis of the paradox in an article entitled 'Reason and habit' (1963) is given in terms of the rationality or otherwise of inculcating habits, would appear to answer that this is not necessarily so, for, as he points out, to speak of an action being habitual does not preclude its being thought about, or the habit being stopped or justified in terms of reasons. It is not necessarily to imply that it is automatic or that it involves merely reflex responses. So far, then, the fact that virtues involve habits does not appear to add anything to the paradox of moral education as we have been considering it. However, Peters goes on to say something about the nature of morality which will ultimately lead us to question the whole analysis of moral behaviour with which we have so far been dealing. In questioning this analysis, new light will also be thrown on moral education and the associated paradox.

Peters points out, first, that moral habits are habits involving actions which require far more understanding on the part of agents than would be required in purely motor skills. Examples of theft or malice, to take Peters's examples, entail that the person doing the action has an understanding of what it is to be another person, to hurt him or her, to deprive him or her of his property, all of which involve a conscious entry into the human world of interpersonal relationships and institutions in a way that understanding how to walk or to feed oneself does not. Peters (1963: p. 36) writes that 'a child, strictly speaking, cannot be guilty of theft, who has not developed the concept of himself as distinct from others, of property, of the granting of permission, etc.', and he goes on to say that all this may take a long time; far longer, in fact, than it may take to get a child not to do certain things of which authority figures disapprove. At this early stage in the child's development we may stop him from taking the toys of his brothers and sisters, but so long as this is seen by the child as a matter of punctilious conformity to the wishes of the authority figures, like toilet training or not bringing dirt into the house, rather than in terms of respect for the property rights of other people, we shall not have taught the child not to steal, properly speaking, but only to inhibit a narrowly conceived range of movements disapproved of by an authority. As Peters (1963: p. 37) says: 'to learn to act on rules forbidding theft, lying, breaking promises, etc., is necessarily an open-ended business requiring intelligence and a high degree of social sophistication.' Acting on such rules, according to Peters, requires considerable intelligence and insight in order to see particular actions as falling under a rule. This fact points to a further element in the dissolution of the paradox of moral education, for the rules we are trying to teach in moral education themselves involve the exercise of intelligence and sensitivity. They cannot be blindly obeyed, but can only be applied in the light of human and social understanding. Hence, in the paradox, the antithesis between the blind execution of the whims of an authority and the intelligent exercise of one's rational will turns out to falsify the extent to which intelligence, and the possibility of moral reflection, are involved in learning not to steal or be malicious and so on. Acquiring virtuous habits, then, is not possible without the exercise of one's reason, even if one is encouraged to acquire such habits by authorities. There is, therefore, no great jump between acquiring the habit and reflecting about it rationally; indeed the possibility of rational reflection on such habits would appear to be opened precisely because the exercise of the habit requires intelligence on the part of the agent.

Someone reading what Peters says about reason and habit might agree with him that learning not to steal must be a procedure requiring the use of reason, and hence that there is nothing paradoxical about being encouraged by authorities to acquire the habit as part of a rational moral education, but suggest that the paradox simply reappears at an earlier stage, when the child does not have the ability to grasp the concepts involved in learning moral rules. Here, surely, there are just orders and obedience, and this cannot be part of a moral education preparing people for moral autonomy. A quick way with this objection might be simply to deny that moral education, properly speaking, can begin before a child has reached a certain level of conceptual sophistication; but this is perhaps too quick, because it says nothing about how children might acquire the concepts of interpersonal life, which I am suggesting are involved in moral behaviour. What is valuable in Peters's article is the way in which he emphasizes that morality and moral concepts are tied into a whole social and interpersonal context, and that moral habits (virtues and vices) are possible only for people who have entered this context. What I now want to suggest is that this fact about morality puts a considerable strain on the Kantian model of the ideal moralist being a rational autonomous will choosing its principles in the light of abstract rational considerations.

The picture of morality which emerges from an appreciation of the habitual nature of virtue, and the way in which the practice of the virtues demands an intelligent sensitivity to the situations in which one finds oneself, in order to see just how a particular virtue might be applied, is one which will place far more emphasis on learning how to see situations in certain terms than on abstract reasoning about, and justification of, principles. Take, for example, the virtue of kindness. In order to be kind, I will have to see just what the feelings of others might be, and just what their good might consist in. Its application will require much sensitivity, both in discovering these things, and in knowing how best to resolve conflicts between what someone wants and what is good for them, and also in knowing how to reconcile kindness to one person with the demands of fairness and justice that others might have on me. Equally, understanding the claims that others might have on me will require on my part not an abstract, quasi-legalistic grasp of principle so much as the ability to see and understand situations from their point of view, and to understand that these beings surrounding me are also people with their own feelings, goals, plans, reasons and desires for self-determination and control of their own destiny.

One of the worrying aspects of looking at morality in terms of freely and rationally chosen principles is the nagging feeling that a man might accept in an abstract way that society as a whole needed a general adherence to such principles as truth-telling, respect for life, respect for individual liberty and so on, and also that it would be good for him if others acted towards him on such principles, while at the same time feeling little or no inclination to act on such principles in his own life, so long as he was strong enough to get away with it. One could easily imagine a man being quite unmoved by philosophical appeals to consistency between the way he treated others and the way he wanted to be treated himself, or by stratagems such as Rawls's thought-experiment, in which everyone is asked to choose for themselves those laws which they would choose if they were legislating for a society in which no one (including they, the legislators) knew anything about their personal strengths, abilities or backgrounds (*cf.* Rawls 1972: p. 12). Indeed, it is unclear why exactly a strong and self-sufficient man who acted only for his own good and never in the light of the needs or rights of others, except in so far as such behaviour might benefit him, would be irrational, as opposed to immoral or inhuman. The problem of moral education and moral choice is not to get people to be rational, but to get them to be human, and getting them to be human is not ideally to be analysed in terms of autonomous agents deciding for themselves the type of life they really want to lead. (Nowell-Smith, for example, says the asking of such questions is part of the connotation of the word 'moral'; 1954: pp. 319–20.)

It is true that the behaviour of a moral man will exemplify a degree of consistency, because he will be habitually virtuous. It will thus be possible to analyse his behaviour in terms of his acting on certain general principles. Indeed, he might frequently appeal in his own deliberations to such principles, in part at least to short-circuit the impossible task he would be presented with if he always had to decide what to do in every new situation, with no preconceptions in the form of general principles to guide his actions. But what we are concerned with here is to see how someone might come to adopt in his behaviour a set of principles which are morally acceptable in having some regard to the rights and feelings of others. I have already said that applying moral principles requires a degree of sensitivity to the human nature of other people. What I now want to suggest is that it is a sensitivity to one's own humanity being shared with that of others, and a corresponding sympathy with them, which forms the basis of moral conduct in the first place, and which gives us the initial and indispensable motivation towards moral behaviour. In other words, part of what is involved in learning what it is to live as a person in a community of other persons is to learn what it is to be treated as a person and to treat others as persons. This knowledge is, above all, the knowledge that people have both feelings and wills of their own, and that it would be inappropriate to regard them as objects to be used and manipulated. No doubt this sense is best learned in a loving family. What is learned may then be extended to others outside one's family, and ultimately find expression in those abstract general principles such as impartiality, fairness and respect for the rights of others which are seen by many writers as characterizing any fully moral system of conduct. What is to be emphasized here is that such principles will not be chosen by lonely, autonomous agents in an emotionally empty state of rational reflection. They will be chosen by those who have some feeling of what it is to be a person among other persons, and only people with this sense will be able fruitfully to apply such principles. We hesitate before Kant's claim that only actions done out of pure duty are truly moral, and that any motivating feeling of humanity or love or shame underlying what one does invalidates its moral purity. The deepest reason for the hesitation is that what gives one the possibility of acting morally (or immorally) is the sense that one is a person among others, and that being a person is to be open to possibilities of hurt, shame, pleasure, self-fulfilment and so on. This sense may well be based in a primitive human sense of sympathy for the suffering and feelings of others, referred to by Rousseau, Hume and many other eighteenth-century moralists. This primitive sense of sympathy, however, will be developed as one learns to live a social life, and to understand the various complex ways in which people can be helped or frustrated. Ultimately, it becomes more a question of perception and awareness than of animal feeling, a matter of perceiving the needs of others, both in remote cases, where one can have no personal experience, and also in cases where a sophisticated sensitivity to the feelings of a difficult, unattractive old person (for example) is required, rather than any immediate emotion of animal love or sympathy, which may in any case be impossible.

As we have seen, one of the most difficult problems confronting both moral philosophers and moral educators is the problem of motivation: how do you get people to accept that they should sometimes act not out of self-interest, but out of respect for the needs and claims of others? From the point of view of education, this problem is sometimes presented as that of how one might bring people to move from a theoretical acceptance of the reasonableness of moral principles to an active acceptance of them in their own behaviour: but this way of posing the problem, as well as the associated picture of the rational agent deliberating his choice of principles, is both untrue to actual moral experience, as well as making the solution of the problem seem more puzzling than it need be. For the picture of the autonomous rational agent deliberating on his principles is indeed difficult to reconcile with the undoubted fact that, on the whole, this is not how people feel when they are confronted with a moral choice: for example, whether to help an injured person. On the whole, they feel that what has to be done has to be done, and there is no feeling of freedom on that, although, of course, they will be free simply to walk away. Moreover, it is rather difficult to see a man as being genuinely fully autonomous over a matter in which he has long been accustomed to act in a particular way and to feel and see things in a particular way. The paradox of moral education is not formally a paradox; there is a solution to it, as it has been stated along the lines suggested earlier, but there is something missing in the picture of morality as being a matter of principles first simply laid down, and later rationally deliberated. What is missing is that morality is based in a way of perceiving situations and of having feelings in them, and that moral education is above all a matter of training in perception and feeling.

Moral principles are tied up with feeling and perception in two ways. First, it is only when we perceive and feel we are in a community of persons that moral principles can begin to seem binding on us, for only then will appeals to our sense of fairness or sympathy or shame or guilt in our dealings with others be at all relevant. So long as we regard others as objects to manipulate and be manipulated by, there is no reason for us to sympathize with their problems and frustrations, or to be fair in our treatment of them, or to feel ashamed of their scorn, or guilty for letting them down. What is really being suggested here is that although the details of various moral codes may vary, the basic impulses on which all morality and moral justification is based, and which give people the feeling that they ought to behave morally to others, in whatever form this comes out, are basically those involved in seeing others as persons rather than as objects. As has often been pointed out, even slave owners and thieves perceive virtue in seeing their colleagues, if not their victims, as persons. This sense, of course, is not something that is achieved by command or by rational choice, but by being part of a human society. So, seeing others as people in a general sense is what provides the motivational background to moral action and the acceptance of moral principles, without which their adoption would remain a mystery. But, second, those moral principles that one does come to accept have to be applied in particular cases, and here again perception of the needs and wants of others is often crucial to their application. A general injunction to respect the feelings or rights of others is hardly much use if we cannot see what the feelings of others are, or how they perceive their rights. I am not saying that we should always go along with how people feel or what they think is their due, but that without understanding these things, we shall not even begin to know how to respect their personhood.

It might be said that this identification of moral principles with the perceptions of others as persons still leaves open the question as to why we should treat each other as persons. To ask this question, however, is to misunderstand the point being made. The point is that human beings do behave like this, at least to those in their own groups or societies, and that this is what makes life, social and personal, possible. If you like, it is the precondition of any genuine social life. As to whether this attitude is ultimately justifiable, outside the actual context of human life, or whether, if we were creatures with different psychologies and traditions, we would have these attitudes, one must remain agnostic. Where reason does have a role to play is not so much in the fact that human beings characteristically, in their behaviour and traditions, manifest this tendency to treat at least some other human beings as persons, but in working out the implications of this fact, so as to see the existence of persons where one had not seen it before, and to find out what treating others as persons might involve outside the context of face-to-face encounters with them. Thus one can come to realize by rational reflection that slaves, too, are people, not relevantly different from one's own relations, or that part of one's income surplus to one's own needs should be given to support handicapped people in the community, even if one had never actually met any slaves or any of the handicapped people in question. But, as Iris Murdoch (1970: p. 66) says in *The Sovereignty of the Good*:

> the more the separateness and distinctness of other people is realized, and the fact seen that another man has needs and wishes as demanding as one's own, the harder it becomes to treat a person as a thing.

That one does have this feeling does seem to be a fact about human nature, and a fact on which our life together is based. It is, of course, true that with human life as it is now, life throughout the world would become intolerable generally were people not to strive to extend the recognition of others as persons, and life does become intolerable where this recognition is absent or its implications flaunted. Educators should attempt to cultivate this feeling in their pupils (and justifications of the general social and utilitarian sort just suggested can be given for doing this), but what is of paramount importance is the way in which the feeling that other people are not to be treated as things is not only basic to all moral motivations and justifications, but also something that is part of our natural endowment, and without which one could not begin to enter a society of persons.

This point about the naturalness of the sense of others as persons remains true, even if, as some psychologists have suggested, it appears only at a certain stage of maturation. If one originally saw the world around one as consisting entirely of objects to be used as best one could for one's own purposes, it is hard to see what additional data emanating from some of those objects could lead one to suppose that they were in fact people, and hence to be seen and treated as entitled to respect, as centres of will and consciousness and sympathy, as subjects of pain and desire. Indeed, if a man had no sense that there are other people in the world, who therefore should be looked at in these ways, it is hard to see how any moral argument or discussion could appear relevant to him or carry any conviction with him. So moral education must work on the natural sense we have to sympathize and feel with others as people. (One might add here that one's own sense of what it is to be a person is itself logically dependent on the recognition of others as people, for a large part of what it is to be a person is to see oneself as entering into relationships of various sorts with other people.) The paradox of moral education turns out, then, to overemphasize the place of free rational choice in moral behaviour. Moral behaviour is not so much a matter of an isolated rational agent acting on freely chosen principles, as a development of one's sense of a shared humanity. It is true, as Peters points out, that in acquiring moral habits one is far from acting irrationally or unintelligently. Also, there will be cases where it is unclear just what the right course of action is (e.g. is it showing more or less respect for others to help them to commit suicide?) and cases where principles conflict (e.g. where keeping a promise to someone might involve hurting someone else). Here, too, reason and intelligence have a part to play. But what I am suggesting now is that abstract reason might not have as central a role to play as the Kantian picture suggests, and that the basic source of morality is something far more like a sense of sympathy, without which moral principles would not even begin to appear rationally compelling. If this is so, then moral educators should pay at least as much attention to the development of a moral sensibility as to the analysis of principles and arguments, and the aim of moral education should be to produce moral insight in people rather than to get them to choose a set of principles for themselves.

What does it mean to produce moral insight and sensibility? The sense of sympathy which is at the bottom of moral behaviour is fundamentally an other-regarding sense, a realization that the feelings and views of others should be taken into account. When you are sympathizing with someone else, you cease to be the centre of your world. In sympathizing, indeed, you begin to feel bound by factors outside yourself, which is something that accords badly with the Kantian ideal of moral autonomy. Iris Murdoch (1970: p. 66), whose criticisms of the Kantian picture of morality have much influenced me, stresses that in our behaviour there is a constant tension between self-centred action, attachment and motivation and the exercise of what she calls 'realism of compassion': that 'unsentimental, detached, unselfish, objective attention' which enables us to see ourselves and others as we really are. Our first tendency in life, as in art, is to opt for selfishness and fantasy (even where these take the masochistic form of self-pity and ineffectual sentimentality), to see things and people with ourselves at the centre merely as they impinge on us and our designs. This, of course, involves the reduction of people to objects of possible manipulations. She argues that the old unregenerate egocentric self is so strong, and such a source of psychic energy, that the rational will (where that is not itself a manifestation of sin) is largely powerless to rid itself of harmful feelings and attachments:

> Where strong emotions of sexual love, or of hatred, resentment, or jealousy are concerned, 'pure will' can usually achieve little. It is small use telling oneself 'Stop being in love, stop feeling resentment, be just.' What is needed is a reorientation which will provide an energy of a different kind, from a different source.
>
> (*ibid.*: p. 55)

What we should do is learn to train our attention on to new objects of attention, which it is to be hoped will lead us to be less egotistical.

It is surprising how little discussion there is in most philosophical treatments of moral education of the fact of selfishness. Perhaps this is because of the stress on moral choice, for, as Murdoch implies, Kantianism in morality may be the supreme assertion of the self. How ever this may be, we can all recognize in ourselves the conflict between selfish and selfless drives. What we want from moral education is habits of selflessness, and it is undoubtedly correct that such habits cannot be acquired by a mere act of will. A habit of this sort is not only continuous; it needs intelligence and sensitivity in practice, and it also runs counter to the strongest drives of our psyche. Murdoch is surely right to see the formation of such habits requiring the systematic directing of one's attention in particular ways. She distinguishes between the clear vision which sees people and things as they really are, with their needs, individuality, strivings and concerns, from the distorted vision which sees only from the point of view of the agent, and is characteristically mean, unjust and lacking in compassion and understanding of others:

> The moral life, on this view, is something that goes on continually, not something that is switched off in between the occurrence of explicit moral choices. What happens in between such choices is indeed what is crucial. I would like on the whole to use the word 'attention' as a good word and use some more general term like 'looking' as the neutral word. Of course, psychic energy flows, and more readily flows, into building up convincingly coherent but false pictures of the world, complete with systematic vocabulary. . . . Attention is the effort to counteract such states of illusion.
>
> (*ibid.*: p. 37)

So, underlying moral acts are habits of thought and attention, which can be cultivated, and which it is the job of moral education to cultivate. This can, not implausibly, be seen as another way of putting what I had described earlier in terms of cultivating one's primitive sense that one is surrounded by persons as well as things. Although Murdoch asserts that unselfishness is not natural to human beings, I have suggested on logical grounds that some degree of unselfishness, at least in the sense of a natural sympathy to the feelings of others, is a prerequisite of the recognition that they are persons. On the other hand, and in line with what Murdoch says, developing what is implicit in this sense certainly requires the development of one's perceptions and sensibilities regarding other people away from oneself and towards how they actually are. This can only be done by a systematic attempt to see things as detached from one's own desires and plans, and in the case of other people this detachment will involve above all a growing recognition of their individuality and personhood.

It is in seeing moral behaviour as behaviour which is freed from the quagmire of self that we find the connection between morality and art, and the place of the study of art in moral education. Of course philosophers in the Kantian tradition are correct to see morality as a matter of impartiality and of treating others as ends in themselves, rather than as means to attain our own selfish ends and obsessions. What they do not tell us is how we might come to see people and situations objectively, and to see them as making demands on us rather than as bridges or obstacles for our desires. Art – good art – can free itself from the obsessions of self and show us

> how differently the world looks to an objective vision. We are presented with a truthful image of the human condition in a form which can be steadily contemplated; and indeed this is the only context in which many of us are capable of contemplating it at all. Art transcends selfish and obsessive limitations of personality and can enlarge the sensibility of its consumer. It is a kind of goodness by proxy. Most of all it exhibits to us the connection, in human beings, of clear realistic vision with compassion.
>
> (*ibid.*: pp. 86–7).

The connection is presumably because the decentring involved in art, as in morality, is, at the same time as being a truthful insight into the idiosyncrasies and failures of others, a sympathetic recognition of them as centres of feeling and consciousness.

Murdoch recognizes the sense alluded to earlier in which all intellectual disciplines are moral disciplines, in their concern with concepts such as justice, accuracy, truthfulness, realism, humanity and so on. Indeed, she suggests that the moral application of such concepts can become clearer through seeing their use in non-moral contexts. However, art and above all literature remain 'the most educational of all human activities' (*ibid.*: p. 88) because they are a place in which the nature of morality can be seen. For not only does good art exemplify the decentring and submission to necessity which is morality, and bad art the obsession with self and fantasy and false or harmful excitement which is the basis of so much wickedness, but an education in literature is above all 'an education in how to picture and understand human situations.' This must be more crucial than an initiation into science, and is the reason why it is more important to know about Shakespeare than about any scientist, for 'we are men and we are moral agents before we are scientists, and the place of science in human life must be discussed in words' (*ibid.*: p. 34).

Miss Murdoch further explores the connections between art and morality, and the distinction between the false consolations offered by fantasy and bad art on the one hand, and the toughness and truthfulness of good art, in *The Fire and the Sun* (1977), but one more theme in *The Sovereignty of the Good* is worth mentioning here because of its relevance to moral education. It is the way in which moral concepts have what Mark Platts (1979: p. 261) calls semantic depth. That is to say, we can understand in a formal way the conditions of their application without realizing experientially what they mean. There can indeed be a merely formal grasp of what the just or courageous thing to do is in a given situation, without any corresponding sense that this is what one should do or what would be admirable to do. As Platts (*ibid.*: p. 262) puts it, we can become like 'a Martian who translates our dictionary but has had no experience of our moral world.' What gives moral concepts life is our seeing the situations to which they apply as compelling a response in a particular direction, and this involves attention and care on our part in the way we see things. Murdoch speaks of value concepts as requiring understanding in depth, that is, through a deepening awareness of what it is that they involve and what it is that gives the situations to which they apply their moral character. This sort of wisdom is no doubt best gained through personal experience and is, as Murdoch (1970: pp. 28–9) stresses, an endless task; for example, our understanding of what 'love' means should be an advance at forty on what it was at twenty, and what it was at twenty was more complicated than that earlier time when all we knew was that Mary was loved by the little lamb that followed her. But experience alone may teach us little without aids in the direction of depth. Here again, literature can be of the profoundest importance, either as a help or a hindrance. How many marriages have been doomed to disillusionment by an uncritical exposure to the view that life is or might be as the wish-fulfilments of romantic novelists would have it? Salvation may not be found in Tolstoy or Proust, but a degree of realism and complexity is there that may help us to understand and be ready for what we will have to suffer.

I have concentrated in the closing part of this paper on the views of Irish Murdoch, both because they are an important corrective to a highly influential strand in moral philosophy, and because they are highly relevant to the question of moral education. The so-called paradox of moral education draws heavily for its force on too rationalistic a conception of morality. This conception stresses to an unrealistic degree the elements of autonomy and choice in ethics. By contrast I have tried to show how morality is founded in certain features of human nature, and how moral education should lay stress on developing those features and the ways of perceiving human life which will foster compassion and justice.

Of course, there will still be room for moral dilemmas, and for discussion of the rightness and wrongness of particular acts and types of act. Moral education has indeed a role to play in introducing people to the principles underlying moral argument. But moral argument is only a comparatively small part of moral behaviour, just as moral differences between men are small in comparison with what are generally regarded, at least within the limits of one's own group, as virtues, such as justice, truthfulness and sympathy, and which are implicit in the recognition of others as persons. Without a common acceptance of such qualities as virtues, moral discussion could hardly begin, while without some predisposition to treat others as persons, moral education would hardly be possible. Given that it is possible, I have argued that its primary task should be to foster the awareness of what is implicit in recognizing others as persons, and that the study of art and literature is an essential means to this end. Apart from the ways in which moral questions are inevitably involved in schooling, which I examined at the start of the paper, it is perhaps in the study of literature and art that school has its greatest contribution to make to the moral education of its pupils.

References

Aristotle, *Nicomachaean Ethics*.

Downie, R., Loudfoot, E. and Telfer, E. (1974) *Education and Personal Relationships*, Methuen & Co., London.

Hare, R. (1964) *The Language of Morals*, Oxford University Press.

Murdoch, I. (1970) *The Sovereignty of the Good*, Routledge & Kegan Paul, London.

Murdoch, I. (1977) *The Fire and the Sun*, Oxford University Press.

Nowell-Smith, P. (1954) *Ethics*, Penguin Books, Harmondsworth.

Peters, R.S. (1963) 'Reason and habit: the paradox of moral education', in W. Niblett (ed.) *Moral Education in a Changing Society*, Faber & Faber, London, pp. 46–65. Reprinted as Volume IV Paper 2 to which all references refer.

Peters, R.S. (1966) *Ethics and Education*, George Allen & Unwin, London.

Platts, M. (1979) *Ways of Meaning*, Routledge & Kegan Paul, London.

Rawls, J. (1972) *A Theory of Justice*, Clarendon Press, Oxford.

2

REASON AND HABIT: THE PARADOX OF MORAL EDUCATION

R.S. Peters

The debate about whether and how virtue can be taught is a longstanding one in the history of ethics; but right at the very start, when Socrates and Protagoras were discussing the matter, Socrates characterically made the point that the answers to the questions depended on what is meant by 'virtue'. Is it the 'correct opinion' and conventional behaviour of well-brought-up people? Or is it conduct based on a grasp of fundamental principles? In more recent times Professor Oakeshott has made a similar contrast between two forms of the moral life.[1] A habit of affection and behaviour, characteristic of the gentleman, is contrasted with the reflective application of a moral criterion. There is a corresponding difference in what is emphasised in moral education. On the one hand there is an emphasis on habit, tradition and being properly brought up; on the other hand there is emphasis on intellectual training, and on the development of critical thought and choice.

It is not, however, necessarily the case either that these divergent accounts of morality are completely incompatible with each other or that there can be no *rapprochement* between their different emphases in matters of moral education. Indeed Aristotle attempted to combine both, but was led into a paradox about moral education which resulted from his attempt to stress the role both of reason and of habit. It is my intention in this paper both to combine these two emphases in moral education and to deal with the resulting paradox.

First of all it is necessary to follow Socrates' advice and attempt to get clearer about what morality is. This might be done by examining the uses of 'moral' and its cognates in ordinary language. But it would be a long and detailed task for which there is little time in this paper; for 'morality', like 'education', means very different things to different people.

Why is it, for instance, that 'morals' suggest something to do with sex and selfishness whereas we speak of 'unethical' conduct on the part of doctors, business

Source: R.S. Peters, *Moral Development and Moral Education*, Allen & Unwin, 1981, ch. 3.

men and advertisers? Does 'unethical' suggest the subtle peccadilloes of the more cultured type of man who misses the mark slightly in the way in which a Greek aristocrat might have done, whereas 'immoral' suggests the more brutish plungings of the Roman? 'Morality', too, can cover the crude rigorous code of the Puritan as well as the more rational intelligent code of the scientific humanist. When Freud expressed agreement with Vischer's saying that 'Morality is self-evident',[2] was he speaking of a crude code whose origin he did much to lay bare in his doctrine of the super-ego, or was he speaking of his own more rational humanistic code?

Behind, however, these vagaries of ordinary usage lies a distinctive form of discourse which has developed to answer distinctive forms of questions. These questions are concerned with what ought to be and with what ought to be done. This is a particular branch of what philosophers call practical discourse. Now practical discourse is not only concerned with answers to questions about what ought to be or what ought to be done. Commands, for instance, are also practical in that they are ways of getting people to do things by means of speech. But they differ from that form of practical discourse in which words like 'ought', 'good', 'right', and 'wrong' occur because there is no implied link with reasons. Saying 'Shut the door' or 'Shut up' has a different social function from saying 'You ought to shut the door' or 'Silence is a good thing'. Words like 'ought' and 'good' guide behaviour: they do not act as goads or stimuli for reactions. And they guide it with the suggestion that there are reasons for doing whatever is prescribed.

This is not, by the way, what is called a linguistic argument, if by that is meant an argument based on how we actually use words. Rather it is an argument of a Kantian form which attempts to arrive at what is presupposed by our use of different linguistic expressions. Nothing depends on using the *word* 'ought' or 'good', just as nothing depends on using the *word* 'moral' or 'ethical'. But once discourse or thought begins to get differentiated, as when, for instance, we begin to distinguish science from mythology and metaphysics, we can try to get behind these verbal distinctions to see what the differences are in the activities which are so picked out. In the particular case of 'ought', 'good' and other such words, if we ceased to use these words and still wanted to get people to do things by means other than twisting their arms, hypnotising them or giving them orders, we would have to devise a new family of words to do this job.

Morality, then, is concerned with what there are reasons for doing or not doing, for bringing into or removing from existence. But this is only the start of the story; for what makes the reasons relevant ones? Supposing it is said that one ought not to slash people with razors, which is to suggest that there are reasons for not doing this. We inquire what the reasons are and are told that people bleed as a result and blood is red and that is why we should not do it. This would be a reason; but it would not appeal much to us as a good reason because it presupposes the principle that the redness in the world ought to be minimised, which most of us would regard as a somewhat bizarre principle. We ought be more inclined to accept a reason like 'it hurts' because we regard the principle that *pain* ought to be minimised as more acceptable than the principle that *redness* ought to be minimised.

It is not my job in this paper to pursue the fundamental problem in ethics of why one such principle is more justifiable than another. I am using this gory example only to bring out the double point that principles are needed to determine the relevance of reasons and that some principles seem more justifiable than others. Our moral principles might be picked out as those which are for us fundamental or overriding in such a structure of rules backed by reasons.

It is manifest enough, however, that in respect of such a structure of rules we can be more or less prepared to justify, revise or adapt them to changing circumstances. We can guide our lives by a host of rules which seem to us self-evident, or which might be backed up by the very general principle that we ought to do what others do or that we ought to do what X, who is in authority or an authority, says. Or we might try to live by a more rational and thought-out code. For men are creatures of habit and tradition in varying degrees. In a similar way we may be more or less intelligent in the application of rules to particular cases. This is the field of judgement, and whereas some men proceed with fine discrimination, others plod along boneheadedly by rules of thumb. Finally we can do what we should mechanically and with heavy hearts without caring overmuch for what we are doing, like reluctant housewives peeling potatoes. Or we can do what we should with more spontaneity because we genuinely care about that for the sake of which we are acting. In brief, the legislative, judicial and executive aspects of our moral life can be more or less rationally, intelligently and spontaneously conducted.

It is important to be clear where we stand in moral matters. Indeed the fact is that I cannot explain what I consider the paradox of moral education to be unless I *do* make clear where I stand.

I am a staunch supporter of a rationally held and intelligently applied moral code. Such a code seems peculiarly pertinent at the present time; for this is a time of rapid social change, of shifting standards both in regard to general social rules and in regard to activities which are thought to be worthwhile, to which we are introduced in the curricula of schools and universities. My objection to intuitionist and traditionalist positions in morals is not based, of course, on these contigent facts about the social situation. My appeal to the social situation is to support the plea of pertinence. For it is just such facts about changing standards and shifting situations which often lead people who think of morality along intuitionist lines to embrace some subjectivist position and to talk about their feelings or commitments as if morality were a matter of private taste, or falling in love.

I was particularly struck by the peculiar phenomenon of American academics who took what sociologists said about moral relativism so seriously that they would never say that anything was right or wrong; instead they would self-consciously produce their blessed 'commitments' rather like the White Rabbit producing his watch from his waistcoat pocket. Of course this existentialist type of reaction is to be seen in the context of the massive pressure to conform in America, about which so much is said in the literature about the 'other-directed' man. The experiments of Solomon Asch and Stanley Milgram have shown the immense force of such social pressures, which can make most men disavow even the plain evidence of their senses. Autonomous judgements require considerable courage in such circumstances and, if asserted, can have a snowball effect which loosens the chains of conformity. These experiments are particularly relevant to the phenomenon of the teenage culture which we have in our midst. But my point is that the assertion of the individual against such pressures need not take the form of rather self-conscious talk about his commitments. After all some things may just be right or wrong, good or bad. The peculiar pertinence of a rationally held moral code is that it can combine a degree of non-relativeness at one level with a degree of adaptability at another. Let me elucidate in a bit more detail both what I mean and where I stand.

To hold a rational code a man must subscribe to some higher-order principles which will enable him both to apply rules intelligently in the light of relevant differences in circumstances and to revise rules from time to time in the light of changes in circumstances and in empirical knowledge about the conditions and consequences of their application. The higher-order principles, which, in my view, are capable of some sort of rational justification, are those of impartiality, truth-telling, liberty and the consideration of interests. For these, I would argue, are presupposed by the very activity of giving reasons in practical discourse. These higher-order principles, though pretty formal in character, provide very general criteria of relevance for justifying particular rules and for making exceptions in particular cases.

Now just as it is possible for a scientist to stand firm on procedural principles like those of putting his theories up for public criticism, going by the evidence in deciding their truth and not cooking evidence, and yet be willing to change the substantial content of such theories, so also is it possible for a man who holds a rational code to stick firmly to his principles at the procedural level – i.e. the principles of impartiality, liberty, truth-telling and the consideration of interests, and yet to revise what he thinks about the substantial content of rules at a lower level – e.g. about smoking, gambling or birth control.

The criticism is often levelled against the advocates of a rationally held moral code that it would lead to moral anarchy. But why should it? For if the higher-order criterion of the impartial consideration of interests affected by rules is applied it will be seen that there are some rules which are so important for anyone living in a society that they could be regarded almost as definitions of a society. For a society is a collection of individuals united by the acceptance of certain rules, and though many of them relate to 'my station and its duties' (e.g. what ought to be done *qua* husband or *qua* teacher) there are also (leaving aside the law) a number of more general rules binding on anyone who is deemed to be a member of the same society – e.g. rules about the keeping of contracts, etc. I imagine that the Natural Law theorists wee attempting to outline such a system of basic rules. It would be difficult to conceive of any social, economic or geographical changes which would lead one to think that such basic rules should be abrogated, though, of course, exceptions could be made to them under special circumstances. Such basic rules are to be contrasted with others which clearly do depend upon particular circumstances. Obviously, for instance, the rule that one should be sparing in the use of water is defensible only in times of drought. The fact that it is difficult to be sure to which category particular rules belong (e.g. about sexual behaviour) does not affect the general usefulness of the distinction. So in a rational code there would be procedural rules which could be regarded as presupposed by the very activity of giving reasons for rules; there would then be basic rules, which would be those which could be justified under any conceivable social conditions; then there would be more relative rules, which would depend, for their justifiability, on more contingent facts about particular social, economic and geographic conditions. From the point of view of moral education it would be particularly important to pass on procedural rules and basic rules. Hence, presumably, the importance which Hare attaches to the question to which he thinks moral philosophers should address themselves very seriously: 'How should I bring up my children?'[3] For in a time of rapid change it is important to pass on both a minimum equipment of basic rules together with procedural rules, without which exceptions cannot be rationally made to basic rules or decisions taken about rules of a more relative status.

And so we pass to moral education. But before we do so I want to draw out one of the implications for moral education which is implicit in the position which I have outlined. If one of the fundamental principles of morality is that of the consideration of interests, moral education will be as much concerned with the promotion of good activities as it will be with the maintenance of rules for social conduct, with what ought to be as well as with what men ought to do. Such good or worthwhile activities were emphasised by the Ideal Utilitarians, such as Moore and Rashdall, who tended also to emphasise things like the pursuit of truth, the creation of beauty, the enjoyment of sensitive personal relationships, which defined the way of life of Keynes and other members of the Bloomsbury set at the beginning of this century. They rightly regarded the extension of such activities and of the outlook which goes with them as one of the main constituents in a civilised life. It would be a very difficult task and quite beyond the scope of this paper either to make a list of such activities or to show conclusively why the pursuit of them is in any man's interest.[4] Nevertheless it is precisely these sorts of activities into which we strive to initiate children in schools. We do, presumably, aim at passing on poetry rather than push-pin. So the promotion of such activities will be as much a problem for those interested in moral education as the passing on of more general rules of conduct.

Now within these worthwhile activities it is generally possible to make the same sort of distinction between matters of procedure and matters of substance which I have made in the case of a rational code. Professor Oakeshott, in his fascinating essay entitled 'The Teaching of Politics in a University', makes a very similar distinction between what he calls the 'language' and 'literature' of a subject. To quote him:

> It is the distinction, for example, between the 'language' of poetic imagination and a poem or novel; or between the 'language' or manners of thinking of a scientist and a text-book of geology or what may be called the current state of our geological knowledge. . . . Science, for example, in a university, is not an encyclopaedia of information or the present state of our 'physical' knowledge; it is a current activity, an explanatory manner of thinking and speaking being explored.[5]

In such 'languages' are implicit various canons, or what I call rules of procedure, which permit the critcism, evaluation and development of the 'literature'. The business of moral education consists largely in initiating people into the 'language' so that they can use it in an autonomous manner. This is done largely by introducing them to the 'literature'. And so we come to the paradox of moral education.

What then is the paradox of moral education as I conceive it? It is this: given that it is desirable to develop people who conduct themselves rationally, intelligently and with a fair degree of spontaneity, the brute facts of child development reveal that at the most formative years of a child's development he is incapable of this form of life and impervious to the proper manner of passing it on. Let me spell out these facts in a little more detail.

First, a fair amount of evidence has accumulated to demonstrate the decisive importance of early learning on later development. I refer here not simply to the evidence of Freudians, Kleinians, Bowlby and Harlow, who have been concerned, roughly speaking, with the importance of early learning on the development of character and personality; I also refer to evidence produced by more physiologically minded psychologists such as Hebb.

Secondly, both the Freudian theory of the super-ego and Piaget's theory of the transcendental stage of the child's development converge to suggest that up to a certain age rules appear to a child as something external and unalterable, often sacred. Freud went further than Piaget in suggesting mechanisms, such as introjection and reaction-formation, by means of which these sacrosanct external rules come to be interiorised by the child and the standards adopted of that parent with whom identification takes place. It is not till later – well after the age of seven or eight – that what Piaget calls the autonomous stage develops when the notion dawns that rules can be otherwise, that they are conventions maintained out of mutual respect which can be altered if the co-operation of others can be obtained.

No doubt a similar point could be made also about a young child's attitude to the 'literature' of subjects such as geography, history and science. In so far as his minimal concepts of space, time and causality enable him to grasp information handed on which belongs to the 'literature' of these disciplines, he will tend first of all to regard them as pronouncements from an oracle. Until he is gradually initiated into the 'language' of the subjects, by means of which he can begin to evaluate the literature, he will remain in the position of primitive people in respect of their attitude to the traditions of their tribe.

Thirdly, there is evidence to suggest – e.g. from Luria's experiments with manipulative tasks – that the giving of reasons has very little educative effect before a certain age. The explanations given by adults bite very little into the child's behaviour, though commands do have an effect at an earlier age.

Nevertheless, in spite of the fact that a rational code of behaviour and the 'language' of a variety of activities is beyond the grasp of young children, they can and must enter the palace of Reason through the courtyard of Habit and Tradition. This is the paradox of moral education, which was first put so well by Aristotle in Book 2 of his *Nicomachean Ethics*.

The problem of moral education is that of how the necessary habits of behaviour and the deep-rooted assumptions of the 'literature' of various forms of good activities can be acquired in a way which does not stultify the development of a rational code or the mastery of the 'language' of activities at a later stage.

I am assuming, by the way, like Aristotle, that children gradually acquire these desirable forms of life by some on-the-spot apprenticeship system. I am also assuming something about the factor which I previously picked out when I stressed the spontaneous enjoyment that goes with such a form of life. Spinoza put this in a very general way when he declared that 'Blessedness is not the reward of right living; it is the right living itself; nor should we rejoice in it because we restrain our desires, but, on the contrary, it is because we rejoice in it that we restrain them.'[6] In the jargon of modern psychology this is to say that a rational code and worthwhile activities are intrinsically not extrinsically motivated.

Now education, at any rate at later levels, consists largely in initiating people into this form of life – in getting others on the inside of activities so that they practise them simply for the intrinsic satisfactions that they contain and for no end which is extrinsic to them. That is why one gets so impatient with the endless talk about the aims of education and the modern tendency to speak about education in the economic jargon of 'investment' and 'commodity'. No one, of course, would deny that many skills and much information have to be passed on to sustain and increase productivity in an industrial society; it is also the case that if money has to be raised from hard-headed businessmen or from an over-taxed and materialistically minded public, the instrumental aspects of what goes on in schools and universities may have to be stressed. But anyone who reflects must ask questions about the point of keeping the wheels of industry turning. And the answer is not simply that it is necessary for survival or 'living' – whatever that means. It is necessary for the maintenance and extension of a civilised life whose distinctive outlook and activities are those which are passed on in schools and universities. In such institutions there is no absolute distinction between teacher and learner. It is a matter of degree of skill, knowledge, insight and experience within a common form of life. So there is an important sense in which 'life', by which is usually meant that which goes on outside the classroom, is for the sake of education, not education for life. This point was well made by the philosopher who was castigated by the Marxist for trying to understand the world rather than to change it. When asked what he proposed to *do* when he had achieved the classless society the Marxist admitted that he might then get round to the sort of thing that the philosopher was doing. To which the philosopher replied: 'I guess I am ahead of my time then!'

Now anyone who has managed to get on the inside of what is passed on in schools and universities, such as science, music, art, carpentry, literature, history and athletics, will regard it as somehow ridiculous to be asked what the point of his activity is. The mastery of the 'language' carries with it its own delights, or 'intrinsic motivation', to use the jargon. But for a person on the *outside* it may be difficult to see what point there is in the activity in question. Hence the incredulity of the uninitiated when confronted with the rhapsodies of the mountain-climber, musician or golfer. *Children* are to a large extent in the position of such outsiders. The problem is to introduce them to a civilised outlook and activities in such a way that they can get on the inside of those for which they have aptitude.

The same sort of problem can be posed in the case of their attitude to rules of conduct. Is it the case that children have to be lured by irrelevant incentives or goaded by commands so that they acquire the basic habits of conduct and the 'literature' of the various activities without which they cannot emerge to the later stage? Is it the case that we have to use such irrelevant 'extrinsic' techniques to get children going so that eventually they can take over for themselves, without needing any longer such extrinsic incentives or goads? Or does the use of such extrinsic techniques militate against intelligent, spontaneous and intrinsically directed behaviour later on?

It might be argued, for instance, that the various maturation levels bring with them the possibility of a variety of intrinsic motivations falling under concepts such as competence,[7] mastery and curiosity. Then there is the ubiquitous role of love and trust; for psychoanalysts such as Bowlby suggest that the existence of a good relationship of love and trust between parent and child during the early years is a necessary condition for the formation of any enduring and consistent moral habits.[8] Whether love, the withdrawal of love, approval and disapproval constitute extrinsice or intrinsic motivations with respect to the development of habits is too complicated a question to consider here. Nevertheless, it may well be that the use of such intrinsic as distinct from extrinsic motivations may be crucial in determining the type of habits that are formed. For the formation of *some* types of habit may not necessarily militate against adaptability and sponta-neous enjoyment. However, it is often thought that, because of the very nature of habits, dwelling in the courtyard of Habit incapacitates a man for life in the palace of Reason. I now propose to show both why this need not be the case and why people can be led to think that it must be the case.

Aristotle was not alone in stressing the importance of habits in moral training. There is William James's celebrated chapter on the subject in which the purple passage occurs:

> Could the young but realise how soon they will become mere walking
> bundles of habits, they would give more heed to their conduct while in
> the plastic state. . . . Every smallest stroke of virtue or of vice leaves its

never so little scar. The drunkard Rip Van Winkle, in Jefferson's play, excuses himself for every fresh dereliction by saying, 'I won't count this time!' Well! he may not count it, and a kind Heaven may not count it: but it is being counted none the less. Down among his nerve cells and fibres the molecules are counting it, registering and storing it up to be used against him when the next temptation comes. Nothing we ever do is, in strict scientific literalness, wiped out.[9]

The evidence from early learning reinforces James's graphic, if depressing, homily. The formation of sound moral habits in respect of, for instance, what I have called basic moral rules might well be a necessary condition of rational morality. It can, however, seem to be antagonistic to rational morality because of an interesting sort of conceptual confusion and because of the development, through a variety of causes, of specific types of habit. I will deal first with the conceptual issue and then proceed to the more empirical one.

What, then, do we mean by 'habits' and is there any necessary contradiction in stressing the importance of habit in moral matters while, at the same time, stressing the intelligent adaptability which is usually associated with reason, together with the spontaneous enjoyment associated with civilised activities?

The first thing to get clear about is that habits, like motives or emotions, are not as it were part of the furniture of the mind in the way in which the yellow, green and black are part of a snooker set. These terms are higher-order ones by means of which we say all sorts of extra things about people's actions, feelings and so on. 'Habit' is a term which we use to say extra things about people's *actions*. They must pick out the sorts of things that we could, in principle, have reasons for doing and the sorts of thing that, in principle, we could stop doing if we tried. It would be odd to talk about a heart-beat or a nervous tic as a habit. Forms of passivity such as stomach aches or feelings of pity or fear are not properly described as habits either.

When we describe an action as a 'habit' we suggest, first of all, that the man has done this very thing before and that he will probably do it again. We are postulating a tendency to act in this way. 'Habit' also carries with it the suggestion not only of repetition but also of the ability to carry out the action in question 'automatically'. A man can automatically stir his tea or puff his pipe while discussing the latest developments in Cuba and if you ask him whether he puts his left sock on before his right, or vice versa, he may say that he requires notice of that question. And if you ask him to pay attention so that he can tell you in what order he makes a series of movements when hitting a good drive at golf he will probably put the ball into the neighbouring wood. This is not a tip for the life-man; it is support for the Duke of Wellington, who proclaimed: 'Habit a second nature! Habit is ten times nature!' The art of living consists, to a large extent, in reducing most things that have to be done to habit; for then the mind is set free to pay attention to things that are interesting, novel and worthwhile.

Of course not all things done automatically are necessarily habits. If a man hears a scrabbling at the window and sees what he takes to be an escaped gorilla peering at him, he may 'automatically' dial 999 while wondering where he has put the bananas. But we would not describe dialling 999 as a habit. Automatic writing need not be one of a person's habits; for 'automatically' picks out only part of what is meant by 'habit' and only in the weak sense that it suggests that is the sort of thing that a man *can* do automatically. Getting up at eight does not cease to be one of a person's habits if, on occasions, he pays careful heed to what he is doing and leaps out of bed briskly the moment the alarm clock tolls the knell of the dawning day.

What are the implications of this analysis for the development of adaptability, which is the hallmark of skilled and civilised activities? What we call a skill presupposes a number of component habits. A fielder at cricket, for instance, may be very skilful and show great intelligence in running a man out by throwing the ball to the bowler rather than to the wicket-keeper. But to do this he would have to bend down, pick the ball up, and contort his body with his eye partly on the ball and partly on the position of the batsmen. But unless these component actions were more or less habits he would not be able to concentrate on using them in the service of the higher strategy of the game. But – and this is the important point – all these component actions would have to be capable of being performed with a degree of plasticity to permit co-ordination in a wide variety of very different overall actions. The concept of 'action' is 'open-ended' in many dimensions. We could describe the man as moving his arm, as throwing the ball at the wicket, or throwing it at the bowler's end, or as running the batsman out, depending on the aspect under which the fielder conceived what he was doing. In what we call 'mechanical' actions a man will always conceive the movements as leading up in a stereotyped way to a narrowly conceived end. In intelligent actions the component actions are conceived of as variable and adaptable in the light of some more generally conceived end. The teachers who have taught me most about golf and about philosophy are those who have insisted on conveying an overall picture of the performance as a whole in which the particular moves have to be practised under the aspect of some wider conception, instead of concentrating either on drilling me in moves which are conceived in a very limited way or going simply for the overall picture without bothering about practising the component moves.

Now the type of habits which would count as moral habits *must* be exhibited in a wide range of actions in so far as actions are thought to be constituted by the sorts of movements of the body that are usually associated with skills. Consider, for instance, the range of such actions that can fall under the concept of theft or malice. What makes an action a case of theft is that it must be conceived of as involving appropriating, without permission, something that belongs to someone else. A child, strictly speaking, cannot be guilty of theft, who has not developed the concept of himself as distinct from others, of property, of the granting of permission, etc. It takes a long time to develop such concepts. In the early years, therefore, parents may think that they are teaching their children not to steal, whereas in fact they are doing no such thing. They may be teaching the child something else, e.g. to inhibit actions of which authority figures disapprove, or to inhibit a narrowly conceived range of movements. At the toilet-training stage, for instance, children may pick up very generalised and often unintelligent habits – e.g. punctilious conformity to rules, unwillingness to part with anything that is theirs. But this is not what the parents were trying to teach them. For the children probably lack the concepts which are necessary for understanding what the parents *think* that they are teaching them, namely the rule of cleanliness. To learn to act on rules forbidding theft, lying, breaking promises, etc., is necessarily an open-ended business requiring intelligence and a high degree of social sophistication. For the child has to learn to see that a vast range of very different actions and performances can fall under a highly abstract rule which makes them all examples of a type of action. If the child has really learnt to act on a rule it is difficult to see how he could have accomplished this without insight and intelligence. He might be drilled or forced to act in *accordance with* a rule; but that is quite different from learning to act *on* a rule.

So it seems as if the paradox of moral education is resolved. For there is no *necessary* contradiction between the use of intelligence and the formation of habits. How then does the antithesis between the two, which is frequently made, come about? Partly, I think, through the existence of certain explanatory expressions such as 'out of habit', and partly because of certain empirical facts about a special class of habits.

To take the point about explanatory expressions first. In explaining particular actions or courses of action we often use the phrase 'out of habit', 'through force of habit', or 'that is a matter of sheer habit'. This type of phrase does not simply suggest that what the man is doing is a habit in the sense that he has a tendency to do this sort of thing and that he can do it automatically. It also implies that in this case:

1   The man has no reason for doing it which would render the action other than one conceived in a limited way. He could of course be raising his arm to attract someone's notice. He might indeed produce such a reason for doing it if asked. But to say that he raised his arm on this occasion 'out of habit' or through 'force of habit' is to deny that, on this occasion, such a reason which he might have, was *his* reason. Raising his arm *simpliciter*, we are saying, is just the sort of thing that he tends to do.

2   The clash with the idea of spontaneity, which is also often associated with 'habit', comes in also because to say that a man cleans his teeth or washes up 'out of habit' or 'through force of habit' is to exclude the possibility that there is any enjoyment in it for him, that he is doing it for pleasure, for what he sees in it as distinct from what he sees it leading on to. It is, in other words, to rule out intrinsic motivation. It is to explain what he does, roughly speaking, in terms of the law of exercise, and to rule out any variant of the law of effect.

It would follow from this that the things which we are wont to do out of habit tend to be pretty stereotyped and narrowly conceived things, which are usually fired off by familiar stimuli. Often a superficially similar cue can release a whole train of such stereotyped movements when the circumstances are relevantly dissimilar. I remember the ghastly sensation of trying to ride a motor-bike and sidecar after being trained on a motor-bike. As I automatically banked my body over and the bike went inexorably towards the gorse-bushes on the moor that stretched beside the road, my brother yelled at me: 'Imagine that you are steering a ship, not riding a motor-cycle.' He was thereby following the correct educative procedure which I have referred to above in order to release me from the force of habit.

Given, then, that the explanation 'out of habit' or 'from force of habit' rules out the possibility of a further extrinsic end by reference to which an action could be deemed to be intelligent and given that 'out of habit' also rules out explanations in terms of pleasure, enjoyment or any kind of intrinsic motivation, it is obvious enough why the intelligent adaptability of a rational code as well as spontaneous delight in practising it and in pursuing worthwhile activities are in stark opposition to things that are done 'out of habit'. But, as I have tried to show, they are not so opposed to habits as mere descriptions of types of action. Habits need not be exercised out of force of habit.

The fact, however, that they very often *are* brings me to my empirical point, which is that there are a great number of things which we do in fact do out of habit, and this is essential if our minds are to be set free to attend to other things. Remember the Duke of Wellington. It is also the case that in some people whom, in extreme cases, we describe as compulsives, the force of habit is so strong that it militates against intelligent performance and disrupts the rest of a man's life. Tidiness and cleanliness are in general sound moral habits because they save time and health and permit efficient and intelligent performance of countless other things. But if a woman is so obsessed with them that she tries to impress the stamp of the operating theatre on the nursery and bedroom of young children, she may well have reached the point where her habits disrupt not only her domestic bliss but also her own capacity for intelligent adaptation and for enjoyment of things that are worth enjoying.

And so we stand at the door of the nursery, which is the gateway to moral education. For it is here, in all probability, that the pattern of character traits and the manner of exercising them is laid down. It is here that habits are first formed in a manner which may lead to the development of compulsives, obsessives, Puritans and impractical ideologues. To explain how this probably happens would involve a careful examination of cognitive development and the role of extrinsic and intrinsic motivation in childhood. I could not begin to tackle this vast subject in this paper. I have only tried to explain and to resolve the *theoretical* paradox of moral education, not to develop a positive theory of rational child-rearing.

Aristotle put the matter very well when he said:

But the virtues we get by first exercising them, as also happens in the case of the arts as well. For the things we have to learn before we can do them, we learn by doing them, e.g. men become builders by building and lyre players by playing the lyre; so do we become just by doing just acts, temperate by doing temperate acts, brave by doing brave acts. This is confirmed by what happens in the State; for legislators make the citizens good by forming habits in them . . . by doing the acts that we do in our transactions with other men we become just or unjust, and by doing the acts that we do in the presence of danger, and by habituating ourselves to feel fear or confidence, we become brave or cowardly. . . . It makes no small difference then, whether we form habits of one kind or another from our very youth; it makes a great difference or rather all the difference.[10]

But from the point of view of moral education it makes all the difference, too, at what age and in what manner such habits are formed, especially under what aspect particular acts are taught. For it is only if habits are developed in a certain kind of way that the paradox of moral education can be avoided in practice. This is a matter about which psychologists and practical teachers will have much more to say than philosophers. For I have only tried to resolve the theoretical paradox of moral education in a theoretical manner.

Bacon once said that the discourse of philosophers is like the stars; it sheds little light because it is so high. But when it is brought nearer the Earth, as I hope it has been in this paper, it still can only shed light on where empirical research needs to be done and where practical judgements have to be made. It is no substitute for either. I hope that subsequent papers in this series will enrich our knowledge and increase our wisdom in relation to these more mundane matters.

References

1 Oakeshott, I.M., 'The Tower of Babel', in *Rationalism in Politics* (London: Methuen, 1962), pp. 59–79.
2 See Jones, E., *Sigmund Freud, Life and Work* (London: Hogarth Press, 1955), Vol. II, p. 463.
3 Hare, R., *The Language of Morals* (Oxford: Oxford University Press, 1952), pp. 74–5).
4 See Griffiths, A.P. and Peters, R.S., 'The Autonomy of Prudence', *Mind*, Vol. LXXI (April 1962), pp. 161–80.
5 Oakeshott, M., *Rationalism in Politics and Other Essays* (London: Methuen, 1962), pp. 308, 311.
6 Spinoza, *Ethics*, Pt V, Prop. XLII.
7 See, for instance, White, R., 'Competence and the Psychosexual Stages of Development', in *Nebraska Symposium on Motivation* (1960).
8 See Peters, R.S., 'Moral Education and the Psychology of Character', *Philosophy* (January 1962).
9 James, W., *Principles of Psychology* (Macmillan, 1891), p. 127.
10 Aristotle, *Nicomachean Ethics*, Bk II, chs 3, 4.

3

CARING

Nel Noddings

The German philosopher Martin Heidegger (1962) described care as the very Being of human life. His use of the term is very broad, covering an attitude of solicitousness toward other living beings, a concern to do things meticulously, the deepest existential longings, fleeting moments of concern, and all the burdens and woes that belong to human life. From his perspective, we are immersed in care; it is the ultimate reality of life.

Heidegger's full range of meanings will be of interest as this exploration continues, but the meaning that will be primary here is relational. A *caring relation* is, in its most basic form, a connection or encounter between two human beings – a carer and a recipient of care, or cared-for. In order for the relation to be properly called caring, both parties must contribute to it in characteristic ways. A failure on the part of either carer or cared-for blocks completion of caring and, although there may still be a relation – that is, an encounter or connection in which each party feels something toward the other – it is not a *caring* relation. Even before I describe the contributions of carer and cared-for, one can see how useful this relational definition is. No matter how hard teachers try to care, if the caring is not received by students, the claim 'they don't care' has some validity. It suggests strongly that something is very wrong.

In *Caring* (1984), I described the state of consciousness of the carer (or 'one-caring') as characterized by engrossment and motivational displacement. By engrossment I mean an open, nonselective receptivity to the cared-for. Other writers have used the word 'attention' to describe this characteristic. Iris Murdoch (1970), for example, discussed attention as essential in moral life, and she traced the concept to Simone Weil. Weil placed attention at the center of love for our neighbors. It is what characterizes our consciousness when we ask another (explicitly or implicitly), 'What are you going through?' Weil wrote:

> This way of looking it first of all attentive. The soul empties itself of all its own contents in order to receive into itself the being it is looking at, just as he is, in all his truth. Only he who is capable of attention can do this.
>
> (1951: p. 115)

Source: Noddings, Nel *The Challenge to Care in Schools*, (Teachers College Press, Columbia University, New York, 1992) ch. 2.

To say that the soul empties itself of all its own contents in order to receive the other describes well what I mean by engrossment. I do not mean infatuation, enchantment, or obsession but a full receptivity. When I care, I really hear, see, or feel what the other tries to convey. The engrossment or attention may last only a few moments and it may or may not be repeated in future encounters, but it is full and essential in any caring encounter. For example, if a stranger stops me to ask directions, the encounter may produce a caring relation, albeit a brief one. I listen attentively to his need, and I respond in a way that he receives and recognizes. The caring relation is completed when he receives my efforts at caring.

As carer in the brief encounter just described, I was attentive, but I also felt the desire to help the stranger in his need. My consciousness was characterized by motivational displacement. Where a moment earlier I had my own projects in mind, I was now concerned with his project – finding his way on campus. When we watch a small child trying to tie her shoes, we often feel our own fingers moving in sympathetic reaction. This is motivational displacement, the sense that our motive energy is flowing toward others and their projects. I receive what the other conveys, and I want to respond in a way that furthers the other's purpose or project.

Experiencing motivational displacement, one begins to think. Just as we consider, plan, and reflect on our own projects, we now think what we can do to help another. Engrossment and motivational displacement do not tell us what to do; they merely characterize our consciousness when we care. But the thinking that we do will now be as careful as it is in our own service. We are seized by the needs of another.

What characterizes the consciousness of one who is cared for? Reception, recognition, and response seem to be primary. The cared-for receives the caring and shows that it has been received. This recognition now becomes part of what the carer receives in his or her engrossment, and the caring is completed.

Some critics worry that my account puts a tremendous burden on the carer and very little on the recipient of care. But we must keep in mind that the basic caring relation is an encounter. My description of a caring relation does not entail that carer and cared-for are permanent labels for individuals. Mature relationships are characterized by mutuality. They are made up of strings of encounters in which the parties exchange places; both members are carers and cared-fors as opportunities arise.

Even in the basic situation, however, the contribution of the cared-for is not negligible. Consider the mother–infant relationship. In every caring encounter, the mother is necessarily carer and the infant cared-for. But the infant responds – he or she coos, wriggles, stares attentively, smiles, reaches out, and cuddles. These responses are heartwarming; they make care-giving a rewarding experience. To see just how vital the infant's response is to the caring relation, one should observe what happens when infants cannot respond normally to care. Mothers and other care-givers in such situations are worn down by the lack of completion – burned out by the constant outward flow of energy that is not replenished by the response of the cared-for. Teachers, too, suffer this dreadful loss of energy when their students do not respond. Thus, even when the second party in a relation cannot assume the status of carer, there is a genuine form of reciprocity that is essential to the relation.

The desire to be cared for is almost certainly a universal human characteristic. Not everyone wants to be cuddled or fussed over. But everyone wants to be received, to elicit a response that is congruent with an underlying need or desire. Cool and formal people want others to respond to them with respect and a touch of deference. Warm, informal people often appreciate smiles and hugs. Everyone appreciates a person who knows when to hug and when to stand apart. In school, all kids want to be cared for in this sense. They do not want to be treated 'like numbers', by recipe – no matter how sweet the recipe may be for some consumers. When we understand that everyone wants to be cared for and that there is no recipe for caring, we see how important engrossment (or attention) is. In order to respond as a genuine carer, one does have to empty the soul of its own contents. One cannot say, 'Aha! This fellow needs care. Now, let's see – here are the seven steps I must follow.' Caring is a way of being in relation, not a set of specific behaviors.

I have put great emphasis on caring as a relation, because our temptation is to think of caring as a virtue, an individual attribute. We do talk this way at times. We say, 'He is a caring person,' or even, 'She is really a caring person, but she has trouble showing it.' Both of these comments capture something of our broad notion of care, but both are misleading because of their emphasis on caring as an individual virtue. As we explore caring in the context of care-giving – any long-term unequal relation in which one person is carer and the other cared-for – we will ask about the virtues that support caring. But for now, it is important not to detach carers from caring relations. No matter how much a person professes to care, the result that concerns us is the caring relation. Lots of self-righteous, 'caring' people induce the response, 'she doesn't really care about me at all.'

Even though I will often use the word *caring* to apply to relations, I will also need to apply it to capacities. The uses should be clear in context. I want to avoid a concentration on judgment or evaluation that accompanies an inter-pretation of caring as an individual virtue, but I also want to acknowledge that people have various capacities for caring – that is, for entering into caring relations as well as for attending to objects and ideas.

When we discuss teaching and teacher–learner relationships in depth, we will see that teachers not only have to create caring relations in which they are the carers, but that they also have a responsibility to help their students develop the capacity to care. What can this mean? For Heidegger care is inevitable; all aware human beings care. It is the mark of being human. But not everyone develops the capacity to care for others in the way described above. Perhaps very few learn to care for ideas, for nonhuman life, for objects. And often we confuse the forms of caring and suppose caring to be a unitary capacity that transfers easily from one domain to another.

42

Simone Weil is a good example of an outstanding thinker who seems to have believed that intellectual caring and interpersonal caring are closely related. In the essay from which the earlier passage was extracted, Weil observed that the study of geometry requires attention and that attention so learned could increase students' concentration in prayer. Thence, we may suppose, Weil concluded that closer connection in prayer would produce more sensitive interpersonal relations; that is, she believed that intellectual attention could be transferred to interpersonal attention. This is doubtful. Evidence abounds that people can attain high levels of intellectuality and remain insensitive to human beings and other living things. Consider the Nazi high command or the fictional Professor Moriarty (Sherlock Holmes's nemesis), who attended lovingly to his orchids but was evil incarnate in the human domain. So the varieties of care need analysis.

Unequal caring relations are interesting not only in the human domain but also in the realm of nonhuman animals. It is doubtful whether any animal can be a carer with respect to humans (although there are those who have argued the case for dogs), but many animals are responsive cared-fors, and taking care of animals can be a wonderful way to learn caring. In our interaction with animals, we also have an opportunity to study the forms of response that we value. Some animals respond with intelligence, and we usually value that. Some respond with affection; they like to be stroked, cuddled, held or scratched. Still others respond vocally. All of these responses affect us and call forth a caring attitude. Further, certain physical characteristics that suggest the possibility of a valued response also affect us. Most of us feel sympathy for baby seals threatened by hunters, because they look as though they might respond in the ways mentioned. Creatures that are slimy, scaly, or spiny rarely evoke a sympathetic response in us. The nature of our responses will be seen as important when we consider the roots of ethical life.

In another sense of care, human beings can care about ideas or objects. An approach to education that begins with care is not anti-intellectual. Part of what we receive from others is a sense of their interests, including intellectual passions. To enhance a student's understanding and skill in a given subject is an important task for teachers, but current educational practices are riddled with slogans and myths that are not very helpful.

Often we begin with the innocent-sounding slogan mentioned earlier, 'All children can learn'. The slogan was created by people who mean well. They want teachers to have high expectations for all their students and not to decide on the basis of race, ethnicity, sex, or economic status that some groups of children simply cannot learn the subject at hand. With that much I agree.

But not all individual children can learn everything we might like to teach them. Further, the good intentions captured in the slogan can lead to highly manipulative and dictatorial methods that disregard the interests and purposes of students. Teachers these days are expected to induce a desire to learn in all students. But all students already want to learn; it is a question of *what* they want to learn. John Dewey (1963) argued years ago that teachers had to start with the experience and interests of students and patiently forge connections between that experience and whatever subject matter was prescribed. I would go further. There are few things that all students need to know, and it ought to be acceptable for students to reject some material in order to pursue other topics with enthusiasm. Caring teachers listen and respond differentially to their students. Much more needs to be said on this highly controversial issue, but for now it is enough to note that our schools are not intellectually stimulating places, even for many students who are intellectually oriented.

Few students learn to care for ideas in school. Perhaps even fewer learn to care for objects. I am not talking about mere acquisitiveness; this seems to be learned all too well. I am talking about what Harry Broudy (1972) called 'enlightened cherishing' and what the novelist and essayist John Galsworthy (1948) called 'quality'. This kind of caring produces fine objects and takes care of them. In a society apparently devoted to planned obsolescence, our children have few opportunities to care lovingly for old furniture, dishes, carpets, or even new bicycles, radios, cassette players, and the like. It can be argued that the care of many tools and instruments is a waste of time because they are so easily replaced. But one wonders how long a throwaway society can live harmoniously with the natural environment and also how closely this form of carelessness is related to the gross desire for more and more acquisitions. Is there a role for schools to play in teaching care of buildings, books, computers, furniture, and laboratory equipment?

Caring for ideas and objects is different from caring for people and other living things. Strictly speaking, one cannot form a relation with mathematics or music or a food processor. The cared-for cannot feel anything for us; there is no affect in the second party. But, oddly, people do report a form of responsiveness from ideas and objects. The mathematician Gauss was 'seized' by mathematics. The poet Robert Frost insisted that 'a poem finds its own way' (see the accounts in Noddings and Shore 1984). And we know that well-tended engines purr, polished instruments gleam, and fine glassware glistens. The care we exert induces something like a response from fields of ideas and from inanimate objects. Do our students hear enough – or anything at all – about these wondrous events?

Finally, we must consider Heidegger's deepest sense of care. As human beings, we care what happens to us. We wonder whether there is life after death, whether there is a deity who cares about us, whether we are loved by those we love, whether we belong anywhere; we wonder what we will become, who we are, how much control we have over our own fate. For adolescents these are among the most pressing questions: Who am I? What kind of person will I be? Who will love me? How do others see me? Yet schools spend more time on the quadratic formula than on any of these existential questions.

In reviewing the forms of care, it becomes clear that there is a challenge to care in schools. The structures of current schooling work against care, and at the same time, the need for care is perhaps greater than ever.

The debate in ethics

No discussion of caring today could be adequate without some attention to the ethic of care. In 1982 Carol Gilligan published her now famous *In a Different Voice*, describing an alternative approach to moral problems. This approach was identified in the voices of women, but Gilligan did not claim that the approach is exclusively female, nor did she claim that all women use it. Still, the avalanche of response from women who recognized themselves in Gilligan's description is an impressive phenomenon. 'This is me,' many women said. 'Finally someone has articulated the way I come at moral problems.'

Gilligan described a morality based on the recognition of needs, relation, and response. Women who speak in the different voice refuse to leave themselves, their loved ones, and connections out of their moral reasoning. They speak from and to a situation, and their reasoning is contextual. Those of us who write about an ethic of care have emphasized affective factors, but this is not to say that caring is irrational or even nonrational. It has its own rationality or reasonableness, and in appropriate situations carers draw freely on standard linear rationality as well. But its emphasis is on living together, on creating, maintaining, and enhancing positive relations – not on decision making in moments of high moral conflict, or on justification.

An ethic of care – a needs- and response-based ethic – challenges many premises of traditional ethics and moral education. First, there is the difference of focus already mentioned. There is also a rejection of universalizability, the notion that anything that is morally justifiable is necessarily something that anyone else in a similar situation is obligated to do. Universalizability suggests that who we are, to whom we are related, and how we are situated should have nothing to do with our moral decision making. An ethic of caring rejects this. Next, although an ethic of care puts great emphasis on consequences in the sense that it always asks what happens to the relation, it is not a form of utilitarianism; it does not posit one greatest good to be optimized, nor does it separate means and ends. Finally, it is not properly labeled an ethic of virtue. Although it calls on people to be carers and to develop the virtues and capacities to care, it does not regard caring solely as an individual attribute. It recognizes the part played by the cared-for. It is an ethic of relation.

In moral education an ethic of care's great emphasis on motivation challenges the primacy of moral reasoning. We concentrate on developing the attitudes and skills required to sustain caring relations and the desire to do so, not nearly so much on the reasoning used to arrive at a decision. Lawrence Kohlberg (1981) and his associates, following Plato and Socrates, have focused on moral reasoning. The supposition here is that moral knowledge is sufficient for moral behavior. From this perspective, wrongdoing is always equated with ignorance. Gilligan explicitly challenged Kohlberg's scale or hierarchy of moral reasoning (suggesting a powerful alternative developmental model), but others of us have challenged the whole idea of a developmental model, arguing that moral responses in a given individual may

45

vary contextually at almost any age. (The language used to discuss what one is doing and why may, of course, depend on intellectual development, but moral behavior and its intellectual articulation are not synonymous.)

Moral education from the perspective of an ethic of caring has four major components: modeling, dialogue, practice, and confirmation (Noddings 1984). Modeling is important in most schemes of moral education, but in caring it is vital. In this framework we are not trying to teach students principles and ways of applying them to problems through chains of mathematical reasoning. Rather, we have to show how to care in our own relations with cared-fors. For example, professors of education and school administrators cannot be sarcastic and dictatorial with teachers in the hope that coercion will make them care for students. I have heard administrators use this excuse for 'being tough' with teachers – 'because I care about the kids of this state' – but, of course, the likely outcome is that teachers will then turn attention protectively to themselves rather than lovingly to their students. So we do not tell our students to care; we show them how to care by creating caring relations with them.

There is a second reason why modeling is so vital. The capacity to care may be dependent on adequate experience in being cared for. Even while a child is too young to be a carer, he or she can learn how to be a responsive cared-for. Thus our role as carer is more important than our role as model, but we fill both simultaneously. We remind ourselves when we are tempted to take short cuts in moral education that we are, inevitably, models. But otherwise, in our daily activities we simply respond as carers when the need arises. The function of modeling gets special attention when we try to explain what we are doing and why in moral education. But the primary reason for responding as carers to our students' needs is that we are called to such response by our moral orientation.

Dialogue is the second essential component of moral education. My use of the term *dialogue* is similar to that of Paulo Freire (1970). It is not just talk or conversation – certainly not an oral presentation of argument in which the second party is merely allowed to ask an occasional question. Dialogue is open-ended; that is, in a genuine dialogue, neither party knows at the outset what the outcome or decision will be. As parents and teachers, we cannot enter into dialogue with children when we know that our decision is already made. It is maddening to young people (or any people) to engage in 'dialogue' with a sweetly reasonable adult who cannot be persuaded and who, in the end, will say, 'Here's how it's going to be. I tried to reason with you. . . .' We do have to talk this way at times, but we should not pretend that this is dialogue. Dialogue is a common search for understanding, empathy, or appreciation. It can be playful or serious, logical or imaginative, goals- or process-oriented, but it is always a genuine quest for something undetermined at the beginning.

Dialogue permits us to talk about what we try to show. It gives learners opportunities to question 'why', and it helps both parties to arrive at well-informed decisions. Although I do not believe that all wrongdoing can be equated with ignorance, I do believe that many moral errors are ill-informed decisions, particularly in the very young. Thus dialogue serves not only to inform the decision under consideration; it also contributes to a habit of mind – that of seeking adequate information on which to make decisions.

Dialogue serves another purpose in moral education. It connects us to each other and helps to maintain caring relations. It also provides us with the knowledge of each other that forms a foundation for response in caring. Caring (acting as carer) requires knowledge and skill as well as characteristic attitudes. We respond most effectively as carers when we understand what the other needs and the history of this need. Dialogue is implied in the criterion of engrossment. To receive the other is to attend fully and openly. Continuing dialogue builds up a substantial knowledge of one another that serves to guide our responses.

A third component of moral education is practice. Attitudes and 'mentalities' are shaped, at least in part, by experience. Most of us speak regularly of a 'military mind', a 'police mentality', 'business thinking', and the like. Although some of this talk is a product of stereotyping, it seems clear that it also captures some truth about human behavior. All disciplines and institutional organizations have training programs designed not only to teach specific skills but also to 'shape minds', that is, to induce certain attitudes and ways of looking at the world. If we want people to approach moral life prepared to care, we need to provide opportunities for them to gain skills in care-giving and, more important, to develop the characteristic attitudes described earlier.

Some of the most fascinating work in contemporary feminist theory is devoted to the study of women's experience and its articulation. It seems likely that women's traditional experience is closely related to the moral approach described in ethics of care. Women, more often than men, have been charged with the direct care of young children, the ill, and the aged. They have been expected to maintain a pleasing environment, to look after the needs of others, and to mediate disputes in ordinary social situations. If we regard this experience as inseparable from oppression, then we might agree with Nietzsche that what I am describing is merely 'slave mentality'. But if we analyze the experience, we find considerable autonomy, love, choice, and consummate skill in the traditional female role. We may evaluate the experience as essential in developing fully human beings.

Women have learned to regard every human encounter as a potential caring occasion. In nursing theory, for example, Jean Watson (1985) defined the moment in which nurse and patient meet as a 'caring occasion'. It is not just that the nurse will provide care in the form of physical skills to the patient. Rather, it is a moment in which each must decide how to meet the other and what to do with the moment. This is obviously very different from defining a medical encounter as a problem-solving event. Problem solving is involved, of course, but it is preceded by a moment of receptivity – one in which the full humanity of both parties is recognized – and it is followed by a return to the human other in all his or her fullness.

If we decide that the capacity to care is as much a mark of personhood as reason or rationality, then we will want to find ways to increase this capacity. Just as we now think it is important for girls as well as boys to have mathematical experience, so we should want both boys and girls to have experience in caring. It does not just happen; we have to plan for it. As we will see, such planning is complex and loaded with potential pitfalls.

Some schools, recognizing the needs just discussed, have instituted requirements for a form of community service. This is a move in the right direction, but reflection produces some issues to worry about. The practice provided must be with people who can demonstrate caring. We do not want our children to learn the menial (or even sophisticated) skills of caregiving without the characteristic attitude of caring. The experience of care-giving should initiate or contribute to the desired attitude, but the conditions have to be right, and people are central to the setting. This is a major point, to which I will return.

Next, practice in caring should transform schools and, eventually, the society in which we live. If the practice is assimilated to the present structures of schooling, it may lose its transformative powers. *It* may be transformed – that is, distorted. If we were to give grades for care-giving, for example, students might well begin to compete for honors in caring. Clearly, then, their attention could be diverted from cared-fors to themselves. If, on the other hand, we neither grade nor give credit for such work, it may inevitably have second-class status in our schools. So long as our schools are organized hierarchically with emphasis on rewards and penalties, it will be very difficult to provide the kind of experience envisioned.

The fourth component of moral education from the perspective of caring is confirmation. Martin Buber (1965) described confirmation as an act of affirming and encouraging the best in others. When we confirm someone, we spot a better self and encourage its development. We can do this only if we know the other well enough to see what he or she is trying to become. Formulas and slogans have no place here. We do not set up a single ideal or set of expectations for everyone to meet, but we identify something admirable, or at least acceptable, struggling to emerge in each person we encounter. The person working toward a better self must see the attribute or goal as worthy, and we too must see it as at least morally acceptable. We do not confirm people in ways we judge to be wrong.

Confirmation requires attribution of the best possible motive consonant with reality. When someone commits an act we find reprehensible, we ask ourselves what might have motivated such an act. Often it is not hard to identify an array of possible motives ranging from the gross and grubby to some that are acceptable or even admirable. This array is not constructed in abstraction. We build it from a knowledge of this particular other and by listening carefully to what she or he tells us. The motive we attribute has to be a real, a genuine possibility. Then we can open our dialogue with something like, 'I know you were trying to help your friend . . .' or 'I know what you're trying to accomplish . . .' It will be clear that we disapprove of this particular act, but it will also be clear to the other that we see a self that is better than this act. Often the other will respond with enormous relief. *Here is this significant and percipient other who sees through the smallness or meanness of my present behavior a self that is better and a real possibility.* Confirmation lifts us toward our vision of a better self.

It is worth repeating that confirmation cannot be done by formula. A relation of trust must ground it. Continuity is required, because the carer in acting to confirm must know the cared-for well enough to be able to identify motives consonant with reality. Confirmation cannot be described in terms of strategies; it is a loving act founded on a relation of some depth. When we consider specific changes that should occur in schooling in order to meet the challenge to care, we need to put great emphasis on continuity. Not all caring relations require continuity (some, as we have seen, are brief encounters), but teaching does require it.

Confirmation contrasts sharply with the standard mode of religious moral education. There we usually find a sequence of accusation, confession, penance, and forgiveness. The initial step, accusation, causes or sustains separation. We stand in moral judgment and separate the other from ourselves and the moral community. In contrast, confirmation calls us to remain in connection. Further, accusation tends to produce denial or rationalization, which we then feel compelled to overthrow. But the rationalization may in fact be an attempt on the part of the accused to find that possible motive and convey it to us, the accuser. Because we have to reject it in order to proceed with confession, penance, and forgiveness, offenders may never understand their own true motives. This sequence also depends heavily on authority, obedience, fear, and subordination. We can be harsh or magnanimous in our judgment and forgiveness. Our authority is emphasized, and the potential power of the offender's own moral struggle is overlooked.

I do not mean to suggest that there is never a place for accusation and confession in moral education. It is not always possible for us to find a motive that is morally acceptable; sometimes we have to begin by asking straight out, 'Why did you do that?' or 'How could you do such a thing?' But it is gratifying how often we really can see a better self if we look for one, and its identification is a first step in its realization.

This whole way of looking at ethics and moral education challenges not only parts of the religious tradition but also the ideas of Freud and like-minded theorists. Freud believed that our sense of morality develops out of fear. The superego, Freud said, is an internalization of authority – of the father's voice – and its establishment results from resolution of the oedipal conflict. Sons fear castration by the father if they disobey or compete with him. Resolution of this desire to rebel and compete involves acceptance of the father's power and authority, and the superego (Freud's guide to acceptable behavior) takes up residence within the son. This account of moral development led Freud to conclude that women must be morally inferior to men. Because girls need not fear castration (having been born in that dread condition), their moral voice never attains the strength and dependability of men's.

Recent criticisms of Freud suggest that more attention should be given to the preoedipal period. Nancy Chodorow (1978) has theorized that girls and boys develop different psychological deep structures because females are almost exclusively the primary care-givers for both. Girls can find their gender identity without separating from their mother and, hence, develop a relational personality structure and perhaps even a relational epistemology or way of knowing (Keller 1985). Boys, however, must construct their gender identity in opposition to all that is female. Here we have the possible roots of the different moral voices described by Gilligan.

Eli Sagan (1988) has also suggested that moral development begins and is strongly affected by preoedipal life. Without rejecting the Freudian framework entirely, Sagan recommends a shift in emphasis. If we give due weight to early childhood, we see that conscience (a sense of right and wrong, not mere internalization of authority) develops as much out of love and attachment as out of fear. Further, the primary fear is not of harm and punishment but, rather, of disappointing a loved parent and, at worst, losing that parent's love. This is a major challenge to masculinist psychology and a suggestion compatible with an ethic of caring and the model of moral education outlined here. Love, caring, and relation play central roles in both ethics and moral education. I suggest that caring is the very bedrock of all successful education and that contemporary schooling can be revitalized in its light.

References

Broudy, Harry (1972) *Enlightened Cherishing*. Urbana: University of Illinois Press.

Buber, Martin (1965) 'Education', in Martin Buber, *Between Man and Man* (pp. 83–103). New York: Macmillan.

Chodorow, Nancy (1978) *The Reproduction of Mothering*. Berkeley: University of California Press.

Dewey, John (1963) *Experience and Education*. New York: Collier Books (Original work published 1938).

Freire, Paulo (1970) *Pedagogy of the Oppressed* (Myra Bergman Ramos, trans.). New York: Continuum.

Galsworthy, John (1948) 'Quality', in J.D. McCallum (ed.) *The College Omnibus*, New York: Harcourt Brace and Co.

Gilligan, Carol (1982) *In a Different Voice*. Cambridge, Mass.: Harvard University Press.

Heidegger, Martin (1962) *Being and Time* (John Macquarrie and Edward Robinson, trans.). New York: Harper & Row (Original work published 1927).

Keller, Evelyn Fox (1985) *Reflections on Gender and Science*. New Haven, Conn.: Yale University Press.

Kohlberg, Lawrence (1981) *The Philosophy of Moral Development*. San Francisco: Harper & Row.

Murdoch, Iris (1970) *The Sovereignty of Good*. London: Routledge & Kegan Paul.

Noddings, Nel (1984) *Caring: A Feminine Approach to Ethics and Moral Education*. Berkeley: University of California Press.

Noddings, Nel, and Shore, Paul (1984) *Awakening the Inner Eye: Intuition in Education*. New York: Teachers College Press.

Sagan, Eli (1988) *Freud, Women, and Morality: The Psychology of Good and Evil*. New York: Basic Books.

Watson, Jean (1985) *Nursing: Human Science and Human Care*. Norwalk, Conn.: Appleton-Century-Crofts.

Weil, Simone (1951) *Waiting for God*. New York: G.P. Putnam's Sons.

4

FINDING A COMMON VOICE

Eamonn Callan

Since the Enlightenment our understanding of moral progress has been mas-
sively influenced by a particular ideal of justice. The ideal can be elaborated in
many very different ways, but its essential features are familiar and widely
endorsed.[1] Justice is identified with respect for a cluster of rights which affirms
both the moral equality of all persons and the autonomy of each. Respect for
those rights has inspired the modern condemnation of racism, sexism, and
similar forms of oppression; it has also shaped many of the intellectual landmarks
of modernity, from John Locke's treatises on government to John Rawls's theory
of justice.

Although the voice of justice is still no doubt the loudest and most insistent in
public moral discourse, feminist scholarship over the last decade has suggested
that it is not the only voice worth heeding. Many have proclaimed the importance of an 'ethic of care' as an alternative moral voice to justice, and one whose
neglect in theories of moral development and the practice of moral education
may be profoundly damaging. Two very obvious questions have to be addressed to
assess the significance of this alleged alternative to the dominant contemporary
moral ideal. First, what is the relationship between justice and caring in a
successful moral life? Second, how do we distinguish morally laudable caring
from caring which is morally indifferent or worse?[2]

I believe that the answers to the two questions I have posed are connected in an
important way. The bifurcation of morality into independent ideals of caring and
justice is a mistake to begin with, because the kind of caring we should want
always requires a supporting sense of justice, and the particular sense of justice we
should prize is itself deeply entangled with a certain kind of caring for others.
This is not to deny that our current moral discourse may contain different voices,
one of which expresses a sense of justice divorced from caring for others and
another a caring which discounts the rights of others. My point is merely that
neither the caring nor the justice worth having can be adequately characterized in
abstraction from the other; and so in the moral life we should aspire to achieve
for ourselves and our children, justice and caring blend into a common voice.

Source: *Educational Theory,* 42: 4, Fall 1992.

Sundering justice and caring

The question of how justice and caring are connected can be answered in several ways which divorce the two and thus foreclose the achievement of a common voice.[3] One might think of them as comprehensive but strictly incommensurable moral orientations in that no objective grounds for declaring one superior to the other are available or even conceivable. On the other hand, if such grounds were available, it could be argued that justice is simply a better moral orientation than caring or vice versa. There is a third way of sundering justice and caring, however, which cannot be so quickly summarized. I want to examine this approach in some detail because it is the most philosophically plausible way of separating the two ideals and thus the most challenging alternative to the view I shall defend.

Justice and caring may be construed not as comprehensive moral orientations but rather as complementary virtues in a life where different virtues are needed for different tasks. One can argue towards that conclusion in the following way. Suppose human relationships at their best are to be found in the unselfish love of parents for their children or close friends for each other. The caring for the good of others which abounds there does not have to end at the borders of intimacy – it can be evinced, for example, in solicitude for the suffering of strangers or, less dramatically, in pleasure at witnessing their joys. Of course, as David Hume and others have thought, there might be formidable psychological obstacles to any substantial extension of the virtues of intimacy beyond the boundaries to which they have traditionally been confined.[4] Yet Humean pessimism on this matter is far from obviously justified. Indeed, current empirical research suggests that the voice of caring can be commonly deployed outside the narrow context of family and friendship.[5] So the expansion of caring responses and attachments would seem to some degree a feasible project, and given the ideal of unselfish love, it can also be advanced as the paramount goal of moral education. Nevertheless, the paramount goal still cannot be the only goal; for even if Humean pessimism were excessive, it would take an insane optimist to have no misgivings about relationships or transactions in which caring cannot take root or is too frail to restrain the power of divisive nonmoral motives. To the extent that such misgivings are warranted, moral agents need virtues in addition to caring, and moral education must encompass those additional virtues. In particular, the limits of caring have to be rectified by a sense that others may have pressing claims upon one's aid or forbearance irrespective of the indifference or antipathy one may feel towards them. To acknowledge such claims is to have a sense of justice.

This third way of divorcing caring from justice makes the latter into what Michael Sandel calls a purely 'remedial virtue'.[6] That is to say, its purpose is to remedy the evils that beset human interaction when caring responses are absent or dangerously weak; but the restoration of harmony which justice brings about may still be a pallid substitute for the harmony whose collapse creates the need for justice. If I have grown indifferent to someone I once cared for as a friend or compatriot, then my sense of justice might restrain me from violating her rights, and thus mutually respectful social cooperation could continue; but that is surely a distant second best to the sense of communion that was possible when I did care.[7] In a revealing metaphor, Loren Lomasky refers to rights as the 'heavy artillery in our moral arsenal.'[8] The image of moral weaponry aptly expresses the ideas, familiar since Hume, that justice is a virtue designed for conditions of conflict and that the equilibrium it establishes may be little more than the peace that enemies reluctantly live with after battle.[9] Yet if justice is nothing more than a remedial virtue, approaches to moral education which pretend otherwise, such as Kohlberg's, threaten to mutilate our moral lives. Once children learn to import justice into moral contexts where reciprocal caring is psychologically feasible, they will give up the best moral response in favor of one that is markedly inferior. Moreover, justice-centered approaches to moral education may foster a tendency to interpret all moral encounters in adversarial terms. If conditions of personal conflict are what appropriately evoke the virtue of justice, then strategies which pretend that justice has ubiquitous moral relevance may beget the illusion that conditions of conflict are similarly ubiquitous.[10]

I believe that this third way of sundering justice and caring is mistaken, and mistaken for reasons which also disclose the inadequacy of the other two ways I have mentioned. I shall argue that even in circumstances where the value of caring is most vividly apparent – that is, in relationships of love – the sense of justice is an essential companion to the kind of caring that is morally admirable. Justice is more than a remedial virtue for confrontations between those who are mutually indifferent or hostile; it has a compelling moral relevance, even at the core of human intimacy.

Rose and Albert: a test case

My claim that the caring and justice worth prizing are enmeshed with each other is best approached through scrutiny of a particular moral response. The example I shall use is from Rose Borris's moving story about learning to read in her mid-forties. When Rose first tried to enroll in reading classes, she was opposed by Albert, her illiterate husband.

> It's hard to get out of home when your man doesn't want you to do this. You're lucky if you can get out the door. That's why I didn't start in September. I had to fight with Albert all the time because he wanted me at home. He said I was never going to learn. Maybe he was afraid. But one day he said, 'It's no use Rose. I can see what you want. I can't stop you.'[11]

Albert's words might express nothing more than the recognition that his wife's will was stronger than his, and in that event, his change of heart would have no moral significance. But then again, claims about what we cannot do are common when we discover our deepest moral loyalties; for example, 'I cannot participate in a war'. So Albert's change of heart may be driven by nobler motives than a pragmatic realization that he would lose the battle; it may signal the triumph of his better self, the power of a love or conscience that would not allow him to continue opposing Rose.

Before exploring the possible character of this 'better self', it will help to look at the worse self it had to contend with. Rose speculates that Albert opposed her out of fear. Perhaps he was afraid that a literate Rose would not want an illiterate husband or that by learning to read her attachment to him would be weakened or altered in unforeseen ways. Of course, these are self-centered fears, but they arise within a context of caring about another person and one's ongoing relationship to her. We care about others under particular descriptions, and sometimes the descriptions are such that the conduct our caring inspires is morally repellent.[12] Albert might care intensely about Rose as one half of a relationship that is the secure and predictable core of his very identity. If so, her educational ambitions will naturally make him afraid, and his fears will incline him to oppose those ambitions.

But we can care about another under a variety of descriptions at the same time, and if this were true of Albert, it could explain his change of heart. Suppose Albert loves Rose as more than one half of a cherished relationship. He cares for her as someone whose good matters for her own sake, even when her good might imperil his relationship with her. I shall call this unselfish caring. Given the presence of this kind of attachment in a sufficiently potent form, it could be enough to countervail the motivational pull of his fears so that eventually he must say 'I can't stop you'. The change of heart might also be prompted by a sense of justice. Albert might be motivated by the growing thought that Rose has a right to pursue an education outside the home, and that he has no right to interfere.

I have identified two possible moral sources of Albert's change of heart: unselfish caring and a sense of justice. These might be reflected in his conduct in three possible ways:

1   Albert ceased to oppose Rose because he cares for her as someone whose good matters for her own sake. The sense of justice is wholly irrelevant to the explanation of his change of heart. I shall refer to this response as pure caring, and this is one way in which a moral response can manifest unselfish caring.
2   Albert relented because he cares for Rose unselfishly and respects her rights. This response exemplifies an integration of unselfish caring and justice.
3   Albert relented because he has a sense of justice. Unselfish caring is wholly irrelevant to the explanation of his conduct. This is pure justice.

The question of which response is best enables us to adjudicate between the three ways of sundering justice and caring and the integrated ideal I have set against them. If justice and caring were incommensurable moral orientations, there could be no objective grounds for preferring pure caring or pure justice, and perhaps the integrated response would not even be a coherent possibility. If one orientation were objectively superior to the other, then either pure caring or pure justice could be shown to be best. If justice and caring were complementary virtues, with justice functioning in a purely remedial role, then pure caring would be the best response. However, I shall argue that there are strong grounds for favoring the integrated response and the ideal it presupposes.

Uniting caring and justice

In what way is the sense of justice 'irrelevant' to the response of pure caring? I take it that those who would favor that response would answer the question along the following lines. Suppose we question Albert about his change of heart, and he is baffled or uncomfortable by our attempt to introduce the language of justice. He relented in his opposition to Rose simply because he cared for her unselfishly. Thoughts of rights and correlative duties did not enter his head, and he does not see how his response would have been any morally better if they had.

But consider a case that parallels this interpretation of pure caring. A slaveholder grows to love the slave he owns, and eventually this leads him to free the slave. The caring for the slave's good which his action expresses is unselfish. The slaveholder knows that the slave will leave him as soon as he is liberated, and that thought grieves him intensely; but he also knows that the slave will never be happy and fulfilled without freedom, and because he values that happiness and fulfillment so deeply he frees the slave. But the slaveholder does not think of his relationship with the slave in general, and the act of manumission in particular, in terms of moral (as opposed to legal) rights and duties. He does not think of the slave's freedom as something to which the slave has a right, and the manumission is conceived as an act of sheer good will rather than the performance of a moral duty.

Something seems radically amiss in the slaveholder's response. But what is it? Consider how the situation might be viewed by a slave who understands the oppressive character of slavery. Perhaps he is grateful for his master's love. Yet he might also think that so long as his right to freedom is not acknowledged, the full measure of his worth as a person has not been taken. Persons have a worth that is not reducible to the relationships in which they are embedded, even when the relationships are constituted by bonds of unselfish caring; and their worth creates peremptory claims upon the aid or forbearance of others – moral rights in other words – which are not contingent upon the affections that may or may not bind particular members of the moral community. The slaveholder does not see the slave in this way, and for that reason there is a sense in which his love, though unselfish, is degrading. It is a love without respect for the other as a person. All this applies equally to Albert, assuming that his response were a matter of pure caring. So long as Albert does not think of Rose's freedom as something to which she has a right, his love too bears the same defect. If there is any truth to this, then justice could not be a mere remedial virtue because its absence would mar our moral responses even when pure caring is enough to secure appropriate action.

Yet this cannot be the whole story. For those of us whose moral socialization has occurred under the shadow of post-Enlightenment ideals of justice – and that, to varying degrees, includes just about all of us – the idea that respect for rights is an essential moral response is bound to command extensive intuitive assent. I have appealed to that intuition, but I have not addressed the alleged moral liabilities we incur when we attempt to live in fidelity to its requirements.

These alleged liabilities can be appreciated if we compare the pure caring which Albert might evince with pure justice. It can be argued that pure justice is morally alienating in a couple of ways which contrast sharply with pure caring. First, pure justice reduces Rose to the status of an anonymous bearer of rights, devoid of individuality and interchangeable with any other bearer of rights. One might call this the problem of abstraction. In giving justice, moral agents filter out of their awareness all the fine detail of the other's identity and context, regarding the other merely as an instance of the universal.[13] Second, pure justice precludes any substantive ties that might bind Rose and Albert in a shared affective commitment to her good. This might be called the problem of emotional disengagement. In giving justice, moral agents confront each other with wholly separate identities, each isolated in the pursuits of its own private ends, impervious to the call of human solidarity.[14] These claims, if they can be vindicated, would be enough to restore the idea that justice is, at best, a remedial virtue.

Of course, in defending the ideal that underpins the integrated response I am not committed to the claim that pure justice is better than pure caring. It would be perfectly consistent to affirm the integrated ideal and say that pure caring is sometimes or always better than pure justice. But the liabilities of abstraction and emotional disengagement which supposedly vitiate pure justice will also, presumably, corrupt the integrated response to the extent that it draws upon the sense of justice. If this were true, then the kind of moral education I am advocating, in which justice and caring blend into a common voice, would be disastrous because insofar as justice is elicited it would induce both a coarsening of moral perception and a dilution of the affective ties that give meaning to people's lives.

I shall argue that these misgivings about the integrated response are groundless. But before pursuing that argument, a caveat is in order. It may well be that the most influential conceptions of justice in recent times have been morally alienating for the two reasons I have specified. There is more than a tincture of abstraction and emotional disengagement in justice as conceived at Lawrence Kohlberg's Stage Six, at least in some of its formulations;[15] and behind Kohlberg stretches a long philosophical tradition, with Immanuel Kant as its ruling patriarch, in which the twin sins of moral alienation are not uncommon.[16] But to reject the integrated ideal because of the defects of that tradition and the educational practices it has sponsored would be a grave error, since justice can be interpreted in a way that escapes the hazards of alienation. I shall sketch that interpretation below. The point I want to stress here is that if we are to assess the ideals of caring and justice as governing ideals of moral education, each has to be explored in its most morally alluring versions. To dismiss caring, as some have done, by portraying it at its sentimental and self-indulgent worst is regrettable;[17]

but so too is the rejection of justice when rejection is based upon nothing more than the excess baggage of the Kantian tradition.

Justice and moral alienation

The dehumanizing absurdity of an abstract moral awareness of others is not an original discovery of recent scholarship: it was brilliantly critiqued almost fifty years ago in Simone Weil's 'Human Personality':

> I see a passer-by in the street. He has long arms, blue eyes, and a mind whose thoughts I do not know, but perhaps they are common place. It is neither his person, nor the human personality in him, which is sacred to me. It is he. The whole of him. The arms, the eyes, the thoughts, everything. Not without infinite scruple would I touch anything of this. If it were the human personality in him that was sacred to me, I could easily put out his eyes. As a blind man he would be exactly as much a human personality as before. I should not have touched the person in him at all. I should have destroyed nothing but his eyes.[18]

The absurd moral abstraction that Weil portrays here is not, I should hasten to add, an attitude she regards as intrinsic to justice. On the contrary, the 'infinite scruples' about respecting the individuality of the other that Weil professes arise from her distinctively theocentric conception of justice.[19] I do not want to defend her conception here or anywhere else. My limited purpose is to show how far the absurd moral abstraction that she contrasts with true justice falls short of our ordinary understanding of what it is to respect others as persons.

Putting out someone's eyes is a violation of human rights, and hence disrespect for persons, if anything is. But if one thinks of respect simply as prizing whatever makes human beings persons, then respect can prosper even if one abuses everything about them that does not constitute their personhood. Eyesight is not a criterion of personhood, and so respect for persons, on this bizarre interpretation, could not ground a right not to have one's eyes put out. Weil is perfectly right on that score. The interpretation is bizarre, however, because our common understanding of respect pertains not merely to what it is to *be* a person but also to the conditions that empower one to *flourish* as a person. Among other things, to flourish as a person is to be capable of the fulfillments of human intimacy and solidarity, to be free to perfect one's talents, to be able to make independent choices about religious affiliation, vocation and the like. To put a man's eyes out would be to block him cruelly in the endeavors which enable him to flourish as a person. He could no longer see the people he loves, he would be hampered in perfecting his talents, and so on.

There are two important aspects of this conception of respect for persons that I want to emphasize. First, if the sense of justice is grounded in respect for others in this sense, then justice is precluded on those occasions when one does not assign ultimate value to the other's good. In order to respect another as a person, one must value her flourishing. But that is merely another way of talking about prizing her good. Therefore, the sense of justice which expresses respect cannot involve any abstraction that would blind us to the other's good. The distinction between pure caring and pure justice is thus a bit less stark than it might initially seem, since each requires that Albert assign ultimate value to Rose's good. (Nevertheless, there is a difference between the kind of valuation entailed by each. I shall return to the significance of this difference later on.) Second, flourishing as a person is not the predictable realization of some uniform attribute; it is rather a condition which varies widely according to the fine detail of particular selves and circumstances. So the concern for the flourishing or good of the other which is internal to the virtue of justice must be attuned to the rich contextual detail that differentiates one moral encounter from another. This does not mean that justice operates independently of all universalistic considerations. My point is that the interpretation of those considerations requires a particularistic awareness. A very simple example of this is the interpretation of the right to medical care when one is ill. The right may be universal, but what it requires of others in particular circumstances is vastly dependent on contextual factors.

If the sense of justice can be understood in the manner I have outlined, then the fear that respect for rights inevitably brings a damanging moral abstraction in its wake is untenable. So one cannot favor pure caring over the integrated response – or over pure justice for that matter – by arguing that any drift towards abstraction must be arrested. To be sure, given that Albert evinces either the integrated response or pure justice, he must see Rose as an instance of the universal, a bearer of the right to freedom, and in that respect like any other person. But that awareness is compatible with sensitivity to the particularity of the other's good. After all, if I gaze upon a picture in an art gallery and say 'That's a wonderful picture', I am regarding it as an instance of the universal; but I do not thereby cease to be engrossed by the unique, particular thing that it is. The same point applies, *mutatis mutandis*, to the universality entailed by either the integrated response or pure justice.

The problem of emotional disengagement cannot be resolved in quite the same way as the problem of abstraction. For here there certainly is a substantial difference between pure caring and pure justice. Even though Albert must value Rose's good even when his response is a matter of pure justice, the emotional poverty of that response may represent an important human loss; and to the extent that the same loss is incurred in the integrated ideal, it too may be deemed inferior to pure caring.

To address the problem of disengagement, it is necessary to distinguish two variations of the integrated response. Suppose Albert exhibits an unselfish caring which is by itself too weak to bring about his change of heart. Thoughts of rights and duties are needed to supplement a rather anemic caring attachment. Otherwise the latter would continue to be overwhelmed by his self-centered fears. In that event, the integrated response would to a degree be infected with the same emotional disengagement that characterizes pure justice, and for that reason it might reasonably be thought inferior to a response of pure caring. But notice that the problem of disengagement in this variation of the integrated response is created not by the presence of the sense of justice but by the absence of caring in a sufficiently potent form. This suggests another variation which captures the moral ideal that I want to affirm. Suppose the unselfish caring in Albert's integrated response is every bit as strong as we might find in an instance of pure caring. There is no loss of affective engagement, and hence no moral alienation. But in addition to unselfish caring, there is the motivational pressure of a sense of justice which tells Albert that Rose is a person in her own right, with claims to freedom that cannot be brushed aside. There is nothing psychologically or conceptually odd about this coalition of deep caring and justice. If I had to fight for an adequate education for my autistic son, I would no doubt be moved by my love for him; but my conduct would also be animated by the thought that he has a right to education, like other children in the same plight. If I did not have the former motive, I would not be responding as a caring parent should; if I lacked the latter, I would be remiss in failing to see him as a person whose worth transcends my affections. The sense of justice need not dampen the power of love, and together they may yield a more complete moral response than either can alone.

Nothing in the argument I have presented obliges us to dispense with the obvious ingredient of fact in the thesis that justice is merely a remedial virtue – namely, the fact that a sense of justice may protect us from a complete moral collapse when caring fails us. My claim has simply been that justice has a role in our lives that extends far beyond any merely remedial function. That larger role cannot be repudiated so long as we want to think of others as having an inviolable worth that is not reducible to the affective attachments in which their lives may be enmeshed with ours.

Justice and caring in public morality

So far I have defended the centrality of justice to the moral life, and hence to moral education, against attempts to reduce it to a purely remedial role at best. Yet even if the defense were entirely successful, it would not be enough to justify a moral education directed towards a common voice, because accepting the centrality of justice is entirely compatible with assigning the virtues of caring to a peripheral or subordinate role.

Consider the following comparative assessment of the integrated ideal and pure justice. One might argue that though there is a moral or quasi-moral perspective which might accord the preferred version of the integrated ideal a higher ranking than pure justice, there is another and more compelling moral standpoint which would regard the differences between them as irrelevant. More precisely, even if the integrated ideal might be applauded and pure justice deprecated within the framework of a personal ethic that celebrates human love, neither response can be favored over the other in a public morality that denies relevance to anyone's private values.[20] After all, for many people the best response on Albert's part would subsume motivating thoughts concerning the love or fear of God, but it hardly follows that religious belief has any legitimate bearing upon public morality. The analogy with religious considerations makes it plain that there is more than innocent conceptual maneuvering in the division of morality into personal and public realms, with caring confined to the personal and justice reigning supreme in the public. For if caring were properly an exclusive matter of personal ethics, a moral education in public institutions that sought to combine justice and caring into a common voice would be as misguided as one that ascribed parity of status to the sense of justice and the love of God.

One way of countering this line of reasoning is to dissolve the distinction between personal and public morality upon which the whole edifice of liberal political thought is erected.[21] But that is a course which creates forbidding difficulties. For one thing, those of us who would like to keep God out of politics without resorting to compulsory atheism cannot do without the distinction between private and public spheres.[22] The question I want to press instead is why the virtues of caring should be relegated to the private sphere, and thereby placed beyond the mandate of public moral education, once we acknowledge the importance of the distinction between private and public values. There are a couple of ways of challenging the relegation of caring to the private sphere without impugning the legitimacy of the sphere itself.

It can be argued, as Charles Taylor has done, that a public morality may be directed towards 'shared goods' which extend beyond the austere notion of respect for rights.[23] These shared goods, such as patriotism (without jingoism) or attachment to local communities, are as much intrinsic values of public life as a common sense of justice.[24] And the realization of such values will require that our children learn to care about others under particular descriptions – as compatriots, neighbors, and the like. Taylor's argument can be developed in a way that does not annihilate the distinction between public and private values because it does not presuppose that every shared good (including religious faith) is a legitimate concern of public morality. There is another route to the same conclusion, however, which I want to concentrate on, and it has the advantage of not depending on the contentious premise that patriotism, say, may be as basic to public morality as respect for rights.

For the sake of argument, suppose that preserving the bonds of justice is the *only* ultimate concern of public morality. No other ties between persons can be considered an intrinsic value, save in the context of a private ethic. Does it follow that an education in public morality must be relentlessly confined to the values of justice, forgoing any attempt to strengthen caring attachments? The answer must be 'no', because such attachments may be necessary to buttress respect for rights against the pressure of opposing motives in public life. Thus the idea that justice is the remedial virtue is turned upon its head once we see that caring may often be needed to remedy the frailties of the sense of justice.

The force of this claim can be brought out by returning to the distinction I alluded to earlier on between the valuation of the other's good which is entailed by the sense of justice and the valuation entailed by unselfish caring. In a case where respect for rights holds without any admixture of caring, the good of the other is wholly distinct from that of the agent who gives respect. For example, if Albert's response were a matter of pure justice, he would have to value Rose's good in a certain sense, but the advancement of her good and his own good would coincide only in purely accidental ways. In caring for someone unselfishly, on the other hand, the advancement of her good becomes partly constitutive of one's own good, so that when hers is thwarted, other things being equal, so too is one's own. The remarkable research of Kristen Monroe and her associates on rescuers of Jews in Nazi-occupied Europe illustrates this identification at a saintly extreme. The terse explanation of one man for his efforts – 'every other person is basically you' – may express a sentiment that most of us can admire but few can emulate.[25] But unselfish caring of a less spectacular kind can still to a degree integrate the good of others with our own in innumerable ways. In moral transactions with strangers, for example, I cannot care for them as friends or loved ones; but I can still care for them as fellow citizens, say, or more fundamentally, as persons whose flourishing is not altogether extrinsic to my own. In addition to identification with the other's good, caring implies that her good commands my emotions in a certain way – her grief is echoed in my sorrow, her joys give me joy, and so on. This is the phenomenon that Carol Gilligan calls 'co-feeling', and it is certainly precluded when all that binds one to another is a reciprocal respect for rights.[26] Again, it is easy to underestimate the scope of the phenomenon by focusing on its most extreme instances, such as a parent's emotional engrossment in the condition of a sick child, while overlooking the more humdrum ways it can permeate our lives. Whenever there is a robust sense of community within a group of people, for example, we could expect co-feeling to be widespread in the way individuals respond to the crises and triumphs in each other's lives, and acts of support and assistance will commonly be explained in terms of that phenomenon.

The hazards of a moral education that takes justice as its exclusive preoccupation become clearer at this point, even for those who insist that justice is our only ultimate concern. At best, such an education leaves respect for rights cut adrift from the agent's own good and the impetus of her emotions; and at worst, it is starkly opposed to them. This poses an acute motivational problem for moral education. 'Why should I respect the rights of others?' is more than part of the ancient philosophical puzzle about why one should be moral; it is also a question that arises urgently in the life of anyone when respecting another's rights is at odds with her own good or the pull of her emotions. Moral education has to give people sufficiently powerful motivating reasons to answer the question in a way that forestalls the violation of rights. But such reasons may be decidedly hard to come by when the good of the other is altogether extrinsic to one's own and her sorrows and joys find not the faintest echo in one's own sentiments. Of course, there has been a tradition in moral philosophy that, since Plato, purports to offer compelling reasons for being moral which apply regardless of the vagaries of human inclination; but that tradition is entirely irrelevant to moral educators whose task it is to control the vagaries of human inclination in the service of justice.[27]

If the sense of justice is aligned with unselfish caring, then it has a formidable ally in resisting any slide toward injustice; and even if one's only interest is the avoidance of the latter, it would be foolish to overlook the power of that alliance. Ironically, the voice of justice would seem liable to fall altogether silent unless it combines with a difference voice.[28]

Notes

1 One obvious source of diversity is the various ways in which rights to freedom and equality can be construed, and another is the problem of how to adjudicate between different rights. The former problem is especially prominent in recent philosophical literature on distributive justice, e.g., John Rawls, *A Theory of Justice* (Cambridge, Mass.: Harvard University Press, 1971); Robert Nozick, *Anarchy, State and Utopia* (New York: Basic Books, 1974); and Joseph Raz, *The Morality of Freedom* (Oxford: Oxford University Press, 1986). The latter problem has not produced such a voluminous body of philosophical literature. But see Jeremy Waldron, 'Rights in Conflict,' *Ethics* 99, no. 3 (1989): 503–19.

2 There is some tendency in feminist scholarship to confine the concept of caring to morally admirable attitudes and conduct. That tendency is evident in Nel Noddings's important work on the ethic of care. Tightening up the word's meaning in that way is perfectly legitimate so long as it is acknowledged that this does not answer but merely recasts the second question I ask here. Given that 'caring' is confined to what is morally laudable, the question then becomes how we are to distinguish authentic caring from morally indifferent or deplorable attitudes and conduct. Noddings is very aware of the need to make such distinctions and carefully differentiates the 'deep sense' of caring she prizes from responses or attitudes with which it might be confused. See Nel Noddings, *Caring* (Berkeley: University of California Press, 1984), 12–13.

3 I hesitate to attribute each theoretical option to particular scholars for a couple of reasons. First, the options are not always as crisply discriminated as one would like. Furthermore, one commonly finds authors sliding from one option to another and back again.

4 See David Hume, *A Treatise on Human Nature*, L.A. Selby-Bigge (ed.) (Oxford: Clarendon Press, 1968), 484–9; Owen Flanagan and Kathryn Jackson, 'Justice, Care and Gender: The Kohlberg–Gilligan Debate Revisited,' *Ethics* 97, no. 3 (1987): 625.

5 See Betty Bardige, 'Things So Finely Human: Moral Sensibilities at Risk in Adolescence,' in *Mapping the Moral Domain*, Carol Gilligan *et al.* (eds) (Cambridge, Mass.: Center for the Study of Gender, Education and Human Development, 1988), 87–110.

6 Michael Sandel, *Liberalism and the Limits of Justice* (Cambridge: Cambridge University Press, 1982), 31.

7 *Ibid.*, 32.

8 Loren Lomasky, *Persons, Rights and the Moral Community* (Oxford: Oxford University Press, 1987), 8.

9 David Hume, *An Enquiry Concerning the Principles of Morals*, J.B. Schneewind (ed.) (Indianapolis: Hackett Publishing, 1983), 20–34.

10 Sandel, *Liberalism*, 34–5.

11 Rose Borris with Paulette Jiles, 'At A Loss For Words,' in *Best Canadian Essays 1989* Douglas Fetherling (ed.) (Saskatoon: Fifth House, 1989), 141.

12 See Eamonn Callan, 'The Moral Status of Pity,' *Canadian Journal of Philosophy* 18, no. 1 (1988): 7–8.

13 See for example, Carol Gilligan, *In a Different Voice* (Cambridge, Mass.: Harvard University Press, 1982), 21–2; Seyla Benhabib, 'The Generalized and the Concrete Other: The Kohlberg–Gilligan Controversy and Moral Theory,' in *Women and Moral Theory*, Eva Feder Kittay and Diana T. Meyers (eds) (Savage, Md.: Rowman & Littlefield, 1987), 154–77.

14 Gilligan, *Different Voice*, 160–5.

15 Irrelevance of all special moral attachments at Stage Six, such as filial duties or the bonds of friendship, is perhaps the most striking symptom of these flaws in Kohlberg's theory. However, in one of his last writings he endorsed an extension of the theory that purported to accommodate these moral phenomena. See Lawrence Kohlberg, 'A Current Statement on Some Theoretical Issues,' in *Lawrence Kohlberg: Consensus and Controversy*, Sohan and Celia Modgil (eds) (London: The Falmer Press, 1985), 532–41.

16 In fairness to Kant, it should be noted that he has been ingeniously defended against the charges of abstraction and emotional disengagement, though in the case of the second charge especially, the success of the defense may be in some doubt. See Barbara Herman, 'Integrity and Impartiality,' *The Monist* 66 (1983): 233–50; Robert Louden, 'Kant's Virtue Ethics,' *Philosophy* 61, 238 (1986): 473–89.

17 See Christina Hoff Summers, 'Filial Morality,' *Journal of Philosophy* 83 (1986): 439–56.

18 Simone Weil, 'Human Personality,' in *Two Moral Essays*, Ronald Hathaway (ed.) (Wallingford, Penn: Pendle Hill, 1981). This essay was originally written in 1942. See Simone Pétrement, *Simone Weil: A Life* (New York: Pantheon Books, 1976), 492.

19 Weil's notion of a particularistic 'attention' to the wholeness of the other was further developed in the moral philosophy of Iris Murdoch, who explicitly acknowledged her immense debt to Weil. Like Weil, Murdoch makes it plain that the necessary attention is not something to be contrasted with the virtue of justice; it is rather an essential feature of the truly just response. So it comes as a surprise when an influential writer on the topic of caring, Lawrence Blum, argues for the recognition of a cluster of 'Murdochian' virtues which are to be *distinguished* from justice because of the particularistic attention they imply and justice allegedly precludes. Invoking Weil's and Murdoch's concept of ethical attention while ignoring the way they connect it with justice is an oversight that is not unique to Lawrence Blum. Gilligan also overlooks this point. Of course, Weil and Murdoch may be wrong in thinking that justice can and should subsume particularistic attention to the other. But we are at least owed an argument to show why they are wrong on this point, and the necessary argument is not provided merely by showing that the dominant contemporary conceptions of justice have neglected particularistic attention. Simone Weil, *Waiting for God* (New York: Harper & Row, 1973), 139–57; Iris Murdoch, *The Sovereignty of Good* (London: Routledge & Kegan Paul, 1970), 17–23, 34; Lawrence Blum, 'Iris Murdoch and the Domain of the Moral,' *Philosophical Studies* 50 (1986): 343–67 and 'Gilligan and Kohlberg: Implications for Moral Theory,' *Ethics* 98, no. 3 (1988): 472–91; Carol Gilligan and Grant Wiggans, 'The Origins of Morality in Early Childhood Relationships,' in *The Emergence of Morality in Young Children*, Jerome Kagan and Sharon Lamb (eds) (Chicago: Chicago University Press, 1987), 287.

20 The attempt to relegate caring to the private sphere was part of Kohlberg's response to Gilligan, though he never, at least to my knowledge, spelled out the educational implications of that relegation as I do here. See Lawrence Kohlberg, Charles Levine and Alexandra Hewer, *Moral Stages: A Current Formulation and a Response to Critics* (Basel: Karger, 1983), 20–7. The relegation of caring to the private sphere is challenged on somewhat different grounds than those I explain here in Joan C. Tronto, 'Beyond Gender Difference to a Theory of Care,' *Signs* 12, no. 4 (1987): 644–63.

21 Feminist scholars with postmodernist leanings have made this move. For a provocative

argument along these lines see Audrey Thompson, 'Friendship and Moral Character: Feminist Implications for Moral Education,' in *Philosophy of Education 1989*, Ralph Page (ed.) (Normal, Ill.: Philosophy of Education Society, 1990), 61–75.

22 See Eamonn Callan, 'Godless Moral Education and Liberal Tolerance,' *Journal of Philosophy of Education* 23, no. 2 (1989): 267–81. It is important to note that the public/private distinction I want to salvage here is between a sphere of legitimate political coercion and a realm of free individual and group choice. There is another public/private distinction which must be carefully distinguished from this one – in other words, the distinction between domestic and non-domestic spheres. The tendency to conflate the two distinctions is a disastrous error which has long bedeviled liberal politics and liberal theory. For example, if I think of the domestic sphere as something that must be outside the range of legitimate political coercion, I will be incapable of recognizing the pressing political relevance of questions about domestic violence and abuse.

23 Charles Taylor, 'Cross-Purposes: The Liberal–Communitarian Debate,' in *Liberalism and the Moral Life*, Nancy S. Rosenblum (ed.) (Cambridge, Mass.: Harvard University Press), 159–82.

24 Indeed, Taylor would seem to believe that a conception of distributive justice will presuppose shared goods. See his 'The Nature and Scope of Distributive Justice,' in Charles Taylor, *Philosophical Papers Volume 2* (Cambridge: Cambridge University Press, 1985), 289–317.

25 Kristen R. Monroe, Michael C. Barton and Ute Klingemann, 'Altruism and the Theory of Rational Action: Rescuers of Jews in Nazi Europe,' *Ethics* 101, 1 (1990): 103–22. The recent research of Samuel and Pearl Oliner on the rescuers reveals the same extraordinary sense of human solidarity as the driving force in many of their lives, though their analysis is marred by a somewhat crude distinction between a justice and caring orientation. See Samuel Oliner and Pearl Oliner, *The Altruistic Personality* (New York: The Free Press, 1988), 142–70.

26 Carol Gilligan and Grant Wiggans, 'The Origins of Morality in Early Childhood Relationships,' 288–9.

27 For a trenchant critique of the tradition see Peter Singer, *Practical Ethics* (Cambridge: Cambridge University Press, 1979), 204–8.

28 There is a more ambitious and speculative line of argument which might begin where mine ends, a line of argument which has been brilliantly pursued by Susan Moller Okin. Suppose that the best conception of justice can only be formulated and understood as warranted from a perspective which involves a diffuse caring for all other members of the moral community – universal benevolence, in other words. The task in moral education of cultivating the right sense of justice would thus be *conceptually* inseparable from cultivating a particular kind of caring. This suggests an even more tightly integrated ideal of justice and caring than I envisage here. An assessment of Okin's work is beyond the scope of this paper. For one thing, a thorough assessment would require answers to thorny questions about how the best conception of justice is to be discerned. My more modest project in this final section of the essay has been to show that even if justice and caring are conceptually independent, there is ample reason to cultivate both together in the context of (public) moral education, given the way they are interwoven in moral motivation. See Susan Moller Okin, 'Reason and Feeling in Thinking about Justice,' *Ethics* 99, no. 2 (1989): 219–49; *Justice, Gender, and the Family* (New York: Basic Books, 1989).

Acknowledgement

Useful comments were made by Nicholas C. Burbules and two anonymous reviewers on an earlier draft. I am suitably grateful.

5

CHARACTER, COMMUNITY, AND EDUCATION

Betty A. Sichel

By living in an intimate, communal society and thus being a member of a moral community, children acquire habits, dispositions, interests, feelings, desires, language, knowledge, attitudes, symbols, ways of treating other human beings, and thus an embryonic form of morality. The more important issue here is not whether some thinkers would use the derogatory terms 'inculcation' or 'indoctrination' for this process of becoming a moral person and a member of a moral community. It might even be argued that all initiation into society and a moral community is some form of inculcation and indoctrination. Instead of disagreeing about the negative denotations and connotations of these terms, it is accepted that education in societies and communities also involves the transmission of certain moral views and values. This transmission some writers might call inculcation or indoctrination. The terms are unfortunate. What alternative could be suggested other than educating children in communities and society? Would those who insist on negative descriptions want to educate children with no roots and no ties? Would they expect that at the age of reason, children will be able to reason abstractly without any taint of the concrete or particular that is nourished in communities? Any such view could only be an exaggerated figment of the imagination. And the creature would not be a human being, but some aberrant organism.

The problem we will study here is how moral education involves two faces – one, the transmission of moral excellences by a moral community, and two, moral education within a large public environment such as the school.

Communities and moral education

The good life, communities, and public policy

Some might be aghast at the assertion here that communities transmit moral knowledge, skills, attitudes, sentiments, and excellences. Critics would wonder

Source: Betty A. Sichel, *Moral Education: Character, Community and Ideals*, Temple University Press, 1988, ch. 5.

whether the stress on community life and the noting of various aspects of communal moral education are posited as a jest. Critics would point to the recent disintegration of so many communities and question whether the present writer slept through a period that witnessed the demise of constitutive communities. This criticism can be answered in the following way. It is true that at present there have been major shifts in communal life, that some communities have disappeared, and some have been scarred beyond recognition. Does this mean that constitutive communities with historical roots and moral traditions have almost wholly disappeared? Does this mean that newer constitutive communities cannot be formed? An examination of some of the recesses of human life and society suggest that perhaps scholars ignore the communities that have survived the strains of twentieth-century social, scientific, and value revolutions. At present, about one-third of the children in the United States are still raised in such communities.

In relation to these surviving constitutive communities, we must address various issues that refer to these communities' ability to provide moral education for their children. First, someone may argue that such communities have a right to exist and their survival requires that they effectively provide moral education to a younger generation. Instead of couching this argument in terms of a language of rights, there is a different way of beginning. We need to question under what circumstances human beings achieve the good and moral life. Is the maintenance of community life one avenue for achieving the goals of the good and moral life? Present criticism of the quality of moral education and of public morality is hollow if certain questions are not answered or if answers only camouflage the problems. Formal education alone cannot resolve the problem of societal morality. The development of reasoning about moral dilemmas in itself cannot be the sole way to promote morality. Many public figures and policy makers assume that schools can resolve all the problems of American society. There are few attempts to examine whether other institutions of society and whether communities should also be expected to contribute in positive ways to moral education. When John Goodlad and Lawrence Cremin refer to educational networks,[1] they refer to all the other places and institutions in which human beings are educated. These other places – communities, institutions, associations, groups, media, and the like – can no longer be ignored. They are places where moral education occurs. Policy makers and theoreticians now need to investigate how various places outside the school can promote moral education.

Someone may wonder why these other places are ignored and not seen as foundational to moral education. One reason for this present omission is that moral education theory and policy have been dominated by one single view of what moral education should be. Even many of those who claim to move beyond the Kohlbergean hegemony of the previous decade still adhere to Kohlberg's basic notions. There is continual reference to abstract reasoning and formal standards as the basis of moral education.[2] These thinkers continue to posit a questionable conceptualization of human nature and reasoning and they ignore fundamental dimensions of the moral life. Unlike the questions asked during the last five decades, philosophers are again asking the question that was fundamental for earlier thinkers. This question is, what is the good life? The good life is inextricably tied to the moral life. Moral education also needs to be broadened to include this question. This question about the good life cannot be answered by schools alone. Schools cannot provide the sole means to transmit and engender morality.

Moral education must begin with induction into a moral community that will give children an intuitive vision of the good and moral life. This induction includes in embryonic form many dimensions of mature moral life. Young children who act and live within a moral community gain unarticulated understanding and skill in this moral world without necessarily gaining moral self-consciousness. A vision of the moral world is best provided by communities and parents who are already members of communities. The question society as a whole must ask is whether it is sufficiently concerned to provide the tools and policy to foster the good life and morality as it develops in communities and in the broader arena noted here. Does society want people who are moral and possess a vision of moral ideals and a moral universe? The issue of moral education is not just an issue resolved by families or schools, but depends on more general, broader social and political policy. In other words, rather than assuming any single institution, political group, or social association can assure the moral climate of society, moral education is a multifaceted endeavor involving all major communities, associations, and groups, involving political and social life, and personal decisions and responsibility.

If society is committed to the belief that communities should initiate children into a moral world, then society must ask which political and social policy can nourish communities and guarantee their survival. What political and social policy will foster the health of communities without requiring these communities to become fanatical political pressure groups? Some of the recent fanaticism and political pressures of communities may well be based on fear of this new age, fear of the changing values of society, and fear that their own communal values and ways of life may be crushed. These communities may see public policy as protecting and nourishing the autonomous individual and privatism and denigrating the worth of communities. Concern with how public policy might promote communities may also neutralize some of the more irrational and potentially fanatical forms of political and social pressure. Any social policy to nourish communities raises other problems. One of these problems is where community interests and a community's moral world should end and where the common good of a larger, more universal public morality should begin. Can a boundary be drawn between the community and the public moral world? The boundary between community and public morality creates especially difficult problems and probably ones that are currently causing excessive political and social consternation. If society as a whole turns away from these various questions and does not foster rational and serious discourse on these issues, then communities will fight for their survival and rely on political partisanship and pressure techniques.[3]

Moral education in communities

Emphasis on communities and communal ties in the first place assumes that moral education at an early stage would aim to induct children into the traditions, values, and morality of the community. Children would acquire the moral excellences of their community. Through education within a community, children would become members of a moral world. Numerous examples of analogous induction in to a community can be given. These examples provide insights into how novices become fully fledged members of communities and can also suggest how communities induct children into their moral worlds. An initiate in some religious order, an apprentice in an art studio, or a doctoral student in a science laboratory is introduced and gradually accepts appropriate excellences, character, and rules of the religious order, the community of artists, or the scientific community. Induction into these and similar communities occurs by having the agent surrounded by and embedded within that community, by the novice taking part in the community's rituals and rites, by imitating exemplar skills and moral behavior, by recognizing the ideal types respected by the community, by having behavior corrected by older members of the community, by having an implicit (or explicit) mentor system, by being guided to develop know-how and acquire appropriate skills, by listening to the stories of the community's history and its moral heroes, and by acquiring knowledge and understanding, appropriate attitudes, and feelings. Through these and other experiences, novices acquire the knowledge and understanding, the skill and expertise, the attitudes and feelings necessary for membership in the community. Membership in a moral community is not achieved by attending courses that explain the community's moral rules and rites, its moral standards and behavior. Induction is not achieved through formal courses to motivate student moral discourse and discussions. Rather, through active participation and engagement within the life of a community, by actually living and practising the skills and morality within some particular community, the novice becomes a competent member of a moral community.

Those who want to become professional painters or dancers, scientists or physicians, violin makers or singers do not create communities for themselves. As Rawls and others have recognized, these artists and scientists seek already formed associations to achieve their goods, purposes, and interests. These associations or communities already exist and have their own histories, traditions, common language and symbolic system, implicit requirements for membership, standards of skillful performance, knowledge, and attitudes, values and morality. The fully fledged members of the community already possess attachment bonds with other members of the community and with the community itself. Membership in these communal associations is not automatic, but requires some sort of induction, initiation, and training by which the novice acquires the values, skills, knowledge, and moral excellences of the community.

A child's moral education should begin within some primary community. The term 'primary' is used to refer to the child's first community membership. For children, induction into a community is both similar and dissimilar to the novice's induction into a professional community of experts. The induction of a child into a moral community is different from novice induction into a professional community in that the novice's interests, desired good(s), and purposes govern the choice of the community membership sought. Children do not choose which communities they will become members of. They do not choose whether to become members of a moral community and moral world. Whereas novices who want to become experts join instrumental communities, children are born into constitutive communities. Membership in a moral community is one criterion for being human. All human beings need to join a moral community. Novices already are members of such moral communities, whereas children by being born and living within communities become members of a moral community. Yet in some ways, it is unfair to distinguish too rigidly between these two types of communities. Though novices may see a community as instrumental to their desires, interests, and purposes, the community itself may actually be a constitutive community in that its members' identities are constituted by the community.

A child's induction into a constitutive community is similar to a novice's induction into an instrumental community in two additional ways. First, both types of community have similar techniques for transmitting the community's values, moral excellences, skills, and knowledge. Through induction into a community the child acquires an intuitive understanding of what it means to see other human beings as cherished members of a larger moral community. Benevolence and altruism are among the many sentiments children may acquire. What else does a community transmit to children? What aspects of moral life do children learn and understand through induction into a community? Only a few of the many moral dimensions transmitted by communities are noted here: admiration for moral heroes; the practice of actual moral life as it occurs in the daily, ordinary aspects of communal living; the development of skill in carrying out moral actions; recognition of the struggles and tragedies of moral life and, simultaneously, respect and admiration for moral grandeur; intuitive understanding of moral excellences; assistance in the first developmental steps in acquiring moral excellences; acquiring the responsibilities of moral life; being loved, nurtured, and cared for by cherished members of the community and thus learning how to love, nurture, and care for others; becoming attached to and bonded within the community, this bonding being one dimension of membership in the moral world of the community; learning the symbols and metaphors, the forms of moral discourses, the rites and the rituals that make up and define the community and its moral world. This transmission occurs through being cherished and nurtured, through living and breathing, speaking and listening, acting, participating, and experiencing within the community. The child becomes a member of the community's moral world both through the great leaps of momentous events and the small steps of unnoticed, unrecognized events.

There is a second way to look at the problem of the survival and nurturance of communities. At different times in human history, new communal structures have formed. These newer communities may even begin as instrumental communities, but in time they eventually may become constitutive communities. With changing values, changing family patterns, new technological developments, questions about values, and shifts in demographic patterns, there are also changes in communal structures and alignments. In other words, newer and undreamed of communal groups and structures could be developed. These need not just be small, elite groups of fortunate people, as Hermann Hesse assumed in *The Glass Bead Game* or in a different way, Alasdair MacIntyre seems to suggest as beyond virtue. Rather, new groups of people in instrumental and sentimental communities need to be provided with the power, social strength, and means to nurture what could become constitutive communities.

For some moral agents, the character acquired during this early period remains a primary aspect of moral life. Even if community moral excellences still seem acceptable in adult life, they acquire different meanings through the diverse styles and moral lives of various moral agents. However, some might still wonder whether during the late twentieth century a primary community's moral excellences can remain the basis of mature moral character and govern all moral judgments and action. Though the instances seem few to intellectuals analyzing present changes in morality and human life, there are still a considerable number of people who live their moral lives within the confines of communal moral excellences. However, the point made by some philosophers is quite different. They claim that moral agents must make autonomous and principled decisions to resolve moral dilemmas. Moral agents cannot use moral excellences that have been transmitted by communities. According to these philosophers, an agent using such moral excellences would not be making a judgment but only following morality dictated by some group or custom. This common assumption has serious defects. First, it assumes that the only people who can be moral are those who have a most highly developed form of reasoning and use formal principles. Second, it assumes that morality exists only when autonomous, fully self-conscious judgments are made. Anyone who acts without autonomously making reasoned judgments with formal principles is not a fully moral person. Third, this common assumption involves an incorrect understanding of how moral excellences, communities, and reasoning function in morality. If a person possesses moral excellences, this does not imply that the person acts without reasoning or judgment.

At times, an agent may modify communal moral excellences. With development, more mature or ideal forms of moral excellences emerge. For many persons, there eventually will be entrance into additional communities. This will often be entrance into the public domain and into the larger political world, where different, more complex moral problems exist. At times, the character and moral excellences of the original community cannot wholly meet the needs of these new communities, of public life, or complex moral dilemmas. This does not negate the formation of character in a primary community during early childhood. With this character, a human being becomes morally rooted and from this perspective acquires a vision of a moral universe. From this perspective, a moral agent also should have the potential to modify, restructure, enlarge, change character, and make informed moral judgments.

Families and moral education

Though newborn babies are helpless and require nurturance and care, they possess abilities, potentials, and reflexes that allow them to reach out and relate to their world. The first moral lessons begin during infancy and continue in early childhood. The world provides the written music, the notes and musical phrases of these moral lessons; the infant directs and interprets this music; the infant combines disconnected notes and musical phrases into a new whole that eventually becomes his or her moral life.

An infant's world is not merely an extreme form of egocentricity. A larger universe that extends through time and place is reflected within the child's narrow world. The mother nursing her infant and the concerned father fondly consoling the sick infant may not at first be known by the infant. But through their constant attention, the glow of their love and warmth, an infant receives the first lessons of morality.

On one level, the positive resolution of Erikson's first psychosocial crisis 'trust' describes one aspect of these first lessons:

> The ontological source of faith and hope which emerges I have called a *sense of basic trust*: it is the first and basic wholeness, for it seems to imply that the inside and the outside can be experienced as an interrelated goodness.[4]

> For the most fundamental prerequisite of mental vitality, I have already nominated a *sense of basic trust*, which is a pervasive attitude toward oneself and the world. . . . By 'trust' I mean an essential trustfulness of others as well as a fundamental sense of one's own trustworthiness.[5]

While speaking of how the development of trust affects the ego,[6] mental vitality,[7] conscious experience,[8] human vitality,[9] and faith,[10] Erikson in his major writings does not explicitly relate the development of trust to morality.[11] However, the implications of acquiring 'a sense of basic trust' for later morality and moral education can be discerned. For example, a 'lack of concern for the interests of others . . . [may result from] the agent's having been psychologically damaged as a result of emotional deprivation in childhood.'[12] The degree of emotional deprivation, the possible lack of trust, and the level of mistrust can influence the morality of the adult moral agent. In an extreme case of such deprivation, the psychopath is found.

How is morality and moral development related to the resolution of this first ego crisis, trust versus mistrust? For example, the mental vitality required for resolving complicated moral dilemmas is related to trust in that a moral agent must trust herself in numerous diverse ways even to embark on the voyage necessary to resolve the moral problem. Furthermore, moral action requires trust in oneself. The moral agent must trust in her own competence and be willing to carry out a moral judgment and to act, even when moral action is fraught with uncertainty. Without trust, the moral agent will withdraw from the moral scene and be fearful about her ability to resolve the problem. When turning to the other dimension of trust, trusting others and trusting the world, we see another way that the sense of basic trust relates to morality. If someone does not trust other people or the world in general, why would that person enter into the moral domain in any way but a timorous manner? If a moral agent does not trust other people (e.g., believes that those others are hostile, manipulative, or self-serving), would that agent be concerned with the welfare or interests of others?

While denying that trust is dependent 'on absolute quantities of food or demonstrations of love,' Erikson stresses the importance of 'the quality of the maternal relationship.'[13] Similarly, psychologists, led by Bowlby, have highlighted the importance of attachment bonds between primary care givers and infants.[14]

An infant's world is not just a subjective or wholly egocentric universe, but contains the symbols, meanings, and messages that are the raw material for the child to fashion into his own world and his own being. In some cases, however, that world may be too distant and separated from the infant. The infant reaches out to embrace the world, and the world's meaning and substance elude his grasp. For other infants, the world is oppressive; it suffocates their attempts to breathe and experience. In this case, some narrow, confining portion of the larger world becomes the infant's world and this limited segment infuses the infant's entire being. But no matter who the infant is, using different styles, the infant extends himself, interprets the world, gives it meaning, and incorporates these meanings into his being.

How can we interpret the first awakening of the infant and how relationships with the world stir within the infant? How can we describe how these stirrings eventually form not only the person's psyche and innermost self, but also her moral world and moral being? The world does not remain William James's 'buzzing, blooming world' for long, but instead must be transformed into a caring, warm, concerned, recognized, and structured world if that infant is eventually to become a moral person and a fully fledged member of a moral community. During these early years, important moral education occurs. Even when personal moral agency is nonexistent, moral education and the development of morality occurs; it occurs from birth, not merely at some arbitrary 'age of reason'.

Character is formed through a reflexive interrelationship between a human being and that being's environment. Even though an infant at birth possesses potentials, these are not components of an inherent moral script that automatically unwinds with increasing age. Even genetic makeup does not *determine* moral character. Simultaneously, the child is not a *tabula rasa* on which the environment writes its moral messages. Dewey argues that habits and thus character are 'outgrowths of unlearned activities which are part of . . . [one's] endowment at birth.'[15] At birth, these impulses are 'as meaningless as a gust of wind on a mudpuddle . . ., a blind dispersive burst of wasteful energy,'[16] and yet these impulses acquire meaning, according to Dewey, through social interaction with a responsive environment and responsive people. Similarly, Piaget refers to the unorganized, unstructured sucking reflex that becomes the infant's first introduction to the world. The infant's reflexes, impulses, and genetic endowment gradually become an organized structure of certain aspects of the larger world, his world reflected through nurturing care givers and society.

It is not blatant romanticism to claim that infants reach out to the world and silently urge a parent to hold and caress them, love and nurture them, talk to and feed them. We cannot underestimate the role of infants' reflexes and impulses in fostering moral development. Through these reflexes, the infant turns a head toward a parent and the parent hears the unsaid words, 'Here I am, your child, to be held and fed, loved and educated. I will discover the world through you. You will introduce me to the world.' These words are not just a flight of fancy. They are believed and cherished by parents. While we can speak of how these reflexes evolve and that they disappear within a few months of birth, still they serve another purpose. The new parent does not merely see the infant as a helpless being in need of caring, but as a responsive person who reciprocates caring behavior. Parents interpret such reflexive behavior by saying, 'She likes me; look how she holds on to me.'

During the first months of life, an infant's development is often interpreted by parents in terms of personal affection and attachment. This is not a far-fetched interpretation, for infants' preference for the contours of a human face, their eye contact, and turning to see where a sound comes from strengthen attachment bonds between child and parents. The cooing and babbling between child and parent are not just educational necessities for language development, but are also among the first steps of the dance of morality. All the neonate's reflexes and the infant's abilities and experiences occur within a social world, with other people, primarily between infant and parents. These parents, however, are part of some society, ethnic group, religious group, or other intimate community. Parents are actually the vehicle for presenting the values and morality of the community and society.

Few would doubt parents' effect on the morality of their children. And yet, it is also commonly recognized that traditional forms of families are in disarray, that there is considerable divorce and large numbers of one-parent families, and that many mothers have entered the work force. We might argue that this is one sign of the tremendous changes occurring in society. But if we expect to improve moral life or provide adequate moral education, then there must be attention to what alternative family forms might be and to what type of social policy might insure the moral education of the very young child that previously had occurred only in one setting, the traditional family.

Schools and communities

We must begin this section on moral education in schools with additional comments about the communities that children come from and the relationship between schools and these communities. Those who have stressed the schools' responsibility for moral education may argue the following:

> Communities may inculcate children with expected forms of behavior and social rules, but these should not be confused with the moral education schools should engender. Acceptance of communal rules and values applies to small kinship systems, what Tönnies called the *gemeinschaft*. The aim of moral education in schools is something quite different in that it should refer to justice and fairness, to the rights and interests of a much wider group of people. The reasoning and principles of formal moral education programs should apply universally.[17] Moral education given in public schools thus requires a different framework and form than that of communities. It is acceptable for communities to induct their children into the moral universe of those communities, but public schools cannot take this course.

Other voices may join in this criticism and say that there must be a wall separating the public school from community, separating induction and moral education.[18] Some may also say that whereas a community will have agreed upon moral standards and values, the public school cannot advocate a single set of moral standards or values. These critics would claim that present society with its rampant individualism requires that moral education in public schools concentrate on abstract reasoning and formal principles. According to this position, communities no longer have moral vigor. Solitary individuals make up society, and these individuals have the sole responsibility of making moral judgments. Therefore they must be given the tools to make these judgments. Their moral reasoning must be improved. They need to acquire moral principles (e.g., neo-Kantian formal principles or a utilitarian maximization of good principle).

Still others champion abstract reasoning and formal principles for an altogether different reason. They claim that moral education that fosters such reasoning and principles does not conflict with a community's fundamental values and morality, but places communal morality within a larger context. Abstract moral principles would sidestep the problem of concrete, particularized moral standards by advocating a form of reasoning and abstract principles. Cognitive processes and rational thought would be the focus of moral education. The content of actual moral decisions would not be as important as the justification of the judgments (e.g., deciding which moral standards should be used in making a moral judgment). However, formal criteria and abstract reasoning cannot either serve communities or curb excessive individualism. Communities are unhappy with highly generalizable, abstract moral principles and argue that

74

principles ethics actually sustain a certain view of morality that they find unacceptable. Instead of being neutral regarding moral content and moral decisions, moral education based on abstract reasoning and formal, highly general principles is often destructive of community life. On the other side, moral education that subscribes to formal ethical principles is deficient for those who have never been raised in communities. A moral education based on abstract reasoning cannot correct excessive individualism. Before agents are willing to subscribe to any morality or ethical principles, they must view other human beings as members of a moral community. These others cannot be outsiders to be manipulated in the quest for private interests and personal success. Recognition of others as equals within a moral community is not dependent on learning to reason abstractly or using certain ethical principles. Rather, the reasoning and principles require prior membership in a moral world and this criterion is fulfilled by communities.

Instead of advocating either community moral education alone or moral education based on highly abstract moral principles, another approach to morality and moral education can be taken. Moral education must include a variety of approaches, two of these being character education based on community affiliations and the development of rational means of solving moral problems.[19]

Saying that both communities and schools must have a role in moral education creates many problems. Children from very different communities with different values and moral excellences may attend the same school. How can a school approach the question of moral education under these circumstances? Are the only two alternatives to be recommended either the development of abstract moral reasoning or moral neutrality? Since both these alternatives are rejected, another course and a different relationship between community and school needs to be briefly sketched.

The school as bridge

It has been said many times that the school is a bridge between the family and the larger society. Thus, the school becomes a meeting place for communities and an intersection between communities and the larger society. For various reasons, schools in recent years have lost touch with communities and communities seem to have little to say about the moral education their children receive in school. How could some balance again be reinstated?

Let us look at one proposal and see how the school and community might jointly further moral education. Numerous philosophers have argued for the priority of moral action over moral reasoning and for the need of moral education to juxtapose moral action and moral reasoning. One form that this could take is to institute a program of public service, by which students tutor and play with younger children, work in senior citizen centers, entertain and give concerts in hospitals, assist the handicapped and help in social organizations, assist in day-care centers and nursery schools, teach religious school, and help those confined to their homes.

The range of a public service program, however, is not the issue here. More often, the issue has been whether a service program should even exist. For example, toward the end of the Vietnam War it was suggested that instead of military service, young people should be required to serve two years in some capacity that could include social service. More recently, when considering the 'Nation at Risk' and other national reports, some states again considered this question of a service program. In this case, their concern in part was with civic education. The mandating of service programs was to ensure civic responsibility. Students in these programs, it was believed, would develop greater awareness and practical understanding of a common social good. Again, this idea to mandate that students contribute a certain number of hours in social and public service was abandoned. A number of public and private schools, universities, hospitals, youth organizations, and churches have service programs. But these are different from what had been proposed. In these various institutions, children and young people volunteer to help others. No one is required to serve.

For a short time, one Northeastern school district mandated service as a graduation requirement. However, when this mandate was challenged and criticized by taxpayers, the board of education withdrew their earlier mandate. The program became voluntary. Service was acceptable providing adolescents chose whether to volunteer for the program. Was this the taxpayers' real criticism? Might the problem have been that a very small group of people, administrators and members of the school board, made the decision to mandate the policy.

The decision to develop a public service program could have been made in another way. There could have been sufficient discussion that included the various community constituencies of the school district and thus taxpayers, administrators, teachers, adolescents, and other concerned persons. These would be discussions, not the hearings that boards of education often have. The difference between discussions and hearings is great. With hearings, each interest group presents its case in the most exaggerated form possible. The goal is to present the most forceful persuasive brief for one's position. There is little or no attempt to find common meeting grounds or solve a common problem. The advocacy of discussions is not a call for each individual or group to do nothing but present his or her unexamined opinion. The discussion noted here refers to networks of communication, to groups of people working to resolve a common problem. In this case, specific skills and knowledge are necessary. The school may need some neutral person with appropriate interpersonal and group skills to conduct these meetings.

These discussions might not only include questions about whether there should be some service program, but also what such service should include. Service might not just be monitored or administered by schools, but by other institutions, agencies, and organizations. Unquestionably, the people of the school district might reject the idea of service, develop a pilot project to test the consequences, or try a service program in some limited form. They may see certain experiences, volunteerism, and work as service, whereas the school previously had not included these as part of the service program. In this case of community involvement in the decision-making process, the idea of some form of service may well have broad support. Instead of waiting to see whether various communities criticize a policy, the school insured that communities contributed to it. Finally, there is also the question of school leadership needed to implement such policy. When decisions are made, school leaders need to have the courage and integrity to implement the policy. This does not mean that a public service problem continues without any evaluation or modifications, but instead that school leaders are committed to the process of developing moral education programs and to the decisions emanating from such policy groups.

Communities and agreement about moral education

It is often assumed that the presence of a number of diverse communities implies that there can be no agreement about the moral behavior, moral standards, and moral ideals fostered by schools. Assuredly, there are differences in the morality and moral excellences accepted by different communities. But admitting this is not the same as saying that there are no agreed-upon moral standards, moral behavior, or moral ideals. What is needed at this juncture is for communities and parents to come together with educators to ascertain where there is agreement. In this quest, parents, communities, and the school became partners. This relationship is not easy to maintain, but the alternative is for schools to claim to be the experts and for parents and communities to remain political pressure groups fighting the unacceptable decisions of educators. The advocacy of partnerships may be particularly difficult in excessively large or comprehensive schools. The answer here is not necessarily a return to neighborhood schools. Other directions could be taken to insure that schools are of a size that allows for extensive community involvement. The control of school size may allow for the fostering of the ethos that Gerald Grant and others claim would improve moral education in schools. The issue here is providing much greater communication networks between diverse groups.

Educational aims: aims of education and aims of moral education

It has not been fashionable to posit far-reaching, long-term educational aims and ideals. Recent criticism of American education and the reports that recommend educational policy have had no time for educational aims. There has been only criticism of declining test scores, a weakened and fragmented curriculum, how American education does not meet the economic and technological challenge of the present age, and the inability of American youth to match the performance scores of students in other highly technological countries. Without reference to educational aims, there have also been statements about what direction specific educational reform should take. Cries about educational excellence have been little more than persuasive slogans without theoretic underpinning or practical denotation.[20] State mandates to test at every level of public schooling and new curriculum requirements have had no relationship with long-term aims. The vision of the 'educated' person has not just been clouded, but has disappeared as the concern of any constituency.[21] Different constituencies march to different drumbeats.

General, long-term educational aims and the goals of moral education are closely related members of the same family. Moral education and its goals not only involve moral virtues, but intellectual virtues as well. The goals of moral education move in many directions and encompass the following: improvement of students' character; the further development of the moral excellences students have acquired in communities; the developing of the emotions, interests, and desires necessary for the possession of moral excellences and for making moral judgments; the fostering of the intelligence and reasoning necessary to evaluate character, enlarge moral excellences, and resolve a wide range of moral dilemmas; the acquiring of knowledge and the means to obtain additional knowledge that contributes to the resolution of complex moral dilemmas. The more general aims of education must also include these same dimensions: questions about the good life, intellectual and moral virtues, the development of the individual, and various criteria – moral criteria, epistemological claims, and aesthetic standards.

One example of general aims of education indicates why long-term, general educational aims are needed and how the goals of moral education and general education are related. After defining culture as 'activity of thought, and receptiveness to beauty and humane feeling,' Whitehead then posits a first statement of what education should aim to produce – people 'who possess both culture and expert knowledge in some special direction.'[22] Through this aim of education, Whitehead integrates the generalist and specialist, the intellectual and the moral, the intellectual and the aesthetic, the past and the future. The 'receptiveness to beauty and humane feelings' describes the aesthetic and moral aspects of culture, and the 'activity of thought' refers to the reasoning and intelligence that cultures and human beings require to insure the good life and then improve life. But Whitehead does not limit the aims of education to this one terse statement. He stresses the importance of appreciating ideas and the interrelationship between ideas. Among the various passages that relate to these educational aims is the following:

> You may not divide the seamless coat of learning. What education has to impart is an intimate sense for the power of ideas, for the beauty of ideas, and for the structure of ideas, together with a particular body of knowledge which has peculiar reference to the life of the being possessing it.[23]

Finally, Whitehead advocates the development of the aesthetic characteristic 'style' that includes both 'attainment and restraint'. With style, the person possesses the power to attain the desired end without distraction, with restraint and with control over diverse events. Style 'pervades the whole being'.[24]

Many policy makers and philosophers of education would argue that long-term, general aims of education now have little currency. Except for sounding pleasant at the beginning of a school handbook, they tell little about what should be done in classrooms or about what curriculum recommendations should be or about which methods should be used. The better way, these critics would claim, is to stop arguing about irrelevant aims of education and begin mandating specific subject requirements that relate to the economic needs of a nation and the work needs of students. It is true that general educational aims do not provide specific educational policy and practice. This does not imply that schools who accept one set of broad, general educational aims would have identical programs. In their practical instantiations, different schools might have very different programs and practices. But all the schools would have programs and practices that in some way reflected the broad educational aims.

What would such aims do to the current arguments about educational excellence and the improvement of schools? Why would broad educational aims be one means of tempering present arguments? Instead of arguments, criticism, and mandates being fragmented and relating primarily to political and economic concerns, there could be a refocusing of educational discourse. By placing educational discourse within a different framework, a different set of recommendations might emerge.

What of the other primary problem that must concern us here, the relationship between general educational aims and the aims of moral education? General educational aims refer to characteristics that generate the good life. For Whitehead, the good life involves the enjoyment of beauty, the beauty of ideas, the attainment of desirable ends without distraction,[25] humane feelings, activity of thought, and the seeking of various perfections. These various dimensions are also basic to the moral life. The various perfections one seeks in the moral life are related to moral excellences, which are not just the virtues implanted in young people by communities. Any moral excellence can be evaluated against a standard of what it would mean for that moral excellence to be a perfection. Activity of thought is necessary to evaluate present moral excellences, to change them, to decide whether they can provide the right or best standard to resolve a moral dilemma, and to judge what action a moral excellence requires in a particular situation. But there is another relationship between general educational aims and the aims of moral education. All formal education is moral education. Even at times when moral education becomes a specific course of study within a school, it is still inimicably interconnected with the larger aims of education. Moral education and its goals are not subsumed under the more general goals of education and are not a component of the larger domain of education. Rather, moral education and its aims are embedded within and overlay all of education.

Notes

1 John I. Goodlad, *A Place Called School* (New York: McGraw-Hill, 1984); Lawrence A. Cremin, *The Genius of American Education* (New York: Vintage, 1965).

2 For example, Oser describes moral education as referring to justice, formal principles, and abstract reasoning. Fritz K. Oser, 'Moral Education and Values: The Discourse Perspective,' in M.C. Wittrock (ed.) *Handbook of Research on Teaching*, 3rd edn (New York: Macmillan, 1986). *Cf.*, Marvin W. Berkowitz, 'Four Perspectives on Moral Argumentation,' in Carol Gibb Harding (ed.) *Moral Dilemmas* (Chicago: Precedent, 1985).

3 In this quest to maintain the integrity and strength of communities, it should be stressed that not all communities have been politically visible. At times, those that have remained comparatively invisible in political terms have suffered the most. Political silence has meant that some communities have become fair game in political battlefields.

4 Erik H. Erikson, *Identity: Youth and Crisis* (New York: W.W. Norton, 1968), p. 82.

5 *Ibid.*, p. 96.

6 *Ibid.*, p. 82.

7 *Ibid.*, p. 96.

8 *Ibid.*, p. 97.

9 *Ibid.*, p. 104.

10 *Ibid.*, p. 106.

11 In one short, infrequently cited article, Erikson briefly examines 'the roots of virtue'. Erik H. Erikson, 'The Roots of Virtue,' in Julian Huxley (ed.) *Humanist Frame* (New York: Harper & Brothers, 1961), pp. 145–65.

12 Ronald D. Milo, *Immorality* (Princeton, N.J.: Princeton University Press, 1984), p. 77.

13 Erikson, *op. cit.*, p. 103.

14 In any human society optimum conditions rarely exist and thus there usually is not the attainment of absolute trust or 'unambivalent attachment'. Robert Hogan, John A. Johnson and Nicholas P. Emler, 'A Socioanalytic Theory of Moral Development,' in William Damon (ed.) *Moral Development* (San Francisco: Jossey-Bass, 1978), p. 9.

15 John Dewey, *Human Nature and Conduct* (New York: Modern Library, 1922/1957), p. 85.

16 *Ibid.*, p. 86.

17 The distinction made here is between social conventions and morality. Communities, it might be argued, teach social conventions, customs and mores. Public schools, however, must be concerned with a different framework, with the development of a fully self-conscious form of moral reasoning and the use of higher-order abstract moral principles. Moral dilemmas, it is argued, are very different from dilemmas involving social conventions. Nucci, for example, argues this position. Larry P. Nucci, 'Conceptual Development in the Moral and Conventional Domains: Implications for Values Education,' *Review of Educational Research* 52 (1982): 93–122. It was argued earlier in this book that this rigid boundary cannot be sustained, and thus the rigid boundary between moral education in communities and schools also should not be sustained. It should not be a matter of whether the social or moral have priority or whether each should be assigned to a different institution. Rather, the social and moral domains overlie each other and are nurtured within all sorts of educational institutions.

18 Thomas Green raised many provocative issues about moral education inside and outside the wall in a paper presented at the fall 1986 Middle Atlantic States Philosophy of Education Society.

19 It is difficult to delineate the development of moral character and excellences not just because of the general difficulty and complexity of moral education, but because of certain present trends in formal education. For example, one such problem is the

current emphasis on a single form of empirical research, testing, and on the evaluation of results. In all formal school subjects, testing is now seen as the only way to judge what a student has achieved, whether a student has succeeded or failed in the course of study. While there are many discussions of the shortcomings of such testing, there has been little attention to how this testing agenda has affected moral education recommendations. Kohlberg for one has argued that perceptible changes in the moral agent's form of making moral judgments occur with appropriate moral education programs. The argument here is not whether Kohlberg's claim is valid, but that his moral education recommendations and theoretical notions are consistent with this present concern of educational policy makers. Students can be tested and can display whether moral cognitive development has occurred. What about character education? A similar means to that currently used for Kohlbergian theory cannot (and should not) be used to test character development. Thus, critics would ask, how would one *know* whether character education had been successful? The response would probably be, the only real proof is the quality of the long-term moral life of the community and society or the quality of life within the school. In the present climate of educational policy, however, this would hardly be a sufficient response. Such a response would not satisfy those who demand hard evidence. But as Mannheim noted during an earlier period, the most important phenomena are possibly those that cannot be caught with our present statistical, scientific tools. And this is as true today of present attempts to quantify moral development as it was of science in general during Mannheim's time.

20 Hacker, for example, in a review of a number of national educational reports, speaks of this problem, that if there are no general educational aims then programs flounder because they wander in every possible direction. Andrew Hacker, 'A Nation at Risk: The Imperative for Educational Reform,' *New York Review of Books* 31 (1984): 35–6.

21 In relation to this, Hawkins, for example, notes that 'public education is in a moral quandary.' Robert B. Hawkins Jr, 'Strategy for Revitalizing Public Education,' in J.H. Bunzel (ed.) *Challenge to American Schools* (New York: Oxford University Pres, 1985), p. 46.

22 Alfred North Whitehead, *The Aims of Education* (New York: Free Press, 1929/1967), p. 13.

23 *Ibid.*, p. 23.

24 *Ibid.* To understand Whitehead's aims of education, we would have to dig deeper and search in his writings on culture, history, aesthetics, science, and symbolism.

25 Whitehead does not use the expression 'desirable ends', but the use of criteria to evaluate ends is implied by his discussion of eternal objects and perfection(s).

6

FRIENDSHIP AND EDUCATION

Patricia White

It is possible to imagine self-respecting citizens enjoying appropriate self-esteem, hope in a democratic future, confidence in their values, and the courage to defend them. With these alone, however, those citizens would suffer a terrible lack, for nothing has been said about friendship. One of the worst things that can happen to you as a child in the playground is to discover that your best friend does not want to play with you, while perhaps the saddest aspect of old age is to be the one who is left. At both ends of life and at all stages in between, Aristotle's view that 'without friends no one would choose to live, though he had all other goods' (*Nicomachean Ethics*, 8.1.1154b) seems to capture the value we place on friendship.

If friendship is so valuable to us, does it have a place among the major aims of education in a democracy? Is it the kind of thing that *could* be fostered by education in the broadest sense? If so, is the encouragement of friendship something that could figure among the aims of *school* education? To tackle these questions, we need, first, to have some idea of what friendship is, of what we value in valuing friendship. Is it a unitary thing? When I mentioned to the director of a firm that I was doing some philosophical work on friendship, he replied, 'Ah, you mean affiliation.' Did he have in mind the same kind of thing as the therapist who recommends that people should have friends because such 'well-connected' people live longer and healthier lives (Bellah *et al.* 1985: p. 135)? Are either of them talking about the same thing as the friendship of Kate and Sue described by Lawrence Blum (1980)?

> Kate and Sue are friends. Both are clerical workers in the same large insurance firm. Sue is a quiet, thoughtful and somewhat moody person; Kate is cheery and outgoing.
>
> Sue and Kate enjoy each other's company. They enjoy talking about people they know and events that take place in the office. They appreciate and value qualities they see in each other. Kate feels she learns a lot from Sue.
>
> Kate cares very much for Sue. Sue has a tendency to get depressed quite often. Kate has learned how to make Sue feel better when she is

Source: Patricia White, *Civic Virtues and Public Schooling*, Teachers College Press, 1996, ch. 5.

in such moods. Sue is not naturally or readily open about what is bothering her; but Kate has learned how to draw her out when she feels that Sue wants to talk. Sometimes she pushes Sue too hard and is rebuffed by her, in a not especially sensitive way. Kate is hurt by such rebuffs. But more often Sue is glad to have such a good friend to talk to, and is grateful for Kate's concern for her, and for Kate's initiative in getting her to talk. Sometimes Kate can cheer Sue up just by being cheerful herself (as she naturally is anyway), but she often senses when such a mood would not be appropriate.

Kate and Sue are comfortable with each other. They feel able to 'be themselves' with each other, more so than with most other people. They trust each other and do not feel that they need to 'keep up a good front' with one another. The women trust each other with personal matters which they do not usually discuss with their husbands. They know that the other will treat the matter seriously, and will not breach the confidence involved. They know each other well and know how to be helpful to the other in discussing intimate personal matters. They care deeply for each other, and they know this about each other, though they do not express it to each other explicitly. Each one appreciates the care and concern which she knows the other has for her. This is part of what enables them to be so open with each other – the knowledge that the response will be a caring one, even when it is not directly helpful in a practical sense.

Kate and Sue are willing to go to great lengths to help each other out. They readily do favours for each other – helping shop, picking up something at the cleaners, making excuses and covering for each other at work, taking care of each other's children.

When Kate is troubled about something Sue is concerned too; and vice versa. Sue thinks about how to help Kate out. For example, she helps her to think about how to deal with her horrible boss.

The relationship between Sue and Kate was not always so close. They came to know each other gradually. Their different temperaments kept them from taking to each other immediately. In addition, Kate often felt, and sometimes still feels, shut out by Sue's reserve, and her rebuffs. She was anxious to please Sue, to have Sue like her, and this often made her forget her own desires and needs. In her insecurities in the relationship she would also not be able to focus attention on Sue's own needs, feelings and situation. In struggling with Sue, and with herself, to reach a deeper level of commitment, she worked through these insecurities. She was thereby enabled to distinguish more clearly Sue's needs and feelings from her own, to overcome tendencies to distort.

(pp. 68–9)

We also need to ask why we think that friendship – whether like that between Kate and Sue or some less deep relationship – is valuable. Is friendship valuable to us for instrumental reasons, even perhaps lofty ones, like its role in the promotion of self-knowledge? Has it, or some forms of it, an intrinsic value? How might the reasons for its value affect its status as an aim of education? Is there a downside to friendship that educators need to take account of?

Kinds of friendship

A good starting point is Aristotle's discussion of friendship in his major ethical works. As Martha Nussbaum (1986) points out, Aristotle devotes more space to friendship than any other single topic. Aristotle's *philia*, though, seems at first sight a more extensive term than *friendship*, covering, for instance, the relationship of mother and child, husband and wife, and other close family relationships. Its emphasis is on sharing and mutuality. But, on reflection, how much *is* Aristotle's concept significantly broader than our own? The idea of parents and children, husbands and wives being friends is not unfamiliar.

As Gabriel Garcia Marquez (1988) says:

> She discovered with great delight that one does not love one's children just because they are one's children but because of the friendship formed while raising them.

(p. 211)

What, then, characterizes these relationships? Certainly not every case in which someone genuinely loves or likes something is a case of *philia*. As Aristotle points out, there are lovers of wine, but clearly it is not friendship that is in question here; and that is the case for two reasons which throw light on the notion of friendship. There is no mutual affection, and the lover of wine does not wish the wine well for its own sake. Friendship seems to involve, as Aristotle suggests in the *Rhetoric* (2.4.1381a), mutual well-wishing and well-doing out of concern for one another, in good times and in bad. We look to friends in times of trouble for support, and we also want to share in our friends' sorrows; we do not want to be spared them (see Wilson 1987). Hugh Campion, an elderly man in Isobel Colegate's (1988) *Deceits of Time*, sees himself as part of a group of friends, but here mutuality is certainly lacking:

> Hugh's reading had always been to some extent a search for friends; his choice of biography of the seventeenth-century Lord Falkland was part of the search. He liked the idea of a group of friends, to which in his imagination he could belong.

(p. 179)

He had been enthusiastic about the Holland House set, the Bloomsbury Group, and 'considered himself more or less in a condition of amitié amoureuse with Lady Wemyss.'

This autumn . . . he was beginning on the Great Tew set. . . . The men who gathered around Lord Falkland at Great Tew seemed so particularly charming, brilliant, careless of worldly advancement, virtuous; if there was anything undesirable about their friendships he had yet to discover it. He was beginning to feel that he knew them a little, though of course being so long ago it was harder to imagine them; still he felt he would have been at home at Great Tew.

(p. 180)

The case of Hugh Campion and his 'friends' may seem quaint and rather sad (though it is certainly better that he has his Great Tew friends than none at all), and I mention it not in a heavy-handed way, to underline the point about mutuality, but because it has some relevance to education. For Hugh Campion's attitude toward people in books is not uncommon, I guess, among readers. If that is right, what might be the role of literature for young readers' understanding of friendship?

Finally, for a case of friendship, Aristotle claims that there must be mutual *awareness* of the inclinations and good wishes of each for the other. It could be that mutual admiration could exist between people who did not know each other at all, but this would not make them friends. Such feelings existed for some time, it seems, between Philip Larkin and Barbara Pym. Only when each knew of the other's warm appreciation of their work and kindly feelings toward the other did their friendship begin to develop.

Three broad and different types of relationships, for Aristotle, meet the conditions of friendship. They are distinguished by the basis of the relationship in each case, which can be pleasure, advantage, or character. In a pleasure friendship, the bond between the friends is simply their mutual pleasure-seeking. The friendship of people who enjoy one another's company and some of the same activities may have this kind of pleasure cement. But, when the relationship meets some obstacles, unlike Kate and Sue, the friends will not feel inclined to try to work through these difficulties. Rather, the obstacles will be seen as reasons for a parting of the ways. An advantage friendship could be, for instance, a professional relationship. Two young teachers may share ideas and materials for lessons, let each other know about professionally useful courses, and so on. They may enjoy each other's company and chat over a cup of tea at the end of the day in the staff room, but if one of them moves away to another school, the relationship may just fade away. In a character friendship the bond is the other's character and the good that the other instantiates. Each partner loves the other for what makes the other the person he or she is, with his or her particular attitudes, aspirations, and dispositions. Since the bond is based on the character of the partners, the friendship, like that of Kate and Sue, is likely to endure.

It is important to appreciate that the first two types are not in any sense exploitative relationships. The *basis* for the friendship is pleasure or advantage, but the end, if it is indeed a friendship, is still, as John Cooper (1980) persuasively argues, mutual benefit. Also, the categories are not mutually exclusive. Character friends can find each other fun, as can business associates or fellow professionals linked by the bonds of an advantage friendship.

In talking of friendship as a relationship of mutual well-wishing and well-doing, it is important to bear in mind that friendship has its downside, too. Character friends may be drawn to each other for what each sees in the other, for what makes each the person he or she is, but what attracts them may not be admirable parts of the other's character. The friendship may in fact be based on a pattern of vices that, reinforced in the relationship, are ever more openly and impudently displayed. Where the vices are mild weaknesses of character, the relationship will be one that fuels rather foolish behaviour; where the vices are more serious the relationship may become a destructive one that, in the extreme, may lead to the mutual ruin of the partners. Such relationships are mirror images, seen in increasingly distorting mirrors, of that between Kate and Sue. Jane Austen has a number of examples of the foolish end of this spectrum, like the relationship between Marianne and Willoughby in *Sense and Sensibility*. In real life, there have been such relationships as that between Oscar Wilde and Lord Alfred Douglas[1] and between Scott and Zelda Fitzgerald. In these latter cases, it is tempting to think that each partner would have done better, would have flourished more, in a different relationship.

There are other aspects, too, to the downside of friendship. For young people, the betrayal that is sometimes involved in friendship, and to which they are especially sensitive, is particularly painful. In a secular world where, for many of us, friends are all we have, this can be an experience of intense misery: We have no friend in Jesus to alleviate the pain.

Tragic conflict is another aspect of the downside of friendship. Far from the Aristotelian conception of a harmonious relationship integrated with one's other responsibilities, it may be that on occasion loyalty to one's friend will overwhelm other obligations. It may lead to painful conflicts, where finally one's love for one's friend may force one, after desperate struggles with oneself, to go against deeply held moral convictions.

The topic of friendship is a vast one, and in this brief paper I shall have to set to one side many aspects of it and issues raised by it. I shall not have much to say about sexual relationships on the one hand or, on the other, the kind of less intimate attachments people might have to fellow citizens. There can, however, be no impermeable barrier between these relations – lovers are usually also friends in one or more of the senses outlined, and the relations between fellow workers and members of the same community can turn into friendship, as in the case of Kate and Sue. I also cannot consider here a number of questions that this treatment raises: does it make sense to talk of degrees of friendship? What is the relationship between friendship and intimacy? Do the Aristotelian categories capture all the main kinds of friendship? What, for instance, of friends brought together by a practice like philosophy? In concentrating, however, on intimate relationships of mutual well-wishing and well-doing between pairs or small groups of people, I am still working on a large canvas where I am aware that I do less than justice even to the main features of my subject.

Why is friendship valuable?

Both pleasure and advantage friendships obviously have value. What of character friendships? Aristotle and later writers offer a number of reasons for their value. Let me indicate what seem to me to be the major ones.

A value that many people would, like Francis Bacon, see as the first 'fruit of friendship' is the sharing of times of joy and sorrow. For this 'redoubleth joys, and cutteth griefs in halfs' (Bacon 1985: p. 141), as the story of Kate and Sue very cleary exemplifies.

Linked to this first fruit is the idea of the friend as a powerful resource. Bacon, echoing Aristotle (*Nicomachean Ethics*, 8.1.1155a) and acknowledging that he is following the ancients, points out that 'a friend is another himself' (p. 144). There are many things that a person cannot do for himself either because he is physically unable to (for instance, carry out a wish after his death) or because it would not be seemly for him to (for instance, indicate his merits), and here a friend can take his place.

Another fruit of friendship for Bacon is that 'it maketh daylight in the understanding' (p. 142). It does this, according to Bacon, in two ways. First, in having to marshal our thoughts to put our problems to our friends, we actually become clearer about the issues and, as a result, wiser. We enjoy this first benefit even if our friends are not able to give us any actual advice. In the best cases, however, our friends will be able to give us advice on moral and also general practical (e.g., business) matters. In the moral case this is invaluable, since such advice cannot be obtained from books and, given in the wrong way, it can often be wounding and hard to accept; a friend may therefore be the best person to help us avert moral disaster. In this Bacon follows Aristotle, who similarly extols the value of friendship in providing moral guidance (*Nicomachean Ethics*, 9.12.1172a). In practical matters, too, a friend's advice is likely to be highly reliable: it will be in one's interest and not twisted to some other end, and also, because a friend will be intimately acquainted with one's situation, it will take into account all aspects of that situation. In this latter respect, it will contrast favourably with advice given by someone not well acquainted with one who may well suggest something that will 'cure the disease but kill the patient'.

More generally, friendship can simply make things go better. At work, for instance, colleagues may not get on badly and relationships between them may be reasonably congenial, but the situation will be transformed if they are real friends. Working with friends can bring all kinds of satisfactions to the experience of going to work, as well as benefits to the enterprise in which the people are working, as Aristotle noted in his remarks on shared activities (*Nicomachean Ethics*, 9.9.1169–1170b). It might be objected that it will not necessarily be good for the enterprise: The demands of friendship may conflict with the demands of work. In school, for instance, teachers may break up groups of friends because they disrupt their own and others' learning. Often in such situations the value of friendship is sacrificed, and without any great misgivings, to the demands of work. It may be, however, as I shall suggest below, that greater efforts should be made, and should be seen to be made, to accommodate both demands.

Friendship can enrich one's life in a less immediately obvious way. One of the worst things that can happen to a person is for a friend to die. Indeed, it is even sometimes recommended that people should attach themselves to more permanent objects, like the pursuit of truth, so that they avoid the pain of losing loved friends. But some people – for instance, Cicero – would claim that the enrichment of life that comes from friendship does not end with the death of a friend. As Cicero puts it:

> And may I attempt an even more difficult concept? Even [when] a friend is dead, he is still alive. He is alive because his friends still cherish him, and remember him, and long for him. This means that there is happiness even in his death – he ennobles the existences of those who are left behind.
>
> (Cicero, trans. 1971, p. 189)

In several important ways friendship with the dead is continuous with friendship with the living. In both there are loyalty, memories of times spent together, and the sharing in imagination of thoughts and perceptions of events. The pleasure that older people find in reminiscence often involves the pleasure, tinged with sadder elements, of reliving the vivid experience of friendship with friends now dead.

A further benefit of friendship mentioned by Aristotle (*Magna Moralia*, 2.15.1213a) is the increase in self-knowledge that an intimate relationship with a friend can bring. Aristotle suggests that it may be hard for us to assess our aspirations and commitments without bias, but if we see some of our own attitudes and desires mirrored in our best friend, we shall be able to consider them more dispassionately. It may be, too, that our friends will help us more directly to self-knowledge with comments on our attitudes and perhaps lifestyle that it would be impertinent, or at least out of place, for a stranger, or even an acquaintance, to make.

The reasons for friendship discussed so far all cite the fruits of friendship, as Bacon calls them. If we want support when we are in trouble, practical help, sound advice, self-knowledge, and so on, we have a reason to make friends. Suppose, however, our ideal is the self-sufficient, independent life in which one relies on one's own resources. In this case will friendship – the intimate relationship of mutual well-wishing and well-doing – have any value for us? It seems to me that the only answer to be given to the fiercely independent person who is sceptical about the value of friendship is the answer that Aristotle gives. He asks a person who has all the other goods to reflect on what she would be giving up in not having friends. In the passage in which he considers this, he emphasises several times how *strange* it would be not to value friendship. He says:

> But it seems strange, when one assigns all good things to the happy man, not to assign friends, who are thought the greatest of external goods. . . . Surely it is strange, too, to make the blessed man a solitary; for no one would choose to possess all good things on condition of being alone. . . . And plainly it is better to spend [one's] days with friends and good men than with strangers or any chance persons.
>
> (*Nicomachean Ethics*, 9.9.1169b)

There is no knockdown argument to convince someone who sees no value in friendship that she is wrong. One can only make the kind of appeal that Aristotle does, an appeal that may in fact be made more successfully in a literary work than in a piece of philosophy. One can only *show* the place of friendship in our lives, showing the goods that come to us through our attachments to others and, as a counterpoint, what we lose in living the solitary life. But this bare statement only illustrates all too graphically the need for literature to come in where the power of philosophy runs out.

Where does this leave educators? Should parents and teachers perhaps soft-pedal friendship, since they cannot provide watertight arguments as to why it should have a place in any human life? This conclusion does not follow, I think, for reasons connected with those John White and I have suggested elsewhere for highlighting shared activities in education (J. White and White 1986). What would be the rationale for underplaying the value of friendship? It should not be concern about what I earlier called the downside of friendship, since most of our values have their negative aspects. However, we do not try to omit these values from, or play them down in, children's upbringing; rather, we educate them to cope with those aspects. It would only make sense to play down friendship if we knew that almost all children were going to be determined loners or Nietzschean *Über-menschen* who might furthermore actually be *harmed* if they were educated in an atmosphere that fostered and celebrated the ties of friendship. As things are, it would be strange, to echo Aristotle, to bring up children in a way that did not acknowledge the very large place friendship has in the lives of most people.

Fostering friendship

How can educators, both teachers and parents, encourage friendship? I am still thinking here not of the friendliness and cooperative atmosphere that any teacher will want to encourage in a classroom, but of friendship – the relationship of mutual well-wishing and well-doing between people – in Malamud's (1968) words, the steak, not the spam: 'Levin wanted friendship and got friendliness; he wanted steak and they offered spam' (p. 111).

First and foremost, teachers and parents can do their best to create conditions in which friendship can flourish. For parents of young children this means, in the early years, providing opportunities for their children to make friends. It means, too, taking their children's friendships seriously, helping them to keep the promises they make to their friends, and indicating and reinforcing the kind of behavior characteristic of friendship ('Yes, that's right; share it with your friend'). Later it may mean that parents respect the privacy of a friendship. It seems to be important to the notion of friendship that there are matters which are private between friends. These private matters seem to be at least of symbolic importance, marking the closeness of the bond. Friends often say, 'I'm not telling everybody but I would like you to know . . .' People also can become quite worried if a piece of information about them becomes public knowledge before they have told their friends. I would like to explore further the role of privacy in friendship. If it has something like the significance I have indicated, however, it is important for parents to recognize the significance of privacy in friendship and not press their children, how ever subtly, for details of their conversations with, and letters from, friends.

What might be the role of the school in creating the conditions for friendship to flourish? In the first place, this seems to me to require that all staff consider what might constitute making space for friendship in their particular context. Here the elementary school will make different demands from the high school. What will be common to both, and to all other educational institutions, is that in making space for friendship an institution will be implicitly supporting many aspects of the education of its students to which it is already committed. For, as we have seen, friends can provide moral advice, support us in our projects, and help us to develop self-knowledge, so fostering friendships will dovetail with a number of the school's other aims.

If the aim of the school is to celebrate friendship as one of the most cherished of human values, it first has to *refrain* from doing certain things. It has to respect friendship and *show* that it does so in its practices. This will mean, for instance, that teachers will need to consider carefully before splitting up friends. In general, presumably they will want to avoid it by finding other ways around the problem that the splitting up of the friends is intended to solve. Sometimes, however, there will be compelling reasons for such a strategy, for instance, where a pair of students is particularly disruptive of their own and others' learning and a number of other solutions have been tried and have failed. If friends have to be separated, though, this should be done with manifest regret – because it is a matter for regret if an important value has to be overridden for whatever compelling reason – and certainly not with the sense of satisfaction a general might have in routing the enemy.

In Michael Carson's *Sucking Sherbert Lemons* (1989), Novvy, the Novice Master, has to discuss in his class with the novices an item in the Rule Book of the Order that he confesses he does not like dealing with – Particular friendships. The Rule runs as follows:

Particular friendships between the Brothers are to be discouraged because they tend to erode the spirit of Universal Brotherly Love which should prevail in all communities of the Order.

(p. 115)

In the world of the Order there is a rationale for the Rule, as Novvy explains. Particular friendships could interfere with the quest to become one with Christ, and they could take away from the love a Brother owes to all the other Brothers. Leaving aside friendships that are woven around the vices, or weaknesses, of the partners to their detriment, it is not clear that in the secular world of the school there is any need to try to restrain or prevent particular friendships. Yet from anecdotal evidence, it seems that some teachers feel that they have to put pressure on particularly close friends to 'join in more with the others', 'to join a group'. Devotion to one or two people, however, seems in itself morally desirable, in that it involves, as Blum points out (1980: p. 80), in varying measure and at different times, sympathy, compassion, concern for others, patience, and so on. It only becomes morally suspect when it involves a deficient stance toward others. Some closely knit couples do indeed take such a stance, but by no means all close friendships involve such attitudes. If and when they do, it is appropriate for the school to condemn the attitudes and take steps to change them, rather than intervene prematurely and cast a suspicious eye on a morally praiseworthy situation.

It would be interesting to know more about teachers' attitudes toward close friendships between students. Is there any evidence, for instance, that there is a widespread wariness about friendship among teachers? If there is, why might this be? Do teachers feel in some way threatened by these relationships? Is it that some teachers have a moral outlook which gives a major place to moral rights and duties and in which there is no prominent place for a value like friendship? If so, perhaps that also explains why some teachers say they feel guilty about the time they spend helping children to cope with the problems their friendships are causing them.

Sometimes it is not the friendship itself that teachers take exception to, but the activities it involves. Respecting friendship and taking it seriously may mean that teachers will have to revise their views about gossip. It is commonplace for teachers to cast severe glances at gossiping girls (girls seem to attract this attention more than boys), even if the gossiping is happening in a break. But is this necessarily a morally reprehensible activity? That question needs a chapter in itself, not least to clarify the notion of gossip, but here let me just suggest that there are reasons for thinking that adolescent gossiping is not automatically to be condemned. There may be moral value in it. Sabini and Silver (1982), who define gossip as 'idle evaluative talk about someone behind his back' (p. 92), see it as 'a training ground for both self-clarification and public moral action' (p. 106). And Sissela Bok (1984), who deals in some detail with the harmful aspects of gossip, which she defines as 'informal personal communication about other people who are absent or treated as absent' (p. 91), suggests that to condemn gossip absolutely is to

> fail to consider its extraordinary variety . . . [to] ignore the attention it can bring to human complexity, and [to be] unaware of its role in conveying information without which neither groups nor societies could function.
>
> (p. 101)

For adolescents, particularly, gossip may have an important role to play in the process of developing more finely differentiated moral attitudes toward the actions and attitudes of others.

It has been suggested that teachers might *show* the value of friendship in the everyday life of the school by being friends with their students. If we are talking here about friendliness, fine. The deeper, more intimate relationship, however, which has been the focus of this chapter, is, generally speaking, ruled out by the norms of impartiality that must govern the teacher's conduct. Just as doctors or lawyers would be likely to create ethical complexities for themselves if they entered into intimate personal relationships with their patients or clients, so it is with teachers. In the case of the teacher, there is the additional consideration of the immaturity of the students. So what does a teacher do if, in the middle of a maths lesson, a tearful six-year-old child raises a hand and says, 'I haven't got any friends'? He responds, 'But you have; I'm you're friend!' And when the child goes on to ask, 'Will you play with me at recess, then?' he says, 'Of course!' This real-life example illustrates superbly for me the kind of wisdom we expect, and usually get, as a matter of course from teachers. We expect that teachers will know just when in a clash of values one value must give way to another and know how to make the appropriate response in the context. This teacher was perfectly well aware of the demands of his professional role, but in this instance these demands had to give way to a response to a child who is feeling the misery of being friendless. A less perceptive teacher might have responded to the child's plea', Oh, I'm sure you have; I'm sure lots of people want to play with you' and then gone on with the maths lesson. In so doing, he would have lost the chance to make a response that recognizes and underlines the value of friendship.[2]

So far the emphasis has been on restraint, on the need for the school not inadvertently to disvalue friendship in upholding other values. But is there anything the school can do *positively* to encourage friendship and the under-standing of and valuing of friendship among students? One might perhaps first question whether it is appropriate for the school to do anything positive about friendship. Friendship, it might be claimed, is simply something that happens to one. Everyone, or almost everyone, comes across people they are particularly drawn to and, as a result, friendships develop and that is that. But, as Blum (1980) points out, friendships can exist at very different levels, and a relationship like the one between Kate and Sue has over time involved considerable effort on both their parts in overcoming obstacles to their deep commitment and care for each other. Such caring, far from being a natural process, is hard to achieve, and it may well be something that the school can help young people to understand and appreciate.

Let me, then, tentatively offer some suggestions about what the school might do *positively* about friendship.

In general, active efforts by the teacher to promote friendship among students will rightly be seen by them as officious meddling and will do more harm than good. Teachers of very young children, however, who are concerned to encourage friendship among their students along the lines that I have suggested parents might do, may from time to time discover this means that they have to take an active role. They may sometimes have to remind children of the obligations of friendship, help friends to resolve their disputes, and console a child who has been abandoned by his or her friend.

With adolescents, the teacher will be concerned not with the promotion of friendship, which would almost inevitably involve an unjustifiable interference in the lives of her students, but with deepening the understanding of the complexities of the phenomenon of human friendship. The teacher can help them to explore what it is to enter into a relationship in which both partners are deeply committed to each other. She can consider the downside of friendship in its various aspects – the conflicts that may exist with other values and those relationships that hinder the flourishing of one or both partners or, in the worst cases, destroy them. Here literature and film may well have an important role to play. Sometimes this may be incidental to the study of, say, a novel as part of the literature syllabus. Sometimes the teacher may deem it appropriate to focus explicitly on questions like those raised by the friendship between the determined Emma and the biddable Harriet in Jane Austen's *Emma*.

This last point raises the question of how desirable it is to encourage young people to become self-conscious about their own friendships in particular. To take a fairly familiar phenomenon, it may be important to young people in some contexts simply to be seen as having a friend, that is, not to be seen as friendless. And anyone who can reasonably respectably fill the role of friend is better than no one at all. Here friendship is clearly serving a purpose beyond itself, but it is one whose object, unlike that of the usual advantage friendship, involves the notion of friendship itself. Sometimes a relationship like this will persist for a while with few of the usual characteristics of a friendship simply because both parties want to preserve the picture of themselves as a person who has a friend. How wise is it for teachers to draw attention to this?

Most of the great classical treatises on friendship – those by Aristotle, Cicero, and Montaigne, for instance – do not allow for the possibility of friendship between women or between men and women. Had the authors not held views about the inferiority of women, it seems to me, they could have applied what they have to say about friendship without difficulty to those cases as well. Today, too, different views exist on the capacities of men and women for friendship. Discussion of views of alleged gender differences in this area also needs to find a place in education.

Conclusion

Dispositions like self-respect, self-esteem, and courage are clearly needed to sustain a democratic community. The fraternal feelings not focused on here that citizens should have toward fellow citizens are also, perhaps more obviously, linked to the democratic community. But the intimate notion of friendship that has been the focus of this paper seems to me just as much to characterize a democratic society. In such a society friendship can be *publicly* celebrated as something of intrinsic value that may on occasion override other values. This would be an impossible public stance in a totalitarian society. In the latter, when friendship competes with the subject's allegiance to the party or state, it can never win out. The depiction of Jung Chang's (1993) father, in *Wild Swans*, perfectly exemplifies this absolutist position. For this man, communist principles and adherence to their interpretation by Chairman Mao always took precedence over his undoubted love for his wife and family. In this respect, in Mao's China, he was doing no more than a good citizen should. By contrast, democratic societies can tolerate the fact that sometimes people, exercising their moral judgment and not without misgivings and regret, will put the values of friendship above their political obligations. Perhaps this is the hallmark of democracy.

Notes

1 I am grateful to Louise White for this example.
2 I am indebted to Cornel Hamm for this example.

References

Aristotle (1984) *The Complete Works of Aristotle* (J. Barnes, ed.) Princeton, NJ: Princeton University Press.

Bacon, F. (1985) *The Essays*. Harmondsworth: Penguin (Original work published 1625).

Bellah, R.N., Madsen, R., Sullivan, W.M., Swidler, A. and Tipon, S.M. (1985) *Habits of the Heart: Individualism and Commitment in American Life*. Berkeley: University of California Press.

Blum, L. (1980) *Friendship, Altruism and Morality*. London: Routledge.

Bok, S. (1984) Secrets: *On the Ethics of Concealment and Revelation*. Oxford: Oxford University Press.

Carson, M. (1989) *Sucking Sherbert Lemons*. London: Black Swan.

Chang, J. (1993) *Wild Swans: Three Daughters of China*. London: Flamingo.

Cicero, (1971) 'Laelius: On friendship,' in M. Grant (trans.) *On the Good Life* (pp. 172–227). Harmondsworth: Penguin.

Colegate, I. (1988) *Deceits of Time*. London: Hamish Hamilton.

Malamud, B. (1968) *A New Life*. Harmondsworth: Penguin.

Marquez, G.G. (1988) *Love in the Time of Cholera*. London: Cape.

Sabini, J. and Silver, M. (1982) *Moralities of Everyday Life*. Oxford: Oxford University Press.

White, J. and White, P. (1986) 'Education, liberalism and human good,' in David E. Cooper (ed.) *Education, Values and Mind* (pp. 149–71). London: Routledge. Reprinted as Volume I Paper 15.

Wilson, J. (1987) *A Preface to Morality*. London: Macmillan.

Part I

(2) Religious education

7

(i) RELIGIOUS UPBRINGING AND THE LIBERAL IDEAL OF RELIGIOUS AUTONOMY

Peter Gardner

On the subject of Émile's religious upbringing Rousseau writes:

> what religion shall we give him, to what sect shall this child of nature belong? . . . We will not attach him to any sect, but we will give him the means to choose for himself according to the right use of his own reason.[1]

John Stuart Mill seems to have subscribed to a somewhat similar liberal approach, for on the subject of religious education he maintains that the

> diversity of opinion among men of equal ability, and who have taken equal pains to arrive at the truth. . . . should of itself be a warning to a conscientious teacher that he has no right to impose his opinion authoritatively upon a youthful mind . . . The pupil should not be addressed as if his religion had been chosen for him, but as one who will have to choose it for himself.[2]

Yet if the goal or the ideal of religious upbringing or religious education were to be seen as involving autonomous decisions about religious matters, would this mean that parents should refrain from bringing up their children attached to a sect and with a faith or creed imposed? In other words, if religious parents succeed in bringing up their children to share their religious beliefs, are they not endangering the future religious autonomy of their children and endangering the chances of the liberal ideal being achieved? To put this another way, if children are brought up by their parents to hold a set of religious beliefs and to engage as believers in the religious practices and rituals of their parents, will this prevent those children from subsequently approaching those beliefs in an autonomous

Source: *Journal of Philosophy of Education*, Vol. 22, No. 1, 1988.

way and deciding for themselves what they think about them or, at least, is such an upbringing likely to be detrimental to their taking this type of decision?[3] The recent debate between T.H. McLaughlin and Eamonn Callan[4] has focused attention on these very questions, McLaughlin's thesis being that a religious upbringing need not endanger autonomy, especially if parents follow the guidelines he prescribes. In this paper I want to explore certain aspects of both McLaughlin's thesis and religious upbringing, but before doing so I should like to clarify two issues.

1 Beliefs, choice and autonomy

There seems to be a tendency in considerations of autonomy to regard beliefs as things we can choose, or, to be more technical, to regard beliefs as intentional. Judging from our opening quotations, perhaps Rousseau and Mill support this view of beliefs, and it is clearly an approach that McLaughlin endorses, for he is concerned that the children of religious parents should be brought up so that they can 'make [their] . . . own choices in due course' amongst and from religious beliefs and their alternatives.[5] However, I think this is an approach we should be wary of. It is not that we should maintain, as some have done,[6] that beliefs cannot be chosen, or that we should support Elizabeth Telfer's claim that 'It does not make any sense to say, "I decided to think that such-and-such is the case".'[7] After all there is no reason why I cannot deliberately organise my environment with tape recordings, graffiti and the like, so as to get myself to believe that I am getting better in some ways. Equally, though it might require an ingenious tale to provide a plausible background to such a case, I see no reason why a person could not arrange to have himself brainwashed or indoctrinated into beliefs which he does not, but would like to, hold.[8] Such a person would seem to have chosen his beliefs, just as a person who gets someome to wash her car may have chosen to have her car washed. So beliefs, I want to suggest, can be chosen; there is neither absence of sense in such a suggestion nor does such a suggestion advance a logical or a contingent impossibility. Nevertheless, beliefs, I would maintain, are very rarely chosen. Indeed, to accept something as true *just* because we want to seems beyond most of us, and, possibly, beyond all of us. There are, of course, lots of things in life we can choose and easily achieve or acquire, but beliefs do not appear to belong to this category. When our consciences prick and we suffer feelings of guilt, it would be a great relief if we could choose to believe that we did not commit the worrying deed, and when our work is going badly or colleagues fall out with us, would it not be nice if we could choose to believe, despite the evidence, that our work is going well and that we have never been so popular? But to come to hold these beliefs just because we want to seems something we cannot manage.

Nevertheless this does not mean that choice and autonomy cannot be exercised in the realm of belief. What we clearly can choose to do is to assess, examine, ponder, reflect and so on. We may not choose the outcome of our deliberations and, hence, we may not choose what we come to believe, but we can choose to deliberate.[9] And such reflections and deliberations as part of a concern to decide things for ourselves as opposed to heteronomously following what others say, has been seen as an important feature of autonomy.[10] Yet what is of particular importance to our inquiry is the outcome of these reflections and deliberations. Developing an idea from R.F. Dearden, we may suggest that if the goal of religious autonomy is to be achieved, then the agents in question need to arrive at beliefs on religious matters where an adequate explanation of why they believe what they do can terminate with *their own* conscious ratiocinations and with what they regard as good reasons.[11] To echo Dearden, this does not mean that the autonomous agent has to be the spontaneous creator of his beliefs any more than it means that his beliefs have to be original;[12] what it does mean is that where this type of explanation of an agent's beliefs is seen as inadequate and a more satisfactory explanation is sought which is couched in terms of, say, upbringing or parental influence, then the implication is that the beliefs are part of the heteronomous make-up of the agent.[13]

In view of the preceding observations, I will in the remainder of this paper talk of reflection about and assessment of beliefs rather than choice of beliefs, and I will understand autonomous reflection and assessment to be of the kind that is to be explained in the way just outlined.

The second introductory issue I want to touch upon concerns autonomy and being informed. There is a tendency within some educational circles to see the autonomous person as well-informed and as someone who has the wherewithal for knowledgeable and well-grounded decisions. J.P. White even attempted to justify a compulsory curriculum that equipped pupils with understanding for subsequent choices in terms of its providing for autonomy.[14] McLaughlin would seem to go along with this sort of tendency, for he sees informing children about alternative faiths and creeds and the like as a way of preparing for autonomy in the religions domain.[15] Now the point I want to make, and it is a point that has been made elsewhere,[16] is that the autonomous person need not be well-informed or knowledgeable about alternatives, opportunities or possibilities. It may be true that for a person to exercise his or her autonomy, that person needs to be faced with what are perceived as options, but any resulting decision need not be well-grounded or well-informed. The ignorant are not *ipso facto* heteronomous and 'well-informed and autonomous' is not a tautology. Consequently, while the goal that McLaughlin wants religious parents to aim for is one that he describes as autonomous choice about religious beliefs and their alternatives. I would suggest that in addition to thinking 'choice' should be replaced by 'reflection and assessment', 'autonomous' should be conjoined with 'well-informed'. These changes, however, do not imply that McLaughlin is tackling a different question to the one we are interested in. After all, Rousseau and Mill want learners to be given the wherewithal for 'choice', by which we may assume they mean that learners should be well-informed, and this, I would suggest, is also part of the liberal ideal, that is to say, the ideal involves informed people reflecting and assessing for themselves.

Having clarified these matters, let us turn to what may seem to be a particularly liberal feature of McLaughlin's case. It is that children should be made aware of beliefs which conflict with their parents' religious beliefs and which, as a result, conflict with beliefs that they themselves hold.

2 Awareness of alternatives

McLaughlin favours what Callan would describe as a strong religious upbringing.[17] It is one in which religious parents bring up their children to share their religious beliefs and in which children participate in the religious practices and events that are part of their parents' faith or creed. But, in addition, McLaughlin wants religious parents to make sure that their children are aware that there are alternatives to the beliefs they and their parents share, and he also wants these children to be made to appreciate that one day they will have to decide for themselves about and between what they have been brought up to believe and these alternatives.[18] This awareness and appreciation are seen as 'liberal features' of the kind of religious upbringing McLaughlin favours,[19] while an account of an upbringing which supposedly lacks these features is said to have 'an illiberal feel to it'.[20] In McLaughlin's guidelines there is, then, what he describes as 'an explicit emphasis on the child's realising that alternatives do exist to the beliefs held by his family; and that he [the child] has a clear responsiblity to make his own choices in due course – including the possibility of rejection of those beliefs'.[21]

So, a supposed liberal feature of the type of upbringing we are considering is that children should be made aware of alternative beliefs. But what will this awareness amount to? And should it be seen as a liberal feature? With regard to the first question, presumably McLaughlin is interested in views which are held by other people which are inconsistent with the religious beliefs shared by the child and his or her parents, for if they were consistent they would not be alternatives. It might be suggested, therefore, that what he is concerned with will involve the child being made aware of what these alternative views are and that there are those who hold those views. Yet such a suggestion surely fails to do justice to McLaughlin's emphasis that children should be made to realise 'that alternatives do exist'. The fact is that a person might consider a belief which is an alternative to one that he holds without realising that it is an alternative, and, similarly, children might be made aware of beliefs which contradict or conflict with beliefs that they already hold without appreciating that this is so. Consequently, in order to satisfy McLaughlin's guideline about alternative beliefs, it seems that parents have not only to make sure that their children understand what certain beliefs involve and are aware that there are those who hold those beliefs, but also that their children appreciate that the beliefs in question conflict with what their parents and they themselves believe. Take, for example, the atheist's belief that there are no gods. Religious parents who try to satisfy McLaughlin's guidelines as far as this belief is concerned will have to try to make sure that their children understand this belief, that they are aware that it is held by some people, and that it conflicts with beliefs that they and their parents hold. Or suppose the parents in question are Jewish; then, in order to satisfy McLaughlin's guideline about alternative beliefs, they will have to inform their children about, say, Hinduism and other alternative systems of religious beliefs to their own, they will have to try to get their children to understand such beliefs, they will have to make their children realise that such beliefs are held by lots of other people, and they will have to try to get their children to appreciate in what way these various systems of belief conflict with what they share and regard as true.

Given the diversity of religious beliefs as well as atheistic and agnostic positions, complying with McLaughlin's guideline about alternative beliefs could prove very demanding. But suppose religious parents go some way along the route he prescribes and get their children to come to understand some alternative beliefs, to recognise that those beliefs are held by many others, and to appreciate that those beliefs conflict with the beliefs they hold and share. Such success prompts the question: what propositional attitude or attitudes will these parents who are trying to follow McLaughlin's recommendations want their children to have towards these alternative beliefs? And to this question we might add: and how will they want their children to regard those who believe in these alternative beliefs? The answers, I suggest, are that they will want their children to believe that the beliefs in question are false and that those who believe them are mistaken.

No doubt some readers will find these answers disquieting and some will say that if these answers are correct, then the kind of upbringing we are examining has an illiberal feel to it. But what alternative answers could there be? Suppose the religious parents we are considering want their children to believe the alternative views that they make them aware of. This would mean that they would want their children to have inconsistent beliefs. Now since McLaughlin lays great stress on parents being committed to developing children who can think rationally,[22] clearly parents who want their children to hold inconsistent beliefs would not be following his guidelines.

Another possibility, and one that might be thought to have something of a liberal feel about it, is that the parents we have been considering will want their children to be temporarily open-minded about alternative beliefs, temporarily open-minded in the sense of not thinking the alternatives true or false at the moment, but being prepared to take an autonomous decision about them later. But can what such parents want for their children be regarded as rational? Can it be thought rational to believe a proposition and to be aware of its negation and to appreciate that what one is aware of conflicts with what one believes, and yet to be open-minded about it while continuing to believe what one originally believed? Surely rational thought cannot be reconciled with being open-minded about a proposition whilst appreciating that it contradicts or is inconsistent with what one believes. This, of course, is not to deride open-mindedness; it is simply to acknowledge that open-mindedness about a proposition requires open-mindedness about its negation. To be open-minded about atheism requires one to be open-minded about theism as well.

Where people fail to meet this requirement, we will look for some special explanation in terms of their failing to understand what they are open-minded about or in terms of their failing to appreciate that what they are open-minded about conflicts with what they believe and so on. However, in the type of upbringing favoured by McLaughlin, in which children are to appreciate alternatives as alternatives, there should be no such failures. All of which means, I take it, that the parents we are considering, in so far as they are committed to rationality, will not want their children to be open-minded about alternative beliefs.

It could also be pointed out that there is a danger in bringing up a child to believe a set of beliefs while encouraging him or her to be open-minded about alternatives. It is that the child might start to view his beliefs and what conflicts with them as not in conflict at all, but just as matters or expressions of personal or social preference. In this way encouraging open-mindedness and discouraging the child from reaching what is a logical consequence of the beliefs he or she holds is to encourage a slide into relativism. And this is a danger which, I suspect, may be encountered in the New R.E., in multicultural education and in other educational ventures where children are made aware of a system of beliefs which may conflict with their own. For in such ventures children may be discouraged from reaching what is a logical consequence of their holding the beliefs they do and, instead, they may be encouraged to be open-minded about alternative beliefs.[23] If we were to label the error involved here, we might call it the fallacy of tolerance. It is the fallacy of refraining from concluding that beliefs held by others are wrong or that certain people are mistaken when such conclusions are a logical consequence of one's position.[24] And if the parents McLaughlin is concerned with were to encourage open-mindedness about alternative beliefs, they would be encouraging their children to commit this fallacy.

In view of the foregoing, we may claim that McLaughlin does not want religious parents to bring up their children to believe alternative beliefs or to be open-minded about them. Instead, as was proposed earlier, he wants them to bring up their children to believe that the alternatives are false and that those who hold them are mistaken. This may seem less liberal than his guidelines might have suggested; for he might have been understood as maintaining that while a child might be brought up to hold certain beliefs and to be aware of alternatives, these alternatives should remain unjudged and unassessed until the child is in a position to reflect on them in an informed and autonomous way. Yet, as we have seen, this is not the route McLaughlin's guidelines prescribe. As for whether McLaughlin realised the full import of his recommendations about alternative beliefs, I am not sure. What we can be sure about is that his concern that children be made aware of alternative beliefs and his concern for rationality mean that he is maintaining that children be brought up to treat alternatives not as options awaiting assessment, but as alternatives about which certain propositional attitudes are required.

Should we, however, support the suggestion that this treatment of alternatives within a child's upbringing ought to be seen as something less than liberal? In other words, should we reply to the question raised earlier by maintaining that what McLaughlin is actually recommending as far as alternative beliefs are concerned should not be seen as a liberal feature of a child's upbringing? If we are to answer in the affirmative, presumably this is because what is being recommended violates a liberal and, possibly, an important liberal principle. Such a principle might be some kind of stricture against one's thinking others are wrong unless one has good reasons for reaching such a conclusion, which, as a prescription for parents might become the advice to avoid bringing up any child to think that others are mistaken unless that child has good reason for so concluding.[25] This advice might be thought of as combining respect for reason and a sort of deference to others, possibly based on the idea that if others believe something, then such a belief might be worth holding or, at least, should not be dismissed without informed and reasoned consideration. Of course, children acquire beliefs without grounds or reasons. In fact, education and learning have to start this way. So, if parents are to discourage children from committing the fallacy of tolerance, it may seem inevitable that they will be failing to comply with the liberal prescription for parents that we have just spelt out. Perhaps this is why such a prescription needs to be taken as a *prima facie* principle, in which case we are into the debate of whether there are good enough reasons for religious parents to override such a principle and follow McLaughlin's guidelines. But this is a debate I do not want to enter, for all I have wanted to do in this section is to show where a concern to make children aware of alternatives coupled with a concern for rationality leads, and to reveal that this feature of McLaughlin's case might not be as liberal as some may have thought.

Just in case it is felt that my inquiries, in a manner of speaking, have been too one-sided, I should add that what has been said in this section can, with appropriate changes, also be said about parents who bring up their children to be atheists and who are concerned with making their children aware of alternatives and with rationality. Agnostic parents might be a little more difficult to deal with. If there are agnostic parents who believe that it can never be rational to adopt either an atheistic or a theistic position, then if they support the concerns just mentioned, they will bring up their children to believe that atheists and theists who think that reason is on their side are mistaken and always will be. Other agnostic parents might believe that as things stand at present it is not rational to adopt either an atheistic or a theistic position and, given that they support similar concerns, they will bring up their children to believe that atheists and theists who think reason is on their side are mistaken; but, unlike the agnostic parents previously mentioned, they could teach their children to be on the look out for new arguments, new evidence and the like. And accusations of subjecting their children to upbringings that have an illiberal feature might be levelled against these atheist and agnostic parents. Some critics might even claim that giving children such upbringings will severely impair the possibility of achieving the kind of liberal goal mentioned at the outset.[26] Such a claim might also be made about the kind of upbringing McLaughlin supports, and the question of whether or not his guidelines will lead to the type of liberal goal he has in mind is what I now want to consider.

3 Beliefs and their persistence

Can we attack McLaughlin's case on the grounds that he is encouraging indoctrination?[27] Well, if we were to argue along the following lines, it might look as though we were advancing a powerful criticism of his case: the strong kind of religious upbringing McLaughlin favours will indoctrinate children and since, as McLaughlin himself agrees,[28] indoctrination involves developing unshakable beliefs, his recommendations will not be successful because they will not lead to the development of those who will eventually decide on their religious commitments for themselves. But is this argument as forceful as it might appear at first sight? For a start we may note, as Callan has done,[29] that it is surely mistaken to think of unshakable belief as a condition of indoctrination; for there is nothing contradictory in talking about someone who was indoctrinated into a set of beliefs subsequently ceasing to hold those beliefs.[30] Similarly, I do not think we are necessarily wasting our time arguing with people over beliefs with which they have been indoctrinated; our gains, if gains there be, may be small, but there is nothing inconsistent in the idea of such gains being made.

Still, even if unshakability or permanence of belief is not a necessary condition of indoctrination, it might be maintained, as I have done elsewhere,[31] that indoctrination involves the production of a certain effect, and that this consists of a reluctance to change even in the face of arguments and reasons to which no response is forthcoming or in the face of arguments and evidence which, to an outsider, may seem overwhelming. In fact, we may see the strength of this reluctance as a measure of the extent to which a person has been indoctrinated, and, after all, a satisfactory account of indoctrination is one that will allow us to explicate the idea that there are degrees of indoctrination and that one person can be more deeply indoctrinated than another.[32] So, although we might abandon the unshakability condition, if we see some degree of reluctance to change as a condition of indoctrination, we might continue to criticise McLaughlin's case on the basis that his recommendations will lead to the indoctrination of children which, since it involves a reluctance to change, will obviously prevent subsequent autonomous reflection and assessment. However, what should be remembered here is that 'indoctrination' is an extremely contested concept, and any accusation employing it may well be contested, with the result that the accusation could lose much of its force. Furthermore, it might be difficult to press home the kind of criticism we have outlined, a criticism whose central premise is simply that a necessary condition of indoctrination is that the recipient acquires a belief which he or she is reluctant to change even in the face of good opposing reasons, counter-examples and so on. For what is being maintained is that a certain effect is a necessary condition of indoctrination, and what we should bear in mind is that no method or approach or process or upbringing, unless defined as such, can guarantee the achievement of such an effect, and, therefore, it is difficult to see how we can accuse McLaughlin of prescribing what is a sufficient condition of indoctrination.

Nevertheless, despite weaknesses in the line of reasoning we have been exploring, I do not think we should abandon our concern with the effects of a strong religious upbringing, though rather than become embroiled in the topic and literature of indoctrination, I want instead to direct attention to an idea which has a long history. It is to be found in Plato's claim:

> the first step . . . is always what matters most, particularly when we are dealing with those who are young and tender. That is the time when they are easily moulded and when any impression we choose to make leaves a permanent mark.[33]

This idea might also be thought to be endorsed by Rousseau's remark:

> The chief harm which results from the monstrous ideas of God which are instilled into the minds of children is that they last all their life long, and as men they understand no more of God than they did as children.[34]

In addition, this would seem to underpin such sayings as 'The child is father of the man', and it receives considerable support from many psychologists and psychoanalysts, who see childhood as formative. The idea in question is that early beliefs, the beliefs we grow up with, especially, some might say, the beliefs we share with our parents or with those who bring us up, have a tendency to stick, or, paraphrasing Plato, the dye of early learning tends to be fast. But if we were asked to explain why early beliefs have this tendency, what sort of explanation would we advance? Given that early beliefs may vary from person to person, the explanation, I take it, is not that these beliefs are so reasonable that they are likely to survive subsequent informed, and autonomous inquiry. Indeed, part of what seems to be at issue here is that these beliefs are able to resist coming under the microscope of such inquiries. In fact, I would suggest that in looking for an explanation of the phenomenon of the persistence of early beliefs, we should move away from matters to do with reasonableness and epistemic status and turn to factors which are external to the conscious mental operations of the reasoning inquirer. Employing an idea raised earlier, it could be further suggested that where we have to have recourse to such explanations, that is where, for adequacy's sake, we have to explain people's beliefs in terms, say, of their upbringing or schooling or their attitudes and dispositions in terms of genetics or potty-training or maternal deprivation, then we are employing a mode of explanation which is indicative of heteronomy. This is why we may claim that the phenomenon of the persistence of early beliefs is indicative of the heteronomous side of our make-up. And in keeping with this claim we may argue that a religious upbringing of the kind favoured by McLaughlin will not enhance a person's chances of subsequent autonomous reflection on and assessment of those religious beliefs acquired in and through that upbringing. This is not to say that such an upbringing will render this type of reflection and assessment impossible. It is simply to emphasise that there is a tendency for early beliefs to stick, and that such beliefs are ones that it seems difficult for their holders to examine in an autonomous way. Consequently, parents who are committed to the type of liberal ideal we mentioned at the outset and who are genuinely concerned that their children should eventually reflect upon religious matters in an autonomous way and who do not want to be responsible for predetermining their children's subsequent religious stances would seem best advised to avoid subjecting their children to an upbringing which inculcates a particular set of religious beliefs. There again, it might be thought irrational for parents who accept that early beliefs tend to persist and who agree that a religious upbringing is likely to predetermine subsequent beliefs to be committed to McLaughlin's approach and his goal. We can say this because it is irrational for people to aim for a goal while pursuing a course of action which they believe may well prevent their achieving that goal, unless, of course, they pursue some additional and compensating courses of action.

Another issue that might be worth raising here concerns a more general matter than the particular phenomenon we have been considering. I say 'more general' because it does not focus on the beliefs of childhood but deals with beliefs in general, and this matter, which we can call the persistence of beliefs, is that people tend to be reluctant to change their beliefs. Often it seems that people need what they regard as good reasons for abandoning what they believe even when they lack good reason for believing what they do; that they believe something would appear, from their point of view, to constitute a *prima facie* case for continuing to believe it. Given this phenomenon, then if one wants individuals to take the kind of reasoned decision about a host of competing views, we should avoid developing in them a commitment to a particular set of those views.

There is a third phenomenon I want to mention and we may call it the persistence of important beliefs. Religious beliefs occupy a most important place in the cognitive and the practical life of the believer; they influence how he or she perceives much of the world and they determine much of what he or she does or thinks should be done. Now beliefs of this kind – and this is what I mean by the persistence of important beliefs – are those which are difficult to dislodge.[35] Furthermore, such a phenomenon, we may suggest, is not to be accounted for in terms of intentions or, at least, it is not to be accounted for in these terms if we wish to continue to support the position on the intentionality of belief outlined above. In other words we may maintain that people do not decide to stick with their religious beliefs because they feel they would be unhappy or directionless without them any more than someone may decide to believe he is popular because this will make him or her feel good. Nevertheless, our important beliefs tend to persist, and alternative ideas are often dismissed just because they are alternatives, or they are scrutinised for errors, and even when none is found we insist, 'There must be something wrong with that idea', or, like believers in a good god or gods who encounter the problem of evil, we intone 'It's inexplicable'. Faced with such a phenomenon, talk of faith rather than belief may not seem out of place, though whatever the description, given this phenomenon, parents who equip their children with a set of religious beliefs are equipping them with what may well persist. The fact is that we do not seem to treat, or be able to treat, our important beliefs as Popperians treat scientific hypotheses; life stances are not things we easily discard and replace with a new model.

It could be suggested that the persistence of beliefs which underpin our life stances, such as religious beliefs, can be explained in terms of those beliefs forming the frameworks within which inquiry and assessment take place, and, as a result, they remain immune to, or above, our reflections and decisions. Now there is no doubt that religious beliefs do form such frameworks for many inquiries, but the point we are making in drawing attention to the persistence of important beliefs is that beliefs which may often provide such frameworks, and might in this respect be thought of as important, have a tendency to persist even when the spotlight of inquiry focuses on them. There may, of course, be an important psychological or ethological issue involved here. It could be that to function effectively people require a set of ideas which occupy a position of some permanence.[36] Still, this explanatory territory is not an area we need explore. All we need emphasise is that this third phenomenon, like the other two we have outlined, could impair the success of McLaughlin's strategy.

In the light of the foregoing we may argue that without talking about indoctrination we can nevertheless consider the effects of McLaughlin's prescription and, on the strength of the phenomena we have described, we may criticise his case. We can point out that given those phenomena, bringing up children to hold certain religious beliefs might well prevent them from subsequently engaging in the kind of autonomous and reasoned reflection that is McLaughlin's goal. In response McLaughlin could argue that people are not prone to the phenomena we have described, though this might leave him open to the charge of operating with an overly rational picture of people. On the other hand he might insist that his guidelines are designed to compensate for the various empirical aspects of belief we have been describing. But it is difficult to see in what way bringing up children to believe that alternatives are false will achieve this. Indeed, the phenomena we have been considering would indicate that the belief that alternatives are false will also be difficult to dislodge, and this will compound the problem and further threaten the achievement of the liberal ideal. McLaughlin could add that we should also remember his insistence that parents should bring up their own children with the understanding that one day they will have to decide about religious issues for themselves. But even if parents try to follow this recommendation, how effective will their endeavours be when they are up against the various tendencies we have outlined? In fact, what might be worth bearing in mind here is that what makes people question their beliefs is doubt, not the injunction to question them. Of course, lots of experiences and encounters and more besides might make a person doubt, but there seems little in McLaughlin's guidelines that would turn believers into doubting Thomases, let alone into free-thinking metaphysical speculators.

There is what many will regard as a tension between a strong religious upbringing and the liberal ideal of autonomous reflection and assessment, and it is a tension which, as I hope we have shown in this section, may be explicated without having to pursue arguments concerned with indoctrination. As to whether similar tensions are to be found in cases where parents subject their children to atheistic or agnostic upbringings, I think the answer might be in the negative. My reason is that an atheistic or agnostic position is not, in our sense, as important as a religious one, in that a religious position, unlike an atheistic or agnostic one, may well provide a variety of frameworks within which social and moral issues are to be assessed and judged. After all, there is no such thing as an atheistic position on, say, abortion, adultery, sex before marriage, the roles of men and women, the upbringing of children, what is not to be eaten, or how one should spend certain days, but many religions provide frameworks within which these and other issues are to be discussed and decided upon. If we accept that a criterion for the importance of beliefs is their influence and pervasiveness,[37] religious beliefs might be seen as more important than a belief in atheism or agnosticism, and given that important beliefs tend to stick, we can see why one can argue that religious beliefs might prove more persistent than many other beliefs. This is not to deny that tensions exist between the liberal ideal and atheistic and agnostic upbringing. It is rather to suggest that stronger tensions are more likely to exist when the upbringing is of a strong religious kind.

Perhaps, then, the message of this section is this: upbringings tend to be influential, but some are more likely to be influential than others. Or, pursuing a similar point: parents are often responsible for what their children subsequently believe, and some are more likely to be responsible than others.

So far we have raised doubts about whether, if followed, McLaughlin's recommendations will lead to the type of goal he has in mind. Yet, readers with a more practical approach to the world and its problems may suggest that there is what they see as a more basic doubt here. It is, in advertising terms, whether there is even a market for McLaughlin's recommendations. This is the next issue I want to consider.

4 Appeal and understanding

Will McLaughlin's prescriptions attract any followers? As one of my students, Jo Maurice, remarked, 'Surely religious parents won't be very much interested in McLaughlin's advice. They will be more concerned that their children become believers than with their children taking autonomous decisions and possibly ceasing to believe.' Now, clearly, if all religious parents thought faith more important than autonomy and were not prepared to run the risk of autonomous rejection, then we might argue that McLaughlin's prescriptions would have no followers. However, some faiths or creeds might embody the view that the benefits of being a believer only accrue to believers who have autonomously reflected and decided. Parents who are committed to such a faith or creed will value autonomy as a means, but they need not value it is an end. In this respect they might be thought of as differing from the liberal, for the liberal, we may suggest, values autonomy as some kind of end, though for all this the religious parents we have described, in so far as they value the instrumentality of religious autonomy, will be concerned that their children's upbringings pave the way for such autonomy and do not determine their children's subsequent beliefs on religious matters.

These considerations might be taken as indicating how religious requirements and autonomy can be reconciled, and McLaughlin has also defended the idea that such a reconciliation is possible. Thus, in reply to the question 'must not parents who are religious believers value *faith* rather than *autonomy* in their children?'[38] (McLaughlin's italics) he says:

> The answer is that the conflict between faith and autonomy in the religious faith of a liberal is a false one. From such a position, what is demanded is autonomous religious faith based on appropriate reasoning and evaluation, not mere lip-service or conditioning. . . . Religious liberal parents may well hope that their child's eventual autonomy will be exercised in favour of faith; but in the logic of their own religious – as well as liberal – position, this must remain a hope rather than a requirement.[39]

The phrase 'the logic of their own religious . . . position' would seem to be of importance here. Presumably it refers to the demands of a religious position in which autonomy has the kind of status and significance it enjoys within a liberal system of values. Looking at it in this way we may understand McLaughlin to be maintaining that there will be no conflict because religious liberal parents will have a faith which is compatible with their liberal principles and, in particular, they will have a faith which embodies the very kind of respect for autonomy that one associates with a liberal position. What this means, I take it, is that religious liberal parents will see autonomy as some kind of end in itself; they will accept, as McLaughlin puts it, that 'the development of personal and moral autonomy is a fundamental value',[40] and so they will differ from religious parents who look upon autonomy as having only instrumental value.

This type of defence could be thought to beg various questions about what faiths are compatible with liberalism, what faiths share the liberal's regard for autonomy, and why, if religion and liberalism are so compatible, they have, as history reveals, so often been at loggerheads. Yet rather than dwell on these sorts of questions, let us consider what the preceding inquiries could be taken as showing, and this is that while religious parents who are more concerned with faith than autonomy and who fear the possibility of autonomous rejection will fight shy of McLaughlin's prescriptions, some religious parents might not. Those, for instance, who place an instrumental value on autonomy together with those McLaughlin calls 'religious liberal parents' might be thought to be those who would follow his advice. But will they? Suppose they believe that early beliefs tend to stick or that beliefs in general tend to stick or that important beliefs are difficult to dislodge, or suppose that they fear that for some other reason a strong religious upbringing could determine subsequent religious stances. Given the high value they place on autonomy, they will surely try to find an alternative to McLaughlin's preferred kind of strong religious upbringing – unless, that is, they believe that awareness of alternatives and believing they are false along with the emphasis that one day their children will have to assess religious matters for themselves will overcome these difficulties. And few, I think, will believe that. In short, it seems that not many religious parents will be attracted by McLaughlin's case. Those who do not value autonomy too highly will not be attracted, and many of those who value it highly will not be attracted because of worries about the effects of a strong religious upbringing.

In response McLaughlin and his supporters might claim that our inquiries into who will or should follow his advice have overlooked the important aspect of understanding and when this is taken into account all who are concerned about informed and autonomous assessment of a religion or religious matters will want their children to be subject to a strong religious upbringing, even atheists! Bizarre as this claim is, it seems to follow from an argument which maintains that a strong religious upbringing is necessary for a certain kind of religious understanding. This argument, which we may call the argument for understanding, is outlined by McLaughlin as follows:

If an account of the nature of the religious domain can be given which stresses the significance of *practice* to religious meaning and understanding and the importance for autonomous choice of being 'on the inside' of a given religion then a liberal parent could argue that giving a religious upbringing is in fact giving the child an experience which will enable him to evaluate religion for himself in a significant way. This could be linked to the point that it is impossible to develop an adequate understanding of religion *in abstractio*, but that this can only be achieved through a particular religion. So it might be argued, far from hindering the child's capacity for autonomy in this field, the provision of an appropriate form of religious upbringing is in fact facilitating it.[41]

Presented like this it may look as though McLaughlin is merely outlining a possible line of reasoning, not advancing an argument to which he is committed. However, we should note that McLaughlin puts this argument forward as one he thinks should be advanced[42] and that in his reply to Callan he maintains that one of the inadequacies of a religious upbringing that is weaker than the one he prefers is that it will not equip children with the understanding necessary for the desired kind of reflection and assessment,[43] the implication being that 'the significance for understanding of experiencing religion "from the inside" is considerable,' and that only something like McLaughlin's preferred strong religious upbringing will provide sufficient understanding for informed reflection and decision-making.[44] It seems, therefore, that the argument for understanding is one to which McLaughlin is committed.

But what does such an argument involve? It could be suggested that judging from the passage quoted above the argument for understanding has a specific and a general form. In its specific form it maintains: children can only understand *a* religion sufficiently well for subsequent informed and autonomous reflection and assessment if they are brought up to believe in that religion, participate in its practices, rituals, etc., that is if they receive a strong religious upbringing in that faith or creed. This type of argument has one of the bizarre consequences mentioned earlier, that atheists who want their children to be in a position to decide for themselves about *a* religion should bring up their children to believe in that religion! If this is not reason enough for rejecting this argument, we can point out that the specific argument might be taken as insulting many converts, including St Paul and the disciples of Jesus, and it could support the distressing accusation that those who turn to a religion after an atheistic or agnostic upbringing will of necessity lack the cognitive wherewithal to make an informed decision about that religion. Of course, these latter criticisms treat the specific argument as claiming that a strong religious upbringing in a religion is necessary to *any person* if that person is to have enough understanding to take an informed and autonomous decision about that religion at any time of his or her life, whereas all a supporter of the specific argument may wish to claim is that giving a child a strong religious upbringing in a religion is necessary if that child is to acquire the requisite understanding about that religion to be in a position to make an informed decision about that religion at some early stage in his or her life, at the age, say, of 17 or 18. Yet this refinement still leads to a bizarre consequence concerning atheist parents, and it raises the question of why belief should be necessary for a 17-year-old's understanding but not for a 37-year-old's. There again, and this might be thought particularly important to our inquiry, McLaughlin cannot accept this refinement, for he accepts that children can grow up to acquire the requisite degree of understanding for informed decisions about alternative faiths and creeds without receiving a strong religious upbringing in them all, and presumably he accepts that children can acquire this degree of understanding before they reach their late teens, for he seems to be of the opinion that this level of understanding can be achieved while children are under some sort of parental control.[45] In fact the specific form of the argument for understanding, whether refined or otherwise, renders impossible the very kind of goal about informed and autonomous assessment of alternatives that McLaughlin wants parents to aim for. In brief, it is not an argument he would endorse.

What, then, of the general form of the argument for understanding? This argument goes as follows: children can only understand religion sufficiently well for subsequent informed and autonomous reflection and assessment about religious matters, including decisions about where they stand with regard to some faiths or creeds, if they have received a strong religious upbringing in a faith or creed. If this argument is understood as claiming that such an upbringing is necessary for everyone if they are to acquire the requisite level of understanding, it would clearly be insulting to many converts and to those who have turned to religion despite having non-religious backgrounds. It could also be insulting to many who, through study and dedication, rather than background, have come to understand religious matters. Perhaps, then, this argument should be understood in a refined way, as just claiming what is necessary if children are to reach the requisite level of understanding by their late teens. But does this argument not also lead to the bizarre consequence that atheist parents who want their children to be in a position by their late teens to take an informed decision about religious matters should ensure that their children receive a strong religious upbringing? And is this type of argument not one that atheists and agnostics might also employ? Could atheists not maintain that to have an informed appreciation of atheism by their late teens, children need to understand atheism from 'the inside', and that confronting life as finite, perceiving the universe as bereft of a divine *logos*, seeing millions of people as having a need for a false metaphysic, and appreciating that man is on his own when it comes to solving problems, cannot be adequately understood *in abstractio*? As for agnostics, could they not present a similar case, albeit one concerned with the necessity of appreciating doubt from 'the inside' and about the impossibility of adequately appreciating their gnawing scepticism *in abstractio*? I must admit I am not convinced by these lines of reasoning, and neither is McLaughlin, at least as far as atheism and agnosticism are concerned, for his thesis requires him to accept that a child can take an informed and autonomous decision about these positions by, say, his or her late teens, without being brought up as an atheist or agnostic. This means that if he supports the refined version of the general argument, he must regard the religious domain as in some way unique, as requiring a strong upbringing in order that the requisite degree of understanding can be achieved by a certain stage. Some might object to this view on the grounds that religions do not constitute a homogeneous domain and that the understanding achieved within one faith or creed need not be transferable to or illuminate other faiths or creeds or religion in general. Yet those who would raise this objection might be thought to have misunderstood the argument under consideration, for the refined version of the general argument only maintains that a strong religious upbringing in a faith or creed is necessary for informed and autonomous decisions by a certain stage, not that such an upbringing is sufficient. Still, if the religious domain lacks homogeneity, why should a strong religious upbringing be necessary to a child's reaching a certain level of understanding about religious matters in general by a certain stage in his or her life? There again, if, as this refined argument concedes, adults can acquire sufficient understanding for informed choice without a strong religious upbringing, why do children require such an upbringing if they are to reach the appropriate level of understanding by a certain age? If a defender of the refined argument were to answer in terms of adults possessing intellectual advantages over children, then we might respond by suggesting that not all children might be disadvantaged in this respect or these respects. This being so, the refined argument would seem to require further refinement, so that it concerns itself with what some children (the less able?) need. But, then, what would happen if extra resources were devoted to the task of trying to raise these children to the level of those who do not need a strong religious upbringing? The answer, I take it, would be that even more children would not need a strong religious upbringing. All of which further discredits what, as we have seen, would seem to be an already discredited version of the argument for understanding.

What I have been considering is an argument that presents a strong religious upbringing as necessary for the kind of informed assessment that is part of the liberal goal. I have considered four versions of this argument and found them all wanting. Other versions may be waiting in the wings, but it is difficult to see how any version of this argument could avoid or withstand the various objections I have raised, and I think I can safely conclude that such an argument ought to be rejected. I can also point out that some versions of the argument for understanding render impossible the kind of liberal goal that McLaughlin wants parents to aim for.

Some concluding observations

In this paper I have tried to show that the type of approach prescribed by McLaughlin need not be successful in achieving the liberal goal at which he wants parents to aim. Making children aware of alternatives within the context of strong religious upbringing, together with a concern for rationality, is not a matter of presenting a shop window of positions that are not to be believed or disbelieved till later. It is to present those alternative positions as false and those who believe them as mistaken – entitled to their own views and possibly kind and decent people – but mistaken. In addition we should note that more phenomena than indoctrination may result in the persistence of beliefs and get in the way of autonomous assessment and reflection, and that the beliefs that may persist could include not just the positive religious beliefs which a child has been brought up to accept, but also various beliefs about the falsity of alternatives. Furthermore, we may have serious doubts about whether McLaughlin's case will have much appeal even amongst those who might be thought likely to warm to its reassurances. Still, having said that, perhaps we should add that there may be some parents who will find McLaughlin's recommendations reassuring, these being religious parents who in the past may have felt the odd twinge of guilt about bringing up their children within a particular faith or creed. They may now feel that providing they make their children aware of alternatives and emphasise that one day their children will have to decide for themselves, they can proceed with a light heart and their customary heavy hand. In this way McLaughlin's thesis could well serve as a green light to the very kinds of parents that he and those who share his liberal ideals should be most concerned about.[46] As for the defence of a strong religious upbringing in terms of its being necessary for understanding, maybe we ought to add to our previous criticisms that we should be on our guard against theories which treat belief as necessary for understanding. Such theories imply that disbelievers do not understand and that disbelievers do not disagree with believers, since for disagreement there has to be agreement about meanings. Now not only may we reject such a conclusion and the theories that lead to it on the grounds, for example, that atheists and theists *do* disagree, we may also be frightened that such an approach to understanding could lead to a kind of isolationism with believers in a faith or creed accepting that anyone who holds alternative views does not understand their faith or creed. Developing on this, we may note that the liberal view of the good society is of a society in which there is discussion, argument and dialogue not just within but between different groups. Theories which see belief as necessary for understanding threaten this picture at a logical level and, in terms of their social influence, they would encourage people to dismiss the views of 'disagreers' and outsiders and so discourage the debates and the interchange and dissemination of ideas which are part of the fabric of the liberal society. Another strand of the liberal view of the good or ideal state is one in which ideas are refined and truth approached through disagreement, discussion and debate. However, theories which regard belief as necessary for understanding render disagreement impossible and so encourage the ossification of ideas. For a variety of reasons, therefore, it would seem that such theories are not ones which liberals will readily endorse.

Finally, I should point out that I am well aware that this paper might be thought to raise more questions than it pursues and tackles. 'What type of upbringing is best suited to achieving the liberal goal?'[47] and 'If the psychology of belief is as we have described it, how attainable is the liberal goal?' are just two of those questions. However, for much of this paper I have been mainly concerned with looking into and exploring a particular thesis. It is a thesis which maintains there need be nothing odd in parents claiming that while they want their child to 'choose' his or her own religion or to be an atheist or agnostic, they are making sure that their child is brought up within their faith, holding their religious beliefs and looking at the world from their point of view. Our immediate response to such a claim would probably be that the parents were being hypocritical or disingenuous, for we would be likely to suspect that they have no desire for their child to engage in subsequent autonomous reflection and assessment. But suppose they were most concerned that their child engage in such activities. What would our reaction be then? We would probably say or, at least, think that the parents in question were misguided, for they are embarking on a course of action that seems likely to prevent their child from getting to the desired goal. Much of what I have been trying to do in this paper is to explain why they are misguided, and why their following the sorts of guidelines prescribed by McLaughlin will not provide the necessary re-direction.

Notes and references

1 J.J. Rousseau (1974) *Émile*, p. 223 (London, Dent).
2 J.S. Mill (1965) Inaugural address, in J.B. Schneewind (ed.) *Mill's Essays on Literature and Society*, p. 399 (New York, Collier-Macmillan). It might be suggested here that Mill, in contrast to Rousseau, would have favoured a wider range of options from which a 'choice' was to be made, for while Rousseau seems to be concerned with religious sects, Mill would have wanted atheism and agnosticism and non-theistic perspectives to be among the options. However, I make no claims about there being exact similarity between Rousseau's and Mill's recommendations in this area, though I do feel that their emphasis on an upbringing or education for subsequent 'choice' is worth drawing attention to. We may also note that the debate between McLaughlin and Callan (see below) seems to have concerned itself with an upbringing for a subsequent 'choice' from amongst the wider range of options favoured by Mill.
3 Even if there is nothing inconsistent in the idea of someone receiving a religious upbringing and subsequently deciding in an autonomous way where he or she stands on religious matters, what may worry the liberal is that such an upbringing may lessen the chance of such decisions being taken. Put this way it may seem that the problem we are to consider is an empirical one (see T.H. McLaughlin (1985) 'Religion, upbringing and liberal values: a rejoinder to Eamonn Callan', *Journal of Philosophy of Education*, 19, p. 124), but this, I would contend, does not mean that it is an issue on which the philosopher need remain silent.
4 See T.H. McLaughlin (1984) 'Parental rights and the religious upbringing of children', *Journal of Philosophy of Education*, 18, pp. 75–83; E Callan (1985) 'McLaughlin on parental rights', *Journal of Philosophy of Education*, 19, pp. 111–18; and T.H. McLaughlin (1985) 'Religion, upbringing and liberal values: a rejoinder to Eamonn Callan', *Journal of Philosophy of Education*, 19, pp. 119–27. It should be noted that the issues explored and debated by McLaughlin and Callan, and this seems true of other inquiries in this area, appear to be couched in terms of two parents bringing up their child or children. Yet clearly those issues and debates could be couched in terms of a single parent bringing up his or her child or children or in terms of a guardian or guardians bringing up a child or children. For simplicity's sake, but for no other reason, I have gone along with the usual way of couching the problems and issues in this area.
5 T.H. McLaughlin (1985), p. 120.
6 See, for example, R.S. Downie and E. Telfer (1971) 'Autonomy', *Philosophy*, 16, pp. 293–301.
7 E. Telfer (1975) 'Autonomy as an educational ideal II', in S.C. Brown (ed.) (1975) *Philosophers Discuss Education*, p. 21 (Basingstoke, Macmillan).
8 Suppose a father realised his children were being persecuted because of his religious beliefs and suppose, try as he might, he could not stop himself revealing his religious beliefs. Might he not arrange to be treated by an indoctrinator or brainwasher so as to disbelieve the tenets of his faith or creed? And if the treatment were successful, could we not say that the father had chosen to believe what he believed as the result of the treatment?
9 See E. Telfer, *op. cit.*, p. 21.
10 See R.F. Dearden (1975) 'Autonomy as an educational ideal I', in S.C. Brown (ed.) (1975) *Philosophers Discuss Education*, pp. 7–8. See also R.F. Dearden (1968) *The Philosophy of Primary Education*, p. 46 (London, Routledge & Kegan Paul).

11 Dearden suggests: 'a person is "autonomous" to the degree that what he thinks and does cannot be explained without reference to his own activity of mind' (R.F. Dearden (1972) 'Autonomy and education', in R.F. Dearden, P.H. Hirst and R.S. Peters (eds) (1972) *Education and the Development of Reason*, p. 453 (London, Routledge & Kegan Paul). I would suggest that the word 'conscious' needs to be added here. Where we explain what a person does in terms of their unconscious, are we not saying that in this respect the person is heteronomous? (See P. Gardner 1985) 'The paradox of moral education: a reassessment', *Journal of Philosophy of Education*, 19, p. 42 and p. 47. Perhaps it also needs to be emphasised that the conscious mental activities that one is concerned with are those that the agent controls, but then it may look as if one's account of autonomy is becoming circular.

12 See R.F. Dearden (1975), pp. 8–9.

13 Of course, being heteronomous, like being autonomous, is something we can be to a greater or lesser extent, and in fact a person might be markedly autonomous in one area of his or her life and markedly heteronomous in another. An academic, for example, may be extremely autonomous in his academic pursuits and inquiries, and, yet, in his domestic affairs be very much under his mother's influence and follow her recommendations in this area of his life with little thought of assessment.

14 See J.P. White (1973) *Towards a Compulsory Curriculum*, especially p. 22 (London, Routledge & Kegan Paul).

15 See for example, T.H. McLaughlin (1985), pp. 120–1; and T.H. McLaughlin (1984), p. 81.

16 See, for example, M. Bonnett (1976) 'Authenticity, autonomy and compulsory curriculum', *Cambridge Journal of Education*, 6, p. 109. See also P. Gardner (1984) 'The compulsory curriculum and beyond: a consideration of some aspects of the educational philosophy of J.P. White', *Journal of Philosophy of Education*, 18, pp. 180–2.

17 Callan has maintained, 'It is important . . . to make a distinction between being brought up within a particular belief system, such as a religious or political creed, and being brought up in a family where one is merely exposed to the fact that one's parents adhere to certain beliefs' (E. Callan (1975), p. 112). The former type of upbringing being seen as a strong religious upbringing, the latter being seen as a weak religious upbringing. It seems to me that, in practice, the effects of a so-called weak religious upbringing might be very similar to the effects of a strong religious upbringing.

18 See, for example, T.H. McLaughlin (1984), p. 81; and T.H. McLaughlin (1985), pp. 120–1.

19 See, for example, T.H. McLaughlin (1985), p. 120.

20 *Ibid.*

21 *Op. cit.*, pp. 120–1.

22 See, for example, *op. cit.*, p. 121.

23 In this context it might be worth considering Jean Holm's claim: 'To encourage pupils to evaluate religions is incompatible with helping them to stand in other people's shoes' J. Holm (1982) 'The ethical value of religious education', in L.O. Ward (ed.) (1982) *The Ethical Dimension of the School Curriculum*, p. 155 (Swansea, Pineridge Press). If by this Holm wishes to be seen supporting some general thesis along the lines that deciding or concluding that a person's beliefs are mistaken is incompatible with understanding that person's point of view or appreciating how it affects their vision of the world or, perhaps, respecting their view, then surely she is mistaken; for there is no reason why it is impossible for me to understand and even respect those who would subscribe to such a general thesis or to appreciate how it affects and colours their view of, say, education, even though I believe they are mistaken. Equally, if Holm does subscribe to such a thesis, I see no reason why she cannot understand and respect my

position and appreciate its significance for me, even though she thinks it mistaken! Indeed, if understanding is a necessary condition of belief and disbelief, then it is difficult to see how one could defend the thesis that disbelief is incompatible with understanding. There again, appreciating the significance of a belief for someone is in no way threatened by accepting that that belief is false, nor need such an acceptance lead to disrespect or dismissiveness. There is after all quite a leap, including a move from facts to values, from finding something false to finding it fatuous, birdbrained or not worthy of any serious consideration. Of course, a defender of Holm's claim might point out that she is talking about those of school age. But if her claim does not hold for adults, why should it hold for those at school? Is it because young people are more likely to accept the principles that we ought never to try to appreciate the world from the point of view of those who have what we regard as false beliefs and that we should not respect those beliefs that we take to be false? If so, I would suggest that what is needed is some attempt to dissuade the young from subscribing to such unacceptable principles, rather than an attempt to dissuade them from appreciating where their other beliefs lead.

24 I am grateful to David Miller for suggesting the title 'the fallacy of tolerance' for this type of error.

25 Principles about what we ought not to believe, in so far as they seem to resemble principles about what actions we ought and ought not to perform, might be thought to lend support to the thesis that belief is intentional. However, if we oppose this thesis or even if we favour the less radical position on this issue outlined earlier, we may wish to suggest that principles about belief should be interpreted in such a way that they do not lend support to the thesis of intentionality. Thus, 'One ought not to think that others are wrong without good reason' might be understood as a recommendation to spend some time considering whether there are good grounds for thinking that someone else is wrong, and this, it may be noted, is something we could encourage children to do without compromising our position on the intentionality of belief.

26 In response to this it might be argued that if early beliefs persist (see Section 3), the second group of agnostic parents just mentioned seem most likely to achieve the kind of liberal goal we outlined at the start.

27 We can note the question of whether a religious upbringing need be indoctrinatory is one that occupies a prominent position in the inquiries of McLaughlin and Callan. See, for instance, T.H. McLaughlin (1984), pp. 77-8; E. Callan (1985), pp. 114–16; and T.H. McLaughlin (1985), p. 124.

28 See T.H. McLaughlin (1984), pp. 77–8. I take it we can safely infer from what he says here that McLaughlin goes along with the thesis that indoctrination involves producing an unshakable belief. We can also note that when he is criticised by Callan for accepting such a thesis (see below), McLaughlin does not argue that he has been misinterpreted. See T.H. McLaughlin (1985), p. 124.

29 See E. Callan (1985), p. 115.

30 See P. Gardner (1982) 'Indoctrination: a child-centred approach', *The Polytechnic Wolverhampton Faculty of Education Journal*, 1, pp. 2–3.

31 See *op. cit.*, pp. 2–5.

32 See *op. cit.*, p. 2.

33 Plato, *The Republic*, 377b.

34 J.J. Rousseau (1974), p. 222.

35 In speaking of important beliefs, I am only speaking of their importance relative to the person who holds them. I should also make it clear that I am not too happy about using 'important' in this context. 'Influential' and 'significant' are some of the terms I have considered using instead.

36 I am aware that there is another and what is in fact a more basic issue that might be

mentioned here, and this might be thought to be of a transcendental or presuppositional nature. It is that in order to reason, examine or speculate one needs to accept something, some principles, rules, fixed points and the like. In this respect, reasoning, speculating, even doubting, presuppose that the agent is committed to or accepts some ideas, concepts and so on; without them the thinker cannot function at all. However, the psychological or ethological matter that I mention in the text is based on a different line of reasoning to this transcendental or presuppositional issue. All I am suggesting in the text is that a human being may need a fairly permanent or settled body of beliefs in order to function effectively; too much change and doubt may leave him or her unsure and uncertain in his or her dealings with the world. And this is different from the more basic issue that the reasoner or inquirer needs a base, a set of ideas, etc., in order that reasoning and inquiry can be possible at all.

37 See note 35.

38 T.H. McLaughlin (1984), p. 79.

39 *Ibid.*

40 *Op. cit.*, p. 75.

41 *Op. cit.*, p. 82.

42 See *op. cit.*, p. 81.

43 See T.H. McLaughlin (1985), p. 122.

44 *Ibid.*

45 In fact as far as I can see there is nothing in his recommendations to suggest that McLaughlin would oppose what I have said here, though I should point out that I am not claiming that McLaughlin's view is that all parents on their own can be successful in their efforts to get their children to the requisite level of understanding by the time their children are in their late teens.

46 Although it was advanced in a different context it might be felt that this is a useful place to remind ourselves of William E. Connolly's observation that 'it is never in itself a sufficient argument against an idea to say that it can be misused' (W.E. Connolly (1983) *The Terms of Political Discourse*, 2nd edn, p. 144 (Oxford, Martin Robertson). Still, even if the parents we have just mentioned would be misusing McLaughlin's thesis, it may be well worth bearing in mind that such a thesis might readily lend itself to this kind of misuse.

47 Yet, while this question has not been tackled in any direct way, it could be suggested that given what was said earlier (see note 26), a certain kind of agnostic upbringing is best suited to the purpose of achieving the liberal goal.

7

(ii) PETER GARDNER ON RELIGIOUS UPBRINGING AND THE LIBERAL IDEAL OF RELIGIOUS AUTONOMY

Terence H. McLaughlin

In his article, 'Religious upbringing and the liberal ideal of religious autonomy'[1] Peter Gardner develops a series of challenging arguments against my claim that it is possible to reconcile a commitment to a central liberal value such as personal autonomy with an acknowledgement of the rights of parents to give their children a (certain sort of) religious upbringing: one where their children are brought up to have an initial determinate religious commitment, but one which is open to, and compatible with, the child's eventual achievement of autonomy.[2]

Gardner's attack on my argument contains a mixture of logical and empirical elements. His own view is that parents concerned with the development of the autonomy of their children should refrain from bringing them up to have an initial determinate religious commitment of any sort. Although he does not outline in any detail a positive account of the form of upbringing which he himself favours in relation to religion, Gardner claims that an agnostic or atheistic upbringing is less objectionable than a religious one as far as the development of autonomy is concerned, and concludes (although rather tentatively) that a certain sort of agnostic upbringing is the one best suited to the achievement of the liberal goal.[3]

In this article, I shall seek to defend my position against Gardner's attack and to show that he has over-stated the tensions between my account of religious upbringing and the liberal ideal. Indeed, I shall claim that certain elements of Gardner's attack, in particular his rather stark and impoverished account of what is involved in 'open-mindedness' and its development, are likely to constitute in themselves an obstacle to the realisation of crucial aspects of that ideal.

I shall adopt throughout the same sub-headings as those used by Gardner for the sections of his article, although for reasons of clarity I shall address the sections in a slightly different order at one point.

Source: *Journal of Philosophy of Education* Vol. 24. No. 1, 1990.

1 Beliefs, choice and autonomy

Gardner begins his article by raising two issues for clarification, neither of which I take significant issue with. The first involves calling into question a 'tendency' in discussions of autonomy (including mine) to regard – or perhaps, more accurately, to give the impression of regarding – beliefs as things we can (simply) *choose*. Gardner is rightly wary of such tendencies. The role of 'choice' in the context of belief has to be sensitively outlined so that the impression is not given that the person is engaging in wholly capricious acts of the will in relation to their beliefs, unconstrained by the demands of rational assessment, truth, etc.

Gardner offers the following account of the (normal) role of choice in the realm of belief: 'What we clearly can choose to do is to assess, examine, ponder, reflect and so on. We may not choose the outcome of our deliberations and, hence, we may not choose what we come to believe, but we can choose to deliberate'.[4] There is perhaps more to be said here about the role of choice and the will in relation both to belief in general[5] and to religious belief in particular.[6] But without entering into a detailed discussion of such matters, I agree that, unless important qualifications are supplied, 'choice' is a potentially misleading way of referring to the kind of judgement about belief that is the outcome of the process of reflection. The terms favoured by Gardner, 'reflection about' and 'assessment of' beliefs, rather than 'choice' of them, cover what is in fact implicit throughout my argument.[7]

The second issue raised by Gardner for clarification is the relationship between being autonomous and being informed. Gardner points out that the autonomous person need not, simply in virtue of being autonomous, be in possession (of well-grounded) information or knowledge about 'alternatives', 'opportunities' or 'possibilities' of various kinds, or be capable of rational decisions in relation to them. For Gardner, 'well-informed and autonomous' is not a tautology, and he seeks to underline this by favouring the conjunction of the terms 'autonomy' and 'well-informed'.[8] Once again, this clarification refers to assumptions that were tacitly contained within my article. 'Autonomy' *simpliciter* does not imply the possession by the person of a rationally grounded perspective on objects of choice, although a notion such as 'rational autonomy' clearly does.[9] It is the latter notion that is presupposed in my article. This is seen, for example, in the stress that I lay on reasoning, etc. throughout.

Since there are no real points of disagreement between Gardner and me on these issues, I turn now to more substantive points of dispute.

2 Beliefs and their persistence

One of the key elements in Gardner's critique of my position involves a claim about the negative *effects* of the sort of religious upbringing I discuss as far as the achievement of autonomy is concerned. Whilst wanting to avoid some of the difficulties involved in invoking the notion of indoctrination,[10] Gardner seeks to characterise the constraining effects of such an upbringing on the autonomy of children by appealing to the alleged (general) phenomenon of the 'persistence of beliefs'. He concludes that, in the light of this phenomenon, parents concerned with the development of the religious autonomy of their children should avoid the inculcation of any particular set of religious beliefs. To do otherwise is, on his view, to run a serious risk of predetermining the subsequent religious stances of the children.

A general claim about the 'persistence of beliefs' needs to be examined carefully. It is not clear that beliefs are, in themselves, the sorts of things which persist. For example, it is certainly not true of first person present tense beliefs such as 'There is a ball coming towards me'. We need therefore to look closely at Gardner's account of the three forms which he claims that 'persistence of beliefs' can take.

1   Persistence of *early* beliefs. Gardner claims that: 'early beliefs, the beliefs we grow up with, especially . . . the beliefs we share with our parents or with those who bring us up, have a tendency to stick . . . the dye of early learning tends to be fast'.[11] Gardner holds that this phenomenon is 'indicative of the heteronomous side of our make-up'.[12]

2   Persistence of beliefs *in general*. Gardner outlines this notion in this way: 'people tend to be reluctant to change their beliefs . . . that they believe something would appear, from their point of view, to constitute a *prima facie* case for continuing to believe it. Given this phenomenon, then if one wants individuals to take the kind of reasoned decision about a host of competing views, we should avoid developing in them a commitment to a particular set of those views.[13]

3   Persistence of *important* beliefs. Gardner writes: 'we do not seem to treat or to be able to treat our important beliefs like Popperians treat scientific hypotheses; life stances are not things we easily discard and replace with a new model.'[14] He takes religious beliefs to be examples of the 'important beliefs' he has in mind here: 'Religious beliefs occupy a most important place in the cognitive and the practical life of the believer; they influence how he or she perceives much of the world and they determine much of what he or she does or thinks should be done.'[15] For this reason, he continues, they tend to persist and alternative beliefs are either dismissed or not critically appraised in any serious way.

Gardner's argument at this point is formulated loosely and in rather a sweeping way. It gives rise to at least four interrelated categories of question. First, what is the character and explanation of the persistence that is being referred to here and in relation to which kinds of beliefs? ((1) (2) and (3) clearly contain beliefs of many different sorts.) Second, what is the justification offered for the claims about persistence? Third, is persistence of belief *per se* always to be seen as a bad thing? And, fourth, if the phenomenon is, as Gardner describes it, a very general one, will not any initial set of beliefs, and not just religious ones, prove an obstacle to the achievement of autonomy? Gardner does not, in my view, provide adequate answers to any of these questions.

An important preliminary point to make is that there is a (broad) category of basic beliefs, falling no doubt mainly under (1), persistence of early beliefs, where the character of the persistence has a fundamental and logical flavour. In relation to such beliefs, ordinary (as distinct from philosophical) doubt is out of place, and it is hard to see that the persistence of such beliefs could be either called into question or seen to be objectionable. The precise characterisation of this category gives rise to some complex questions, but perhaps for my purposes here I can sketch it roughly. It includes beliefs about what is logically self-evident and other basic beliefs which are fundamental in another way, if not strictly logically founded. For example, Quinton describes propositions such as 'the sun will rise tomorrow' as of a kind which 'only an epistemologist, in a state of occupational imbalance brought on by over-indulgence in hyperbolic scepticism, would regard as matters for reasonable doubt'.[16] Although it is true, he continues, that such beliefs 'rest on inductive generalizations which are necessarily not susceptible of complete verification,' it is reasonable for us to base our practical lives on beliefs of this kind since all such living depends upon judgements of probability of one sort or another.[17] In a similar vein, Anthony Kenny discusses a category of fundamental truths, such as the propositions that human beings sleep and die, which are unshakable in that there could never be a reason for disbelieving them which did not call into question the possiblity of there being such a thing as evidence at all.[18] Gardner seems to acknowledge that there is nothing objection-able in encouraging children to have persistent beliefs of this kind.[19] Presumably (2), persistence of beliefs in general, can also be seen as 'basic' in character, since it seems to be a requirement for the coherence necessary for human agency.[20] The 'basic' category is also expandable to include basic moral beliefs, although here the character of the fundamentality and the persistence might be thought to be rather different. Presumably, Gardner has no objection to children being brought up to have fairly persistent beliefs of a moral sort. For example, despite his suspicion in other writings of paternalism and compulsory curricula, Gardner makes exceptions in the case of moral beliefs and upbringing, and indeed other kinds of belief, on the basis of the kinds of harm that might otherwise result.[21]

What seems common to this (roughly delineated) category of basic beliefs is an element of *inescapability*, although the character of the inescapability needs to be sensitively and variously characterised in the light of the different kinds of beliefs involved. In relation to these 'basic beliefs' the four questions outlined earlier can receive an answer. First, with regard to the character of the persistence, this can be seen in the case of 'basic beliefs' to have a kind of fundamentality to it. It is important, however, to be wary of giving a (merely) causal account of this. There is, after all, nothing to prevent a person reflecting upon these persistent beliefs, even though, in some cases, they may well conclude that in calling such beliefs into question they are straining, in different ways, at the limits of what can be criticised. For practical purposes, too, it might be thought that encouraging such reflection in children might not be a priority, unless they were being introduced to philosophy.[22] It is nevertheless true that the persistence of such beliefs can be seen as rational in its general character. Second, there seems little difficulty in justifying claims that such beliefs do indeed persist in the vast majority of people, although the claims need to bear in mind the character of the persistence that is at issue. Third, the persistence of these beliefs as a result of their being held unreflectively can scarcely be seen in negative terms. Gardner seems to hold that the persistence of beliefs is *per se* a danger to autonomy and part of the 'heteronomous side' of our make-up, but it is hard to see that this is true in the case of 'basic beliefs'. Fourth, since it would seem that the persistence of such basic beliefs is actually *necessary* for the achievement of autonomy, there need be few worries about a set of initial beliefs in this category frustrating it. Indeed, the notion of alternative competing sets of initial beliefs here seems problematic.

Gardner's main worry is surely more specific, concerning the persistence of *certain kinds* of beliefs,[23] ones which are controversial and open to serious doubt, and which cannot be seen to be conclusively justified or legitimately seen as fundamental or basic.[24] Another way of identifying such beliefs would be, perhaps, in terms of what goes beyond the 'necessary minimum' needed to give a child an initial 'primary culture', which Bruce Ackerman characterises as requiring 'the least restrictive environment consistent with . . . dialogic and behavioural development.'[25] The category of 'basic' beliefs identified so far could be argued to be part of this 'necessary minimum' in a way that a determinate religious formation is not.[26] Let us focus therefore on Gardner's specific concern about the persistence of *religious* beliefs, and see how the four questions posed earlier might receive an answer in this context.

First, what is the character and explanation of the persistence that is being claimed in this case? The logical or fundamental flavour to persistence characteristic of some of the basic beliefs discussed earlier is not easily applicable here. We can also safely assume that Gardner is not advancing a form of deterministic or causal thesis. We must also note that Gardner is not concerned with persistence which is the result of autonomous rational assent, but rather that which is unreflective and heteronomous. Claims about this kind of persistence seem to be essentially empirical in character, and Gardner seems explicitly to acknowledge this in his statement that he has been describing 'various *empirical* aspects of belief.'[27] This is also seen in his remark that the phenomenon of 'persistence of beliefs . . . *could* impair the success of McLaughlin's strategy,'[28] and in his concern to make it clear that he is not claiming that the form of religious upbringing I discuss will render reflection and assessment *impossible* but merely, granted 'persistence of beliefs', inadvisable.[29] He also admits that a psychological or ethological issue is relevant to the phenomenon of 'persistence of beliefs',[30] although he does not explore this 'explanatory territory'.

If all this is so, the answer to the second question, about the justification of the 'persistence' claims, comes into focus. Gardner's claims depend on the empirical (particularly psychological) evidence that can be adduced in support of them. An assessment of this evidence would need to take into account, for example, the widespread phenomenon, in the case of religious beliefs, of the many people who, in fact, turn away from, and reject, their initial religious formation,[31] or at least put it into critical perspective.[32] It is important to remember too that my argument is situated in the context of a pluralistic society, where the child will not only be surrounded constantly by a range of religious and non-religious perspectives, but will also be inevitably drawn into the open debate about such matters which is part of the tradition of such societies, particularly through liberal education, the provision of which I enjoin on parents as a responsiblity. Above all, however, the parents in my argument are specifically charged with the task of being alert to the danger Gardner has identified, and of taking steps to counteract them as part of their active commitment to the development of the autonomy of their children. This includes encouraging the children to hold their beliefs on the basis of reasons. In sum, further justification needs to be provided of the character and significance of Gardner's claim that 'upbringings tend to be influential, but some are more likely to be influential than others',[33] and, in particular, further justification is required for his claims about the negative character of a religious upbringing in relation to the development of autonomy. It is therefore open to me to re-state my point that judgements about the empirical effects of strong religious upbringing are complex, and that there are (at least) two sides to the story.[34] This is not, of course, to deny or overlook the possibility that the phenomenon of 'persistence of beliefs' does constitute a risk, but merely to point out that it is one which parents, on my argument, are conscious of, and is only one of a number of risks that they need to bear in mind.

One line of argument which might be thought to strengthen Gardner's position is the claim that there is something of a logical character to the persistence of *religious* beliefs, because they are not, or cannot, be held in the same critical, rational manner as other beliefs, since they have a kind of absolute status which preserves them from being called into question or being seen as subject to the demands of justifications, grounds, reasons, foundations, and so on. One such line of argument might be of a Wittgensteinian sort.[35] Another way in which the persistence of religious beliefs might be shown to have an explanation linked to the logical character of such beliefs is if it could be shown that *in principle* religion is immune from significant rational criticism, religious belief therefore having an inherently dogmatic and fetishistic character.[36] A full examination of such lines of argument would involve us in a long digression. Suffice to say that Gardner does not support his position by arguments of these kinds, say by a development of the hint in this direction in his account of (3), persistence of important beliefs, above. It is a presupposition of my argument that religion is a domain which is amenable to reason in a sense which makes the concept of rational autonomous judgement applicable.[37] In the absence of a convincing argument from Gardner against this position, it seems that he is open to the challenges I have outlined arising from the empirical basis of his claims about persistence.

The answer to the third question, about whether persistence of beliefs in this category is a bad thing from the point of view of the development of autonomy, depends upon the sort of persistence that is at issue. If it is indeed unreflective or heteronomous it does cause concern for the liberal, since, given the status of religious claims, those committed to autonomy cannot be as content with religious beliefs being held in this way as they might in the case of 'basic' beliefs.

What of the fourth question? Given Gardner's account of 'persistence of beliefs' will not *any* set of initial beliefs in the 'controversial' category be equally persistent and equally problematic as far as the development of autonomy is concerned? Does not an atheistic or agnostic upbringing present the same problems? Gardner rather tentatively claims that the answer to this '*might* be in the negative'[38] on the grounds that neither of these alternatives are as *influential* or as pervasive as a religious upbringing, because they do not provide 'a variety of frameworks within which social and moral issues are to be assessed and judged.'[39] Gardner supports this point by observing that, for example, there is no such thing as an atheistic or agnostic view of abortion, adultery, and so on.[40] Several points need to be made here. A preliminary point is that caution needs to be exercised in relation to the claim that there is such a thing as a 'religious' view of such matters in general. There are, notoriously, within and between religions, different and conflicting views. What the religious views have in common, despite many particular differences, is a set of fundamental assumptions or presuppositions which articulate the basic 'framework' of thought and practice within which the problems or issues are conceived and approached. Atheists and agnostics operate similarly with 'frameworks' of the same formal kind. Must not Gardner describe an atheist, for example, as a person with a persistent belief in the *non*-existence of a deity? It is therefore wrong to single out religious belief as uniquely generating a framework. But is it a framework of a more substantial kind, such that it is more generally significant or influential across the person's life as a whole?

It might well be admitted that religious positions do have more ramified and complex implications, say of an ethical sort, than their atheistic or agnostic counterparts, and in this sense are more substantial than they. But a move should not be made too quickly from this substantiality to the notions of 'significance' and 'influence'. In the light of my earlier discussion, the pervasiveness or degree of influence of a form of upbringing is essentially to be seen as an *empirical* matter (a matter, say, of a person's *reaction* to a given set of beliefs rather than (necessarily) anything about the logic or character of the beliefs themselves). It might be argued that the very complexity of religious positions makes them harder to grasp and to adhere to in the conditions of modernity. Further, it cannot be denied that atheistic and agnostic frameworks, if less ramified, nevertheless provide a clear perspective within which particular matters are viewed, a perspective also open to the 'persistence of beliefs' danger. Perhaps the most important thing at issue between these various 'world views' is their fundamental presuppositions. The kind of upbringing I discuss should help these to be reflected upon.

Another point to insist upon is that such 'frameworks', and the traditions which house them, should not be seen as immutable, fixed, givens. There are, in relation to many such traditions, resources within the tradition for rationality, and for calling the tradition itself into question,[41] and it is only traditions of this kind which fall within the terms of my argument. So to bring up children in a particular tradition is not necessarily to entrap them.

Gardner concedes that 'tensions exist between the liberal ideal and atheistic and agnostic upbringing'[42] but needs to provide further defence of his claim that 'stronger tensions are more likely to exist when the upbringing is of a strong religious kind,'[43] and of his overall (tentative) conclusion[44] that a *certain kind* of agnostic upbringing is particularly suited to the promotion of the liberal goal. In specifying a certain kind of agnostic upbringing Gardner seems to be appealing to a distinction between two kinds of agnosticism[45] similar to that drawn by Kenny, who distinguishes 'necessary' and 'contingent' forms of it. 'Necessary' agnosticism is characterised by Kenny as 'the belief. . . that knowledge whether there is a God or not is in some sense impossible because of the limits of the human mind.'[46] Agnosticism in this sense is seen as inevitable and inescapable in that it is 'something which is built into the human condition rightly understood.'[47] In contrast, 'contingent' agnosticism, Kenny's own position, is more open and provisional, as seen in the case of a person who says 'I do not know whether there is a God, but perhaps it can be known; I have no proof that it cannot be known.'[48] The suggestion that 'contingent' agnosticism is the most 'neutral' initial belief position in the 'controversial' category to give a child might appear attractive. But there are difficulties here. One problem is that, granted the phenomenon of 'persistence of beliefs', is not 'contingent' agnosticism going to persist and dominate the child's mind? A further difficulty is that the child may be unable, when young, to distinguish between 'contingent' agnosticism on the one hand, and on the other either 'necessary' agnosticism or the belief that religious matters are unimportant.[49]

A vital consideration which Gardner does not refer to in his discussion is the beliefs that the *parents themselves* hold. I shall refer to this matter later. One aspect of the parental dimension which Gardner does not ignore, however, is his anticipation of my claim that parents can avoid the 'persistence of beliefs' problem by taking the steps I recommend as part of the upbringing I characterise. He argues, however, that there is a hidden implication in the strategy for parents which I recommend which greatly affects its chance of success in this respect. I turn now to his arguments about this.

3 Awareness of alternatives

Gardner notes that an important feature of the form of religious upbringing that I discuss is that, in addition to being brought up to share their parents' religious beliefs and practices, children should be made aware of alternative beliefs, as part of what is needed to facilitate the development of their autonomy. He raises two questions in relation to this. First, what will this awareness amount to? And, second, should this feature of my argument be seen as a liberal one? In the light of the answer he offers to the first question, Gardner delivers a negative answer to the second.

He begins his critical argument by interpreting my position in relation to alternative beliefs as implying that 'parents have not only to make sure that their children understand what certain beliefs involve and are aware that there are those who hold those beliefs, but also that their children appreciate that the beliefs in question *conflict* with what their parents and they themselves believe.'[50] There is considerable complexity in the notion of 'conflict' when applied to differing religious beliefs,[51] in contrast perhaps to differences between religious and non-religious positions, although even here caution is necessary. However, let me accept for the purposes of argument both that a fairly straightforward notion of 'conflict' does apply to the differing sets of beliefs referred to in my position and that, unless the children are aware of these conflicts, they will be unable to grasp the significance of the beliefs for the development of their autonomy. What follows from this?

Gardner holds that if the parents are concerned with (1) bringing their children up to share their religious beliefs, (2) making them aware of alternative, conflicting beliefs which ought to be evaluated in due course, and (3) concerned with developing the rationality of their children, they must (or should), as a consequence, (4) want their children to believe that the alternative beliefs 'are *false* and that those who believe them are *mistaken*.'[52] Any other possibility, Gardner claims, involves children being led to have inconsistent beliefs (*viz.* that both their own beliefs and the alternative, conflicting, beliefs are true), and that this will frustrate (3). Once this import of my conception of religious upbringing is realised, Gardner continues, its illiberal character becomes clear. For how can the danger of the 'persistence of beliefs' be ameliorated, and autonomy facilitated, by parents leading their children to see alternative, conflicting, beliefs in terms of falsity and mistakenness?

But is Gardner correct about this import of my position? Let us look more closely at each element of the argument, beginning with (3) the development of rationality. Gardner lays great emphasis on the avoidance of inconsistent beliefs in his characterisation of a rational state of mind. This seems to follow from a logical point about the nature of belief. The term 'belief' can refer, of course, both to the psychological state of a person who believes something and to what is believed. Let us look first at belief in the sense of 'what is believed'.

Let us suppose that a child believes the following proposition:

Santa Claus is an existent entity who has a direct causal relationship to the delivery of Christmas gifts (SC).

It would seem to follow that, from a strictly logical point of view, a child believing in SC is committed to at least the following two beliefs:

- Not-SC is false, and
- Those believing not-SC are mistaken.

This logical point can be accepted, given that the beliefs at issue satisfy some conditions such as the following:

(a) that they are significantly identifiable and understandable in terms of their meaning and implications;
(b) that they do genuinely conflict with each other in terms of truth and falsity. Granted the satisfaction of conditions such as these about belief in the sense of 'what is believed', it seems to follow that a child believing both SC and not-SC would have inconsistent beliefs in the 'psychological state' sense of belief, provided:
(c) that the child is aware (to an appropriate degree) of (1) and (2).[53]

Such inconsistent beliefs constitute an obstacle (though only one sort of obstacle) to the child's achievement of rationality, and this seems to be reinforced by observations such as those by Bernard Williams that, regardless of the status of the opposition of different beliefs to each other at the level of 'what is believed', it is possible under certain conditions to see their opposition in the mind of the believer as logical in character.[54]

It is important to stress, however, that consistency of beliefs is only a *part* of rationality or a rational state of mind understood more fully. For example, consistency in itself says nothing directly about the truth or justifiability of the particular beliefs involved, as distinct from underlining a formal point about the implications of accepting that to believe *p* is to believe that *p* is true. Williams puts the major formal point as follows: 'it follows from the nature of beliefs that a conflict presents a problem, since conflicting beliefs cannot both be true, and the aim of beliefs is to be true.'[55] Williams goes on to remark that 'A rational man in this respect is one who (no doubt among other things) so conducts himself that his aim is likely to be realised.'[56] But the principle of consistency, in itself, is unin-formative about what is involved in such conduct. Little can be derived from the principle about the *way* in which beliefs should be held by the person (e.g. dogmatically?, in the light of relevant reasons which have been personally assessed after a process of reflection?, in a way which leaves them open for future reconsideration and revision?, etc.). Nor is anything said by the principle about what is necessary in terms of qualities of mind and character for the person to assess their beliefs in an appropriate way and to achieve a rational mind in its fullest sense. One such quality, I have argued, is that of 'open-mindedness', which – crucially – seems to be mis-characterised and neglected by Gardner. The principle also has little to say about the *process* by which rational beliefs ought to be formed in a child. I shall be arguing shortly that an undue stress on consistency during this process is not necessarily a good thing from the point of view of the development of rationality. This range of considerations about ration-ality and its development can now brought to bear upon (4).

In (4) Gardner attempts to derive directly from the principle of consistency the conclusion that a child being confronted with beliefs which conflict with their own must be brought to regard these beliefs in terms of falsity and mistakenness. There are a number of things wrong with this conclusion, many of them related to what has been said about rationality.

The conclusion involves an unduly static and 'finished' view of the state of mind and beliefs of the child. As noted above, conditions of the sort (a), (b) and (c) need to be satisfied before the principle of consistency can be applied with confidence. Further, before such an application, if one were seeking to develop the rationality of the child, one would be concerned about the child's existing beliefs in terms of their justifiability, the way in which they are held and their capacity for development. The child's existing beliefs cannot be treated in an unduly sacrosanct way. It is not easy to see that beliefs which are still in a relatively ill-formed and developing state can easily satisfy the conditions which would lead one to confidently invoke 'the principle of consistency'. Too much stress on this principle by parents at early stages of the formation of the beliefs of their child may lead the child to an undue confidence in, and complacency about, the beliefs that they currently hold in such a way that they fail to fully understand the nature of the beliefs and their implications before they are settled[57] and also fail to see alternative, conflicting, beliefs as worthy of consideration and critical evaluation. One of the complexities here is that beliefs in, and about, the religious domain are complex in terms of their meaning and structure, and judgements are rarely made about the truth and falsity of isolated propositions. A given belief is typically part of a web of beliefs which constitute a person's 'noetic structure'.[58] Gardner's insistence that a child be asked to see an alternative, conflicting set of beliefs as false when compared with their existing beliefs glosses over considerations of this kind.[59] Surely it is better to get a child to be aware of the need to subject their own beliefs and their alternatives to critical scrutiny rather than to insist on them regarding the alternatives as false and mistaken, which will surely invite (too hasty) dismissal of them. This is not, of course, to suggest that concepts of 'truth', 'conflict' and 'mistake' should be avoided during the process of belief formation, and invoked only at a later stage when the child's beliefs are more fully formed. Such concepts are clearly necessary for the coherence of belief formation itself. What is at stake is a matter of emphasis. My general point here is vividly illustrated by another paper by Gardner's: 'Believing others are mistaken – a rational consequence of multicultural education'.[60] Here Gardner poses the question: 'How should students who experience multi-cultural education regard the beliefs they have been introduced to which conflict with their own?' As in the case of my argument, he concludes that, for consistency's sake, the students should neither believe these conflicting beliefs, nor be open-minded about them, but believe that they are false and that those who hold them are mistaken. He wonders why such a conclusion should be thought to be objectionable. After all, he argues, is not the point being made a strictly logical one about the nature of belief? Apart from the limitations of the application of the logical point which I have referred to above, what is wrong with Gardner's argument, here, is precisely the neglect of a developmental perspective on the child's formation of beliefs. The child's existing beliefs, regardless of their status, are given undue respect. Allowance is not made for the point that the achievement of a rational state of mind requires that a child be encouraged to subject their existing beliefs to critical question and challenge, a process which involves the sympathetic consideration of (conflicting) alternatives, and an exploration of, for example, the concept of prejudice in its various forms. It is one of the important aims of multi-cultural education to facilitate this process.

It is clear that concepts such as truth, consistency, falsity and mistakenness must play a part in the child's formation of beliefs and their reflection on them, particularly in relation to the assessment of alternatives. For example, if the child's beliefs are to develop and not merely change, the process must take place under the norms of rationality, which cannot simply be put on one side. However, care must be taken to apply these concepts and norms sensitively during the child's upbringing if the child is to achieve a rational state of mind in the fullest sense.

Another aspect of the way in which the conclusion presents the beliefs of the person in an 'all or nothing' way concerns the *way* in which the beliefs are held. Gardner seems to be one of those philosophers whom Quinton would want to criticise for having 'an exceedingly constricted view of possible belief-attitudes.'[61] Quinton insists that, just as evidence and justification can vary in strength, so can belief. For him, the ethics of belief 'concerns continuously variable degrees of belief and not just the decision between believing a proposition, believing its contradictory and suspending judgement.'[62] To fail to accept the notion of degrees of belief, Quinton claims, is to risk the vice of 'intellectual intemperance', 'of asserting beliefs without qualification when some measure of qualification is rationally in order, when we have some reason, but not conclusive reason for taking them to be true.'[63] Another problem arising from a failure to acknowledge the existence of 'degrees of belief' is that the characteristic notions of faith and doubt in the religious domain cannot easily get a purchase.[64] The notion of degrees of belief is a complex one, which Gardner does not consider, although what he has to say elsewhere about the similar notion of degrees of indoctrination[65] is arguably relevant. The significance of the notion for my criticism of Gardner is that it calls into question the seemingly monolithic notion of belief which he employs both in relation to a person's existing beliefs and beliefs which conflict with them. The notion of degrees of belief signals that beliefs can be held in different kinds of ways, and that conflict of beliefs can be seen in a much more nuanced manner. It indicates a range of possible responses to a conflicting belief beyond the response of judging it false. One such response is that of exploration, on the (provisional) assumption that it may contain some truth, or be only *partly* false, and therefore that it may be partly compatible with the existing belief; or that it may indeed call for the existing belief to be abandoned or modified. This general point can be made in a slightly different way without invoking the notion of degrees of belief, but rather that of open-mindedness. It is precisely this attitude to alternative, conflicting beliefs which I regard as an appropriate one to develop in children, and which I take to be compatible with the development in the child of (initial) determinate beliefs.

130

Gardner rejects this as a coherent consequence of a commitment to (1) (2) and (3) because he claims that a person cannot be 'open-minded' whilst holding a determinate belief. He therefore regards the parents in my argument aiming at open-mindedness as seeking a state of mind for their children which is irrational. He asks:

> Can it be thought rational to believe a proposition and to be aware of its negation and to appreciate that what one is aware of conflicts with what one believes, and yet be open-minded about it while continuing to believe what one originally believed? Surely rational thought cannot be reconciled with being open-minded about a proposition whilst appreciating that it contracts or is inconsistent with what one believes . . . open-mindedness about a proposition requires open-mindedness about its negation.[66]

Gardner seems to hold that (merely) 'being aware' of a conflicting proposition must damage commitment to the existing belief with which it conflicts. But surely this depends on the outcome of the evaluation of the conflicting belief. Perhaps what Gardner means is that it is irrational to maintain one's original commitment whilst seriously evaluating an alternative position.

But Gardner is surely wrong in his claim that open-mindedness is incompatible with holding firm beliefs. William Hare, in 'Open-mindedness and education', illustrates how open-mindedness does not necessarily imply either neutrality on the part of the agent in relation to their existing beliefs or doubt or lack of commitment concerning them: (certain kinds of) commitment are compatible with open-mindedness.[67] Paul Hirst makes a similar point in his paper 'Education and diversity of belief'. He insists that 'Commitment and holding to the revisability of the commitment are in no sense incompatible. True, critical assessment of a belief demands entertaining the idea of rejecting that belief, but the "suspension of belief" for the purpose of critical assessment is not of itself to withdraw commitment, or to enter into a state of doubt for any purpose other than that of critical review.'[68] Similar points are made by other philosophers, for example, Roger Trigg.[69] Given this conception of open-mindedness it does not seem that, in principle, parents who follow my guidelines are encouraging their children to enter into an irrational state of mind. And therefore nor is it the case, as Gardner wants to suggest, that 'the parents we are considering, in so far as they are committed to rationality, will not want their children to be open-minded about alternative beliefs.'[70]

Although Gardner does not give a clear account of his own concept of open-mindedness it seems to be a particularly narrow one. A clue to this is given in his speculations on how I might characterise the intentions of parents seeking open-mindedness for their children: 'the parents . . . will want their children to be temporarily open-minded about alternative beliefs, temporarily open-minded in the sense of not thinking the alternatives true or false at the moment, but being prepared to take an autonomous decision about them later.'[71] The clue is given here in the word 'temporarily'. Gardner seems to be employing a definition of open-mindedness as 'being aware of a given proposition but neither believing nor disbelieving it', and this is certainly the way in which he uses the term in the paper on multi-cultural education referred to. But this is a very specific and limited conception of open-mindedness. Do we not speak coherently of being open-minded in relation to our existing beliefs and commitments? And if we cannot, how can we explain the process of our developing and changing our rationally held beliefs in the light of our consideration of alternatives? Open-mindedness, as I understand the notion, would seem to be a crucial part of an ethics of belief. Quinton argues that 'open-minded readiness to consider beliefs that are inconsistent with or count against one's own'[72] is constitutive of the virtue of intellectual justice or fairness.

But even if the fuller sense of 'open-mindedness' is accepted, Gardner may still ask how it is possible to reconcile a concern for open-mindedness as I understand it with a form of upbringing which seeks the development of initial determinate beliefs in the 'controversial' domain. He may insist that there is an important distinction to be made between open-mindedness as an *achieved* state of mind (albeit never a wholly achieved one) and the activities that are proper to its *promotion*, particularly in a child. Gardner may concede that open-mindedness, in my sense, is compatible (in principle) with (rationally held) determinate beliefs. But this, he may caution, should not lead us to be blind to crucial difficulties arising in relation to the development of determinate beliefs in the *promotion* of open-mindedness.

Exploration of this issue requires more to be said about (2), parents making their children aware of alternative, conflicting beliefs which ought to be evaluated in due course, and (1), parents bringing their children up to share their own religious beliefs. Does not (2) conflict with (1), and does not this conflict have implications for the coherence of both the intentions of the parents and the experience of the children? With regard to the intentions here, it might be asked: how can a parent coherently want their child both to believe *x* and to see (conflicting) *y* as a genuinely open alternative? What sense can be made of this?

One aspect of this problem of coherence concerns the fundamental question of whether religious parents must, in virtue of their being religious, favour the development of faith rather than autonomy in their children. I say something about this briefly at the beginning of the next section. My own characterisation of the intentions of the parents in my argument is that they are aiming at autonomy via faith.[73] The conflict between (2) and (1) seems a sharp one if both are seen as being pursued too crudely in practice *at one and the same time*, and is eased if a developmental and temporal perspective is adopted in relation to the upbringing, and if it is seen as a whole. Roughly speaking, the approach of 'autonomy via faith' demands that an initial faith be developed, sustained by the principle of 'tenacity of engagement'.[74] At a later point,[75] the child is encouraged to put their faith into critical perspective, which involves (among other things) the child's exposure to alternatives in a gradual and co-ordinated way. Over a period of time, the parents encourage the child to reflect upon the beliefs that they have been brought up with and to put them into critical perspective. What place does the parents' presenting alternative beliefs as false or mistaken occupy on my view? Clearly, in the light of my earlier comments, I do not consider that it has the very general salience given it by Gardner. It must nevertheless play a part in my overall view, not least because of my acknowledgement that concepts of truth, consistency, falsity and mistakenness must be brought to bear on the child's reflective formation of beliefs. So for that reason (4) will always be part of the picture. But it will be sensitively invoked according to circumstances, and not in the rather sweeping way that Gardner suggests. It may well be that at the earlier stage, for example, the development of the initial distinctive beliefs involves the parent at least implying that alternatives are false, so that the child has a clear sense of the distinctiveness of the initial beliefs to which they are being introduced. Further it is part of a regulative ideal which governs the whole process in that the teacher ought to be prepared to bring out the implications of a child's beliefs. But here (4) is conducted in a sensitive relationship with a wide range of other measures being conducted to ensure the child's development of rationality in the fuller sense.

Why is it thought necessary for children to be encouraged to develop initial determinate religious beliefs at all? Exploration of this issue requires more to be said about (1), parents bringing their children up to share their own religious beliefs. Gardner ignores the fuller context that I supply to (1) and the implications arising from it. This context is one of religious parents who are also committed to liberal values. They are faced by something of a dilemma in the upbringing of their children. No one unproblematic course of action is open to them in relation to this. They have to achieve a balance between two sets of considerations. On one side of the balance are their own religious beliefs and their implications in terms of commitments, practices, lifestyle, etc., together with (for example) the need for the family to constitute an organic unity. On the other side is their concern for their children to become autonomous. How is the balance between these sets of considerations to be struck? Gardner indicates that his objection to strong religious upbringing is *prima facie* in character, and that there is need for a debate about whether there are good enough reasons for parents to override liberal concerns (as he characterises them), and to follow my guidelines for religious upbringing.[76] Gardner states that 'this is a debate I do not want to enter.'[77] It is important to note that Gardner characterises the necessary debate as one about justification for liberal demands being overridden. My own view, of course, is that the form of religious upbringing I discuss does not override liberal demands but seeks to fulfil them in a distinctive way. But there is still a need for a more nuanced debate about why parents would seek this option, granted its coherence. This debate centres upon the need for parents to establish the balance which I have characterised, and to make the complex judgements that are involved in this. Gardner's advice to parents is given in something of a vacuum, and without sufficient acknowledgement of the context of my argument.

Gardner considers that another danger of the kind of upbringing I discuss is that children will slide, as a result of their exposure to alternative beliefs, into a form of relativism, coming to think that all beliefs are a matter of (mere) personal or social preference. Gardner identifies a 'fallacy of tolerance' here: 'the fallacy of refraining from concluding that beliefs held by others are wrong or that certain people are mistaken when such conclusions are a logical consequence of one's position.'[78] I offer two responses to this suggestion. The first is that the danger which Gardner identifies is, on his own admission, only a *danger*. Some of the features of my argument (for example, the insistence of the importance of rational assessment, and on not merely following convention, etc.) might be thought to militate against it. My second response concerns the alleged 'fallacy of tolerance'. There is a need here to distinguish between *epistemological* and *practical* tolerance. I take Brenda Almond to be making a distinction of this sort in her paper 'Positive values'. She criticises 'an extension of the notion of tolerance from the sphere of action where it properly belongs, to the sphere of thought and belief where it is essentially incoherent.'[79] She claims that the notion of tolerance in relation to (for example) a person holding beliefs about matters of fact known to be false is 'specific' and 'limited', extending only to matters such as not taking steps to get the person to change their beliefs. She claims also that there is a clear limit beyond which tolerance cannot go: 'it cannot extend to an acceptance or endorsement of the beliefs themselves. For that would be to contradict my own thought and belief.'[80] I would contend that my recommended form of upbringing would help to make this distinction clear in the minds of children (without falling into the trap I identified earlier of giving an undue status to the existing beliefs of the child). It should be noted, however, that this does not require that children be brought up to think that alternative beliefs are mistaken. Such a judgement should be the conclusion of their own reflections, and not pre-empted by a pedagogical dictum derived from an abstract consideration relating to the logic of belief.

My conclusion is that Gardner has failed to show that a necessary consequence of the form of upbringing I discuss (arising out of considerations relating to rationality) is the illiberal one that the children involved will (in fact) be brought up to believe that beliefs alternative to their own are false and that those who hold them are mistaken. If this is so, then the strategies I outline in relation to the kind of upbringing I discuss, unencumbered by worries about this alleged consequence, can be brought to bear to avoid the dangers of 'persistence of beliefs'.

4   Appeal and understanding

Gardner begins this final section of his critique by posing the question, 'Will McLaughlin's prescriptions attract any followers?'[81] This question arises from the perception that religious parents are likely to be more interested in developing *faith* rather than *autonomy* in their children. Obviously parents giving a clear priority to faith would be unattracted to my position, and I have never claimed that it has application to all cases of religious beliefs and the concepts of religious upbringing to which they give rise. Gardner notes that my reply to the faith/autonomy intention in my original article refers to religious positions 'in which autonomy has the kind of status and significance it enjoys within a liberal system of values.'[82] Gardner does not challenge my claim that there are such faiths,[83] but argues that even parents subscribing to them would find unattractive the form of religious upbringing I discuss because of the danger it poses to autonomy. This conclusion, of course, depends on the adequacy of Gardner's arguments to substantiate his claims about these dangers, and I have called these into question.[84]

Why might liberal religious parents be attracted to this form of upbringing? Gardner speculates that one answer to this question concerns the claim that 'a strong religious upbringing is necessary for a certain kind of religious understanding,'[85] and therefore, for 'the kind of informed assessment that is part of the liberal goal'.[86] Gardner refers to this claim as 'the argument for understanding', and concludes (after some reflection) that I am committed to it.[87] He offers several versions of the argument,[88] but common to all of them is the claim that a strong religious upbringing is *necessary* for the achievement of understanding and autonomous reflection. He then subjects this general claim to a range of effective criticisms.

These criticisms do not damage my argument, however, because I am not in fact committed to any form of the 'argument for understanding' which involves claims of a strong sort about necessity. I outline a crucial aspect of the version to which I am committed in part of my reply to Callan, which Gardner appears to have overlooked. Callan argued that I had based an argument which is 'clearly fallacious' on the claim that religious understanding may be impossible without religious practice.[89] In reply, I rejected Callan's accusation on the grounds that I had made the more modest claim that practice may be significant or important in relation to religious understanding[90] rather than necessary. (My more nuanced claim is evident too elsewhere in my reply to Callan[91].) What exactly does this claim about 'significance' or 'importance' amount to? In exploring this, I hope to outline the weaker version of the argument for understanding to which I am in fact committed, and which is not vulnerable to Gardner's criticisms.

It may be helpful if I approach it by way of a central misunderstanding of my argument by Gardner which is implicit in his characterisations above, Gardner interprets me as holding that, in the light of the 'argument for understanding', 'all who are concerned about informed and autonomous assessment of a religion or religious matters will want their children to be subject to a strong religious upbringing.'[92] But I do not hold this. In reply to Callan I acknowledged that his 'weak' religious upbringing is an alternative to mine which liberal religious parents might adopt.[93] Both forms of upbringing have their advantages and disadvantages. The decision confronting parents regarding choice of upbringing is a complex one in which there are risks of many different kinds to be weighed against each other. Philosophical considerations cannot have an exclusive or final say in the overall adjudication of these. My argument is designed to show that my notion of 'strong' religious upbringing is a legitimate and coherent possibility, not a necessity.[94]

This illuminates my claim about 'significance'. One of the advantages of the 'strong' form of religious upbringing is that it enables children to gain an understanding of religion 'from the inside', and the points I made about the rights of the parents and the coherence of the family life of the child are important here too. What is needed to license my argument is merely *doubt* about the adequacy of 'weak' religious upbringing to provide sufficient understanding for these purposes.[95] My argument needs to depend only upon that doubt, and not upon some more questionable general thesis about the necessity of the relationship between religious understanding and a 'strong' religious upbringing.

5 Concluding observations

Gardner concludes by observing that the form of religious upbringing I discuss 'need not be successful'[96] in achieving the liberal goal that the parents in my argument are aiming at. This conclusion is something of an anti-climax to Gardner's argument, not least because it states something with which I do not disagree. The qualification 'need not' is significant, for nothing in Gardner's argument shows that my position is philosophically incoherent. His concerns about the effects of such an upbringing are essentially empirical in character. I hope to have shown that Gardner has failed to substantiate these either by appeal to the notion of persistence of beliefs or to the alleged constraints on parents' capacity to develop open-mindedness arising from what is involved in introducing a child to alternative, conflicting beliefs. I therefore conclude that Gardner has not established his contention that the parents described in my argument are misguided, and that the guidelines I recommend will not help them to achieve the autonomy of their children. On the contrary, it is the parents who follow Gardner's guidelines who are perhaps more likely to be misguided in this respect.

Notes and references

1 Gardner, P. (1988) 'Religious upbringing and the liberal ideal of religious autonomy'. *Journal of Philosophy of Education*, 22, pp. 89–105. Reprinted as Volume IV Paper 7(i) to which all references refer.
2 McLaughlin, T.H. (1984) 'Parental rights and the religious upbringing of children', *Journal of Philosophy of Education*, 18, pp. 75–83; Callan, E. (1985) 'McLaughlin on parental rights', *Journal of Philosophy of Education*, 19, pp. 111–18; McLaughlin, T.H. (1985) 'Religion, upbringing and liberal values: a rejoinder to Eamonn Callan', *Journal of Philosophy of Education*, 19, pp. 119–27.

   Throughout this discussion, both Gardner and I focus upon *beliefs*. This might be thought to involve an unduly abstract and unreal account of upbringing, which does not do justice to the fact that upbringing involves the shaping of persons in a general way, including their dispositions, virtues, character, and so on. For reasons of space, however, I must concentrate in this article on beliefs, and cannot explore the additional complexities arising in relation to the other (interrelated) aspects of upbringing.

It is important to note that references to 'strong' religious upbringing both in Gardner's criticisms of my view, and in this article, refer to the specific sense in which that concept is used in the debate between myself and Callan.

3 See, for example, Gardner, *op. cit.*, pp. 103; 108; 111–13; 117, footnote 26; 118, footnote 47.

4 Gardner, *op. cit.*, p. 98.

5 See, for example, Dearden, R.F. (1974) 'Education and the ethics of belief', in R.F. Dearden (1984) *Theory and Practice in Education* (London, Routledge & Kegan Paul), ch. 8. Dearden makes the point that an ethics of belief (and therefore the notion of the will) is relevant not directly to the *content* of our beliefs (in relation to which logical appraisal is appropriate), but rather to normative requirements for the proper formation of beliefs. (See especially p. 106, where Dearden provides an outline of vices and virtues relevant to praising or blaming a person for thinking as they do.)

See also Williams, B. (1970) 'Deciding to believe', in W. Bernard (1973) *Problems of the Self* (Cambridge, Cambridge University Press), ch. 9. Williams's discussion of the coherence of a person deciding to make themselves believe something (pp. 147–51) makes an important distinction between two kinds of motives that a person might have for such a decision, 'truth-centred' and 'non-truth-centred' motives. Such a distinction is relevant to the assessment of Gardner's rather sweeping claim that the notion of a person choosing their beliefs involves 'neither absence of sense . . . nor . . . a logical or a contingent impossibility' (Gardner, *op. cit.*, p. 98). For a further relevant discussion see Helm, P. (1989) 'Belief as action', *Cogito*, 3, pp. 127–32.

6 See, for example, Pojman, L.P. (1986) *Religious Belief and the Will* (London, Routledge & Kegan Paul).

7 I agree with Gardner that, to satisfy the demands of autonomy, such deliberation should be (to a significant degree) heteronomous and explanatory of the eventual beliefs held by the child. (See Gardner, *op. cit.*, p. 99).

8 Gardner, *op. cit.*, p. 99.

9 For recent discussions of the notion of autonomy, see Haworth, L. (1986) *Autonomy: An Essay in Philosophical Psychology and Ethics* (New Haven, Conn., Yale University Press); Lindley, R. (1986) *Autonomy* (London, Macmillan); Young, R. (1986) *Personal Autonomy; beyond negative and positive liberty* (New York, St Martin's Press); Dworkin, G. (1988) *The Theory and Practice of Autonomy* (Cambridge, Cambridge University Press).

10 Gardner, *op. cit.*, pp. 104–5. One can concede, as I did to Callan (McLaughlin (1985) *op. cit.*, p. 124) that the 'unshakable belief' criterion is perhaps too strict an account of what is involved in the indoctrinated state of mind, or at least a state of mind which, whether we describe it in terms of 'indoctrination' or not, is nevertheless inimical to the ideal of rational autonomy. For Gardner 'indoctrination involves the production of a certain effect . . . a reluctance to change even in the face of arguments and reasons to which no response is forthcoming or in the fact of arguments and evidence which, to an outsider, may seem overwhelming' (Gardner, *op. cit.*, p. 104). Gardner's stress on a degree of 'reluctance to change' as a feature of indoctrination is similar to Callan's account, where the indoctrinated state of mind is characterised as one involving beliefs maintained without due regard for evidence and argument and in the absence of a 'serious' concern for critical evaluation (Callan, *op. cit.*, pp. 114–16). It is important to note, however, that it is an attitude towards (the possibility of) change of belief, rather than change itself, which characterises the indoctrinated state of mind. Gardner is aware of this, and concedes, in his earlier article on the indoctrination to which he makes reference, that 'adopting a critical attitude to one's . . . beliefs may lead to, but does not necessitate, rejection. The person who was indoctrinated into Christianity may cease being an indoctrinated person, but still be a Christian. What has changed are not his beliefs, but the way he holds them and his grounds or reasons for accepting

them' Gardner, P. (1982). 'Indoctrination: a child centred approach', *The Polytechnic Wolverhampton Faculty of Education Journal*, 1, p. 3. But Gardner's general characterisation of indoctrination in terms of a 'reluctance to change' might, in emphasising the notion of *change* rather than critical evaluation, obscure this point to some extent. In this respect, perhaps Callan's characterisation of the indoctrinated state of mind is preferable to Gardner's.

11 Gardner, *op. cit.*, p. 105.

12 Gardner, *op. cit.*, p. 105.

13 Gardner, *op. cit.*, p. 106 (emphasis in original).

14 Gardner, *op. cit.*, p. 107. It should be noted that Popperians do not discard and replace their scientific hypotheses lightly.

15 Gardner, *op. cit.*, p. 106.

16 Quinton, A. (1985) 'On the Ethics of Belief', in G. Haydon (ed.) *Education and Values. The Richard Peters Lectures* (London, Institute of Education, University of London), p. 47.

17 Quinton, *op. cit.*, p. 47.

18 See Kenny, A. (1983) *Faith and Reason* (New York, Columbia University Press), esp. ch. 1, 2. Kenny writes: 'it may be rational to accept a proposition though it is neither self-evident nor evident to the senses, nor held on the basis of any reasons' (p. 15) and 'there are some beliefs which must be basic for everyone. Among my basic beliefs is the belief that other human beings sleep. If this is false then my whole noetic structure collapses . . . including the whole methodology of distinguishing true from false. . . . Let me try to suppose that no one else has ever slept: that throughout my life anyone who has appeared to me to be sleeping has in fact been awake, and that everyone has been united against me in a gigantic and unanimous hoax. If I could seriously entertain that supposition, what reason would I have to trust anything I have ever been told by others, or to trust the ways I was taught to tell one thing from another, or the meanings I have been told of the words I use? . . . Because of this, my belief in a fundamental truth such as this is unshakable. . . . In the noetic structure of anyone who has reached the use of reason such truths have a role which is incompatible with their resting as conclusions on the basis of evidence which is better known' (pp. 21–3). See also Wittgenstein, L. (1969) *On Certainty* (Oxford, Blackwell). I have no space to enter into more detailed discussion of criteria for the basicality of beliefs. One issue which arises concerns the question whether a particular *content* of beliefs is to be seen as basic, or merely that *some* beliefs must fulfil the logical role of basicality.

19 Gardner, *op. cit.*, p. 117, footnote 36. On a point of related significance, Gardner also holds that reasoning requires certain habits: see Gardner, P. (1981) 'On some paradoxes in moral education', *Journal of Philosophy of Education*, 15, pp. 65–76: 'In the practical sphere, for example, thinking before leaping, considering the consequences, considering whether anyone is likely to be hurt by a proposed course of action, remembering what happened last time and so on have to become second or ten times nature if we are to reason successfully and effectively' (p. 72).

20 More needs to be said by Gardner about exactly what is meant by 'persistence of beliefs in general'.

21 On this see, for example, Gardner, P. (1981) *op. cit.*: Gardner, P. (1983) 'Liberty and compulsory education', in A. Phillips Griffiths (ed.) *Of Liberty* (Royal Institute of Philosophy Lecture series 15) (Cambridge, Cambridge University Press); Gardner, P. (1984) 'Defending moral education', *Journal of Moral Education*, 13, pp. 75–82.

In Gardner (1983), there is the admission that 'valuing freedom is not incompatible with favouring some cases of paternalistic interference' (p. 127). Gardner concedes that some features of a compulsory curriculum might (under certain conditions) be justified on the grounds of the prevention of harm. Included here is 'moral education, education about the environment and political education in order to prevent or guard against learners harming others and in an attempt to cultivate learners who will act to prevent harm, just as one might recommend health education to prevent individuals from harming themselves' (*ibid*). Presumably Gardner is not unduly concerned about children developing some persistent beliefs about these matters.

In Gardner (1981), there is some discussion of the implications of the alleged long-term effects of childhood experiences. Of these, Gardner writes 'Someone might respond . . . by saying that we will avoid the undesired long-term consequences if we avoid inculcating habits in the young. But . . . if early childhood experiences shape the subsequent adult, then the adult will be shaped, in some way or other, whatever we do, and the attempt to inculcate some good habits, while it may not facilitate the achievement of the desired end (autonomy), will, or so it can be argued, enable us to achieve the best of the available alternatives' (p. 69).

In Gardner (1984), criticisms are made of the notion that teachers (and presumably parents also) can coherently adopt a neutral approach with regard to moral education (pp. 77–8).

22 Compare Matthews, G.B. (1980) *Philosophy and the Young Child* (Cambridge, Mass., Harvard University Press).

23 That Gardner is not really concerned with the sort of basic beliefs we have been discussing is seen in his remark that 'early beliefs may vary from person to person' (Gardner, *op. cit.*, p. 105), which could hardly be the case, at least to any great extent, with basic beliefs as I (roughly) characterise them here. His real concern is shown, for example, in his statement that: 'if one wants individuals to take . . . a reasoned decision about a host of competing views, we should avoid developing in them a commitment to a particular set of those views'. (Gardner, *op. cit.*, p. 106).

24 For Kenny's claim that a belief such as 'God exists' cannot be seen as basic or fundamental in the same sense as the beliefs discussed earlier see Kenny, *op. cit.*, chs 2–4.

25 Ackerman, B.A. (1980). *Social Justice in the Liberal State* (New Haven, Conn., Yale University Press), p. 152. See also McLaughlin (1984) *op. cit.*, pp. 81–2.

26 See Gardner, P. (1980) 'Religious education: in defence of non-commitment', *Journal of Philosophy of Education*, 14, pp. 157–68: 'some form of moral education seems unavoid-able in education, although this is not true of religious education; furthermore, although it may be paradoxical to argue against moral education on the basis of problems about establishing what is true, no such paradox arises when we consider similar objections to the teaching of religious beliefs' (p. 164). We can assume that what Gardner says here about education he would be willing to apply also to upbringing.

27 Gardner, *op. cit.*, p. 107 (my emphasis). See also p. 115, footnote 3.

28 Gardner, *op. cit.*, p. 107 (my emphasis).

29 See Gardner, *op. cit.*, p. 117, footnote 36. Also in Gardner, P. (1981), *op. cit.*, p. 69. Gardner points out that a deterministic perspective on such matters may lead to an end such as 'autonomy' being seen as impossible, regardless of the means used to bring it about. In view of Gardner's commitment to the development of autonomy, we can safely infer that he eschews such a perspective.

30 Gardner, *op. cit.*, p. 107.

31 On this see, for example, Michael Goulder's contribution to Goulder, M. and Hick, J. (1983) *Why Believe in God?* (London, SCM Press), esp. ch. 1.

32 It is clearly important that, in the case of both rejection and criticism of religious faith, the person should not be subject to a residue of negative emotions, etc., such as guilt. Several of the features of my concept of religious upbringing are designed to guard against this. (See McLaughlin (1984), *op. cit.*, p. 81.)

33 Gardner, *op. cit.*, p. 108.

34 McLaughlin (1985), *op. cit.*, pp. 124–6. I do not underestimate the complexities involved in any empirical research into this matter. One of the many complexities here is how empirical research could distinguish between beliefs which persist because of rational assent and those which persist for non-rational reasons.

35 See, for example, Philips, D.Z. (1988) *Faith after Foundationalism* (London, Routledge), esp. ch. 1; Kerr, F. (1986) *Theology after Wittgenstein* (Oxford, Basil Blackwell). For criticisms of the Wittgensteinian perspective see, for example, O'Hear, A. (1984) *Experience, Explanation, and Faith. An Introduction to the Philosophy of Religion* (London, Routledge & Kegan Paul), ch. 1; Mackie, J.L. (1982) *The Miracle of Theism. Arguments for and against the existence of God* (Oxford, Clarendon Press), ch. 12.

36 See, for example, O'Hear, *op. cit.*, ch. 6.

37 McLaughlin (1984) *op. cit.*, p. 79. On this matter see, for example, Hepburn R.W. (1987) 'Attitudes to evidence and argument in the field of religion', in R. Straughan and J. Wilson (eds) *Philosophers on Education* (London, Macmillan).

38 Gardner, *op. cit.*, p. 108 (my emphasis).

39 Gardner, *op. cit.*, p. 108. Gardner may be tempted by Flew's 'presumption of atheism' argument. For a challenge to Flew's argument see Kenny, *op. cit.*, pp. 85–7.

40 Gardner, *op. cit.*, p. 108.

41 See, for example, MacIntyre, A. (1988) *Whose Justice? Which Rationality?* (London, Duckworth), esp. ch. 18.

42 Gardner, *op. cit.*, p. 108.

43 Gardner, *op. cit.*, p. 108.

44 See note 3 above.

45 See Gardner, *op. cit.*, p. 103.

46 Kenny, *op. cit.*, p. 88.

47 Kenny, *op. cit.*, p. 88.

48 Kenny, *op. cit.*, p. 88.

49 On this see Barrow, R. (1974) 'Religion in the schools', *Educational Philosophy and Theory*, 6. pp. 49–57.

50 Gardner, *op. cit.*, p. 91–2 (my emphasis).

51 On this issue, see for example Hick J. (1985) *Problems of Religious Pluralism* (London, Macmillan), esp. ch. 6.

52 Gardner, *op. cit.*, p. 92 (my emphasis).

53 The qualification 'to an appropriate degree' is important here because there are obvious difficulties in the suggestion that the child must be aware of the full meaning and implication of their beliefs and the conflicts between them. This is intensified when it is noted that what is at issue are (complex) *systems* of belief. On the notion of systems of belief see, for example, Mitchell, B. (1973) *The Justification of Religious Belief* (London, Macmillan): 'It is characteristic of any such system that it is highly ramified, and that it is capable of further articulation and development. Moreover, no single individual can comprehend all of it, even to the extent that it has at present been worked out: no one can fully apprehend its intellectual structure or completely appropriate the attitudes that go with it. There are, therefore, great variations in the way individuals are related to it. Some have a more synoptic view than others; some have penetrated more deeply than others; there are differences of interpretation and emphasis as well as varying degrees of practical involvement'(p. 135).

54 See Williams, B. (1965) 'Ethical consistency', in B. Williams (1973) *Problems of the Self* (Cambridge, Cambridge University Press).

55 Williams (1965), *op. cit.*, p. 177.

56 Williams (1965), *op. cit.*, p. 177.

57 My use of the term 'settled' here is not intended to imply any inappropriate degree of rigidity or fixedness, but rather a degree of relative stability following reflection, etc.

58 Anthony Kenny defines 'noetic structure' as 'the assemblage of beliefs a person holds, together with the various logical and epistemic relations that hold among them' (Kenny, *op. cit.*, p. 12).

59 One implication of this consideration is the need for sensitive exploration of complex webs of belief involved, not immediate judgements about truth and falsity.

60 Gardner, P. (1989) 'Believing others are mistaken – a rational consequence of multi-cultural education', forthcoming in *Wolverhampton Educational Bulletin*. This paper was presented to a conference of the West Midlands branch of the Philosophy of Education Society of Great Britain, Gregynog, University of Wales, July 1988. There are a number of other problems facing Gardner's thesis about multi-cultural education. Gardner emphasises the notion of truth. But many matters with which multi-cultural education deals do not concern matters of truth at all (at least in any straightforward way), e.g. questions of custom such as dress, diet, etc. To present these as involving matters of truth or falsity is to invite misunderstanding and offence. Further, there are problems of a moral sort here. In his paper Gardner (1989), Gardner claims that thinking that other people are mistaken is compatible with respecting their beliefs. (See also Gardner (1988) *op. cit.*, p. 104, note 23.) It is not easy to see quite why, and in what sense a person should respect a belief they regard as false. And this has implications for the broader question of respect for the persons holding the beliefs.

61 Quinton, *op. cit.*, p. 46.

62 Quinton, *op. cit.*, p. 48.

63 Quinton (1987), *op. cit.*, p. 49. See also Robinson W.D. (1983) 'Partial belief', *Neue Zeitschrift Fur Systematische Theologie Und Religionsphilosophie*, Vol. 25, No., 3, pp. 244–58. (See also Kenny, *op. cit.*, p. 6). Kenny writes 'It is important for human beings to strike the right balance in belief. One can err by believing too much or believing too little. The person who believes too much suffers from the vice of credulity or gullibility; the person who believes too little is guilty of excessive incredulity or scepticism. If you believe too much, your mind will be cluttered with many falsehoods; if you believe too little you will be deprived of much valuable information. . . . The rational human being is the person who possesses the virtue that is in contrast with each of the 'opposing vices of credulity and skepticism' (p. 5). See also pp. 43–4.

64 On the role of doubt in the religious domain, see, for example, Ferreira, M.J. (1980) *Doubt and Religious Commitment. The Role of the Will in Newman's Thought* (Oxford, Clarendon Press).

65 Gardner, *op. cit.*, p. 94. See Gardner, (1982), *op. cit.*, esp. pp. 2–3. Gardner here claims that the notion of degrees of indoctrination is one of the most neglected aspects of the topic. Gardner rejects as unacceptable the claim that all indoctrinated beliefs must be equally deeply and resolutely held. There are degrees, for example, of 'reluctance or preparedness to question and reject beliefs' (p. 2). This would seem to apply to beliefs in general, and not merely to indoctrinated ones.

66 Gardner, *op. cit.*, p. 92.

67 Hare, W. (1979) *Open-mindedness and Education* (Montreal, McGill-Queen's University Press), ch. 2, esp. pp. 29–40.

68 Hirst, P.H. (1985) 'Education and diversity of belief', in M.C. Felderhof (ed.) *Religious Education in a Pluralistic Society* (London, Hodder & Stoughton), p. 13.

69 Trigg, R. (1973) *Reason and Commitment* (Cambridge, Cambridge University Press), esp. ch. 3. On this issue, Trigg writes 'I can remain committed while my beliefs are being challenged. If my doubt reaches the point where I lose my beliefs, it is true that I must lose my faith . . . [but] faith does not imply certainty. It is much more a determination to remain committed in spite of apparent difficulties. Although it must involve the belief that the difficulties do not provide genuine obstacles to faith, if the faith is to be rational, faith can exist in spite of seeming facts as well as because of them. There is no contradiction in my facing up to the possibility that my beliefs may be mistaken,

while in the meantime holding firmly to my faith. I can be totally committed and at the same time admit that I might be wrong. I am however basing my life on the assumption that I am not' (p. 55).

70 Gardner, *op. cit.*, p. 102.

71 Gardner, *op. cit.*, p. 101.

72 Quinton, *op. cit.*, p. 51.

73 On this, see McLaughlin (1984) *op. cit.*, p. 79.

74 I describe this principle as follows: 'in seeking to provide their child with a stable set of initial beliefs, parents may well have to urge their children to engage significantly with practices and ideas which are not immediately and continuously congenial to them, and which may go against their current inclinations or beliefs . . . this is with the aim of ensuring for the child a *significant engagement* with the beliefs, so that their subsequent assessment – perhaps rejection – of them will be based on appropriate understanding and acquaintance.' (McLaughlin (1985), *op. cit.*, p. 121) See also British Council of Churches Consultative Group on Ministry Among Children (1984) *The Child in the Church: reports of the working parties on 'The Child in the Church' and 'Understanding Christian Nurture'* (British Council of Churches) para. 185; Mitchell, *op. cit.*, p. 122; Hare, *op. cit.*, pp. 55–8.

75 The precise timing of this cannot of course be specified in detail in the abstract, but is a matter for sensitive judgement by the parents.

76 Gardner, *op. cit.*, p. 103.

77 Gardner, *op. cit.*, p. 103.

78 Gardner, *op. cit.*, p. 102.

79 Almond, B. (1983) Positive values, in: B. Almond (1987) *Moral Concerns* (Atlantic Highlands, NJ, Humanities Press), p. 143.

80 Almond, *op. cit.*, p. 143.

81 Gardner, *op. cit.*, p. 108.

82 Gardner, *op. cit.*, p. 109.

83 For an outline of the claim that 'critical openness' is compatible with, and demanded by, (certain forms of) Christian faith, see British Council of Churches Consultative Group on Ministry Among Children, *op. cit.*

84 Gardner also makes the claim that it would be 'irrational' 'for parents who accept that early beliefs tend to persist and who agree that a religious upbringing is likely to predetermine subsequent beliefs to be committed to McLaughlin's approach and his goal . . . it is irrational for people to aim for a goal while pursuing a course of action which they believe may well prevent their achieving that goal' (Gardner, *op. cit.*, p. 106). The second part of this quotation states a truth, but the first part does not accurately represent the beliefs held by the parents in my argument about the effects of a religious upbringing of the sort I discuss. It does not seem to me, therefore, that in giving their children such an upbringing, they are being irrational.

85 Gardner, *op. cit.*, p. 110.

86 Gardner, *op. cit.*, p. 113.

87 Gardner, *op. cit.*, p. 110.

88 Gardner, *op. cit.*, pp. 111–13.

89 Callan, *op. cit.*, p. 118. Presumably, 'practice' here is to be construed richly, as involving more than say, (mere) conformity to the requirements of religious ritual and observance.

90 McLaughlin, *op. cit.*, pp. 126–7.

91 McLaughlin, *op. cit.*, pp. 122; 126.

92 Gardner, *op. cit.*, p. 110.

93 McLaughlin, *op. cit.*, p. 123.

94 McLaughlin, *op. cit.*, pp. 122–6.

95 McLaughlin, *op. cit.*, p. 122.

96 Gardner, *op. cit.*, p. 113.

Part I

(3) The arts and education

8

WHAT KNOWLEDGE IS OF MOST WORTH IN THE ARTS?

Bennett Reimer

The Spencerian view

The title of this paper asks the central curriculum question as it applies to the arts. It is intended to start my attempt to deal with this question on an ironic note.

Herbert Spencer wrote his famous essay 'What Knowledge Is of Most Worth?' (first published in 1859 and then in 1860 as the first chapter of *Education: Intellectual, Moral and Physical*)[1] as a critique of the prevailing values of liberal arts study, which focused on the great aristic and intellectual achievements of Western culture. He effectively achieved his aim of starting a revolution in how education should be conceived. On the basis of his application of Darwin's theory of evolution to education, Spencer argued that the values then current needed to be reversed, so that the arts and humanities were no longer to be regarded as the finest fruits of civilization but should be relegated to leisure-time pursuits. '*As they occupy the leisure part of life, so should they occupy the leisure part of education.*'[2] What should occupy the primary position? That which is of most functional value in ministering to self-preservation directly and indirectly, followed by those activities related to child-rearing, followed still further behind by concerns for maintaining proper social and political relations, and finally, in the basement, 'those miscellaneous activities which make up the leisure part of life, devoted to the gratification of tastes and feelings.'[3] And what, specifically, best ministers to self-preservation and therefore should be regarded as of the highest value?

> What knowledge is of most worth? – the uniform reply is – Science. This is the verdict on all the counts. For direct self-preservation, or the maintenance of life and health, the all-important knowledge is – Science. For that indirect self-preservation which we call gaining a livelihood, the knowledge of greatest value is – Science. For the due discharge of parental functions, the proper guidance is to be found only

Source: Bennett Reimer and Ralph A. Smith (eds) *The Arts, Education and Aesthetic Knowing NSSE 91st Yearbook*, NSSE, Chicago, 1992, Section 2, Chapter II.

in – Science. For that interpretation of national life, past and present, without which the citizen cannot rightly regulate his conduct, the indispensable key is – Science. Alike for the most perfect production and highest enjoyment of art in all its forms, the needful preparation is still – Science. And for the purposes of discipline – intellectual, moral, religious – the most efficient study is, once more – Science. The question which at first seemed so perplexed, has become, in the course of our inquiry, comparatively simple.[4]

The shift from an older notion of liberal education conceived as appropriate for a small elite to a functional, utilitarian view of education as necessary when the masses are to be schooled reflected historical changes occurring not only in intellectual paradigms but in social-political life as well. When education was conceived as being for all rather than for a privileged few, it could no longer afford the luxuries of the leisured class – 'the gratification of tastes and feelings'. Science, representing those subjects dealing with the hard realities of survival and success, would have to become basic. The cultivation of intrinsically qualitative and therefore nonutilitarian dimensions of individual experience would have to be given up (at least, of course, for the masses) in exchange for social and political democracy.

Spencer's view of what is real and what is valuable, historically determined as it was, has had continuing influence because it is persuasive at a certain level of analysis, and the Spencerian argument continues to be made to this day. So it is remarkable that in the face of its strong influence over the past century of education in Western culture, a counterargument continues to be offered and is by some people passionately advanced (and to some degree heeded). That argument is that the primary reality and value of human life remains its inherent quality as immediately experienced. 'Science' – the utilitarian dimension of life and education – is, in this view, valuable not only or even primarily for its functionality (necessary as this is) but as a mode of understanding by which humans know and therefore incorporate into experience an important dimension of their reality. Yet there are other domains of knowing which constitute the multidimensional reality of human experience, including, out of the basement, the persistent and often insistent domain of the arts.

Justifying the arts

In the United States, the major burden of justifying the arts in education in the face of the dominant Spencerian value system has fallen to the professional fields devoted to the arts in education – music education and visual arts education primarily and in recent years also the slowly growing fields of dance education and theater education. Of course, an active community of professional philosophers and aestheticians has produced a wide-ranging literature on all aspects of art and its role in culture. That literature remains a significant dimension of

Western intellectual life. And a fair number of these professional intellectuals have offered ideas and guidelines for education in the arts, ranging from broad general principles to moderately detailed prescriptions for how the arts should be taught in schools. Yet despite such ongoing work at the level of professional scholarship the arts education professions tended, until about three decades ago, to go their own ways little influenced by that literature, to fight their own battles for survival and recognition, and to manufacture their own justifications for why they should be included in schooling (if only in the basement). And they did so with little if any cross-fertilization between art fields, each of which tended to be a self-contained unit not only operationally but intellectually as well. That situation continues to the present.

It will be instructive to look briefly at the ways the professional art education fields went about the task of justifying their existence in a period of history dominated by utilitarian values, because the question of what knowledge is of most worth, while having the most practical consequences for curriculum building, is essentially a philosophical question. A good school curriculum is likely to be conceived as one that is in consonance with a dominant belief and value system. What philosophical stances have been devised not only to justify the presence of the arts in education but also to answer the practical question of what about them is most worth knowing?

A good many attempts have been made to answer that question, because it is itself rather complex and can be approached in a variety of ways.[5] I focus here on three influential arguments.

The claim for functionality

The first argument adopted a Spencerian value structure. What is most valuable is that which best functions to secure the most important needs for humans – self-preservation, productive work, parenting, and so forth. While science (broadly conceived) may fulfill such functions most effectively, anything else contributing in some way to fulfilling them might be perceived as also useful to some degree and worthy, therefore, of being included in schooling.

A host of functional claims have been made for the arts in education over the century and a half that they have been included as part of school programs. The specifics of such claims have reflected the general value system that good education is utilitarian in the broad sense, but they have also focused on particular values that crop up from time to time. If 'discipline' is a matter of great concern at a particular time (as it seems to be in fifteen- to twenty-year cycles), then it must be shown that involving students in art activities provides them with it, and instruction in art should therefore emphasize its demands for regularized, concentrated accomplishment of tasks. If social skills are highly valued at particular times, the contribution of art study to developing such skills can be pointed out. Programs then shift to an emphasis on socially interactive aspects of art involvement. If 'the basics' are being touted as primary, the arts need to be shown to contribute to better learning of them. Instruction accordingly emphasizes the conceptual, numerical, symbol-system dimensions of arts study. Needs for security, moral development, self-esteem, self-expression, mental growth, emotional catharsis, knowledge of history and cultural mores, identification with a particular culture, ability to solve problems, leisure-time activities, and on and on, can all be met by art instruction catering to them. The more of such functions the arts can be shown to serve, and the more pertinent they can be shown to be to favored values, the more important they might become as an integral part of education.

Given the general acceptance of functionality as a major value basis for education as a whole, a certain degree of effectiveness has been achieved by utilitarian approaches in justifying the arts in education and building programs based on them. But a good many problems have also arisen on both sides of the justification–application coin. A deep scratch on the surface of the argument is hardly necessary to uncover the disconcerting fact that no such functional claim can establish the arts as necessary to achieve it. In all cases the value can be realized by a great many other and often far more direct means. In addition, it is hard to establish persuasively that the study of any art actually does contribute to the value in question, except as a result of instructional style rather than any inherent characteristic of art itself. Therefore, instructional style in any other subject would contribute to the value as effectively.

While the arts can then be conceived as more or less useful as one means to foster important values, they cannot themselves be conceived as important or valuable in any essential sense, or as requiring instruction endemic to their own nature. The many attempts to secure a place for the arts in education based on the argument for functionality have left them both poorly justified and without a valid curriculum basis, how ever much they may have won the day in this or that particular advocacy skirmish.

The claim for talent development

The second way an attempt has been made to secure a place for the arts in American schools has also had a utilitarian cast but in a different sense from the first. This has been the argument that a society to be and remain viable requires a system for identifying and fostering the variety of competencies needed to fulfill all its specialized roles. In our society the need for professional artists is generally recognized as both legitimate and important. It is also recognized that individuals who are blessed with what seems like a mysterious talent for creating art deserve to have their talent noticed and developed, to have their personal potentials fulfilled, and to be enabled to contribute as professionals to the communal artistic life. As our major institution for enculturation, the public school would seem to be the logical place to provide opportunities for nurturing artistic talent. Supplementary experiences can then be offered outside the school, but to rely entirely on nonschool arts involvements would be to deprive all children of an equal opportunity to have their talent incubated.

148

When conceived in this way, art instruction logically consists of apprenticeship training in that its purpose is to develop artistic talent. This might seem to be at odds with the claims that art study is instrumental to procuring a variety of other values. In fact, statements of purpose for school arts programs often propose both rationales with little if any awareness that they may be contradictory in their implications for how the arts should be studied. Usually, if thought about at all, the dichotomy is glossed over; after all, if students are learning how to be artists perhaps those other values will also be achieved. What is not brought to consciousness (and not mentioned by art teachers or other advocates for education in the arts) is that many people in our culture do not hold an image of artists as paragons of social virtue. The behavior of artists is often regarded as divergent if not deviant, a degree of leeway being tolerated for them (especially when they happen to be successful). Generally, however, it may be assumed that most parents do not expect that school art instruction will make their children either social deviants or professional artists. They are likely to view such instruction as generally beneficial for a variety of ancillary reasons, and as a way to develop their children's artistic creative talent to some modest degree. Some few children, of course, will take hold in an art and give promise of a professional career.

When Spencer said that the best preparation to both enjoy and produce art is 'science', he meant that the essentials of the arts curriculum are (1) training in the techniques, craft, and processes required to be a functioning artist, and (2) a supportive knowledge about what science has to say about human behavior, human biology, human physiology, and so forth, as they are related to producing art.[6] Given his influence, given the high value many people place on creativity and the widely shared belief that the arts are the paradigm of creativity, and given the variety of other individual and social values ascribed to the activity of creating art, the model of education in art as training to be an artist has been dominant in American schools. This model accounts for the most common historical answer to the question of what is most worth knowing about the arts – knowing how to create them.

The claims of aesthetic education

The third argument has been more philosophically as well as experientially grounded than the previous two.

Some three decades ago a shift in thinking about education in the arts began to take place in both music and visual arts education. An extensive literature detailing the changes in both theory and practice of music and visual art education during the 1960s and afterward testifies to the magnitude of what occurred.[7] Under the influence of the curriculum reform movement, several educational thinkers began to argue that the qualities of experience mediated by the arts, the meanings they make available through their various modes of representation, and the ways those qualities and meanings are generated and shared, are peculiar to the arts. Thus the aesthetic dimension of human experience is seen as a distinct cognitive domain requiring to be understood and valued on its own terms and taught in ways relevant to those terms. In addition, creating art, although valuable and necessary as one aspect of experiencing and knowing aesthetically, is not sufficient to gain the breadth and depth and variety of meanings available from the arts. To be literate in the aesthetic domain requires a broad-ranging array of responses to the arts. Such responses depend on refined capacities and dispositions (1) to perceive, discriminate, feel, and evaluate works of art; (2) to understand them as objects and events with distinctive cognitive characteristics; (3) to be aware of the historical, social, cultural, political, and religious contexts in which they reside; and (4) to be cognizant of the many issues and controversies surrounding them. Education in the arts, if it is to influence the development of such learnings, would have to be essentially different from an instrumentality for achieving a variety of aesthetically ancillary values or from professional training to be an artist. Both may be included and provided for, but the broader goal or aim of education in the arts would have to be the development of aesthetic literacy in a sense neither of the previous rationales was able to define. And the question of what is most worth knowing about the arts would have to be addressed by including for consideration a far more comprehensive selection of subject matters than had previously been identified.

The striking movement in the school arts fields over the past three decades toward an image of arts education as focused on the aesthetic nature of the arts, and as responsible for cultivating aesthetic sensitivity/awareness/literacy as its primary mission, soon began to be known by the term 'aesthetic education'. (The *Journal of Aesthetic Education* began publishing in 1966.) For some this was a confusing phrase in that it seemed to signify an interest in teaching conceptual material from or about the branch of philosophy called aesthetics, which lies outside the training of most arts teachers. But as curricula claiming to be instances of aesthetic education appeared and more books and articles on it were published, the term became ubiquitous and a general sense of its nature became more pervasive. This is not to say that the meaning of the term 'aesthetic education' is entirely clear to its theoreticians or to arts teachers in the schools.[8] It is also not to say that its applications in school arts programs have been consistent or unanimous. Many teachers continue to follow models of arts education based on a variety of assumptions, including that its purpose is to assist in the promotion of extra-aesthetic values or to train incipient artists (neither of which purposes is necessarily ruled out by many conceptions of aesthetic education). And, of course, some theoreticians simply did not and do not find this point of view attractive.

Several characteristics associated with the term 'aesthetic education' became extremely influential in the school arts education fields over the past thirty or so years. Recent important influences have reinforced the belief that education in the arts requires tuition in a broad range of disciplines relevant to the cultivation of the characteristic mode of cognition the arts represent.[9]

The arts as cognitive

What knowledge, then, is of most worth in the arts according to the general point of view often called aesthetic education? Another important intellectual movement in recent years bears on how this question might be answered. This is the growing recognition that traditional conceptions of cognition, equating it with verbal and symbolic conceptualization, are inadequate to describe or explain the variety of modes in which human knowing occurs and by which human knowing may be represented. We can trace to Plato the history of the idea that cognition, to be considered authentic, must be as abstract – that is, free from the vagaries and errors of the senses and the intuitions – as it is possible for rationality to make it. The most dependable, most genuine knowledge therefore is achieved through a movement away from the concrete toward the abstract. 'Basic' subjects are those fulfilling the assumption that cognition is essentially a function of abstract thinking achieved through higher and higher levels of verbal and symbolic conceptualization.

In education, the equation of cognition with rational conceptualization is most dramatically apparent in the influential *Taxonomy of Educational Objectives*,[10] in which the 'Cognitive Domain' consists of progressively higher levels of conceptual functioning, ranging from knowledge (of specifics; of ways and means of dealing with specifics; of the universals and abstractions in a field) to intellectual abilities and skills (comprehension; application; analysis) to synthesis, and finally to evaluation. The 'Affective Domain' (construed in the taxonomy to include primarily attitudes and values) and the 'Psychomotor Domain' are not, *ipso facto*, cognitive. The assumption, then, that cognition exists only when the mind is processing conceptual materials in the ways the 'Cognitive Domain' handbook outlines them is so widespread that few recognize that this is but one way to conceive of cognition. It has, in short, become a dominant myth of our times.

That myth has begun to unravel. Ironically, a major tear in its fabric occurred with the dramatic rise during the 1950s of skepticism about the epistemological foundation of the basic sciences. As D.C. Phillips summarizes it,[11] John Dewey had much earlier raised the issue of whether the warranted knowledge claims of science were more authentic than other types. But the middle of the century brought together several lines of thought inimical to the previous belief system. Popper argued that scientific knowledge claims cannot be proved or fully justified but only refuted. The credibility of logical positivism, which provided a foundation for the traditional scientific epistemology, was eroded. Thomas Kuhn explained how contextual factors determine what qualifies as scientific truth. Lakatos, Feyerabend, and others severely criticized the notion of scientific objectivity. All these constitute a significant literature that questions the myth of rationalistic scientific truth. As W.H. Newton-Smith suggested,

> The scientific community sees itself as the very paradigm of institutionalized rationality. It is taken to be in possession of something, the scientific method, which generates a 'logic of justification'. . . . For

Feyerabend, Kuhn, and others, not only does scientific practice not live up to the image the community projects, it could not do so. For that image, it is said, embodies untenable assumptions concerning the objectivity of truth, the role of evidence, and the invariance of meanings.[12]

The atmosphere created by challenges to the concept that truth is unitary and peculiar to 'objective science' has led to a more relativistic stance toward what can be known, how knowing is generated, and what are appropriate representations for what is known. A striking example is found in the 'Editor's Preface' to the Eighty-fourth NSSE Yearbook, *Learning and Teaching the Ways of Knowing*: 'The roads to knowledge are many. Knowledge is not defined by any single system of thought, but is diverse.'[13] The contributors to this volume described numerous modes of cognition: aesthetic, scientific, interpersonal, intuitive, narrative and paradigmatic, formal, practical, and spiritual. Is it possible that a conception of knowing different from the prevailing one is being born?

The notion of aesthetic cognition as one among several *bona fide* cognitive modes holds great promise, and one is led to ask once more the persistent, contentious, puzzling question, 'What is aesthetic cognition?' Stretching back at least to Plato, the history of the issue of aesthetic cognition has been a tortuous one. I have no intention of tracing that history here.[14] I will, however, offer some selective reflections about it in light of possible educational implications. I will concentrate on one dimension of aesthetic cognition, often called 'knowing of' or 'knowing within'. A second dimension, frequently termed 'knowing how' (about which I will remark only briefly), is intimately related to 'knowing of'. The two together, I shall argue, constitute the nature of cognition in the aesthetic domain. Supplementary to these ways of knowing are two further dimensions of cognition, relevant to improving the quality of knowing of and knowing how – 'knowing about' or 'knowing that', and what I will term 'knowing why'. These must also be treated briefly. I will then offer some suggestions about effective curricula in aesthetic education based on these four dimensions of cognition.

Knowing of or within: the role of form

'Knowing of' or 'knowing within' consists of a particular combination of involvements of the self with particular qualities of an encountered object or event. Any object or event may be encountered in an aesthetic way; my discussion will emphasize encounters with works of art.[15] A work of art in some cultural settings is generally conceived to be a product while in others it is more widely construed to be a process. Both meanings are included in my explanation.

One necessary (but not sufficient) aspect of aesthetic involvements is the directionality of attention or discrimination required. To perceive an object or event in the aesthetic mode, one's focus must include, to some degree, attention to its intrinsically interesting qualities. This kind of focus requires an awareness of such qualities as being not entirely 'about' something for which they act as signs, but as yielding a set of meanings contained *within* the qualities.

The term most often used to refer to the 'within-ness' of intrinsically related events (colors, sounds, actions, and so forth) is 'form'. The form of a work of art is in this sense its sum total of interrelated events. The qualities that constitute the interrelationships may be described at several levels. One may speak of repetitions, contrasts, variations, developments, tensions, resolutions, unities, disjunctions, expectations, deviations, uncertainties, symmetries, distortions, energies, and so forth. Such terms call attention to the dynamic nature of aesthetic form – the sense it gives that forces are at work (across the broadest range from tremendous activation to stillness and quietude) – and to their effects on us when we internalize them. 'Repetition' is an identifiable, objective quality of an object or event, while 'expectation' is an internal, qualitative state of a person. But since expectation (of sounds, of actions, of movements, and so forth) is generated by conditions within the work, we tend to ascribe it to the perceptual qualities we are noticing as well as to its effects on us. Careful distinctions between the two can indeed be made, as in phenomenological analysis: in common language the distinctions are often conflated because cause and effect are so closely tied to each other in experiences of art.

At another level of description of the intrinsic qualities to which one attends when one is attending aesthetically, one may enumerate the characteristic means by which each art achieves the interrelations constituting its forms. In music, for example, relations between pitches heard successively are called 'melody', while relations of pitches heard simultaneously are called 'harmony'. In poetry, relations are established by the use of rhyme, meter, alliteration, imagery, and so forth. Each art has a comparable list of elements by which it establishes its forms. At this level of description of the qualities one has an experience 'of' when perceiving aesthetically, the terms include the relational dynamics they capture and display but refer to the means by which they are so captured and displayed.

Some works of art or types of art present to the percipient nothing more than formed qualities (a Mozart symphony, a late Mondrian painting, a Merce Cunningham dance, a John Coltrane improvisation). In such cases our perception can be of form as such – of sets of relations which have meaning when meaning is conceived as a function of purposeful structure. The purpose of the structure of a work of art is to embody, through the use of perceptual qualities, implications, connotations, intentions, suggestions, possibilities. When we perceive such relationships they function as meaningful with no need for meaning in its more limited and more common sense as requiring conventional denotative signs or symbols. The fullness of meaning in an aesthetic structure is often referred to as its significance or import or expressiveness. Precisely because such meanings are not literal, or are not limited to the literal, aesthetic cognition is *sui generis*.

For example, when a theme from the exposition section of the first movement of a Mozart symphony is treated in a variety of ways in the subsequent section, we recognize that it is being 'developed': that is its meaningful effect. Upon hearing it in the recapitulation section we encounter it in light of its revealed potentials as Mozart chose to develop them. Its 'meaning' has changed from its initial statement, and we find this change – this 'hearing as' or 'knowing as' – to be meaningful. The theme is 'heard as' imbued with the structural associations that were at first only implicit but were then made explicit. It is now 'known as' it has been revealed – as richer with implications than it would first have seemed. We do this analogously with the Coltrane improvisation as he develops musical ideas, with the Mondrian painting as the shapes, colors, and lines structurally define balances, imbalances, implications of bounded with unbounded spaces, and tensions of ambiguities against resolutions of symmetries, and with the Cunningham dance as it unfolds through more and less determinate events.

It is important to recognize that the perceptible structure presented by these and all other works of art includes every interaction between every detail, and that hierarchical patterns of interactions emerge out of particular interactions. In a highly successful work of art *nothing* exists unrelated to and unessential to its total structure of interconnecting events at different levels of complexity and inclusiveness. That is why the perceptual processing of a work of art is not likely to occur once and for all with any one particular interaction with it. Important works of art, no matter their style, type, genre, are those with the maximum richness and integration of interrelationships possible within that style, type, genre. Perception of such works requires an ongoing program of engagements in which the potential meanings in a work – its sum total of meaningful interactions – are revealed more fully to and experienced more subtly by the percipient. The active contribution to the process by the percipient is also an essential factor in aesthetic engagements. A competent percipient does not simply recognize structured events but also determines what will be perceived, in what degrees, and at what levels of discriminative precision. Aesthetic experiencing requires a reconstruction by the imagination of the percipient of the imagined interplay of occurrences built into the form by the artist.

I will discuss later the kinds of knowing that assist us in performing these cognitive operations with form. The point here is that the scope, detail, perspicacity, and ingenuity of one's perceptual structuring of formal qualities are essential determinants of what one knows within an aesthetic interaction. Such knowing, I suggest, is an essential component of aesthetic cognition, and is an essential component of aesthetic intelligence construed as a capacity to gain such cognition. Such knowing is amenable to improvement through learning.

Knowing of or within: the role of content and function

In addition to form-making qualities such as those discussed above, most works of art contain some manner and degree of reference to people, things, ideas, issues, places, and events. Whether called figurative or representational or programmatic, they are often said to contain 'content' or 'subject' in addition to 'form'.

According to one view in aesthetics, called 'formalism', such material is entirely or at least largely irrelevant to the kind of knowing appropriate to works of art. One must ignore or bypass content because the only aesthetically valid way to perceive a work is to perceive its form-causing qualities devoid of referential associations. As Roger Fry, an archetypal formalist, put it:

> No one who has a real understanding of the art of painting attaches any importance to what we call the subject of a picture – what is repre-sented . . . all depends on *how* it is presented, *nothing* on what. Rembrandt expressed his profoundest feelings just as well when he painted a carcass hanging up in a butcher's shop as when he painted the Crucifixion or his mistress.[16]

An opposite view focuses on content as the essential ingredient of knowing in an aesthetic interaction. Often called 'referentialism', this position argues that form is merely a way to point up or enhance the associations a work of art presents, and the goodness or effectiveness of a work is a function of the desir-ability of its explicit message and how well (clearly, powerfully) a work transmits that message. Socialist Realism is a clear, if extreme, referentialist doctrine.

Content, I suggest, is an important ingredient in the knowing of art, because content is an important determinant of the form of the work in which it is contained. That is, when one interacts aesthetically with a work of art, the form of the work as perceived is the determining factor of the knowing one gains from it, but the knowing now includes the role of content as one ingredient of the form.

In a crucifixion scene, for example, the shape of the cross is seen not as an abstract set of two lines intersecting at right angles but as a cross, its intersecting lines being a function of the object we recognize. But in a painting, unlike an actual event (except when the event is being perceived aesthetically), the size of the cross, its placement in the composition, its width, color, texture, and relation to other shapes in the painting are all essential aspects of the form of the painting and of our aesthetic perception of the painting. If any change is made in any of them the aesthetic meaning is changed concomitantly.[17] We see the intersecting lines as an object, but as an object which is part of a 'composition' – a form 'composed' to be meaningful as form. We judge the painting good or mediocre or bad, not on the basis that it contains a cross, as thousands of others equally do, but on the basis of how the cross has been incorporated as an element of meaningful structure. A great painting of a crucifixion is considered great – that is, to yield meaning of a profound, endur-ing nature – not because it has an object called a cross in it but because the object, while recognized to be one, has been 'trans-formed' by its contributing role within the larger structure of interrelationships of which it is a part. The cross as an object is 'seen as' or 'known as' aesthetically meaningful in light of its structural associations within the complex of visual events with which it interacts. Art transcends content through form.

But in addition to the recognition of the cross as a particular object, it is also recognized, if one has been so acculturated, as an object with particular symbolic significance. Because of its association with an important religious event (and for other reasons of interest to archetypal psychologists) the cross is an object so saturated with symbolic meanings as to resist being seen neutrally. The values and affects we attach to it, whatever they may be, are inevitably called into play when we recognize the object in the work of art, adding their impact to our experience of the work. Such impact is also transformed by structure, while at the same time contributing to the impact of the structure.

This holds for all the other layers of associations, values, attitudes, beliefs, symbolic meanings in the crucifixion scene, including the body of Christ, his crown of thorns, the spear piercing his side, the grieving figures at the foot of the cross, and so forth. Each contributes to the total aesthetic cognition available from the painting as meaningful ingredients which have been metamorphosed, that is, changed in and by form to have meanings generally called aesthetic. A different painting containing identical content – even by the same painter – will yield different aesthetic meanings by virtue of differences in its form. That is why every crucifixion painting is unique in aesthetic meaning despite identical or similar contents. It is such meanings that painters – all artists – pursue. As Francis Sparshott explains in his discussion of programmatic music:

> Perhaps we should say that (as in painting) the most approved uses of the [extramusical] devices are those in which what is recognized and relished as referential is at the same time experienced as musical – that is, in which we feel that what we hear would be formally justified even if nothing were being referred to . . . The characteristic musical delight in all such devices, for composers as much as for audiences, lies in the way *music is being made of them*: the exact way in which, having been what they were, they have now become completely music.[18]

The principle raised by this example applies to all the arts (given the necessary adaptations each would required), and to all manners and types and levels of content in the arts.[19] Aesthetic cognition, then, requires knowing about content, given the contributory role content plays, but also, and most importantly, requires the ability to go beyond such knowing to the knowing of or within yielded by meaningful structure. I will discuss later the kinds of learnings that would be useful in order to help students gain the aesthetic knowings available from art, including the knowings about content which contribute to them.

Another factor implicated in aesthetic perception is the variety of uses to which works of art are often put and the various functions they are expected to perform. It is a convention of modern Western culture that works of art, usually as products but also often as processes, are often regarded primarily or solely as a source of the kind of experience called aesthetic (one aspect of which I am here attempting to clarify). Symphonies being performed in concert halls; jazz improvisations listened to in clubs; paintings displayed in museums, galleries, homes; theater productions and dances and movies performed for audiences, and so forth, are understood as being occasions for aesthetic experiencing (how ever many other motives people may have for engaging in them). But throughout Western history and in many other world cultures, art has been associated with other activities.

For an example let us return to the crucifixion painting. Displayed in a cathedral the painting clearly serves a function emphasizing its content, calling the attention of worshippers to the religious meanings depicted in that important event. In this case the form of the painting – its intrinsically meaningful structure of interrelated visual events – is contributory rather than focal, reversing the relationship between form and content as it obtains in aesthetic experiencing. Because that relationship is usually a matter of *degree* of focus, rather than an exclusive focus on form or content devoid of influence from the other, it may be envisioned as occurring on a continuum. At one far extreme, a devout worshipper, glancing briefly at the painting in the cathedral to which she has come to pray, is reminded of the event depicted by the painting and thinks of and is affected by its religious significance, the form of the painting being minimally influential in or perhaps entirely absent from the experience. The painting has in this case served a largely religious function. At the other extreme, a museum curator of Renaissance art, on closely examining the painting displayed in a museum she is visiting, is struck by the power of the artist's use of color as an aspect of structure in relation to other such paintings by this and other Renaissance artists. The religious content is likely to be minimally influential if not entirely absent in her experience, which would seem to be entirely or largely of intrinsic formal relations. And, of course, every possible degree of balance between focus on function and form exists along the continuum.

Just as content is likely to influence form to at least some degree, function is also likely to play a role in how form is perceived. And while I am suggesting the principle that aesthetic meaning requires going beyond content and function to that which form adds to them, I am unable to stipulate the degree to which that must occur in order for an experience to qualify as aesthetic. Nor am I suggesting that there is some optimal balance, or that an experience is 'aesthetically better' if it is 100 per cent of form, as formalists would say. It is possible that different works, with different contents (or none) and different functions (including entirely aesthetic ones), can be experienced across a broad range of foci on various aspects of perceptual processing and be understood to be aesthetic in experience when form plays a significant role. Aesthetic cognition requires involvement in form to some degree, and with meanings from content and function as they have been modified by form.[20]

Aesthetic education, I would propose, is the systematic attempt to influence the degree to which students can incorporate aesthetic meanings in their experience of works of art and other phenomena.

Knowing of or within: the role of feeling

A second necessary aspect of aesthetic engagements has to do with the role of affect or feeling in the knowing of or knowing within yielded by such engagements. The treatment of aesthetic reaction here must be selective, especially given the vast and venerable literature on it. That literature has existed as long as the concept of art has existed[21] because it seems to be an essential characteristic of art that we care about it in a way involving ourselves as creatures who feel. So from the writings of Plato to the latest issues of the various scholarly journals devoted to the arts, the relation of the arts to feeling remains an ongoing point of contention. It is a particularly recalcitrant one because of the difficulties entailed in conceptualizing about awarenesses that are essentially internal, unobservable, unquantifiable, and ineffable. The point I want to focus on here has to do with ineffability.

Feelings, or affects, as I use the terms, are experiences at the level of internal awarenesses of subjectivities.[22] Although we are aware that we are undergoing subjective events we are not able to express or describe them in words (they are ineffable) for a variety of reasons. First, words, by their nature (I am referring here to words as discursive symbols in common language) are unsuitable to express the dynamically evanescent and fleeting character of feelings. Further, feelings are complex amalgams of a variety of felt qualities undergone simultaneously, and the mixtures of qualities are also transitory in that they shift among their combinations and interrelations from moment to moment. Language syntax is not constituted to represent this kaleidoscopic quality of feeling. And feelings are in constant motion in their intensity, each change of degree of intensity changing the nature and quality of what is being experienced. In depth as well there is a constant movement, as feelings are experienced as more or less significant or portentous from moment to moment. All such characteristics of feeling and their sum account for the gap between the richness and density of our inner subjective reality of felt awareness and the limited capacity of ordinary language to mediate or represent it.[23]

What language *can* do is represent those broad classes of feeling clusters which share sufficient common characteristics to constitute inclusive feeling categories. Words such as *love, joy, fear, anger, sadness, happiness* name 'the emotions'. These are broad, classificatory concepts, each of which subsumes the infinite numbers, qualities, gradations, and combinations of what is actually experienced as 'feeling' or 'affect'. The emotion category symbols (the names of emotions) bear the same relation to feelings as experienced as names of diseases bear to the actualities of what is experienced by someone undergoing them. Experience is 'of' or 'within' feeling. Words are 'about' feeling.

With Dewey, Susanne K, Langer, and many others, I agree that the structures of forms of works of art are the most apt, cogent representations of the reality of human experience as being subjective – as being feelingful. The qualities constituting the meaningful, purposive interrelationships of aesthetic form are able to capture the inherent dynamics of feeling (not 'emotion') with a level of precision, fidelity, complexity, and subtlety unavailable in any other mode of mentation. In experiences of meaningful form the 'knowing of', then, includes, as an inseparable aspect, an internalized awareness of expressiveness – that is, feeling constituting an essential component of what is being experienced and known. Interrelations between qualities are not just noticed. They are felt, and do not reach the fullness of meaning of which they are capable unless and until they are felt. But because of the widespread confusion of *feeling* as I am using the term with *emotion* as that term is ordinarily used, and because of the association of art with emotion that we have inherited from nineteenth-century Romanticism, it is important to reiterate that art is not 'emotional'. The distinction is essential. Emotions are classificatory concepts while experiences of feeling are undergone subjectivities, no one of which, as such, is classifiable conceptually.

This distinction is particularly pertinent in cases where the expressive gestalt of a work of art seems to be aptly categorized by an emotion term. Many works of art are simply not amenable to such categorization: no emotion term applies comfortably to a Brahms symphony or to a Cézanne still life or to a Balanchine dance. But one can so categorize them if one chooses. Little disagreement would arise if one characterized the second movement of Beethoven's Third Symphony ('Marcia funebre') as sad, or if one called the entire symphony, as Beethoven did, 'heroic' (Eroica). It would seem as easy and obvious to call Picasso's *Guernica* 'anguished' and Hemingway's *The Old Man and the Sea* 'tragic'.

I suggest that emotions serve the same purpose in works of art as content does, and in fact may be conceived as another type of content. Just as the symbolic meanings of the crucifix influence its aesthetic meanings, the emotion 'sadness' in the 'Marcia funebre' influences the ineffable feeling caused by the form of that movement.

This is not to say that the aesthetic meanings of these works are limited to or equatable with or in any way contained within or to be understood as essentially *caused* by the object (the cross) or the emotion (sadness). Aesthetic cognition transcends any content – including emotional content – through form. The 'Marcia funebre' is, as Beethoven designates it, also '*adagio assai*', and this 'quite slow' is where aesthetic feeling as 'knowing of' begins to exist. It exists as well in the contour of the first theme and its minor modality, in the contrasting contour of the subsequent theme of the trio (in major), in the tone colors of oboe against strings as contrasted with violins against the other strings, in the ritards at ends of sections, in the recurring dotted-note figure and its suggestions and implications in other rhythmic motives and on and on with all the infinite, subtle, expressive, and meaningful details that constitute the purposive structure of this movement. Further, a different *performance* of the movement will inevitably alter its aesthetic meanings, because the slightest change in, say, how the dotted-note figure beginning the first theme is articulated, will change significantly what is perceived and felt.

To explore within all the meanings of form as perceptually and subjectively processed, including the general quality of sadness as one dimension influencing that which is perceived and undergone, is to gain the aesthetic cognitions available from this music. It is not enough to hear the music 'as sad', which is like seeing the object in the painting 'as a cross'. The 'knowing as' required in aesthetic engagements must transcend, through form, the designations, including objects and emotions, which may be present in particular works. When commentators on art dwell on the emotions art designates (and argue endlessly about how art manages to designate emotions[24]), they are fixated at the not yet expressive level of how art functions aesthetically. The notorious difficulties in explaining how perceived qualities can be identified as emotions arise, I suggest, from the inherent differences between form as expressive and language as denotative. Emotions exist at the level of concepts; feelings exist at the level of experiences which by their very nature are ineffable. Attending *in the direction of* meaningful, expressive form allows one to be influenced by but to *pass through* designations of whatever sort, including designated emotion categories, and reach their aesthetic conclusions in cognitions form has substantiated. In such conclusions emotion terms give way to qualitative subjective states ineffable in essence.

Aesthetic education, I propose, is the systematic attempt to influence the degree to which students can incorporate yet transcend any kind or type of content (including emotional content) employed by works of art as one aspect of their ineffable meanings, and thus approach closer to meanings perceptually and affectively experienced as qualities of purposeful structure. Mikel Dufrenne described feeling as a 'capacity of receptivity, a sensibility to a certain world, and an aptitude for perceiving that world.'[25] I would argue that this capacity, sensibility, and aptitude are amenable to improvement by effective education, which focuses on the distinctive cognitions art exists to provide and the distinctive way art provides them, through perceptual/affective processing of formed qualities and contents.

Feeling as proactive. Such processing engages feeling as more than reactive to perceived interrelations in formed events. Feeling also serves a proactive role in aesthetic involvements, a role not given sufficient attention in the literature. For if it is an act of cognition to feel, through absorbed perception, the implied subjectivities an artist has imagined within a perceptual structure, it is cognitive as well to employ attentive feeling as a major means for discovering those implied subjectivities. Feeling, here, is not just the effect of a cause (the work's structure including its content as an aspect of its structure) but is the cause of experienced effects.

The proactive role of feeling as an inherent dimension of cognition in aesthetic involvements is likely to be multidimensional. Feeling is probably implicated in processes of making discriminations between events, classifying event-clusters, abstracting parts from wholes, integrating levels of hierarchical interrelations, comprehending relations, anticipating incipient events, synthesizing wholes out of parts and forming gestalts at higher levels, and so forth.[26] The point is that opportunities to employ feeling in these cognitive operations, and the experience of the expansion of the self such engagements afford, are at the core of the value of the arts and of aesthetic education. The central function of education in the arts is to help all students develop their capacities to gain such cognition, which is likely to be what is of most worth from the arts.

Knowing how

People who bring meaningful forms into existence are generally called artists and anyone so engaged is, at the time of engagement, being an artist. Given that art cannot exist without people being artists, and given that what artists essentially produce are works (whether construed as products or processes) which are a source of aesthetic meanings, an understanding of the nature of artistry as a cognitive endeavor would seem to be important for any viable concept of aesthetic education. However, I will limit my remarks here to a few concerning the knowings entailed in knowing how to create art.

I suggest that to be an artist is to know of or within through the act of causing such knowing to come into being as work, whether as a product or a process. In this discussion I follow common practice in using the terms 'artistic knowing' or 'artistic cognition' or 'artistic experience' to refer to interactions with art while creating it. The terms 'aesthetic knowing' or 'aesthetic cognition' or 'aesthetic experience' refer to those interactions occurring when experiencing a work that someone else has created.[27] Other terms generally used to make this distinction are 'expression/impression' or 'production/appreciation'. What does one need to know how to do in order to cause the coming into being of meanings as a product of formed interrelations between qualities and contents?

First, one needs to know how to imagine such interrelations. 'Imagine' implies the ability to form a mental image of potential or actual relations between some sets of qualities. That image requires two interdependent ingredients – having 'in mind' the materials out of which the relations are to be made (sounds, shapes, movements of the body, people acting, verbal images, etc.) and having 'in mind' the feeling of the ensuing relation. Relations do not exist as abstract: they are brought into existence by some interplay of one thing with another, and the relation is imaged as how one thing interacts with another, the 'interaction' being the 'feeling'. Artists, then, know how to imagine relationships between qualities of the materials they have 'in mind', and how to imagine the affect of those related qualities.

But for artists, 'in mind' is not in the ideal mind Plato envisioned. It is a mind in which the body and its actions, the feeling of the body in action, and the critical, discerning response to the images and feelings caused by the involvement of the body in action are all essential dimensions of knowing. In dance, the 'body in action' can be taken literally, as it can be in any other artistic involvement in which skillful use of the body is an essential aspect of engagement with material being formed (playing an instrument, singing, painting, sculpting, acting, shaping clay). But even in less obviously physical artistic acts (writing a poem, composing, designing a building) the inward 'embodiment' or 'sensuosity' of the experience of the relations being formed is an essential ingredient in what is known and how it is known – the knowing Dufrenne terms 'presence'.[28]

Inasmuch as artists think in terms of meaningful relations between qualities, including how any content may be cast in terms of such relations, the effectiveness of such thinking depends in large part on how well the artist can envision potential relations, and respond opportunely to discovered relations, in the materials out of which the work is being formed. At base, after any considerations of content influence, of functionality or practicality, of any other related factors impinging on the creative act, artists think directly in terms of materials being organized so as to be meaningful. The ability to think this way is tied intimately to the grasp, control, and mastery of the materials *in terms of which* the artist is thinking. The quality of artistic thinking depends on the richness of an artist's 'vocabulary' of available gestures in the materials being formed, control over the subtleties and complexities of the form the material is taking, and ability to take the material in whatever direction the unfolding meaning requires. The term denoting such artistic mastery of material is 'craftsmanship'.

Craftsmanship includes skill but transcends it: craft is the ability to think in terms of meaningful material – material which has taken on and is taking on meaning as a function of its created structure. To know how to create art is to know how to think in this mode. This accounts for the centrality of developing craftsmanship in any attempt to teach people how to be artists; one's ability to 'think art' is tied directly to one's ability to control the material within which one is thinking. To the degree that aesthetic education is concerned with helping students become artists and understand how artists think, it must engage them in the development of their craftsmanship with one set or several sets of materials the arts generally employ.

Two other 'knowings how' to be an artist should be mentioned; knowing how to be sensitive and knowing how to be authentic.

Since the exercise of artistic imagination requires thinking in terms of and through control over the materials in which thinking is taking place, the sensitivity of an artist to the possibilities of meaning emerging from this thinking is a crucial factor in what the artistic result will be. Sensitivity is the level of discernment of rightness or convincingness or meaningfulness of each decision an artist makes as a purposive structure unfolds. Each decision has its consequences in what the form is becoming and what it cannot therefore become. A sensitive artist is guided to decisions leading in fruitful directions – directions productive of the meaningful gestalt being brought into life. Sensitivity to such meaning, perceptually and affectively and sensuously, is, I suggest, cognitive – a way of knowing the significance coming into being in the creative act as one is causing that significance to occur. Imagination, craft, and sensitivity are interdependent dimensions of knowing in artistic creation; each contributes its essential character yet each is dependent on the others for its existence.

Finally, all this must take place in a context of devotion to the inner integrity of the form coming into being, a form which is uniquely meaningful and which therefore makes its demands on the artist bringing it into existence. Knowing how to submit oneself to the requirements of the emerging form as they become apparent through one's sensitivity to what is occurring is knowing how to be an artist authentically. Authenticity, here, is the capacity to serve the needs of artistic meanings in their demands to be created honestly, that is, to be realized not only by the needs of the artist but also by the needs of the form to be whole and meaningful and genuine. In the maelstrom of complex decision making constituting the artistically creative act, it is so easy to make false moves – to do what is convenient or adventitious or unchallenging to one's imagination and sensitivity and craftsmanship, forcing or allowing the result to be less than it has demanded one to make it be. Knowing how to be authentic is, in artistic creation, knowing how to be artistically moral. Artists who act 'in the service of their art' are, in this sense, acting morally, and this moral posture in turn pervades the quality of the imagination, sensitivity, and craftsmanship they exercise as they create.

Artistic knowing, or 'artistry', is the sum of these four knowings how. Such knowing is a component of cognition dependent on but additional to knowing of or within and is amenable to improvement through learning. Such learning requires the exercise of this cognition through engagements of the four dimensions of knowing how in the actual creation of meaningful forms. One can, of course, 'know about' these dimensions just by reading about them. But that is not artistic cognition, just as 'knowing about' the qualities of aesthetic experiencing does not constitute aesthetic knowing. Yet conceptualizating about the ingredients of aesthetic experience and creation can be a powerful aid in developing people's capacities to know of and to know how. This leads to the final two knowings aesthetic education should impart.

Knowing about or that

Knowing of or within and knowing how are ends of aesthetic education. Knowing about or knowing that (and knowing why, discussed next) are means. This distinction between ends and means is crucial. It is a common error to think that people are aesthetically educated to the degree they have a great deal of conceptual knowledge about art, so that education *about* art in the sense of verbal learnings about art replaces the education *in* art I am insisting must take place in order for education to influence the cognitions available from art. A major and well-deserved anxiety in the arts education community about the Getty Discipline-based Art Education project is that verbal knowing might be emphasized over aesthetic/artistic knowing, thereby undermining the very reason for the existence of education in the arts.[29]

By 'knowing about' or 'knowing that' I refer to the conceptual understandings most germane to the enhancement of one's ability to know of or know how. These understandings about art exist at several levels but all focus on the actual interaction of a person with a work. Since this interaction requires perceptual, affective, and sensuous discernment, knowings about what to discern and how to discern are implicated directly in what can be discerned and at what levels of complexity discernment can take place. Aesthetic education consists, in important part, of bringing students' conceptual attention to that which can be known aesthetically and artistically in works of art.

The activity of calling attention to various aspects and levels of meaningful forms may be called 'analysis'. As I use this term it applies to widening concentric rings of examination, description, and integration of aesthetic and artistic materials and processes.

Closest to the work itself is the scrutiny of the components of its form, in as much detail as is possible for the age and experience of particular students. Such scrutiny, when supportive of the inward knowing of the form of a work as immediately experienced, can clarify what is presented in a completed work and what is becoming in a work being created. As a means toward heightened awareness, such analysis is essential. But it fulfills its role in heightening both aesethetic cognition and artistic cognition when the knowings *about* form become submerged in consciousness within the knowings *of* form. That is, *thinking about* meaningful details of form must lead to *thinking with* what has been brought to conceptual awareness in order for the experience to yield the kinds of cognition available from engagements with art, which are always 'knowings within' and, additionally, 'knowings how'. I cannot here discuss the ways to teach art to best insure that thinking about what is going on in a work will become transformed into the thinking with or within which constitutes cognition in art. Such matters fall into the domain of method. I want to make the general point here, applicable to the rest of this section, that all knowings about or knowings that (and knowings why), at any level of generality, must become, through processes of internalization, integrated within aesthetic and artistic cognition as I have tried to explain them, operating as tacit or subsidiary elements of such cognition.[30]

Connected with and widening out from analysis of significant formal details at increasingly higher hierarchical levels of complexity are all the matters relating to the role of content in particular works. Given the important influences of content on form, those influences must be clarified as to how content impinges on what a particular form could be and the corresponding impact of content on what an experience of a particular work might include.

Expanding further, analysis will include the particularities of historical and cultural contexts surrounding this or that work or body of work, influencing or determining its artistic choices and aesthetic contents. For example, to experience more deeply what is available to know from a particular performance of jazz, one needs to understand what was happening in jazz at the time of, say, John Coltrane's performance of 'One Down, One Up'. One needs to understand where Coltrane was in his own development as an artist and where that was to lead, and how jazz was reflecting in this work in particular and in Coltrane's style as a whole a changing sense of musical possiblities rhythmically and harmonically and tonally.

An aesthetically astute experience of 'One Down, One Up' is a cognitive achievement, just as it is a cognitive achievement to create it. Aesthetic education is obligated to influence positively the capacities of mind that make possible both aesthetic cognition and artistic cognition.

Knowing why

What I have termed 'knowing why' adds a broader dimension to knowledge about the contexts in which particular aesthetic and artistic processes occur. This dimension has to do with general understandings about art as a cultural–psychological phenomenon. Here one conceptualizes matters such as these: why art exists; why all cultures have developed arts in some ways like and in some ways different from arts of all other cultures; why standards for judging art might be both general and also dependent on particularities of this and that art, style, genre; why the experience of art and why creating art seem to be so important for people; why different groups of people have different beliefs about art, what it is good for, and how it should be used; why philosophers of art have debated for centuries every conceivable issue related to art, its nature, its value; why some people think education in the arts is essential for all; why some students choose to engage themselves in special efforts to develop creative capacities in an art.

While the experience of a specific work is determined in large part by its specificities of form and content as they are structured by a percipient who brings to it particular habituations, capacities, and knowledge, the beliefs and understandings that person possesses about what art is all about in the first place will color all that happens in the interaction. Art, after all, is a human construct. Its meaning is a function of what one believes it to mean as one's culture has led one to adopt and adapt such beliefs. Aesthetic education, as a culture's mechanism for sharing an important cultural value, must include examinations of that value in its many complex dimensions. Knowing why provides a value structure – a logically consistent system of examined beliefs – within which the other knowings can be experienced as meaningful.

General and special curricula in the arts

Given the preceding discussions (about knowing within, knowing how, knowing about, and knowing why), a curriculum in the arts would be the playing out of their implications in the myriad details to be attended to in building a coherent program of instruction. In the context of this paper only one issue relating to curriculum development can be addressed – the issue of general learnings essential for all students and special learnings for particular students who choose them.

By general education in the arts I mean programs of instruction required of all students in schools, or electives providing the same learnings. By special education in the arts I mean arts electives that concentrate on a particular aspect or related set of aspects of the general arts curriculum and that are conceived to be appropriate only for those students interested in developing particular competencies or understandings.

General education in the arts should be as comprehensive and as extensive as possible. The four basic dimensions of cognition should all be included and should stress the development of each student's capacities to know of and know how. The contexts for such learnings can be single art classes as have traditionally been available or (as I would prefer) comprehensive arts classes in which interdisciplinary learning episodes would be used as (occasional) unifiers for the learnings about particular arts. These classes should concentrate on the unique ways each art functions cognitively, and also call attention at strategic points to the general characteristics of cognition all the arts share.[31]

Whatever the context, learnings related to knowing of or within will provide the unifying core. The experience of many works (from one art if a single art is being taught or from several arts if a comprehensive context exists), representing various historical periods, regions of the world, styles, genres, types, including folk, popular, 'classical', ethnic, and so forth, will be the central activity, supported by the knowings about or that and knowings why essential to make aesthetic sense of them. In my view, emphasis should be placed on works of high quality (works demonstrating high levels of imagination, craftsmanship, sensitivity, authenticity) within each type or genre. Comparisons of the relative value of differing types of art should be avoided. Works of lesser quality can be used to heighten the sense that higher and lower levels of aesthetic value exist in particular examples of art.

Knowing how – creating art – serves both as an end and as a means in general education. As an end it engages all students in the mode of cognition called upon to be an artist – a way of thinking and knowing unavailable except by being (or acting as) an artist. All students need to share this cognition for the sake of knowing what it uniquely allows one to know.

In addition, attempts to create art by using qualities one is experiencing in already created works (for example, attempting to paint distorted figures as related to distorted figures one is perceiving in a painting) can illuminate powerfully the meaningful form(s) created by an artist who chose to use distortion as one element. So it is important that creating art be included in general education both as artistically meaningful in and of itself and as adding an educative dimension to aesthetic meaning.

The balances between experiencing and creating works, and of how much and what levels of conceptual learnings about and learnings why will be included, will largely be determined by developmental factors. The mix for second graders will be different from the mix for eleventh graders, especially because as students get older their abilities to know of, about, and why will far outstrip in depth and breadth their ability to know how (even if they have chosen to elect special study in creating art). But given that age-related and individual capacity-related factors will be an important influence on the balances between the modes of cognition, the principle for general education in the arts remains to aim for as inclusive a program of studies as is possible.

The special learnings segment of the arts curriculum is, on the other hand, essentially selective and intensive. From the several dimensions of aesthetic and artistic cognition, particular ones are chosen as foci for study. The selective nature of such study allows it to be intensive, with more thorough study of one or a few aspects of art than is possible in the general education segment. What is lost in breadth is gained in depth, but the necessary restrictions on how much and what can be studied in depth makes such study appropriate as electives for particularly interested individuals or groups.

The most popular selection from among the various knowings in art has been and is likely to continue to be knowing how. In special programs devoted to creating art, learnings how will appropriately dominate instruction. Experiences of already created works serve here primarily as a means for heightening growth in the understanding of creating, rather than as an end as they do in the general program. Similarly, knowings about and knowings why are selectively focused toward those relating to and helpful for developing creative abilities. A much more restricted range of styles or types of art will be studied than those encountered in the general program – a chorus, after all, deals with choral music, a ceramics class with shaped clay, a play production with acting and staging, and so on, and each of these with only those instances capable of being handled within the constraints of the students' creative skills and the time available.

All these factors make artistic creation appropriately an elective when conceived as the primary mode of interaction with and study of art. (Most students do not choose to devote the time and energy necessary to achieve even modest levels of success in creating art.) Approaches to general education in an art that consist entirely of creating are misconceived and unfortunate. They narrow unconscionably the range of knowings that general education in the arts should provide and give the impression that arts education consists of a limited set of learnings related to one particular mode of engagement and that the study of art is a special endeavor for only those students especially interested or talented.

Other appropriate special art program electives might emphasize aspects other than creating – a high school course devoted entirely to the plays of Samuel Beckett, or to how to be a music critic, or to the arts of Africa, or to issues of avant-garde art, or to the role of technology in the arts. Such foci could be included as specific *parts* of general education, as, for example, units in a required or elective course on 'All About the Arts'. What separates special from general education is the difference in *degree* of extensivity, general education aiming toward one end of the whole-part continuum, special education toward the other.

Education in the arts, I suggest, required of and available to all students in schools as part of general education, and available to all those who choose to study particular aspects of art, exists to serve the needs of all to share the cognitions available only from art. Some few students will go on to become professional artists or professionals in other aspects of the arts, and such students need a broad general education in the arts as the foundation for their special study and special vocation. The rest, for whom the arts can provide a singular dimension of cognition in their lives, deserve to be helped to learn what is most worth knowing in the arts – the ways to share the vividness, clarity, significance, and depth of experience the arts provide.

Notes

1 Herbert Spencer, *Education: Intellectual, Moral and Physical* (New York: D. Appleton, 1896). My discussion of Spencer's influence on education draws on Herbert M. Kliebard, 'The Liberal Arts Curriculum and Its Enemies: The Effort to Redefine General Education,' in *Cultural Literacy and the Idea of General Education*, eds Ian Westbury and Alan C. Purves, Eighty-seventh Yearbook of the National Society fo the Study of Education, Part II (Chicago: University of Chicago Press, 1988).

2 Spencer, *Education: Intellectual, Moral, and Physical*, p. 75. Emphasis his.

3 *Ibid.*, p. 32.

4 *Ibid.*, pp. 93–4.

5 A helpful overview of aesthetic and psychological orientations influential on concepts of art and the teaching of art is given by Arthur D. Efland, 'Conceptions of Teaching in the Arts,' in *The Teaching Process and Arts and Aesthetics*, eds Gerard L. Knieter and Jane Stallings (St Louis: CEMREL, 1979).

6 Spencer, *Education: Intellectual, Moral and Physical*, pp. 75–81.

7 For treatments of the changes that took place in music education, see Michael L. Mark, *Contemporary Music Education* (New York: Schirmer, 1986). For a concise summary of changes in visual art education, see two articles in the *Journal of Aesthetic Education* 21, no. 1 (Summer 1987): Ralph A. Smith, 'The Changing Image of Art Education: Theoretical Antecedents of Discipline-based Art Education,' pp. 3–34, and Arthur D. Efland, 'Curriculum Antecedents of Discipline-based Art Education,' pp. 57–94. Both give useful bibliographies.

8 For a discussion of various assumptions about aesthetic education, see Harry S. Broudy, 'Some Reactions to a Concept of Aesthetic Education,' in *Arts and Aesthetics: An Agenda for the Future*, ed. Stanley S. Madeja (St Louis: CEMREL, 1977), and Bennett Reimer, 'Essential and Nonessential Characteristics of Aesthetic Education,' *Journal of Aesthetic Education* 25, no. 3 (1991): 193–214.

9 'Discipline-based Art Education' is a concept supported by the Getty Center for Education in the Arts, an operating entity of the J. Paul Getty Trust. It is an important attempt to expand traditional curricula in the direction of greater comprehensiveness of learnings. For an overview, see Ralph A. Smith (ed.) *Discipline based Art Education: Origins, Meanings, and Development* (Urbana: University of Illinois Press, 1989), originally published as the Summer 1987 issue of the *Journal of Aesthetic Education*.

10 Benjamin S. Bloom *et al.*, (eds) *Taxonomy of Educational Objectives, Handbook I: Cognitive Domain* (New York: David McKay, 1956); David R. Krathwohl, Benjamin S. Bloom, and Bertram B. Masia (eds) *Taxonomy of Educational Objectives, Handbook II: Affective Domain* (New York: David McKay, 1964); Anita J. Harrow, *A Taxonomy of the Psychomotor Domain* (New York: David McKay, 1972).

11 D.C. Phillips, 'On What Scientists Know, and How They Know It,' in *Learning and Teaching the Ways of Knowing*, ed. Elliot W. Eisner, Eighty-fourth Yearbook of the National

Society for the Study of Education, Part I (Chicago: University of Chicago Press, 1985), pp. 38–9.

12 *Ibid.*, p. 39.

13 Elliot Eisner, 'Editor's Preface,' in *Learning and Teaching the Ways of Knowing*, ed. Eisner, p. xi.

14 For an overview of concepts of aesthetic cognition until the early 1960s, see the index listings under 'Knowledge and art' and 'Truth and art' in Monroe C. Beardsley, *Aesthetics from Classical Greece to the Present* (New York: Macmillan, 1966). For discussions of concepts of aesthetic cognition held by a variety of important contemporary thinkers, see Ralph A. Smith, *The Sense of Art: A Study in Aesthetic Education* (New York: Routledge, 1989).

15 The distinctions between art and other phenomena are important (and complex) but cannot be explored here. It should be mentioned that works of art are generally conceived to be human creations in which their aesthetic meaning is their major or sole reason for being. Anything else – a mathematical formula, a sunset – when regarded for aesthetic meaning is being regarded 'as if' it were art, that is, for meaning as a function of its perceived significant structure rather than as a function of its mathematical proof or its indication of the pollution content of the air. Aesthetic education should clarify this distinction and sensitize students to aesthetic meanings in works of art. Yet it should not neglect other things not conceived primarily to exist for aesthetic meaning but able to offer it as one aspect of their nature.

For an influential discussion of the role of social tradition and authority in determining what counts as art, see Arthur Danto, 'The Artistic Enfranchisement of Real Objects: The Artworld,' in *Aesthetics: A Critical Anthology*, 2nd edn, eds George Dickie, Richard Sclafani, and Ronald Roblin (New York: St Martin's Press, 1989). In this same volume see also George Dickie, 'The New Institutional Theory of Art' for another view of the role of institutional sanctions in defining art.

16 Roger Fry, *The Artist and Psycho-Analysis* (London: Hogarth Press, 1924), p. 308.

17 Several characteristics or 'symptoms' of art described by Nelson Goodman, *Languages of Art* (Indianapolis: Bobbs Merrill, 1969), pp. 252–5, are included in my description – 'syntactic density', 'semantic density', 'relative repleteness', 'multiple and complex reference'. The characteristic of 'exemplification' also figures in my view when construed as responses to aesthetic events reaching to a 'knowing as'.

18 Francis Sparshott, 'Aesthetics of Music: Limits and Grounds,' in *What Is Music?*, ed. Philip Alperson (New York: Haven, n.d.), pp. 66–7.

19 As with any claim applied generally to art, there will be exceptions, such as the attempt by 'conceptual art' to achieve aesthetic meaning through content alone or by emphasizing content. We can understand what this attempt entails, and admire its aspiration, only on the basis of a generality to which it aspires to be an exception. Generalities should be construed, then, to apply 'in most cases' or 'in practically all cases', given the historical propensity (or compulsion) of artists to challenge any generality about art. Aestheticians, driven to generalize, attempt to fend off artists' attacks on generalizations by settling for concepts such as 'art enough', or 'when' rather than 'what' art is, or 'symptoms' rather than 'preconditions' of art. When generalizations are understood to be 'generally applicable' they allow us to make general sense of phenomena – including those phenomena which challenge the generalizations.

20 Compare the treatment in Ralph A. Smith, *The Sense of Art*, chapter 2, in which the views of Beardsley, Osborne, Goodman, and Kaelin are brought to bear on the issues I am discussing here.

21 Chapter 1 of Beardsley's *Aesthetics from Classical Greece to the Present* speculates on the origin of the concept of art.

22 For a detailed and exhaustive treatment of the many meanings of 'feeling', 'affect', 'emotion', and their relevance to the experience of art, see W. Ann Stokes, 'Intelligence and Feeling' (Ph.D. diss., Department of Music Education, Northwestern University, 1990).

23 For an early yet trenchant discussion of the gap between experienced feeling and conceptual language, see Otto Baensch, 'Art and Feeling,' in *Reflections on Art*, ed. Susanne K. Langer (New York: Oxford University Press, 1961).

24 The literature on this issue is so extensive that one hesitates to select examples. For a historical overview, see Beardsley, *Aesthetics from Classical Greece to the Present* under the index listings 'Expression' and 'Emotion'. See also, Marcia M. Eaton, *Basic Issues in Aesthetics* (Belmont, Calif.: Wadsworth, 1988), under the index listings 'emotion', 'feeling', 'expression', 'formalism', formal properties', 'intrinsic properties', 'regional qualities', 'representation', 'resemblance', 'subject matter'.

25 Mikel Dufrenne, *The Phenomenology of Aesthetic Experience* (Evanston, Ill.: Northwestern University Press, 1973), pp. 379–86.

26 Stokes, 'Intelligence and Feeling,' chapter 8.

27 Compare Dewey's discussion of this point in *Art as Experience* (New York: Capricorn Books, 1958), p. 46, in which he deplores the fact that there is no word in English which includes both aspects of involvements with art.

28 See Dufrenne, *The Phenomenology of Aesthetic Experience*, pp. 335–44, in which he richly describes the role of the body in aesthetic knowing.

29 One need only browse in *Art Education*, the journal of the National Art Education Association, over the past half dozen years, to find article after article devoted to accusations and defenses on this issue.

30 For a helpful explanation of how these processes occur, see Harry S. Broudy, 'Tacit Knowing and Aesthetic Education,' in *Aesthetic Concepts and Education*, ed. Ralph A. Smith (Urbana, Ill.: University of Illinois Press, 1970), pp. 70–106.

31 My arguments for why a comprehensive arts curriculum would be desirable, and suggestions for how it might be carried out, are given in Bennett Reimer, 'A Comprehensive Arts Curriculum Model,' *Design for Arts in Education* 90, no. 6 (July/August 1989), pp. 2–16.

Acknowledgement

I am grateful to Philip Alperson for his reflections and to Forest Hansen for his detailed and perspicacious suggestions.

9

THE ARTS AND THE
EDUCATION OF FEELING
AND EMOTION

R.W. Hepburn

If one studies some current philosophical writing on emotion, and then turns back to problems about *educating* the emotions, it is not hard to work out a plausible and attractive story of how such education can be furthered. I should like to outline this story and examine it critically – not the whole story, however, for the subject is vast. I shall look only at one special but important part of it – the part that concerns the educating of emotion through the appreciation of art; and I shall have to be selective even there. Much more will be said about literature than about the other arts.

On the traditional view of emotion, it is difficult to see how an emotion is educable at all. That view suggests that emotion-words are the names of wholly inner experiences, distinguished from each other by their feeling-quality alone. It is hard enough to know how we could learn to use these emotion-words, on such an account, and to communicate about such purely private inner occurrences – as we have to if education is to be possible. But it is equally difficult to understand how, on that view, we could do anything to, and with, our emotions that could count as educating them. We might speak of checking, controlling and suppressing private, inner feelings. But what about transforming and civilizing emotions, or rendering them more discriminating, appropriate, reasonable, sensitive? If these questions are intractable, it is because that traditional view of emotions as inner feelings is inadequate.

Today, we have been made aware that the concept of emotion is complex: that, for instance, emotions have *objects*, and have them necessarily. My fear is fear of *x*, my rage rage at *y*, my delight is delight at *z*. Part of what it is to be afraid is to perceive my situation as threatening: that is, a cognitive element enters necessarily into the having of that emotion. In emotions like jealousy and

Source: *Education and the Development of Reason*, R.F. Dearden, P.H. Hirst and R.S. Peters (eds): Part 3 Paper 6, Routledge, 1972.

nostalgia, the cognitions or judgments are themselves quite complex. Now, if there is an essentially cognitive element to the having of an emotion, then reason and reasoning can after all gain purchase in this area. We can argue about the correctness, reasonableness, of seeing one's situation in this or that way, and thus of having this or that emotion. Emotions can have adequate or inadequate grounds, be justified or be absurd. If so, they are educable.

To have certain emotions involves not only perception or misperception of the facts; it involves also evaluation of the facts. Part of what it is to feel nostalgia is to compare the desirability of being at home and of being where you are. Likewise, understanding *another* person's emotions is partly a matter of understanding how he evaluates elements in his situation – what he sees as an improvement or an impairment of that situation.

These cognitive and evaluative elements can be brought together in the notion of 'seeing as'. To feel gratitude involves seeing so-and-so as one's benefactor; feeling apprehension, seeing such-and-such as possibly dangerous. There are no theoretical limits of complexity or scope in emotional 'seeings-as'. A religious or metaphysical view, for instance, may seek to mediate and control emotions directed at nature as a whole – nature as divine handiwork, or as ominous and inhospitable.

Were emotions wholly inner, quasi-sensations of varying quality, we should be altogether *passive* under them. Recent analysis emphasizes that, in part at least, having an emotion is an active affair, since it involves selective attention, the grouping or interpreting of perceived features of one's situation, and the making of judgments of value.

In the light of all this, we can begin to give some meaning to the task of educating the emotions. It will be concerned, for a start, with ousting vague and imprecise or crude emotions by more specific, appropriate and discriminating ones; with preventing emotion-experience from stagnation – replacing jaded and repetitive habit-emotions with fresh and keen emotions, coupled logically to new individualized ways of seeing.

Now, the story goes on, developments like these are furthered most effectively if, among the objects of a person's emotions, are some so contrived as to control his ways of seeing and feeling with unusual accuracy, and to facilitate quite unhackneyed and richly variegated emotions: that is to say, if they are works of art.

To have something before us by way of illustration, think of the well-known passaage in *Anna Karenina* (pt VII, ch. 16), where Levin expresses his emotion at seeing his new-born child for the first time:

> What he felt towards this little creature was utterly unlike what he had expected. There was nothing cheerful and joyous in the feeling; on the contrary, it was a new torture of apprehension. It was the consciousness of a new sphere of liability to pain. And this sense was so painful at first . . . that it prevented him from noticing the strange thrill of senseless joy and even pride that he had felt when the baby sneezed.

How can the reading of a passage like this be emotionally educative? Because emotion is being made the object of a sensitive, attentive study in its own right – not simply being lived through unreflectively: not classified in the rough and distorting way our normal practical, utilitarian interests encourage. Most of all, the individuality, unexpectedness and intricacy of emotion are not denied, in the way the generalizing clichés of everyday life deny them and reduce them to greeting-card emotion-stereotypes.

In the passage I quoted, Tolstoy retains the emotion-words 'joy', 'apprehension', etc. But a writer need not do so. He may express an emotion with great precision without naming it at all. He describes, rather, how the object of the emotion is seen and interpreted, whether by himself or by a character. Recall, for instance, Shakespeare's marvellously condensed and evocative phrase, 'The dark backward and abysm of time'.[1] Moreover, the words a writer uses may be very closely related to the emotion expressed – we might say 'internally related' to it: the precise emotion may be dependent on a precise way of seeing, and that way of seeing be expressible only by certain words in a certain order. A corollary: literature (and, in different ways, other arts) can be creative of new emotions, not in the sense that a new drug might elicit a new inner feeling-state, but by eliciting a new way of seeing, a way that is logically inseparable from a way of feeling. A work of art is not constructed for the titillation of feelings we already have known, but for the *enlargement* of our emotional experience. Recall Eliot's familiar words from his essay on Dante: 'in developing the language, enriching the meanings of words, . . . [the poet] is making possible a much wider range of emotion and perception for other men, because he gives them the speech in which more can be expressed.'[2]

A second corollary is this: the resources of literature – all the devices (such as metaphor and symbolism) by which a poem can be both intricate and unified – make it possible for a reader to experience quite precise emotional responses to complexes normally beyond his powers to hold together in perception or imagination, and about which he therefore tends to have confused and anxious emotions.

The value and *point* of all this talk about precision, particularity and freshness of emotion is to be brought out, then, by comparison with the normal state of affairs – where, like opinions and judgments of value, emotions too are characteristically blurred and hackneyed, are emotion-clichés, determined or conditioned by popular culture. In day-to-day life it is continually suggested to us that '*this* is what one feels, in *this* situation'. And the 'this' (both times) stands for something blunted, generalized and crude. But why, and by what authority, should one's inner life be constructed out of shabby clichés, and the range of one's emotion restricted to a sort of lowest common denominator of human response to generalized human situation – a slavish mimesis of the mediocre?

There are moral as well as aesthetic issues here: questions of honesty and sincerity. If I accept the stereotypes, I prevent my emotions from reflecting at all accurately how things actually stand in my particular case. Or rather, I suppress, with a mixture of self-deception and apathy, the complexities of my incipient actual response (a response, which, if allowed to develop, might become no less individualized than Levin's *vis-à-vis* the baby); and I substitute instead the easy, conventionalized response, the greeting-card stereotype. Tolstoy, one can say, is emotionally educative, in that his reader is much less likely to disavow the complexity of his own emotions and insincerely suppress them; and is far better equipped to acknowledge, and find words to articulate, fugitive and unmapped forms of feeling. It is not simply that a reader finds verbal expression in literature for life-emotions of his own; but even where this is not so, his reliance upon emotion-clichés is constantly called in question. It is called in question by the skilful presentation of *any* clearly individualized complex of emotion.

These moral implications are vigorously brought out in a very relevant essay of D.H. Lawrence: 'A propos of *Lady Chatterley's Lover*'.[3] 'Our education from the start,' Lawrence wrote, 'has *taught* us a certain range of emotions, what to feel and what not to feel.' What we do feel is thus 'counterfeit feeling', 'false feeling'. In particular, he claimed, 'all love today is counterfeit. It is a stereotyped thing.' As such it cannot satisfy us: with counterfeit emotion 'nobody is really happy, nobody is really contented, nobody has any peace.'

It is not only against insincerity and apathy that emotional education through the arts contends. Another very proper target is *sentimentality*. Sentimentality is essentially *undiscriminating*. Sentimental patriotism, for instance, blurs all differences of value between the various aspects of one's country's way of life: it is wilfully unheeding of valuable aspects in the life of other nations. In general, sentimental emotion is unperceptive of, and insensitive to, the detailed nature of its object, and to that extent it is *irrational* emotion. Excess of excitement makes one unaware of the lack of clear-sightedness. There is a drunkenness of sentiment, where the object is allowed to fall quite out of focus – self-indulgently allowed, since then the emotion can be wallowed in, free from the obtrusive individuality and independence of the object itself. Once again, the emotion-control of an effective work of art can help, by contrast, to show up and can provide a yardstick for measuring the integrity of one's own emotions.

I want now to go further and say that the role of art in delivering one from emotion-clichés is not connected only with questions of sincerity, honesty and perceptiveness, but also with an aspect of one's personal *freedom*. Let us call that aspect 'emotional freedom'. The connexion with freedom is this. The emotion-cliché, the stereotype, can be seen as a trap; for it says, implicitly, that this is the only option for feeling in this sort of situation. In contrast, an aesthetic education is an introduction to countless *alternative* possibilities for feeling: the options are shown to be immeasurably more diversified than the clichés allow. And, in general, freedom is increased in direct proportion to the increase in options. In *Thought and Action*[4] Stuart Hampshire makes the point very clearly: 'Human creativeness in art prevents the recognized varieties of feeling, and established conceptions of the mind, from ever hardening into a final pattern.' In a sense – a weak sense – some of these alternatives were open to us before ever we encountered the works of art in which they are set forth; but they are unlikely to become *live* options; our freedom will not become an *effective* freedom until we have a concrete image and a vivid realization of the options: and this art can supply.[5]

In a more obvious way also, literature can be an agent of freedom. One does not have to be a wholehearted Freudian to know that the less a person understands the feelings and urges in him, the more he tends to be their prey, and the less free he is with regard to them. To be free to modify a pattern of feeling, it is essential to have a grasp of its origins, objectives and affiliations. Nor again do we have to be thoroughgoing disciples of Croce or of Collingwood to see that the explorations of emotion in art can enormously add to our grasp of such patterns, and by so doing lessen our vulnerability to ill-understood emotions, give us an increased dominance over them and thus enhance our freedom. The very pole of un-freedom here, as Plato well knew, is a state of obsession, where only *one* undiscrimating, reality-distorting type of feeling is in command. But well short of that pathological extreme are states where a life is impoverished through the tyranny of a few repetitive, blinkering, undiscriminating emotions. This kind of impoverishment may very well be mitigated by exposure to art-emotions in their variety and particularity.

The logical interconnectedness of feeling and perceiving means that the emotionally impoverished and unfree is also the perceptually impoverished and unfree. As Dewey put it,[6] 'Any predominant mood automatically excludes all that is uncongenial with it . . . [an emotion] reaches out tentacles for that which is cognate, for things which feed it and carry it to completion. Only when emotion dies or is broken to dispersed fragments, can material to which it is alien enter consciousness.' Or, we can add, when the range of available emotion-patterns is increased, as art can increase it.

To attribute an emotion to oneself is not simply to speak of a brief episode of one's mental life, a way of apprehending one's world-at-an-instant. If I say that I am jealous or in love, for instance, I implicitly forecast a range of appropriate *futures*. Love and jealousy have a course or courses to run. The education of emotion involves, importantly, the extending of a person's expectations about possible courses, careers of emotion. Once again – and here is the relevance of these remarks – gratuitous denials of freedom occur where an over-simple popular myth dominates one's understanding of how some emotion 'must' work itself out. The stereotype can bring a sense of inevitability to what is not inevitable at all, and a person be made to feel an actor in a play written by another – allowed perhaps a little improvising, but no tampering with the main emotional plot.

To speak of emotional freedom is a very different thing from speaking of freedom from emotion. The first is highly desirable: but the second is very undesirable indeed. There is in fact a close link between freedom and emotional vitality, keenness of feeling. The person who lacks emotional energy is like a ship that cannot manoeuvre because it is becalmed or because its engines have failed. 'Free choice', in a minimal sense, is still possible (the rudder itself can be moved); but it is not efficacious. This point, though obvious, is often buried by misleading theories of emotion: for instance, a theory that sees emotion as essentially primitive and vestigial and thus unfitted to play a main part in civilized, rational life: or sees the occurrence of emotion as signalling disorder, defect or deficiency. William James has an eloquent response to such accounts. He invites his reader to imagine the world as it would look to one who had eradicated or withdrawn all emotions and emotional qualities. It would be 'almost impossible', he wrote, 'to imagine such a condition of negativity and deadness.' There would no longer be any importance, 'significance, character, expression, or perspective'. 'As the excited interest which these passions put into the world is our gift to the world, just so are the passions themselves *gifts*'; 'and the world's materials lend their surface passively to all the gifts alike.'[7]

Most people are, in fact, familiar enough with the unhappy experience of at least a partial withdrawal of emotional vitality. It has been argued that the conditions of contemporary life make such withdrawal depressingly easy. For instance, the adopting of an objective, scientific attitude to the objects of our study and manipulation requires a deliberate withholding of emotional projection from the objects or the people we are dealing with. To Schiller 'the spirit of abstraction stifles the fire at which the heart should have warmed itself.'[8] Or, as Stuart Hampshire recently put it: 'The price of full rationality is a separation of argument, and of systematic understanding, from the primary emotions.'[9] Now, the argument goes on, it is art that provides objects so fashioned as to engage precisely this whole range of experience, so much held in abeyance elsewhere. J.S. Mill's recovery from his state of emotional deadness, through the poetry of the Romantics, gives us a familiar parable. And Franz Kafka wrote in a letter: 'a book must be an ice-axe to break the sea frozen inside us.'[10]

We can link this theme of the emotion-reviving power of art-experience to my earlier remarks about the numbing effect of emotional habit, the treadmill of generalized emotional expectations. Proust fashions a link for us in the passage in *A La Recherche*, where Marcel sees a peasant girl from a train at dawn:[11]

> I felt in her presence that desire to live which is reborn in us whenever we become conscious anew of beauty and of happiness. We invariably forget that these are individual qualities, and, substituting for them in our mind a conventional type at which we arrive by striking a sort of mean amongst the different faces that have taken our fancy, the pleasures we have known, we are left with mere abstract images which are lifeless and dull because they are lacking in precisely that element of novelty, different from anything we have known.

Finally, although the points I have been mentioning concern mainly the enhancing of self-knowledge and individual emotional freedom, they carry implications of more than one kind for our understanding of other people and the managing of our relations with others. For instance, most of what was said about knowledge

176

of one's own emotions can be transferred without fundamental change to knowledge of other people's emotions. Education of emotion through art is a learning how to make sense of patterns of behaviour in others – patterns that can otherwise lack unity and intelligibility. A wide understanding of emotional possibilities is at least as important to the moral life as a tenacious holding to principle and maxim. Indeed, a too-exclusive stressing of principle can thwart emotional understanding. In Schiller's words again: 'We cannot be just, kindly, human to others – without the power of feeling our way into the situation of others, making others' feelings our own: but,' he goes on, 'this power gets repressed, as we strengthen character by means of principles.'

So far I have been trying to put together a plausible, reassuring and optimistic account of the benign effects of art-education in respect of the emotions and feelings. From now on, I shall refer to this as the 'initial account'. It has been a one-sided account, deliberately so: and a counter-case can easily be mounted. In the rest of this paper I shall state and try to appraise such a case, and work in this way towards a more balanced view.

One set of objections can come from philosophers who are not satisfied that the analysis of emotion, sketched in the initial account, is an adequate one. Emotions (it was said) are controllable, and hence educable through the arts, because all emotions necessarily have objects, and the work of art functions as object in the context of art-appreciation. Against this it may be insisted that some emotions do not have objects. For instance, one's life may contain episodes of melancholy emotion or of buoyant, euphoric emotion – undirected at any object at all.

The account is also much too blandly optimistic about the possibility of achieving the goal of a perfectly refined, discriminating expression of emotion. Numerous writers testify rather to the obstacles in the way of expression, and are more conscious of these than they are of any success in overcoming them.

> Words strain,
> Crack and sometimes break, under the burden,
> Under the tension, slip, slide, perish,
> Decay with imprecision . . . [12]

Let us take stock so far. First, on the analysis of emotion and object-of-emotion. I do not think that the incompleteness of the recent philosophical accounts makes as much difference as the objector suggests. Even if not all emotions have objects, at least on all instances of their occurrence, there remain ways in which these emotions can be expressed discriminatingly, without reference to any specific object. They can be expressed through describing how the world looks, how things seem to be the subject. In the absence of a determinate object, we are not thrown back, that is, on the impossible task of describing wholly inner, private sensations. I describe neither a specific object nor a sensation when I say, to give an example,

the odds is gone
And there is nothing left remarkable
Beneath the visiting moon[13]

or

from this instant,
There's nothing serious in mortality:
All is but toys . . .
The wine of life is drawn . . . [14]

It is useful to be reminded that artists and writers themselves are not always optimistic about the possibilities of perfect and complete communication of emotion. There are bound to be limits to the emotional particularity that is attainable – in literature anyway – when we have to rely upon concepts. Concepts are public and shared, and hence general. But the limits can none the less be pushed back much further by art than in the communication of ordinary life. So much is familiar and trite. What is worth stressing, however, is the way in which experience of art involves awareness *both* of unusually effective communication of feeling, *and* of the presence of limits even here. To come to accept these limits realistically is an important part of the education of feeling. Here, two extremes need to be avoided, and art-experience can help one to avoid them. On the one side, a person may have quite unrealistic aspirations for precise and complete emotional communication. He moves to the other extreme, if, when that hope is disappointed, he withdraws in thoroughgoing disillusionment, and laments that no one can begin to understand how anyone else feels, or tell anyone about his own feelings. The reader of Tolstoy or Henry James or Proust has seen too much expressed, and expressed with accuracy, to have room for such thoroughgoing scepticism: but he is also aware, no less acutely, of what it is like to be brought up against limits and opacities.

Our objections and replies have been discussed in the context of literature and the explorations of emotions in literature. A harder task for the initial account – and one that space will not permit me to develop here – would be to describe the place of emotion in certain of the other arts, particularly in music. Apart from the cases of descriptive (or programme) music and song, music depicts no situations. It follows that if emotions are expressed in the music, it must be not only without objects, but also without situation-appraisals and seeings-as. On the initial account, these are logical essentials of any emotion; and so if that account is accepted, absolute music must be judged incapable of expressing emotions.

Three brief comments may be offered.

1   It could be argued that music expresses not emotions but moods and the dynamics of feeling, its surging and relaxing, its tensions and releases from tension, expectations and fulfilments.

2   The reply will come, however, that music-criticism is full of ascriptions of emotions proper to music: and some at least of these are plausible. If this is accepted, I suspect that a very complex story would be needed to account for it. It would have to refer to bodies of association between musical and emotional data built up in a long-developing tradition, in which vocal music and programme music play an important role, and in which a work is constantly mindful of its predecessors. Interacting with this are 'natural' or semi-natural factors like correlations between rhythms and bodily processes, pitch changes and their analogies with calling, weeping, murmuring and so on.

3   Lastly, musical emotion *does* show the current account to be incomplete and over-simplified, if that account postulates a more-or-less undifferentiated excitement in addition to the appraisals of situation. It seems simply undeniable that, even in the absence of a precise or determinate situation-description, musical feeling can be highly individuated.

I want now to consider a different and (educationally) more worrying objection to the initial account. That account had much to say about the power of the arts to make available new emotional responses and attitudes, whereby to overcome the dominance of emotion-clichés. It may be countered, however, that those new responses and attitudes are themselves particularly liable to become hackneyed; and that, paradoxically, the arts can function as high-class purveyors of stereotypes.

Works of art may replace one set of clichés with others of their own creation, in the end no more or less flexible, discriminating or fit to cope with the complexities of real life than the clichés they displace. One thinks of the literary *schema* of courtly love, or the procession of trend-setting hero and heroine types, down to the existentialist rebels of today. And the existentialist rebel – the opponent of all bourgeois role-playing, all denying of the particular, all stereotyping – is himself now a stereotype, a very pattern of conformity.

The optimistic initial account saw one of the educative functions of art as the overcoming of a tendency to fashion the life of the emotions upon prefabricated or second-hand forms of feeling. The state of affairs that we are now considering is one in which an emotion may not be trusted, or may even be disowned, unless it is found expressed in some work of serious literature, and is thus authorized and vetted. One interrogates the current drama and novel to find, as it were, what one is permitted to feel, what emotional attitudes are sanctioned or mandatory. At one time it will be *angst*: at another a sense of the absurd.[15]

The 'phoneyness' and dishonesty of feeling here need not be spelled out. Lawrence was aware of these dangers. In the passage quoted earlier on 'counterfeit emotion', he adds, 'radio and the film' mediate 'mere counterfeit emotion all the time, the current press and literature the same.'[16]

This objection can, I think, be sustained, though doubtless Lawrence's language is exaggerated. The more we stress the value of art in education of emotions, the stronger may be the temptation to draw our emotions once more second-hand – but with reassuring 'authority' – from art. Again, the teacher needs to devise strategies for minimizing the danger. One such strategy, an obvious one, is to ensure exposure to as wide a range of art-works as possible – to many different periods and idioms – so as to remedy the one-sidedness of particular works and the dominance of any particular authors. The prestige of the authors of one's own day can, on occasion, provide a megaphone or projector for intensifying the current emotion-clichés, making them seem inescapable and 'necessary', rather than submitting them to any critique. Hence the importance of not concentrating too exclusively on contemporary arts, or too readily according the status of *sage* to a contemporary writer.

Hence the importance also of asking, and arguing over, the following questions, questions too much neglected. Is it true that the roles, forms of emotion, patterns of feeling shown as dominant in some works of art, are in fact inescapable, inevitable, the only ones 'available' in the contemporary situation? Or is their supposed inevitability most often a myth, a literary fabrication, but one presented with enough imaginative force as to be in danger of becoming *subjectively* inescapable to many who are exposed to it? To keep raising these questions helps to mitigate the risks of absorbing new clichés for old, and also usefully inculcates an attitude of questioning, of taking and retaining an initiative with regard to one's own emotions and emotional attitudes outside art altogether.

These reflections have carried us into the topic of emotional freedom once again, and suggest obvious objections to the initial account of that. It will be claimed that the account greatly exaggerated the extent to which the arts can be emotionally liberating: for we have opposed to freedom and self-determination, determination by cliché and stereotype. To have one's image of human possibility grossly restricted by a diet, say, of Beckett or Genet, is to have one's freedom diminished, in so far as degrees of freedom are proportional to awareness of options. And, once more, it can be its very imaginative forcefulness (together with the reappearance of the same attitudes and emotions in a succession of works) that imparts a false appearance of inevitability to the view of life expressed. 'Today *this* is how you must feel.'

Clearly, what I am calling an 'image of human possibility' or a 'view of life' has philosophical as well as literary relevance. Philosophical *relevance*, yes: but plays, poems and novels rarely contain philosophy as such. Philosophy is essentially argument, the presenting and defending of grounds for claims made and views presented. In a work of art, however, a view is presented, characteristically, *without* its grounds, without a systematic sifting of evidence and alternatives. The art-work is none the worse for that; but imaginative vitality is liable, in such cases, to be mistaken for philosophical soundness. The point being made is anything but new: although the idiom is different, it repeats the core of Plato's critique of the arts in *The Republic*. Only the philosopher, not the epic poet or tragedian, takes proper account of the Forms.

Emotional freedom – like any other aspect of freedom – is both attractive and uncomfortable, disturbing. Though the enhancing of it can be one motive for a concern with the arts, the clichés offered by art-works themselves can be clutched with relief, and freedom in a measure willingly lost again – in an agreeable lapse into *mauvaise foi*.

Without question, the arts can be enhancers of freedom; but far from automatically – their powers need to be appropriated intelligently. For this, it is of first importance to make clear and vivid that distinction between imaginative force and philosophical necessity or adequacy of grounds. On the one hand: 'This is how things would look if . . . ' or 'to one who believes that . . . '; on the other hand: 'Things can be seen truly in no other way, because . . . .'

It is no less important to combat a tacitly popular view of their *development* of the arts – a determinist or historicist view of their development. (The topic relates closely to the group of arguments just discussed.) It is assumed, often far too readily, that the dominant emotional complexes and attitudes expressed in the arts at any one time are the results of a dialectical process by which all alternatives have been rendered unavailable. In actual fact, changes in the arts – their content, idiom and style – are due to a large number of diversified factors in interrelation. They include unpredictable changes in media and techniques – the discovery of oils, for instance, the inventing of the valved horn, and so on; the rediscovery of earlier art-styles, the impact of inventions in other fields – for instance the impact of photography upon the visual arts; and the equally unpredictable appearance of individual, innovating, artistic genius. The danger to freedom from the over-simplified, historicist account can be averted by attending to just these (untidy, undialectical) details of actual aesthetic changes. To fail to be alerted to this complexity is to be so much the more vulnerable to emotional *conditioning* and *indoctrination* by art – these being strongly contrasted with emotional *education*.

The distinction between indoctrinating and educating may not be self-evident where the emotions are concerned: but we are now in a position to see that it does have an important application. The recent philosophical analyses of emotion help one to understand just how it can apply. To be indoctrinated is to be prompted non-rationally to a belief or attitude or other state of mind: without, that is, being given or encouraged to seek good grounds. To be educated is to be put in a position to choose, knowing the alternatives, the pros and cons, the strength of the case. If emotions were simply inner feeling-states, then possibly at best they could be *induced*: a subject could be conditioned to have them. But, as we saw at the outset, there would be no room for the language of educating, or of providing grounds: no points either for rational appraisal or for the inserting of will. But there *is* room for these, if we realize (and teach) that emotions involve interpreting situations, and a selective directing of attention.

In the initial account, we moved by a gentle transition from the topic of emotional freedom to that of emotional vitality. In particular, it was claimed that art revivifies emotions that are custom-jaded, suppressed or held in abeyance; that it provides a remedy for over-objectifying attitudes, through offering artefacts that are made precisely to *be* the objects of emotion.

I can conceive various directions from which criticisms of this claim are likely to come. First, a preliminary remark. Hampshire has been quoted as saying: 'The price of full rationality is a separation of argument, and of systematic under-standing, from the primary emotions.' Such a remark (in isolation) may suggest, though it does not entail, a misleadingly sharp dichotomy of reason and emotion. If our account is at all on right lines, conceptualizing, interpreting – i.e. activities of reason – remain essential features of emotion-experience itself. Furthermore, intellectual activities can carry their own, often powerful, emotional charge, even if the emotions involved cannot be called 'primary', instinctive ones. But Hamp-shire (and Schiller) may none the less be correct in saying that some intellectual and technical activities can coexist with a greatly attenuated emotional response to the objects of our study and attention, and may even encourage the attenua-tion. In what follows, I shall tentatively suppose that to be true.

We can anticipate objections of two contrasted kinds. If it is true that art elicits powerful emotional responses, can such response be classed reliably as *educative* of the emotions? Can one be confident that it is not equally liable to be emotionally *corrupting*? The point is familiar, but it cannot be prevented from arising in a study of art and education. Is it true, in any case, that when art is properly understood, its resources properly appropriated, it functions primarily as an emotion-stimu-lus? A good deal of twentieth-century aesthetics strongly suggests the contrary.

No one denies that art can be used (misused) in order to arouse all manner of emotions. Erotic literature can be taken simply as pornography: so can passages of Scripture. Sadism can be nourished on an anthology of Renaissance revenge-tragedies. Ability to excite specific strong emotions, however, is only contingently and haphazardly correlated with aesthetic merit.

It is not at all obvious, moreover, that if art is able in some way to give vitality to the affective life, it must be through the converting of particular selected emotions into life-emotions. There are other possibilities. Schiller, for instance, wrote of the 'equanimity and freedom of the spirit, combined with power and vigour' which to him was the mood with which a genuine work of art should leave us. He added: if afterwards 'we find ourselves disposed to prefer some one particular mode of feeling or action, but . . . disinclined for another, this may serve as infallible proof that we have not had a *purely aesthetic* experience.'[17] Schiller was realistic enough to recognize this purity as a goal never fully realized in practice. We can put the point like this. The emotional enlivening proper to the arts may be far less a matter of stimulating particular, specific emotions in the spectator than of dispelling his emotional torpor and inculcating an alert, mobile, exploratory attitude to the play of feeling in the work of art as a whole. All this can certainly be transferred from art-experience to life-experience, and without the fragmentation of the work of art that is usually involved in treating it as a mere stimulus of, say, hate or fear.

This way of putting it might elicit some support even from writers who give much more stress to the formal features of art works than they do to emotion-evocation. When such writers come to describe their experience of art – synoptically grasping the work as a unity in which the quality of any one part is determined by all the other parts – they are describing an activity at the opposite pole from the sluggish or coldly analytical. They speak rather of mobility and alertness of mind, of faculties at full stretch: and they may even see part of the value of the tight, formal organization of a work of art as lying in its power to facilitate such intense and affectively vital activity.[18]

Despite all that has been said, it would be misleading to suggest that the mere presence of beautiful objects is a sufficient condition of emotional vitality for everyone all the time; and the initial account may be further faulted if it suggested the contrary.

Alongside the story of J.S. Mill's emotion-reviving has to be set that of Coleridge in 'dejection'. Neither art nor natural beauty could guarantee emotional vitality (or 'joy' as he called it) to Coleridge. A pre-existing joy was a necessary condition of aesthetic responsiveness. That is to say, recalcitrant factors of individual psychology, as well as social and technical pressures towards objectivity, can lead to the withdrawal of emotion. But to pursue that topic – to do more than just acknowledge it – would take us quite beyond the philosophy of art and of education. Instead, I shall end on a more distinctly philosophical note: for philosophical arguments and beliefs can also cause or partly cause the withdrawal of emotion.

Recall again William James's invitation to imagine a world from which all emotional quality has been abstracted: with it goes all 'significance, character, expression', and so on. Someone may react by saying, 'that, then, is how the world *really* is: the rest (value, emotion, expression) is colourful illusion, decoration, veneer that we apply to it.' One who even dimly feels like saying this will not give a high place on his agenda to the education of the emotions, or to the arts as furthering that end. For such a person the power of art to revivify feeling may be thwarted or sabotaged by the persistent thought – art masks the truth and seeks to undermine our loyalty to it.

What could be said in reply to him? First, consider the problem of discriminating between (1) the value of what is ontologically prior (the world minus its emotional colouring, as fundamental), and (2) the value of what has been worked upon by the energies of man. Even if the emotional and expressive qualities belong to the latter (to the interpreted, fashioned or projected), it does not follow that the person with most integrity and the most sensitive intellectual conscience must opt to live in a world stripped again of all we have contributed. In any case, it could hardly be called 'living'. The enterprise would require, for thoroughness, the stripping off also of all concepts, the abandoning of language, the withholding of all that we bring to the perception of a moment from memory-derived experience. If the enterprise *could* be carried through, it would amount to a form of self-destruction. Could one have an intellectual obligation to bring that about? Could one even speak of 'obligation' here at all – without inconsistency? To feel an intellectual obligation to hold to the austere, de-emotionalized picture of the world as the 'fundamentally true' picture is to feel an *obligation* – it is to have an interest and to make an evaluation: and that is to say – *not* to carry through a programme of removing these from the world.

Although this promised to be a field for philosophical analysis, and not a matter of individual psychology only, it seems the two cannot be kept entirely apart. There is a wide difference of attitude, only partly amenable to philosophical persuasion, between two types of person. The first type feels the life of the emotions to be downgraded and vilified if it turns out that non-human nature itself does not possess emotional qualities, or acknowledge values, or (in a more grandiloquent idiom) manifest a spiritual life. We can see him in the Romantic poet who seeks confirmation or endorsement of his emotion in the metaphysics of post-Kantian idealism or neo-Platonism. The second type admits that emotional qualities are essentially projected by man; but he is not at all downcast about this. He finds it an interesting, even an astonishing, fact that (in James's phrase) 'the world's materials lend their surface passively to all our projectings, and take on inexhaustibly many aspects, expressions, lights, as they do so.' These endless transformations of aspect are among our most distinctive and valuable contributions to the world. The proper account is not in terms of a masking or concealing of the alien, colourless reality, but of exercising a basic form of human creativity.

I have done little more here than set against each other two rhetorics – the one rhetoric disparaging, and the other defending, subjectivity and the life of the emotions. It would take more than a paper to argue out the point between them, and conclusiveness may not be attainable. One thing, however, is clear. If educating the emotions involves first of all taking the life of the emotions with seriousness – and surely it does – then the analysis and appraisal of these rhetorics must be a vital and continuing part of its task.[19]

Notes

1 *The Tempest*, I, ii, 50.
2 *Cf.* John Casey, *The Language of Criticism*, Methuen, 1966, pp. 107f.
3 'A Propos of *Lady Chatterley's Lover*', Phoenix edn, II, Heinemann, 1968.
4 Chatto & Windus, 1969, p. 246.
5 It must, of course, be added that in those cases where the emotion depends for its very existence upon precisely chosen words marshalled in one precise order, we cannot speak of that emotion as in any way available to us before we encounter the work – a necessary truth.
6 *Art as Experience*, Allen & Unwin, 1934, pp. 67f.
7 *The Varieties of Religious Experience*, Longman, 1902, p. 150.
8 *On the Aesthetic Education of Man*, eds E.M. Wilkinson and L.A. Willoughby, OUP, 1968, letter 6, para. 6.
9 *The Morality of Scholarship*, ed. M. Black, OUP, 1967, p. 36.
10 Quoted in G. Steiner, *Language and Silence*, Faber, 1967, p. 88.

11 *A L'Ombre des Jeunes Filles en Fleurs*, Paris, 1929, II, 2, p. 77; *Within a Budding Grove*, trans. C.K. Scott-Moncrieff, I, pp. 326f.

12 T.S. Eliot, *Four Quartets*.

13 *Antony and Cleopatra*, IV, xv.

14 *Macbeth*, II, iii. Someone may argue that in any case the examples of objectless emotions are more properly instances of *moods*, and that to have an object is in fact a necessary condition of being an emotion. Our vocabulary is certainly fluid in this area. We can mark the differences between, say, an obsessive, objectless melancholy and a fear of being arrested for a specific offence, by calling the first a matter of mood and the second an emotion in the full sense. There are similarities, however, as well as differences between the two sorts of case. If it is accepted that emotion may be discriminatingly expressed by a literary presentation of its object, then we can hardly avoid being perplexed whether there can be discrimination between affective states, when no object exists.

15 G.H. Bantock writes interestingly on this general topic, in his *Education, Culture and the Emotions*, Faber, 1967. And he finds apposite quotations in Stendhal, on the 'extent to which the realities we inhabit are themselves in part the creation of the books we have read, of the mythical formulations we have encountered' (p. 97). The present paper is indebted to Bantock's study at several points.

16 'A Propos . . . ', *op. cit.*, p. 493.

17 *Op. cit.*, letter 22, para. 3.

18 This is not primarily an essay in aesthetics; and I am not here concerned to decide between rival aesthetic theories. It needs to be said, however, that I have not been presupposing an 'instrumental' theory of art, according to which the chief (or only) value of art is its power to communicate emotion. The powers of art are multiple; and they are interrelated in complex ways.

19 Further bibliographical notes (some, but not all, of the following have been drawn upon in the chapter): J. Hillman, *Emotion*, Routledge & Kegan Paul, 1960; J.C. Gosling, 'Emotion and object', *Philosophical Review*, 1965; G. Pitcher, 'Emotion,' *Mind*, 1965; J. Benson, 'Emotion and expression', *Philosophical Review*, 1967; M. Tanner, 'Philosophy and criticism', *Oxford Review*, 1967; G.D. Marshall, 'On being affected', *Mind*, 1968; H. Morris-Jones, H. Osborne and R.W. Hepburn, *Aesthetics in the Modern World*, Thames & Hudson, 1968, pp. 81–124.

10

THE ARTS, WELL-BEING
AND EDUCATION

John White

What should be the purposes of education in the arts? This is a big question.
Fully to deal with it – and bearing in mind the kinds of art activities most
commonly found in educational institutions – would require asking why, if at all,
students should make art (write poems, paint pictures, compose music), perform
on musical instruments, engage in literary and other forms of art criticism. In
this paper I shall not be exploring these questions, but limiting the investigation
to what we might call sensuous engagement with works of art and why it should
be held to be educationally desirable.

The starting point for this enquiry, as for so many contemporary philosophical
enquiries about the content of education, must be Paul Hirst's article on 'Liberal
Education and the Nature of Knowledge' (1965). At the time of writing, Hirst's
interest, too, lay exclusively in engagement with the arts, 'literature and the fine
arts' constituting one of the forms of knowledge into which every liberally
educated person was to be inducted. The justification of the artistic form of
knowledge, like that of the others, lay in its indispensability for personal well-
being. For Hirst, as for the Greek philosophers, this resided in the flourishing of
the mind, which in turn consisted in being in a state of knowledge rather than
mere belief; and since knowledge was not all of a piece but was found in logically
discrete forms, individual flourishing depended on induction into *all* these forms.

While I see difficulties both in the view that art is a form of knowledge and in
tying personal well-being so closely to the possession of knowledge, I find Hirst's
claim that engagement with the arts is an essential ingredient of personal
flourishing intuitively appealing. If true, it may give us a powerful argument
for the place of the arts in education, including their place in the school
curriculum. In this paper I shall begin to put this wider claim of Hirst's to the
test, drawing also on recent philosophical writings about the arts which likewise
emphasise the latters' role in human well-being.

Source: From: Robin Barrow and Patricia White, *Beyond Liberal Education: Essays in Honour of Paul H.
Hirst*, Routledge, 1993.

Osborne's argument

Harold Osborne (1986: 298–9) has sought to justify the 'expansion and enhancement of aesthetic sensibility' as an educational aim. This goes further than, but includes, a justification of engagement with the arts, since it also covers aesthetic experience of nature and of the human environment. Osborne sees the current transition towards a society in which work loses its old salience as enabling the cultivation of 'cultural values' not only in a leisured elite but in the population as a whole. 'Culture' consists in the cultivation for their own sake of faculties originally developed for purposes of evolutionary survival, such as intelligence, intellectual curiosity and altruistic fellow-feeling. Another of these originally practical faculties is perception of the environment. In its intrinsic form it has become aesthetic experience: this is virtually definable as perception for its own sake.

Aesthetic experience is thus in the same category as the cultivated pursuit of intelligence in mathematics and logic, of intellectual curiosity in science and history, of religious awe and reverence in organised religion. The increasingly leisured individuals of the future will be able to devote themselves to one or more of such cultural activities. Will aesthetic concerns have any privileged place among them? On this Osborne states that 'aesthetic appreciation is the most important (cultural value) and has an even more general appeal than the acquisition of knowledge for its own sake' (p. 299). He does not say why it is the most important value. If he had done so, we might – it is not clear – have had a reason for making aesthetic experience an indispensable ingredient in human flourishing as distinct from an option which some might adopt and others ignore.

As it stands, Osborne's position and would seem to point to an educational justification of aesthetic engagement which consists in acquainting pupils with cultural pursuits, between which they will later choose which they prefer. The arts would presumably be an important element within the wider field of the aesthetic because of their 'high cultural value' (p. 298), in that it is in aesthetic experience of works of art that perception for its own sake is most fully developed.

The 'opening-up-options' justification of educational, including curriculum, activities is in its general form a familiar, and to my mind sound, argument, given some kind of background commitment to the value of personal autonomy as an element in personal well-being. It may, *inter alia*, be relied on to justify engagement with the arts. But it falls short of what is needed to support Hirst's stronger claim, to which this essay is directed, that such engagement is a *necessary* part of our flourishing. Can this stronger position be defended?

On the way to tackling that question, we need to look more closely at Osborne's account of aesthetic experience. For him it comes close to the exercise of our perceptual powers for their own sake. This would seem to imply that the aesthetic qualities of a work of art – or natural object – are confined to those which can be perceptually discriminated. But this is a contestable claim about the scope of the aesthetic. Others have held that this also covers other features of a work, its expressive powers, for instance, or its capacity to reveal truths about the world or about human nature.

If we accept the narrower account of the aesthetic, it is indeed hard to see engagement with the arts as anything more than an option for those drawn in that direction. It will be a matter of developing ever more skilful powers of discriminating such things as patterns of musical sound and their interrelationships, or connections and contrasts between lines, tones, spatial forms and colours in visual art. Those who do not choose to cultivate such connoisseurship need not feel that they are excluding themselves from something vital to their well-being – any more than they need feel this if they decide not to go in for chess or bacteriology.

The conclusion *seems* to be that if the arts are to have any deeper significance in our lives as objects of aesthetic concern a broader account of the aesthetic must be adopted. Whether this conclusion is true will occupy us through the next section.

Beyond options: further claims for the arts

It is often claimed that engagement with the arts can contribute to personal and social well-being in ways beyond its value as an option for those attracted by it. It has been variously said to help resolve psychological tensions and foster inner harmony; to help us to understand our own existence; to promote mutual sympathy and understanding; to break down feelings of isolation from the rest of mankind; to reinforce socially accepted values; to promote morality. Some writers see it as performing the redemptive role in society today which religion played in earlier times.

If valid, these claims provide educational justifications of some moment. We will be examining them in more detail in the rest of this paper. Many of those philosophers who make them hold the wider view of the aesthetic just mentioned. But not all do. In addition, some people would argue that the benefits referred to depend on a specifically *aesthetic* engagement with works of art; while others would agree that reading literature, looking at paintings and so on might have moral or psychological spin-off, but urge that this need have nothing to do with relating to the works as aesthetic objects. We need to separate these different strands.

Beardsley's argument

First, let us look at the position of Monroe Beardsley (1958). He writes about the 'inherent values' of works of art, that is, their 'capacity to . . . produce desirable effects by means of the aesthetic experience they evoke' (p. 573). He has in mind such effects as the relief of tension, the refinement of perception, the development of the imagination, the fostering of mutual sympathy. Unlike other writers with whom we will be dealing, Beardsley holds the narrower view of the scope of the aesthetic. Like Osborne, he restricts aesthetic qualities of a work to certain perceptual features, in his case broadly classifiable under the headings of unity, complexity and intensity of human regional qualities in the work (p. 462).

Although the third of these, which he exemplifies by such things as vitality, forcefulness, tenderness and irony, seems to point beyond perceptual qualities to emotions expressed in the work, he emphatically denies this, attracted by the thought that what we call the sadness or joyfulness of a piece of music is an objective feature of the work, dependent on perceptual qualities like tempo, rhythm, interval and pitch.

Beardsley's view is, then, that aesthetic experience as so defined can produce the desirable effects he describes. How sound are his arguments?

1   He admits that the claims that aesthetic experience relieves tensions, quiets destructive impulses and helps to create an inner harmony are speculative rather than soundly supported by empirical evidence, although he does mention a remarkable feeling of clarification that we feel when aesthetically absorbed – 'as though the jumble in our minds were being sorted out' (p. 574). We will come back to views about tension and harmony when we turn to writers with a wider view of the aesthetic.

2   His next claim is that aesthetic experience refines perception and discrimination. This seems to follow logically from his perception-based conception of the aesthetic. He further contends that 'if we can be made more sensitive and perceptive by aesthetic experience, then this would have a wide bearing upon all other aspects of our lives – our emotional relations with other people, for example' (ibid.). For this he produces no evidence and *prima facie* the claim seems implausible: just as a developed skill in throwing darts can remain a self-contained achievement with no spill-over on to the improvement of one's personal life or social relationships, should we not say the same of the skills of aesthetic discernment? We must not be misled by language in all this. When Beardsley says that aesthetic experience can make us 'more sensitive and perceptive', this is obviously true if we take these terms in a perceptual sense; but whether it makes us more sensitive to others' needs and more perceptive in our judgements of character is quite another matter.

3   A similar verdict should be passed on the statement that 'aesthetic experience develops the imagination and with it the ability to put oneself in the place of others' (ibid.). It is true that in aesthetic experience (in Beardsley's sense) 'we must be open to new qualities and new forms'; but the kind of imaginative capacity which this requires has to do solely with aesthetic perception and is not the same as the sympathetic imagination which enables us to put ourselves in others' shoes. One cannot assume a transfer of learning between one kind of exercise of the imagination and another: to show this, too, empirical evidence would be needed and Beardsley does not provide it.

4   He then argues that aesthetic experience 'fosters mutual sympathy and understanding'. We have to be careful here. We will come across similar claims when we turn to authors with a wider conception of the aesthetic.

The latter are talking about sympathy and understanding among people generally, or at least among people generally within the same community or culture. But Beardsley's claim is more limited. He has in mind people listening to the same music or seeing the same paintings and so on. 'Insofar as they have learnt to make similar responses, they share an experience' and this tends to bring them together in friendship and mutual respect, to create a bond between them. In adjudicating Beardsley's argument, we should not think of aesthetic experience in individualistic terms, as a transaction between a solitary person and an aesthetic object. If we did, then it would become an empirical matter, and one where evidence is probably not forthcoming, whether lovers of art tend to develop friendship and respect among them-selves. We should rely, rather, on MacIntyre's concept of a 'practice', as a co-operative activity with its own internal goods, included among them the recognition of various personal qualities among participants. If we conceive engagement with works of art as a practice, then it follows logically that those who pursue it are bonded together by ties of co-operative endeavour, respect for each other's abilities and that broad sense of friendship, transcending intimacy, to which Aristotle has drawn our attention in the *Nicomachean Ethics*. In sum, we can accept this claim of Beardsley's as conceptually true – as long as we remember that it has only to do with attitudes and behaviour among the aesthetically initiated and has no bearing on whether aesthetic experience fosters mutual sympathy and understanding outside this circle.

5   Beardsley's last claim is that aesthetic experience offers an ideal for human life – of an activity 'in which means and ends are so closely interrelated that we feel no separation between them' (p. 575). He counterposes this to the gap which often exists between means and ends in other parts of our social life, especially in more boring kinds of work. Aesthetic experience gives a clue as to how this undesirable state of affairs can be transformed.

I find this argument attractive, but wonder whether it gives aesthetic experience any privileged place in presenting this ideal over other activities where partici-pants see what they are doing as intrinsically rewarding, such as theoretical enquiry, sports, community service. If it is not so privileged, we come close to Osborne's position, described above. We may have a good reason for including engagement with art in the content of education in that it helps to extend the range of life-options; but we are not helped in our search for its *further* contribu-tion to personal and social well-being, which is the topic of this section.

Taking all five of Beardsley's arguments together and assessing the light they shed on this further contribution, we can rule out (5), as we have just seen. (2), (3) and (4) fail to deliver what they seemed to promise: where they are at their most convincing, the sensitivity, perceptiveness, imagination, sympathy and understanding which they mention are not qualities found in ordinary human intercourse, but are confined within the circle of aesthetic experience itself. This leaves (1), the speculative, empirically unsupported argument about the relief of tension and the promotion of inner harmony. All in all, Beardsley has given us next to no reason to think that engagement with the arts has any value for human life outside its own autonomous domain.

Other arguments

Osborne and Beardsley both adhere to the narrower conception of aesthetic experience which confines it to acquaintance with perceptual features of aesthetic objects, detaching this from everything lying outside the work itself. Not everyone sees the aesthetic as belonging to a world of its own – Anthony Savile (1982: 86), for instance, quotes with approval Stuart Hampshire's remark that empiricist philosophies 'have detached aesthetics as an autonomous domain, only contingently connected with other interests. . . . The enjoyment of art, and art itself, is trivialised, as a detached and peculiar pleasure, which leads to nothing else. Its part in the whole experience of man is then left unexplained' (Hampshire 1959: 246).

On a broader conception, the objects of aesthetic experience are not limited to perceptible features, still less to such formal features as Beardsley describes, like the complexity and unity in which sensuous phenomena – tones, colours, sounds, etc. – are bound together. The work of art is not, or is not always, an objective, completed entity, requiring only our trained aesthetic perception to yield its aesthetic fruit. On the contrary, for the latter to be possible we must often make a contribution of our own in the shape of an imaginative involvement with the work which brings it to completion. On one such conception, that of R.K. Elliott, one role of imagination is to enable us to experience works 'from within', as if we were participants in their worlds, or were entering into intimate communion with the characters portrayed in them or with their creators. In these ways we experience works as delivering situations (as in painting) or as expressing emotion (as in music) or both (as in poetry) (Elliott 1972: 157).

If one conceives aesthetic experience as not only of perceptual, including formal, features of works themselves, but also, at least in many cases, of imagined human feelings and situations, this helps to provide that non-contingent link between aesthetics and other human interests of which Hampshire wrote. Educationally, it enables us to see cultivating in young people a love of art not only as opening up new options, but also as helping them to live a fuller human life.

In what way? In recent writings, both Anthony Savile (1982) and Anthony O'Hear (1988) have discussed the wider value to us of engagement with the arts. I will now examine and assess some of their claims. As we shall see, several of them are superficially reminiscent of those of Beardsley; unlike Beardsley's, however, they do not shepherd us back inside a narrow perceptual fold.

O'Hear writes:

> Art, on the other hand (i.e. unlike science), is intimately involved in our sense of the value of things. First, by means of its sympathetic

re-enactments of anthropomorphic perspectives on the world, it can play a central role both in value enquiry and in coming to an understanding of the nature of one's own existence and the meanings available in it. And, then, through its ability to resolve, at least for a time, certain fundamental tensions in our existence, it is well fitted to play a role in fostering harmony in one's own existence.

(pp. 162–3)

The first of these claims is that art promotes value-enquiry and self-understanding; the second that it resolves certain tensions and fosters harmony. Are they both sound?

The first claim might seem to suggest that art is valuable to us for theoretical reasons, i.e. that it helps us to uncover truths with which we were not previously acquainted. It certainly can do this. In the field of value-enquiry, we can come to learn about the ethical values of other cultures or sub-cultures or other historical periods through their art, especially through their literature. But putting things like this underrates the importance that the arts can play in our ethical life. It appears to make engaging with them instrumental to something else, the pursuit of knowledge; and to suggest that if non-aesthetic evidence about values were superior to that furnished by art, the latter might prove dispensable. In addition, it is not even clear that in order to attain these theoretical benefits, one needs to engage *aesthetically* with a work, as distinct from mining it, as a scholar, for the light it might shed on other things.

But perhaps O'Hear has other things in mind than theoretical enquiry. He also writes of the contribution art can make to self-knowledge, and self-knowledge is perhaps more a form of practical wisdom than a theoretical achievement. As David Hamlyn (1977) has implied, it can scarcely be modelled on forms of understanding, like science or mathematics, where a distinction can be drawn between the knowing subject and an independent known object. Knowing oneself better is to have got one's priorities more into order, to have come more clearly to see what concerns weigh with one more than others. It involves having dwelt not on one's scheme of values, or hierarchy of desires, as a whole – for this would take us back to the misconception of self-knowledge as confrontation with some kind of inspectable object; but on particular values and on conflicts between them. One role of art is to enable us to dwell on, or better, perhaps, to dwell in our values or desires and their associated emotions in this more particular and less global way. Since works of art are produced to be enjoyed by a public, the desires, emotions and conflicts between them which they express are typically those which many have experienced; and one mark of the greatness of a work is its ability to strike such chords in all of us. In aesthetic engagement with art we come to a profounder self-awareness, of ourselves as unique individuals and at the same time of ourselves as members of a particular community or culture, and as human beings in general. We come to dwell not only in what we *do* feel but also in what we *would* feel if our circumstances were different, or became different. Art both reinforces feelings and priorities we already have and also shakes them up, unsettles established patterns and allows us imaginatively to entertain alternatives – a state, for instance, where grief dominates over everything, or where murder no longer belongs to the unthinkable.

This kind of argument for the ethical import of art may be charged with turning it into a vehicle for moral improvement, and therein treating it just as instrumentally as it is treated in the claim, examined earlier, that art can help in theoretical value-enquiry. We have to tread carefully here. There is no suggestion in this context that through the arts we may come to possess values that we did not possess before, e.g. altruistic values where previously we were egoistical. It may or may not be true that art, or some art, can have this power: to determine this would require empirical investigation. The point to be made is not that engagement with the arts gives us *new* values – although it might do this, but that we have to bring to it desires, feelings and the values they enshrine, which we *already* possess.

Even so, the claim may still look instrumental – it may seem to be saying that we sometimes have recourse to art so as to dwell on our desires and feelings and the conflicts and priorities between them. Does this not overlook the intrinsic interest in it which we must always have if we are to engage with it aesthetically? It is important to defuse this charge of instrumentalism. Aesthetic engagement with a work *is* something pursued for its own sake. But on a broader conception of the aesthetic, since part of what we *understand* by aesthetic engagement is imaginatively dwelling in feelings and desires, the experience of art cannot be divorced from ethical contemplation. We do not choose to read poems as aesthetic objects *in order to* reflect on the ethical life, where the latter is a further goal to which the former is a means; but in choosing so to read them we may well have such ethical ends in mind, accruing as part of our intrinsic experience of the work.

This kind of relationship between the aesthetic and the ethical can be obscured by too narrow a conception of either or both of these terms. Just as objects of aesthetic experience can be confined to perceptual qualities, so the ethical can become restricted to that sense of the moral, recently identified by Bernard Williams (1985), in which duty or obligation becomes the central concept: on a wider view of the ethical, this would cover all aspects of how we are to live our lives, including not only obligations into which we have entered, but also our commitments and enthusiasms for our own projects as well as, what is often inseparable from these, our attachments to persons and communities. If we work with a narrow conception of both terms, the aesthetic and the ethical do indeed constitute seemingly impermeable different worlds: of, on the one hand, a rarefied kind of perception, and on the other of attention to certain kinds of obligation. It is hard to see how aesthetic perception, pursued for its own sake, could be expected to have anything to do with our adhering to moral principles of, say, fairness or non-maleficence. On a broader view of both, however, they come much closer, so close that the aesthetic comes to presuppose the ethical in the way we have seen above (which is not to say that the ethical presupposes the aesthetic, although it may do). What is significant about the conceptions of both the aesthetic and the ethical in their narrow senses is the negligible place both have for the emotions. Just as aesthetic experience on this view has nothing to with expression, so in moral experience the emotions are seen not as motivators of moral conduct – for only the sense of duty could fill that role, but as forms of passivity which have the potential to interfere with our acting morally and so must be kept firmly under control. (A modern version of this Kantian theme is found in R.S. Peters' account of the education of the emotions in Peters (1972)). On a wider view of both areas, the emotions become of central importance: in respect of expression, in the cases of the aesthetic, and in the shaping of our fears, hopes, joys and sorrows into settled dispositions of behaviour and response in the case of ethics.

It is because we bring to our experience of art concerns that we already possess in life that art can play an often-remarked role in binding us together. Beardsley's claim in this area is confined to mutual understanding among the aesthetically initiated; but we now see how this circle can be both deepened and widened: deepened, because those who engage with a particular work of art can become conscious not only of a shared exercise of skills of discrimination but also of the shared life-emotions and values they bring to the work; and widened, because the sharing now goes beyond the initiated and includes others in society unacquainted with this work, or perhaps, indeed, with any works of art. The public character of works of art, their role as a focal point for shared experience, is from an ethical perspective an important feature of them. Since the ethical values which individuals possess come to them, often in complex ways (see Taylor 1990), from the cultures and communities in which they live, art can help to bind us not only as fellow human beings, but also as members of more localised groups. As O'Hear puts it: 'through art, indeed, the individual can come to a powerful realisation of the truth of Bradley's claim that a community enters into his essence' (1988: 148). This adds a further dimension to O'Hear's point about the role of art in fostering self-understanding. This mutual binding is not exclusively a matter of shared awareness; for experience of art, in encouraging us to dwell on the springs of our ethical life, recommits us to what we value, thereby strengthening their role in our life, both individually and communally. Savile (1982: 107), drawing on Hume, gives an interesting example: the tapering of pillars upwards from a broader base insensibly reinforces a shared desire for security.

In these ways, through their common roots in our desires and emotions, art reflects and fosters our ethical life. It has not been proposed, so far at least, that all art does this. Music, and among it the greatest, can be aesthetically interesting for its patterns and complexities of sound, even when we do not hear it as expression. This said, it may still be the case that the patterns and complexities themselves are ethically relevant, but in a different way. I shall be taking up this point in the next section.

O'Hear's second claim is that art can play a part in resolving certain fundamental tensions in our existence and thereby foster harmony. He has in mind such tensions as those between the self and the objective world, between feeling and reason, between the natural and the conventional, between the individual and the community. He writes of the redemptive powers of art, its ability to save us from 'gazing into the horrors of the night' (p. 140).

Elsewhere he makes a significantly different claim to do with tensions, that 'art can help us creatively to express and explore the tensions caused in us by the fundamental dualisms of our nature' (p. 148). Expressing and exploring tensions is different from resolving them. Can art do either?

A claim about resolution we also noted in Beardsley. Quite what resolution means in O'Hear's context would need further exploration, but, as with Beardsley, the claim in question, whether applicable to a narrower or a broader conception of the aesthetic, would seem to depend on evidence, which O'Hear does not provide. For him art seems to have powers once ascribed to religion – redemptive powers, as he puts it, of transforming our life from a meaningless jumble of conflicting elements into a harmonious unity. This may well bring art *too* close to religion. It suggests perfectibilism. The ideal of human perfectibility, as Passmore (1970) has reminded us, has deep roots in our history, not least in the history of our religious and political ideas, from ancient times, but is in his view to be shunned, not welcomed. 'To achieve perfection in any of its classical senses, as so many perfectibilists have admitted, it would first be necessary to cease to be human, to become godlike, to rise above the human condition' (p. 326).

Quite another outlook on human life sees conflict and tension as ineradicable from it. In contemporary ethics one sees this in writers like Williams (1985) who stress the irreducible diversity of values. From this perspective, O'Hear's second suggestion, that art helps us to express and explore basic tensions, may be more fruitful: it seems a surer vehicle of self-understanding than when viewed from the perfectibilist standpoint, since there it may lead us into a false conception of what we are.

At the same time, in any individual's life conflicts have to be managed somehow. Balances have to be struck, values weighted, all within some kind of personal system of psychological regulation. On this view of human flourishing, conflicts coexist within a unitary framework, one which is constantly changing with experience as balances are struck in different places. This has its obvious parallel in the contrasting elements held together within the framework of a work of art. Like a self, a work of art is nothing fixed. Both are endlessly open to being seen from new perspectives, to new features coming to the fore while others recede. Art may speak to us not only in its sensuous delights and its links with our emotional life, but also in its mirroring of our psychic constitution as a whole. If this is on the right lines, then even the least expressive music may still be ethically important to us. Music, indeed, may be a more faithful mirror of ourselves than painting. In the latter, the whole work is laid before us simultaneously for our contemplation. But we never see ourselves at any one time as a complete entity; to think in this way is to resort to that misconceived notion of self-understanding with which we dealt above. Music, flowing through time, never graspable *in toto*, but only in more local stretches and contrasts, is closer to our self as we know it.

Perhaps, after all, O'Hear has something more like this, and not perfectibilism, in mind in writing about art's contribution to our inner harmony. If so, it would be better not to link this with talk of redemption and salvation. Art may indeed have replaced religion in our age as a central element in our flourishing and in our self-understanding; but what it can do for us should not be exaggerated: our lives are not in danger without art, only vastly poorer.

Conclusion

The purpose of education in the arts cannot be restricted to enlarging options. They can have a more intimate connection with our flourishing – with fostering self-knowledge, reinforcing our ethical values, binding us together as members of communities. For these reasons alone, acquaintance with works of art should have a central place in the school curriculum, although not necessarily to an equal extent for pupils of different ages. This essay agrees with Paul Hirst, but for different reasons, that engagement with the arts is, at least, an *important* element in personal well-being. Whether it is an *indispensable* element, as his theory may suggest, is, after all, another question. Given that flourishing is not an all-or-nothing matter and that there can be different degrees of it, it would be hard to show that people could not flourish at all without art. With respect to poetry at least, Kit Wright (1989) is sceptical:

> When they say
> That every day
> Men die miserably without it
> I doubt it.

References

Beardsley, M. (1958). *Aesthetics*. New York: Harcourt Brace and World.

Elliott, R.K. (1972). 'Aesthetic Theory and the Experience of Art', in Osborne, H. (ed.), *Aesthetics*. Oxford University Press.

Hamlyn, D.W. (1977). 'Self Knowledge', in Mischel, T. (ed.), *The Self*. Oxford: Blackwell.

Hampshire, S. (1959). *Thought and Action*. London: Chatto & Windus.

Hirst, P.H. (1965). 'Liberal Education and the Nature of Knowledge', in Archambault, R.D. (ed.), *Philosophical Analysis and Education*. London: Routledge & Kegan Paul. Reprinted as Volume I Paper 12(i).

O'Hear, A. (1988). *The Element of Fire*. London: Routledge.

Osborne, H. (1986). Review of H.B. Redfern *Questions in Aesthetic Education. Journal of Philosophy of Education*, 20 (2).

Passmore, J. (1970). *The Perfectibility of Man*. London: Duckworth.

Peters, R.S. (1972). 'The Education of the Emotions', in Dearden, R.F., Hirst, P.H. and Peters, R.S. (eds), *Education and the Development of Reason*. London: Routledge & Kegan Paul. Reprinted as Volume II Paper 8(i).

Savile, A. (1982). *The Test of Time*. Oxford: Clarendon Press.

Taylor, C. (1990). *The Sources of the Self*. Cambridge University Press.

Williams, B. (1985). *Ethics and the Limits of Philosophy*. London: Fontana.

Wright, K. (1989). 'Poetry' in his *Short Afternoons*. London: Hutchinson.

Part I

(4) Critical thinking

11

(i) McPECK, INFORMAL LOGIC AND THE NATURE OF CRITICAL THINKING[1]

Harvey Siegel

There is at present an unprecedented interest in critical thinking (henceforth CT). National Commissions on the state of education decry the lack of emphasis on the development of reasoning ability in schools and call for the inclusion of reasoning in the curriculum as the fourth 'R'; educators of all stripes belittle rote memorization in favor of educational programs which teach students how to think; entire university systems require their students to take courses in CT before graduation. It is a good time to be in the CT business.

Alongside the rise in interest in CT, recent years have witnessed the growth of the Informal Logic Movement (henceforth ILM). ILM arose largely as a response to the domination of logic by formal methods, and with the conviction that formal logic did little to enhance the reasoning ability of students, especially with regard to the sort of reasoning required in ordinary, everyday situations. Within the ILM it is widely held that logic, construed informally, has much to contribute to the educational task of enhancing students' reasoning ability. Consequently, many persons within ILM consider it to be a leading force in the general educational effort to enhance reasoning ability, and construe it as a focus both for the intellectual clarification of the nature of reasoning and argument, and for the practical, political and pedagogical tasks of establishing critical thinking as an effective and central curricular effort.[2] In short, ILM and CT appear to be inextricably intertwined.

So there appears to be, at least in the minds of some, a close connection between CT, informal logic, and education. While some attention has been paid, in the literature of ILM, to the role of reasoning in education and to other aspects of CT, that literature has not, in my view, paid sufficient attention to questions concerning the nature of CT, the connection between informal logic and CT, or the larger questions of educational aims and ideals which a commitment to CT inevitably

Source: *Philosophy of Education 1985*, Urbana, Illinois, Philosophy of Education Society.

raises. ILM's commitment to CT is, I think, fraught with philosophical difficulties, difficulties which the movement neglects at its peril. In what follows I focus on one particular problem area ILM faces, for I believe that ILM, if it is to continue to construe itself as centrally concerned (either theoretically or pedagogically) with CT, must face much more squarely the important task of developing a satisfactory account of that notion. The remainder of this paper is an attempt to develop such an account.

John McPeck's recent work has also challenged ILM, and has similarly suggested that ILM endeavor to improve its problematic conception of CT. It is therefore appropriate to consider McPeck's analysis alongside the development of my own. This I do, throughout the following discussion.

I The nature of critical thinking

Much of the literature of ILM regards CT as a generalized skill or ability (or set of such skills and abilities). In his recent book *Critical Thinking and Education*,[3] however, John McPeck challenges this conception of CT. McPeck argues that CT cannot be properly regarded as a generalized skill, because there is no – and cannot be any – single critical thinking skill that can be applied generally across subject-area domains. This is because, according to McPeck, thinking (critical or otherwise) is never thinking *simpliciter*, it is always thinking about something or other.

> thinking is always thinking *about* something. To think about nothing is a conceptual impossibility.[4]

On the basis of this point, McPeck criticizes the sort of informal logic/CT course associated with ILM, namely a course which seeks to enhance students' thinking ability *in general*, i.e., without regard to any particular subject matter:

> In isolation from a particular subject, the phrase 'critical thinking' neither refers to nor denotes any particular skill. It follows from this that it makes no sense to talk about critical thinking as a distinct subject and that it therefore cannot profitably be taught as such. To the extent that critical thinking is not about a specific subject X, it is both conceptually and practically empty. The statement 'I teach critical thinking', *simpliciter*, is vacuous because there is no generalized skill properly called critical thinking.[5]

There are some obvious difficulties with this argument. Most fundamentally, it confuses thinking generally (i.e., as denoting a *type* of activity) with specific *acts* (i.e., tokens) or instances of thinking. McPeck's claim that 'Thinking . . . is logically connected to an X'[6] belies this confusion. A given act of thinking may, as McPeck suggests, always be about something or other; it may make no sense to say of a given episode of thinking that the thinker was thinking, but not about anything in particular. But it hardly follows from this that thinking, conceived as a general sort of activity which includes as instances all cases of particular acts of thinking about something – and such a conception must be possible, on pain of inability to identify all the specific acts as acts of *thinking* – must itself be construed as about something or other. It is not the case that the general activity of thinking is 'logically connected to an X', any more than the general activity of cycling is logically connected to any particular bicycle. It is true that any given act of cycling must be done on some bicycle or other. But it surely does not follow that the general activity of cycling cannot be discussed independently of any particular bicycle. Indeed, we can state, and teach people, general skills of cycling (e.g., 'lean to the left when making a left-hand turn', 'slow down before cornering, not during cornering', etc.), even though instantiating these maneuvers and so exhibiting mastery of the general skills requires some particular bicycle. As with cycling, so with thinking. Thus McPeck's suggestion that teaching CT *simpliciter* is a conceptual impossibility is mistaken. As we can teach cycling, so we can teach CT. It makes perfect sense, for example, to claim that one teaches CT, *simpliciter*, when one means that one helps students to develop reasoning skills which are general in that they can be applied to many diverse situations and subject matters. Contra McPeck, there is nothing vacuous or unintelligible about such a claim. This point is supported, moreover, by the fact that there are readily identifiable reasoning skills which do not refer to any specific subject matter, which do apply to diverse situations, and which are in fact the sort of skill which courses in CT seek to develop. Skills such as identifying assumptions, tracing relationships between premises and conclusions, identifying standard fallacies, and so on do not require the identification of specific subject matters: such skills are germane to thinking in subject areas as diverse as physics, religion, and photography. So McPeck's argument that CT is necessarily subject-specific and not generalizable, so that educational efforts (e.g., courses) aimed at developing general critical thinking skills are conceptually confused, is not compelling. It fails to distinguish between specific acts of thinking, and thinking conceived as a general type of activity (which allows the identification of those specific acts as acts of *thinking*), and it fails to take seriously obvious examples of general, i.e., not subject-specific, critical thinking skills and abilities.[7]

Having criticized the conception of CT as a (set of) generalized skill(s), McPeck offers a positive account of that notion. Noting that CT 'involves a certain skepticism, or suspension of assent,'[8] and that such skepticism must be reflective and judicious, McPeck suggests that CT is 'the appropriate use of *reflective skepticism* within the problem area under consideration.'[9] Applying his earlier contention regarding the necessity of subject matter for CT, McPeck argues that CT is properly understood as subject-specific:

> Since critical thinking is always, 'critical thinking about X,' it follows that critical thinking is intimately connected with other fields of knowledge.

Thus the criteria for the judicious use of skepticism are supplied by the norms and standards of the field under consideration.[10]

After chiding informal logicians for neglecting or denying this 'simple insight'[11] regarding the connection between CT and specific subjects or fields, and so for conceiving CT/informal logic as subject-neutral, McPeck suggests that 'the core meaning of critical thinking is the propensity and skill to engage in an activity with reflective skepticism.'[12] McPeck emphasizes that this propensity and skill requires thorough familiarity with the subject matter defining the activity; simply knowing some subject-neutral logic is not sufficient for CT: 'There is no set of supervening skills that can replace basic knowledge of the field in question.'[13] And McPeck offers the following 'more formal' expression of the concept of CT:

Let X stand for any problem or activity requiring some mental effort.

Let E stand for the available evidence from the pertinent field or problem area.

Let P stand for some proposition or action within X.

Then we can say of a given student (S) that he is a critical thinker in area X if S has the disposition and skill to do X in such a way that E, or some subset of E, is suspended as being sufficient to establish the truth or viability of P.[14]

Notice first that the notion of 'reflective skepticism' is opaque. A skeptic might be reflective, and yet her skepticism unjustified. And it will not do to justify skepticism in terms of its appropriateness, such appropriateness being determined by disciplinary or problem-area criteria, for often it is just those criteria which one needs to be reflectively skeptical about.

The act of suspension McPeck highlights in his 'formal' expression of the concept of CT is worth a bit more scrutiny. Here I think McPeck is importantly right about something, although his concern with grinding his 'subject-specific' axe has obscured the important point he makes. Appreciating this point clearly, moreover, leads the way to an incisive reformulation of the concept of CT.

What is it for a critical thinker to have 'the disposition and skill to do X in such a way that E (the available evidence from a field) is suspended (or temporarily rejected) as sufficient to establish the truth or viability of P (some proposition or action within X)?'[15] It is simply to say that the critical thinker has the disposition and skill to question the power of E to warrant P. That is, the critical thinker has the disposition and skill to ask whether E actually provides compelling reasons for P, or justifies P. This is, I think, the defining characteristic of CT: the focus on reasons and the power of reasons to warrant or justify beliefs, claims, and actions. A critical thinker, then, is one who is *appropriately moved by reasons*: she has a propensity or disposition to believe and act in accordance with reasons, and she has the ability to assess the force of reasons in the many contexts in which reasons play a role. McPeck rightly notes the two central components of this conception of CT. There is, first, the ability to assess reasons properly. Call this the *reason assessment* component. There is, second, the willingness, desire, and disposition to base one's actions and beliefs on reasons, that is, to *do* reason assessment and to be guided by the results of such assessment. This I call the *critical attitude* or *critical spirit* component of CT. Both components are, I claim, essential to the proper conception of CT, the possession of which is necessary for the achievement of CT by a person. They are jointly sufficient as well. The concept of CT is captured by this 'appropriately moved by reasons' (henceforth 'AMR') conception.[16]

Although McPeck's conception of CT hinges on the notion of 'reflective skepticism', which I have argued is defective in certain ways, it is important to note that McPeck's analysis does recognize the components of, and is largely compatible with, the AMR conception. As has already been pointed out, McPeck's formal expression explicitly mentions the critical spirit component of the concept of CT, and his subsequent discussion emphasizes this component: 'It is sufficient for our purposes to recognize that training in particular critical thinking skills is not sufficient to produce a critical thinker. One must also develop the disposition to use those skills.'[17] McPeck also emphasizes the central role of the reason assessment component in CT. He labels his approach to CT 'epistemological' rather than 'logical', because it focuses on the epistemology of various subject areas rather than on subject-neutral logic, and he notes that 'the epistemological approach to critical thinking involves little more than providing . . . [an] understanding [of] what constitutes good reasons for various beliefs.'[18]

McPeck's detailed articulation of his conception of CT thus approximates the AMR conception. However, his discussion often obscures this, for that discussion emphasizes issues which are tangential to the nature of CT, and in which he takes positions which are problematic – thus focusing attention on the tangential issues and his problematic positions on those issues and thereby obscuring his correct identification of the two central components of the AMR conception of CT. I wish now to (1) consider three such tangential issues, (2) show how McPeck's discussion of them is problematic, and (3) argue that the AMR conception is independent of these issues, and stands untouched by criticisms of McPeck's discusson of them.

II The relation of logic to CT

McPeck is emphatic in his insistence that logic (formal or informal) is either largely or entirely irrelevant to CT. He writes that:

> the real problem with uncritical students is not a deficiency in a general skill, such as logical ability, but rather a more general lack of education in the traditional sense. . . . I shall attempt to show why courses in logic fail to accomplish the goal of developing critical thinkers and how the

epistemology of various subjects would be the most reasonable route to that end . . . there is both a conceptual and a pedagogic link between epistemology, critical thinking, and education, but the study of logic or critical thinking as such has no part in this linkage.[19]

The standard approach for developing critical thinking . . . has been to teach logic and various kinds of general reasoning skills. Presumably, the rationale for this approach is that since logic plays a role in every subject, and logic is intimately related to reasoning, the study of logic should improve one's ability to assess arguments and statements in any subject area. What I wish to argue is that the plausibility of this reasoning can be sustained only by seriously underestimating the complexity of the different kinds of information used in arguments and by overestimating the role of logic in these assessments. That is, even when the problem at issue is the rational assessment of some statement or argument, the major requirements for such assessment are epistemological, not logical, in character.[20]

(I note in passing McPeck's ambivalence as to whether logic is *entirely* irrelevant to CT, or only *largely* irrelevant (so that logic is at least somewhat relevant). The former citation makes the first, stronger claim; the latter makes only the second, weaker claim.)

As noted earlier, McPeck agrees that reason assessment is a central component of CT – indeed he emphasizes the point, since his 'epistemological approach' places reason assessment at the heart of CT. Thus logic can be irrelevant to CT for McPeck only if logic has nothing to do with reason assessment. But this is false on its face: even if many, or even most, reasons are properly assessed only with reference to subject-specific criteria, some (and perhaps many or most) reasons are properly assessed at least partially in accordance with subject-neutral logical reasons. The fallacies furnish obvious examples here. To take just one: When Jehovah's Witnesses come to my door, and argue that I should believe in the divinity of the Bible because (for the reason that) the Bible proclaims itself to be the divine word of God, it does not take any theological or other subject-specific information or criteria to realize that the reason offered does not in fact support the claim it is offered in support of. Rather, it begs the question. Here logic is relevant to reason assessment, and so is relevant to CT, even on McPeck's own terms. This example illustrates the relevance of *informal* logic to reason assessment, and so to CT as McPeck construes it.

Similarly, *formal* logic is relevant to CT. First, formal logic can be seen as providing a paradigm of good argumentation. A deductively valid formal argument is as strong an argument as it is possible to have; the connection between the premises and conclusion of such an argument is as tight as any such connection can be. To put the point slightly differently: formal argumentation may profitably be seen as constituting an 'ideal type' of argument, which (like ideal types in social science, or 'ideal laws' like the ideal gas laws in physical science) may not be typically, or ever, encountered in everyday discourse, but which nevertheless are central to our theoretical understanding of argumentation. Thus formal logic is a crucial component of an adequate conception of CT.

A second reason for thinking formal logic to be relevant to CT is that the latter is fundamentally concerned with the proper assessment of reasons, and formal logic provides an excellent source of clear reasons. For example, it is hard to imagine a more compelling reason for accepting some proposition 'q' than the proposition '$pvq.-p$' ('p or q, and not p'). Given the latter proposition, we have conclusive reason for accepting the former. In fact, propositions which deductively entail some other proposition seem to me to be the most compelling reasons for accepting the latter proposition that there can be. Thus formal logic is relevant to reason assessment, and so to CT (and exposure to formal logic is desirable for the CT student, for it illustrates well the fundamental property of 'being a reason for').[21]

Thus logic (both formal and informal) is relevant to reason assessment, and so to CT, on McPeck's terms as well as my own. Logic is relevant to the determination of the goodness of reasons. Such determination is central to CT. Thus his claim that logic is irrelevant (either largely or totally) to CT is mistaken.

III The relation of logic to information

McPeck draws a sharp distinction not only between logic and CT. He also[22] distinguishes sharply between logic and (non-logical, subject-specific) information, and argues that the assessment of good reasons is determined (largely or wholly) by the latter. We have already seen that McPeck claims that 'the major requirements for [the rational assessment of statements or arguments] are epistemological, not logical, in character.'[23] His view is that the assessment of good reasons is dependent, not on logic, but on specialized, feld-dependent knowledge:

> typically we are in a quandary less about the logical validity of an argument than about the truth of the putative evidence. We frequently cannot determine whether evidence is good or not, because such a judgement depends upon special knowledge. One has to be a fellow participant in the particular domain of meaning to appreciate the proper significance of the evidence.[24]

> critical thinking is linked conceptually with particular activities and special fields of knowledge.[25]

> specific content, knowledge and information cannot be coherently demarcated from critical thinking.[26]

McPeck is at least partly right here: the assessment of reasons often involves essential appeal to information which is subject-specific or field-dependent. But there are difficulties here as well. First, McPeck shifts, as earlier, between stronger and weaker claims: that logic is entirely irrelevant to reason assessment, or that it is only somewhat irrelevant (and so somewhat relevant) to such assessment; that information is sufficient for reason assessment, or only necessary for such assessment; that information is always necessary for reason assessment or only sometimes necessary. McPeck writes, for example that

> a minimal condition for understanding a good reason in any field is that one understands the full meaning of the specialized and often technical language in which such reasons are expressed.[27]

True enough, in cases in which reasons are expressed in specialized and technical language. But frequently reasons are expressed in non-specialized, non-technical language. In such cases full understanding does not require mastery of specialized language. Reasoning occurs in specialized and technical, but also in non-specialized and non-technical, areas. Thus McPeck's weaker claim that specialized information is sometimes required for reason assessment is sustained, but the stronger claim that it is always required is not. (How typical each sort of case is is an empirical matter.) Moreover, the weaker claim is an important point for critical thinkers to appreciate, but it is not itself a subject-specific point; it is rather a general point about reason assessment that could well be made in a general critical thinking course. Thus McPeck's weaker claim is well-taken. But it must not be confused with the stronger claim. Nor does it cast any general doubt on the utility of a general course in CT. Indeed, points like the ones McPeck is concerned to make, e.g. that specialized knowledge is often required for reason assessment, themselves belong to no specific field; to the extent that they are important points for critical thinkers to grasp, it seems highly appropriate to present them in a domain-neutral CT course. Thus McPeck's argument does not only not undermine, it actually suggests the practical necessity or utility of, general CT courses: such courses are important if there is general information – like McPeck's point, and like logic – that it is important for students to have.

If there is a viable distinction to be drawn between logic and information, they are both relevant to reason assessment and so to CT. McPeck does well to remind us of the importance of specialized information for CT. But this in no way establishes the non-importance of general information, or the inappropriateness of general CT courses.

IV   The relation of CT to rationality

We have already seen McPeck's emphasis on the role of good reasons in CT. This naturally raises the question of the relation of CT to rationality. McPeck suggests that CT is a sub-species of rationality, but that the latter far outstrips the former:

> While critical thinking is perfectly compatible with rationality, and with reasoning generally, we should not regard the terms as equivalent. The concept of critical thinking denotes a particular type of thinking . . . no injustice to rationality will result from simply construing it as the *intelligent use of all available evidence* for the solution of some problem. There are, of course, difficulties with the notion of evidence (what, for example, is to count as evidence?). Also, rationality may sometimes countenance the disregarding of certain types of evidence. But it is precisely from these problematic junctures in reasoning that critical thinking derives its conceptual content and it is here the employment of critical thinking is perhaps most useful. Indeed, it requires critical thinking even to recognize that one has arrived at such a juncture. All of this does not make critical thinking distinct from, much less incompatible with, rationality; rather rationality includes critical thinking as a particular aspect (or subset) of itself. The concept of critical thinking merely marks out the facet of rationality that comprises the disposition and skill to find such difficulties in the normal courses of reasoning.[28]

McPeck seems to suggest here that rationality is broader than CT in that, while rationality includes within its domain all instances of the intelligent use of evidence in the solution of problems, CT involves only some of those instances: namely, those instances in which the determination of relevant evidence is problematic. When one is engaged in intelligent problem solving, one is within the domain of rationality; when one is engaged in such a way that it is necessary to raise 'meta-questions' about the constitution, relevance, or appropriateness of putative pieces of evidence to the solution of the problem at hand, one is in the sub-domain of CT within the larger domain of rationality. CT is a particular sort of rational thinking which takes place in a particular sort of problem-solving context.

The distinction McPeck draws here between CT and rationality is untenable. McPeck limits the range of CT to cases in which reasons or evidence are in some ways problematic, and to reasoning about the problematic nature of the reasons or evidence in question. But this restriction is not argued for. It is, moreover, incompatible with McPeck's earlier articulation of his 'epistemological approach' to CT, according to which CT involves the skill and disposition to seek out, understand, and base belief and action upon good reasons. If McPeck is to maintain his 'epistemological' or 'good reasons' approach to CT, then he must reject the limitation he seems to want to place on the range of CT in his distinction between CT and rationality. The reason assessment component of CT extends to the assessment of all reasons, not just 'meta-reasons' concerning the constitution, relevance or appropriateness or problematic 'ground floor' reasons.

Once one rejects this limitation on the range of CT, the distinction between CT and rationality collapses. CT is coextensive with rationality, not merely a dimension of it, for rationality is 'coextensive with the relevance of reasons,[29] as is CT. The connection between rationality and reasons is as tight as can be. As Laudan puts it:

> At its core, rationality . . . consists in doing (or believing) things because we have good reasons for doing so . . . if we are going to determine whether a given action or belief is (or was) rational, we must ask whether there are (or were) sound reasons for it.[30]

Insofar as rationality consists of believing and acting on the basis of good reasons, and insofar as we accept McPeck's epistemological approach to CT (or any approach which makes reason assessment central), we must perforce regard CT not as a dimension of rationality, but as its equivalent or educational cognate. Thus the distinction McPeck draws between CT and rationality cannot be sustained.

It is time to regain the thread of the overall argument. I have been arguing that McPeck's discussions of the relations between logic and CT, logic and information, and CT and rationality are in their various ways problematic. This should not obscure the fact that we are fundamentally agreed that CT centrally involves reason assessment and the disposition to engage in it, that is, that CT involves both the reason assessment component and the critical spirit component of the AMR conception. That conception is unbesmirched by the difficulties with McPeck's analysis which I have been belaboring for the last few pages. In the end McPeck is importantly right about the nature of CT, despite those difficulties.

V Conclusion

If the AMR conception of CT is correct, two large sets of philosophical issues are of crucial importance for the analysis and theory of CT, and so for ILM. The first involves the relationship between CT and the philosophy of education; the second the relationship between CT and epistemology. The first of these sets of issues, concerning the relationship between ILM, CT and the philosophy of education, the justification of CT as an educational ideal, and the justification of educational interventions aimed at the fostering of CT skills and dispositions in students, is particularly germane for this audience. I regret that space forbids pursuit of these important and exciting issues.[31]

I hope, however, that our time here has not been wasted. For central to these issues is the notion of CT, a notion which is far from clear. Important theoretical and practical work hinges on it. To the extent that light has been shed on it, work in informal logic, educational psychology, educational policy, curriculum development, and pedagogy all stand to benefit.

McPeck's book has been fundamental to the clarificatory project. While not without its difficulties, *Critical Thinking and Education* has shaken ILM from its complacency with respect to the notion of critical thinking, and also with respect to its obliviousness to central issues in the philosophy of education. For philosophy of education, it has breathed new life into classical questions concerning, among others, educational aims and their justification, the role of logic in education, and the relationship between subject-specific information and 'domain-neutral' information and their respective roles in the curriculum. Such breaths of fresh air do not come our way very often. We are all in McPeck's debt for sending this happy and refreshing gust our way.

Notes

1 This paper is taken from Part One of my 'Educating Reason: Critical Thinking, Informal Logic, and the Philosophy of Education.' Part One, 'A Critique of McPeck and a Sketch of an Alternative View,' is to appear in the *American Philosophical Association Newsletter on Teaching Philosophy*, 1985. Part Two, 'Philosophical Questions Underlying Education for Critical Thinking,' is to appear in *Informal Logic* 7 (1985).

2 As Richard Paul puts it, ILM 'ought to move to become the professional group that superintends the teaching of logic-critical thinking skills in the public schools and so universalize its influence in education.' Richard Paul, 'An Agenda Item for the Informal Logic/Critical Thinking Movement,' *Informal Logic Newsletter* 5 (1983): 24. Similarly, Blair and Johnson offer as one of the attitudes which characterize ILM the following: 'An orientation that treats the teaching of reasoning skills as a key part of education, integral . . . to preparation of youth for responsible social and political roles.' J. Anthony Blair and Ralph H. Johnson, 'Introduction,' in *Informal Logic: The First International Symposium* (Inverness, Calif.: Edgepress, 1980) [henceforth *IL*], p. x.

As Blair has forcefully pointed out to me, it is misleading to speak to ILM as a monolithic group with universally shared viewpoints. On the contrary, philosophers who identify themselves with ILM differ widely on virtually every matter of group interest. Indeed, the very identification of ILM and its members is problematic. Roughly, I have in mind those persons who read *Informal Logic*; belong to the Association for Informal Logic and Critical Thinking (AILACT), which is affiliated with the American Philosophical Association; attend conferences on critical thinking and/or informal logic held periodically at the University of Windsor, Sonoma State University, and elsewhere; and teach courses in informal logic and/or critical thinking. The diversity of opinion among such a wide collection of persons is, I agree with Blair, very great. Nevertheless, some generalizations, such as the ones which appear in this paragraph, seem to me appropriate.

3 John McPeck, *Critical Thinking and Education* (New York: St Martin's Press, 1981). In subsequent references to this book, emphases are in original unless otherwise noted.

4 McPeck, p. 3.

5 *Ibid.*, p. 5.

6 *Ibid.*, p. 4.

7 *Cf.* Richard Paul's similar criticism in his review of McPeck's book, in *Educational Leadership* (forthcoming), Stephen P. Norris' excellent discussion of this issue in his 'The Choice of Standard Conditions in Defining Critical Thinking Competence,' *Educational Theory* 35 (1985): 97–107, and Perry Weddle's review of McPeck's book in *Informal Logic* 6 (1984): 23–5.

8 McPeck, p. 6.

9 *Ibid.*, p. 7.

10 *Ibid.*, pp. 7–8.
11 *Ibid.*, p. 8.
12 *Ibid.*
13 *Ibid.*, p. 9.
14 *Ibid.*
15 *Ibid.*, p. 13.
16 Further discussion of this conception of critical thinking may be found in my 'Critical Thinking as an Educational Ideal,' *The Educational Forum* 45 (1980): 7–23; and my 'Educational Ideals and Educational Practice: The Case of Minimum Competency Testing,' *Issues in Education* 1 (1984): 154–70. Robert W. Binkley also holds something like this two-part conception of critical thinking/good reasoning. Robert W. Binkley, 'Can the Ability to Reason Well be Taught?' in *IL*, pp. 79–92.
17 McPeck, p. 19.
18 *Ibid.*, p. 22.
19 *Ibid.*
20 *Ibid.*, p. 23.
21 In the paper mentioned in note 1 above, Part Two, I argue that the development of an epistemological account of reasons, and of the relation A bears to B when A is a reason for B, is one of the central philosophical tasks to which ILM must address itself. The above discussion of formal logic is taken largely from my 'Educational Ideals and Educational Practice: The Case of Minimum Competency Testing.'
22 The two distinctions McPeck draws are closely related: logic is to be distinguished from critical thinking precisely because it is not logic, but information, which is relevant to reason assessment. They are of a piece. Nevertheless, it serves clarification more fully to separate the distinctions and discuss each in turn.
23 McPeck, p. 23.
24 *Ibid.*, p. 28.
25 *Ibid.*, p. 56.
26 *Ibid.*, p. 64.
27 *Ibid.*, pp. 23–4.
28 *Ibid.*, p. 12.
29 Israel Scheffler, *Conditions of Knowledge* (Chicago: Scott Foreman and Company, 1965), p. 107. *Cf.* further discussion of Scheffler and of the relation between critical thinking and rationality in my 'Critical Thinking as an Educational Ideal.'
30 Larry Laudan, *Progress and Its Problems* (Berkeley: University of California Press, 1977), p. 123. Critical discussion of Laudan's application of this point to the problem of the rationality of science can be found in my 'Truth, Problem Solving and the Rationality of Science,' *Studies in History and Philosophy of Science* 14 (1983): 89–112.
31 I take them up in the papers mentioned in note 1 above.

11

(ii) RESPONSE TO HARVEY SIEGEL

John E. McPeck

First, Siegel presents an argument which is designed to show that 'thinking' can, and should, be considered a general skill with a general range of application. He argues:

> It is not the case that the general activity of thinking is logically connected to an X, any more than the general activity of cycling is logically connected to any particular bicycle ... As we can teach cycling, so we can teach thinking.

It seems to me that this analogy with cycling falls wide of its mark for one crucial reason: 'cycling' does denote a specific skill, whereas 'thinking' does not. All manner of things *can* and *do* count as effective *thinking*, but not all manner of things can count as effective *cycling*. Cycling has a rather limited, if not unique, set of standards and criteria which determine what counts as effective cycling. But there is no similar set of finite criteria which determine (or define) effective thinking. Furthermore, Siegel keeps using the awkward phrase 'the general activity of cycling', and this locution hides an important confusion: cycling is not a 'general activity' but a rather specific one. The only sense in which it is *general* is that you can go to different places, and for different purposes, but cycling, *qua* cycling, is a specific activity. Different destinations and purposes do not change the specific nature of the skill of cycling. But different problems and purposes *do* change the inherent nature of the skills required in thinking. No one set of skills can encompass 'thinking', but one set of skills does encompass cycling.

Furthermore, in order to teach someone to be an effective cyclist, one specific bicycle is sufficient. But to teach someone to be an effective thinker (whatever that might mean) one specific thought or, indeed, type of thought, is not sufficient. I do not, therefore, believe that thinking can be effectively taught as if it were a specific skill.

Source: *Philosophy of Education 1985*, Urbana, Illinois, Philosophy of Education Society.

The next point in Siegel's paper which I will briefly comment upon is his claim that:

> There are readily identifiable reasoning skills which do not refer to any specific subject matter, which do apply to diverse situations, and which are in fact the sort of skill which courses in CT seek to develop. Skills such as identifying assumptions, tracing relationships between premises and conclusions, identifying standard fallacies, and so on do not require the identification of specific subject matters.

First, let me say that I have analyzed and discussed these kinds of skills at length, both in my book and in subsequent papers, so I shall not repeat myself here. But very briefly, I have argued that phrases like: 'the ability to identify assumptions', 'the ability to draw valid conclusions from premises', 'the ability to define a problem', etc. are phrases which semantically masquerade as descriptions of general abilities, but upon analysis, none of them actually denotes a generalized ability. Rather, each phrase subsumes a wide variety of *different* instances under its rubric, such that no singular ability could account for its diverse range of achievements. Take, for example, 'the ability to recognize underlying assumptions'. That this is not a singular ability can be appreciated by considering the fact that to recognize an underlying assumption in mathematics requires a different set of skills and abilities from those required for recognizing them in a political dispute, which are different again from those required in a scientific dispute. Thus, the phrase 'ability to recognize underlying assumptions' does not denote any singular uniform ability, but rather a wide variety of them. Assumptions are not all cut from the same cloth. And even trained logicians cannot (to use Siegel's phrase) 'readily identify them' within the various domains of human knowledge. You can, of course, logically characterize assumptions for students, that is, tell them what an assumption *is*, but this logical knowledge will not enable them to discover the diverse assumptions in the various knowledge domains and contexts. In general, I think many people, including Siegel, are actually bewitched by the grammar of these phrases into thinking that they denote singular, teachable skills, and that these skills can be 'readily' applied no matter what the subject matter or context. In actual practice, these phrases refer to a wide variety of skills, which logicians (and sometimes ourselves) give a common nomenclature to. But we should not think that these collective descriptions refer to a singular skill.

Having said this, I should also point out (as Siegel has observed) that I do not regard the study of logic as totally without point. There is certainly something to be said for understanding what an assumption is, what a deductive inference is, etc. But I do object to such understandings being cashed-out as providing general 'critical thinking skill'. Anyone generally familiar with the critical thinking literature knows that this is not merely a paranoid worry on my part. Though not his intent, perhaps, Siegel's interpretation of these general phrases as describing 'general abilities' inadvertently provides aid and comfort to the army of false advertisers out there. Knowing what an assumption *is*, and knowing what a valid argument *is* is far from sufficient for enabling people to engage in effective critical thinking, at least, in any significant context. In a sense, the study of logic is a bit like studying formal linguistics by people who are about to study a foreign language: it is perhaps interesting, has *some* relevance, but is largely beside the *practical* point.

The longest single discussion in Siegel's paper has to do with the 'relations of logic to CT'. In my book I have argued that the informal logic movement (ILM) overestimates the role of logic in CT. In particular, I argued that the business of *reason assessment* is primarily an epistemic inquiry, since it has to do with truth, evidence, and beliefs. And logic, as such, has little (and perhaps often *no*) role to play in such endeavors. Siegel, on the other hand, wants to make a case that a subject-neutral logic plays a much larger role in reason assessment than I acknowledge.

In any case, I have argued that reason assessment, *per se*, is primarily an epistemic matter (not a logical one), because reasons are the premises *within* arguments which we must assess for their truth or plausibility. And when we are assessing the truth or plausibility of premises we are engaged in an *epistemic* and not a logical endeavor. However, Siegel believes, that more often than not (?), logic itself plays a substantial role in the assessment of reasons *per se*. He says:

> The fallacies furnish obvious examples here. To take just one: When Jehovah's Witnesses come to my door, and argue that I should believe in the divinity of the Bible because (for the reason that) the Bible proclaims itself to be the divine word of God, it does not take any theological or other subject-specific information or criteria to realize that the reason offered does not in fact support the claim it is offered in support of. Rather, it begs the question. Here logic *is* relevant to reason assessment.

Even in this example, however, which is offered as a clear-cut case of logic assessing a reason, I would insist to the contrary that the assessment of the reason given is still epistemic rather than logical. If you examine the reason given by the Jehovah's Witness, you will see that the reason given *does support* the conclusion (how ever weakly) that the Bible has divine origin. Indeed, we should be surprised if the Bible did *not* assert of itself that it has divine origin. Of course, we would not believe this grand assertion simply for that reason, but it does constitute *some* evidence (how ever weak) for its divine origin. We remain skeptical of the assertion because we would want other corroborative evidence of some kind which would help support the authenticity or veracity of the assertion – without such we must remain skeptical. But notice that our skepticism is based upon *epistemic*, not logical, considerations having to do with what constitutes good reasons for this claim. If, in a parallel example, the FBI received a letter which read: 'I, John Doe, do hereby confess that I am the authentic assassin of Jimmy Hoffa, etc., etc.,' the FBI would and should take this as *some* evidence of the claim asserted in the letter. The same holds for the Bible case. In both, we are assessing the veracity or authenticity of evidence (albeit weak), but *logic* does not reveal the weakness of such evidence. Thus, I still regard epistemology, and not logic, as the major tool of reason assessment. What has gone wrong in the ILM generally, and to a lesser extent in Siegel's paper, is that both seriously *underestimate* the complexity of ordinary information or knowledge and they seriously *overestimate* the role of logic in helping to unravel such complexity.

And finally, Siegel challenges and rejects my claim that CT is a dimension, or sub-set, of rationality generally. He claims that CT and rationality are 'coextensive' and 'equivalent'. He says:

> The distinction McPeck draws here between CT and rationality is untenable. CT is coextensive with rationality, not merely a dimension of it, for rationality is 'coextensive with the relevance of reasons', as is CT. The connection between rationality and reasons is as tight as it can be.

I have two comments to make about this position. First, I would argue that the concept of 'rationality' is not only broader than 'CT', but it is also broader than 'reason assessment'. Thus, contrary to Siegel, it is not coextensive or equivalent with either of them. Let us begin with 'reason assessment'. While the assessment of reasons (indeed any kind of reason) *can, in principle,* be the object of rationality, it does not follow that rationality always consists in the assessment of reasons. Sometimes it is rational merely to accept certain reasons *without* assessing them. For example, it would be rational merely to accept directions to an address from a stranger when in a strange city (i.e., it is better than wondering). Also, I might rationally believe that it is going to rain this evening just because the weatherman said so. In neither of these rational actions is the assessment of reasons involved. While it is possible *in principle* to provide assessment of these reasons, the rational actions themselves do not involve such assessments: the reasons are here merely accepted. Thus, unless one is going to stretch the meaning of 'reason assessment' beyond recognition, since there is no *process of assessment* going on here, I do not see how these rational actions could be seen as cases of 'reason assessment'.

Furthermore, consider the very large class of rational acts that we routinely engage in, sometimes even out of habit, where 'reason assessment' plays no part. For example, when I use a calculator to do sums, I rationally rely upon it without questioning or thinking about whether its answers are correct. With more complex calculations, we might not even understand the reasons if they should be provided, yet we routinely, and rationally, rely on such things. But even in those cases where we were once provided with reasons which we understood, we do not continue to assess those reasons *each time.* Indeed, to the contrary, it would be considered irrational to do so. Even when I brush my teeth, which is now a rational habit (just as smoking is an irrational habit), I seldom rehearse the reasons why it is rational. But it is nonetheless rational for that. Therefore, not all cases of rationality are cases of 'reason assessment'. And *a fortiori*, not all cases of rationality involve CT. My position is, and has been, that CT and reason assessment are a sub-class of rationality. Therefore, they are not equivalent or coextensive notions, as Siegel argues.

Secondly, my analysis of the concept of CT as 'the disposition and skill to engage in an activity with reflective skepticism', specifically tried to capture this particular dimension of rationality, and to set CT off from the other kinds of rational behavior. I believe this partitioning is consistent with the ways we talk about CT in our daily language, and with our pre-analytical intuitions about CT. Just as we, and our language, recognize that not all cases of thinking are cases of CT, we also recognize that not all cases of rational behavior are cases of CT. To argue, as Siegel does, that rationality is coextensive with CT, not only flies in the face of ordinary language, but it leaves one to defend the view that brushing one's teeth is an instance of CT.

Part I

(5) Gender and education

12

IS WOMEN'S STUDIES A LEGITIMATE SCHOOL SUBJECT? AN OUTLINE OF AN AGENDA FOR DISCUSSION

Lyn Yates

For some time now the question of the range of appropriate offerings for the secondary curriculum has been the subject of debate and soul-searching in Australia. Arguments have been forged in school-based discussions, in various state government inquiries and accreditation committees, and in the federal-level attempt by the Curriculum Development Centre to develop a core curriculum[1] and promote discussions by academics, teachers and the press. At the same time there has been vigorous work by Equal Opportunity Units and by concerned workers at all those levels mentioned above, to consider the issue of sexism in schools and the ways in which the curriculum fails to do justice to the work and interests of women and girls. Nevertheless, although 'equal opportunity' work is accepted as legitimate, and the purging of sexist references in textbooks is seen as necessary, when the question of teaching 'women's studies'[2] arises the response is far from a unanimous support. Responses range from bitter hostility and sarcastic jibes concerning the validity of the subject as an area of knowledge and the political values it is seen as expressing, to the passionate advocacy of those who feel that this is the central knowledge to be taught. And somewhere in the middle are those who are supporters of equal opportunity issues, but, for a variety of reasons, are doubtful that the teaching of women's studies is the best line of action to take.

Although there has been considerable discussion both of women's studies and of the nature and legitimacy of subjects in the school curriculum, the two types of discussion commonly take place in different worlds: they are published in different places, read by different audiences and address different concerns. Theorists of knowledge and the curriculum generally take questions relating to girls and women as a side issue, something that might require a particular

Source: *Journal of Curriculum Studies*, 1986, Vol. 18, No. 1.

working-out in the light of their general principles but which is not fundamental to their formulations. They usually have, at best, a superficial understanding of feminist critiques. Advocates of women's studies on the other hand, while they might describe the nature and value of their own concerns, rarely do so in the context of an explicit consideration of the general role of public schooling. Most of the discussion and theorizing concerning women's studies has in fact been concerned with the situation of adult women and with institutions and educational forms which cater for them.[3] At secondary school level, although many reformist teaching projects have been embarked upon, in theoretical terms far more attention has been directed by feminists to what is wrong with the curriculum than to what should be done about it.[4]

The arguments which follow attempt to draw together the rationale and concerns that have motivated the development of women's studies with the rationale and concerns that have been asserted by 'mainstream' theorists and practitioners of the school curriculum. My concern is with the institution of compulsory public schooling. More specifically, the context of what follows is that of discussions and activities in Australian schooling. The forms and cultural context of Australian schooling are not identical to those in other countries, though the points to be discussed here are largely those which have some general relevance.

The two major sections of this article are somewhat different in form. The first takes the form of arguing a case concerning the legitimacy of women's studies as an area of study. It briefly establishes the nature of the area of study in question, sets out the types of argument about legitimacy that have been made by curriculum theorists, and suggests how the specific arguments about women's studies are, and should be, interpreted here. The purpose of the second section of the article, however, is not to argue to a particular conclusion but rather to set out some of the types of argument about whether and in what way women's studies might be offered in the curriculum. These arguments indicate the range of fields of study that may be relevant to answering this question and show the complexity of the concerns inherent in a particular curriculum question. The arguments developed here are only some of a number of ways the issue of women's studies might be addressed. My emphasis here is on relating the question of women's studies to some general concerns of educationalists and to lines of research and analysis of the curriculum. I am not able to elaborate here some of the discussions and disagreements among those concerned with women's studies as to its nature, methodology, etc. Nor will I treat at length the question of what 'works' with students, or the question of student or 'community' demands for certain types of teaching rather than others, though these are all important concerns.

In some ways the deliberations in this paper may be an illustration of a particular idea of what curriculum theorizing is about. I am taking the position that curriculum theorizing is not a form of theory whose questions are in the first place derived from theory, or one which should be characterized by strict adherence to a single disciplinary framework of discussion. Rather it should be sensitive to the issues raised by practice and seek to elucidate these in a variety of ways. It must be tolerant of complexities and ambiguities. To some extent this position is similar to the approach which William Reid has characterized as 'the deliberative' model of curriculum theorizing.[5] However, in comparison with Reid, I am trying here to take seriously insights from a number of fields (feminism, liberal philosophy, neo-Marxist sociology), and do not agree that such theorizing need be 'diametrically opposed to . . . the radical perspective'.[6]

The legitimacy of the subject matter

What is the content of women's studies?

In terms of its content or subject matter, the premise on which women's studies is based is that previously existing subjects are inadequate ways of understanding individual experience and the world, and that the studies grouped under this new heading are both a corrective of previous misunderstandings and a source of new enlightenment.[7]

It is argued that previous subjects have been inadequate because they left women out, they made women invisible. More importantly, however, it is said that this omission has *distorted* the frameworks that have been developed. For one thing, research in many fields has been carried out by male researchers on male subjects, yet written up in a way which implies that the knowledge thus gained applies to everyone; at the same time the rare pieces of research done about girls are assumed to be related to a special subcategory of humanity, and are by no means portrayed as representative of the whole.[8] Again, if we look at the conceptualization of a problem in a discipline, we can see how an insensitivity to women's experience and their specific contributions affects the types of analysis and framework developed. To take one example: in sociology and the sociology of education a significant focus of interest has been the relationship between the socio-economic status of individuals and outcomes such as examination success, subject choice, post-school career patterns, and so on. Traditionally, 'socio-economic status' has been measured by the job that the father has (or, in the case of a married woman, that of her husband). This leaves out and distorts a number of important things. It can classify a woman who is totally economically dependent on her husband as of a higher socio-economic status than a woman who is economically independent, in that she is in the paid workforce.[9] Again, notwithstanding the fact that sociologists and psychologists in other contexts stress the importance of the *mother* in the bringing up of children, here, when they correlate statistics about the success rate of children at school, they are likely to ignore the mother's experience of and relation to the paid workforce and to categorize children solely on the basis of the father's occupation. So the omission of women's experience leads to some clear anomalies in the sorts of framework of explanation that have been developed.

It has also been shown how language itself has contributed to the processes of omission and distortion referred to above.[10] I am not suggesting here that there is a simple and automatic relationship between words and thought. However, there are empirical demonstrations that language can influence the understandings people have developed. For example, the existence of non-equivalent adjectives to describe men and women (such as 'hysterical', whose non-existent simile 'testerical' is amusingly discussed by Miller and Swift)[11] helps shape the interpretations of their role. Again, the use of the generic 'he' and 'mankind' encourages a slide from the abstract discussion of everyone to a concrete concern with male experiences.[12] In recent years, the counter-sexism campaigns in Australian schools have drawn attention to this issue in relation to teaching style and classroom strategy, but what women's studies as a field of study also wants to emphasize is that language is not just an issue relevant to who might readily identify with the subject matter, but has actually affected and distorted how disciplines have developed. For example, a basic text on the sociology of education, in describing socialization, says that:

> any child may be expected to prepare himself so that when he is older he can play the role of pupil, worker, father, and voter. Any adult may be expected to behave at more or less the same time as a father, worker, and a voter.[13]

And the picture on the front cover of the book also happens to be of a boy.

In terms of its content, then, women's studies has been concerned with the way in which existing subjects, if they are to give equal attention to women, require some quite fundamental reforms. For example, we mght need to alter or modify the periodization used in history. Traditionally, history has been organized around major events of public life: wars, political change or changes in modes of non-domestic production. Taking women's experience and contribution seriously might lead to some new organization of historical narrative around changes in modes of childbirth and rearing and of changing relations of private and public life.[14] Again a variety of writers have suggested that taking women seriously would lead to reforms and modifications to the particular types of abstraction from the world that have been central in disciplines such as mathematics, economics and philosophy.[15] To put this in positive terms rather than in the form of a critique, it is suggested that women's studies attempts to investigate women's experience in a way previous subjects have not. Various writings by those engaged in this field set out ways in which this can be done, both by example and by theoretical reflection.[16] They discuss such characteristics of the field as its core values (valuing women), its methods (for example, inter-disciplinarity, reflexivity, qualitative methods), its substantive concepts (patriarchy, perhaps). I am trying here to outline the forms of discussion and work being done. The specific examples I have given are the subject of discussion and debate in the field, just as journals of history and sociology bear testimony to the debate over values, methods and concepts in those disciplines.

To date, I have indicated briefly what women's studies tries to study and how it claims to be different from other subjects. I have also given some indication of the body of literature which illustrates, discusses or reviews this area. But what does all this mean in terms of the validity of women's studies as a subject for the curriculum?

How do we assess the legitimacy of women's studies as a subject for the school curriculum?

To consider the question of the legitimacy of women's studies as a subject for the curriculum, it is necessary to ask how, in general, subjects are deemed to be acceptable. In the second half of the twentieth century the grounds on which practitioners and curriculum theorists (or, rather, teacher theorists and non-teacher theorists) assess legitimacy have multiplied. At the school level the grounds are often left implicit, and many people, both in practice and in theory, effectively disown the term by seeing it simply as an outcome of power among the contenders.[17] Others disallow discussion of the issue by presuming that legitimacy necessarily resides in what was taught in the past.[18] In response to either of these positions, the task for supporters of women's studies would not be to prove a case but to manoeuvre politically to gain numbers and power. However, the discussion which follows presumes that many people concerned with schooling do not see the issue in such cynical and closed terms, and tries to say something about where the characteristics of women's studies might stand in relation to the concerns people have.

I am not trying to imply here that issues of politics and power are not part of the working-out of legitimacy claims, or that philosophers can work out answers in a way which is untouched by the interests of the practical world. However, I am agreeing to some extent with the position taken by John White where he says that:

> in assessing curricular objectives, one should not just *assume* that objectivity will be impossible. One must simply work through the arguments presented for the objectives, see if they are valid, and press for further arguments to support the premises on which they rest. It is only when people begin to discuss the rationale for curriculum objectives, only when they begin to press the argument back to more fundamental values and assumptions, that we shall be able to judge how objective or subjective the issues are. It is remarkable how little of this *fundamental* questioning there has been in the recent movement for curriculum reform.[19]

The writers who seem to have something to say on the issues of legitimate offerings in the school curriculum discuss theories which range from philosophically and epistemologically derived theories about the range of legitimate disciplines,[20] culturally located versions of this,[21] and theories derived from a concern with oppression and divided class interests.[22] There are of course major differences between these approaches, but in some ways there is a significant overlap too. All of these theories, I would argue, can be interpreted as having a concern firstly with the idea that education should embody the full range of culturally relevant knowledge; secondly, with a way of delineating the minimal areas of approaches necessary to encapsulate that; and, thirdly, with the idea that what is taught *is* real or powerful to the students in question, that is, that it does connect with them, and that it gives access to something beyond a surface relevance.[23] It is the claim of the growing body of feminist theory and research that its inclusion is essential on the grounds just outlined.

Here, since I am trying to deal with the main sources of opposition to women's studies rather than try to deal with the varied frameworks of the approaches I have mentioned, I will refer to the classic statement of the defence of the existing disciplines, that of Paul Hirst in 'Liberal Education and the Nature of Knowledge'.[24]

Since Hirst's paper was written two decades ago, and since in recent years his work has been less the subject for discussion than the work of writers like Skilbeck in Australia and Lawton and White in England, it may seem that I am choosing a 'straw man' on which to test the argument. However, the reasons for looking at Hirst's work here are two-fold. Firstly, it might be argued that the case for opposition to women's studies is not as strong or as clear on the basis of other writers' arguments as it is with Hirst's. If we take the Australian Curriculum Development Centre framework of 'cultural mapping' for example,[25] it might be argued that questions of legitimacy would in the end reduce to a political struggle as to who was to control the mapping and selecting. Insofar as there is more to the mapping claim than this, it could be argued, this would have to be in some way analogous to Hirst's attempt to outline fundamental forms of knowledge. In other words, Hirst's is the strongest case of the notion that the basic and most important forms of knowledge can be worked out in a way which is detached from the whims of those doing the working-out.

The second reason I have chosen to focus on Hirst is related to the passage from John White's work quoted above – that is, I am suggesting that in Australia in recent years there has been too little attention paid to the types of overview question that Hirst raised. The emphasis in discussions has been on why particular subjects or areas of study would be desirable, rather than on why a certain range of subjects might be seen as necessary, that is, as basic, vital, and sufficient. (The 'back to the basics' movement by no means does this.) It is true that the Curriculum Development Centre project did try to raise the broader approach but, among many teachers in Victoria at least, its rationale has been little regarded. So I am focusing on Hirst's argument because this way of addressing the issue has some importance. It has implications too for whether the claims for women's studies should be seen as any different from those of a host of other special interest groups which would like their subjects to be taught in schools (driver education, first aid, etc.)

Although Hirst argues neither that schools need to be *restricted* to the areas he lists nor that his identification of key areas needs to be represented in the school curriculum as distinct subject areas (though the reader could be forgiven for drawing such conclusions), he tries to set out the grounds on which the fundamentals of the school curriculum should be built. He argues that the minimal range of learning needed to give access to important knowledge and ways of knowing can be assessed by working out which disciplines have distinctive and significant questions and concepts, have reliable and particular ways of testing for the truth of what they are investigating, and are not reducible to another. (He claims, for example, that a subject like geography is not basic in this sense.)

In response to considerations of this type, those supporting women's studies would argue that it meets the criteria outlined. The distinctive concern of women's studies is with the ways issues of gender have influenced history and social life. Women's studies develops theories of women's oppression (or if that formulation seems too political, theories of the ways in which the situation of women and the relation between women and men have been mediated in and have mediated history and contemporary life). Women's studies' ways of testing the truth of an analysis includes attention to whether the account fits with women's experience, a distinctive form of testing of propositions which is in contrast, for example, to research in disciplines which may be done on women and girls but with concepts which reflect a male-centred analysis. To give an example here: Gilligan's work[26] takes cases of moral reasoning by women which would be interpreted as immature in terms of the hierarchy of moral development developed by Kohlberg. Gilligan's analysis tries to show that it is not that women's ways of operating here do not measure up, but that the form of measurement itself is faulty: it is based on or tested against male experiences and concerns rather than those of women. In many other fields too, measurements and interpretations of empirical phenomena in relation to such concepts as economic activity, psychological adequacy, behaviour of interviewers and interviewees, etc., are made differently once women are given equal centrality.[27] And the content of these various analyses makes clear that the distinctive form of analysis here is something more than giving rein to the individual subjectivities or idiosyncrasies of the researcher: it arises out of some general new orientations and ways of proceeding. Nevertheless, those who contend that women's studies does not meet Hirst's criteria would argue either that it is not a distinctive study in itself but a subbranch of existing studies in history, literature, etc., and/or that it is not a disciplinary field but a partisan and ideological perspective.

Here it is important to look back at the types of argument which were developed in the quite lengthy debate over Hirst's original proposition.[28] Coming both from general philosophers and curriculum theorists and from those working in particular subject areas, the arguments reiterated a doubt that Hirst's criteria could be used in any pure form. Either the criteria allowed that a huge range of studies might be fundamental (not just science, but microbiology, genetics, physical chemistry, etc., since all might be argued to have distinctive concepts) or they allowed the possibility that none would meet the criteria, since all could be reduced to or were based on the language and logic of the Western tradition. As Sandra Coyner argues in proposing that women's studies should be self-consciously developed as a discipline:

> We create a 'legitimacy gap' between Women's Studies and the traditional disciplines, to our own disadvantage, by comparing our practice to their ideals.[29]

Coyner's point is supported by the testimonies of historians, musicians, and others who responded to Hirst by pointing out that the reality from within the discipline was far messier than he acknowledged.

In fact, as a variety of writers have pointed out,[30] the reason that some areas and types of study are recognized as disciplines and others not is historical and social: it reflects dominant interests at the time modern universities were established and subsequent power over funding of departments. Hirst to some degree concedes this point by acknowledging that forms of knowledge are not timeless entities and that change is possible.[31] He also acknowledges that one of the tests for working out the basis of school knowledge is whether a form of study has endured and built up a body of intellectuals trained in and committed to it. However, although Hirst seems to dispute this idea,[32] the underlying rationale for his approach would seem to be that the development of the disciplines reflects some sort of cumulative move towards truth and/or that approaches and questions which gained their impetus in the past are to be valued above those which are gaining their impetus today.

Today, although there are arguments over the details of his exposition, probably the most widely influential account of the nature of the development of knowledge within the disciplines is that of Thomas Kuhn.[33] In Kuhn's terms, the development of knowledge takes place as a paradigmatic, puzzle-solving activity, in which theories are exhausted and replaced by those which embody a *competing* set of assumptions to interpret the same subject matter. It may be that the competing theories are as related to social circumstances and political values as they are to the nature of the 'scientific' puzzle in question, and it may be that lines of acceptability and change are more complex than Kuhn's initial exposition suggested. But whichever version of Kuhn's ideas is accepted, the value of confining the school curriculum to that which has proved itself in the past becomes a more open question. I am not trying to argue a completely relativist position here, nor do I think that Kuhn's work need imply this: 'paradigms' are accepted not just on the basis of intersubjective consensus but because they have some successful relation to a world out there. What I am suggesting is that if we take some of the points made by Kuhn, which have now been very widely accepted, then a women's studies perspective may be seen as a valid means of gaining insight into problems which are not solvable in other ways, even though it may embody values which are at odds with some existing approaches and may therefore appear 'ideological' to them.

To put this in the rhetoric of the staffroom discussion, in response to the question 'If we are going to have women's studies, why not have men's studies too?', one answer is that we already do have men's studies, in that a great deal of traditional subjects like history and literature are about men (for example, the host of novels on adolescent boys which are so favoured for general teaching purposes). However, an alternative answer, which I am suggesting here, is that 'women's studies' *incorporates* men's studies. Although existing ways of investigating the world focus on men, in that they treat men as some sort of universal individuals representing everyone, they also make men invisible – that is, they make their gender invisible.

What I have been trying to show in this part of the paper is that in relation to a range of theoretical concerns about the basis and range of the school curriculum, there are grounds as to why women's studies should be taken seriously. It embodies a range of concerns that are distinctive and of *general* significance. Moreover, the types of argument which have been raised concerning whether it meets the norms which distinguish existing subjects are not signs of its illegitimacy, but are illustrations of the normal processes and political interests involved in having an area recognized as a field of study.

It might seem that I am taking a rather strange line of argument by suggesting that women's studies meets Hirst's criteria for a fundamental area of knowledge, while arguing also that those criteria take an overly static and positivist view of knowledge. Nevertheless both points – the significance of the contributions being made by women's studies and the dynamic and contested nature of knowledge – are very relevant to the issues of the content-base of the school curriculum.

This first section, then, has primarily addressed the first two points raised by theorists of the curriculum which were outlined earlier: the importance of the area as an area of knowledge and its importance relative to other areas. I have not dealt so far with the third point of concern to theorists of the curriculum: how the subject will work in the setting of the school and the teacher–student relationship.[34] This third point is not third in some hierarchy of importance. What is meaningful and relevant to students is of course central to schooling as a reality, and a good defence of women's studies could equally have begun from this point. Sociologists of knowledge in recent years have also made a valuable contribution in showing that a focus on what is happening to students in the classroom can help avoid confusing the rhetoric of curriculum with the reality. Such a focus is a necessary corrective to abstracted theorizing about the aims or scope of the curriculum. In the next section of the article, then, I am taking as given that a number of proposals as to the relevance and meaningfulness to students of concerns with gender in the curriculum have been made, and will focus on some issues related to how schooling works. I will look here at some of the arguments about whether and how women's studies should be introduced as a new subject in the curriculum, what some possible lines of action are, and what their likely consequences are.

Should women's studies be a subject, or elective, or an option, or a topic, or a perspective, or . . . ?

The new insights and perspectives developed by women's studies make a case for a general reform of subjects that are taught in the curriculum. But schools, especially in systems which are committed to school-based curriculum development, are rather messy places. Change is likely to be piecemeal and might come from a variety of sources (for example, centralized changes to the prestigious Higher School Certificate syllabi, the development of new textbooks, inspirations derived from in-service education, curriculum development worked on within the school by individuals, departments, or the staff as a whole). Given that general transformation of knowledge to accord with the valuing of women and girls promoted by women's studies is unlikely to take place overnight, this section discusses some ways in which people might argue about the value of offering women's studies as a distinct subject.

As in the first section of this paper, I am not trying to explore the different values people may hold about the purposes of schooling and the type of individual and social development they would like to produce. Rather, I am trying to indicate some sources of the different *understandings* they hold about how processes of schooling work. These understandings, which are part of the positions taken on whether women's studies should be a separate subject, involve both questions of principle and pragmatic considerations. They require attention to the effect of forms of the 'framing' of knowledge on the development of that knowledge, to mechanisms of the teaching–learning situation (that is, how students are likely to operate in different types of situation), and to the implications of the school being a social institution located in a particular social context.

The arguments I will set out here are drawn from my experience of discussions that have taken place on the issue in a number of sites: feminists outside the school system who are concerned with women's studies; academics whose concerns touch on this area; teachers involved in conference, in-service and in-school discussion. The arguments which follow are not tightly documented both because this is not possible and because the intent is to draw attention to some lines along which the issue may be thought about. In setting out three types of discussion of this issue, I want to indicate both the complexity of the problem (as of all curriculum issues) and to suggest some types of research that may aid our discussion.

Concerns about whether women's studies can be pursued at school level

In the first section of this paper, I outlined claims for women's studies which teachers and advocates of women's studies would generally hold in common. However, there is not a common position on how women's studies achieves its distinctive form of knowledge. One interpretation of this process would argue that, while the issues here are of legitimate and vital concern for students, to try to teach women's studies in the school setting is a contradictory exercise.[35] That is, they would argue that, central to developing knowledge in a way which does not incorporate the oppression of women is that it be totally democratic, and controlled equally by those engaged in it. Given the constraints of the school system (requirements for assessment, the institutionalized authority of the teacher), it might be that women's studies should not be presented as a school subject because the form in which it would have to be taught would hopelessly compromise its distinctive value.

The arguments above are more likely to be put by those not employed as teachers, but echoes of these arguments are taken up by those teaching in schools. One such line would be the argument that women's studies should not be offered unless certain controls over such areas as the form of assessment can be granted – for example it should not be an externally examined Higher School Certificate subject.[36] Another such line might be the insistence that the subject be taken only by those who wanted to do it, or those who had some common interests to pursue.[37]

However, the argument above is a particular interpretation of women's studies, not one which is held in common by all those concerned with this area. Other advocates of women's studies would question whether an attempt to avoid the normal structures of disciplinary/school-subject knowledge *should* be seen as necessary characteristics of the area.[38] There are also those who accept the characterization above as a sort of ideal to which reforms would be directed, but accept that other considerations in the school context make compromises essential.

Framing and marginalization

A second line of concern is one which takes up lessons derived from the work of sociologists of knowledge and of the curriculum over the last two decades regarding the effects of the way subjects are bounded and related to each other. Basil Bernstein's work,[39] especially 'On the Classification and Framing of Educational Knowledge', has attempted to show the types of identity, control and power which are developed when the curriculum is organized into separate subjects as compared with more integrated forms, both as far as the effects on individual students and the development of knowledge are concerned. Theorists working at the tertiary level have also discussed at some length the effects of developing women's studies as part of existing subjects as compared with developing a new subject.[40] Bowles and Duelli Klein, for example, argue that attempting to work within existing subjects is likely to involve a dissipation of energy and a less sustained attention to developing the central concerns of the new area.[41] Analogously, Bernstein[42] had argued that if the development of new knowledge in the traditional form of the university Ph.D. is preceded by an enforced lengthy period of socialization into existing identities as historians, physicists, etc., then this will constrain the types of breakthrough made.

To extrapolate this issue to schools, it might be considered that taking occasional units on women in history or women in literature as part of general courses in history or literature would constrain both the time devoted to issues related to girls and women (and to gender as an issue) and the way they were taken up (since the main attention would need to be on what these contributed to the *subject* rather than on what these contributed to our understanding of men and women and their relation to each other and to society).

On the other hand, a sustained line of opposition to the development of women's studies as a separate subject (including that from some supporters of feminism or equal opportunity) argues that development of that type is a means not of the subject becoming more powerful, but of its being contained and marginalized. That is, if there exists a subject that is said to deal with the area of women's studies, this might be taken by others as an excuse not to reform existing subjects. In this way women's studies may be isolated in a limited part of the curriculum – and almost invariably one which is not part of the core (at junior level) or of the prestigious subjects (at senior level). Thus women's studies can be 'marginalized' and 'ghettoized' by not being part of what teachers, students and parents see as the central matters that the school deals with. Coyner[43] and Bowles and Duelli Klein,[44] discussing the situation at tertiary level, contest the 'marginalization' claims: they argue that these are not a necessary consequence of separation and cite subjects which have split off without losing status in this way (biochemistry, linguistics). In the school situation one might predict that the likelihood of marginalization is higher depending on the level and way in which women's studies is offered. If it is introduced as a year 12 subject, one which is acceptable for gaining entry to tertiary institutions, then some traditional processes of gaining acceptance are begun. On the other hand, if it is offered as, say, an elective at year 9, especially one which competes with 'serious' subjects, the way is open for its treatment as a hobby subject, a course which may be of great benefit to the few students who take it, but which is generally devalued by their peers and parents.

The points being made here are that the way in which the subject is offered affects both the depth and the way in which issues within it may be pursued, and also the way in which the value of its content is assessed and related to other school and non-school learning.

Opportunism might also be powerful

A third line of argument might be drawn from many feminists who write about curriculum. It stems both from a concern with pragmatic realities as to what individual activists might do and from certain ideas about the effects of working with the small groups which might be drawn to take women's studies at any level. Here it is suggested that if girls and women are to build knowledge and structures relevant to their interests, the way to begin is not by trying to take on the daunting task of general reform or reform of the most highly regarded areas, but rather to take any opportunity to offer a subject which may be of interest and power to some students. This incorporates a different view of social change, one which bears more resemblance to symbolic interactionism and a belief in individuals as constructors of their world[45] than to a belief in the effects of 'structures' implicit in much of the earlier discussion of framing and marginalization. Here writers argue that it is possible for a committed group to concentrate on their own concerns, no matter how these are viewed from outside, and that general change can develop outwards from this rather than needing to come from initial general reforms.[46] Moreover, writers here draw attention to a range of recent research which suggests that girls and women teachers can teach and learn more effectively if they are not in a mixed-sex group.[47]So the line of argument here is that in principle any chance to offer a women's studies course should be seized, and that a separatist, not commonly taken subject has its own value.

Further research on some of these issues is needed. There has been little evaluation of reactions by students at the school level to women's studies courses. In terms of some initial impressions, I have observed individuals and classes which seemed to enjoy, learn and develop from their women's studies courses. Elsewhere some teachers have found that an attempt to confront issues of gender in a relatively direct fashion through a women's studies course has produced counter-productive responses from the students and boredom. These are in part empirical questions which are related to knowing more about teaching–learning processes and the specific conjunction of circumstances that exists in particular schools and groups of pupils.

In this second section of the paper I have been suggesting that, given that the general concerns of women's studies are a valid and important area of study, the question of the way in which reforms should be introduced is not a simple one. The position people might take here will depend on their pragmatic assessment of the situation in their school and their state, their understanding of how change comes about in the school system, and consequently whether attempts to work from below or from above are the more viable strategies. Associated with all this, there is also the question of what relative emphasis reformers want to place on the need to reform the understandings that all students are getting, as compared with the need to work with girls to develop and strengthen their understandings of themselves and develop their own power to produce change in the future.

References and notes

1 Curriculum Development Centre (1980) *Core Curriculum for Australian Schools* (Curriculum Development Centre, Canberra).
2 Although I have not capitalized the term 'women's studies' throughout the article, I do (as I will argue later) want the referent of this term to be understood as a subject matter with a certain coherence and quality, not just a meaningless conglomeration identified only by who does the study or by the study being 'about women'. I decided not to

capitalize the term as I do not want it to be interpreted as an ossified and dogmatic testament to be learnt and revered (as we might interpret the capitalized forms of 'History', 'Literature', and 'Science'). It is rather, as other subjects should be, a body of living concerns, questions and information whose content may be contested and will change.

3 See, for example, journals such as *Women's Studies International Forum*, *Signs* and *Harvard Educational Review*, 49, 4 (1979); Boxer, M.J. (1982) 'For and about women: The theory and practice of Women's Studies in the United States'. In Keohane, N.O., Rosaldo, M.Z. and Gelphi, B.C. (eds) *Feminist Theory* (Harvester Press, Brighton), pp. 237–72; and Bowles, S. and Duelli Klein, R. (eds) (1983) *Theories of Women's Studies* (Routledge & Kegan Paul, London).

4 Some further discussion of this can be found in Yates, L. (1983) 'The theory and practice of counter-sexist education in schools'. *Discourse*, 3, 2; and Yates, L. (1984) ' "Curriculum becomes our way of contradicting biology and culture" – an outline of some dilemmas for non-sexist education'. *Australian Journal of Education*, (forthcoming).

5 Reid, W. (1981) 'The deliberative approach to the study of the curriculum and its relation to critical pluralism'. In Lawn, M. and Barton, L. (eds) *Rethinking Curriculum Studies* (Croom Helm, London), pp. 160–87; and Reid, W. (1978) *Thinking about the Curriculum: The Nature and Treatment of Curriculum Problems* (Routledge & Kegan Paul, London).

6 Reid (1981), p. 167 (see note 5).

7 See, for example, Bowles and Duelli Klein (1983) (see note 3); Boxer (1982) (see note 3); Gilligan, C. (1982) *In a Different Voice: Psychological Theory and Women's Development* (Harvard University Press, Cambridge, Mass.); Howe, F. (1979) 'Introduction: The first decade of Women's Studies'. *Harvard Educational Review*, 52, 2, pp. 413–21; Martin, J.R. (1982) 'Excluding women from the educational realm'. *Harvard Educational Review*, 52, 2, pp. 133–48; Roberts, H. (ed.) (1981) *Doing Feminist Research* (Routledge & Kegan Paul, London); Rosaldo, M.Z. and Lamphere, L. (eds) (1974) *Woman, Culture and Society* (Stanford University Press, Stanford); Spender, D. (ed.) (1981) *Men's Studies Modified* (Pergamon Press, Oxford); and Westkott, M. (1979) 'Feminist criticism of the social sciences'. *Harvard Educational Review*, 94, 4, pp. 422–30.

8 See on sociology, Acker, S. (1980) 'No women's land: British sociology of education 1960–1979'. Paper presented to the British Sociological Association Conference, Lancaster; on psychology and moral development, Gilligan (1982) (see note 7); on philosophy, Martin (1982) (see note 7); on language, Spender (1981) (see note 7).

9 See Delphy, C. (1981) 'Women in stratification studies'. In Roberts (1981), pp. 114–28 (see note 7).

10 For example, Miller, C. and Swift, K. (1977) *Words and Women* (Anchor, New York); Spender, D. (1980) *Man Made Language* (Routledge & Kegan Paul, London); Spender (1981), pp. 155–73 (see note 7).

11 Miller and Swift (1977), pp. 59–61 (see note 10).

12 *Ibid.*, pp. 17–48.

13 Musgrave, P.W. (1972) *The Sociology of Education* (Methuen, London, 2nd edn), p. 18.

14 See Summers, A. (1975) 'An object lesson in women's history'. In Mercer, J. (ed.) *The Other Half* (Penguin, Harmondsworth, Middlesex), pp. 49–62; and Lewis, J. (1981) 'Women lost and found: The impact of feminism on history'. In Spender (1981), pp. 55–72 (see note 7).

15 Spender (1981) (see note 7); Martin (1982) (see note 7); Bowles and Duelli Klein (1983) (see note 3); Roberts (1981) (see note 7).

16 See note 7.

17 This is a tendency in much of the 'new sociology of education' and its heirs: see Young, M.F.D. (ed.) (1971) *Knowledge and Control* (Cassell, Collier and Macmillan, New

York); and, especially, the debate between Young and John White over whether knowledge is socially relative in White, J. and Young, M.F.D. (1975) 'The sociology of knowledge: I'. *Education for Teaching*, 98 (Autumn); and White, J. and Young, M.F.D. (1976) 'The sociology of knowledge: II'. *Education for Teaching*, 99 (Spring).

18 Again both teachers and outsiders, such as many of the contributors to the *Australian Council of Educational Standards Review*.

19 White, J. (1975) 'The concept of curriculum evaluation'. In Golby, M., Greenwald, J. and West, R. (eds) *Curriculum Design* (Croom Helm, London), p. 392.

20 See, in particular, Hirst, P.H. (1965) Liberal education and the nature of knowledge. In Archambault, R.D. (ed.) *Philosophical Analysis and Education* (Routledge & Kegan Paul, London), pp. 113–38; and Hirst, P.H. (1974) *Knowledge and Curriculum* (Routledge & Kegan Paul, London). This paper reprinted as Volume I Paper 12(i). Other variants on this can be found in Pring, R. (1974) *Knowledge and Schooling* (Open Books, London); White, J. (1973) *Towards a Compulsory Curriculum* (Routledge & Kegan Paul, London); Schwab, J.J. (1964) 'Structure of the disciplines: Meanings and significance'. In Ford, G.W. and Pugno, L. (eds) *The Structure of Knowledge and the Curriculum* (Rand McNally, New York); and Phenix, P.H. (1964) *Realms of Meaning: A Philosophy of the Curriculum for General Education* (McGraw-Hill, New York).

21 Reynolds, J. and Skilbeck, M. (1976) *Culture and the Classroom* (Macmillan, South Melbourne); Curriculum Development Centre (1980) (see note 1); Lawton, D. (1975) *Class, Culture and the Curriculum* (Routledge & Kegan Paul, London).

22 For example, Ashenden, D., Blackburn, J., Hannan, B. and White, D. (1984) 'Manifesto for a democratic curriculum'. *The Australian Teacher*, 7 (February); Freire, P. (1972) *Pedagogy of the Oppressed* (Penguin, Harmondsworth, Middlesex); and Midwinter, E. (1972) *Projections: An Educational Priority Area at Work* (Ward Lock Educational, London).

23 Some further discussion of this is given in Yates, L. (1981) 'Varieties of curriculum theorising'. In Centre for the Study of Innovation in Education, *Core Curriculum and Values Education: A Literature Review* (Curriculum Development Centre, Canberra); and Yates, L. (1981) 'Theoretical oppositions to core curriculum'. In Centre for the Study of Innovation in Education, *ibid*.

24 Hirst (1965) (see note 20).

25 Curriculum Development Centre (1980) (see note 1); Reynolds and Skilbeck (1976) (see note 21).

26 Gilligan (1982) (see note 7).

27 See Roberts (1981) (see note 7); Spender (1981) (see note 7); Miller, J.B. (1976) *Toward a New Psychology of Women* (Penguin, Harmondsworth, Middlesex).

28 See Hirst (1974), pp. 84–100 for some discussion of and references to this (see note 20).

29 Coyner, S. (1983) 'Women's Studies as an academic discipline: Why and how to do it'. In Bowles and Duelli Klein, p. 47 (see note 3).

30 For example, Bowles and Duelli Klein (1983) (see note 3); Spender (1981) (see note 7); Young (1971) (see note 17); and Kuhn, T.S. (1970) *The Structure of Scientific Revolutions* (University of Chicago Press, Chicago, 2nd edn).

31 See Hirst, P.H. (1974) 'The forms of knowledge re-visited'. In Hirst, pp. 92–6 (see note 20).

32 *Ibid.*, pp. 95–6: 'The thesis is simply about the present state of affairs, but that state of affairs is not to be regarded as either a transient articulation of a merely socially relative concept of knowledge, or the latest expression of an absolute and invariant framework implicit in knowledge.'

33 Kuhn (1970) (see note 30).

34 The type of considerations that, for example, led Pring (1974) (see note 20) to argue for some important modifications of Hirst's approach.

35 For example, Humphreys, D. (1975) 'School and the oppression of women'. In Mercer (see note 14); Spender, D. (1981) 'Education: The patriarchal paradigm and the response to feminism'. In Spender (see note 7); and Spender, D. (1982) *Invisible Women: The Schooling Scandal* (Writers and Readers, London).

36 For example, see the arguments by Fowler, R. (1983) 'Sexually inclusive curriculum'. *The Victorian Teacher*, 2, 5, pp. 12–17, although she is not arguing for the teaching of women's studies as such.

37 For example, to teach girls and boys separately, see Joint TTUV, VSTA and VTU Counter-Sexism Project (1984) 'What about the boys?' *Ms Muffett*, 22 (April).

38 For example, Freeman, J. (1974) 'The tyranny of structurelessness'. In Jaquette, J.S. (ed.) *Women in Politics* (John Wiley & Sons, New York), pp. 202–14; Coyner (1983) (see notes 29 and 3); and Yates (1983) (see note 4).

39 Bernstein, B. (1971) 'On the classification and framing of educational knowledge'. In Young (see note 17); Bernstein, B. (1975) *Class, Codes and Control, Vol. 3* (Routledge & Kegan Paul, London).

40 Especially the contributions to Bowles and Duelli Klein (1983) (see note 3).

41 Bowles and Duelli Klein (1983), p. 7 (see note 3).

42 Bernstein (1971), p. 57 (see note 39).

43 Coyner (1983) (see notes 29 and 3).

44 Bowles and Duelli Klein (1983), pp. 1–26 (see note 3).

45 See Dawe, A. (1970) 'The two sociologies'. *British Journal of Sociology*, 21, 2; Stanley, L. and Wise, S. (1983) *Breaking Out: Feminist Consciousness and Feminist Research* (Routledge & Kegan Paul, London).

46 Spender (1982) (see note 35); Bowles and Duelli Klein (1983) (see note 3).

47 For example, Spender (1982) (see note 35); Spender, D. and Sarah, E. (eds) (1980) *Learning to Lose: Sexism and Education* (The Women's Press, London); and Kelly, A. (ed.) (1981) *The Missing Half: Girls and Science Education* (Manchester University Press, Manchester).

13

WOMEN'S PHYSICAL EDUCATION: A GENDER-SENSITIVE PERSPECTIVE

Ann Diller and Barbara Houston

Active exercise was my delight. . . . No boy could be my friend till I had beaten him in a race, and no girl if she refused to climb a tree, leap fences, and be a tomboy.[1]

Louisa May Alcott

Why should one talk about *women's* physical education? Why not talk about physical education for both women and men, for children, for adolescents, for adults, for persons? Some would argue that to raise the separate question of women's physical education is to already affirm and perpetuate a detrimental distinction based on biological sex where such a distinction is neither required nor desirable.

There is no question that physical education has been differentiated for the sexes for reasons having to do with perceived biological and social differences between them.[2] Women have played an active role in the development of their own formal physical education since its modern beginnings in the mid-nineteenth century, and it has differed in character from men's physical education in the following ways:[3]

1   The philosophy of physical education for women has emphasized the impor-
    tance of securing 'the greatest good to the greatest number'[4] and has all along
    placed a greater emphasis on amateur as opposed to professional sport, on
    cooperation rather than competition, and on the basic benefits to be gained by
    everyone rather than pursuit of the scarce benefits affordable to the few.
2   Women and men have differed in their conceptions and administration of
    competitive athletics. In women's programs extramural sport has been devel-
    oped within the educational context, with goals and staff allocations the same
    for general education, professional preparation and intramural and extra-
    mural programs. Men's physical education has been characterized by a sever-
    ance between physical education and extramural competitive sport.

Source: Postow, B. (ed.) *Women, Philosophy and Sport*, Metuchen, N.J.: Scarecrow Press, 1983.

3   There have been different explicit curricula for women and men. Although sport has been a major ingredient of both programs, the selection of sports has been different; and when the sports were the same, women developed them differently 'by way of such affectations as shortened matches, divided basketball courts and special rules and techniques.'[5]

4   Curriculum development has borne a different emphasis in the two programs with dance and movement education developed primarily by women and given more attention within women's programs and colleges.[6]

A more significant observation to make, however, is that in contemporary American society it is obvious that equality has not been realized through gender-differentiated physical education programs. Women's physical education has received less money for programs and personnel, and women have had unequal access to facilities. In general, women's sports have been underfunded, and less well coached and equipped, and players have not had equal fringe benefits such as medical benefits, housing, food and travel allowances. Women have not had equivalent opportunities for athletic scholarships. In schools and in society, women's sports have been accorded much less status and attention than men's.[7]

In short, it is fair to say that the gender-differentiated programs have suffered from sexism; they have been different and unequal. This has made many educators properly skeptical of proposals that we continue to take sex and gender differences into account when designing physical education programs.[8] But there is still fierce debate about the best way to realize sex equality.

On a general level the disagreement about sex equality has a dual focus. In part it concerns our interpretation of the concept of sex equality.[9] Does sex equality entail the elimination of activities in which there might be significant sex differentiation by virtue of natural and ineradicable sex advantages? Or does it allow for significant sex differentiations and merely require the elimination of sexist attitudes and values now associated with these differences?[10] Additional disagreement arises over the best means to realizing the ideal of sex equality, how ever it is interpreted. Should we, need we, take account of gender in the methods we propose for the realization of our ideal?[11] In physical education this controversy takes the form of a debate over the extent to which physical education programs should be sex-integrated or sex-segregated.

In this paper we assume the viewpoint of an educator who is already strongly committed to sex equality and to equal educational opportunity but recognizes that this still leaves a number of practical questions and policy problems undetermined. In Section I we examine the physical education debate over sex integration in an effort to identify central legitimate concerns on each side. In Section II we introduce the concept of a gender-sensitive perspective as one way of doing justice to the concerns of both sides. We then take this gender-sensitive perspective as our viewpoint on women's physical education for the rest of the paper. In Section III we apply this perspective to our definition of physical education and discover the importance of the hidden curriculum. Section IV

236

sketches some prominent features of the hidden physical education curriculum for girls and women. In Section V we address the question of the educator's responsibility for dealing with undesirable hidden curricula and suggest a number of alternative approaches. Section VI is a brief summary of our conclusions on what it means to take a gender-sensitive perspective toward women's physical education.

I Sex-integrated physical education: for and against

In this section we will examine some of the major arguments for and against sex-integrated physical education. We shall start with those that favor integration.

1

In addition to the *prima facie* case against sex segregation in physical education[12] there are strong considerations that favor sex integration. Integrationists argue that we will never come to have an accurate knowledge of the abilities of girls and women until we have sex-integrated classes and similar expectations for the two sexes. Many constraints have been unfairly imposed on girls and women because of erroneous beliefs about physiological differences between the sexes. Specialized rules for girls have circumscribed their play and women are still kept from competing in certain events.[13] These sorts of constraints have led to serious confusion about the causes of the differential in female and male sports performance. Differences arising from unequal experience have been mistakenly attributed to natural or physiological differences.

A well-known example of this mistake is captured in the phrase 'throwing like a girl'. The implication is that girls throw badly by nature. Dr Jack Wilmore of Arizona University devised an ingenious experiment which is easy to replicate:

> When he asked boys and girls to throw the ball, the boys did much better than the girls. Then he asked each of them to throw with their non-dominant arm (i.e. right-handers throw with their left hand and vice versa). On this occasion both boys and girls threw the same distances.[14]

The point this simple experiment makes is that physiological differences alone obviously do not account for performance differences. We cannot know what accounts for performance differences until we give equal training to girls and boys. The same point might also be made with respect to attitudinal differences. For example, women's attitudes toward competition may have been so thwarted or distorted by our continually being forced to compete in unfair circumstances that these attitudes may be more a testament to our imposed disadvantages than to our moral superiority.

The general failure to differentiate between performance discrepancies attributable to physiological differences and those resulting from training has also given us inaccurate estimates of the gap between the athletic potential of the two sexes. Very few women have ever had training equivalent to that of many men. Consequently, women are nowhere near exploring the limits of their potential. As more women become involved in sports and their training is taken seriously, we see amazing improvement in their world records. For example, when Don Schollander won his Olympic medals for men's swimming in 1964, no one would have predicted that ten years later his times would not be good enough to win the women's gold medal.[15]

The integrationist concludes that since we do not and cannot know for some time what a realistic estimate of the sex distinction in athletic potential might be, it is premature to think of having anything other than coeducational physical education.

A second argument posed by those favoring integration is that the differences in athletic potential, once we do know more about them, will deserve relatively little attention in physical education. As with research on sex differences in general, more attention has been paid to the differences than to the relevant similarities. Even if we were to rely on our currently available estimates of sex differences we should beware of exaggerating their significance for physical education.

Granted that some physiological differences between the sexes are relevant for the sports performance of equally well-trained world-class competitors, there are several points more salient for physical education. Whatever their differences, 'neither sex has a structure that is unsuitable for sports,'[16] and both sexes have physiological advantages dependent upon the choice of sport. A physical education program designed to include only or mostly activities favoring one of the sexes would be a poor program. There are other activities one should want to include for a variety of reasons such as their appeal to student interest, their contribution to physical fitness, their lifetime playability, the facilities they require, and their expense.

Further, females and males are similar physiologically in such areas as coordination and the ability to learn particular skills. These similarities, along with other considerations, are more relevant to the design of physical education programs than are the sex differences in the performances of world-class competitors. It is not the point of physical education classes to train top-level sports competitors.

Another argument in favor of sex integration is that it offers girls a better opportunity to realize their potential. This view is expressed rather clearly by two fifteen-year-old girls, who explain in a recent study why they prefer coeducational physical education:

> I feel I have to set higher goals when playing with the boys. . . . I do better, too, when I compete with them.

> When I was in an all girls class I knew I was the best and it was easy to slack off. Now I really have to work to stay near the top. It's better that way.[17]

It might be argued that integration provides a better opportunity only for the very best girls and not for the others. But this argument relies on assumptions about the overall ability of girls as a group in comparison with boys and this is the very point at issue. The expectations of performance for girls have generally been lower than for boys and this itself may account for most of the differences at a physical education class level.[18] Sex-integrated classes and ability groupings within these classes should reduce the chances that sex, rather than individual abilities and interests, will determine the performance expectations.

2

Those who favor sex-segregated classes or a gender-differentiated physical education curriculum acknowledge many of the points raised by integrationists, but still remain unconvinced of the desirability of coeducational programs. They are concerned not only with the advantages any physiological differences might give boys and men but also with the social power advantages which males hold in our sexist culture. They call attention to the fact that males dominate coeducational interactions in ways that limit female participation, undermine women's values, and discount their concerns.[19] They argue that integration will, contrary to what has been claimed, bring about a *greater* loss of opportunity for girls.

Recent empirical research reported by Griffin legitimates this concern that sex-integrated physical education classes will not necessarily eliminate sex bias. Solomons' observations of game interactions among fifth grade integrated classes showed that

> girls tended to be left out of game interactions by the boys. This was true even when the girls had a higher skill level than the boys did. Additionally, both girls and boys regarded boys as better players even when the girls were more highly skilled. Boys preferred to pass the ball to an unskilled boy rather than to a skilled girl. Girls tended to give away scoring opportunities to boys. Unskilled girls were almost completely left out of game action. However, both skilled and unskilled girls received fewer passes than boys did.[20]

A second argument against sex integration is a straightforward political argument about male dominance. There are more men than women involved in physical education and athletics; they are better established in the hierarchy; and men are and will continue to be regarded more favorably by the general educational administration which is also male dominated. Therefore, whatever we think of it in principle, in *practice* integration in physical education is a bad political strategy if we are concerned to further women's interests and increase their autonomy in this field.

Among women physical educators a further worry is that women's distinct interests and values will be submerged in integration so that coeducational programs will be shaped in a masculine mold. A frequently cited example is the way in which cooperative participation may be devalued in the face of a male preoccupation with competitive excellence.[21]

Another argument arising from concern about male dominance is somewhat more complex. In its most sophisticated version the argument is a plea for diversity and pluralism. It rests on the contention that women and men have distinct cultures which need to be preserved. The strong segregationists argue then that we can better realize equality by opting for an organizational arrangement that recognizes genuine differences and provides protection for them.[22]

II A gender-sensitive perspective

In philosophy of education this same tension, between the case for sex integration and the apparent need for some gender differentiation, finds its expression in the search for a just and unbiased conception of the educated person. In her Presidential Address to the Philosophy of Education Society, Jane Roland Martin speaks to this issue. She talks about the evolution of her own views on the 'ideal of the educated person'. Martin concludes that at this time we need what she calls a 'gender-sensitive ideal'. She summarizes her position as follows:

> For some time I assumed that the sole alternative to a biased conception of the educated person was a gender-free ideal, that is to say an ideal which did not take sex or gender into account. I now realize that gender may *have* to be taken into account if an ideal of the educated person is not to be biased according to sex. Plato was wrong then, in Book V of the *Republic*, he said that sex is a difference which makes no difference. I do not mean by this that there are inborn differences which suit males and females for separate and unequal roles in society. Rather I mean that identical educational treatment may not yield identical results so long as that treatment contains a male bias. And supposing it were to yield identical results, so long as those results themselves involve the imposition of a masculine mold, sex bias will not be overcome. To opt at this time for a gender-free ideal is to beg the question. There are sex differences in the way people are perceived and evaluated. There may be sex differences in the way people think and learn and view the world. A conception of the educated person must take these into account. What is needed is a gender-sensitive ideal, one which takes sex or gender into account when it makes a difference and ignores it when it does not. Such an ideal would truly be gender-just.[23]

Martin raises two separate questions: (1) should our ideals of the educated person be different for the sexes? and (2) should our way of going about the realization of even a common ideal be different for each sex? In this paper we shall concern ourselves with the second question and argue in favor of a *gender-sensitive perspective*. We use the term 'perspective' to indicate a particular point of view, or standpoint, which is taken in order to give proportional importance to the component parts, in this case those having to do with gender.

We shall use the term 'gender-sensitive' in the spirit outlined by Martin, namely as an alternative both to a gender-free perspective, which completely ignores gender, and to a sex-differentiated approach, which chooses to perpetuate sex differences. Thus, one should take gender into account when doing so makes a difference by furthering sex equality or by preventing sexist bias.

What would a gender-sensitive perspective mean for physical education, especially for women's physical education? The rest of our paper will be an extended answer to this question.

III The domain of physical education

Up to this point we have talked of 'physical education' in an ordinary-language sense without defining it precisely. It is time now to look more closely at our concept of physical education. How would a gender-sensitive perspective view the domain of physical education? What is included? What ought to be included? This is an important question because the issue of which gender differences need to be taken into account will be determined, in part, by what one includes within the domain of physical education.

Definition 1: deliberate physical education or what is taught

What is 'physical education'? What are we talking about when we talk of anyone's physical education, whether woman or man, girl or boy? A first, perhaps obvious, clearcut answer is to say that physical education consists of the formal instruction given in 'physical education classes'.

Since physical education classes are usually required of all high school students, these classes are the one instance of deliberate instructional efforts to attend to physical learning for all young persons. But there are numerous other instances of deliberate physical education. Within formal schooling itself, the 'extracurricular' sports often include effective teaching. Physical education in non-school settings is done in classes at summer camps and playgrounds, fitness classes, Y programs, Little League baseball, private and group lessons in tennis, swimming, etc.

What all of these instances share is a deliberate, intentional effort to do physical education; almost everything else about these classes varies. The expectations, the participation levels, the facilities, and staffing all range from high quality levels to the barest minimum.

What is of more philosophical interest is the wide variety of educational aims and curriculum emphases. Physical fitness and physical health have been a more or less constant theme and concern of all physical educators. But the form these have taken and the additional emphases have varied considerably.[24] As noted above, some women's programs have developed movement education and have included dance, neither of which has been emphasized in male programs.

The role of sports has been varied and controversial. In some cases sports and physical education have been entirely separate, recognizing that physical education need not entail sports. On the other hand, many physical education programs consist almost entirely of a combination of intramural and extramural sports. But even where sports are dominant, different ideals are reflected in the emphases which vary from competitive sport to lifetime sports to the non-competitive 'new games'.

Anyone addressing educational questions from a gender-sensitive perspective would want to consider how these different educational aims have affected each sex. This then requires us to ask a further question: What does each sex actually learn from their physical education?

Definition 2: what is learned

So far we have defined physical education from the point of view of the educator – i.e., in terms of what is taught. If we consider the student's point of view as well, then we must broaden our definition to include what is actually learned by the students.

For many students, especially those with able teachers or high motivation, their education includes a large amount of what is deliberately taught – the physical skills, the knowledge and information, as well as attendant values and attitudes. But this is not the sum total of any student's physical education. A more inclusive view must also ask what else students have learned about their physical selves, their physical abilities and capacities. What physical propensities have they acquired? What have they learned about their physical being in the world? A gender-sensitive perspective needs to know whether these learning outcomes are different for girls and boys.

If we want to know what girls and women learn about themselves as physical beings in a physical world, especially from informal settings and situations, we must turn to the 'hidden curriculum'.

IV The hidden curriculum

In *Memoirs of an Ex-Prom Queen*, Alix Kates Shulman describes, with wit, humor, and incisive accuracy, much of the hidden and not-so-hidden curriculum for girls' physical learning. Shulman's account of minimally supervised school play-ground activities and their cumulative effect for girls and boys provides us with an instructive microcosm of the informal, incidental, and exceedingly powerful lessons girls learn about their physical being in the world. If we read Shulman's description from an educational point of view, we can see that it captures the major features of many girls' informal physical education.

Once I started school I learned I would have to choose between hair ribbons and trees, and that if I chose trees I'd have to fight for them. The trees, like the hills, belonged to the boys.

Before and after school, the boys would fan out over the school grounds and take over the ball fields . . . we played girls' games under the teachers' protective eyes. We could jump rope, throw rubber balls for a-meemy-a-claspy, practise tricks on the bars nestled in the ell of the building, play jacks or blow soap bubbles – all safe, dependable and sometimes joyous games which the boys disdained because we did them. . . . Though in my summers and on my street I had wandered freely, taking to the woods and the very tips of the trees, in my first weeks of first grade I learned to stay uncomplainingly in my place on the steps or in the shadow of the school. I learned masculine and feminine.

'Go on to the Mountain, girls, it's a gorgeous day,' Mrs. Hess would urge us as we stood on the steps at recess trading cards. Or, 'Why don't you play some freeze tag? You need the exercise.' But we knew better. We knew that going near the ball fields or behind the backstop or near the basket hoop or in among the fruit trees or around the Mountain or near the skating pond were extremely dangerous expeditions, even if we went in a pack – for that was all boys' territory, acknowledged by everyone. Despite Mrs. Hess's prods and assurances, we knew that at any moment out there a pair or trio or more of boys might grow bored with their own game and descend on us with their bag of tricks. If a girl was spotted on their territory the boys felt perfectly free to: give her a pink belly, or lock her in the shed or not to let her down from a tree, or tie her to the flagpole or. . . .

We knew better than to tell Mrs. Hess. The one time I ran crying to her with my dress ripped after Bobby Barr had pulled me out of an apple tree, she hugged and comforted me with a double message: 'I know, dear, those are rough boys. Why don't you play with the girls?' . . . from the moment we got kicked out of the trees and sent into the walk-in doll house back in kindergarten, our movements and efforts had been so steadily circumscribed, our permissible yearnings so confined, that the only imprint left for us to make was on ourselves. By the third grade, with every other girl in Baybury Heights, I came to realize that there was only one thing worth bothering about: becoming beautiful.[25]

One thing to notice in Shulman's account is the extent to which these informal sex-segregated playground activities mirror the standard forms of sex discrimination and the undesirable outcomes we have already discussed as part of our historically sex-segregated formal physical education programs; the unequal distribution of resources, facilities, and 'territory'; the reification of gender differences; the stratification with male dominance; and finally the attendant loss of opportunities for girls. Shulman's passage illustrates how the hidden curriculum for girls includes, indeed demands, their acquiescence to these inequalities.

The girls learn to accept gender-differentiated constraints on their physical movements, while male-imposed limits on their rights to physical space are established and maintained by physical intimidation. The girls' physical being in the world is 'circumscribed' and 'confined' in direct contrast to the physical freedom of the boys. And the girls soon learn that their games are devalued, while the one and only physical priority for their own sex is physical beauty.

What is of further interest to us here is the way in which the school setting both allows for and contributes to a hidden curriculum which runs counter to the explicit values and directives for physical education. So Mrs Hess urges the girls to go to the mountain, to play freeze tag because they 'need the exercise'. Thus we have a deliberate physical education directive for girls – *exercise*. But the situation, the setting, and the girls' own experiences, as well as Mrs Hess's unguarded comments about 'rough boys' teach the girls that for them to engage in any interesting or strenuous physical activity will be difficult, dangerous, and costly.

In most contemporary schools the hidden curriculum is presumably less blatant and the deliberate physical education program is better organized. We nevertheless have reason to suspect not only that it still exists but also that the essential content of the hidden curriculum for many, if not most, girls remains substantially the same, whether from school or non-school settings.[26] If we take a gender-sensitive perspective we must address this problem: what should the educator do about hidden sexist curricula?

Before we attempt to answer this question, there are several remarks that need to be made about our use of the term 'hidden curriculum.'[27] We use the term in a broad, but nontrivial, sense to refer to learning that is not openly intended. Our usage allows us to speak not just of the hidden curriculum of the school but also of the hidden curriculum in other settings, whether overtly educational or not. But more importantly our usage allows us to focus on the hidden curriculum there may be for an identifiable group of learners. We are specifically interested in what women learn, from a variety of settings, which can interfere with the success of physical education programs designed for them.

One might well object to our use of the term '*hidden* curriculum' to cover this informal learning. In particular, in the case of the hidden curriculum of sexism, it could be argued that it is no longer hidden, it has been found and articulated rather clearly. Thus, if we mean to discuss unintended educational outcomes perhaps the term 'informal curriculum' might seem preferable. But we shall purposely keep the term 'hidden' for two reasons: first, the existence of a sexist curriculum may be clear to some but there are many who are quite unaware of it still; second, and more importantly, the term 'hidden' indicates a concern for recognizing that we have not agreed upon or chosen to teach this 'curriculum' and students have neither been asked nor told about these learning outcomes.

V Confronting the hidden curriculum

Hidden curricula are, of course, not confined to physical education; and we can ask, in general, what educators should do when the content of their students' hidden curricula runs counter to the aims and values of the deliberate formal curriculum which they are trying to teach. Let us consider, for a moment, the general problem of hidden curricula and the possible alternatives open to the educator. We will then return to the particular problem of hidden curricula for women's physical education.

1

Faced with an undesirable hidden curriculum, an educator or educational institution can make one or more of the following moves:

1   *Give up.* The educator can simply give up and change the deliberate curriculum to bring it in line with the hidden curriculum so as to eliminate any inconsistency.[28]

2   *Do nothing.* In this case one merely goes about one's business as usual, teaching the deliberate curriculum and ignoring what is not a direct part of it, assuming either that these other influences already get too much time and attention, or that they are not serious impediments.

3   *Create a more desirable alternative.* A more positive move is to alter the emphasis of the deliberate curriculum or create a new deliberate curriculum to counterbalance the undesirable effects of the hidden curriculum.

4   *Reform the organizational structures.* A more drastic move is to intervene directly in the educational setting, altering structures and organizations so as to eliminate as much as possible those practices and situations which contribute to or perpetuate the undesirable learning that arises from or occurs under the jurisdiction of the educational institution itself. This might involve changes in formal classroom instruction, teacher–student interactions, administrative organization, or changes within the institutional environment affecting rules, procedures or informal relationships.

5   *Study the hidden curriculum.* In this case one addresses the hidden curriculum directly by making articulation and critical scrutiny of it an integral part of the deliberate curriculum. In short, make the hidden curriculum part of the subject matter to study.

6   *Take the offensive.* Perhaps the most far-reaching move is to teach students self-defense skills 'against the onslaught of unasked-for learning states'[29] i.e., teach students how to identify hidden curricula, how to discover the sources, and how to avoid the learning outcomes one does not wish to acquire.

2

These six alternatives sketch what the educator can do in response to undesirable hidden curricula. But we have yet to answer the question of what an educator should do. In particular, what is the educational responsibility toward hidden curricula as seen from a gender-sensitive perspective? In order to answer this question we shall distinguish three types of cases. Our criterion is the extent to which the locus of control for an undesirable hidden curriculum lies within the educational institution:

(a) the hidden curriculum is a direct outcome of educational practices or in-school procedures;
(b) the hidden curriculum comes from the larger society but manifests itself within the school in ways which are amenable to direct educational intervention and control;
(c) both the source and the control of the hidden curriculum lie outside the school, but the learning outcomes constitute a serious impediment to the achievement of educational goals.

3

Let us start with the first case. Whether one finds sexism hidden in the explicit curriculum or in the institutional practices, the educator's responsibility for direct intervention is clear. This responsibility is generally acknowledged; and a number of appropriate reforms, which exemplify our fourth alternative, have been proposed and undertaken; for example, efforts to arrange a fairer allocation of resources and attempts to redress the blatant inequalities in physical education expenditures and facilities for women. Reallocation of resources is also necessary to prevent perpetuation of the assumption that men's programs are more important and valuable than women's.

Equalizing the numbers of women and men who teach physical education, coach, and carry administrative responsibilities is another example of organizational reform. But we still need to change the pattern in which males frequently coach females while females rarely coach males if we are to avoid the implicit message that sports is a male domain in which males have the expertise.

The proposal to integrate sport activities using ability groupings is often seen as an important way to counter the belief that biological sex is relevant to athletic participation. Heide makes this point:

> Girls and boys, women and men must participate together in sports with decisions about participation of individuals and groups to be based on current skill, agility, experience, strength, size, weight, interest, speed and/or relevant criteria, not the irrelevant factor of biological sex.[30]

246

Our discussion so far indicates that the most obvious way of countering undesirable learning outcomes from in-school hidden curricula is to reform the organizational structures. But the third approach of curriculum change in order to create a more desirable alternative may also be necessary and useful. Suggestions that we introduce new sports for which women are naturally advantaged would be another way to counter beliefs that male biological sex determines general athletic prowess.[31]

The efforts of many women physical educators to preserve a sex-differentiated curriculum in order to avoid what they believe to be immoral or unhealthy attitudes toward competition and violence hidden in men's programs might plausibly be seen as examples of either the Do Nothing or the Create a More Desirable Alternative approach.

4

Let us turn now to case (b), in which the manifestations of the society's hidden curriculum are amenable to educational intervention. Patricia Griffin's examples of teacher–student interactions illustrate ways in which teachers can intervene to offset standard sexist stereotypes and to discourage sexist comments:

(MALE STUDENT to another male student who is crying):
    John, if you're going to act like a girl, get off the field.
TEACHER: Tom, anyone, boy or girl, who gets hit and knocked down that hard might cry.
STUDENT: Why do the girls have to play?
TEACHER: John, the girls want to play as much as you do. Everyone will have a fair turn to play.
STUDENT: Mark throws like a girl.
TEACHER: No, Jane, Mark throws like he needs practice throwing. Lots of girls throw well and lots of boys don't.[32]

Thus a gender-sensitive perspective would emphasize the important difference between saying that 'Mark throws like he needs practice' and 'Mark throws like a girl' even though both comments are criticisms of Mark's throwing.

Another pertinent example of behavior that manifests standard sexist presumptions is male students poaching from female students' territories in games, also cited by Griffin. Notice the difference between a teacher who encourages poaching: 'Susan, if you can't catch it, back off and let Steve get it' and a gender-sensitive approach: 'John, that was Susan's ball' or 'Don't crowd her out, Dan.'[33]

These are examples of a gender-sensitive perspective because they illustrate ways in which a teacher takes gender into account in order to further sex equality or to prevent sexist bias. But how does a teacher come to notice these numerous incidental cases of gender bias in the first place, especially when they are part of the prevailing culture? It seems likely that many teachers will neither notice nor intervene unless they themselves have studied the hidden curriculum.

Thus one might argue that the first students to study the hidden curriculum, and take the offensive, ought to be teachers themselves. If curricular and organizational changes are to succeed, teachers must know what the hidden curricula are, how to identify sources and how to make the necessary interventions. Courses and workshops on 'sexism in education' and on 'sex roles' are needed for teacher education and in-service teacher training.[34]

Once teachers are prepared to notice and intervene in sexist interactions, the case for sex integration becomes stronger. Since the interactions in sex-integrated programs are more likely to reveal sexist hidden curricula, an attentive teacher can then address this explicitly. Furthermore, one of the findings on coeducational teaching in university physical education is that both teachers and students are challenging and correcting one another's biases.[35] Griffin shows that similar corrections could also occur with younger students:

STUDENT: I'm the third base person, not the third base man.
TEACHER: You're right, Sue. Thanks for correcting me.[36]

5

We believe there is also a strong educational case to be made for extending alternatives (5) and (6) above, i.e., the study of the hidden curriculum and teaching students to defend against it, whenever we suspect that the hidden curriculum for a group of students is a direct impediment to these students' learning. This brings us to case (c). Here the issue of responsibility is much less clear than in cases (a) and (b); and our discussion must be somewhat speculative. Indeed it is important to emphasize at the outset that study of the hidden curriculum cannot and should not take the place of able teaching, sound training, regular practice, and equal opportunities for participation, all of which have been historically unavailable to most girls and women.

But what if we do have good pedagogy and relatively equal opportunities for women, can we then discount the hidden curriculum? Not if we believe the literature on female physicality. In her book *Body Politics*, Nancy Henley quotes and then verifies Marge Piercy's description of the different ways women and men move and occupy space. Piercy describes Wanda teaching a theater group about movement:

Wanda made them aware how they moved, how they rested, how they occupied space. She demonstrated how men sat and how women sat on the subway, on benches. Men expanded into available space. They sprawled, or they sat with spread legs. They put their arms on the arms of chairs. They crossed their legs by putting a foot on the other knee. They dominated space expansively.

Women condensed. Women crossed their legs by putting one leg over the other and alongside. Women kept their elbows to their sides, taking up as little space as possible. . . . Women sat protectively using elbows not to dominate space, not to mark territory, but to protect their soft tissues.[37]

But what does this have to do with impediments to women's physical education? Let us compare Piercy's description with Iris Young's phenomenological description of the difference between the movements of untrained males and untrained females when they engage in athletic activity.

Now most men are by no means superior athletes, and their sporting efforts more often display bravado than genuine skill and coordination. The relatively untrained man nevertheless engages in sport generally with more free motion and open reach than does his female counterpart. Not only is there a typical style of throwing like a girl, but there is a more or less typical style of running like a girl, climbing like a girl, swinging like a girl, hitting like a girl. They have in common, first, that the whole body is not put into fluid and directed motion, but rather, in swinging and hitting, for example, the motion is concentrated in one body part; and second, that the women's motion tends not to reach, extend, lean, stretch, and follow through in the direction of her intention.

For many women as they move in sport a space surrounds them in imagination which we are not free to move beyond; the space available to our movement is a constricted space. Thus, for example, in softball or volleyball women tend to remain in one place more often than men, neither jumping to reach nor running to approach the ball.[38]

The point here is that the restrictions women have learned to accept or to impose on their physical being in the world may explain why many so-called 'unathletic' women seem unable to move freely in athletic activity. If this is true, then it is hard to imagine how such deep-rooted physical inhibitions can be altered without direct attention to both their sources and their behavioral manifestations. In other words, one would need to study the society's gender-differentiated physical norms and help students identify the ways in which these norms can interfere with physical self-determination on a basic level.

But the question of educational efficacy as well as educational responsibility remains problematic in these (c) cases, where both the source and the control of the hidden curriculum lie outside the scope of formal education. We can urge the importance of studying the impact of society's physical norms on women's physicality; and we can attend to the ways in which our norms may even prescribe physical vulnerability for women. But we must also recognize that educational efforts alone are bound to be limited when women's ability to protect themselves depends in large part upon social and political conditions.

The prevalence of rape and physical violence against women is a case in point. Although it is difficult to determine the precise impact of such conditions, it is also unrealistic to ignore the complex connections between physical freedom and educational equality.[39]

6

Our discussion of educational responsibility for hidden curricula leads us to conclude that alternatives (3), (4), (5), and (6) are all necessary for women's physical education. But different approaches need to be taken at different times.

In elementary school less reification of gender differences has occurred and the creation of a concrete alternative model of coeducational physical activities should be relatively successful. Children's conceptions about what is and is not sex-role appropriate are still comparatively loose. However, because of their limited experience and less developed reasoning abilities, children are more dependent upon the examples in their immediate environment than are older students, who have better abilities to imagine alternatives and to avoid over-generalizing from single cases. We also have a greater degree of control over the young child's environment.

Thus the emphasis in elementary school should perhaps rest on the energetic and thorough construction of a better alternative. We can, to a great extent, more systematically control the sexism in elementary school through this method than we can later on. But a gender-sensitive perspective for elementary schools would also require us to notice that between the ages of four and twelve, boys usually have a number of outside-school advantages, including additional athletic practice, coaching, advice, information about sports, many male role models, and general encouragement for their physical feats. We would recommend, therefore, that in addition to integrated physical education classes and sports there be opportunities for extra activities for girls, such as additional coaching and teaching. This is especially important in elementary school, because most sports and physical activities which one engages in as an adolescent or an adult require early development of physical motor skills and build on these.

In the present situation, at the older ages this structural intervention is probably not adequate to deal with the sexism that has become entrenched. At this level one must both create an alternative and address the hidden curricula from other settings. At adolescence whatever sex differences there are emerge most obviously; and much social attention is given to accentuating them. The socialization literature on girls consistently reports that although there is some tolerance for 'tomboys' and a greater latitude in expectations of gender role comformity given to prepubescent girls, with adolescence there is increasing pressure for girls to come to terms with their physical femininity and to develop the 'properly feminine' beliefs, attitudes and behaviors.[40]

Gender roles are, however, interdependent; and as Money noticed early on, one only learns what girls are supposed to do and be like by simultaneously learning what boys are supposed to be like, and vice versa.[41] This symbiotic interplay of norms defining femininity and masculinity means that we cannot hope to alter one without having the other come under critical scrutiny as well. Although there may be a greater need for girls to examine the hidden curriculum for themselves because of a greater incongruity between the socialization message and the developmental objectives of the physical education programs, we know that in general sex roles can be limiting to educational achievement for both females and males.[42]

VI   Beyond sexism in physical education

In essence we have tried to address the transitional problems of moving from a sexist education in a sexist culture to a non-sexist education that will nevertheless continue for some time to be influenced by a wider sexist culture.

We have argued that inasmuch as it will affect the success of educational practices, one cannot separate the sexism in the larger context of society from the educational setting. Hence, educators must, if they are to be responsible, adopt a gender-sensitive perspective. A gender-sensitive perspective on physical education requires that we be sensitive to what the larger society is teaching that is relevant to its subject matter, what girls and women are learning about their physical selves. It requires that we attend to this learning, recognize its influence upon our goals and find ways of dealing with it that are appropriate to each level of education.

A gender-sensitive perspective is not a blueprint for physical education that will answer all our questions about particular practices. Rather, it is a perspective which reminds us of conditions that must be met before we are entitled to hold our physical education theories up for admiration or even for adoption. We have contrasted a gender-sensitive perspective with a gender-differentiated ideal, suggesting that the latter is often negligent with respect to sex equality. We are now in a position to indicate what the concept of gender sensitivity might require of any women's physical education. It requires, among other things, that

1   theories or proposals for women's physical education should be formed in the knowledge of the sexism that has been associated with the history of women's physical education;
2   theories or program proposals can demonstrate that they are non-sexist;
3   theories or program proposals acknowledge some responsibility for foreseeable educational outcomes, even when these are partially attributable to hidden sexist curricula from other settings.

Our gender-sensitive perspective is like the 'Pushmi-Pullyu' in the Dr Dolittle story. It has two heads that look in different directions, one ahead to our ideal of sex equality, one backwards to the social realities from which our ideal has emerged. It is useful to have two heads, for the ideal of equality has been with us a long time, but there is an equally long history of its failure in practice. It is only by constantly exploring the tension between the views from both heads that physical education can help women achieve physical freedom as well as physical well-being.

Notes

1 Quoted in Gerda Lerner, *The Female Experience: An American Documentary* (Indianapolis: Bobbs-Merrill, 1977), p. 7.

2 The historical documentation of attitudes towards women's physical education and, in particular, women's own views about what their physical education should be can be found in several articles. See: Roberta J. Park, 'Concern for the Physical Education of the Female Sex from 1675 to 1800 in France, England, and Spain,' *Research Quarterly AAHPER* (May 1974), pp. 104–19; Roberta J. Park, '"Embodied Selves": The Rise and Development of Concern for Physical Education, Active Games and Recreation for American Women, 1776–1865,' *Journal of Sport History*, 5, no. 2 (1978), 5–41; Patricia Vertinsky, 'Sexual Equality and the Legacy of Catherine Beecher,' *Journal of Sport History*, 6, no. 1 (1979), 38–49.

3 This summary of characteristics is drawn from June A. Kennard, 'The History of Physical Education,' Review Essay in *Signs: Journal of Women in Culture and Society*, 2, no. 4 (1977), 835–43.

4 Betty Spears, 'Prologue: The Myth,' chapter 1 in *Women and Sport: From Myth to Reality*, ed. by Carole A. Oglesby (Philadelphia: Lea & Febiger, 1978), p. 11.

5 Kennard, *op. cit.* p. 836.

6 For a more elaborate discussion of the history of these developments within physical education see Daryl Siedentop, *Physical Education: Introductory Analysis* (Dubuque, Iowa: Wm C. Brown, 1972), especially chapter 6.

7 Documentation of the inequality of opportunity in physical education and sports may be found in: A. Fishel and S.J. Pottker, 'Sex Bias in Secondary Schools: The Impact of Title IX,' in A. Fishel and S.J. Pottker (eds) *Sex Bias in the Schools* (New Brunswick, N.J.: Rutgers University Press, 1977); T. Saario, C. Jacklin and J.C. Tittle, 'Sex Role Stereotyping in the Public Schools,' *Harvard Educational Review*, 43, no. 3 (1973), 386–416; B. Gilbert and N. Williamson, 'Sport is Unfair to Women,' *Sports Illustrated* (May 1973); B. Gilbert and N. Williamson, 'Are You Being Two-Faced?' *Sports Illustrated* (June 1973); B. Gilbert and N. Williamson, 'Programmed to Be Losers,' *Sports Illustrated* (June 1973). See also D. Stanley Eitzen, *Sport in Contemporary Society: An Anthology* (New York: St Martin's Press, 1979), chapter 11, 'Sexism in Sport.'

8 One of the common distinctions employed in the literature on sex roles is that between sex and gender. When the distinction is drawn, 'sex' refers to the biological differences between females and males and 'gender' refers to the social differences between the sexes. However, the matter is far from simple; usage of the terms is often inconsistent and some have argued that the distinction itself is unsuccessful because of the complex linkage between biological and social aspects of sex. Granted the difficulties, we will, nevertheless, employ the distinction in this essay. We use the term 'gender-sensitive perspective' precisely because we believe that not just biological differences between the sexes are relevant to the development of physical education programs. We do not wish to beg any questions about the nature or causal explanation of gender differences. We are interested in the implications we think they should have for educational practice. Hence, we invoke the concept of gender, but we use it solely as a descriptive term. For an insightful discussion of the difficulties with the distinction between sex and gender

see Margrit Eichler, *The Double Standard: A Feminist Critique of Feminist Social Science* (London: Croom Helm, 1980), pp. 10–19.

9 A good general introduction to the problem of the interpretation of the ideal of sex equality may be found in Jane English (ed.) *Sex Equality* (Englewood Cliffs, N.J.: Prentice-Hall, 1977), Section II. For a discussion of whether this ideal requires the abolition of sex roles see: Alison Jagger, 'On Sexual Equality' in that volume.

10 An interesting discussion of this controversy and its implications for sports activities is set out in two papers: Richard Wasserstrom, 'Racism, Sexism, and Preferential Treatment: An Approach to the Topics,' *U.C.L.A. Law Review* (February 1977), pp. 581–615; and Bernard Boxill, 'Sexual Blindness and Sexual Equality,' *Social Theory and Practice*, 6 (Fall 1980), 281–99.

11 The philosophical discussion of this point occurs in the context of debate about the morality of affirmative action programs. See: S. Bishop and M. Weinzweig (eds) *Philosophy and Women* (Belmont, Calif.: Wadsworth, 1979), chapter 7; C. Gould and M. Wartofsky (eds) *Women and Philosophy* (New York: G.P. Putnam's Sons, 1976), Section IV; Barry Gross (ed.) *Reverse Discrimination* (Buffalo, N.Y.: Prometheus Books, 1977).

12 The *prima facie* case against sex-segregated sports is summed up by Mary Anne Warren in 'Justice and Gender in School Sports.' The same case holds against sex-segregated physical education classes.

13 For a chronicle of the limited participation permitted women in the Olympic Games see: Ellen Gerber, Jan Felshin, Pearl Berlin and Waneen Wyrick, *The American Woman in Sport* (Reading, Mass.: Addison-Wesley, 1974), chapter 4.

14 This experiment is reported in Jean Cochrane, Abby Hoffman and Pat Kincaid, *Women in Canadian Sports* (Toronto: Fitzhenry and Whiteside, 1977), p. 81. See also Jack Wilmore, *They Told You You Couldn't Compete with Men* (Toronto: University of Toronto Press, 1969). It is doubtful that one can overestimate the powerful impact early sex-role socialization has on a child's sense of her own physical abilities. From the moment of birth we are subjected to biased judgments and expectations of our physical abilities. One study, for example, reports that as early as twenty-four hours after birth parents have different expectations for infants based on sex alone. Among infants who did not differ on any physical or health measures, fathers judged sons as 'firmer, larger featured, *better coordinated, more alert, stronger* and hardier'; daughters were judged as 'softer, finer featured, *more awkward, more inattentive, weaker,* and more delicate' (emphasis ours). J. Rubin, F. Provenzano and Z. Luria, 'The Eye of the Beholder: Parents' Views on Sex of Newborns,' in A. Kaplan and J. Bean (eds) *Beyond Sex Role Streotypes* (Boston: Little, Brown, 1976), p. 183.

15 Reported in Jackie Hudson, 'Physical Parameters Used for Female Exclusion from Law Enforcement and Athletics,' in *Women and Sport*, ed. by C. Oglesby, p. 52. See this article for scientific refutation of many myths about women's natural inferiority in sports. In addition to the tremendous increase in women's performances in conventional Olympic events, Hudson reports on women's world records in endurance events such as long-distance running and swimming.

16 Jean Cochrane *et al.*, *Women in Canadian Sports*, p. 80.

17 May Domb Mikkelson, 'Co-ed Gym – It's a Whole New Ballgame,' *Journal of Physical Education and Recreation* (November/December 1979), p. 63. Something akin to this sentiment was expressed long ago by Elizabeth Cady Stanton. She recalled her own experience in an all-girls school: 'The thought of a school without boys, who had been to me such a stimulus both in study and play, seemed to my imagination dreary and profitless.' Quoted in Roberta J. Park, '"Embodied Selves": The Rise and Development of Concern for Physical Education, Active Games and Recreation for American Women, 1776–1865,' *Journal of Sport History*, p. 39.

18 For a discussion of the literature on sex bias in teacher expectations in physical education see Patricia Scott Griffin, 'Developing a Systematic Observation Instrument to Identify Sex Role Dependent and Sex Role Independent Behavior Among Physical Education Teachers,' Doctoral Dissertation, University of Massachusetts, 1980 (*University Microfilms International* No. 8101326). See also R. Allard, 'Teacher Behavior Directed Toward Individual Students in Physical Education Classes: The Influence of Student Gender and Class Participation,' unpublished doctoral dissertation, University of Massachusetts, 1979.

19 A recent report, 'The Classroom Climate: A Chilly One for Women,' issued by the Project on the Status and Education of Women, Association of American Colleges, 1982, documents this sort of male domination in coeducational settings. For a recent review of the literature on the role of social power in coeducation and on the differential effects of single-sex education and coeducational settings on the educational attainments of girls and boys see: J. Finn, J. Reis and L. Dulberg, 'Sex Differences in Educational Attainment: The Process,' *Comparative Education Review,* 24, no. 2, part 2 (June 1980), s33–s52.

20 Griffin, *op. cit.* p. 10.

21 For a concise exploration of the ambivalence some women coaches have about women adopting so-called male attitudes towards competition see: Joanna Rohrbaugh, *Women: Psychology's Puzzle* (New York: Basic Books 1979), chapter 17.

22 This argument is put forth by both women and men physical educators and it appears in its sophisticated form in Boxill, 'Sexual Blindness and Sexual Equality.' Interestingly, those male and female physical educators who argue against coeducation do so on the same grounds, but their interpretation of the reasons differs. Both contend that it will mean a loss of opportunity and a change in the valuation of the activities. However, women contend it will mean a loss of opportunity for all but the very best girls; men contend that it will mean a loss of opportunity for the better male athletes. Women worry that girls will pick up what they consider to be morally questionable male attitudes towards competition; men worry that the girls' participation will trivialize or devalue the activities or increase the risk of male humiliation in defeat. It should, of course, be noted that the sex differences in those attitudes are not clear-cut. There are many men who defend coeducation in this area and deplore the dominant combative model for sports. There are also women who argue that girls should not infringe on male sports territory. A good discussion of these general attitudes can be found in Jan Felshin's chapter, 'The Social View,' in Ellen Gerber *et al.*, *The American Woman in Sport.*

23 Jane Roland Martin, 'The Ideal of the Educated Person,' presidential address, *Philosophy of Education Society Proceedings* (1981), forthcoming.

24 For an extended discussion of the different conceptions of physical education that have influence in contemporary education see Daryl Siedentop, *Physical Education: Introductory Analysis* (Dubuque, Iowa: William C. Brown, 1972). For a less systematic, but fairly representative sampling of contemporary influences see R. Cobb and P. Lepley (eds) *Contemporary Philosophies of Physical Education and Athletics* (Columbus, Ohio: Merrill, 1973).

25 Alix Kates Shulman, *Memoirs of an Ex-Prom Queen.* Copyright © 1969, 1971, 1972 by Alix Kates Shulman. Reprinted by permission of Alfred A. Knopf, Inc. and Granada Publishing Limited. The passage quoted is from pages 18–21.

26 The sexist hidden curriculum of schools is fully documented in Frazier and Sadker, *Sexism in School and Society* (New York: Harper & Row, 1973); Judith Stacey *et al.* (eds) *And Jill Came Tumbling After: Sexism in American Education* (New York: Dell, 1974); and Bonnie Cook Freeman, 'Female Education in Patriarchal Power Systems,' in P. Altbach and G. Kelly, *Education and Colonialism* (New York: Longman, 1978), pp. 207–42.

See also a special issue, two parts, on Women and Education, *Harvard Educational Review*, 49, no. 4 (November 1979) and vol. 50, no. 1 (February 1980). A good general introduction to what we call the sexist hidden curricula for women in non-school settings can be found in V. Gornick and B. Moran (eds) *Woman in Sexist Society: Studies in Power and Powerlessness* (New York: Basic Books, 1971). The best general introduction to a systematic explication of sexism in society can be found in the chapter 'Theory of Sexual Politics,' in Kate Millett, *Sexual Politics* (Garden City, N.Y.: Doubleday, 1970).

27 Our usage of the term 'hidden curriculum' follows closely that employed by Jane Roland Martin in her paper 'What Should We Do with a Hidden Curriculum When We Find One?' *Curriculum Inquiry*, 6, no. 2 (1976), 135–51. Reprinted as Volume IV Paper 24. To our knowledge Martin is the first to draw a distinction between the hidden curriculum of a setting and the hidden curriculum for a learner. For a further discussion of the hidden curriculum see Elizabeth Vallance, 'Hiding the Hidden Curriculum,' *Curriculum Theory and Network*, 4, no. 1 (1973–1974).

28 Enactment of the proposed Family Protection Act could, in effect, force the deliberate curriculum into even greater alignment with sexist conventions in the larger society. The Act, if passed, would prohibit the use of federal funds for educational materials that 'do not reflect a balance between the status role of men and women, do not reflect different ways in which women and men live, and do not contribute to the American way of life as it has been historically understood.' Ann Pelham, 'Family Protection Act: Dear to New Right, but Unlikely to Get Out of Committees.' *Congressional Quarterly Weekly Report*, 39 (Oct. 3, 1981), p. 1916. This Bill (S1378, HR3955) has been referred to five different Senate and House Committees.

29 Jane Roland Martin, 'What Should We Do with a Hidden Curriculum When We Find One?' p. 149. Reprinted as Volume IV Paper 24, pp. 453–69.

30 Wilma Scott Heide, 'Feminism for a Sporting Future,' in *Women and Sport*, ed. by Carole Oglesby, p. 197.

31 Jane English, 'Sex Equality in Sports,' *Philosophy & Public Affairs*, 7, no. 3 (Spring 1978), 269–77.

32 Griffin, pp. 137–8.

33 Griffin, p. 136.

34 Projects funded by the Women's Educational Equity Act Program (WEEAP) have developed materials to aid teachers in addressing sexism in education. A complete listing of these can be found in the catalog of materials published by WEEAP.

35 Linda L. Blair, 'Implementing Title IX: Concerns of Undergraduate Physical Education Majors,' *Journal of Physical Education and Recreation* (November/December 1979), p. 77.

36 Griffin, p. 139.

37 Nancy Henley, *Body Politics* (Englewood Cliffs, N.J.: Prentice-Hall, 1977), p. 38. The quotation is originally from Marge Piercy, *Small Changes* (New York: Doubleday, 1973), p. 438.

38 Iris Young, 'Throwing Like a Girl: A Phenomenology of Feminine Body Comportment Motility and Spatiality,' *Human Studies*, 3 (1980), p. 143.

39 Adrienne Rich eloquently reminds us of this: 'Women and men do not receive an equal education because outside the classroom women are perceived not as sovereign beings but as prey. The growing incidence of rape on and off campus . . . is certainly occurring in a context of widespread images of sexual violence against women, on billboards and in so-called high art. More subtle, more daily than rape is the verbal abuse experienced by the woman student on many campuses. . . . The undermining of self, of a woman's sense of her right to occupy space and walk freely in the world, is deeply relevant to education. The capacity to think independently, to take intellectual risks, to assert ourselves mentally, is inseparable from our physical way of being in the

world, our feelings of personal integrity.' Adrienne Rich, *On Lies, Secrets, and Silences* (New York: W.W. Norton, 1979), pp. 241–2.

40 There is an enormous literature on sex role socialization. Some frequently cited books include these: Shirley Weitz, *Sex Roles* (New York: Oxford University Press, 1977); Lenore J. Weitzman, *Sex Role Socialization* (Palo Alto, Calif.: Mayfield, 1979); A. Kaplan and J. Bean (eds) *Beyond Sex Role Stereotypes: Readings Towards a Psychology of Androgyny* (Boston: Little, Brown, 1976); and Irene Freize *et al.*, *Women and Sex Roles* (New York: W.W. Norton, 1978). A short summary of the literature may be found in Lenore J. Weitzman, 'Sex Role Socialization,' in Jo Freeman (ed.) *Women: A Feminist Perspective* (Palo Alto, Calif.: Mayfield, 1979), pp. 153–216. Much research and writing on sex differences and sex role socialization is fraught with bias. A good explication of some of the difficulties plaguing the literature can be found in Margrit Eichler, *The Double Standard: A Feminist Critique of Feminist Social Science* (London: Croom Helm, 1980).

41 John Money and Anke Ehrhardt, *Man & Woman Boy & Girl* (Baltimore: Johns Hopkins University Press, 1972), p. 19.

42 E. Maccoby, 'Sex Differences in Intellectual Functioning,' in E. Maccoby (ed.) *The Development of Sex Differences* (Stanford, Calif.: Stanford University Press, 1966), pp. 25–55.

Suggestions for further reading

In addition to the works cited in the notes, the following are suggested for further reading:

Diana Nyad and Candace Lyle Hogan. *Basic Training for Women.* New York: Hogan and Hilltown Press, 1981. Especially chapter 1, 'The Mind.'

Margrit Eichler. *The Double Standard: A Feminist Critique of Feminist Social Sciences.* London: Croom Helm, 1980.

Carol Gilligan. *In a Different Voice: Psychological Theory and Women's Development.* Cambridge, Mass.: Harvard University Press, 1982.

M. Ann Hall. 'Sport, Sex Roles and Sex Identity,' *The CRIAW Papers.* Ottawa, Canada: CRIAW, 1981.

Kathryn Morgan. 'Androgyny: A Conceptual Analysis,' *Social Theory and Practice* (forthcoming).

Dale Spender. 'Education: The Patriarchal Paradigm and the Response to Feminism,' in Dale Spender (ed.) *Men's Studies Modified.* New York: Pergamon Press, 1981.

Part II

EDUCATIONAL PRACTICES

14

THE CONCEPT OF TEACHING

Israel Scheffler

A Restrictions of manner

Every culture, we may say, normally gets newborn members to behave according to its norms, how ever these are specified, and many cultures have agencies devoted to this job. But not every way of getting someone to behave according to some norm is teaching. Some such ways are purely informal and indirect, operating largely by association and contact, as languages are normally learned. But not every formal and deliberate way is teaching, either. Behavior may be effectively brought into accord with norms through threats, hypnosis, bribery, drugs, lies, suggestion, and open force. Teaching may, to be sure, proceed by various methods, but some ways of getting people to do things are excluded from the standard range of the term 'teaching'. To teach, in the standard sense, is at some points at least to submit oneself to the understanding and independent judgment of the pupil, to his demand for reasons, to his sense of what constitutes an adequate explanation. To teach someone that such and such is the case is not merely to try to get him to believe it: deception, for example, is not a method or a mode of teaching. Teaching involves further that, if we try to get the student to believe that such and such is the case, we try also to get him to believe it for reasons that, within the limits of his capacity to grasp, are *our* reasons. Teaching, in this way, requires us to reveal our reasons to the student and, by so doing, to submit them to his evaluation and criticism.

To teach someone, not that such and such is the case, but rather *how* to do something, normally involves showing him how (by description or example) and not merely setting up conditions under which he will, in fact, be likely to learn how. To throw a child into the river is not, in itself, to teach him how to swim; to send one's daughter to dancing school is not, in itself, to teach her how to dance. Even to teach someone *to* do something (rather than how to do it) is not simply to try to get him to do it; it is also to make accessible to him, at some stage, our reasons and purposes in getting him to do it. To teach is thus, in the standard use of the term, to acknowledge the 'reason' of the pupil, i.e. his demand for and

Source: *Concepts of Teaching*, Macmillan, C.J.B. and Nelson, T.W. (eds) Rand McNally & Co., Chicago, 1968. Ch. 3.

judgment of reasons, even though such demands are not uniformly appropriate at every phase of the teaching interval.

The distinctions here discussed between teaching and fostering the acquisition of modes of behavior or belief are, we may say, distinctions of *manner*. They depend on the manner in which such acquisition is fostered. The organic metaphor, as we have seen, focuses on the continuity of the culture's life – in effect, on the behavioral norms and beliefs forming the *content* of the culture. It makes no distinctions in manner of acquisition of this content, of the sort we have illustrated by referring to the concept of 'teaching'. It is these distinctions, however, that are central to moral issues concerning social and educational policy. The usefulness of the organic metaphor in certain contexts cannot be taken to show that the distinctions of manner referred to are of no practical or moral moment, that, for example, teachers ought, by any means and above all, to adjust students to the prevailing cultures (specified in any way you like) and to ensure its continuity (no matter how specified). Whether teachers ought or ought not to do just that or some alternative is an independent and serious moral question that requires explicit attention. That it receives no emphasis in the organic metaphor indicates not that the question is unimportant, but that this metaphor is inappropriate in practical contexts.

We shall end this discussion by trying to show how fundamental the question of manner is, and we shall refer here again to the concept of 'teaching'. We have already taken pains to indicate that the notion of teaching is considerably narrower than that of acculturation. The fact that every culture may be said to renew itself by getting newborn members to behave according to its norms emphatically does not mean that such renewal is everywhere a product of teaching in the standard sense we have discussed. To favor the widest diffusion of teaching as a mode and as a model of cultural renewal is, in fact, a significant social option of a fundamental kind, involving the widest possible extension of reasoned criticism to the culture itself.

That this option may, in particular societies, lead to great changes in funda-mental norms, beliefs, and social institutions, with respect to the prevailing culture, is indeed possible, even highly likely. But such a consequence need not always follow. In particular, it is not likely to follow where the culture itself institutionalizes reasoned procedures in its basic spheres, where it welcomes the exercise of criticism and judgment, where, that is to say, it is democratic culture in the strongest sense. To support the widest diffusion of teaching as a model of cultural renewal is, in effect, to support something peculiarly consonant with the democratization of culture and something that poses a threat to cultures whose basic social norms are institutionally protected from criticism. Such support is thus consistent with the vision of a culture where understanding is not limited and where critical judgment of policy is not the institutionalized privilege of one class, where policy change is not perforce arbitrary and violent, but channelled through institutions operating by reasoned persuasion and freely given consent. Many, even most, social thinkers have shrunk before such a vision and argued that culture cannot long survive under democracy in this sense. Others have urged the fullest institutionalization of reasoned criticism, fully aware that such a course indeed threatens societies with rigid power divisions, but denying that all societies are therefore threatened and that *no* culture can survive which rests on free criticism freely interchanged. The issue, in short, is not whether culture shall be renewed, but in what *manner* such renewal is to be institutionalized. It is this fundamental practice issue that must not be obscured in practical contexts by metaphors appropriate elsewhere.

B Teaching

We have indicated how the notion 'teaching' suggests a crucial distinction with regard to the manner in which learning may proceed. What was involved in this phase of our discussion was, of course, the everyday, standard use of 'teaching,' and not some stipulated use. This standard use deserves further, detailed attention, for the word figures centrally in numerous discussions of education where the context makes plain that it is to be taken in the ordinary way. We turn then to an examination of the term 'teaching', in an effort to understand the ways in which it is typically applied, and that to which it typically refers. Our concern is thus to provide an account of the accepted meaning of the notion 'teaching'. We shall not, however, attempt to provide here an explicit definition, but only an informal discussion of certain elements of this accepted meaning.

We may begin by recalling the difference between 'success' and 'intentional' uses of the verb 'to teach'. In the 'success' use, a word refers to more than just the doing of something; it refers also to the successful outcome of what one is doing or has done. To have built a house is more than to have been occupied in building activity; it is also to have gained success in this activity. So, to have taught someone how to swim is more than to have been occupied in teaching someone to swim; it is also to have succeeded.

Let us now, for the sake of simplifying the process of our analysis, abstract from considerations relating to success, and restrict our inquiry to 'intentional' uses of the verb. With such a restriction understood, we may classify the teaching referred to by the verb as an activity: it is something that one normally engages in or is occupied in doing. Jones may be engaged in teaching Smith how to operate an electric saw, just as he may be engaged in painting his house. Indeed, to say of Jones that he is teaching is normally to convey that he is engaged in teaching.[1] Teaching is, further, directed toward a certain result: it is a goal-oriented activity.

It is worth noting that not everything true of Jones and expressible by a verb form can be so described. Jones is not normally said to be engaged in breathing, sitting, or strolling, though he breathes, sits, and strolls. Though he owns property, he is not said to be engaged in owning property; although he has reached the age of 57, he is not ordinarily described as having been occupied in reaching the age of 57. Teaching is engaged in, it is directed toward a goal the attainment of which normally involves attention and effort, and provides a relevant definition of success. Breathing, sitting and strolling are not oriented toward goals in specifiable ways; we do not speak of success in breathing, sitting or strolling. To own property and to reach the age of 57 do not embody strivings for certain goals; they are not even described as things being done. 'What is he doing?' may be answered by 'He is sitting', '. . . is strolling', '. . . is hunting', '. . . is teaching', but not by 'He is owning property', '. . . is reaching the age of 57'. In the latter cases, indeed, the present continuous is normally inapplicable altogether. We may say 'He owns', but not 'He is owning'; we may say 'He has reached the age of 57', but not '. . . is reaching the age of 57'.

By contrast, if Jones is working on a puzzle, he is trying to solve it; if he is said to be painting his house, he is normally understood to be trying to get it painted; if he is described as teaching Smith how to operate an electric saw, he is normally taken to be trying to get Smith to learn its operation. What he is doing is thus tied to a goal striven for, which may or may not in fact be attained. Jones' working on the puzzle may be fruitless; it may be too hard for him. He may succeed and, moreover, do a fine job in painting his house and he may, furthermore, be successful in teaching Smith how to work the saw. In each case, the activity engaged in is oriented toward some goal defining its success and normally requiring extended effort for its attainment. In each case, too, such attainment provides one index of proficiency.

Now one may, of course, try to do many things, not all of which are themselves activities which involve further tryings. One may, for example, try to sit (on a particular chair), or try to breathe (in a room with little oxygen or with an injured lung) or try to stroll (but be interrupted by unexpected guests). Such tryings are themselves oriented toward goals and may or may not be successful. It does not follow that sitting, breathing and strolling are species of trying or involve trying generally. One cannot try to sit without trying but we often sit without trying.

It is, furthermore, true that on particular occasions sitting itself, for example, may be associated *in some way* with trying. A man may be sitting in an effort to relax and catch his breath, knowing that too much exercise is bad for his heart. Nevertheless, people often do sit without trying thereby to relax or to do any-thing at all. To describe someone as sitting is not, in itself, to convey that he is trying to accomplish something in particular. By contrast, to describe someone as working on a puzzle is to convey that he is trying to solve it, to describe someone as painting his house is normally to convey that he is trying to get it painted, to say of someone that he is teaching a pupil how to work an electric saw is ordinarily to convey that he is trying to get him to learn how to work it.

One misunderstanding must here be forestalled. To work on a puzzle all afternoon is not, in every case, to try to solve it during the afternoon. The puzzle may be a very difficult one and known to be difficult, and the man working on it may have no hope of solving it in a few hours; he may in fact not be trying to solve it in a few hours. But he cannot be said to have been working on it even during the afternoon unless what he was doing was done in an effort to solve it, with or without some special time restriction. Similarly, one may be painting one's house all day without trying to get it painted by nightfall. But if one were not trying to get it painted at all, ever, one could hardly be said, without considerable qualification, to have spent the day painting one's house. Finally, learning to operate an electric saw may in fact require many lessons. Jones may thus be teaching Smith for an hour or two without trying to get him to learn the operation of the saw in an hour or two. But, unless what Jones does is done in the attempt to get Smith to learn its operation, he cannot well be said, in normal circumstances, to be teaching him how to operate an electric saw. The goal of an activity, in sum, may lie beyond the boundaries of the activity or some segment of it or may lack temporal conditions altogether. Nevertheless, engaging in the activity involves trying, generally.

Finally, it should be noted that teaching has here been said normally to involve an effort to achieve learning, but the converse is, as a matter of fact, false. Efforts to achieve learning cannot generally be said to involve teaching. Thus, though the achievement of learning is indispensable to teaching success, it is not in itself sufficient; the learning must, in addition, be accomplished in the appropriate manner.

That teaching, as normally understood, is an activity, requiring effort and allowing for the exercise and development of proficiency, and oriented toward a goal that may lie beyond any segment of it, we have already seen. We must now try to make clearer its temporal characteristics. As an activity, teaching takes time. Suppose I told you I had been teaching John, and you asked, 'When?' If I said 'Yesterday, at exactly 3: 15 p.m., but neither before nor after,' this answer would be thought absurd. Teaching is no instantaneous occurrence, like a thunderbolt or the flash of a falling star across the sky. Thus the question, 'At exactly what moment were you engaged in teaching John?' makes no obvious sense, while 'For how long were you busy teaching John?' is a perfectly legitimate question.[2]

It should now be noted that the question, 'For how long have you been teaching John?' may receive, roughly, two sorts of answers. One answer may refer to relatively short intervals, for example 'two hours'. Another answer may refer to longer intervals, for example, 'three weeks', or 'two and a half years'. Let us call all such intervals 'teaching-intervals' and notice that not every part of every teaching-interval is also a teaching-interval. If Jones has been teaching Smith how to drive an automobile for the last three weeks, he has still, surely, not been teaching him, even during these last three weeks, while Smith has been having his lunch, during his working hours, or while he has been asleep or visiting friends. Rather, this three-week interval is characterized by a certain pattern of relatively unitary teaching-intervals, which we may here call 'lessons'.

If a continuous teaching-interval is one all of whose interval parts are themselves teaching-intervals of the same sort, then we may here construe a lesson as a continuous teaching-interval that is not itself part of some other continuous teaching-interval. A patterned sequence of lessons may then go to make up a complex teaching-interval such as a course of instruction or part of such a course. Though lessons are smaller than courses, every lesson is still an interval and not a moment, despite the fact that such important happenings as a pupil's seeing the point may indeed be momentary events highlighting the lessons during which they occur.

Let us now attend to the single lesson. What characterizes teaching during the lesson? What must we observe in order to decide that what is going on before us is a case of teaching? We have already stressed that teaching is an activity involving the attempt to achieve a certain sort of learning within certain restrictions of manner. But the implications of this point deserve to be spelled out in answer to the questions posed above.

For it is often supposed that all activities are construable as distinctive patterns of bodily movement. We have already denied that everything expressible in verb forms, as a truth about anyone, refers to some activity. Surely it takes a little further reflection to see that some such descriptions are not readily amenable to analysis into statements about movement. That Jones now owns 740 acres in Texas is completely independent of his present patterns of bodily movement. That he has just turned 45 is equally independent of his present motions, though, presumably, some general connection with his physiological condition may be expected. Such cases are relatively easy to segregate, however, and to label 'states', in order to succumb to the temptation to maintain that all activities, by contrast, *are* construable as distinctive patterns of bodily movement. For activities, so the argument runs, are after all things we do, and what is doing but effecting some change in the environment by producing some movement?

The latter argument is, indeed, plausible but nevertheless misguided. It is, to begin with, true that the states in question are *not* normally classified as things we do. The question, 'What is he doing now?' can hardly be answered by 'Owning 740 acres in Texas' or 'Just turning 45'. It is, further, true that of the things that do answer this question, *some* are readily seen to refer to distinctive patterns of bodily movement. For example, 'Just sitting', 'Breathing regularly' (said by a nurse of a patient), and 'Strolling through the park' are all appropriate answers and indicate some pattern of movement (where this is taken broadly as including posture or orientation as well as motion).

It is, however, also true that other appropriate answers to the question 'What is he doing now?' include, for example, 'Working on a geometry problem', an activity description which turns out to be quite resistant to the attempt to interpret it as referring to some distinctive pattern of movements, as I shall try to show in a moment. The point to see now is that 'doing' is a broad category including things that *prima facie*, at least, are construable as movement patterns as well as things that are not. It is this fact that undermines the argument that activities must be patterns of movement since they are things we do.

But this fact must be examined concretely by reference to examples. Let us compare the case of breathing with that of working on a geometry problem, both admittedly doings, in contrast to what were above called 'states'. How is it possible to tell that a person is breathing during a given interval? We observe a certain repetitive pattern of movement associated with the sequence of air intake and expulsion during the interval. Compare the case of a boy working on a geometry problem during a given interval. He must, of course, be doing something reasonable with the aim of solving the problem. To be working on it, he must be trying as well as doing. What is observably done may, furthermore, vary with the situation, and will be associated with reflection in any event. To know that the boy before us is really working on a geometry problem and not simply playing with the paper, we need to judge that he is in fact thinking but, furthermore, we need to judge that whatever he is doing involves the hope of solving a problem. To judge that he is thinking is already to go beyond his manifest bodily movements (though not perhaps beyond certain unobserved internal changes). To judge what he is trying to do, moreover, we should ordinarily have to go beyond his bodily movements during the present interval. We may, for example, know that he is enrolled in a geometry course at school, that he has been assigned the problem as homework, that the solution is to be handed in the next day, that he has always turned in his homework promptly in the past, that he has frequently expressed the desire to major in mathematics.

All these external items of information are clues to his present intent in the light of which we interpret what he is doing (including his present movements) as 'Working on the problem'. His observable motions might be any of an indefinite number. He may pace the floor, stare out the window, look at a diagram, turning the paper sideways, frown, etc. Each of these motions is, furthermore, frequently duplicated in cases having nothing to do with working on a geometry problem. None is thus either a necessary or a sufficient condition of such working. (It follows that all taken together cannot be necessary and that all taken alternatively cannot be sufficient.) Here, then, is a case of an activity that is not identifiable with some distinctive pattern of movements despite the fact that it is a 'doing', something done. Aside from the fact that thinking is involved, the doing of the interval requires interpretation in terms of its environing context.

Returning now to the previous questions concerning teaching during the single lesson, it seems obvious that the case is parallel to that of working on a geometry problem during a given interval. Teaching, too, involves trying as well as doing – trying to get someone to learn something. Here too, what is observably done in the way of patterns of movement varies indefinitely and is duplicated in contexts where no teaching is involved at all. The teacher may talk or he may be silent, he may write or he may not, he may ask questions or not, he may use special materials or equipment, or he may not. Anything of this sort, furthermore, may be done by people not engaged in teaching. Whether a man is teaching or just criticizing, meditating, arguing, sulking, entertaining, etc., is thus not something that can be read off directly from the movements of the teacher during the lesson. Aside from the question of ascertaining the teacher's thinking, the interpretation of what is done during the lesson depends on the intent with which it is done, and the determination of such intent varies with information about the lesson's context. Teaching cannot thus be construed as some distinctive pattern of movements executed by the teacher.

In the light of this analysis, it appears that attempts to think of teaching in extreme behavioristic terms are, at best, ambiguous and, at worst, totally misguided. Returning to the geometry example, it may plausibly be argued that the boy has, in fact, not solved the problem unless he can produce proof in stated or written form. Proofs can be checked for validity, once produced. In this weak sense, it may be admitted that 'behavioristic' evidence (with respect to the stated or written product of the boy's motions) enters into our judgment as to the success of his activity. It does not follow that the *production* of proofs can be generally characterized in advance, that we can say generally what pattern of speaking or writing movements constitutes a sufficient condition for problem-solution in geometry or mathematics. That such a characterization is impossible is demonstrable on mathematical grounds alone. This situation is general in science as well, where, though theories, once produced, may be evaluated as to their scientific worth, we have no general rules for the production of worthwhile theories. To think of problem-solving as a complex sequence of movements governed by rule is thus a myth.

It surely does not follow that the boy's mere working on the problem (as distinct from his solving it) can be construed as such a sequence. It is mistaken to suppose that learning geometry is a matter of mastering some distinctive pattern of movements or that teaching geometry consists in prescribing the movements to be made.

Analogously, that a given instance of teaching activity has been successful in achieving learning may plausibly be argued to admit of behavioral test in the form of some standard examination of pupils' knowledge, skills, or attitudes. It does not follow that teaching may be described as a standard pattern of movements even where it is successful, let alone where it is not. It is thus mistaken to think that one may learn to teach by mastering some distinctive pattern of movements, or that we can teach people to teach by prescribing such a pattern for them, formulated in general rules. What can reasonably be done in the way of teaching people to teach presents, indeed, a crucial problem. Suffice it for the present to remark that whatever rules can profitably be applied here are likely to be comparable to rules profitably used in the teaching of geometry or science rather than to rules of spelling.

To conclude, if we are to decide whether or not Jones is engaged in teaching activity during a specified interval, we can neither rely merely on one momentary observation nor rely merely on observations of Jones' movements during the interval in question. Rather, in the light of information that normally goes beyond the interval in question, we have to see whether what Jones is doing is aimed at getting someone to learn something, whether it is not unreasonably thought to be likely to achieve the learning aimed at, and whether it falls within the restrictions of manner peculiar to teaching as ordinarily understood – in particular, whether acknowledgement of the alleged pupil's judgment is made, whether, e.g. the pupil is not systematically precluded from asking 'How?' 'Why?' or 'On what grounds?'

Notes

1 This matter of what is normally conveyed or understood by a statement concerns something weaker than what is implied by the statement. Nowell-Smith has discussed such a notion under the label of 'contextual implication'. See P.H. Nowell-Smith, *Ethics* (London: Penguin Books, Ltd, 1954), p. 80. He writes, 'I shall say that a statement *p* contextually implies a statement of *q* if anyone who knew the normal conventions of the language would be entitled to infer *q* from *p* *in the context in which they occur.*' He also stresses that contextual implications may be expressly withdrawn, but that unless they are withdrawn, we are entitled to presume that the inference holds in the context in question. The notion of what is normally conveyed though not implied by a given statement need not, of course, be interpreted just in the way Nowell-Smith interprets it; the present text uses the notion but is neutral with respect to variant explanations of it. For other recent analyses of teaching, see B.O. Smith, 'On the Anatomy of Teaching,' *Journal of Teacher Education* (December 1956), 7: 339 and 'A Concept of Teaching,' *Teachers College Record* (February 1960) 61: 229.
2 Related questions are discussed in Z. Vendler, 'Verbs and Times,' *The Philosophical Review* (April 1957), 66: 143.

15

INSTRUCTION AND
LEARNING BY DISCOVERY

R.F. Dearden

I Introduction: 'teaching'

The purpose of this article is to examine and compare two conceptions of teaching which have often been set in sharp contrast to each other. The contrast which I have in mind is that between the teacher as an instructor and the teacher as a facilitator of the children's own creations and discoveries. This contrast has been much more prominent in discussions of primary education than of education at any other stage and is representative of two distinct traditions of teaching which are present at that stage. These might be called, as Blyth calls them in his recent book,[1] the elementary school tradition and the development tradition, which latter is especially associated with Froebel and those theories often referred to as 'child-centred'. There are, of course, many aspects to the contrast between these two traditions. One could discuss it in terms of personal relationships, pupil motivation, creativity, classroom climate and so on, but the aspect which I want quite specifically to focus attention on is that of knowledge and the passing on of that knowledge. It is for that reason that the title 'Instruction and Learning by Discovery', which has a strong cognitive flavour to it, seemed most apt.

Now it might well seem to some that a misleading twist or bias is already being imported into the discussion at the start by insisting that instruction and learning by discovery pick out two conceptions of *teaching*. For the point about learning by discovery, it might be objected, is precisely that the teacher does not teach: the children find out everything for themselves. The answer to this is immediately to grant the point of the objection, namely that being told something is quite different from finding it out for oneself, but to deny that it is only in the case of instruction that we can properly speak of 'teaching'. This 'finding out for oneself' which is contrasted with being instructed is of a peculiar kind. No sane person really supposes that children are going to rediscover the whole of what they need to know quite apart from the teacher's agency; if that were possible we should not need schools at all. In other words, it is not by chance

Source: R.S. Peters (ed.) *The Concept of Education*, Routledge, 1967, Ch. 9.

that these discoveries are made but as a result of the teacher's deliberate contrivance, in 'structuring the environment' for example, or in practising discovery 'methods'. Both in the case of instruction and in the case of learning by discovery, then, the teacher's agency and influence are present, though admittedly they are present in very different ways.

Behind the objection to allowing that learning by discovery involves 'teaching' there lies a confusion over what sort of concept 'teaching' is. It may seem that for a variety of operations all to be called 'teaching' there must be some one nuclear operation common to them all on account of which the concept is applied. In that case instruction might readily suggest itself as the most promising candidate for this nuclear role, and then there would be some justice in denying that learning by discovery involved teaching. But the assumption at work here is mistaken, and the way in which it is mistaken merits attention. It can be brought out by some examples which I have adapted from Ryle's *Concept of Mind*.

If we were to consider 'farming' as an activity, we might note that ploughing was one farming job and tree-spraying another, while applying fertilizer is a third job and milking is a fourth, yet there is no one common nuclear operation by virtue of doing which alone a man is to be called a farmer. Similarly with solicitoring, drafting wills is one job and arranging for the transfer of property another, while defending a client in court is a third and explaining some point of law is a fourth, but again there is no one common nuclear operation present in all. So with teaching, I suggest, there is a whole range of operations any of which may, under suitable conditions, be examples of it, such as writing on a blackboard, correcting exercises, punishing, answering questions, demonstrating a procedure, setting material for reading, supervising practical work and so on. Teaching is what Ryle has called a 'polymorphous' concept: it can take many forms, and instructing is only one of them.

What, then, is characteristic of teaching as an activity, if it is not some nuclear operation such as instructing? This question is not to be answered by a review, even a very extensive review, of the particular things which a teacher might do, but by considering the central *intention* which lies behind his efforts. That intention is to bring it about that someone learns something. Teaching is not just placing things before people for their consideration, or informing, or telling, or conversing, or narrating, but taking such measures as will bring it about that something envisaged by the teacher is learned, by which I mean that it is both understood and remembered. What we teach is intended not just to be registered, but to be kept in mind: teaching involves the deliberate equipping of a person in some way, whether in respect of knowlege, skill or settled habit.

The next question to ask is whether there are any restrictions to be placed on this process vaguely called 'bringing it about'. Since it is necessarily the aim of the teacher to get someone to understand and remember something, such measures as he adopts must be consistent with achieving that aim. But nothing more specific than that is implied. What *method* to adopt in teaching or what kind of *approach* to use is not further indicated by the concept, but depends on the specific sorts of thing we wish to teach and the various psychological and other conditions which bear upon being effective in teaching. If we know that a person has been teaching, and we have no other clues supplied by the context as to what in particular he has been teaching, or how, then we know very little indeed of the form which his activities took. Such images as come to mind will reflect the idiosyncrasies, experience or prejudices of the particular individuals whose images they are and will be in no way warranted by the information here given. But what people customarily think of when they hear a word is of no philosophical interest; it is what they are entitled to think that matters, and that is a question of what is implied by a concept. Knowing that a person has been teaching entitles us to think only that he has been active in such ways as are consistent with the intention to bring it about that someone will learn something. That way may have been to instruct, or to have staged the making of discoveries by someone – discoveries relative to the learner and not to the teacher, that is – so that we return once again to the point that it is two conceptions of teaching that are being compared here.

II Instruction

If we turn now to consider instruction, we shall have to be on our guard against the very same mistake that was pointed out in connection with the concept of teaching. On hearing the word 'instruction', we may form a picture of a brow-beating, hectoring, offensive teacher of a sort admittedly sufficiently common in the past to have formed a public stereotype, and in rejecting this *picture* we may think that we have validly rejected all instruction. But that would be so only if it could first be shown that all instruction must necessarily be of this bullying and insensitive kind. A further feature of this picture which is no necessary accompaniment of instruction is that of baldly telling someone something, for example who followed whom on the throne of England, or what the exports of South Wales are, so that things are learned by rote. Instruction *need* not be confined to such a bald exposition of various items of information, but may include a reasoned explanation of something or an experimental demonstration of it. The principle of 'learning by experience' may be interpreted here as acquiring *sense*-experience and be satisfied by a reference to what can be seen in some visual aid, or by an excursion to some instructive museum, gallery or historical site. Again, instruction *need* not be given by word of mouth, but may be given by referring the learner to a lesson in a textbook or to the appropriate programme in a machine. Far from being tied to some particular form which the accident of tradition has given to it, instruction may take many forms and be given in more than one manner. Furthermore, an important distinction often unmade in discussing instruction is that between formal instruction and incidental instruction, the former implying a set time when the teacher or teacher-substitute delivers some planned lesson, while the latter may be present in a much more loosely structured classroom régime. The one may be defensible where the other is not.

If we ask what is distinctive of instruction as a way of passing on knowledge, the answer would seem to be that in instruction this knowledge is directly imparted.

Instruction does not hint at, or seek to elicit, or guide one in finding out for oneself, but directly imparts, and hence in this respect stands in sharp contrast as a way of teaching to contriving that children learn by discovery. Instruction stands in contrast also, though this is often overlooked, to other forms of verbal teaching. The fact that instruction, as the imparting of knowledge, requires the use of language, does not entail the converse that all use of language by the teacher must be instruction. In Plato's dialogue the *Meno*, Socrates teaches a slave that a square double the area of a given square is to be constructed on the diagonal of the given square, and not by doubling the length of its sides, but he does not actually impart this information: he elicits it. At one point he comments to Meno as follows:

> Now notice what, starting from this state of perplexity, he will discover by seeking the truth in company with me . . . . Be ready to catch me if I give him any instruction or explanation instead of simply interrogating him on his own opinions.[2]

Though all instruction may require the use of language, then, not all teaching by the use of language is instruction, and though this may seem obvious enough when once it has been pointed out, it has nevertheless escaped the notice of the more extreme reactionaries against the teacher as instructor who dominates the elementary school tradition. To argue that a teacher ought not to teach by instructing him does not mean that he must be silent, which would make him about as effective as a boxer with his hands tied behind his back, or an Alpine guide forbidden to use his feet, but leaves a great range of linguistic uses open to him, such as eliciting by questioning, hinting, commenting and even professing ignorance.

If teaching by instructing implies the imparting of knowledge, or more briefly if it is teaching by telling, what are we to think of it? No doubt there are many things to be said here about pupil motivation and so on, but I shall confine comment to an appraisal of the adequacy of instruction as a way of passing on *knowledge*. From this point of view it would seem sensible enough, if teachers have to pass on in a few years what has taken the labour of centuries and often the insight of genius to arrive at, to set up special institutions called schools and to make them places of instruction, though instruction doubtless enlightened by psychology and less harsh in manner than in the traditional picture. How better than by instruction could you teach French, handwriting, how to read, swimming, technical drawing or metalwork, assuming that you wanted to teach these things? Especially where *skill* is concerned, whether physical skills like swimming, or practical skills like carpentry, intelligent instruction, whether formal or incidental, together with practice, would seem to be quite the best way of teaching, and we may notice that wherever a teaching job is specifically that of passing on such a skill we do talk of 'instructors', such as driving, gunnery and flying instructors, or instructors in various crafts.

There are, however, kinds of knowledge not normally referred to as 'skills' which require the acquisition and operational mastery of concepts, principles and criteria of critical appraisal, as for example in mathematics, science and history. To teach subjects such as these solely by instruction would be to treat them as collections of information, an error which was in fact conspicuously perpetrated in the elementary school tradition. Learning science or history, for example, was a stocking up with a mass of information imparted by the teacher, a conception of teaching which the Hadow Report of 1931 (Section 75) made famous in the phrase 'knowledge to be acquired and facts to be stored'. What are we to think of instruction, then, not in relation to French, handwriting, swimming, metalwork and so on, but in relation to such subjects as mathematics and science?

From the point of view of knowledge still, and not that of motivation, it might seem that instruction was to be criticized because the knowledge passed on was 'knowledge' only as being based on the authority of the teacher and not as being seen by the learner to be appropriately justified by proofs, evidences, arguments and so on. But this will not do, because there is no reason at all why proofs, evidences and arguments could not be made the content of instruction quite as much as what they are the reasons for. Nor is it the case that instruction must be limited to material of a fairly low level of generality. In primary school mathematics, for example, the laws of arithmetic and the concepts of place-value and of a base *could* all be made the objects of instruction. So long as there is something definite to be imparted, then it can be made the content of instruction. If instruction is to be found inadequate, therefore, it cannot be from the point of view of the instructor, but from the point of view of the learner's mastery of the instruction.

If not just memorization of the content of instruction is desirable but an intelligent mastery of it, involving judgment in its application, then instruction cannot be wholly adequate. But the implication of this is that instruction needs to be supplemented, not supplanted. It needs to be supplemented by opportunities for trying out for oneself how the knowledge which is being imparted is to be applied. Just as instruction in a skill needs to be supplemented by practice if performance is to be raised to the level of being 'good at' whatever skill it is, so with instruction in the various academic subjects opportunities need to be given for exercising judgment in applying the concepts, principles and criteria in a suitable variety of cases. And when that is done, then instruction would seem to be at its most intelligent, and from the point of view of knowledge and passing on that knowledge, would seem not to be open to any important objection. We might next consider, then, the much canvassed alternative to it of learning by discovery, in which what is to be learned is not imparted and then mastered but is found out by oneself in the first place.

III Discovery

In discussing discovery methods, or 'finding out' as opposed to being told, not a great deal turns on analysis of the meanings of these words. It is the particular conception of *how* one is supposed to discover, or find out, that is crucial. But there are one or two points perhaps worth making about discovery in general before proceeding to a more particularized discussion. In the first place, the frequently rhapsodic description of making a discovery in terms of thrills and glows is apt to suggest that discovery is essentially an exciting psychological experience, perhaps the sort of experience that we have on finding a cherished object we thought we had lost, or on finishing a difficult piece of work with a sigh of deep satisfaction. But such a connection between making a discovery and glows of satisfaction is purely contingent, since one could have all of these feelings in the *false* belief that one had discovered something, and on the other hand one really could have discovered something yet without feeling anything in particular about it.

'Discovery' and 'finding out' are what Ryle has called 'achievement words' like winning, seeing and hearing, which are to be contrasted with 'task words', such as running, travelling, looking and listening. In using an achievement word we are asserting there to be some state of affairs over and above the person's activity or state of mind, and a biographical account of a person's efforts and feelings does not by itself tell us whether he has brought about that state of affairs or not. We may try in vain, or try and rashly claim success, but whether what we do is to count as an achievement depends on how things are in the end, not on how we feel or the effort we exerted. Faced with finding the area of a parallelogram for the first time, I may have the most thrilling and deeply satisfying experience you can imagine of seeing how it is to be done, but unless I have got it *right* this cannot count as a discovery, or a finding out, or an insight, in spite of all the thrills and glows, because 'discovery' carries an implication of the *truth* of what is put forward. A false or mistaken discovery is a contradiction. The achievement implied by discovery, then, is that of getting at the truth in some sought-for respect, and this is a matter independent of our pleasure or pains.

The consequence of ignoring this point is that 'discovery methods' of teaching may be made to sound more reliable than they really are, but the illusion of guaranteed success engendered by the proleptic use of 'discovery' here is like talking of 'creative writing' before anyone has yet had a chance to have a look at it. The upshot of a lot of bustling activity might be confusion, muddle, uncritical acceptance of first ideas, or failure to have any ideas at all, as well as possibly having the result of making a discovery. Evidently this teaching method must involve considerable art if the chances of success are in fact to be high. But having noticed that the epithet 'discovery' could easily falsely prejudge the issue, I shall pass on to consider some particular conceptions of *how* success is to be reasonably assured, since it is here that the really important issues are likely to lie. One of the main points of what follows will be to try to show that the blanket term 'discovery methods' conceals and confuses certain crucial distinctions, distinctions of which we ought to be sharply aware if muddled practice is to be avoided.

IV Learning by discovery

1 The pre-school model

A convenient point at which to begin is with what is frequently held up as the very paradigm of how children should learn, namely the learning of the pre-school child as he trots round the garden, plays with his friends or explores the neighbourhood. He discovers in this way a bird's nest in a hedge, that worms wriggle, that table tops are slippery, where the milkman goes, and so on. School learning, it is said, should be just like that, or as near like it as possible: a discovering for oneself under the pressure of real interest and in the course of a spontaneous activity. Finding out about mathematics and science should be an eager lighting on one fascinating fact after another, just like exploring a wood or seeing what is in a pond; for mathematics and science, it is pointed out, are not confined to the study or laboratory, but are 'all around us'.

Now what needs to be questioned here is not the validity which this conception may have for the learning of various miscellaneous facts about the world. There would seem to be no reason to deny that a child would, in normal circumstances, almost inevitably learn many facts about himself and his situation simply as a condition of forming and carrying out purposes. It is the validity of this as a conception of how we could learn such subjects as mathematics or science which is questionable. To take the case of science first: if all that is meant is a pottering about in which one may or may not notice that reflections in a spoon are distorted, what things look like when seen through coloured glass, that some objects float while others sink and so on, then no doubt this account is unexceptionable. With very young children especially there is an important place for this kind of learning, but such limited and undirected curiosity does not amount to science. All of this could and did and does go on where science has never been heard of. Such finding out does not even begin to resemble science until problems start to present themselves which cannot be solved without putting forward, and then testing experimentally, suggested solutions of a non-obvious kind.[3] Even the perception of a scientific problem requires more than naïve curiosity, and the concept of an experiment implies more than pushing and poking at things. This point tends to be obscured by the belief that science discoveries are accidents which could happen to anybody. Certainly a scientific discovery might be made by accident, but the point to notice is that these accidents only happen to people with a certain kind of training and with certain things preoccupying them. 'Discovery, like surprise, favours the well-prepared mind.'[4]

If elementary scientific investigation was as natural as this account likes to make out, it would require explaining how it is that this tradition of inquiry is historically so late to get started and geographically still so limited in extent. Even to try to classify what floats and what sinks, quite apart from trying to arrive at the general conditions for flotation, marks a sophistication which would still be strange to many. Far from being like trotting round a garden, learning science and what is characteristic of a scientific inquiry involves initiation into a particular social tradition of inquiry and is therefore something which, one way or another, has to be taught. In case this should now seem so obvious as not to be worth pointing out, it must be added that not only is it thought by some that science somehow just arises out of pottering about with things, but it may also be thought not even necessary that the teacher should know any science for this to happen. According to a recent article in *Educational Research*,[5] 'such is the interest among our young children that even the non-scientist can do a great deal by merely providing opportunities and encouragement.' How it is that a person himself ignorant of science is nevertheless able to 'provide opportunities' and reliably to ascertain that scientific 'discoveries' are in fact begin made by his class is left unexplained in this article. But there cannot be many practising teachers who suppose that ignorance of anything is a qualification for teaching it. To teach something in ignorance of it is not just difficult: it is logically impossible.

With mathematics, the pre-school model is even less adequate, since the concepts and truths of mathematics are not even empirical, and hence can even less plausibly be represented as wide open to the curious gaze of tireless young investigators. Indeed, there have been and are societies which have never progressed beyond such primitive forms of counting as the tally-stick, though they probably all noticed that worms wriggle, what floats and a similar mixed assortment of empirical facts. But although a spontaneous generation theory of mathematical knowledge might seem to be implicit in the doctrines of the more extreme reactionaries against instruction, if these theorists were faced with the implications of their view, they would probably disown it, at least verbally. Much more usual, and at least apparently less extreme, is a conception of learning by discovery in terms of 'planned experience'. That is to say, the teacher is to contrive situations or to present materials which are so 'structured' that appropriate experiences must be provided for the children. What we do, on this theory, is to embed a conceptual structure in some materials, or in a 'concept kindergarten', from which it can then be 'abstracted' in the course of play. The child is to 'notice' the common features which certain things have, or the relationships which they have one to another, and 'abstract' them, this 'abstraction' being regarded as a *process*.

2 *Abstractionism*

A clear example of abstractionism as a theory of concept formation is provided by the writings of Dr Z.P. Dienes, whose wooden blocks for forming concepts of place-value and of a base are now quite well known. Dienes writes of the child as 'extracting' the requisite features and as 'discarding' irrelevances, almost as if a mental prising off of what the designer had embedded in the blocks were going on. The process, he writes, 'should probably run as follows: an abstraction process, followed by a symbolization process, followed again by the learning of the use of the symbols.'[6] The 'abstraction process', it should be added, is allotted by Dienes to a period of a few weeks of free play with the materials. Again, the recent publication *Mathematics in Primary Schools* similarly speaks of 'abstractive teaching methods',[7] the 'abstraction of an idea'[8] and of what happens 'once a child has abstracted the concept'.[9] And just as Dienes writes of following up the abstraction process with 'symbolization', so here there is a process of 'making explicit' what has already been learned in the 'planned' experience provided.

This theory is, of course, at least quite as old as John Locke, whose *Essay Concerning Human Understanding*, published in the seventeenth century, based a whole theory of knowledge on abstraction. It lies behind the view that science is 'inductive', in the sense that the scientist is supposed to proceed by gathering instances and then moving to cautious generalizations based on them, rather than by boldly setting up hypotheses and then testing them experimentally. It was implicit also in the didactic apparatus of Montessori and the idea of 'sense training', so that it is not some brand new theory that we are here invited to espouse. A convincing refutation of abstractionism as a theory of concept formation, however, was recently given by Geach, so that only a few points specifically tailored to this as a theoretical basis for discovery methods of teaching need to be made here.[10]

To begin with, we may agree that any situation or state of affairs can always be conceived of in a great variety of ways, depending for example on the present interests and past learning of those who come to it. Assuming that a certain moving object in a field has been discriminated, we may conceive of it as an animal, a quadruped, a horned creature, a ruminant, the mother of a calf, a menace to our safe passage, a milk production unit, or indeed just as a cow. In fact, the potential variety of the ways in which something may be conceived is now being exploited in the so-called 'creativity tests', in which the person tested is called on to conceive of some object, such as a brick, in as many different ways as possible. Suppose we take as a further example a child's toy, say a set of bricks. What conceptions of the bricks will he develop in the course of playing with them? Here again we may agree that the potential variety is enormous. He may conceive of a tower, a ship, a train, a pattern of colours, a sorting of the bricks into various kinds, their use as missiles, and so on, depending on the concepts which he has acquired and his present interests.

Now the point I want to make is this. When a teacher presents a child with some apparatus or materials, such as Cuisenaire rods, Dienes blocks or an assortment of objects on an investigation table, he typically has in mind some one particular conception of what he presents in this way. But then the incredible assumption seems to be made that the teacher's conception of the situation somehow confers a special uniqueness upon it such that the children must also quite inevitably conceive of it in this way too, even though they may not even possess the concepts involved. In some mysterious way, a special potency is thought to inhere in teaching apparatus such that if children play with it or manipulate it, significant experiences must be had, and important concepts must be abstracted. For example, if we let children play with Cuisenaire rods, then in building houses with them and so on it is reasonable to suppose that they will find out that two sticks placed end to end give the same length whichever way round the sticks go. But because the *teacher* sees this fact as a concrete illustration of the commutative law that $a + b = b + a$, the *child* is credited with having had an important mathematical experience. Far from having just played with sticks, he is seen as being poised on the brink of, or even as having made, a major mathematical discovery. Again, a child given a block of Plasticine to play with naturally breaks it up for modelling purposes and later puts it together again. But he has not just fingered Plasticine it is thought. The sage onlooking of the hovering teacher has conferred a special significance on his manipulations such that important steps have been taken in this episode towards abstracting the concept of the conservation of volume. To put the point quite generally, an unconscious assumption behind the advocacy of *this* notion of discovery methods is that in spite of the variety of ways in which any situation may be conceived, the teacher's conceiving of it in one particular way is somehow thought to confer a special uniqueness on it such that children must come to conceive of it in that way too.

The explanation of this strange belief seems to be twofold. In the first place it is reasoned, quite correctly, that instead of just *telling* children about various things they ought to know, it would be valuable to provide concrete examples or models of those things. We can provide a set of sticks which supply a model of the natural numbers from 1 to 10, or a set of blocks which model the relative values of different places in number notation. This is correct and important. But then it is falsely assumed that a person who does not possess the knowledge that we possess must still see the materials as *examples* or *models*, and hence will be able to 'get back' to the way in which we conceive them. Yet without possession of our concepts in the first place, it makes no sense to talk of examples or models, because an example, or a model, or an instance, or a feature, is always an example, model, instance, or feature *of* something, and unless you know what follows this 'of' you logically cannot perceive the thing *as* an example, model, and so on. This is not to say that there can be no value in a short initial period of play with new materials, for example to satisfy curiosity, but that such value as there may be is quite different from what it is here being claimed to be.

Suppose I wish to teach someone syllogistic logic, and to do this I require to make clear to him the logical powers of expressions such as 'all S is P', 'some S is not P', 'no S is P' and so on, where S and P stand for classes of things. I might do this by drawing various circles, some overlapping and some wholly outside or inside others. This would be a model of the various class relationships involved. But instead I issue compasses to a class and instruct them freely to draw circles. Can I say that important experiences in syllogistic logic are being provided here? Can I say that during four weeks or so of play with circles, important abstractings have been going on and now need merely to be symbolized, or just to be made explicit, as logical relationships? Surely this is no more likely, short of divine intervention, than that advances have been made in the design of spectacle frames, or that the symbol of the Olympic Games has been arrived at, or that a value for π has been discovered? While freely drawing circles may look to *me*, with my preconceptions, to be an important logical or pre-logical experience, and I may write books on the abstraction of formal logic from play with circles, the fact remains that from the child's point of view the truest description of what occurred is probably that fun was had just drawing circles. To return to the real case, we may well ask why it is that although children have played with blocks and bricks for years, it is only now, when they are provided in schools, that important mathematical concept-abstractings are supposed to accompany play with them. Perhaps it is the sign of a new state of mathematical grace which has now descended upon children.

A second explanation of the belief in abstractionism may lie in the experiments which psychologists have carried out on concept-formation. Bruner, for example, has done a famous series of experiments[11] in which sets of cards, each set patterned in such a way as to have some one feature which makes it a set, are presented to subjects who are then asked to find the feature which the cards have in common. In this way, Bruner has produced interesting results about the strategies adopted by different people in setting about this task. Now it might be said that in giving children apparatus which illustrates or exemplifies some concept or relationship, we are doing nothing very different from what Bruner did, so why is abstractionism so plainly erroneous? The answer is that there is all the difference in the world between experiments such as Bruner's and free play with concept-forming blocks of wood. In Bruner's case it is a requirement of the experimental set-up that the subjects shall have clear instructions as to what they must try to do. They do not just play, while Bruner hovers in the background weaving stories round their play, but at the very start of the experiment, when they are instructed what to do, they already have a vague concept of what they are looking for; they know the *sort* of thing it is, and their task is to specify that vague concept more precisely. There is no abstractionism here, but the usual guess-and-test of purposeful inquiry. But a child who is presented with apparatus which *we* call structured, and who is then left to 'have experiences', is not in this position at all. He is not searching for anything of which he has been given a rough idea already, but is just playing as he pleases, and only the belief in innate ideas and a natural tendency towards mathematical understanding could lead us to suppose that he will do more than learn a few very obvious empirical facts about the materials with which he is playing.

Even if a child has some mathematical knowledge, however, all sorts of unconscious assumptions on our part may blind us to the possible variety of conceptions open to him. For example, if we take this arrangement of Cusenaire rods

it is by no means obvious that this is a structured representation of anything mathematical. It may be just a pattern of colours, the start of a model wall, a test to see whether the two layers are exactly the same in length, and so on. Even if we give the rods their usual values in the Cuisenaire system of 2, 4 and 6, and say that this arrangement presents $2 + 4 = 6$, all sorts of conventions of representation are being presupposed here. For example, we could as well regard this as a representation of $2 + 4 + 6 = 12$, so bringing out the assumed convention of what represents 'equality'. We could regard it as $\frac{1}{3} + \frac{2}{3} = 1$, or as $40 + 80 = 120$, so bringing out the assumed convention of what represents a unit. In short, the situation is 'structured', not in some sense 'by itself', but only in the eyes of the person who has been specifically taught how to conceive of it, though how he conceives of it may come to seem so natural and obvious to *him* that he may assume that anyone must conceive of it in this way too. In just the same way it is often assumed that if we put pictures over the sentences in a reading primer, it must be just *obvious* to the child what the sentence 'says' from looking at the picture, whereas it may be doubted how many adults would respond in the way required if someone presented them with a picture and just said 'What sentence does this depict?'[12]

'Mathematics is all around us', the advocates of this sort of discovery say. And of course mathematics is all around us; so too are atomic physics, gravitation, molecular biology and organic chemistry. They are all, in a sense, though not all in the same sense, 'there'; but the point is that you need more than eyes to see them, and if children are to conceive of their environment in mathematical or in scientific ways, they will have to be more than placed in contact with it. They will have to be taught *how* to conceive it, though the fact that other influences besides that of the school are always at work may blur the issue by making it really seem that some child has just spun it all out of his head, or 'abstracted' it from apparatus. Children are not, as seems often to be assumed, like a teacher on a refresher course who enjoys finding all sorts of new and interesting ways of applying his already *existing* knowledge to the latest apparatus, but are more like such a teacher faced with set theory, if he has never met that before. Even this, however, is an unfair analogy, since such a teacher has at least a notion of the sort of thing that a mathematical relation or structure is, whereas in all of this young children are complete beginners.

3 *Problem solving*

The two conceptions of learning by discovery which have been considered so far, and strongly criticized, do not exhaust the possibilities, however. 'Learning by discovery' can be given another, and much more plausible, interpretation besides the interpretations based on the model of pre-school learning or on abstractionism. What this alternative is we can begin to see by returning to the point, made earlier in discussing instruction, that not all use of language by the teacher need be instruction. For example, in questioning Meno's slave, Socrates drew attention to what the boy was discovering. This alternative conception, in which the teacher much more actively participates, is often present alongside the conceptions that have already been criticized, but is rarely distinguished from them. Yet the resemblance is in fact slight. *Mathematics in Primary Schools*, for example, vacillates throughout between 'providing experience' and something like the Socratic method. In that recent publication of the new Schools Council, the Socratic method is in fact in one place explicitly endorsed,[13] and *discussion* is stressed in several places. For instance, after citing an example of the discovery of the commutative law of addition, that $a + b = b + a$, the text continues: 'It was quite clear that if the teacher had not discussed the number patterns with the boy, and questioned him, he would not have made the discovery at all.'[14] But the writer seems to be quite unconscious of the fact that this is a very different sort of 'discovery method' from the 'planned experiences' of abstractionism.

In this third conception of discovery methods, the teacher is much more than the hovering provider of materials, or the structurer of an environment from which new concepts are supposed to be abstracted in the course of undirected activity. In this third conception, the teacher questions, discusses, hints, suggests and instructs what to do to find out. But this way of teaching is not, or not predominantly, a way of instruction, because what has actually to be learned is not imparted. The stress is on the individual's mastery of knowledge, so that throughout all this teacher activity what the teacher says is specific enough to focus attention and effort in the desired direction, but at the same time open enough to leave genuine discoveries still to be made, discoveries which the teacher can be reasonably confident will be made on the basis of what he knows has already been learned in the past and the deliberate guidance he is now giving. For example, he may instruct that squares of numbers be drawn and that the answers to some multiplication tables be shaded on them, but leave open the discovery of the patterns so revealed. He may instruct in the conventions governing the representation of cardinal numbers and the four processes of arithmetic with certain materials, but leave open the discovery of a multitude of particular number relationships which can then be made. Posing the problem of how to find the area of an irregular shape, he may alternately prompt, tell, question, encourage and then watch, in a subtle interplay of minds which follows no set pattern. Where elementary science is concerned, he may suggest, orally or on a card, a certain problem and indicate or discuss how the solution might be found, but leave open the finding of the answer. For example, he may suggest an enquiry into how a bean extends itself in growth, and suggest marking it at intervals as a way of finding out; but he does not say what will be found out, whether the bean extends at its tip, emerges from the ground or stretches like elastic, for example. Similarly, it may be suggested in discussion that electric bulbs could be wired in series or in parallel, but without actually saying how this affects brightness, or how the failure of one of the bulbs affects the others: that can be left to be found out. He may give instructions for the use of a hydrometer in fresh and salt water and in paraffin, but leave it to be discovered how flotation is affected in each case. And once the concept of an experiment has been taught, there is no reason to doubt that a few children at least will be able sometimes to devise simple experimental tests for themselves to answer questions that have come up.

This interpretation of 'learning by discovery' has to be set in the strongest possible contrast to the interpretations based on pre-school learning or on abstractionism which have already been discussed. This kind of discovery is not a romantic sailing forth into the unknown on a journey which will bring who-knows-what ecstatic joys and thrills, nor is it the illumination of the soul by an intellectual grace which somehow proceeds from apparatus. The teacher does not 'provide experiences' but *guides* experience, by the subtle use of language, towards learning something that is regarded as educationally valuable. In its recognition of the crucial role of language this conception is more like instruction than it is like abstractionism, though the centre of attention is the individual's mastery of what is to be learned rather than the instructional imparting of it. Again like instruction, this conception of teaching involves the planning of work, both to ensure steady progression and to allow for practice or revision, though the planning is more flexible than with a course of instruction, since the sequence of learning is deliberately less closely controlled and can be adapted to any useful side-interests that may arise. The only resemblance of this conception to abstractionism lies in its recognition of the importance of instances or examples of what is learned.

What are the merits of teaching by this kind of 'discovery method' as against teaching by instruction? Plainly it would be far too time-consuming for *everything* to have to be found out in this way.[15] Before trying to answer this question any further, however, it needs to be pointed out that we do not have to make an exclusive choice between these two; and presumably the intelligent teacher, as opposed to the doctrinaire who fervently adheres to the dogmas of a particular ideology, will make his own judgment as to what a particular occasion requires in the light of all its special circumstances. To vary what one does according to the situation is part of what it means to be intelligent. But the merits of the alternatives have to be appreciated to do this, so that the virtues of the discovery method have to be known.

Much is often said on the merits of learning by discovery from the point of view of improved motivation and the better retention of what is learned, though to discuss these points would fall outside the restricted scope of the present discussion. We might note, however, that in the midst of the acclaim for a new golden road to knowledge there are cautious and informed voices that doubt the factual basis of some of the claims which are being made.[16] What has to be considered here, however, is the possible merit of learning by discovery from the point of view of the *knowledge* gained by it. Is it superior in any important way to knowledge gained by formal or incidental instruction, for example?

One way in which learning by discovery is often thought to have merit is that in this way children do not just learn, but they 'learn how to learn'. The source of this popular, if somewhat obscure, phrase can be traced back to some experiments performed on monkeys by Harlow.[17] Harlow set a long and varied series of discrimination problems to his monkeys and found that their ability to solve them improved very considerably as the experiment proceeded. They were somehow using past experience to cope more easily with new problems. In short, they had done something, called by Harlow 'forming a learning set', which made the solution of new but similar problems much more efficient. The notion would therefore seem to be a variant on our old friend, transfer of training, the special point of this new experiment having been to refute the reduction of all learning to the formation of stimulus–response bonds by trial and error. Where school learning is concerned, what we would seem to have to suppose is that in learning by discovery children form certain general heuristic principles which enable them to get onto the right track with new problems much more rapidly and efficiently than would have been the case if the knowledge had been imparted by instruction. Two points need to be made about that.

First, whether there could be such general principles is not an empirical matter for psychologists to settle, though contentment with showing a correlation without seeking its explanation may make it seem otherwise. It is not obvious, for example, how discovering the area of a parallelogram would later facilitate discovering which numbers are prime, or how discovering which materials are electrical conductors would later facilitate finding out the conditions governing the period of a pendulum. A person might do better through greater confidence of interest gained from the previous success, but that is not 'learning how to learn' in any conceivable sense. The second point is that in so far as there could be general principles which would facilitate later learning, there does not seem to be any reason why they should not be made part of the content of instruction, as done by people who lecture and write books on how to study, for example. The fact that instruction has in the past often been uninformed by the psychology of learning, and has been of a narrow and mentally limiting kind, is no argument at all against all possible forms of instruction, as was stressed earlier.

Another alternative, however, is that learning by discovery may have an advantage over instruction in respect of the mastery of what has to be learned, and for the kind of reason that Dewey gave. A pupil being instructed is in a receptive role which requires that the pace at which he goes and the sequence of what he attends to are determined by someone else, whereas a pupil working to find something out for himself can proceed at a pace individually suited to him and by a sequence of acts intelligently ordered in view of the end towards which he sees himself as moving. In short, learning by discovery allows more room for individual differences and permits a more intelligent appreciation of what one is doing. But to offset this gain a little is the greater chanciness which then necessarily enters into learning, since a teaching method which genuinely leaves things open for discovery also necessarily leaves open the opportunity for not discovering them. It would seem, however, that there really is the possibility here of a superiority over instruction in learning by discovery.

What I have tried to distinguish, then, is a conception of teaching by discovery which draws in the active verbal participation of the teacher in framing pro-blems, suggesting, discussing, or instructing what initially to do, but which leaves the result of the learner's activity open in some important respect, so that what is to be learned has indeed to be found out, and is not imparted. The only resemblance between this conception of learning by discovery and the concep-tion based on abstractionism is in the stress on first-hand experience wherever possible, but apart from that it is analogous more to instruction. The possible superiority of this third conception of learning by discovery over learning from intelligent instruction would need to be shown empirically, though one can see that on some occasions at least it might well be superior on account of its greater adaptation to individual differences and greater scope for intelligence. But whether this possibility is in fact realized is something that a philosopher ought to realize is not possible for him to say. In fact, with some idea of what we are looking for in mind, it is precisely the sort of thing that we could usefully set out to discover.

Notes

1 Blyth, W.A.L., *English Primary Education* (1965), Vol. 2, Ch. 2.
2 Plato, *Meno*, 84 c.d. (W.K.C. Guthrie's translation).
3 Toulmin, S.E., *The Philosophy of Science* (1953), Ch. 2.
4 Bruner, J.S., 'The Act of Discovery' in *Readings in the Psychology of Cognition* (1965), eds Anderson, R.C. and Ausubel, D.P., p. 607.
5 Barker, D., 'Primary School Science', *Educational Research*, Vol. VII, No. 2 (Feb. 1965), p. 157.
6 Dienes, Z.P., 'Research in Progress' in *New Approaches to Mathematics Teaching* (1963), ed. Land, F.W.
7 HMSO, *Mathematics in Primary Schools* (Curriculum Bulletin No. I. of the Schools Council, 1965), p. 8.
8 *Op. cit.*, p. 53.
9 *Op. cit.*, p. 92.
10 Geach, P., *Mental Acts* (1957), sects 4–11. Geach criticizes abstractionism as giving an impossible account of how we could *learn* new concepts, i.e., by supposedly noticing and abstracting common features of things. For: (1) How could *logical* concepts such as 'not' and 'or' be abstracted in this way? Where are the features of 'nottishness' or 'alternativeness' to abstract from? (2) With *arithmetical* concepts we must first conceive of things as being of a certain kind, e.g. people or molecules, before it is even intelligible to talk of their number. Moreover, the concept of number is much wider than just of how many in a visible group. (3) With *relations* abstractionism fails, for where is that feature, e.g. of bigness, possessed by big fleas and big elephants, but not by little elephants, which we are to abstract? (4) Even with *colour* concepts the theory fails, for where are the three separable features in an object which might truly be described as its being yellow, lemon and coloured? Geach stresses that such distinctions and classifications as our concepts mark do not just hit us when we open our eyes but are *made* by the mind. Language, of course, is crucially important in leading us to make such distinctions. Far from 'symbolization' being a trivial capping of concepts already formed, it would be truer to say that forming a concept *is* learning the use of a symbol. *Cf.* also Wittgenstein, L., *Philosophical Investigations* (1953), Pt. I, sects 1–43.
11 Described in Thomson, R., *The Psychology of Thinking* (Pelican, 1959), pp. 67–70.
12 *Cf.* Daitz, E., 'The Picture Theory of Meaning' in *Essays in Conceptual Analysis* (1956), ed. Flew, A.G.N. Of course, pictures may be a considerable aid to someone already able to read *part* of the sentence, since then the picture particularizes something of which he already has a rough idea.
13 *Op. cit.*, p. 86.
14 *Op. cit.*, p. 12 (see also pp. 7 and 92).
15 *Cf.* Ausubel, D.F., 'In Defence of Verbal Learning', *Educational Theory* (1961), p. 15.
16 E.g. Friedlander, B.Z., 'A Psychologist's Second Thoughts on Concepts, Curiosity and Discovery in Teaching and Learning', *Harvard Educational Review* (Winter 1965).
17 Harlow, H., 'The Formation of Learning Sets', *Psychological Review* (1949), p. 51.

16

TEACHING BY DISCUSSION

David Bridges

1 Analysis of the concept of discussion

'Discussion' is a word applied to an activity involving a number of people (in e.g. group talk) or a single person (in a disquisition upon a subject). It is also applied to a product, for example a scholarly article or newspaper editorial. All these cases have certain features in common which I shall try and present as the necessary and, together, sufficient conditions for something to count as discussion.

Centrally, discussion requires the putting forward of more than one point of view upon a subject. The different points of view may be expressed by different people or by one person, in speech or in writing, but they must be expressed or put forward or there is no discussion. The expression of more than one point of view, of alternative or different angles on a matter, is independently a necessary feature of discussion. Lectures, articles or editorials may be simple expositions of a single point of view upon an issue. These are not discussions of that issue. They become discussions only if they present the pros and cons of that single point of view, or if they explore alternative points of view.

One cannot simply 'discuss' or 'have a discussion'. Discussion is always a discussion of, about or on something. There is always a subject, question, matter or issue which is 'under discussion', and the central function of discussion is the improvement of knowledge, understanding and/or judgment on the matter which is under discussion.

This last distinction is important because it emphasises that discussion is not necessarily restricted, as seems sometimes to be supposed, to the pursuit of truth (knowledge) but is an activity which can be associated with the illumination of alternatives in an area which does not admit of fully objective and rational conclusion; with the development of understanding for its own sake and without commitment to a final judgment between alternatives; and with the evolution of judgment through mutual accommodation and adjustment of opinion rather than by straightforward reference to evidence and indeed in the absence of

Source: Bridges, David, *Education, Democracy and Discussion*, [orig. Humanities Press, 1979] University Press of America, 1988. Chs. 1 and 7.

such evidence. These distinctions need, and will receive, further explanation. For the moment let me simply use them to indicate why we need to formulate the function of discussion as the improvement of 'knowledge, understanding and/or judgment' on the matter which is under discussion.

Discussion differs from the social art of conversation in that what the talk is about is a matter of some serious importance in discussion and to discussants, whereas conversation and conversationalists may, and perhaps are conventionally expected to, address their subject lightly or indeed playfully. In staff rooms and common rooms in educational institutions the uninitiated or the obstinate create all sorts of social tensions by approaching conversations with the seriousness of discussion or discussions with the playfulness of conversation. I think the distinction between what I have called 'serious' and 'playful' group talk is a recognizable if not altogether unproblematic one. Ordinary language is not however entirely consistent in treating conversation as a playful activity. Much of what Ruth Shaw says about conversation (Shaw, n.d.) parallels what I would want to say about discussion. Nevertheless I shall maintain the distinction in the terms I have described, hopefully purchasing clarity and consistency at the price of a minimal degree of prescriptiveness.

Discussion requires those engaged (whether one or more) to be prepared to examine and be responsive to the different opinions put forward. By 'examine' here I wish to embrace a range of dispositions including, weakly, a readiness to understand and appreciate differences (Ruth Shaw suggests that it is a necessary condition for A and B to be conversing that they are 'each interested in the experiences, attitudes and opinions of the other') and, strongly, an inclination to adjudicate or decide upon their merits.

Two things are important here. The first is the mutual responsiveness of contributions to a discussion, such that what is said at one stage may be affected by what has been said before. In this respect a discussion differs from e.g. a symposium of pre-prepared papers or the presentation to a meeting of set-piece speeches. The second important thing is the readiness or disposition of the contributors to be affected by opinions one way or the other insofar as (on some criteria) they merit acceptance or approval. The difference between the first and second point here is I think reflected partly in the difference between discussion proper and for example the disputation between barristers in a court of law, debate between rigidly opposed political adversaries or domestic argument between an estranged couple who 'refuse to listen to each other'. In each of these last three cases those participating may be mutually responsive in the first sense. They have to answer each other's points; their own case has to take into account what the other has presented; they have to shift with each other's changing moods and styles – all this is going on. But it is possible for them to do all this without having their own stance, their own beliefs, their own understanding or position shifted in the least by what the other side has said, precisely because their intentions are singlemindedly to defend one position, or attack another with a view to shifting the opinion of their adversary or a third party (the judge, jury or electorate in the first two cases). They are entirely resistant to the merits of the opposing opinion or demerits in their own except insofar as these represent tactical problems in their task of persuasion.

By contrast, to enter discussion is, I want to say, necessarily to bring to the presentation of different points of view not a completely open mind perhaps but at least some minimal disposition to understand, to appreciate and to be affected by the range of opinion which is presented. (It is of course quite compatible with being so disposed to be in the event unaffected by other opinions if they lack merit). Discussion in this respect, whether it be oral or written, is paramountly the activity not exclusively of rational persons as Bailey has come close to suggesting (Bailey 1973), but of reasonable persons, such as are amenable to reason above all but also to the illuminative potential of the intuitions, received common sense, and passions upon which alternative opinions may be based.

I wish to offer as a conceptual point, then, the observation that to enter discussion is to be disposed to understand, to examine and to 'take', or be affected by, opinions other than one's own. Furthermore I think one can claim that discussion would have no point unless there was reason to suppose that in general people's understanding or opinion was in fact modified by the consideration of alternative perspectives. (Just as one can in the 'task' sense 'teach' without bringing about learning, but it would be logically odd to engage indefinitely in teaching in this sense when one had no reason to believe that one was teaching in the 'achievement' sense of the word, i.e. actually bringing about learning.)

The conceptual point is I believe in accord with common experience that you simply cannot discuss something with someone who has closed his mind to the possibility that you might have something to contribute to his understanding. At least this is something that this student, interviewed on the Small Group Teaching Project, has plainly realized:

> If there's any inkling about the fact that they are right and you're completely wrong, then I just don't think about it, and I try to shut it off and say, 'how much longer have we got of this?'
>
> (Bridges 1974)

My answer, then, to the question 'what are the necessary and sufficient conditions for saying that people are engaged in the discussion of something? is:

1   they are putting forward more than one point of view upon a subject;
2   they are at least disposed to examine and to be responsive to the different points of view put forward; with
3   the intention of developing their knowledge, understanding and/or judgment on the matter under discussion.

It is perhaps worth noting that this analysis satisfies the two requirements indicated in my preliminary paragraphs. It seems to cover both the case of the group discussion (e.g. in a seminar or meeting) and the individual discussion (e.g. in a lecture or paper), though I am inclined to take the first as the primary and paradigmatic case. The analysis also allows both for oral and for written discussion.

The analysis also draws attention to the twofold obligation of those who wish properly to engage in discussion in its group form – to proffer opinion and to examine responsively opinion offered by others. Merely to listen in silence may be to attend, attend to or observe a discussion: it is not to engage in discussion (unless it is a related private discussion with oneself). Merely to proffer one's own opinion without any inclination to learn from others may be to contribute to discussion, and indeed to do so valuably, but again it is not to engage in it. Engagement in discussion is essentially a 'give and take' activity of a highly reciprocal and paradigmatically gregarious character. This necessary characteristic of discussion is something which I will show to have important implications for the use of discussion in teaching.

2   Teaching and discussion

There is something slightly odd in the whole idea of 'teaching by discussion'. This arises, I think, from the essential reciprocity in the concept of discussion which I want to insist on. Discussion places each of its participants in the position of both contributor and responsive listener, of 'teacher' and learner. To accept for oneself only one of these roles is to disengage from discussion proper and to embark on something else. So, if a 'teacher' adopts for himself (as he may well be justified in doing) the single purpose of bringing about learning in others and surrenders, sacrificiously, dutifully, or arrogantly, the purpose of pursuing knowledge or understanding for himself, then he ceases to be engaging in discussion, and we need to reconceive what precisely he is up to. To express the point in terms which are not paradoxical but which have the ring of paradox: all those who engage in discussion are 'teachers'; but any who are concerned exclusively to teach cannot be engaged in discussion. A teacher may of course *use* a discussion situation in all sorts of ways to help in his task of bringing about learning in others – and these different ways will place him in different kinds of relation to the discussion and to the discussion group. In this paper I want to indicate and comment on a few of the different uses of discussion in teaching.

3   Facilitating discussion

At the very least – but still very importantly – a teacher may provide the opportunity for, facilitate, encourage, organize or convene a discussion in which, in the extreme case, he need have no further role. In other words, he would simply be providing some measure of administrative or motivational support for a discussion which in all respects could be the occasion for a reciprocal learning experience.

There is a wide spectrum of possible teacher activity here related to the strength of the student motivation. The weakest form of teacher activity may be simply that of the convenor who finds a suitable place and a convenient time for the meeting of a group, which in this case has all the motivation and purposefulness which is needed. At the other extreme the teacher may seek to compel attendance at a discussion on an unwilling group – though it seems most unlikely that his intervention could end there if anything like a discussion was to take place. Between these two extremes there will be all sorts of different measures to which the teacher can be responsible for providing the stimulus or raising the questions for discussion. While such initiatives are widely regarded as helpful, constructive and non-directive, they need to be treated with some caution by anyone concerned to protect open enquiry. 'Providing the stimulus or basis for discussion' can be readily translated as 'choosing what it is important to discuss'; and 'raising the questions for discussion' as 'defining the problem'.

Ivan Illich is among those who are deeply suspicious of the way discussions are typically organized in educational institutions in which, as he believes, 'presumed common interests are pre-packaged' and in which 'it requires an authoritarian presence to define for the participants the starting point for their discussion.' His own suggestion is that people should be able to phone in to a computer to arrange for partners with whom to discuss a book or film or recording (Illich 1971).

Of course, any group engaged in discussion has either to agree on what to discuss and on a definition of the problem or (what amounts to the same thing at a second-order level) to discuss what it will discuss or the problem of defining the problem. Those concerned to protect open enquiry and open discussion must however be cautious, as Illich warns, of begging these important questions and they must resist attempts to impose an artificial answer to them upon the group.

In principle, however, it is quite possible for a teacher to promote learning by *facilitating* the kind of open discussion which is in all relevant aspects that of the simple learning group.

4   Controlling the traffic

There is another function which a teacher can perform with a view to facilitating discussion without necessarily interfering with its 'pure' enquiry character. This is the procedural function of controlling the traffic of contributions to the discussion, indicating for example who is next in order to speak.

It is possible to dispense with this function – particularly in a small group – but in a group of any size it is simply easier for would-be contributors to signal to a single, agreed person that he wants to speak than to do so simultaneously to the group as a whole. The same function is of course commonly associated with any necessary timekeeping on the discussion or on stages of the discussion. More importantly it may be coupled with a positive socially allocated responsibility or personal concern to protect more timid, sometimes perhaps divergent, voices from interruption or suppression by the louder or stronger ones.

Even these minimal functions may however be exploited for the purposes of guiding the substantive drift of the argument and not merely the procedural order of contribution. The deliberately or unselfconsciously manipulative chairman may exhibit an obtuse blindness to the signals of those whose opinions he dislikes and an ever ready eye to the voice he approves of or the barely restrained comment which was what he would have really wanted to say himself at that moment had he had the liberty to do so; formal procedural control over a discussion may be sufficient to allow such a chairman to produce the argument he wants in much the same way that an organist who is properly in control of his stops and pedals calls forth a Bach fugue. To do this is to destroy the openness of the discussion, and thence its capacity to promote proper enquiry.

We need to be aware that this may be the case but it does not need to be the case. A chairman may equally well act scrupulously on the principle of everyone in turn and a fair hearing for all or, if this is more productive to the purposes of the group, on the principle of seeking and protecting divergence of opinion, or insisting upon the fullest examination of one point at a time (or whatever). As I have already suggested, however, effective enquiry may be assisted by an insistence that the principles of procedure are made clear and that they are accepted by those whose enquiry they are intended to support.

5 Developing the quality of the group's discussion

The first two functions that I suggested the teacher might fulfil in discussion are ones which, in principle anyway, leave the character and quality of the group's argument untouched. They are the functions of, so to speak, the administrative and procedural officials of the group, analogous to those of the secretary and chairman in certain kinds of committee. The person performing these functions could be said to be promoting the learning of the group in only a rather indirect way – which is why perhaps someone who thinks of himself as having a responsibility to 'teach' will either feel that these functions are insufficient to his responsibility or will exploit them in the ways I have described in order to exert a more active influence upon the group.

Typically, teachers intervene in group discussion with a wider range of purposes than those I have so far described. Among these additional purposes is a set which is still basically supportive of group enquiry but which is concerned to improve the quality of the process of that enquiry.

Thus the teacher may either offer the group some sort of evaluation on the manner in which they have tackled a problem or, more typically, intervene directly in the discussion to ask:

- why someone holds a particular opinion;
- how one point follows from another;
- what is the relevance of some point to the issue at hand;
- what alternative opinions might be presented;
- whether one claim does not contradict another;

to call for more

- clarification;
- explanation;
- illustration;
- precision;
- conciseness;
- reasons, evidence or argument;

to seek

- a more systematic pooling of information;
- a more sympathetic hearing to divergent opinions;
- a more imaginative and open-minded conjecture;
- a more vigorous critical attack;
- a more ready and tolerant adjustment of their own opinions to other people's;

or to encourage

- orderliness;
- reasonableness;
- respect for different points of view.

In any of these ways the teacher may contribute to the quality of the particular enquiry in which the group is currently engaged. But, equally, the teacher may be seeking to develop in his students both understanding of and competence in the epistemological and the social form of argument which they are practising.

Again one has to say that *in principle* such intervention is supportive to the purposes of group enquiry through discussion and that it is not necessarily obstructive even to open discussion. But whether this remains the case on any particular occasion *in practice* will depend on the satisfaction of a number of conditions.

One set of these conditions is rooted in theory of knowledge. The teacher's interventions in the cause of the quality of the argument can be viewed by his students as constructive and justifiable only if they share in or aspire to the teacher's criteria of 'quality' and if they accept his interpretation of those criteria in their application to their own discussion. If these conditions are satisfied the interventions are, so to speak, *intersubjectively* validated. However, the possibility of their further validation against something approaching *objective* standards would rest on their being in accord with some more widely established tradition or conventions of good, proper or correct argument and with the application of these in practice. (I need to add this last phrase because people may for example like clarity in principle but disagree in terms of what they would count as clear argument in a given instance.)

Now some conditions or criteria of good argument may be fairly uncontroversial – e.g. The law of non-contradiction. But many others are not, in particular in certain areas of the curriculum. The relevance or otherwise of introspection to psychological argument or of personal experience and feeling to literary, moral or religious judgment are on record as matters of controversy even among those who might have been expected to be the priestly preservers and givers of the epistemological law. Indeed a large part of, in particular, aesthetic and moral argument is about, precisely, what does constitute a relevant reason. Moreover, should some disciplines be naive enough to assume that their form of enquiry and judgment is epistemologically unproblematic or uncontroversial, attendant bands of philosophers and sociologists will rapidly demonstrate that the case is otherwise.

The best that can be looked for then is as wide as possible an intersubjective agreement as to the criteria of good argument.

That the teacher's interventions in the interests of the quality of discussion are supportive to the purposes of group enquiry is also dependent upon certain social psychological conditions. Let us note for example that students will not necessarily give a teacher's interventions the interpretation which is intended. Experience on the U.G.C. Small Group Teaching Project suggested that even students in higher education could be almost frightened into silence by tutors' interventions which were intended and interpreted by tutors as simple requests for more explanation or justification. The students' language in talking about their tutor's challenges and questions evoked the atmosphere of the jungle rather than that of the seminar room. Tutors were perceived as 'pouncing' on them (this very frequently), 'attacking' them, 'trapping' them and getting them 'in a corner'.

I present these examples simply to show that if teachers/tutors are to improve the quality of argument in an actual world rather than a hypothetical world of purely and successfully rational animals then they will have to take into account the kind of psychological and socio-psychological conditions which obtain in their class.

Nevertheless, let us note that in principle there is an important function for the teacher to perform in relation to a discussion which is supportive to its enquiry – and that is to help to develop the quality of argument of its participants and indeed to develop in them the range of capacities and dispositions which successful discussion requires.

6 Guiding the enquiry to a predetermined conclusion: (closed discussion or indirect instruction)

For many teachers the activity which they like to call discussion represents a change in style and pace from formal instruction, but no significant change in terms of the learning objectives or the outcomes which they seek. They may feel perhaps that students will be able to concentrate better if they can talk as well as listen, may understand better if they can ask questions, and may remember better if they have something which at least resembles the experience of discovering for themselves the solution to a problem or arriving at their own judgment upon a controversial question. And indeed the teachers may find their expectations fulfilled as long as their students tolerate or fail to detect the inescapable phoniness of the enterprise.

It is important to recognize the very real difference between the character of this kind of teacher intervention and the kind that I described in the previous section. In the case that I was examining there the teacher's concern was with the *process* or processes of enquiry. The enquiry itself remained a genuine enquiry, the substantive discoveries, conclusion or learning outcomes of which could only be guessed at. It was in this sense an open discussion. In the role that I am now concerned with, the teacher's intention is pre-eminently to teach the group a particular set of substantive beliefs, opinions or conclusions. Thus the activity which the group is engaged in ceases to be anything properly describable as an enquiry, unless it is an enquiry into what the teacher has in mind. It is clearly not open in at least one respect (in that the outcome is 'fixed') and will typically cease to be open in other respects, e.g. where the teacher attempts to conceal his real purposes in order to create a more vivid illusion of discovery or self-generated judgment.

The production of the desired 'answer' in this kind of discussion may be a very direct or an extended process; it may be in an area where the criteria for 'getting it right' are uncontroversial or where they are problematic and in dispute; and the criteria may be overt, explicit and shared (between teacher and students) or covert, implicit and the object of some uncertainty. Such distinctions generate a wide variety of closed question-and-answer or pseudo-discussion transactions with different kinds of problems, moral and functional. I shall illustrate and comment on just a few of these.

Perhaps we can first note briefly that to ask a question as if it were a genuine enquiry when it is not, or to engage people in what purports to be a genuine enquiry while actually manipulating the whole process to your own ends, is to be at best covert and at worst downright dishonest. It is difficult to see how to defend such practice when there are perfectly practicable alternative patterns of behaviour open to one.

Beyond this the argument gets more complicated – and it concerns the ways in which, in 'guided discussion' situations, 'reasoning' becomes defined as 'teacher's reasoning', which may be highly personal, idiosyncratic and perhaps even erroneous. This is especially a problem in areas where opinions rest upon problematic value judgments and where what would count as correct reasoning is a matter of social and academic controversy. But it can also be a problem in less obvious areas. Douglas Barnes quotes the following exchange from a comprehensive school biology lesson:

T. How does the fish contain the oxygen from the water? What happens . . . ? Stephen?

P. It allows the water to run over its gills and the . . . er . . . and extracts the oxygen.

T. First of all think of it in stages, Stephen. Where does the water go first of all?

P. Miss, it enters the mouth and then it passes over the gills taking out the oxygen. Then it comes out of the gills.

T. Comes out of the back of the gill-cover.

(Barnes *et al.* 1969.)

Barnes' comment here is particularly relevant to the concern I am trying to illustrate:

> The difficulty for the pupil seems to rise not only from the nature of the subject matter. If he were explaining this to an equal for a given purpose his choice of items would be determined by that purpose and the extent of his knowledge. But he is explaining it to a teacher who already knows it, and for an unstated purpose, so he can only construct a criterion for choosing items by projecting himself into the teacher's mind, partly in response to her signals of acceptance or rejection. The teacher seems to be demanding more specific references; the problem for the pupil must be to determine what will be relevant and acceptable – by what criteria the teacher is judging relevance.

Another example which Barnes offers is from the first form religious education lesson in a secondary school – a lesson concerned with life in New Testament Palestine:

T. How did they get the water from the well? . . . do you remember? . . . Yes?

P1. They. . . ran the bucket down . . . er . . . and it was fastened on this bit of string and it . . . (here the words become inaudible for a phrase or two) . . . other end to the water.

T. You might do it that way . . . where did they put the water . . . John?

P2. In a big . . . er . . . pitcher.

T. Good . . . in a pitcher . . . which they carried on their . . . ?

P2. Heads.

Barnes' commentary on this piece is again very revealing:

> The question 'How did they get the water from the well?' has signalled to Pupil 1 that this is a relatively open question to which an improvised sequence would be appropriate. His reply, the quality of which is here irrelevant, is met by 'You might do it that way' spoken with an intonation expressing doubt. That is Pupil 1's answer rejected, though in a

polite form of words. Pupil 2 suggests an answer *of a different kind*; he intuits – or remembers – that his teacher does not want improvised reasoning but the name of an object. His reply 'In a big . . . er . . . pitcher' is accepted and carried further with a promptness which signals to both pupils that this was what was required in the first place . . ..
This is an example of the kind of question which the investigators have come to call a 'pseudo-question', in that while it has the form of an open question the teacher's treatment of replies shows that he is willing to accept only one answer.

We may observe, incidentally, that it is difficult to see why on any objective grounds P2's answer should be deemed more reasonable than that of P1. On the face of it the class is taking an early lesson (they are in their sixth week in a new school) in, as Barnes puts it, 'the kinds of reciprocal behaviour appropriate to a teacher–pupil relationship – that is, *learning when not to think.*'

The other thing that happens in this sort of context – and this is a logical consequence of the situation which the teacher has set up, not merely a contingently related phenomenon – is of course that since it is the teacher's thought process that has become the object of the pupil's enquiry it is in the psychology of the teacher's behaviour rather than the logic of the argument that are to be found the clues to the required answer. Indeed students become remarkably skilful in reading the clues which the teacher gives, often unconsciously, so that, as Bullock observes, 'class discussion is often no more than a series of disconnected endeavours to read the teacher's mind' (DES1975).

The kind of examples I have quoted here – and analogous ones are to be found in the reports of the Humanities Curriculum Project and the Ford Teaching Project – go to illustrate the way in which this kind of closed 'discussion' ('closed' at least in the sense that the outcome is predetermined) is destructive of enquiry and of reason. They support the recommendation contained in the Bullock Report, *A Language for Life*, that the teacher might watch that the questions he asks are open-ended rather than closed, and that the synthesis he brings about is seen to be the end point of the pupil's own thinking under his guidance. 'Genuine thinking,' the report suggests, 'may be more readily provoked when the teacher poses a genuine problem than when he asks a question to which he knows the answer' (DES 1975).

7 Some further functions of discussion in teaching

Sections 3, 4 and 5 above were concerned with some different ways in which a teacher might support or enhance the quality of a group's learning in discussion. In section 6 I commented on the kind of intervention in which the teacher replaces the dynamics of the group's own enquiry with a form of indirect instruction. This kind of transaction resembles discussion proper in some ways but Barnes' researchers preferred to call it 'pseudo discussion' and even Bullock felt compelled to refer to it as 'class discussion' in inverted commas.

A teacher may of course exploit the learning possibilities of group discussion in other ways. He may take advantage of the different kinds of information about people in the group which a discussion affords to help, for example, a new group of students to get to know each other, by making this either the subject of or an incidental pay-off to the discussion. He may exploit the social and inter-personal values implicit in group discussion to promote certain moral, social or political ideals. I see no reason why either of these purposes need interfere with the central enquiry function of the group – though it seems to me that here, as elsewhere, it is honest and avoids confusion if one makes explicit the secondary as well as the primary purposes of the discussion, if, in the terms that I have chosen to use, these are 'open'.

There is a further popular use of group discussion in teaching, however, which can easily raise the same sort of problems as its use in 'guided discovery' – and this is its use (or abuse) as a way of assessing students' knowledge or understanding. At one extreme this assessing can take a form which is properly described as inter-rupting discussion rather than contributing to it. I mean where the teacher intervenes, for example, to ask a student if she can recall something from a previous lesson, or asks a question like the one about the pitcher in the example quoted earlier, which, even if it is not put explicitly as 'Can you remember what I said about "x" last lesson?' amounts to the same thing. This kind of intervention leads to all the problems that I indicated in the last section, especially if it is, as is commonly the case, the dominant mode of questioning in the group.

At the other extreme (to the teacher assessing by direct questioning) the teacher may get a lot of information about what students do and do not understand by simply listening in on their discussion. To one degree or another this is a common practice in higher education where, for example, a seminar follows a lecture. Discussion in this context will commonly help the lecturer to see what he failed to make clear in his lecture – where a student either simply says he does not understand or, more revealingly perhaps, demonstrates his misunderstanding when he attempts to use some of the ideas from the lecture in his own contributions to discussion.

For a teacher or tutor to attend to a discussion with this in mind is not necessarily obstructive to his students' enquiry *provided* they do not feel awed into either concealing their possible misunderstanding under a cloak of silence, or hiding their disagreement with the tutor in, again, silence, or perhaps even worse, a pretence at consensus.

To set inside or alongside a discussion group, someone whose enquiry is not into the subject under discussion but into the ignorance and misunderstanding of other members of the group is not necessarily to obstruct the enquiry, but there is evidence to suggest that it may well obstruct it in practice. Certainly this is the case in the cruder forms of intervention which turn the whole activity into a series of examining questions and answers.

The point is that reciprocity and the 'give and take' character of discussion imply that it is the activity of 'seekers' rather than 'knowers', and the presence of a 'knower' in the group will inescapably be an antipathetic one. If the 'knower' seems to be wresting control of the discussion or its outcomes from the 'seekers' he will almost inevitably generate a sense of alienation equivalent in the learning situation to that experienced by frustrated members of pseudo-democratic school councils. As one college of education student explained:

> If there's any inkling about the fact that they are right and you are completely wrong, then I just don't think about it, and I try to shut it off and say 'how much longer have we got this?'

> (Bridges 1975)

8 Neutrality and openness in teaching

One of the most significant contributions in recent years to the development of group discussion in schools has been the work of The Schools Council/Nuffield Humanities Project, which took discussion as its basic teaching strategy in the development of understanding of controversial value issues in the classroom.

The project invited the teacher to 'accept neutrality as a criterion by which to criticize his performance' and it is this invitation in particular which has prompted controversy among teachers and educators. It is not my concern in this context to explore all dimensions of this controversy. I wish simply to relate the values and practice of procedural neutrality as expressed in the Humanities Project, to the values and practice of open discussion as I have identified it.

There is a *prima facie* sense in which a discussion in which one member of the group, albeit the teacher, is deliberately constrained from 'taking sides' or from 'expressing his own opinion' is not an open one. And indeed this is very much the kind of thing that some critics of HCP's suggested teaching strategy have found unacceptable. Thus the Schools Council Moral Education Project has argued that:

> The easy identification of teachers' value positions is a good thing from the pupils' point of view and not something to be regretted. Our principal reason for believing this, for favouring commitment, is that 65 per cent of boys and girls between thirteen and sixteen (in a survey referred to elsewhere) . . . expected adults to 'come off the fence', to be willing to reveal their views when asked. Adolescents in the survey claimed, and we believe they were right, that to refuse to state what you think about an issue while expecting others to do so is to adopt a superior position in which you treat others as less than persons.

> (McPhail *et al.* 1972)

And later the project echoes an argument close to the basic liberal argument for free or open discussion. Without the kind of contribution that the teacher can make, children are likely to receive from their peer group or the mass media 'a selection of points of view which is in no sense exhaustive.' This is not enough.

> They badly need criticism and expansion which can only come from individuals, including teachers, who are willing to take the trouble . . . .
> It is not that a particular teacher's comment is necessarily right minded and valuable, but rather that we need variety of comment from people who care and are willing to speak.
>
> (*Ibid.*)

It might be argued then that for the teacher to adopt the role of procedural neutrality is for him to deny the group opinions which the group is in some sense entitled to as part of the reciprocal engagement of discussion; which the group requires as one among the range of significantly different points of view that are socially available; and which the group requires as a basis for challenging and criticizing the opinions received from, for example, the media or their peers. Insofar as this is the case – and I think something like this denial *is* implied in the practice of procedural neutrality – then procedural neutrality seems to require something less than the properly open discussion.

However, there is a good deal more that needs to be said before one can conclude that neutrality is hostile to open discussion. Indeed I shall want to suggest that this is far from the case.

The first point to note is that the purpose of the teacher's self-denying ordinance is precisely to allow the students in the group greater actual freedom to express and evaluate their own opinions. The experience of the Humanities Project was that *as a matter of observation* where a teacher did put forward his opinions – even (or especially?) where he put them forward 'modestly, yet sincerely and with conviction' – children found it really very difficult not to treat these as having special authority. As a result, they tended to be discouraged from either putting forward or giving proper attention to divergent opinion and from making up their own minds about questions on the basis of a proper weighing of reasons, evidence and argument. At least, the project found sufficient evidence of this kind of difficulty to suggest that teachers who found this a problem in their own classroom should explore the effects of adopting the style of procedural neutrality. If it is the case, as the project suggests, that the teacher's deliberate restraint in withholding his own opinion has the effect of opening up the discussion in which his students can then engage, then this may be regarded as a strategy designed to maximize rather than to reduce openness of discussion. As John Elliott points out:

> If his students persist in ascribing an uncritical authority to his views, then some kind of closure is put on the range and depth of viewpoints explored.
>
> (Elliott 1975)

There is interesting confirmation of the experience of the Humanities Project in the literature associated with case-work by social workers in which what has been referred to for some time as 'neutral discussion' is advocated in circumstances in which a case-worker is trying to get a client, for example, to express reactions which he is ashamed of or fears will be ridiculed and where the case-worker is 'trying to make clients self-supporting again'. (See, for example, Moffett 1968.)

The second point to note in defence of procedural neutrality is that it has to be seen in developmental terms. The second of the project's five major premises is that 'the teacher accepts the need to submit his teaching in controversial areas to the criterion of neutrality *at this stage of education*' (Schools Council/Nuffield Humanities Project 1970, my italics).

The teacher's reticence can be interpreted[1] as a weaning operation, drawing the student from his subservience to the opinion of authorities and developing his capacity for independent evaluation of opinion until he is genuinely capable of treating the teacher's opinion with the respect demanded by the evidence and argument which supports it, and its capacity to illuminate, rather than the social authority of its source. That students should develop the capacity to handle arguments in this way would be one of the central concerns of the humanities teacher. Evidence that his students *are* able to separate the teacher's expressions of his views from his authority position might justify the teacher in expressing his opinion openly in the discussion. The main reservation to this is the very important cautionary and practical one made by John Elliott:

> Years of educational conditioning may make it extremely difficult for students to understand and accept the teacher's renunciation of the role of 'expert', so ingrained is the notion by their past educational experiences . . . [the teacher] can so easily deceive himself into believing that students are not ascribing authority to his views, when in fact they are.
>
> (Elliott 1975)

The teacher's 'neutrality' may be interpreted, then, as assisting in a developmental stage in the student's weaning from dependence on authority to independence of judgment. It may become redundant as soon as a group of students show themselves able to separate the teacher's opinion from the teacher's authority – but we must be cautious of assuming too readily that students have made what appears in practice to be a very difficult step.

A third point that deserves emphasis in this context is that there is nothing manipulative or covert about the procedures associated with procedural neutrality. Throughout the project handbook it is emphasized that the teacher must make sure his students understand his, and their own, roles, the nature of the discussion and the reasons for its particular mode of conduct.

> The chairman should explain to the students the nature of the task they are engaged upon, its aim and the need for rules in a discussion group.

The nature of controversiality needs to be explored and the chairman must make it clear why he will attempt to be neutral. He should invite students to discuss with him from time to time how far he is succeeding in filling the role he has defined for himself.

(Schools Council/Nuffield Humanities Project 1970)

This concern for explicitness and overtness in relation to the pattern of teaching and learning is in obvious accord with ideals of openness, as well as the more basic requirement of clarity of purpose.

Finally, let us note that the Humanities Project is attached to open discussion in another and very significant way. This is in the sense that it insists that the discussion is a genuine enquiry, the learning outcomes of which are therefore unpredictable and unpredetermined. Indeed it has been his concern with the development of this kind of teaching and learning (among other things perhaps) which led the project's director, Lawrence Stenhouse, to criticize models of curriculum planning which are formed on the basis of pre-specifiable learning outcomes, and which similarly led the project's evaluation team to devise evaluation strategies other than those (fashionable in its early days) which interpreted curriculum evaluation in terms of some measure of the extent to which pre-specified learning outcomes were achieved (Stenhouse 1975).

All in all, then, the four points considered here lead me to the conclusion that, far from being antipathetic to open discussion, the strategies recommended by the Humanities Curriculum Project seem to offer a contribution to the protection and development of open discussion of considerable importance. Whether there are significant numbers of teachers who will share the project's commitment and have the stamina really to test out its demanding strategies, time will show. Such teachers have it in their power, I believe, to initiate significant improvement in the quality of academic and also political discussion in our community.

I have placed myself thus firmly in support of the strategy of procedural neutrality primarily because I share what I believe to be its aspiration to wean students from dependence upon the authority of their teachers and because I am persuaded by the experience of the Humanities Curriculum Project, (and, following this, the UGC Project on Small Group Teaching in Higher Education, and the Ford Teaching Project) that this is in practice a very difficult thing to do, but yet something in which the strategy of procedural neutrality may be able to assist.

I am conscious however that the notion of the neutral teacher is not without its contradictions and limitations and perhaps I should give fuller recognition to these. I believe however that many criticisms of the strategy in addition to those I have already described turn out to be less fundamental than they might at first appear if we conceive of the strategy of procedural neutrality as a 'weaning' one, to be used at a particular stage in students' development and not as a once and for all recipe for the teacher's role in group discussion.

Mary Warnock's criticism of the neutral teacher is a case in point. Though she ignorantly or obtusely fails to refer to the Humanities Curriculum Project, much of her argument could be interpreted as a criticism of the project's aspirations and recommended teaching strategy. This applies particularly to her central point, which is as follows:

> Unless the teacher comes out into the open, and says in what direction he believes that the evidence points he will have failed in his duty as a teacher. For what his pupils have to learn is not only, in an abstract way, what counts as evidence, but how people draw conclusions from evidence . . . . Thus the teacher must if he is to teach his pupils to assess evidence fairly, give them actual examples of how he does this himself. His pupils may disagree with him. The more adult they become, and the better their earlier experience of arguments, the more capable they will be of weighing the probabilities differently. But unless they see before them the spectacle of a rational man drawing conclusions rationally, they will never learn what rational probabilities are.
>
> (Warnock 1975)

Now, of course, insofar as what is under discussion is something upon which it is possible to draw conclusions rationally then this is something a teacher should teach (at some stage). Moreover it may be, though this would be something requiring empirical investigation, that it can be well taught by the example of 'a rational man drawing conclusions rationally'.

However, two qualifications must be made to the conclusion that Mary Warnock reaches. First, not all questions upon which discussion may intelligently take place lend themselves to *rational* conclusions; some may not even allow *conclusions* to be drawn; and on others, which may *allow* conclusions and even rational conclusions to be drawn, a group may be concerned not to reach a conclusion but, for example, merely to understand the variety of opinion which is entertained upon the question.

Secondly, and more importantly in this context, Mary Warnock seems to lack any psychological perspective on how a group of related competences may best be developed. Presumably if we *are* to draw conclusions rationally we must in any case first engage in some kind of honest and impartial attempt to understand the different arguments, evidence and points of view on the question under discussion. But, says the Humanities Project, it is not so easy to get students to do this. In particular the process is commonly obstructed by the busy demonstrations offered by the teacher of his own point of view and of his conclusions. So, the very demonstration which Mary Warnock is calling upon teachers to make may very well turn out in practice to be obstructive to that kind of learning which she wants to encourage. Or, to get closer to the point, there is good reason to believe that the practice she recommends will be obstructive to her own purposes unless the students concerned have already achieved the kind of independence of mind which procedural neutrality is intended to develop.

The actual advocates of procedural neutrality, then, as opposed to Mary Warnock's imagined or unidentified ones, are not recommending anything which is *necessarily* in contradiction with what Mary Warnock wants. They are merely rather better informed than she appears to be about how to organize one's teaching in order to pursue it.

A different set of problems about the role of the neutral teacher in discussion bothered me more deeply. They are puzzling not least because they involve in a very substantial way the 'paradox of openness' to which I have already referred.

To adopt the strategy of procedural neutrality in discussion is itself to adopt, to demonstrate and quite possibly to promote a specific and substantive set of values. The Humanities Project has of course never pretended that this was other than the case. Lawrence Stenhouse describes three ways in which the project was value-committed – in its decision to include controversial issues in the school curriculum; in the values (respect for persons, a preference for rational procedures, etc.) which govern its teaching procedures; and in its assertion of 'the democratic values' which call for open debate and dialogue on those issues 'for which society has not found a solution that can be universally or almost universally accepted' (Stenhouse 1970).

John Elliott writes similarly and pointedly of 'the values of the neutral teacher'. 'Procedural neutrality,' he explains, 'expresses a teacher's commitment not to use his authority to promote judgments which go beyond impartial criteria of rationality. Within the field of controversial value issues such a commitment is synonymous with a commitment to democracy as a worthwhile form of life' (Elliott 1975).

The project acknowledges unequivocally then that, in choosing to submit certain matters to discussion in the classroom rather than to authoritative instruction and in confining the teacher to the discipline of procedural neutrality, it is committing itself to a specifically 'democratic' value position – one which in the event turns out to be far too radically democratic for many parents, teachers or pupils to accept!

Now, if it is the case that by his mode of handling of discussion in the classroom the teacher is demonstrating his commitment to democratic values, including for example the value of open discussion, a concern for rationality and reasonableness, a commitment to fairness and a respect for other people's opinions, feelings and interests, if, as seems to be suggested, all this is involved in being procedurally neutral, then it is difficult to see in what sense the teacher can avoid giving his (authoritative) support to some rather than to other positions upon the examples of controversial issues which the Humanities Project offers. Surely the ethical commitments of the neutral teacher *must* lead him to substantive commitments on issues which are raised by the project's packs – for example on the place of women in society, capital punishment, religious toleration, wars of colonial oppression etc.? Indeed at the time of the heated debate about the project's (eventually withheld) 'Race' pack this was precisely the point made by NUT Secretary Fred Jarvis. After reminding Stenhouse of his own statement concerning the axiomatic and *un*controversial nature of certain values, including 'respect for persons', Jarvis went on:

> I believe 'respect for persons' is the essence of race relations and I cannot see how a teacher can be neutral where this is concerned.
>
> (Jarvis 1972)

The project's strategy was subsequently defended on a number of grounds – but, most interestingly, on an argument which confirms the point that the project had substantive as well as procedural moral commitments of a liberal/democratic character – for it was pointed out that there was some evidence, albeit marginal in character, that procedural neutrality was a strategy which helped to generate attitudes of greater tolerance and respect about and between racial communities than did direct proselytization on behalf of a liberal 'tolerant' standpoint (Verma and Macdonald 1971).

But are we then to conclude that the 'neutral' teacher is merely a liberal/democrat who is more intelligent than most in the manner in which he promotes his values – or that the 'open' discussion is merely a more subtle and effective means than instruction of promoting a certain kind of substantive ethical position?

I think in part that this has to be accepted – though the point could be presented without quite so much of the air of unveiling a conspiracy. Another way of expressing it would be to say that procedural neutrality and open discussion are teaching strategies appropriately employed by a liberal democrat who wishes his 'hidden curriculum' and the means he takes to be consonant with his explicit curriculum and the ends he pursues. This is to acknowledge the ideological basis of procedural neutrality and of open discussion (i.e. their moral/political affiliations) – but to my knowledge this is a basis which nobody who has written about either has attempted to conceal.

This conclusion needs some qualification however, for as I have already argued, one feature of the liberal-democrat's beliefs is to hold his own beliefs with some scepticism – to wish among other things to submit them to continuing critical discussion and to accept that that discussion may cause him to modify or even to change them. Moreover, he is also committed to respecting other people's rights to disagree with his opinions and to tolerating and even valuing opinion which differs from his own. This respect and this tolerance has of course some limits – as critics of the liberal position are very quick to point out. But nevertheless the liberal's honest interest in other people's points of view (an interest due to them for their own sake and not merely for the purpose of their exploitation or refutation) is something which can communicate itself and encourage individuals to express their own views and to share in discussion in the persuasion that what they say will receive attention, respect and consideration.

In more concrete terms I believe that this is what the strategy of procedural neutrality can achieve. Students who are all too accustomed to being expected to be the silent auditors to a teacher's wisdom, to accepting beliefs on the teacher's say-so, to being invited to contribute only that which they are supposed to have remembered from a previous lesson, to having their own thoughts snubbed, ignored or manipulated to the purposes which the teacher has in mind – these students find instead that they are in the presence of a teacher who is prepared to hold his tongue, to listen attentively and to encourage others to do the same and to let one's faltering opinions speak for themselves. Perhaps by so doing the teacher immediately identifies himself with a certain set of (liberal) values, but it seems plausible to expect (and there is a certain amount of evidence to support this expectation in case studies of procedural neutrality in action) that the overwhelming effect is to encourage students in a new sense of the dignity and worth of their own opinions.

There will be those of course – I have rather gained the impression that Mary Warnock is among them – who will be reluctant to credit the opinions of mere students with 'dignity' or 'worth'. However, the thrust of my whole argument leads me to the conclusion that those with such opinions will be compelled not merely to eschew procedural neutrality but to fail to engage in anything properly describable as discussion with those whom they so regard.

9 Group discussion as a democratic form of teaching and learning

Those associated with the Humanities Curriculum Project were not the first and are not alone in seeing some connection between a preference for learning by discussion and 'democratic' values. Indeed, a number of writers on education have identified discussion as a characteristically democratic mode of teaching and learning. W.H. Kilpatrick, for example, has written of

> the democratic educative process, where young and old discuss and consider unsettled matters in order to learn through study and concluding how better to study and conclude.
>
> (Kilpatrick 1937)

A Bureau of Current Affairs pamphlet on discussion methods claimed that

> What can be said in general terms is that discussion is a democratic way of acquiring and examining knowledge.
>
> (Bureau of Current Affairs 1950)

H.J. Hallworth has indicated the double significance of discussion in the context of teacher training:

> The object of group discussions is to teach by example . . . to establish a democratic situation for the teacher in training . . . the hope being that he will then create similar democratic situations when he is himself engaged in teaching.
>
> (Hallworth 1957)

In what sense, more precisely, can discussion in the context of the classroom or university seminar be held to be a 'democratic' teaching or learning procedure?

The first point that one might make is that a preference for group discussion in decision-making and a preference for group discussion in the context of teaching and learning can be rooted in some common epistemological premises concerning the status of knowledge and understanding and the way in which these may be developed. It seems to me that a preference for group discussion over, for example, the authoritative lecture in teaching and a preference for democratic deliberation over authoritative decision in the political context can both be rooted in a common epistemological scepticism and, more positively, in the same opinion that the fullest and most sound understanding is the product of group processes (pooling of information, exchange of perspectives, criticism and refutation, creative stimulation, mutual negotiation) rather than, or at least in addition to, individual judgment. Discussion in the classroom might then be held to be a democratic pattern of learning in the sense that like democratic decision-making procedures it makes the outcome dependent not upon the opinion of someone acknowledged as an or in authority but on the co-operative endeavour and judgment of the group as a whole.

John Dewey makes very much this point in complaining of the inconsistency which exists between the democratic method of forming opinions which we employ in political matters and the methods in common use in forming beliefs in other contexts.

> The real trouble is that there is an intrinsic split in our habitual attitudes when we profess to depend upon discussion and persuasion in politics and then systematically depend upon other methods in reaching conclusions in matters of morals and religion, or in anything where we depend upon a person or group possessed of 'authority'. In homes and in schools, the places where the essentials of character are supposed to be formed, the usual procedure is the settlement of issues, intellectual and moral, by appeal to the 'authority' of parent, teacher, or textbook.

And then Dewey goes on to warn,

> Dispositions formed under such conditions are so inconsistent with the democratic method that in a crisis they may be aroused to act in positively anti-democratic ways for anti-democratic ends.
>
> (Dewey 1940)

Michael Fielding has related the same argument more directly to the inconsistent practices of schools and sees that a genuine concern to equip students for participation in democratic decision-making must require changes in traditional 'authoritarian, teacher-dominated classroom methods'.

> If school councils are to try to encourage people to participate in the running of their own lives rather than letting others do it for them, then the old idea of the teacher as the sole fountain of knowledge, imparter of facts and omniscient director of all activities within the classroom must go. Pupils must be given the opportunities to develop social skills and the variety of skills associated with the making of choices within a variety and multiplicity of situations. So many teachers and Heads appear to expect pupils miraculously to be able to participate fluently and maturely and be critical and discerning in their intellectual and social behaviour when they leave the fifth or sixth year without having been offered any genuine opportunities or encouragement to do so in the previous ten years of their school lives. Often people have expressed horror at the docility and disinterest of fifth or sixth formers and have then gone on to suggest that this intellectual lethargy was either proof that school councils could never work or the root cause of their frequent failure. Such critics seldom, if ever, pause to consider that there might be some connection between such sheepishness and the authoritarian, teacher dominated classroom methods still typical of most secondary schools today.
>
> (Fielding 1973)

My first point leads already into the second, which is that the discussion situation in the classroom requires the establishment of a set of social relationships different from many traditional classroom relationships and corresponding significantly with those associated with the idea of a democratic community. The teacher's role has effectively to change either to one in which he is one of the group in a more or less equivalent position to everyone else or to one in which he is some sort of procedural chairman. Either way he abandons his traditional position *vis-à-vis* his students as *the* authority on the subject under discussion. He also submits his, so to speak, political authority to a system of rules determined by the purposes and requirements of the discussion rather than his person.

Thirdly, and even more significantly perhaps, the students' relations with each other are affected. Discussion is an activity of which the success depends essentially on the reciprocal efforts of those taking part. It *requires* social involvement, co-operation, mutual attentiveness and responsiveness, respect and appreciation of individual divergence, reasonableness, etc. – the kind of qualities and relations which, one might argue, lie at the heart of democratic community. Again it is worth noting that pedagogic procedures like the lecture or other form of authoritative instruction or individual study could not be expected to generate the same kinds of relationships or values.

There does seem then, to be some kind of justification for considering a preference for discussion in the classroom as a 'democratic' preference. An important proviso to this conclusion is that it does depend on the discussion being a genuine discussion in the terms which I have laid out. To substitute for the lecture a highly directive or subtly manipulated form of group talk is in no way to embrace the principles and procedures which I have called democratic. Indeed it may be an effective way of preventing any such tendencies. But then, neither is it, in the terms which I have defined, to engage in anything which is properly describable as discussion.

Note

1 I say 'can be interpreted' because I am conscious that members of the project team have stressed different arguments in support of the concept of the neutral teacher. Lawrence Stenhouse, for example, the project's director, has stressed the importance of the *political* argument concerning the Project's responsibility to teachers (and teachers' responsibility to parents), who may be deeply attached to a diversity of values.

References

Bailey, C.H. (1973) 'Teaching by discussion and the neutral teacher', *Proceedings of the Philosophy of Education Society of Great Britain*, VII, 1. Oxford: Basil Blackwell.

Barnes, D., Britton, J. and Rosen, H. (1969) *Language, the Learner and the School*. Harmondsworth: Penguin.

Bridges, D. (ed.) (1974) *Homerton Pilot Project on Small Group Teaching: Evaluation Report*. Norwich: University of East Anglia, Centre for Applied Research Education (University Grants Committee Small Group Teaching Project).

Bridges, D. (1975) 'The silent student in small group discussion', *Education for Teaching*, 97, Summer.

Bridges, D. (1976) 'The silent student in small group discussion', in Group for Research and Innovation in Higher Education. *Small Group Teaching*. London: Nuffield Foundation.

Bureau of Current Affairs (1950) *Discussion Method: The Purpose, Nature and Application of Group Discussion* (pamphlet). London: Dennis Dobson.

Department of Education and Science (1975) *A Language for Life* (Report of the Bullock Committee). London: HMSO.

Dewey, J. (1940) *Freedom and Culture*. London: Allen & Unwin.

Elliott, J. (1975) 'The values of the neutral teacher', in Bridges, D. and Scrimshaw, P. (eds) *Values and Authority in Schools*. London: Hodder & Stoughton.

Elliott, J. and Adelman, C. (1973) 'Teachers' actions and their effects on pupils'. Norwich: University of East Anglia, Centre for Applied Research in Education (Ford Teaching Project, Document G).

Elliott, J. and Adelman, C. (1974) *Towards a General Methodology of Enquiry/Discovery Teaching*.

Norwich: University of East Anglia, Centre for Applied Research in Education (Ford Teaching Project, Document 1).

Fielding, M. (1973) 'Democracy in secondary schools: school councils and "shared responsibility"', *Journal of Moral Education*, 2, 3.

Group for Research and Innovation in Higher Education (1976) *Small Group Teaching*. London: Nuffield Foundation.

Hallworth, H.J. (1957) 'Group discussion in its relevance to teacher training', *Educational Review*, 10.

Illich, I. (1971) *Deschooling Society*. London: Calder and Boyars.

Jarvis, F. (1972). Letter to *The Times Educational Supplement*, 11th February.

McPhail, P., Ungoed-Thomas, J.R. and Chapman, H. (1972) *Moral Education in the Secondary School*. London: Longman.

Moffett, J. (1968) *Concepts in Casework Treatment*. London: Routledge & Kegan Paul.

Ruddick, J. (1973) Small Group Teaching Project: Handbook 2, Small Group Teaching and Learning. Norwich: University of East Anglia, Centre for Applied Research in Education (mimeographed).

Schools Council/Nuffield Humanities Project (1970). *The Humanities Project: An Introduction*. London: Heinemann.

Shaw, R. (n.d.) *Conversation and Communication*. Inaugural Lecture, Birkbeck College, London.

Stenhouse, L. (1970) 'Controversial value issues in the classroom', in Carr, W.G. (ed.) *Values and the Curriculum*. A Report of the Fourth International Curriculum Conference, National Education Association Center for the Study of Instruction, Washington, DC.

Stenhouse, L. (1975) *An Introduction to Curriculum Research and Development*. London: Heinemann.

Verma, G.K. and Macdonald, B. (1971) 'Teaching race in schools: some effects on the attitudinal and sociometric patterns of adolescents', *Race*, 3, 1.

Warnock, M. (1975) 'The neutral teacher', in Brown, S.C. (ed.) *Philosophers Discuss Education*. London: Macmillan.

17

(i) INDOCTRINATION AND INTENTIONS

Ivan Snook

According to White (1967), indoctrination requires an intention of a certain sort, namely the intention that the child believes what is taught in such a way that nothing will shake his belief. I want to argue that this is close to being a correct analysis of 'indoctrination' but that, as stated and discussed by White, the criterion is still inadequate.

1   The intention to inculcate unshakeable beliefs may be a necessary condition but it is certainly not sufficient. Teachers of mathematics, chemistry, and Latin have to teach many things which they do not expect to be questioned, much less rejected. White's account does not cover our unwillingness to call those teachers indoctrinators.

2   His main example deals with a false proposition ('Melbourne is the capital of Australia'). He then has to carry on the argument in terms of a series of falsehoods. Since the point of the intention criterion is to shift attention from content. It is unfortunate that his examples suggest that what is true cannot be indoctrinated. His examples also deal with what the agent himself knows to be false or doubtful. He makes no allowance for the application of 'indoctrination' to the teaching of what is true and certain or to the teaching of what is false or doubtful when the agent does not know that it is false or doubtful.

These two criticisms are partially in opposition. On one hand, I criticize White because he seems to have 'indoctrination' cover the teaching of what is true and certain (mathematics, Latin, chemistry) and on the other, because he suggests that it does not. I seem to say that the analysis is both too strict and too lax. In the tension between these two positions the main problem of indoctrination lies. What has to be allowed for is (1) that it is *conceptually* possible to indoctrinate what is true and well established, and (2) that *in fact*, most of the

Source: Ivan A. Snook, *Indoctrination and Education*, Routledge & Kegan Paul, 1972, ch. 3.

time, we do not want to apply the term 'indoctrination' in these cases. An adequate analysis must be able to account for both these facts.

I suggest that the following provides a necessary and sufficient condition of indoctrination: *A person indoctrinates P (a proposition or set of propositions) if he teaches with the intention that the pupil or pupils believe P regardless of the evidence.*

This paper will be devoted to explicating the various sections of this 'definition' and to showing how it can account for the various facets we have so far considered.

Indoctrination and teaching

To separate 'teaching' and 'indoctrination' is I think mistaken conceptually and dangerous in practice. Far from it being the case that 'teaching' excludes 'indoctrination', there is a *necessary* or *conceptual* relationship between them.

There is an ambiguity about 'teaching' which is important in the analysis of indoctrination. A small child may teach his mother, or a student teach his professor. Yet we would not say that the child indoctrinated his mother or the student his professor, regardless of the nature of the belief or the method used. Similarly, we can say that I taught the class a particular theorem on Tuesday afternoon: 'indoctrination' seems to resist close specification of time.

The reason for this is that 'teach' can refer to any intentional attempt to foster learning but that its other and more usual use is narrower. In the narrower sense, it suggests: (1) that the person teaching stands in a special relationship to the person taught, a relationship of some authority which gives the teacher a privileged role in the transaction; (2) that there are teaching activities extended over a period of time. The noun 'teacher' captures this better than the verb. We do not call someone a teacher simply because on an occasion he 'teaches' someone something.

'Indoctrination' is related to this narrower sense of teach. It implies (1) some degree of authority–control and (2) performance extended over time. In the formula given above, 'teaches' should be understood in this way.

This connection with 'teaching' helps to solve certain problems which continually crop up in discussions of indoctrination. For example, it has been suggested that a person who engages in an argument with a friend on a contentious issue might be an indoctrinator. Gregory and Woods (1970: p. 103) tell us that the two authors split company on the question whether or not a devout Catholic who tries to convince another person of the truth of the Catholic religion must be an indoctrinator. They parted company on the question because one argued that this could be done rationally while the other said it could not. Surely they both missed the point. The answer must be 'no' because 'indoctrination' does not figure in *any* interplay of ideas but only in teaching situations. Certainly if all attempts to persuade others in contentious issues constitute indoctrination, most of us are indoctrinators. In fact, however, there is a world of difference between arguing a case in the drawing room, the philosophy seminar, or the executive suite and arguing it before one's students.

We might even (though with some hesitation) go further and suggest that 'indoctrination' is restricted to what is done to children. Perhaps the notion of indoctrinating adults makes little sense unless (1) it is the continuation of a process begun in youth *or* (2) special psychological weapons are used, making 'brainwashing' an appropriate term.

Even more absurd are the scruples of Gregory and Woods that they themselves might be indoctrinating in their article on indoctrination (1970: p. 103). If one can indoctrinate by writing a paper directed to one's academic colleagues, then it seems evident that the concept has been stretched beyond recognition. Part of this distortion can be attributed to their stress on doctrines: if any reliance on doctrine constitutes indoctrination then there *are* problems with any presentation of controversial statements. This is one reason why the notion of doctrines cannot be central to the concept. The other source of confusion is the neglect of the intimate connection with teaching. There is a distinction to be drawn between what we are entitled to say to our colleagues and what we can legitimately say to those who are our students.

Teaching and intentions

The phrase 'with the intention' leads us to examine the concept of 'intention'. 'Intention' is a difficult term to analyse since it is used in many different contexts, each of which has its own problems. It is used here in the context of moral evaluation: only if there is the intention to impart beliefs regardless of the evidence can we apply the term 'indoctrination'. This moral context helps us to specify more accurately the phrase 'with the intention'. In the context of moral responsibility, 'intention' can connote (1) what is desired, and (2) what is foreseen as likely. Thus, I want to argue that a person is indoctrinating if (1) in his teaching he is actively desiring that the pupils believe what he is teaching regardless of the evidence, or (2) he foresees that as a result of his teaching such an outcome is likely or inevitable. That is, there is a strong and a weak sense of 'intend' (and 'intention') and the concept of indoctrination includes both.

In everyday usage, 'intention' is often restricted to the strong sense. We commonly use 'intention' to refer only to what we want to do, not to the inevitable by-products of what we do. If I am hammering nails, and disturbing the neighbours, it is legitimate to ask what I am doing. My answer ('fixing the fence') specifies my intention and you may then say 'he does not intend to disturb the neighbours'. However, if the consequences involve harm to someone, it then becomes appropriate to speak of intentionally causing the harm even if I do not in any way desire that harm. If I persist in firing a rifle in a populated area, the fact that I intend (strong sense) to shoot birds does not excuse me if I should kill or injure a human being. It can be said that since I foresaw that possibility, I intentionally brought it about. It is my contention that the results of indoctrination are a matter for moral concern, and to act with the realization that they will follow is to act intentionally and so render the agent liable to moral criticism.

Arguments against intentions as the criterion

A number of objections can be raised to this criterion of intention and my rendering of it.

1 It might be objected that there are cases which we would term indoctrination which this criterion does not cover. The following examples might be suggested:

a   A mediaeval teacher is teaching that the world is flat. He is not intending (strong sense) that the pupils hold false beliefs nor does he foresee this. And yet, they are being led to hold beliefs which evidence does not support: they are being indoctrinated. To this, the reply must surely be: how is 'indoctrination' relevant here? The matter is not disputed, the evidence that exists confirms what is being taught. Why call it indoctrination *in any sense*? To accuse the mediaeval teacher of indoctrinating when no evidence contrary to his beliefs was available would be rather like accusing a nineteenth-century doctor of malpractice because he did not prescribe penicillin. In short, any reply to this example is that it would be unreasonable to call it indoctrination and hence the criterion is unaffected.

b   A more difficult problem is raised by the case of a person working within a system in which certain ideas are generally accepted as beyond question, although in a wider connection they are subject to dispute. Examples would be a Communist teacher in a Communist country, a Catholic teacher in a Catholic school, a racist teacher in a racist community. It will be objected that these people can be called indoctrinators despite the fact that they can claim that they do not desire or foresee that their beliefs will be held 'regardless of the evidence', for they have no reason to think that there is anything wrong with the evidence. I want to leave for a later section the problems associated with the connection between evidence and consensus but the objection against 'intention' as a criterion has to be dealt with here.

The problem, in brief, is this. An observer outside the system calls it 'indoctrination' (and in a pejorative sense). Yet an indoctrinating intention does not seem to be present. The intention criterion is, therefore, faulty.

The following lines of defence are open:

a   It could be said that in these cases a full-blown intention *is* present, i.e. the teachers in the system are devoted to the cause and their main intention is that the beliefs be held. The evidence they give is secondary to the main purpose – the handing on of certain beliefs. So, they do in fact intend that the pupils believe P regardless of the evidence, although they are unaware of any evidence to the contrary.

b   The observer's charge of indoctrination can be viewed as an ascription of responsibility. Standing outside the system and aware of the insufficiency of the evidence, he judges that the inevitable result of the teaching will be that the pupils will hold beliefs for which the evidence is dubious. Consequently, he accuses the teacher of indoctrinating. It is rather like an observer who describes someone as a thief. The accused can then attempt to rebut the charge by reference to the facts ('these things are mine'), or to his state of mind ('I did not know they belonged to someone'). Similarly, the person accused of indoctrination can argue that because of his lack of knowledge, he could not be said to be acting intentionally. If the charge is valid, he then becomes aware of what he is doing, and if he continues, the charge of indoctrination is applicable in the full sense. He now foresees the results and 'intention' becomes appropriate.

At this point, my critic might argue that in 'solving' his initial problems two further ones have opened up.

2   'Come on now,' he might say, 'you insisted that intentions could save the day. Now you write content and method into *your* notion of intention. How is your analysis in any way superior to any other?'

It is true that my notion of intention is grounded on what and how the teacher teaches. I would deny, however, that it is just another way of talking about content, method, or consequences. It has the advantage over these in that it can subsume any one of these singly or two or more of them conjointly. For example, if a teacher sets out to win a class for Christianity or 'democracy', he is indoctrinating because of his intention (strong sense) even if his method is totally 'rational'. If a teacher twists the evidence for his own purposes, he is indoctrinating, even if the content is quite undisputed. His intention (strong sense) is indoctrinatory although the content might seem to be excluded from that label. If a person in good faith teaches in such a way that the students are led to hold strong views on disputed issues, the charge is again appropriate because of the consequences which are intended (weak sense). That is to say, the intention is detected in content, method, or consequences but is not equivalent to any particular one, or any particular combination.

3   Another critic could argue that the intention criterion is totally useless. 'Surely,' he might say, 'the best judge of someone's intention is the agent himself. But you have suggested or implied that in some cases the agent may not even know he has the intention.'

I would agree that in normal circumstances the agent is the best judge of his intentions. However, this is not so where moral criticism is involved. 'I gave my excuse,' says the schoolboy. 'You lied,' says the teacher. 'I am resting,' says the employee. 'You are wasting time,' says her boss. 'I'm having a fling,' says the gay husband. 'You are being unfaithful,' says his frank friend. Each gives a description of sorts, the observer merely adding a moral criticism. Similarly with indoctrination. A person *might* say 'I am indoctrinating' but normally he would not. Indoctrination is intentional but the intention need not be one to indoctrinate in the sense that he would answer 'indoctrinating' when asked what he was doing. He would normally state his intention as one to teach.

This brings out again the connection between teaching and indoctrination. 'Indoctrination' is inappropriate unless the agent is teaching. This rules out chance happenings, unconscious influence, and events over which the agent has no control: indoctrination involves intention. However, because of the pejorative nature of 'indoctrination', the agent is not the best judge of what he is doing.

Indoctrination and beliefs

The indoctrinator teaches with the intention that the pupil or pupils *believe* P. This aspect brings home the point that indoctrination is concerned with beliefs. Crittenden (1968) found in his search of several dictionaries that their one point of agreement was that all implied that 'indoctrination' is inappropriate in reference to behaviour. Expressions such as 'indoctrinated to clean their teeth', 'indoctrinated to salute the flag', 'indoctrinated with etiquette' are a misuse of the term. Where behaviour is uppermost, the term 'conditioning' or 'training' is more normally used.

Indoctrination is concerned with propositional knowledge (knowing *that*), with statements which can be true or false. When the charge of indoctrination is made it is appropriate to ask what beliefs are involved.

This distinction can help in the solution of the problem of the moral training of the young child. This involves the inculcation of habits rather than beliefs and the term 'indoctrination' is not appropriate. In so far as morality becomes a matter of beliefs ('because it is your duty', 'because God wills it'), the intention criterion must come into play: is this a step towards evidentially held beliefs or is it the beginnning of the inculcation of one set of beliefs? In the latter case, the term 'indoctrination' becomes appropriate.

Indoctrination and evidence

I have argued that the indoctrinator intends that the pupil believes P 'regardless of the evidence'. In full-blown cases of intention, this captures very well the difference between the indoctrinator and the educator. For the educator, the beliefs are always secondary to the evidence: he wants his students to end up with whatever beliefs the evidence demands. He is concerned with methods of assessing data, standards of accuracy, and validity of reasoning. The answers are subsidiary to the methods of gaining answers. The indoctrinator, however, is typically most concerned with the imparting of the beliefs: these are what he strives to hand on. It is the evidence that is of subsidiary importance. The indoctrinator will himself make use of evidence, logic, and proof – but it is a *use of*, in order to further his aim: the beliefs are more important than the evidence.

313

The cavalier treatment of evidence is exemplified most obviously in those systems which are called ideologies. Corbett (1965: pp. 121–3) has documented this aspect of Marxism. In Marxist social theory, the proletariat (wage earners) is seen as an oppressed class, growing poorer until it inevitably spearheads revolution. When the facts turn out otherwise, the claim is not denied but simply reinterpreted. When it is established that the workers are getting richer not poorer, the Marxist answers that *relatively* they are getting poorer. When it is suggested that in some countries workers are not oppressed, the reply is that they are oppressed in more subtle ways. Remark that the peasants, not the proletariat, have spearheaded revolution, and the 'proletariat' is redefined as 'the workers and peasants'.

Roman Catholicism, another 'ideological' system, adopts similar tactics. The claim is made that the Church cannot make a mistake about faith or morals and cannot therefore change a ruling on these matters. Point to an obvious change (usury was once condemned and is now accepted) and the reply is either that this was not a matter of morals or that the teaching did not change: something else changed (the nature of money). The Pope is infallible. Pius IX condemned the proposition that men are free to worship according to their conscience; Vatican II affirmed this freedom. Solution: Pius IX was not being infallible on this matter. The result is that evidence can never go against the claim: *any* evidence is compatible with the claim.

Examples of ideological thinking can also be found within psychology. A strict behaviourist asserts that 'all learning occurs by means of reinforcement' and means to assert something quite significant. Point out that a child seems to learn some words solely by imitation and the reply is that the child is being reinforced 'automatically'. Indicate that we frequently keep on at a task just because it is hard to solve, and the behaviourist answers that care in problem solving is 'self-reinforcing' (Chomsky 1959: p. 37). In due course, the term 'reinforcement' becomes so attenuated that the original claim is empty. The behaviourist (like the Marxist or Catholic) can *always* sustain his case by rewriting it to suit the evidence or by reinterpreting the evidence so that the case remains untouched.

In an ideology, the claims are more important than the evidence. Small wonder that when an ideology is being taught, evidence plays only a minor role. We do associate indoctrination with ideologies and with good reason. The misuse (not necessarily the suppression or denial) of evidence is one of the main reasons why this is so.

Criticism of the evidence criterion

If it is granted that the manner in which ideologies use evidence is to be deplored, the question can be raised as to the role of evidence in other matters. The following criticisms might be made of the attempt to link 'indoctrination' so closely with the concept of 'evidence'.

1   The connection can be criticized on the grounds that the concept of evidence finds its place in empirical claims. The notion of evidence is inappropriate for example in mathematics and morality. Here we seek for logical argument, deductive proof, and good reasons. We do not demand evidence. Hence, the argument runs, my analysis of indoctrination cannot cover cases where proof or good reasons rather than evidence are required.

   Two strategies are open to us:

a   We can go along with this and assert that indoctrination *is* restricted to factual claims about the world and that where evidence is inappropriate, the notion of indoctrination is also out of place. Hence we could not talk of indoctrinating mathematics or morals. This reply works rather well for mathematics, which is a self-contained system of axioms and demonstrations. For morals, it works to some extent: morals are concerned with behaviour and to that extent 'indoctrination' is not apposite. On the other hand, many of the reasons given for a moral decision are empirical claims ('this will injure him') and the evidence criterion *is* appropriate. However, it is almost certainly true that ultimately there is a gap between facts and values: moral reasoning has a style and validity of its own and evidence is only partly a cogent factor (people can agree on the evidence and still *logically* disagree about what is to be done). The handing on of moral points of view seems to be open to the charge of indoctrination even though 'evidence' does not seem to fit.

b   A second possible strategy is that used by Scheffler in his discussion of the evidence criterion in analyses of 'know' (Scheffler 1965: p. 59). The objection can be met, he suggests, by construing 'evidence' as including proofs and reasons in the areas in which these are more appropriate than evidence in the strict sense. A person has adequate evidence for Q when he has good reasons for believing Q. What 'good reasons' consist of will vary with the subject concerned.

2   It might also be objected by one of strong philosophical bent that evidence cannot be had for any proposition and that the demand that people hold their beliefs on the basis of evidence is an unrealistic one. This objection might be stated in the following ways. (1) The demand that a belief be based on evidence leads to an infinite regress: for we must have adequate evidence for accepting the evidence, etc., etc.: i.e. we believe P because of Z, Z because of Y, Y because of X, and so on. (2) Empirical propositions are at best *probable*: there is no certainty in any knowledge which is gained by means of induction.

   This is not the place to enter into the philosophical justification of knowledge itself. Nor is it necessary. What we are interested in is an investigation of an educational problem and this sets limits which entitle us to avoid the deeper issue. Machan (1970: p. 262) has argued for an epistemology of education and although some of his assertions are open to serious question he does stress that education requires an account of the evolutionary nature of human knowledge. In brief, what is vitally necessary is some understanding of what can be legitimately taught at any particular stage in history. In our terms, we need some convention, according to which we can meaningfully say that teaching X was not indoctrination last century, but is today. We want, further, a criterion which as far as possible is neutral towards the various philosophical positions. If one's account of indoctrination rests on a particular view of reality and knowledge, it will be open for others to reject it if they hold a different metaphysical or epistemological view.

Evidence and the schools

It would be pretentious to suppose that in a discussion of this nature I could map out anything approximating to an 'epistemology of education', but something has to be said or else the criterion of evidence will not be useful in the analysis of 'indoctrination'.

I would argue that schools are concerned not so much with 'truth' (over which men differ philosophically and factually) but with what is 'established' by those who are regarded as competent in the area in question. This does not mean that the man in the street has no part to play at all. He plays his role by the acceptance of certain experts as experts. A proposition in chemistry is supported by evidence if those who study chemistry accept this evidence; the layman's acceptance of such men as experts justifies his acceptance of their authority and justifies the teacher's teaching even if he himself is not in a position to evaluate the evidence. However, if the biologists were to agree that biological warfare is militarily justified, this would not constitute evidence since they are not regarded as experts in *that*. That is to say, evidence is related to consensus, although truth is not.

It might be objected at this point that if my analysis is accepted the classroom teacher cannot safely teach anything. Even in mathematics or physics there are controversies on the boundaries of the discipline, and in subjects such as history and literature, there are always current and well-known disputes. The teacher may not be aware of these or, if he is, may judge that they are too subtle for the age or intelligence of those he is concerned with. In so far as a dispute belongs only to the higher reaches of the subject, the teacher cannot be held responsible for not conveying it. He neither desires nor foresees that the pupils will believe regardless of the evidence, and he cannot be accused of indoctrinating.

When the doubt is integral to the study even at the level the teacher is concerned with, it could be argued that the teacher *should* be aware of it. However, there is so much that a teacher ideally 'should' be familiar with that we are inclined to be cautious about demanding such requirements on pain of moral fault.

The point being made is this: while many things are desirable in teaching, criticisms such as 'you are indoctrinating him' cannot rest on these idealistic requirements. They must be based on minimal demands. I would assert therefore that the teacher at any level is at least bound to take account of those matters in which the doubtful validity of the evidence is common knowledge in the community: political, social, and religious statements are doubtful in this sense. Indoctrination is most likely to occur in these areas.

Intention and motive

A brief discussion of motive is necessary for four reasons:

1   the possession of a good motive does not excuse one from the charge of indoctrination;
2   the fact that a particular teacher has a motive for indoctrinating does not entitle us to say that he is indoctrinating;
3   however, the possession of a motive is strongly suggestive of the possibility of indoctrination, and the teacher with such a motive should take particular care; and
4   it is unlikely that a person is indoctrinating if he has no conceivable motive for doing so.

I have attempted to distinguish intention from motive by suggesting that intention specifies what the teacher is doing, motive explains why he is doing it. There are cases in which this distinction will not hold up and some would argue that the logical distinction cannot be sustained. Nevertheless, it is a useful distinction in the analysis of indoctrination.

Wilson (1966: pp. 391–2) confuses the two. He argues that the teacher's aim (intention) cannot be the criterion of indoctrination since a person might think that it is right to indoctrinate children with certain myths in order to give them security, 'and however liberal the aim or intention, it would still be indoctrination'. On my distinction, this is a misguided objection. It is clear that what the teacher intends is that these myths be believed. The motive (security) is irrelevant to the charge of indoctrination. Whether this teacher was indoctrinating or not would depend not on his motive for propounding the myths but on the nature of the myths. There is little likelihood of the child growing up with the belief that his father can cope with every problem in the world. Nor is the child likely to cling for ever to a belief in Father Christmas. Since the teacher neither intends nor foresees that there will be any long-term effect on the child's mind, the charge of indoctrination is not appropriate. On the other hand, unscientific notions about sex, dogmatic views of religion, and prejudices about social position are likely to persist and be inimical to the later considerations of evidence. If one taught these 'myths', with the knowledge of their doubtful status, he would be indoctrinating. The motive for propounding the myths has no effect on the charge of indoctrination.

Holbrook (1963: p. 111), writing about the teaching of religion in universities, protests against the tendency for other faculty members to charge professors of religion with indoctrinating without providing any warrant for the charge. The charge, he argues, is frequently gratuitous 'since suspicion of motive is neither evidence nor proof of the charge.' This is certainly correct, although a subject like religion is suspect because it is not clear what else the teacher can intend other than belief or commitment. Nevertheless, something more is required for sheeting home the charge of indoctrination than the fact that the teacher has a motive.

An interesting illustration of this is provided by an actual case (*A.A.U.P. Bulletin* 1967: pp. 278–91). The administration of a university hired a sociology professor, knowing that he had strong Marxist sympathies. He was subsequently dismissed on the following grounds: (1) Marx was the only reading prescribed for his courses; (2) his examinations covered only polemical questions; and (3) he had announced his intention to continue to teach in this manner. The administration concluded, with some justification, that he was indoctrinating. The reader will notice how the criteria I outlined are operating: (1) he had a motive (he was a Marxist); (2) his style of teaching gave evidence of an intention (weak sense, at least); and (3) he admitted an intention (strong sense).

We might profitably compare this case with two hypothetical cases. Suppose another Marxist were to give fair consideration to other social theorists: the motive would not be grounds for assuming an indoctrinating intention. What about a non-Marxist who also restricted his reading list to Marx on the grounds that he had found this the best way to launch into a discussion of social theory: in the absence of any motive for indoctrinating Marxism, we might accept that no reprehensible intention was involved.

So, in actual cases in which indoctrination is alleged, the application of the intention criterion will require skill. Nevertheless, it is argued, the intention of the teacher is the crucial factor.

Some cases

Any analysis of indoctrination must take account of cases which actually occur in an educational setting. It must clearly cover those cases which are recognized as indoctrination, must exclude those which we do not want to label indoctrination, and provide a way of handling the doubtful cases in a consistent and useful manner.

1   Cases which are clearly indoctrination:

   a   Teaching an ideology as if it were the only one with any claim to rationality.
   b   Teaching, as if they are certain, propositions which the teacher knows are uncertain.
   c   Teaching propositions which the teacher knows to be false.

2   Cases which may seem like indoctrination but which are not:

   a   Teaching young children acceptable behaviour.
   b   Teaching facts (the tables, or Latin verbs) by rote.
   c   Influencing the child unconsciously.

3   Problematic cases:

   a   Inculcating beliefs which the teacher believes are certain but which are substantially disputed.
   b   Teaching any subject without due concern for understanding.

On the criterion I have put forward, all cases under 1 are adequately covered. The teacher intends fixed beliefs, in the strong sense. If he denies such an intention, he can be shown that it is an area of doubt and uncertainty (at the very least) and that what he is doing is sure to result in fixed beliefs. Once alerted, he can foresee the outcome and 'indoctrination' is appropriate. A rough guide to his intention will often be the attitude he takes towards one who rejects these beliefs. If this rejection is seen as a failure, a rejection of all he has taught, he has been indoctrinating.

Case 2a is ruled out: beliefs and evidence are not relevant to this early training and the question of indoctrination does not arise. Case 2b is excluded since there is little chance of the tables or verbs impairing the child's later assessment of evidence ('evidence' is not really relevant to things like tables or verbs anyway). Since there are no consequences liable for moral review, intention does not arise as an issue. Case 2c is ruled out because unconscious influences are (by definition) not intentional.

Case 3a is a case of indoctrination if the teacher knows that the beliefs are disputed: he foresees that what he is teaching is likely to be believed despite the fact that the evidence is inconclusive. Case 3b might be indoctrination if (1) there were positive intent to make the child incapable of impartial appraisal of the subject or (2) non-rational methods were so consistently used as to lead to contempt for the evidence. The charge could always be rebutted by showing that both (1) there was no intention (strong sense); this might be done by showing there was no motive; and (2) in the main, rational methods were used. This line of defence is open also to the busy teacher who must often neglect to give reasons; the overall intention is the key.

In this way there is provision for a distinction of content on the grounds of whether fixed beliefs are more or less appropriate. There is also scope for the realization that dogmatic teaching even of an exact science can warp the students' thought.

Conclusion

'Indoctrination' implies a pejorative judgment on a teaching situation. It suggests that someone is taking advantage of a privileged role to influence those under his charge in a manner which is likely to distort their ability to assess the evidence on its own merit. The positive intention to bring about this state of mind is sufficient for the application of the term to his teaching, even if he should fail in his task: 'indoctrination' is both a task and an achievement word. Such a desire is not necessary, however, if it is foreseen that this state of mind is likely as a result of what is being done. In all cases, some action must be intentional in the strong sense. A person cannot indoctrinate if he is not doing anything intentional at all: one cannot indoctrinate by omission. One can be held responsible for omissions, but 'indoctrination' is not an appropriate term for them.

Intentions are paramount but content and method are important. From a consideration of method, an observer can detect the intention to indoctrinate. Content is important because not all content is equally susceptible to indoctrination. Drill in Latin verbs is far less likely than drill in patriotic sentiments to result in 'beliefs regardless of the evidence'. Doctrines in the sense of ideologies are not essential to the concept but they often provide the motive for indoctrination. Because we find it difficult to imagine a motive for indoctrinating physics we tend to exclude the teaching of such subjects from indoctrination. I have argued that the concept can include them, but a motive is needed to explain why anyone would want to indoctrinate them.

Bibliography

A.A.U.P. Bulletin (1967), 'Academic freedom and tenure: Adelphi University'. 53, September.

Chomsky, N. (1959), Review of B.F. Skinner's *Verbal Behaviour in Language*, 35: 1.

Corbett, J.P. (1965), *Ideologies*, London: Hutchinson.

Crittenden, Brian S. (1968), 'Teaching, educating and indoctrinating', *Educational Theory*, 18, Summer, 237–52.

Gregory, I.M.M. and Woods, R.G. (1970), 'Indoctrination', *Proceedings of the Annual Conference, January*, Philosophy of Education Society of Great Britain, 77–105.

Holbrook, C.A. (1963), *Religion: A Humanistic Field*, Englewood Cliffs, NJ: Prentice-Hall.

Machan, J.R. (1970), 'Education and the philosophy of knowledge', *Educational Theory*, 20, Summer.

Scheffler, I. (1965), *Conditions of Knowledge: An Introduction to Epistemology and Education*, Chicago: Scott Foresman.

White, J.P. (1967), 'Indoctrination', R.S. Peters (ed.) *The Concept of Education*, Routledge and Kegan Paul.

Wilson, J. (1966), 'Comment on Flew's "What is indoctrination?"' *Studies in Philosophy and Education*, IV, Summer, 390–5.

(ii) ON THE CONCEPT OF
INDOCTRINATION

Henry Rosemont Jr

Certain issues are difficult to treat simultaneously from the vantage points of philosophy and education. The disinterestedness with which the philosopher is supposed to confront problems may in some cases be construed as an unjustifiable lack of concern for the immediacy of an issue as it must be faced by the educator. At present (and perhaps at all times), indoctrination is an issue of this kind.

In theory it should be possible to treat the concept of indoctrination philosophically in a general and abstract way, using analytic methods, with a minimum of subjectivity; but in fact the difficulties Americans are having in facing up to the ugly realities of Vietnam, racism, and poverty show clearly that the public schools – in consonance with other institutions – have generated and perpetuated an idealized account of America's past and present which can only be characterized as indoctrination.

The issue is thus an immediate one for the American educator: the continuance of a 'U.S.A. über alles' type of indoctrination severely cripples the ability of the American people to come to grips with the manifold evils that confront and threaten to destroy them and is therefore a dangerous roadblock to the quest for a more decent and humane society. And the immediacy of this issue easily causes the philosopher discomfort because it blurs the distinction between his being disinterested and his being uninterested; indeed, it suggests that his aura of objectivity is illusory. Again in theory, the philosopher's nonpartisan attitude, if attainable, is considered an important and desirable step down the road to Utopia; but whether attainable or not the step is of little moment if in fact we are in the suburbs of Armageddon.

The above remarks may be disputed by philosophers and educators alike. I will attempt to provide some justification for them in the pages to follow; they are offered at the outset so that the reader may at least understand, if not appreciate, the perspective from which this response to Mr Snook's paper was written.[1] No claim of disinterest is made herein, and none is intended. If Mr

Source: *Studies in Philosophy and Education*, 1972, Vol. VII, No. 3.

Snook's concept of indoctrination is correct the analysis has little to tell us about what is wrong with the public schools, and even less to tell us about improving them. It seems to me, however, that the concept of indoctrination is crucial for understanding and alleviating our educational maladies, and therefore I believe it is important to show how and why his analysis is mistaken.[2] Several points of more narrowly philosophical interest wil be taken up in the footnotes.

A fundamental point of disagreement between Mr Snook and myself lies in the importance he attaches to intention in determining indoctrination. He proffers the following as a *necessary* (and sufficient) condition for applying the term: '*A person indoctrinates P (a proposition or set of propositions) if he teaches with the intention that the pupil or pupils believe P regardless of the evidence*' (100; Snook's italics). A direct implication of this criterion is that if there is a person X such that X has been indoctrinated, then there must be another person Y such that: (1) Y is a teacher of X; (2) Y has a specific intent; (3) Y's intent is morally blameworthy. Because of this implication Snook must reject my characterization of the public schools as institutions of indoctrination, for that characterization – when coupled with his criterion – entails that the vast majority of public school teachers have engaged in morally deplorable acts, and I assume that Mr Snook no less than myself is reluctant to affirm such a conclusion.

The argument can be put another way. If Mr Snook's criterion is correct, and if very few teachers act from malevolent motives, then there is no large-scale indoctrination going on in the public schools. I adhere to my characterization but refuse to hold an almost totally misanthropic view of teachers; therefore, I must reject his criterion (as he would undoubtedly reject my characterization).[3] More specifically I am rejecting his emphasis on intention as the crucial determinant in deciding whether or not an act of indoctrination has taken place.

One reason that he gives such weight to intention (as he correctly points out in the beginning of his paper) is the fact that the term *indoctrination* always has pejorative connotations, that we deplore all instances of indoctrination. But to move from this observation to a dominant focus on intention obscures the important point that we often deplore actions or events without holding anyone responsible for their occurrence. Thus any event described by (substituting into) the sentential function 'X was killed' will undoubtedly be deplored, but in many cases no one will be found guilty of *moral* wrongdoing. 'By accident', 'In a case of justifiable homicide', 'While charging the enemy position', and so on, would all be descriptions of such cases.

By parity of argument it seems that we can also deplore all actions described by 'X was indoctrinated' without at the same time always finding someone with a morally culpable intention. Hence we can agree with Snook that all forms of the word *indoctrination* have pejorative connotations, but deny that there must always be a person or persons whose intentions are deserving of our moral pejorations.

This same point can be seen in another light by an example. Teachers A and B each teach a set of students A' and B', respectively. Teacher A has the indoctrination intention and strongly advocates a set of propositions which he knows are not true; as a result, students A' are (become) indoctrinated. Teacher

B teaches exactly the same set of propositions in the same way, with the same results. Enter two qualifications: (1) Teacher B believes the propositions are true; (2) He does not believe his teaching methods will lead students B' to believe those propositions 'regardless of the evidence'. Now if someone asks why students A' think and act as they do, it would be correct to say, 'Because they were indoctrinated'. But what of students B' who think and act in the same way, and do so because they were taught by teacher B? Clearly they, too, have been indoctrinated, and teacher B has functioned as an indoctrinator even though his intentions may have been most praiseworthy.

This example illustrates two important points. First, it shows that when considering task-achievement terms like *indoctrination* we must look not only at the actors but also at the acted upon; and if the acted upon have been indoctrinated, then there must be an indoctrinating actor – lack of intention notwithstanding. Secondly, the example shows that the charge of indoctrination is not solely a *moral* charge; our pejorations can also involve the teacher's professional competence or intellectual capabilities. Putting these two points together, if students A' and B' think and behave in the same way and their behaviors are due to the same causes (i.e., they were formally taught), and if 'indoctrination' correctly describes the one case, it correctly describes the other, and both teachers are indoctrinators subject to criticism. What we criticize and deplore, however, will not be the same in both cases; with teacher A we criticize and deplore his moral turpitude, whereas in the case of teacher B the opprobrium is directed at his professional ineptness or his intellectual inadequacies.

In just the same way, we can withhold moral judgment on public school teachers – in the USSR, China, and other countries as well as the United States – while at the same time maintaining that most or all of them are liable to the charge of indoctrinating the young in their respective countries. On this account, then, teachers must be willing to assume professional and intellectual as well as moral responsibility for what and how they teach. They are, after all, professionals, and looked upon as intellectuals. Snook, however, has a rather different view of teachers.

> Teachers are specifically concerned with ideas, beliefs, facts, propositions: their job is to impart knowledge. It is a hazard of such an occupation that some pupils will hold beliefs regardless of the evidence, and to an outsider such results will often be in some sense foreseeable. *To hold the teacher guilty of indoctrination in these cases would stultify his whole work. It would be safer for him to impart no knowledge and so avoid any suspicion of indoctrination.*
>
> (103; italics mine)

But the extent of teacher temerity is clearly an empirical question; perhaps teachers will indeed cower at the prospect of accountability, but there is no way of telling in advance whether they might not feel and behave more like individuals and less like tools if they were allowed to assume full responsibility for their pedagogic actions. (I will return to this point at the end of the paper.)

To strengthen the case for taking the whole teacher and pupil relationship into account when discussing indoctrination it will be useful to examine a few of Snook's cases in some detail. Snook excludes the teaching of correct behavior to children from the concept of indoctrination: 'if the teacher sincerely desires that the child exercise his critical faculties in disputed areas and provides the best reasons he can when these become acceptable to the child' (105).[4] It might be noted first of all that the notion of 'correct' does not have any direct relevance to Snook's intention criterion. As long as the requisite desire is present, it does not make any difference whether correct or incorrect behavior is being taught; in neither case can the teacher be liable to the charge of indoctrination if intention is paramount (necessary). On the other hand, if correctness is really at issue, what is needed is some standard of correctness and not an investigation into the teacher's desires.

Moreover, introducing the concept of indoctrination into a discussion of correct behavior shows that not all early training can be excused as social conditioning, a point which Snook de-emphasizes: 'Whatever the final verdict on the methods in *Brave New World*, it is clear that much of this sort of training does consist in social conditioning rather than in indoctrination' (83). True enough; but to say that *much* of this training is social conditioning is a long way from saying that *all* of it is. Certain attitudes and behavior that are taught will limit the educational experiences of the pupils, making it difficult or impossible for them to consider certain subjects on the merits of those subjects alone; and to the extent that these attitudes and behavior are caused by the teacher, the relevant pedagogic acts are instances of indoctrination. But obviously some attitudes and behavioral patterns are taught without reference to any particular proposition or set thereof (as, e.g. pledging allegiance to the flag in the primary grades), so on Snook's grounds any teacher focusing on inculcating behavior (have respect for authority and symbols thereof) could avoid a charge of indoctrination simply by denying that she intended to have the children hold any *specific* beliefs regardless of the evidence.[5]

As Snook points out in another context, two people might describe the same event differently (104). In questioning a teacher about what she is doing, she might reply, 'I am teaching the children the correct behavior.' Our description, however, might be, 'You are indoctrinating them.' Admitting that a teacher's intentions will not always allow us to decide a case of indoctrination – it is difficult to imagine that the teacher would say or believe that she intended to teach incorrect behavior – Snook must fall back on another test, namely whether untoward effects on the children can be foreseen by the teacher (105).[6] This test is important, for it shows not only that intention alone is insufficient for determining indoctrination, it also shows clearly that moral responsibility is not the sole issue involved in the pejorative application of the term. In response to further interrogation the teacher in our example above can assert there is only a 15 percent probability that the children will be affected adversely by her teaching techniques. We might reply (if such were the case) that the probability was actually 85 percent, but now we are no longer calling the teacher's ethical motives into question; it is her professional competence that is under examination. And how do we know when to question a teacher's competence or intelligence? – in the same way that we know when to question his or her morality: whenever we believe indoctrination is going on.

Another case taken up by Snook reinforces this conclusion. He maintains that influencing a child unconsciously in certain directions is not indoctrination, because *ex hypothesi* the acts are unconscious, and hence the crucial intent is missing (105). But a lack of awareness about what one is doing does not always absolve the person of responsibility – moral or otherwise – for the consequences of his actions. To return to our hapless teacher B, suppose that he unconsciously influences some children to think and act precisely like other children who have been influenced by an intentional indoctrinator. Again we must describe all the children as indoctrinated, and teacher B is an indoctrinator, unconsciously or not. Further, a parent who subtly but not willfully influences his child to look upon the members of another ethnic group as inferior may avoid opprobrium by saying he was not conscious of what he was doing, but this defense is not always open to the teacher, except perhaps to avoid a charge of racism; for the rest, the teacher might well be held responsible for the child's attitudes because as a professional the teacher is expected to have a fairly sophisticated knowledge of how and why children are influenced in various ways.

As a final illustration of the extent to which indoctrination involves questions of teacher competence and intelligence no less than morals, we may consider Snook's case 3a: inculcating beliefs believed by the teacher to be certain, but which are substantially disputed. His comment here is that 'case 3a is a case of indoctrination provided the teacher knows that the beliefs are substantially disputed' (105). Now every philosopher knows that there is no belief or view that will not be disputed by someone, so 'substantially' is a key term in this case. Fundamentalists deny Darwin's views; does this mean the teacher cannot inculcate the theory of evolution? Perhaps he can, because few fundamentalists are biologists (i.e., they are not 'experts'). But what of Lamarck and Lysenko?[7] Do their writings provide 'substantive' disagreement to the view that evolutionary change in a species is a function of random genetic mutation? Pass to genetic differences between ethnic groups. Does Jensen provide grounds for seriously disputing the view that there are no genetic differences with respect to cognitive capacities between the races?[8] Worse, was it proper in 1965 for a teacher to inculcate support for the policies of the United States in Vietnam because relatively few people disagreed with those policies, but is it now, in 1971, indoctrination because a majority of the American people believe those policies disastrously mistaken? I will return to these questions again; for now it must be noted that until the notion of 'substantially disputed' is tightened up considerably it would not seem possible for anyone ever to be found guilty of indoctrination – which may be a *reductio ad absurdum* argument against any criterion of indoctrination based on intention.[9]

By now it probably is obvious that whereas Mr Snook sees very little indoctrination going on, I see a great deal. Indeed, I would go further – with some of the progressivists – and maintain that it is not possible to teach without engaging in *some* indoctrination; therefore, the basic question is not whether to indoctrinate, but rather (1) how to minimize it and (2) which indoctrinating materials and methods of those which cannot be avoided will have the minimal mischievous consequences.

Snook, however, will have nothing to do with this phrasing of the question, for the thrust of it is to mitigate evil and he seems more anxious to promote the good; for him, indoctrination occurs but rarely, and with moral purification can be eliminated altogether. The discrepancy, however, between this conceptualization of indoctrination and the teaching prevalent in the schools is even noted by Snook on occasion, as for example when he says, 'The fact that all societies form their young in some desired image is a problem for anyone concerned about indoctrination' (69). Why is this a 'problem' except to the apologist? If all societies devote much time and energy to molding the ideas, attitudes, and behavior of their young in highly specific ways, then those responsible for the molding are indoctrinators, and the fact of indoctrination must be faced squarely and not analyzed away. Take another example: 'While consistent, Kilpatrick's discussion has a weakness: by locating the *meaning* of the term in method, Kilpatrick is forced to concede that some indoctrination is inevitable' (70; Snook's italics). This is a curious way of countering an argument. Kilpatrick offers several premises regarding method, from which the inevitability of indoctrination follows as a conclusion. Hence Snook should be showing what is wrong with one or more of Kilpatrick's premises; instead he merely says he does not like the conclusion. Again, if it is a fact that some indoctrination is inevitable everyone concerned about education should attend to the fact and not to the 'weakness' of critiques strong enough to point it out.

Snook is consistent in his efforts to exorcise the spectre of inevitable indoctrination from the educational host.

> A further complication arose from the realization that society forms individuals to a desired pattern. From this fact two corollaries were drawn: (a) Indoctrination is going on all the time in hosts of ways; b) To refuse to deal with controversial issues is to indoctrinate in the status quo.
>
> The first corollary merely confuses the issue; if all human education (in its broadest sense) is indoctrination there is no point in getting upset by the accusation of indoctrination. Such confusion can only be dispelled by insisting that 'indoctrination' is a term to be applied to certain human actions, and implying moral criticism of them.
>
> (73–4)

It has already been argued that 'indoctrination' does not only imply *moral* criticism; it can also imply a professional and intellectual challenge. Even more misleading, however, is Snook's contention that there is no reason to get upset about indoctrination if it is going on all the time.[10] If the great majority of students who come out of the American public schools think and act just like those few students who have been indoctrinated intentionally into believing their country holds a monopoly on virtue, beauty, truth, and industry, the great majority of teachers must be *doing* just what the intentional few are doing. Thus it is of the utmost importance to 'get upset' about this point if *teachers do not understand that they have ever engaged in indoctrination* (either as transmitters or receivers). By showing that and how teachers themselves have been indoctrinated, and indoctrinate in turn, we may facilitate a needed re-examination of textbooks, teacher views and attitudes, methods, and the social control function served by the schools.[11] This re-examination may lead to an alteration of the kinds of indoctrination that currently obtain; alterations which may, for instance, treat war as cruel and insane rather than necessary and occasionally glorious. Or alterations which create an intellectual and aesthetic environment such that the people who pass through it will forever find repugnant the use of terms like 'dink', 'nigger', 'like', and 'gook' in referring to other human beings.

Perhaps Mr Snook would endorse these and other suggested alternatives, but in order to do so he must accept the fact that the schools are not neutral with regard to social change (or social stagnation), and if I read him correctly he would be reluctant to accept this fact. In commenting on the second corollary quoted above he says:

> If there are two views on a social issue, one conservative and one liberal, refusal to consider the issue favors the conservative side. This surely is not a logical claim but an empirical one: to my knowledge there is no evidence to support it. It is an assumption which is freely asserted and can, therefore, be freely denied. As Ennis points out, if the school does not consider social problems, the liberal can claim that this is a vote for the status quo; the conservative can reply that it is a voice in favor of change since the school is failing to condemn socialism.
>
> (74)

This quotation contains three related errors. In the first place, it is interesting that Snook endorses Ennis's point about the conservative, because in the paragraph following this quotation he employs an argument which is effective against Ennis – but is not applied. In claiming that the omission of text materials does not usually constitute indoctrination Snook points out that if we ask 'When did I indoctrinate him?' the answer 'When you did not teach him X' is usually unacceptable (74–5).[12] With regard to Ennis we ask a similar question, 'When were the schools voices of social change?' And we get in response, 'When they did not condemn socialism.' In this case the conservative's argument can be defended against a charge of *petitio principii* only by claiming that it is *ignoratio elenchi*.

Second, what Ennis calls a 'claim' by the liberal might be a true empirical statement. To take one brief example from personal experience, a student member of the faculty senate at a small midwestern university brought up the subject of the purchase of table grapes by the school for use in the cafeterias in the dormitories.[13] A faculty member responded with the comment that the issue of the grape boycott was beyond the range of interest and competency of the university as a whole; therefore the university should not take a stand on the matter. It is clear, however, that the stand had already been taken for them, because the university was purchasing the grapes and, therefore, supporting the grape growers against the migrant workers (in the strongest sense of 'support', namely, the economic one). The issue, then, was not whether to take a stand on the matter, for that was a *fait accompli*; rather the issue was whether to continue to support the growers or stop purchasing grapes and thereby support (to a lesser extent) workers. This example clearly is not an isolated curiosity.

The third error is closely related to the second. The charge that refusal to consider an issue favors the conservative side is seen by Snook to be merely an empirical claim, which he says can be 'freely denied'. I do not know whether he will deny it as freely after taking cognizance of the above example, but more importantly, the charge is first and foremost a *logical* and not an empirical claim. Except for those matters determined by administrative fiat, proposed changes involving the schools must first be taken up and deliberated by an appropriate governing body (e.g., school board, faculty senate, PTA, etc.) before those changes can be effected. This is no more than to say that new policies do not spring full-grown from a chairman's gavel if rules and regulations are being followed. In more logical terms the point would be expressed: changes can occur in the schools if and only if those changes are first deliberated. It is, then, a logical equivalence, and by denying the right side of the equation (refuse to deliberate the issue), the conservative is simultaneously denying the left side as well (no changes can occur).[14]

It might be admitted at this point that the schools have never been neutral, but retorted that they can become so. Even if this possibility is granted for the sake of the argument we then face the question of whether the schools *should* be neutral, and here the 'neutralists' are faced with a dilemma. On the first horn, if they say the schools should not be neutral there is no longer any dispute between them and the partisans except about which side of a particular issue to take. On the other horn, if it is maintained that the schools should be neutral – admitting that they are not now in that position – what means can be found for making them neutral except to have them take a stand on an issue which demands social and institutional change?

It might appear that an escape from the second horn is possible by arguing that the schools are permitted to take stands on issues that relate to their own aims and purposes.[15] But the aims and purposes of the schools have never been widely agreed upon, nor have any aims and purposes, how ever narrowly decided, ever been divorced from the aims and purposes of the larger society. Until such agreement and possibility of separation is demonstrated we can be excused for suspecting that the answer to the question 'What are the issues which relate to the aims and purposes of the schools?' will be, 'Those issues on which the schools do not remain neutral.'

Continuing as a sceptic, then, I remain as unconvinced that the schools have ever been or can be neutral as I am unconvinced that they are or can be innocent of indoctrination; and to argue that they *should* be both neutral and innocent seems to me a plea for privileged sanctuary at best, and at worst, a clear indication that an integral part of the disease has been mistaken for the cure.

To conclude on a more positive note, it does seem to be possible, with great personal effort, to have the school function in such a way as to enhance man's ability to get along with his fellows and to survive on this earth; but if the possibility is to be realized, much of the required effort will have to be expended by teachers who will be as willing to defend their choice of subject matter and methodology as they are their motivation. Perhaps no one should teach biology who does not know of Lamarck, and perhaps teachers should not endorse the policies of their government unless they are willing to defend those policies on grounds other than the fact that they are the policies of the government. If it is argued that this position is wholly idealistic because school and other bureaucracies make a personal assumption of instructional responsibility impossible, it can be replied that no more compelling reason can be given for reducing the size of those bureaucracies below the level of instructional interference. By diffusing responsibility throughout impersonal institutions instead of apportioning it to persons, we will lose not only our professional and intellectual standards but the sense of moral responsibility as well – and I believe that in wanting to avoid such losses Mr Snook and I are in fairly close agreement.

Notes

1 J.A. Snook, 'The Concept of Indoctrination,' *Studies in Philosophy and Education* 7 (Fall 1970): 65–108. Hereafter references to Snook will be cited by page number within my text.

2 Another assumption made herein is that in his reply Mr Snook would prefer to address criticisms rather than acknowledge compliments, and as a consequence I will pass over in silence those portions of his work with which I am in agreement, concentrating instead on those areas where there are substantive differences between us. Not all of these differences involve matters of fact as much as they involve matters of emphasis. Without digressing to a metaphysical critique of linguistic analysis, it may nevertheless be said that the results of such analyses are at least partially to be seen as persuasive; in this particular case, Mr Snook would persuade us to see indoctrination in one way, and I in another.

3 As will be seen below, this characterization follows from attending to the indoctrinated as well as the indoctrinator, and it does not therefore require an unusual definition of *indoctrination*. I would settle for the definition in Webster's *New World Dictionary*: '1. to instruct in doctrines, principles, theories, or beliefs. 2. to instruct; teach.' Thus to whatever degree ordinary language is an appropriate sanction, it would seem to favor the present view over Snook's. It might also be noted that the term has not always been used pejoratively. I remember that my first two days in boot camp in 1952 were called 'indoctrination period' and the Marine Corps must not have looked upon these sessions as immoral.

4 Snook can perhaps be excused for his use of the word *sincerely* in this passage because of its relation to his central concern of intention. It is nevertheless an inappropriate adjective to use with the verb 'desires'. Whatever I can be sincere about I can also

be insincere about; but I do not know what it would be like to insincerely desire some object or state of affairs.

5 It might be noted here that Snook does not make clear the relation between propositions and beliefs either in his criterion or defense of it. To see why this relation is important, consider his case 1 c (104): 'Teaching propositions which are false and known by the teacher to be false.' This would be an interesting case for someone who held a noncognitivist (emotive) theory of ethics. On this theory value statements (expressions of beliefs?) are neither true nor false because they do not express facts. But if they are neither true nor false, then they cannot be *known* to be either true or false, and trivially, they cannot be known to be false. Now until a clarification of the relationship between propositions and beliefs is forthcoming we are driven to the rather counterintuitive conclusion that no teacher could be accused of indoctrinating as long as he confined himself to making such assertions as 'The infliction of cruelty on human beings should always be rewarded.' The noncognitivist (and Snook) might want to invoke the proposition–statement distinction here, but it will not, by itself, solve the philosophical question of the relationship between value beliefs and propositions without begging it, and it surely will not solve the problem confronting a harried principal who has an eloquent disciple of the Marquis de Sade on his faculty.

6 On page 103 he says the results must be 'clearly' foreseen by the teacher.

7 Although Lamarck is usually taken to be in opposition to Darwin, their two views are logically compatible. We need only ask, 'What is the probability that a mutation wherein acquired characteristics were genetically transmitted would survive?' As long as this probability is not zero, the two views are not in contradiction.

8 A.R. Jensen, 'How Much Can We Boost IQ and Scholastic Achievement?' *Harvard Educational Review* 39 (Winter 1969): 1–123.

9 Regarding the question of establishing guilt Snook says, 'I am not concerned about how we would in practice make the charge of indoctrination stick but about what is meant by the charge' (106). This disclaimer notwithstanding, Snook does appear concerned to establish guilt or innocence. 'He can point out the likely results and *argue that since method is under the teacher's control such results are intentional*' (107); 'The charge could always be *defeated* by showing . . .' (105); 'the person *accused* can *rebut* the charge by showing . . .' (106). (All italics mine.) Further, in arguing that content and method are important for *establishing* intention Snook is clearly more concerned with legalistic than philosophical issues.

10 To see that this form of argument is generally weak, consider another example. It might be argued that because Skinner's behaviorism describes *all* behavior (including linguistic behavior) as a function of reinforced conditioning there is no reason to get upset about conditioning; the whole concept becomes so general as to be vacuous. But the charge of vacuity can blur the (philosophical) perspective from which Skinner is asking us to view the entire world. One may applaud the simple elegance of this perspective or recoil from its physicalistic implications; vacuous, however, it is not.

11 For the control functions of the schools, see Joel Spring, 'Education as a Form of Social Control,' mimeographed.

12 It is not, however, *always* unacceptable.

13 These events occurred in 1968.

14 The choice of modals here is important. It is not being argued that if issues are deliberated, changes *will* occur; the point is that deliberation is a precondition for changes, and hence the term *can*.

15 I am indebted to my colleague Walter Feinberg for the clarification of this point in particular and, more generally, for his many and keen insights into the discrepancy between the ideal and the actual functions of the schools.

18

(i) COMPETITION IN EDUCATION

R.F. Dearden

Competition is a topic which has been all but totally ignored in the educational literature of recent years. And this neglect is surprising, since competition is evident in our educational arrangements at many points. There is competition for class positions and grammar school places, for prizes and entrance to universities, to be first, best, top, fastest and so on. Opinions divide, and hackles quickly rise, over the virtues and vices of such arrangements as these, but the attitudes expressed typically cluster with attitudes to other things in a way which has conveniently been called child-centred or traditional. At one extreme, competition is regarded with horror and much is said about the virtues of cooperation. At the other extreme one finds the tough-minded approval of competition as a crucial necessity, not just in schooling but in life generally.

Clearly there will be points in this controversy at which factual findings should be decisive. An instance would be whether some form of competition does or does not in fact have certain envisaged consequences. Yet one suspects in advance that here is a topic which could be seen as giving some persuasive force to an emotive theory of ethics. Facts there may be, but in the end divergences of attitude may well remain which can rationally be neither justified nor attacked: they just are the attitudes of those who express them. But before that stage of irreconcilable difference is reached, if it must be reached, there is much scope for rational argument and not only argument over the truth or falsity of research findings. There are, for instance, at least two conceptual questions which can be rationally pursued, and with some profit, before the value question is faced. These two conceptual questions concern what competition is, and what things can in consequence be competed for.

What is competition?

I take as a conveniently simple schema for analysis and discussion the situation where A and B are in competition for X. In this schema, A and B will normally

Source: R.F. Dearden *Problems in Primary Education*, Routledge, 1976. ch. 9.

be individuals, or else associations of individuals such as schools, classes, houses, teams, companies, or nations. Nevertheless, theories, policies and ideals may also properly be said to be in competition with each other when they are canvassed or championed by people as being singularly entitled to be called true, correct, right or perhaps most suitable for funding. But granted this conveniently simplifying schema, I want to suggest three conditions as being separately necessary and jointly sufficient for A and B to be in competition for X.

First of all, A and B must both want X. There must be some common object desired by both, such as the best seat, Mary's favours, the largest share in the market, the job just advertised, the prize, to be first away from the traffic lights, to sit nearest to God, and so on. For without a common object the paths of A and B will not necessarily cross.

The second condition is that A's gaining possession of X must exclude B's gaining possession of it. For if both A and B can have their desires satisfied, e.g. because Mary has an identical twin sister or because there is a whole row of the best seats still vacant, then there is no need for or point in competition. Thus we do not normally compete for air to breathe since there is enough available for everyone. But in a wrecked submarine or a collapsed coalmine there could conceivably be competition, and the space in which to enjoy fresh air, or in which to enjoy the air on the upwind side of a big city, are often very much competed for.

Yet a third condition is that both A and B should persist in trying to gain exclusive possession of X even when they know that one of them must be excluded. They must become and remain competitors. For, realizing that they are in a situation of potential competition, A and B might both volunteer to forgo X, or agree to distribute it equally between them, or take turns in having it, instead of becoming competitors for its exclusive possession. These alternatives are common enough amongst friends, close colleagues and families. Of course, A and B may be in competition with each other without yet knowing it, as when institutions recruit from the same pool of ability without being aware of each other's existence. Companies seeking a particular market may have to do some market research to find out just who their competitors are, while Mary's several boy-friends may not even guess at first that they are in competition with anyone at all. This third condition, however, indicates what is necessary when A and B do know, or do find out.[1]

For and and B actually to be in competition for X, then, A and B must both want X, A's getting it must exclude B from having it, and they must both persist in trying to get it even if they know that one's getting it must exclude the other. When fifty pupils enter the school chess club's tournament, or when 1,000 eleven-year-olds sit the eleven-plus examination to determine the 250 of them who will go to grammar schools, we do indeed have a complication of the simple schema I have adopted for analysis, but nothing essential is changed. But before passing on to the second of the two conceptual questions raised at the beginning, there are some educationally relevant comments which can already be made in the terms of this suggested analysis.

It seems often to be assumed that competition and cooperation are themselves in competition with each other. To embrace the one, it is assumed, is wholly to exclude the other from a place in our educational arrangements. But this is manifestly not so. Competition does in fact normally require various forms of cooperation. Wherever A and B are groups of individuals, such as school houses or teams, then competitive advantages will usually accrue to the group which can muster a high degree of internal cooperation. The best football teams are not necessarily those composed of eleven star players. Furthermore, whether A and B are individuals or teams, they must normally cooperate with each other at least in observing the rules governing the competition. These rules may be the conventional rules of a game, the rules of war, state laws governing industrial and commercial practices, or school rules related to some test situation. Even when competitive testing in a classroom reaches such a pitch that each child jealously guards what he writes with a hedge of books and crooked arms, still there are no-cheating rules to be jointly observed if the competition is to be fair. Competition, whatever one may think of it, does require cooperative observance of its own shared ethic in all cases short of total ruthlessness. Of course, it does make sense to urge the replacement of competition by a much greater degree of cooperation, but cooperation in less degree is still normally required where competition still prevails.

Those who wish to eliminate or greatly to reduce the amount of competition in education often make what they think is an important concession. Competition is all right, they say, provided that each child is competing only with himself. But is this a conceptual possibility if the earlier analysis is correct? Can one compete with oneself? Taken literally, competition with oneself would involve a contradiction: I myself must both win and lose in the same competition. If this contradiction is avoided by dissociating my present from my past self, then presumably it is not myself after all but someone else with whom I then compete. The reality of what is approved here, of course, is simply that I should now try to improve on my own past performances: I should try to play the piano better than I did last week, or try to get more sums right or to write more neatly. Doing one's best and trying to improve are doubtless central to learning situations, but they are not perspicuously described as competing with oneself.

Nevertheless, a reason can I think readily be discerned for favouring this illogical description. Consider an educational climate in which true competition is rife. If a reformer then wishes to shift the motivational emphasis away from interpersonal rivalry to a spirit of individual self-improvement, then the notion of 'competing with oneself' is an admirably persuasive device. Instead of blocking or opposing an existing attitude it seeks more economically to redirect it. Though strictly lacking in sense, the phrase may therefore be thought to be justified by its effects in helping to shift a well-entrenched practice towards something else thought to be more acceptable.

Close in spirit to competition, but not quite the same as it, is emulation. The emulous person strongly wishes to approach, or match, or even perhaps excel another person in some respect, for instance in abilities, achievements, position, or wealth. He takes another as a standard to try to equal or surpass. But this desire does not necessarily place the emulous and the emulated people in competition with each other. To try to emulate Russell's clarity, or Rothschild's business success, is not to try to gain exclusive possession of anything. But emulation is like competition in that what one thinks of it will probably be in part determined by one's opinion of the emotions by which it is normally accompanied, such as admiration or envy, liking or hatred.

What things can be competed for?

If the analysis of competition so far given is correct, then the range of possible objects of competition will be co-extensive with the range of things that can satisfy the three conditions laid down. Of these conditions, the first two seem by far the most important. That is to say, to be a possible object of competition something must (1) be capable of being desired, i.e. of being thought good, an advantage worth having, etc; and (2) be capable of being exclusively possessed, whether by its very nature or by virtue of some rule or convention. For instance, in relation to being desired, it is hard to imagine how simple possession of a saucer of mud could be a possible object of competition, while the exclusiveness condition would find a difficulty in the idea of competing to believe that God exists. But the interesting question now is: can education be a possible object of competition?

Let us grant that being an educated person is certainly a state that can be desired. But can it be exclusively possessed? Roughly speaking, to be educated is to possess certain attitudes, knowledge and abilities, for instance to care about truth, to understand the principles of magnetism, or to be able to see irrelevance. These items are suggested as an indication of the general sort of thing, rather than as obviously essential items. But possessions of this mental sort do have two features which seem to rule them out as possible objects of competition. First, they are logically non-transferable. Though I may share with you my under-standing of the Industrial Revolution, I cannot give it to you or be dispossessed of it as if it were a car, coat or can of beer. A second and closely related feature is that these mental possessions represent infinitely repeatable achievements. My possession of them in no way debars you from exactly similar achievements, within the limits of your personal educability. We can all know the facts about Tudor England, know the declension of *mensa*, believe in God, have the skill to play the violin, or respond appreciatively to literature, without exhausting a limited stock of anything. There are not fewer facts left for you to learn if I gorge myself on Tudor history, or less skill available for you if I quickly master the fingering of the 'cello.

These features of educational achievements should not be confused with the open-endedness of those same achievements. It may indeed be silly to think of anyone as having an absolutely complete knowledge of history or science, since there will always be more that could be known. But it would not matter if there were only 148 historical facts that could be learned. The essential point is that this learning is infinitely repeatable, and not that what is learned is infinitely extendable.

A very similar point to that made here was also made by Spinoza in his *Ethics*. Spinoza argued there that virtue and happiness together lay in increasing our understanding of God-or-nature. But in that case, he further argued, 'the greatest good of those who follow virtue is common to all, and all can equally enjoy it.'[2] The greatest good in life was thus presented as a goal which could be pursued by all without competition or strife.

Being educated, then, is a state for which it makes no sense to compete, since it represents a logically nontransferable and an infinitely repeatable achievement. And this result, if it is true, seems to me interesting and important if we are to place competition in proper perspective in our educational arrangements. Nevertheless, since competition plainly does occur, it must obviously be capable of having some place in education. What place, then, could it have, if the state of being educated is not something for which it makes sense to compete?

There are, I think, two main ways in which competition can have a place in education. Each is related to one or other of the main conditions for being a possible object of competition, namely that an object be capable of being desired and that it be capable of being exclusively possessed. It would not be sensational news to any practising teacher to say that children do not always want to be educated, either at all or in some particular respect. If we nevertheless persist in the desire to educate them, there then faces us a serious motivational problem. And so arises one main way in which competition may enter education. We can so arrange things that educational achievements are inseparably linked with some other artificial achievements for which children can readily be induced to compete. We can thus hold out prizes, team points, privileges, places of prestige, carefully hoarded approval, or the bliss of being top or first or fastest as restricted rewards, available to some few who satisfy sufficiently, by their personal effort, the levels of educational achievement we set for all. Knowledge, abilities, attitudes are infinitely sharable, but honours and rewards by design are not. The hope is that by competing for the latter something of the former may also be gained. The justification would be that human nature rather than the nature of what is to be learned is what makes competition necessary here. Whereas children do not by nature seek to be educated, it will be said, fortunately they are naturally competitive.

Since I am at the moment concerned to explore what is possible rather than what is desirable, I shall leave the matter there and turn to a second main way in which competition can have a place in education. Children may want to be educated in some respect, but access to the necessary means may be restricted and have to be competed for. It is of course a familiar fact of social life that although knowledge is infinitely sharable, people may not be willing to share it. Teachers often jealously guard their ideas from the imitative intentions of colleagues. Researchers may set up a dummy scientific experiment to put others off the real scent. Trades and professions guard access to their special expertise and confer its benefits only at a price. Though knowledge is infinitely sharable, access to it can be restricted and artificially made an object of competition.

Now education is normally to be gained only by having access to certain institutions, where the attentions of teachers and the use of such equipment as books, laboratories and instruments is available. But these means represent very finitely sharable allocations of a community's resources. These allocations in turn reflect political decisions to train so many teachers and no more, to provide so many nursery, grammar school or university places and no more, and so on. With resources and access to them thus limited, competition for those resources and that access is certainly one way of distributing them.

When children leave their school and walk down the path or across the playground to the road outside, they take with them in varying degree that invisible but infinitely sharable achievement which we call being educated. But it is an achievement that has been made possible by having greater or less access to very finitely sharable resources, which can readily be made into objects of competition. In this way, as in motivating reluctant learners, competition can and often does have a place in education.

What things ought to be competed for?

In the previous section it was argued that competition can have an important place in education both as a motivation for learning and as a means of determining access to educational resources. In turning finally to consider whether it ought to have either of these possible places, it is convenient to take first the simpler case of competition for access.

Access

Concerning access, then, there are two questions which need to be distinguished: (1) How much in the way of educational resources, e.g. university places, is it both possible and desirable to provide? (2) If demand for access exceeds supply, how is entry to be determined? Now competition between pupils is relevant only to the second of these questions. Increase the educational provision and competition as a distributive device ceases to be necessary. The question of the merits and demerits of competition must therefore be separated from the prior and primarily political question of how much of our resources to allocate to some aspect of education.

Granted an excess of demand over supply, or a degree of scarcity of educational provision, competition is of course not the only way of determining access. The principle adopted could be that of first come first served, or random selection by lots, or teachers' recommendations, or being able to afford fees set so that only the required percentage can afford them. No doubt there are other possibilities too. But granted the institutional arrangements making selection necessary, then competition as a distributive device can be both the fairest and the most efficient. It can be fairest because it can most successfully restrict determination of the outcome to the candidate himself and his relevant abilities. And it can be most efficient because it can select those most able to profit from access to the resources provided. Furthermore, since the central point is to gain access, and only contingently to defeat rivals, then those aspects of triumphing over others and glorying in their defeat which may make competition objectionable for some are at least minimized if not wholly excluded.

It certainly seems to me that competition can be the most efficient way of allocating resources, but whether it is the fairest depends on one's conception of what it is necessary to be fair to. Competition is fair to the candidates as they now present themselves, but unfairness may lie behind how they now are, for instance in how they came to possess or be able to develop their present abilities. Tinkering with the system may partially satisfy an enlarged conception of fairness here, but serious doubts will almost certainly transfer the issue to the political question of how much educational provision to supply, i.e. it will by-pass the distributive device and bring into question the size or type of the institutions provided. And that is indeed another question.

Motivation

The evaluation of competition as a motivation for learning is highly complex, and probably not in the end wholly rationally decidable. It is not just a question of accurately describing different sorts of competitive arrangements and then empirically discovering their different consequences. There is also the problem of knowing which consequences are to be relevant and what weights to attach to them. Whatever is officially approved, however, there will doubtless always be some unofficial competition between children: to be first on to Book Two, to have the biggest collection of fossils, to be most fashionable in hair or clothing, and so on. The question here is rather what a considered staff attitude should be. Competition is intrinsic to many games but it is not intrinsic to gaining possession of educational achievements, for these mental possessions are infinitely sharable. Should, therefore, a situation be artificially contrived in which children are moved to learn by the educationally extrinsic motivation of competitive success?

The use of competition in education is often defended by analogy with its approved place in games. A standard staffroom reply to the objector to competition is that he surely would not want it excluded from football, cricket, athletics or hockey. But how valid an analogy is this? Competitive games have two features which seem relevant here: (1) Competition is intrinsic to those games, and has indeed been deliberately introduced into them in order to make them more enjoyable. A game of sport can still be a good one through competing even if one loses. (To illustrate: I personally recall enjoying my first organized cross country race, in which I came 185th.) (2) Playing games, in the spirit of a game, is voluntary, so that if one does not enjoy that sort of competition one can choose to stick to bird-watching, hiking or playing patience.

As an argument by analogy, however, this is unconvincing, for in both the respects mentioned educational learning frequently differs from games. First, as has already been argued, the intrinsic goals of education are non-competitive achievements with their own appropriate intrinsic motivations. Education is not a factitious goal set up just to provide an enjoyable field for the exercise and display of competitive skill and striving. Secondly, learners often do not have much choice as to whether or not to participate in the classroom arrangements which teachers institute. These, of course, are not by themselves objections to using competition in education, but to basing its use on an analogy with games and sports. Nevertheless, it must be admitted that there are some activities of learning in schools which may with great advantage be turned into games. If some tasteless pill of learning can be sugared by competition into being willingly taken, then why not? If some important spellings are thus learned, or some indispensable arithmetical facts are thus memorized, perhaps by minds which do not noticeably sparkle and flash with the intelligent perception of pattern or relation, then some good has been done which probably would not otherwise have been done. And if some children should occasionally choose to enter into a musical, painting or handwriting competition, then it would seem a doctrinaire restriction of liberty to stop them from doing so. But it is not these genuinely game-like activities which we have mainly to consider. What we have to consider, and what is not game-like, is the deliberate adoption of competitive arrangements in a school as a prime source of motivation for much educational learning.

And here, I think, at the heart of the matter lie different views of human nature. Where we find a classroom regime of competitive testing, class lists, comparative grading and ranking, prizes and other such rewards, then these will be upheld as a necessary spur to stimulate efficient learning and to 'keep up standards'. Without them, it will be said, children (and perhaps staff too) will flop back into idleness and desultory learning. The argument can be developed by pointing out that competition has two great virtues which admirably suit it to this role of spurring on our slacking natures.

First, competitiveness is *natural*. The young display it without ever being taught, as we see in sibling rivalry. Such basic human endeavours as getting parental approval and attention and, later, getting sexual attention, automatically elicit a tendency to compete with any others who are seen as wanting the same attentions. Another aspect of this naturalness is that if it is suggested to children that they compete, then they very readily rise to the suggestion, competing the more vigorously the younger they are. No doubt cultures may have been heard of where non-competitiveness is regarded as a virtue, but again it could not be thought of as a *virtue* if competitiveness did not exist as a natural tendency to be curbed and controlled. Of course, simply being natural does not make anything desirable: selfish greed, jealousy, spite and envy are probably natural inclinations, but we do not approve of them on that or any other account. The argument is that because competitiveness is natural, it is available to serve as a means to learning, and it acquires value instrumentally from the value of what has to be learned.

Still further developing the argument, it may be said that a second admirable feature of competition is its wide applicability. It is like money. True, even with money you cannot buy a place in heaven, but you can buy a splendid funeral and the best plot in a cemetery, not to mention food, transport, entertainment, clothes, houses, works of art and promises. Rather similarly, such factitious goals of competitive success as getting prizes, coming top of the form, sitting in prestigeful seats and heading the star charts are attachable to the learning of anything that is learned alongside others, e.g. French, mathematics, history and even religious knowledge. And with such powerful arguments as these to make the case, one can then go on to point out certain additional bonuses. Through competition with others, it may be said, we come to know ourselves better and so form a truer self-concept, and we are prepared for what will later be a prevalent feature of much in adult life, especially in our work.

There are, I think, three possible moves open to anyone who wishes to oppose the general use of competition as a motivational device in education, and who therefore has to rebut the preceding arguments. The first and perhaps most obvious move would be to contest the facts relied upon in making the case for competition. It is not really necessary here to deny that competitiveness is natural. Suppose it could be shown that there are in fact *other* motivations available, perhaps just as natural. Then this would falsify the previous argument's implicit reliance on supposing competitiveness to be the only motivation available to accomplish the necessary learning. In the conveniently simplifying traditional or child-centred line-up of attitudes, competition is favoured by the traditionalist. But child-centred educationists would argue that children can be intrinsically motivated by educational learning and its standards as readily as they can be extrinsically motivated by competition. Furthermore, they can be motivated by less individualistic and more cooperative modes of learning, and by non-competitive personal goal-setting. More neutral in their partisan affiliations would be such further sources of motivation as perceived vocational utility, and the approval and encouragement of respected adults.

How could this seemingly factual dispute be settled? It might look as if a traditional teacher had only to try the alternative regime to determine its truth or falsity. But a common reaction to such a change is a confirmation of the traditionalist's fears. And a common further child-centred reaction to that apparent failure is that the children have for years had the old regime institutionally reinforced in them: they cannot change their nature overnight, and nor can the teacher change his. Now this dialogue really passes over into a distinct second move open to those who oppose competition. This move is to deny any significant fixity at all to 'human nature' in its relevant respects, and to assert instead that motivation follows upon rather than precedes the school's arrangements. Institutions make acting from some sorts of motive easy and acting from others difficult. They thus soon present a corresponding phenomenon of 'human nature' by a kind of Darwinian selection. Educationally formative institutions may therefore even be seen as subtly indoctrinatory in making it seem natural to suppose that people are inevitably of the nature that the institution itself engenders. Social psychological experiments into the different effects of different social climates show that there is at least some truth in the main propositions characteristic of this move. Yet these experiments never demonstrate the omnipotence of the experimenter. Limits and resistances to modifiability are found, though whether they are due to a core of genetic factors or to the effects of yet other institutions is unsettled.

There is yet a third possible move to make. This is broadly to accept the facts adduced by those who favour competition, but to argue that the consequences of adopting the practices based on those facts nevertheless do more harm than good. It may therefore overall be thought better to accept less efficient learning and some lowering of intellectual standards on account of the moral harm that is thus avoided. Whatever one thinks of this move, it does have the merit of explicitly drawing attention to what many people find objectionable in competition as a motivation. And the objection is not just that motivation is then extrinsic to the standards, skills and sensitivities of the educational goals that are set. After all, these may eventually become instrinsically motivating in the manner made familiar by Allport's principle of functional autonomy, e.g. we first go to sea for profit, but then come to love seafaring itself.

But there are strong moral objections, so far unheard, concerned with the effects of competition on interpersonal relationships. Roget's *Thesaurus* supplies the clue in classing competition under 'active antagonism', while Hobbes in the *Leviathan* placed it first amongst the three principal causes of quarrel among men.[3] Competition, it will be said, excludes many opportunities for cooperation. It stifles sympathies and erodes the sense of fraternity with our fellows. Seeing them as rivals, we see the price of their success as being our own self-esteem. Very naturally wishing to preserve that self-esteem, we are relieved by others' defeat, and even find ourselves glorying in others' failures. Emotions and attitudes towards others are engendered and released which are little, if at all, removed from malice, for others' loss may be our gain. And wanting to triumph over others can itself become functionally autonomous. In a predominantly competitive school regime, some must be unsuccessful and be consequently threatened by a general loss of self-esteem. To protect this, they will, if they do not despair, withdraw their concern from success in learning and locate it elsewhere. For competition will motivate learning only if there is some chance of relative success. One pointed way of putting this line of moral objection, then, is to ask where teachers can possibly get the right to organize the humiliation of some for the benefit of others, or to make it psychologically necessary for some to withdraw their concern from learning in order to preserve some self-esteem.

Not only are the issues involved in evaluating competition now seen to be complex beyond any hope of settling them in a single article, but also I think it must now be apparent that value-loadings and priorities may be differently distributed over this issue. It is doubtful whether the notion of 'the right answer' is applicable, though certainly many answers can be seen to be ill-considered, too narrow in what they take into account, based on false or dubious premises, or resting on doubtful presuppositions. Again, some of the bad effects of competition can in many ways be mitigated without abandoning competition altogether. For instance, if only the top five of thirty are identified, no one has the humiliation of being laughed at by classmates, or found a shameful disappointment by parents, for coming bottom of the class. These mitigating arrangements further prevent a final answer by blurring the issue.

The function of philosophy here, it seems to me, cannot therefore be to try to settle this question in just one way for everyone who will only attend to the arguments. Its function is rather the liberalizing one of drawing out presuppositions, clarifying concepts and examining validity. This can, I think, be liberalizing both in widening awareness of what is relevant to a personal decision, and in helping to create a larger field for reasoned discussion in place of what is often a rather bitter controversy. Small gains, it may be thought, if what we wanted was definitive solutions, but nevertheless gains for all that.

Notes

1 I stress that this third condition is necessary only if A and B are consciously to compete. But it might be said that conditions one and two are together sufficient, without condition three, in cases of unconscious competition, as in applying for a job in ignorance of the fact that there are other applicants. This distinction might be called that between 'objective' and 'subjective' competition. But condition two, concerning exclusiveness, is the most interesting of the three, I think, and is common to both objective and subjective competition.
2 Spinoza, *Ethics*, 1677, part 4, proposition 36.
3 Hobbes, *Leviathan*, 1651, part I, chapter 13.

18

(ii) AGAINST COMPETITION

In praise of a malleable analysis and the subversiveness of philosophy

Michael Fielding

Of schools in all places, and for all ages, the healthy working will depend on the total exclusion of the stimulus of competition in any form or disguise.[1]

John Ruskin.

A Introduction

A willingness to commit oneself to unconditional support or rejection of competition in education is seldom encountered amongst educational writers in Britain today. Not surprisingly, modern philosophers of education are even less willing to embrace 'extreme' positions than classroom teachers or colleagues writing in other disciplines. Of course, many would suggest that such caution is quite proper to the philosophical enterprise and that, in any case, raucous shouts for commitment from the effervescent young ignore the likelihood that to advocate a simplistic black-and-white portrayal is to substitute caricature for analysis. Certainly, if one looks at the four most recent contributions by philosophers concerned with competition in education it[2] is at once obvious that the issues involved are highly complex and that heavy-handed treatment would be entirely inappropriate. Dearden in particular is very much alive to the obduracy of the disputes; whilst there is, he suggests, little doubt about what is *meant* by competition, there are ferocious disagreements to the appropriateness or desirability of competition in specific instances and in its more general motivational role in schools.

Whilst retaining allegiance to counsels of care and sensitivity to the complexities that underlie most issues of importance, I do wish to advocate an 'extreme' position on the issue of competition. Like Ruskin, though for different reasons, I would suggest that competition should be totally eradicated from schools. I hope to show that my advocacy is not merely a seizure of intellectual overexuberance or a naively simplistic steamroller operation, but rather that there is considerable

Source: *Proceedings of Philosophy of Education Society of Great Britain*, Vol. X, 1976.

philosophical and historical support for such a view despite the fact that it has been subject to massive neglect from the philosophical community on both sides of the Atlantic for decades.

It is my purpose in this paper to establish two negative and two positive theses, thence to offer my own suggestions towards an analysis of competition, and finally to draw out a number of implications that accrue from the paper as a whole. My negative theses are, firstly, that what I shall call an 'essentialist' approach to competition is inherently unsatisfactory; and, secondly, that any philosophical analysis of competition that hopes to arrive at an insightful account without paying attention to the historical career of the concept is likely to prove limited and, quite possibly, mistaken: my positive theses are, firstly, that competition is an 'essentially contested' concept; and, secondly, that historical perspective is of paramount importance both in analyzing a concept like competition and in philosophical activity as such.

B Negative theses

Competition: the essentialist approach

An essentialist approach is one which, as the name suggests, seeks out necessary and sufficient conditions for meaningful use. It is concerned to establish the meaning of a term, to identify particular features which must be present on every occasion of its use; there is an assumption that there is a substantial essential core which gives the notion stability and which contains its referential nexus. Dearden's account of competition provides a substantive example of just such an essentialist analysis. Adopting as a simple schema a situation in which A and B are in competition for X, Dearden posits three separately necessary and jointly sufficient conditions for A and B to be in competition for X:

1 'A and B must both want X. There must be some common object desired by both.'
2 'A's gaining possession of X must exclude B's gaining possession of it.'
3 'Both A and B should persist in trying to gain exclusive possession of X even when they know that one of them must be excluded . . . . Of course A and B may be in competition with each other without yet knowing it. . . . This third condition, however, indicates what is necessary when A and B do know, or do find out.'[3]

There are many things about this account of competition which are unsatisfactory; each of the three conditions Dearden lays out can be sensibly challenged and there are numerous disputes over the notion of competition which are not dealt with. Considerations of space preclude a detailed critique, the raw materials of which interested readers can in any case glean from Clinton Fink's compendious paper[4] on conflict theory in sociology. What would, I think, be pertinent to my enterprise is to focus on some of the issues a satisfactory account of competition ought to include and to illustrate why these distinctions which Dearden omits make a difference to a consideration of competition in education.

The first of these omissions concerns the relationship between competition and conflict, an issue about which considerable dispute raged amongst sociologists in the mid-sixties. Is there a conceptual distinction to be made here, as Raymond Mack[5] suggests, and what of the further questions, e.g. as to which is the genus of which the other is one species, as to whether both competition and conflict are two distinct species of struggle, or whether the two are synonymous?

The importance of making some kind of decision on these matters can be illustrated by considering a number of other related but distinct issues also omitted from the Dearden analysis. Firstly, there is the debate over the relationship between competition and regulation. Dearden makes passing reference to the issue when he talks about competition requiring 'co-operative observance of its own shared ethic', but this observation is given the status of something of additional interest rather than being an integral part of the definition.[6] Certainly there is no recognition on Dearden's part that the history of the concept betrays considerable disagreement as to whether competition is rule-governed, and even where there has been agreement on this matter the further queries as to the nature of the regulation. Quite clearly, the position one adopts here is likely to affect debate on the role of competition in schools, for the spectrum of possibilities encompassed by this issue ranges from a revamped Social Darwinism on the one hand to very firm restrictions on general modes of behaviour and stipulations about what may or may not be done to other competitors on the other.

Equally important in its implications for discussion amongst educationists are the disputes over the relationship between competition and rivalry, the characterization of competition as either direct or indirect struggle, and the disagreement as to whether competition is object-centred or opponent-centred. Again, depending on which of the many possible positions one could legitimately adopt, approval of competition in schools could quite conceivably sanction behaviour within whose boundaries there thrived a form of compulsive narcissism whose staple diet consisted largely in the humiliation of fellow pupils and which at no time made reference to a non-instrumental view of knowledge. So far as I can see, there is nothing in Dearden's account to help resolve these issues, yet evidently they must be resolved before debate about competition in schools can get under way.

There are many other long-standing disputes over the necessary conditions of competition, three of which I should like to mention as particularly significant with respect to the debate about competition in education: these concern distinctions between voluntary and involuntary competition; the fundamentally important demarcation between the competitive process and the competitive motive; and the highly contentious but equally important assertion that competition is a morally normative concept. I will touch on these issues again at a later stage in the paper: suffice to say here that the last two, perhaps more than any of the other distinctions made about competition so far, are at once profoundly controversial and of considerable importance, yet these too are omitted from Dearden's analysis.

Whilst I have taken issue with his paper on substantive grounds, it is my view that the limitations of Dearden's account are largely attributable to the limitations of essentialism itself. What comes over very strongly from a reading of the considerable literature on the subject of competition is not merely the sheer number of issues over which disagreement persists, but the very nature of the disagreements themselves: very often the disputants can and do take up *diametrically opposite positions such that no resolution is possible* other than in the highly unlikely event of the capitulation of one party. To put it another way, the hard core of the disagreement is conceptual, not merely terminological, and it is precisely because of this that the kind of issues I raised in the preceding paragraphs are simply not open to solution on the basis of an essentialist approach, for such an approach inevitably involves ruling out of court, not merely an isolated or idiosyncratic use, but what in many instances amounts to a whole tradition of use stretching back over tens and in some cases hundreds of years. To approach an analysis of competition in terms of necessary and sufficient conditions is to embrace defeat before one has begun. Dearden's omissions are significant not just because they are omissions, but because those issues not mentioned (and, indeed, those criteria he does specify) are all fundamentally contested: every single criterion of competition that has ever been put forward as a necessary condition of its use can be and has been challenged.

Competition: the ahistorical approach

I wish now to establish my second negative hypothesis concerning philosophical analysis of competition and historical perspective by taking a brief look at Professor Perry's paper 'Competition and Co-operation'.[7]

There are four points which seem to me to be central to Perry's case: firstly, that the notions of competition and co-operation are necessarily interdependent – Perry talks of 'the essential connection of the one to the other';[8] secondly, that co-operative and competitive arrangements each involve behaviour usually thought to be characteristic of the other – 'people co-operate competitively and compete co-operatively';[9] thirdly, that educationists need to recognize that competition and co-operation 'are no more psychologically incompatible than they are logically contrary'[10] and that it is high time we stopped bandying about large claims concerning the merits or otherwise of competition and co-operation and indulging in loose and muddled talk about so-called competitive and co-operative motives; lastly, that there is an important distinction to be made between the 'social interaction' and the 'individual action' meanings of competition, a distinction which enables one to recognize the ubiquity of involuntary competition in education and in society.

Most of what Perry has to say is by no means new. This is not necessarily a fault, especially if what is said needs reiterating, which, by and large, it does. However, there is an occasional suggestion that we are witnessing a new phenomenon or new distinctions are being precised whereas, in fact, neither is the case. Whether competition in education is, as Perry suggests, more of a cockpit of contention today than it was, say, in the mid-fifties and sixties is, I would think, doubtful. All Perry's major distinctions, with the possible exception of his remarks on the tendency to approach problems of motivation with insufficient regard to their sophistication and complexity, have precedents in the history of the concept.[11]

In itself, this failure to acknowledge relevant historical precedent is not necessarily of major importance. However, if, as is too often the case and is the case here, that very failure leads to an unsatisfactory analysis it becomes highly significant. I have cited in the notes writers on competition who have put forward ideas similar to Perry's as much as 75 years before him, but, of course, those writers did not find their views meeting with universal acceptance; it would have been equally possible to cite counter-examples rather than corroboration, thus giving rise to a completely different account of competition and co-operation.

There are three such counter-arguments I should like to put forward here. Firstly, his talk of the 'essential connection' between competition and co-operation has a long history of opposition and is, in any case, too vague to be of much help. Perry clearly does not mean that the concept of competition is logically dependent on the notion of co-operation in the sense that the one is the obverse of the other. But if he does not mean that it is not at all clear what he has in mind by an 'essential connection' between the two. It seems that Perry intends us to believe that any acceptable definition of competition must characterize those who compete as in some way co-operating and those who co-operate as in some way competing.

Whilst one might agree that in one possible sense of co-operation people must co-operate in order to compete, Perry's attempts to substantiate the reverse contention are less successful. He says

> co-operative undertakings, of whatever kind, normally assume persons capable of competing for individual advantage within the limits imposed by the conventions of co-operation which are being applied.[12]

But what are we to make of such a contention? It is avowedly contingent in a way that his remarks on the co-operative basis of competition are not; it begs a multitude of socio-economic and cultural questions; and it obscures rather than clarifies what might count as an answer to the fundamental question which it sets out to solve – namely, 'What is the nature of the "essential connection" between competition and co-operation?'

My second objection to Perry's basic position is that his contention that we 'co-operate competitively and compete co-operatively', whilst being arguable, remains largely unargued. I am very much more in sympathy with writers like Dahlke and Luschen[13] who argue that to use these terms in this way is to substitute self-contradiction for subtlety and that a perfectly good conceptual vocabulary exists (or can be put forward) to cope with the kind of nuances which hybrids like 'co-operative competition' are attempting to grasp.

In the light of these worries I have expressed, Perry's third twin contention that it is merely confusing and muddle-headed to talk of a competitive motive and that

> What would really move educational discussion forward is some exploration of the uncharted territory of how competition and co-operation interact in teachers, pupils and adults in later life[14]

turns out to be highly questionable.

In connection with the latter part of the contention I would suggest that Perry's educational explorers should give priority to the double task of toughening up their conceptual hardware and spending a little time studying previous exploits before attempting to map out an 'unknown' which might, without these precautions, turn out to be either familiar or illusory. Educational discussion (and the lamentably omitted educational practice) would, I suggest, benefit a great deal from gaining a working knowledge of its historical antecedents and allowing that knowledge to imbue ensuing philosophical activity. Only then would the kind of psychological and sociological work to which Perry rightly attaches so much importance be able to figure significantly in 'educational discussion' and educational action. With regard to the former part of the contention, I would agree with Perry that motives are not 'neatly isolable states of mind', but I do not see myself thereby committed to jettisoning the notion of a competitive motive.

Perry's account, then, whilst not implausible, lacks the kind of detailed philosophical underpinning necessary to substantiate its validity. An awareness of the historical career of the concept of competition would have made the obligatory nature of such an underpinning evident, for there exists an entire tradition of political and educational thought which calls his analysis into very serious question. Likewise in sociology – following the Dahlke/Luschen line of thought there is a perfectly good case to be made for competition and co-operation being irreconcilably antagonistic and not 'essentially' interdependent as Perry maintains. To give my contention substantive form within the educational debate I would instance Alex Bloom's rhetorical query

> How can children reconcile the opposing concepts of competing *against* and co-operating *with*? Do you help your brother over one stile and push him away at the next?[15]

Let it be noted too that such remarks are very far from a careless spectatorial aside or the utopian clarion call of a pedagogic adolescent. Bloom's school in the East End of London bore living witness to the tenability of an utterly non-competitive education for ordinary pupils within the state system.

Having laid out, albeit in abbreviated form, my arguments to substantiate my two negative theses that either an essentialist or an ahistorical approach to philosophical analysis of competition are bound to prove unsatisfactory, I should now like to provide some antidote to negativity by endeavouring to establish my positive theses that competition is an 'essentially contested' concept and that historical perspective is centrally important in analysing a concept like competition and in philosophical activity as such.

C Positive theses

Competition as essentially contested concept

It might well be objected, even by those who have up to this point retained some sympathy for my enterprise, that if my theses were correct they would surely lead to some sort of latter-day version of the Tower of Babel, thus ensuring not merely that we would not get anywhere fast but that we would not get anywhere at all. My reply would be two-fold: firstly, such a despairing response is only entailed if one refuses to countenance anything other than an essentialist approach to the problem. If one were to take a line like that of, say, John Kleinig in his 'Punishment and Desert' the prospects would look a good deal more promising. Kleinig maintains

> just as verbal definitions are not appropriate in the case of colour words, definitions comprising a set of necessary conditions jointly sufficient for the use of a term are frequently inappropriate for the words we use to characterize human activities.[16]

Setting forward similar views to those advocated in Michael Scriven's 'The Logic of Criteria,[17] Kleinig suggests that

> Many of our activity words are partially defined in terms of conditions which are typically or characteristically, but not always necessarily, implied in their use. . . . The general idea is that they are defined in terms of a set of conditions which are jointly sufficient for their use but some of which are necessary only in certain circumstances.

Expressed in schematic terms this reads as follows:

Let A be an activity word; then

$$A =_{df} a, b, c, d, e, \text{ and } f$$

where a and b are necessary conditions for the use of A and c, d, e, and f are typically or characteristically but not always necessarily implied in A's use.[18]

A second string of my reply would be to direct the objector to the historical career of the concept of competition and suggest that in the light of the nature of the disputes one might seriously consider, not merely accepting the validity of the Kleinig/Scriven thesis, but extending it to embrace even more fully the implacability of the disagreements and thereby, paradoxically, resolve our methodological and conceptual dilemmas.

Competition as a morally normative concept

Perhaps I could unpack some of the philosophical baggage contained in this rather cryptic remark by elaborating a little on my earlier contention that competition has been and can still be legitimately regarded as a morally normative concept.

To my mind this is one of the most interesting and most important areas of dispute, yet it is one which is totally neglected by contemporary philosophical and sociological writers. Dearden suggests that the 'value question' can be satisfactorily faced *after* one has analysed the concept, but this exclusion of value questions from the analysis itself, whilst having sound historical and philosophical precedent, is very far from being self-evidently legitimate. My own position is roughly that I understand competition to be an open-textured concept; there is thus the possibility that it has an evaluative as well as a descriptive dimension. This general philosophical stance is neither new nor unsupported; a recent example of such an approach is Raymond Plant's treatment of the notion of 'community' in his book, *Community and Ideology*.[19]

By way of historical substantiation of my position I will cite two instances of what I take to be normative definitions of competition which will, I hope, illustrate my point; both are typical of the approach which the bulk of writers within the socialist tradition adopt. Sidney Reeve in his book *The Cost of Competition* writes as follows:

> The competitive relationship is not and *cannot* be a pleasant or a wholesome or an unselfish, Christian one, whatever may be the nature of the results. It is *in its very essence* an egotistical, overbearing thing, conceivable with the doer only in relation to the overcoming of other people.[20] (My italics.)

Ira Howerth, a much-neglected writer on the ethical and social aspects of competition, affirmed six years later that

> All competition is *essentially selfish*. That is its condemnation. No matter how much competition is 'regulated' by forbidding the practice of objectionable methods the selfishness of it remains. . . . The eternal and insuperable objection to competition from the ethical standpoint is the state of mind involved.[21] (My italics.)

The point about these two excerpts is not whether one agrees with them or not, but, firstly, that the value issues are not brought into the discussion after one has defined what one means by competition – these issues are taken account of and incorporated in the definition itself; and, secondly, that they are but two examples of a whole tradition of thought.

The notion of 'essential contestability'

The normative approach to accounts of competition is not, of course, the exclusive mode of one particular political tradition. Thus, in opposition to Reeve *et al.*, one could cite a view like the following, which boldly asserts that

If nothing suppresses competition, progress will continue for ever.[22]

As any normative account of competition can be, and usually is, challenged by those operating in a rival tradition of political thought; as the very notion of a normative account is itself challenged; and as there seems little or no agreement among 'wertfrei' analysts on a satisfactory account of competition, I am led to suggest that this kind of bedrock disagreement opens up the possibility of considering competition as an 'essentially contested' concept, that the search for meaning in the essentialist sense is bound to prove illusory.

Competition is not, I would suggest, an 'essentially incomplete' concept, i.e. one about which people have agreed to close debate temporarily, nor is it what might lightheartedly be termed an 'essentially confused' concept, i.e. one which in some mysterious way encourages people to talk at cross-purposes or about different things! An 'essentially contested' concept is one about which disputes do not resolve themselves even when the contestants are aware of rival interpretations. Indeed, disputants seek to establish further arguments and justifications to back up their claims in order to establish even more firmly their own particular interpretation. In this kind of situation some philosophers have tended to take the view that the issues are resolvable and that resolution is likely to be brought about by examining the metaphysical presuppositions of the participants. However, W.B. Gallie, who first coined the notion of an essentially contested concept, suggests that, although endless disputes do remain endless precisely because of metaphysical or indeed psychological recalcitrance, this need not necessarily be the case. With certain concepts that are central to aesthetics, political philosophy and philosophy of religion these apparently endless disputes

> are perfectly genuine: [and] although not resolvable by argument of any kind, are nevertheless sustained by perfectly respectable argument and evidence. . . . These mutually contesting, mutually contested uses of the concept [make] up its standard general use.[23]

350

A similar thesis has also been put forward by Alasdair MacIntyre, who shares Gallie's concern that we regard seemingly perpetual debates about certain concepts, not as indications of intellectual slovenliness or as the inevitably confused manifestations of an essentially confused field of inquiry, but rather as activity quite proper to the understanding and development of notions which are by their very nature essentially contested. With certain social concepts 'institutional argument, debate and conflict'[24] are, MacIntyre suggests, part of the continuity and identity of these concepts.

Although I have neither enumerated in detail the kind of features a concept has to possess in order for it to be essentially contested, nor said anything about how wide an application such a notion has, I do not intend to go into these matters in any more depth here, much less will I attempt to resolve the latter issue.[25] What I hope to have established thus far in this paper is that there are good reasons for thinking that the notion of an essentially contested concept is illuminating and legitimate, and also, in view of the range and the nature of the disagreements touched on earlier, that there are strong *prima facie* grounds for supposing that competition provides us with an example of just such a concept.

On the importance of historical perspective

In his 1956 paper on essentially contested concepts Gallie made another point of major importance which is pertinent to my present purposes; he drew specific attention to the necessity of recognizing that any philosopher who wished to undertake an adequate analysis of appraisive concepts should not ignore the historical career of the concept under consideration, and that this historical aspect of a philosophical undertaking should not be regarded as some sort of appendage to be included or excluded according to the contingencies of a particular philosopher's intellectual training. In recent years this position has received increasing support from philosophers like Richard Bernstein, Abraham Edel, Alasdair MacIntyre and Raymond Plant.[26] MacIntyre puts it thus:

> We cannot investigate a philosophical subject matter adequately unless we take seriously the fact that such a subject matter always has a historical dimension. That dimension is missing in most work by philosophers within the analytic tradition.[27]

It seems to me that this view is both importantly true and worth re-emphasizing frequently, and it is to some of the shortcomings of analytic philosophy highlighted by writers like MacIntyre that the limitations of the Dearden/Perry analysis can be traced. One of the things which I find worrying about their articles is that the analyses are offered and often received as the impartial teasing out of characteristics and implications of certain concepts, whereas, if I have understood their arguments correctly, they are far from neutral. Whilst both writers offer certain insights and clarification they accomplish this at the expense

351

of a more global understanding: their insights are only partial and their clarification is limited to a particular ethico-political view of man which, whilst perfectly legitimate, can neither claim to be neutral nor comprehensive. Dearden's article, despite its sharpness and sensitivity, by-passes much of the important debate on the subject and ends by offering a traditional liberal view as if it were analytically true. Perry's paper has similar shortcomings, and the fecundity of his metaphors and the vehemence of his assertions tend to smother rather than take cognizance of a long and complex debate.[28]

In praise of a malleable analysis

As I see it, the controversy about competition has ranged in the past over four distinct but related issues: (1) Competition at the level of social ideal; (2) Competition as a procedural device; (3) Competition as a motive, and (4) The act of competing itself. I would maintain that one's characterization of (3) will depend on what one builds into (2), and further (and perhaps more contentiously) one cannot give a clear account of (4) except in terms of (2) and (3).

Competition as social ideal: A society based on a competitive ideal would in all probability be characterized by exaltation of largely individualistic values.[29] Personal success would be held up as the *summum bonum* of such a system regarded by its supporters as inherently progressive. Such a vision of an ideal society would be anathema to the traditional socialist, who would approach its advocacy with the kind of incredulity which led Robert Blatchford to remark:

> Imagine it! The Ideal of Human Brotherhood to be built on a foundation of egotism and self-interest![30]

For a socialism incorporating an ethical network of fraternal values such suggestions make little or no sense. Competition and co-operation at the level of principle are utterly irreconcilable.[31]

Competition as a procedural principle: As was evidenced by the complex debate in the earlier part of this paper, to give a non-contested characterization of competition as a procedural principle is not merely a tall order but an impossible request. All one can do is stipulate what one means by competition, state in which context one intends using the term, and buttress one's account with a coherent and convincing justification.

The competitive motive: An important part of my thesis is to establish that the competitive motive and formal competitive procedures are distinct. That there is an important and meaningful distinction to be made seems to me plain: the thousands of fidgeting, prodding, sniggering, shuffling recalcitrants who make up a goodly proportion of those attending the compulsory morning act of worship in the schools of Britain might legitimately be described as irreverent, inattentive, irreligious, deeply bored and/or a host of other choice epithets denoting some form of incomprehension, antagonism or spiritual malaise; but they could hardly be said to be worshipping. For them to have been worshipping they would have had to have done more than go through the motions. They would have had to have actually wanted to worship; their motives would have had to have been religious. Likewise, some unfortunate bedraggled specimen in baggy football shorts and borrowed plimsolls toiling across sodden fields and braving swollen streams to come 194th in the annual inter-house cross-country into which he was speedily press-ganged is hardly competing. He does not want to do it, hates the rain, cannot run any faster than more portly relatives five times his age, has no interest in winning and does not even know the course. One might legitimately say he was taking part in a competitive activity, but one would be hard pushed to make out a case for saying that he was competing; for, quite clearly, he did not have a competitive motive.

One's characterization of the competitive motive will, it seems to me, depend on one's account of competition as a process. For the individualist a description of the competitive motive might be in terms of striving against others to establish one's meritorious superiority; for the socialist it might be in terms of the selfish desire to excel at the expense of others, whilst a 'neutral' description might merely be in terms of the desire to win.

The act of competing. I am suggesting that one cannot compete outside a competitive situation, nor can one compete in a competition without a competitive motive. This rules out the notion of competing against one's will; it is, however, possible to take part in a competition without a competitive motive, e.g. we may not wish to take part or to win, or we may not even be aware that there is a competition going on. Indeed, some, if not all, of these kinds of 'involuntary' competition occur frequently in our society, but we are not entitled, I would suggest, to describe people involved in such activities as competing any more than we are entitled to say of a sullen schoolboy yawning his way through a morning assembly he neither cherishes nor understands that he is worshipping.

The kind of distinctions I am endeavouring to establish here are, I believe, backed up not merely by academics like Dahlke and Luschen, but also by common use.[32] Talk of 'real co-operation' entails the underlying assumption that for something to be properly called co-operation the external relationship needs to be informed with co-operative motives and values. If one 'co-operates' with another person merely to advance self-interest, or greed, or to seek revenge then one is not co-operating: pursuing the Dahlke/Luschen line of argument one might properly term it 'association'; co-operation has been appropriately described as 'the machinery of fellowship'. What I am suggesting is that the same line of argument holds good for competition. To be involved in a competitive situation unwittingly or against one's will or with some end in view other

353

than winning is not to compete but to take part in or be a part of a competitive process.

Given the validity of my emphasis on the act of competing as the key to understanding and assessing the notion of competition, I would further suggest that if one is to give a satisfactory analysis one must adopt a particular ethico-political standpoint. The fact that one's description of competition includes or omits references to, say, selfishness can only depend on one's axiological preferences. I, personally, would insist that the fundamental moral character of competition is selfish. This does not mean that I would not admit my opposite number in the individualist tradition could characterize competition as intrinsically desirable or as essentially neutral. He can, and no doubt would do so, but I am not bound to accept the validity of his viewpoint even though I might well admit its consistency within its own particular terms of reference. I regard competition as an essentially contested concept and this entails that whilst putting forward my own definition as the proper characterization of competition I recognize that there is a rival definition which, like my own can point to a tradition of ethical, social and political thought to substantiate its validity.

In addition, I would suggest that even when one has made such an ethico-political choice one is still not in a position to offer an adequate characterization of competition unless one specifies for what purposes one wishes to use the term. The concept of competition offers an example of the tenability of the Kleinig/Scriven thesis: unless one makes it clear in what sense and in what context one intends to use the concept there is no way of justifying inclusion or exclusion of, say, a rule-governed condition or the omission or insertion of, say, rivalry as a part of the concept. A social anthropologist may wish to include the rule-governed criterion to differentiate competition from conflict, or an economist may want to build in similar restriction to clarify the distinction between, say, fair and unfair competition or between trade and piracy. Both are entitled to do so and would, no doubt, cite numerous historical precedents within their own areas of study to justify their assertions. What they could not do, however, would be to pronounce an alternative use in a different field as illegitimate.

D Philosophy as a subversive activity

I reject the use of competition in schools: competition as a social ideal seems to me abhorrent; competition as a procedural device is morally repugnant because whatever other criteria one wishes to include or omit I would insist that part of one's characterization contain some reference to working against others in a spirit of selfishness; for that reason I would also deplore any fostering of a competitive motive; the act of competing is thus irremediably objectionable, as is the social ideal which forms a substantial part of the political backcloth against which such practices are set.

Advocacy of such views, or views which have close affinity with them, are unlikely to endear one to the many and various supporters of the status quo. No doubt, too, such suggestions will be branded as either hopelessly utopian or doubtfully philosophical or both. Charges of utopianism require an answer which can, I think, be given, though not within the confines of this paper. With regard to the role of philosophy in this debate I would comment by contrasting my own views with those expressed by Dearden and Perry when, at the end of their papers, they make broad recommendations for the future.

Dearden suggests that philosophical inquiry, whilst not being able

> to settle this question (concerning the evaluation of competition) in just one way for everyone who will only attend to the arguments

might nonetheless have

> the liberalizing (function) of drawing out presuppositions, clarifying concepts and examining validity.

Such a liberalizing process Dearden conceives as

> widening awareness of what is relevant to personal decision, and in helping to create a larger field for reasoned discussion in place of what is often a rather bitter controversy.[33]

For Perry the main task of future thought on the subject of competition is to turn its attention to psychology and sociology in order to investigate with greater precision and in greater depth the interaction of co-operation and competition in education and in later life.

Supra Dearden I would suggest that philosophical inquiry into the nature of competition involves the inquirer, not merely in the important tasks of unearthing hidden premises and the clarification and evaluation of previously little examined arguments, but also in the sometimes painful business of descending from the railings of neutrality on which so many philosophers endeavour to remain so lovingly impaled. It may well be, too, that such commitment which I think is necessarily bound up in a philosophical account of competition does little to alleviate the bitterness of the controversy. I would also suggest that increased awareness and clarity can as easily widen wounds and inflict new incisions as it can heal existing ones.

Contra Perry, I would advocate that practising teachers, and especially those who by virtue of present organizational structures have considerable influence in the formulation and finalization of policy decisions, think hard and long about the nature of competition. Although Perry would doubtless abhor such an interpretation, I suspect many teachers would see his recommendations as, if not sanctioning then certainly doing little to prohibit, the tendency to shelve fundamental political and ethical questions and turn to sociology and psychology as some sort of axiological polyfilla. Alasdair MacIntyre has suggested that philosophy is the solvent of ideology; hopefully, it can also be the solvent of an increasingly ubiquitous 'managerial' pedagogy.[34]

Other writers have ably argued that in a number of important ways competition is incompatible[35] with most current philosophical notions of education. The primary purpose of this paper has been to attend to the inadequacy of contemporary philosophical accounts of competition, hopefully offer a more satisfactory alternative, and draw a number of conclusions of a philosophical and practical sort with regard to education.[36] As I have intimated, this alternative, far from offering a cosy settlement of outstanding issues, reaffirms their intractability and uncovers additional contentious points frequently operating as suppressed premises in contemporary discussion. If, as I suggest, teachers and others acknowledge that one can only arrive at an understanding and view of competition if one is prepared to make and acknowledge some sort of commitment about the nature of man and the good life, then the staffroom will be less likely to remain a hothouse of pedagogic and political banalities and the activities of the teacher within classrooms and on playing fields more likely to be thought out and considered. Much of the discussion about competition that goes on at present is concerned with issues to do with its appropriateness or otherwise to certain activities as if it were some sort of motivational chameleon; but any prescriptions about its use in education must necessarily wait upon the outcome of prior deliberations concerning fundamental issues in social and political theory. That debate and decision-making in schools should make explicit reference to contentious, bedrock questions in these areas seems to me highly desirable, for in the uncertain event of discussion addressing itself to the socio-political presuppositions of current educational practice many who pride themselves on their unadorned neutrality will be revealed splendidly clothed in handsomely embroidered ideology.

Notes and references

1 *Fors Clavigera*. Vol. viii, p. 255. Quoted in W. Jolly, *Ruskin on Education*, London: Allen 1894, p. 131.
2 W.E. Brownson, 'The Structure of Competition in the School and its Consequences', *Proceedings of the Thirtieth Annual Meeting of the Philosophy of Education Society* (USA), 1974, pp. 227–40; R.F. Dearden, 'Competition in Education', *Proceedings of the Philosophy of Education Society of Great Britain 1972*, Vol. IV, No. 1, pp. 119–33, reprinted as Volume IV Paper 18(i) to which all page references refer. L.R. Perry, 'Competition in Education', *Montefiore Memorial Lecture*, Froebel Educational Institute, 16 May 1972; L.R. Perry, 'Competition and Co-operation', *British Journal of Educational Studies*, Vol. XXIII, No. 2 (1975), pp. 127–34.
3 Dearden (1972), p. 332.
4 C.F. Fink, 'Some Conceptual Difficulties in the Theory of Social Conflict', *Journal of Conflict Resolution*, Vol. XII, No. 4 (1968), pp. 426–56.
5 R.W. Mack, 'The Components of Social Conflict', *Social Problems*, Vol. 22, No. 4 (1965), pp. 388–97.
6 Dearden (1972), p. 333.

7 Perry (1975).

8 *Op. cit.*, p. 128.

9 *Op. cit.*, p. 133.

10 *Op. cit.*, p. 132.

11 Perry's important insistence that we recognize that all behaviour in a competitive situation is not necessarily competitive was strongly made by F.C. Sharpe, 'Some Problems of Fair Competition', *International Journal of Ethics*, Vol. 31, No. 2 (1921), pp. 123–46, and was regarded by M.A. May and L.W. Doob as the linchpin of their pioneer work, *Competition and Co-operation*, New York: Social Science Research Council, 1937; his assertion that in an important sense it is misleading to talk of a competitive motive, though one I would strongly disagree with, again has a respectable historical lineage, *viz.* C.H. Cooley, 'Personal Competition: its place in the social order and effect upon individuals; with some considerations on success', *American Economic Association Economic Studies*, Vol. IV, No. 2 (1899), pp. 71–173; likewise a version of Perry's notion of involuntary competition was proffered by J. Harvey, J.St.G.C. Heath, M. Spencer, W. Temple and H.G. Wood, *Competition: a Study in Human Motive*, London: Macmillan, 1917, still the only full-length book devoted largely to the ethical, social and political aspects of competition.

12 Perry (1975), p. 128.

13 H.O. Dahlke, 'Co-operation', in J. Gould, W.L. Kolb (eds) *Dictionary of the Social Sciences*, London: Tavistock, 1964, pp. 140–1; G. Luschen, 'Co-operation, association and contest', *Journal of Conflict Resolution*, Vol. XIV, No. 7 (1970), pp. 21–34.

14 Perry (1975), p. 133.

15 A.A. Bloom, 'Compete or Co-operate?', *New Era*, Vol. 36, No. 10 (1955), pp. 210–12 (originally published in *New Era*, Vol. 30, No. 8 (1949)).

16 J. Kleinig, *Punishment and Desert*, The Hague: Martinus Nijhoff (1973), p. 15.

17 M. Scriven. 'The Logic of Criteria', *Journal of Philosophy*, Vol. LVI (1959), pp. 857–68. Cited in Kleinig (1973), p. 16.

18 Kleinig (1973), pp. 15–16.

19 R. Plant, *Community and Ideology*, London: Routledge & Kegan Paul, 1974.

20 S.A. Reeve, *The Cost of Competition*. New York: McClure, Phillips, 1906, p. 92.

21 I.W. Howerth, 'Competition, Natural and Industrial', *International Journal of Ethics*, Vol. 22 (1912), p. 415.

22 J.B. Clark, *Essentials of Economic Theory* (1907), p. 374, cited in R.T. Ely, 'Competition: its nature, its permanency, and its beneficence', *Publications of the American Economic Association*, Third Series, Vol. 2 (1901), pp. 55–70.

23 W.B. Gallie, 'Essentially Contested Concepts', *Proceedings of the Aristotelian Society*, N.S., Vol. LVI (1956), p. 169.

24 A. MacIntyre, 'The Essential Contestability of Some Social Concepts', *Ethics*, Vol. 84, No. 1 (1973), p. 5.

25 I think there would be disagreement on the issue of breadth of application even amongst those like Gallie and MacIntyre who strongly maintain the importance of the notion of an essentially contested concept. See Gallie's *Philosophy and the Historical Understanding*, London: Chatton & Windus, 1964, p. 190, for a brief discussion on this issue. See also N.W. Care, 'On Fixing Social Concepts', *Ethics*, Vol. 84, No. 1 (1973), pp. 10–21 for a critique of MacIntyre's thesis.

26 R. Bernstein, *Praxis and Action*, London: Duckworth, 1972; A. Edel, 'Analytic philosophy of education at the crossroads', in J. Doyle, *Educational Judgements*, London: Routledge & Kegan Paul, 1973, pp. 232–57, reprinted as Volume I Paper 2.; A. MacIntyre, *A Short History of Ethics*, London: Routledge & Kegan Paul, 1967; A. MacIntyre, *Against the Self-Images of the Age*, London: Duckworth, 1971; Plant (1974).

27 MacIntyre (1971), p. 95.

28 To state that 'educationists have to face the fact that people co-operate competitively and compete co-operatively' without so much as a sideways look at alternative characterizations strikes me as extremely odd; to end his article by juxtaposing his own position with the familiar decrepit caricature of 'perfectly co-operating' man or 'the lonely egoist exploiting mankind' as if these were our only alternatives surpasses the merely odd.

29 I am aware that some socialists, e.g. the Webbs, and some societies, e.g. the Soviet Union, have advocated 'socialist competition'. One's position on this issue depends on which strand of socialist thought one feels most at home with. The conflict between Marx and Proudhon on the subject was exceedingly bitter – see Proudhon's *System of Economical Contradictions or the Philosophy of Misery*, Ch. 5, and Marx's response in his *Poverty and Philosophy*. For an insightful treatment of this thorny issue see I. Deutscher, 'Socialist Competition', *Foreign Affairs*, Vol. 30, No. 3 (1952), pp. 378–90.

30 R. Blatchford's 'Altruism: Christ's glorious gospel of Love against Man's dismal science of greed', London: Clarion Newspaper Co., 1898, p. 5.

31 In the words of William Temple, 'Brotherhood and competition are not only distinct, they are contradictory.' See his 'The Church and the Labour Party: a consideration of their ideals', *Economic Review*, Vol. XVIII, No. 2, 5/4/1908, pp. 190–202.

32 Consider the following extract from Krishnamurti's *Education and the Significance of Life*: 'It is essential that this feeling of equality prevail in the right kind of school, for there can be real co-operation only when the sense of superiority and its opposite are non-existent', p. 92.

33 Dearden (1972), p. 341.

34 For a witty but nonetheless hard-hitting article revealing the nature and extent of the threat of the 'managerial fallacy' see Robert Thornbury's 'Management by Mafia', *Times Educational Supplement*, 7/11/75, p. 2. Such a fallacy leads one to suppose that 'Discussion of the school's educational philosophy seems unnecessary. The head sees himself as a trouble-shooter whose response to staff debate is personnel management'.

35 Recent additions to the literature include D. Aspin, 'Games, Winning and Education: Some further comments', *Cambridge Journal of Education*, Vol. 5, No. 1 (1975), pp. 51–61; C. Bailey, 'Games, Winning and Education', *Cambridge Journal of Education*, Vol. 5, No. 1 (1975), pp. 40–50; P.E. Daunt, *Comprehensive Values*, London: Heinemann Educational, 1975; J. McCann, 'Competition in Education', Unpublished M.A. Dissertation, University of London Institute of Education, 1975.

36 I should like to thank everyone who has offered help and criticism in connection with this paper; particularly Scott Carson, Suzanne De Castell, Professor R.S. Peters, Jim Tarrant, Paddy Walsh, Pat White. My debt to John Kleinig is permanent.

19

PUNISHMENT, DISCIPLINE AND THE MORAL ORDER

Richard Smith

PUNISHMENT AND DISCIPLINE

Among those who work in difficult or dangerous jobs, for example in coal-mines, there is often a discipline that comes not from being subject to the will of any person, how ever rational and well-intentioned, but from the work itself. If it is to be done successfully and with the minimum danger and discomfort to all those engaged in it certain procedures must be followed and safeguards observed. Because the workers can see that the nature of the work demands this there is correspondingly less need for discipline to be imposed on them by some other agency. This is an ideal situation, as far as discipline is concerned: where the discipline is inherent in the work or activity, and where rules or procedures are followed because they are perceived as appropriate if the work is to be done. In the same kind of way it does happen, and fortunately not all that rarely, that a class of pupils appears collectively to accept the idea that learning some arithmetic, say, is a good thing and that if they are to learn then various routines, such as doing the homework set out and not interrupting the teacher when he is explaining a difficult point, have to be kept to.

I am not concerned to argue about the definition of 'discipline'. Some writers would reserve the word for the following of rules because they are seen appropriate to the task in hand (thus P.S. Wilson 1971) and would reserve the adjective 'disciplined' for the class like the one above but not apply it to a group of pupils which has been brought to order by some external factor such as the teacher's threats of punishment. Other writers take a wider view of discipline in which it is perfectly proper to speak of one person or group of persons being 'disciplined', that is brought to order, by another's imposing of his authority. I think there is nothing to be gained by attempting to stipulate that the word should be used in one way or another. I only want to insist that whatever words we use there is clearly a difference between three sorts of cases: one, where we follow rules

Source: Richard Smith, *Freedom and Discipline*, Allen & Unwin, 1985, chs 6 and 7.

willingly because we perceive them as right or appropriate; two, where we follow them under manipulative coercion, such as when we are persuaded that there is no alternative to the rules; and three, where we follow them under what may be called punitive coercion, being threatened with punishment or in general some unpleasant consequences if we do not.

It seems clear enough that the first sort of case, whether or not we call it 'discipline', is what we would prefer to find in our schools. The question of course is what we are to do when this ideal breaks down or has no chance to develop. What kind of action can we take to bring about the order necessary for teaching and learning, and indeed for civilized relationships in general, to take place? One may be heavily critical of manipulative modes of treatment, yet it is likely that one reason for the growth of manipulative practices, particularly in schools, is the feeling that punishment is somehow a bad thing: that it is repressive or psychologically unhealthy, or that to punish a pupil is in itself tantamount to an admission of failure of some kind. Consequently there is, I think, a reluctance in some quarters of the educational world even to think about punishment. Sometimes this is rationalized by saying that anyone who teaches well should have no need to punish. But there can be few teachers who have *never* found themselves forced to issue a punishment. It therefore seems a good idea to devote some careful thought to what is involved in punishment.

Sometimes punishment has been regarded as a practice in keeping with the values most civilized people would probably support. For a start, it can be said to be respectful of the individuality of persons: it is usually individuals that we punish, whereas manipulation and other methods of control characteristically are designed to influence groups. Then too punishment respects freedom: on at least some views of punishment, as I shall describe later, punishment offers us the choice between on the one hand committing an offence and incurring the punishment and on the other observing the rules and keeping our liberty (or our money or whatever). Manipulation gives us no such freedom of choice: it may not even allow us to realize our behaviour is being influenced. Punishment is also connected to the values of justice and fairness: I shall call punishment *fair* if it falls on offenders (as opposed to the innocent) and *just* if it is a response to the breaking of rules which are good and sensible ones. Manipulation, however, makes no distinction between those who would and those who would not have behaved in the desired way if left to their own devices.

It cannot therefore be assumed from the beginning that punishment is an unmitigated evil, to be avoided at all costs in a community. This assumption is perhaps easier to make because in a wide sense a lot of 'punishing' goes on all the time in ordinary human relationships. That is, we often feel aggrieved by another person and, particularly when they are close to us, we make them suffer in return. Often we do this only half-consciously, dimly feeling that we have been hard done-by and retaliating without being at all clear about what we are doing. No doubt this sort of behaviour is a great evil and source of unhappiness in people's lives. But this wider kind of 'punishing' is not what I am writing about here. The need to distinguish this from the kind of punishment which is the subject here may make a rough definition helpful at this point.

I follow what has become known as the Hart account (Hart 1968), with appropriate modifications, which I shall defend presently, for the case of schools rather than courts of law. Punishment consists in the intentional infliction of some sort of unpleasantness, by one somehow entitled or authorized to do so, on an offender for a wrong voluntarily done by him. The point of this definition is simply to make clearer the subject under discussion. It is not meant in itself to pre-empt argument or to solve any problems. However, it does help to distinguish the sort of punishment I am concerned with here from the sort mentioned in the previous paragraph, for obviously there can be no question of anyone being entitled or authorized to inflict punishment in ordinary human relationships between, say, husband and wife. Beyond this, however, the definition leaves many questions open.

What, for example, is the purpose of stipulating that punishment should only be for offences committed voluntarily? This is certainly the case with the majority of offences liable to punishment under criminal law. There the advantages of allowing it as an excuse that a person did not know he was committing an offence, or was forced to commit it against his will, are, according to Hart (1968: pp. 45 ff.), those of choice and confidence or security. If I am liable to be punished only when I have acted willingly and wittingly then my own choice is effective in determining my future. I assume a responsibility for my own life, and experience the satisfactions of one who feels in control of his own destiny, that I could not have if from time to time I found the course of my life diverted by the requirement that I pay the penalty for offences I did not know I had committed. In addition to this I am thus better able to predict the future with greater confidence that my plans can be carried through.

In schools, on the other hand, teachers do not always feel similarly obliged to establish that offences are voluntary before they punish them. The child's failure to do his homework may indeed be due to factors at home outside his control, or he may quite genuinely have been trying to be friendly rather than insolent to the teacher, but it is the experience of many pupils that they are punished without account being taken either of intentions or extenuating circumstances. Why should this be any more tolerable in schools than it is in the world outside? Admittedly teachers do not have the resources for making investigations which are available to those who enforce the criminal law, and decisions in the classroom sometimes have to be made quickly. Perhaps, however, this just means that we should not punish unless we are reasonably sure about an offender's motive and the truth of any excuses that are offered. After all, it is possible to require, in the examples above, homework to be produced without fail the following night, when yet another sister's birthday party would be stretching misfortune beyond plausibility; it is possible to have the apparently insolent child stay after the lesson to discuss his behaviour with you. Such measures are often inconvenient for the teacher, but inconvenience has to be weighed against the likelihood of resentment on the part of a pupil who feels his intentions have been misinterpreted.

This is connected with an important way in which punishment in schools differs from judicial punishment in the wider world. Judicial punishment is incurred for an offence against laws or rules, which can be inspected in statute books and elsewhere. The connection of course is that when a person can know in advance, because rules have been published, what he is liable to be punished for it is possible for him to exercise the choice and live in the security that are supposed to be the advantages of order being maintained through punishment rather than through manipulation or sophisticated bullying. In schools, on the other hand, teachers commonly punish pupils for offences that are not expressly forbidden by rules. The danger in this is obvious: pupils may come to feel that punishment is less a result of their own intentions, choices and actions than of the whim of the teacher. Yet it is hardly an attractive solution to increase the number of rules so greatly that punishment can always be shown to be the consequence of breaking an explicit rule. For then children would very likely come to regard the wrongness of wrong conduct as consisting simply in the breaking of rules, rather than in being inconsiderate or endangering the safety of others or whatever it is that the rules are intended to prevent. That is, a heavily rule-bound institution engenders in its members what might be called a kind of moral immaturity in which they cannot see beyond the rules to the reasons for them. Moreover, where there is a proliferation of rules the disregard or even contempt into which some of the petty or trivial ones fall may begin to infect the more important ones. An apparently pointless rule against leaving the school by a certain door is widely ignored, and no one can be bothered to enforce it; then the rule against crossing the main road other than by the footbridge falls into contempt, with perhaps fatal results. It might be some answer to distinguish between the importance of rules by the scale of the punishment. One problem here is that teachers often seem convinced that by mounting a purge against relatively minor misdemeanours they will somehow eradicate the major ones: as if a successful campaign against infractions of school uniform regulations will mysteriously cause general improvements in behaviour. I know of no evidence to support this belief. It seems at least as likely that children will at best resent being harassed over matters they see as of little importance and at worst become seriously confused about whether the length of skirts and width of trousers is more or less central to the proper running of a school than bullying or stealing.

How ever many rules we have they clearly cannot in any case cover everything for which schoolchildren have customarily been liable to be punished, unless some are catch-alls such as 'Never annoy a teacher'. This of course is precisely the sort of regime which children see themselves as enduring in schools: one where they get punished merely for contravening teachers' wishes, how ever capricious and unreasonable they may be. Corrigan's study (1979), for example, of adolescent pupils shows the extent to which they saw school punishments as just a matter of their being 'picked on' and 'pushed around', victims of the arbitrary will of the teachers. Here is none of the predictability, the confidence that one's own choice will determine the course of his life, that is supposed to characterize the proper operation of punishment. Catch-all rules therefore seem no answer to the problem of how children are to know what they are liable to be punished for. Might we perhaps simply abandon in schools the connection made in the world outside between punishment and explicit rules? This seems to be the policy of a comprehensive in Essex, which declares in literature sent to prospective parents and staff 'School regulations are kept to a minimum . . ... The school demands high standards of work and behaviour . . . any deviation from expected standards comes into the area of punishment.' The wording is unfortunate, suggesting (though no doubt not meaning) that straightforward lack of academic ability may be punished. But an attempt might be made to justify punishing without explicit rules having been infringed in two ways, as far as I can see. First, it might be argued that punishment in the case of children has a rather different function from punishment in the case of adults. Children are less mature and less rational: we cannot assume they know what they are doing in the way we normally can with adults. Children are punished less because they have knowingly broken rules than so that they may know the correct standards in future: punishment thus has a teaching role. I discuss this argument in the next section. Secondly, it could be said that in schools established routines can take the place of rules. We are then justified in punishing a pupil who without excuse contravenes a routine we have reason to believe he is familiar with: he enters the classroom when he should have waited in the corridor, for example, or fails to bring the appropriate books to the lesson. Everything depends, of course, on these routines or expectations being made sufficiently clear, as well as the consequences of failing to comply with them. Otherwise there will be nothing to distinguish these routines from others (such as the routine the class has drifted into, unasked, of always sitting in the same desks) where, to borrow the Essex school's wording, deviation does not come into the area of punishment. This is the ordinary practice of many teachers: they establish known routines, rather than publish rules. Punishment of infringements of such routines will certainly meet the criteria of predictability and security that I have mentioned. But these routines are beginning to look very much like rules: the only difference is that they are not written down. Yet clearly it is quite possible for them to be more familiar to children than many articles of criminal or civil law are to the average adult.

It is important to be clear about the direction of the argument so far. I am not claiming that as teachers we are justified in establishing any rules or routines we like and punishing children for breaches of them. Rather my argument is that, when we wish to prevent certain sorts of action (and therefore to promote others), first a case can be made out for preferring punishment over other means, notably manipulation, of achieving our end, and that secondly punishments in school can be relatively like judicial punishments in being incurred only by those who have offended voluntarily against known rules or routines. I have several times stressed that punishments, properly understood, have the advantage of minimizing resentment on the part of the pupil. This is not just liberal or permissive thinking. It is obvious enough that we do not want any devices we adopt for achieving order in schools to end up by increasing disaffection and alienation. Of course even where rules (from now on I shall use this term to include known routines) are well-known and offenders against them are punished only where they have done so voluntarily and without excuse it is still possible for pupils to consider the rules themselves trivial, absurd or merely the expression of teachers' idiosyncratic or selfish wishes. The pupils may even be quite right in this. But there is no solution to that problem to be found in the nature of *punishment*, and I think it is a big mistake to put pressure on the notion of punishment in the attempt to make it yield such a solution. For example, P.S. Wilson (1971) tries to ensure that punishment cannot be a means simply of enforcing whatever the teacher likes by tying it logically to specifically *moral* rules, as we shall see in the next section. On my account of punishment, enforcing a rule through punishment certainly does not guarantee that the rule is sensible or just. Rather, on my view, the merit of punishment lies in the *way* it enforces, in its having, so to speak built-in, the protections such as predictability that I have already mentioned. Arriving at just rules is a different and additional task. A healthy society has procedures for doing so, for challenging unjust rules and laws, and similarly a good teacher explains and discusses rules and routines with his or her pupils, occasionally even changing ones that are objected to with good reasons. Even where rules are unjust the punishment may be fair in being impartial between pupils, in taking account of relevant excuses, and so on.

It is obviously very important that teachers should be clear when they are inflicting, and pupils when they are suffering, a *punishment*, and when something different but confusingly similar is intended. Punishment is deliberately inflicted unpleasantness: it is not punishment if the unpleasantness is incidental. I do not punish a pupil whom I set extra work to improve his chances of passing an examination, how ever tiresome he finds the work. Nor am I punishing the class if at the end of a lively and enjoyable art lesson I ask them to spend a few minutes making the room usable by the class that comes in there after the break. In these cases I must make clear, by the wording of my request, the tone of my voice and so on, that this is not punishment, for the class that made a mess accidentally while working well will very likely resent the implication that they were ill-behaved if they think they are being punished, with consequent damage to our future relationship. There are other occasions which may resemble punishment and must be distinguished from it if punishment is not intended. Reproof may be meant more as a reminder ('You must remember to bring the vocabulary book in future') or in a more elaborate form as an extended telling-off it may be meant rather to cause discomfort and shame, in which case it is surely a kind of punishment. Again a teacher does well here to be clear about his intentions, for the child who experiences as punishment what was intended as no more than a reminder may feel that he has been treated unfairly. Where no distinctions are made it is no wonder that teachers are seen as sources of undifferentiated unpleasantness, fond of 'getting their own back' on pupils or 'throwing their weight around'.

It is particularly confusing, in my view, to attempt to make a distinction between punishments and penalties. Those who do usually claim that a penalty is an appropriate response to a breach of the regulations designed for the smooth running of an institution when no real wrong is done – examples given are often those of fines for overdue library books or for parking on double yellow lines – while a punishment is the reply to significant wrongdoing. Accordingly there are some teachers who like to impose a battery of impositions, unofficial detentions and other minor 'penalties' on pupils who arrive late for lessons, default on homework, forget pens and rulers, and so on. I take it that the point of thinking of these as 'penalties' and the significance of their being imposed often seem more or less automatically without discussion is to avoid the morally charged atmosphere of guilt and shame that is often felt to surround the notion of punishment. Perhaps that is commendable, but I do not see why we have to think of punishment as inevitably accompanied by a crippling burden of shame and guilt. Nothing in my own account implies this. In any case, the distinction between punishments and penalties seems to me misguided in two ways.

First, where the distinction is made on the basis of the kind of rule breached, as above, it appears incoherent even on its own terms. For why do we 'penalize' the sorts of things we do unless there is something wrong with them? The double yellow lines outside my house are there because the road narrows and bends at this point, and if I leave my car there for the sake of convenience, confident that police or traffic-wardens rarely come past, I am acting selfishly and risking causing an accident. If I keep my one-week loan for longer, deciding it is well worth the fine, I am keeping it from another reader who might well have planned his work on the assumption that the book would be back when it was due. Similarly with offences against the smooth running of the classroom or school: if they really matter, if for example they selfishly cause inconvenience to other people, let us think of the detention or whatever as a *punishment*. Apart from anything else, doing so may help keep before our minds the need to consider motive and intentions. If on the other hand they matter only a little or not at all let us scrap the relevant rule or respond with remonstrance, reminder, reasoning or in some other way. Thus penalties are confusing because they convey the message that the behaviour penalized does not really matter, while the child still finds itself on the receiving end of what looks remarkably like a punishment.

Secondly, recall that punishment is supposed to have the merit of respecting the individual's responsibility, of giving him the choice of whether both to offend and to pay the price or observe the rule and preserve his freedom, so conferring the benefit that he is in charge, in this respect at least, of his own life and destiny. If we make school a place of *penalties*, conceived as being imposed for offences 'which neither you nor your judge necessarily regard as being of any *intrinsic* importance' (P.S. Wilson 1971: p. 117), we offer children this autonomy while at the same time denying them it. We do not offer children the chance to begin to take responsibility for their own lives if we regard this freedom as extending only over things that do not really matter. This makes school not so much a part of life (and so a place where the world is explored and tested) as an eccentric, self-contained game of its own. For the remainder of this paper I shall write of punishments and penalties, punishing and penalizing, interchangeably.

To insist that it is precisely where matters of importance are concerned that people must be given significant responsibility may seem strange in the context of punishment. For it may be thought that what we want to do is to *prevent* crimes and offences, not leave people with the choice of whether to commit them or not. The reader may be inclined to agree with Rawls (1972: pp. 314–15), who declares that punishments are 'not simply a scheme of taxes and burdens designed to put a price on certain forms of conduct . . . it would be far better if the acts prescribed by penal statutes were never done.' Certainly laws and rules are intended to prevent offence taking place: to quote Hart, it is not 'a matter of indifference whether we obey the law or break it and pay the penalty. Punishment *is* different from a mere "tax on conduct"' (1968: p. 44). The point of punishment, however, is that while it aims to prevent offences it does this in a way that leaves room for other principles and goods that we value, which a more single-minded, draconian system of preventing offences would not. To quote Hart again, 'More is at stake than the single principle of maintaining the laws at their most efficacious level' (*ibid.*). If that was *all* we wanted, we would behave very differently. We might for example take measures to isolate or even exterminate those sections or age-groups of the population statistically most likely to commit crimes; we would no doubt institute curfews and compel people to carry identity cards. If we have reservations about measures such as these it is because as well as freedom from crime we value other things, like freedom of speech, of movement and association. All this applies with equal force to schools, where we value not only obedience to rules but also the individuality, initiative and readiness to experiment that often characterize the process of learning but may conflict with rules being maintained 'at their most efficacious level'.

I have so far been concerned to justify punishment by pointing to the benefits and safeguards that it incorporates. That is one way of justifying punishment: there are other, separate and distinct, questions about the justification of punishment still to answer. In particular there is the question of the purpose or general justifying aim, as it is sometimes put, of punishment. That is, punishment may be a way of achieving a particular end that incorporates various safeguards, but what exactly is the end that it is meant to achieve?

As may already be clear, I accept that the general justifying aim of punishment is to secure greater obedience to laws and rules by deterring offenders, both those who have already offended from doing so again and those who so far have not but might if not deterred. If this seems too obvious an answer to be worth making, I do so at this point because different answers have been offered, such as that the general purpose of punishment is to reform offenders, or to visit retribution on them, or to reveal the moral order. I discuss some of these in the next section. Although it might seem that the question of the general justifying aim ought logically to have come first I have left it until now both in order to sharpen the contrast with manipulative means of securing order by indicating the procedural advantages of punishment, and in the hope of minimizing confusion among the various different justifications of punishment. Where an account begins by stating that deterrence is the purpose of punishment it is all too easy to get the impression that this answers all questions of justification. That is why those who regard deterrence as the general justifying aim are often taken to have committed themselves to savage exemplary punishments or to the punishment of the innocent, for the former might deter very effectively and the latter might be necessary to maintain deterrence where for some time no offences had actually taken place.

Deterrent punishments in schools can raise a number of problems, but there is one particular reason why, I believe, many writers are reluctant to conclude that deterrence is the general justifying aim of punishment. This looks like justifying punishment by reference to its beneficial consequences for a society or community, as, in a sense, it is. However, to justify a practice solely by pointing to its consequences is regarded by many philosophers as tantamount to removing that practice from the moral dimension of human life altogether. To take an over-simplified example, if I consider myself obliged to keep a promise to you, not simply because I *promised* but only to the extent that the consequences appear, when I weigh them up, more beneficial to all involved than those of breaking it, then I have failed to understand the specifically moral nature of promising. The obligation to keep a promise does not derive only from the consequences of doing so. To deny this is to be a consequentialist, or perhaps the particular kind of consequentialist called a utilitarian, who holds (again I simplify) that actions are only good or right to the extent that they promote the greatest good of the greatest number of people. Now even where philosophers have been prepared to concede that consequentialism is a moral outlook at all, rather than one actually antithetical to morality, many of them have wanted to insist that punishment cannot be viewed in purely consequentialist or utilitarian terms. They have felt that there is a moral element to punishment which we do not do justice to if we justify it purely by talking of its beneficial results for the individual or even his society as a whole.

I agree that punishment is not to be justified exclusively by its consequences, and in general my view of ethics is far from consequentialist or utilitarian. In saying that the general aim of punishment is deterrence I have not appealed only to its consequences to justify the institution of punishment, for I have repeatedly emphasized that we are justified in deterring offenders through *punishment*, rather than other means, because punishment, properly understood, respects the individual's capacity for choice and his responsibility for directing his own life. Then too punishment, by characteristically falling on offenders and not on the innocent, is in harmony with our moral sense of what is just and fitting. I have certainly spelled out some of the *advantages* of this, in terms of security and confidence for example, partly in order to de-mystify notions such as 'responsibility', but the point is not simply that being allowed to take responsibility for your own life, through the institution of punishment, tends to have a pleasant outcome rather than the reverse (for this might equally be brought about by other means). Rather, the nature of the value of such responsibility is revealed by its connection with other moral values such as freedom and the capacity to consider reasons.

To talk of deterrence in answering *one* sort of question about the justification of punishment does not imply a general justification of punishment in purely consequential terms. The supposition that it does mean this simply shows how easily various *different* questions about the justification of punishment can become confused and treated as one.

PUNISHMENT AND THE MORAL ORDER

One way of expressing a central argument of the last section is to say that punishment is related to morality (or ethical considerations, or the moral life, or the moral order of things) in a way that many other means of achieving order are not. Responsibility and choice, which punishment respects, are linked to the notions of right and wrong which lie at the heart of morality. For it would make no sense to commend a person for doing right, or blame him for doing wrong, if he had no choice in the matter or could not properly be said to be responsible. A pupil is not blameworthy for an involuntary (and unexaggerated) fit of coughing, how ever much it disrupts the lesson, since he did not choose to be seized by it. (He might of course be to blame for coming to school in that state, or his parents might be to blame for letting or making him come.)

The unease which talk of morality sometimes provokes is such that a degree of reassurance may be helpful here. In talking of 'the moral order' I do not mean to convey that I think there is some fixed, unvarying array of commands and prohibitions that we all have to obey. Rather the phrase indicates the moral dimension to life, the range of considerations about what we ought to do, what is for the best and what sort of life we ought to live, that human beings can escape from only by resigning their powers of deliberation and choice and becoming automata. To talk of moral issues is not necessarily to insist that we ought to do this or that, or that people should live their lives in any particular way. But it is to insist that ideas of duty, of what ought to be done, of right and wrong, justice, fairness and other virtues, simply could not be eliminated from the thought and practice of creatures recognizably like ourselves.

The purpose of this section is to investigate two aspects in particular of the relationship between punishment and morality: the claim that punishment brings about moral learning, and the role of retribution. First, however, it may make for greater clarity if I emphasize that my argument so far has been about the general practice of punishment or, as it is sometimes put, the *institution* of punishment. That a society or community employs the institution of punishment means that it characteristically attempts to secure order by punishment as I have defined it rather than by pre-emptive psychological treatment, periodic purges of 'unreliable elements' or simple bullying. It is the wholesale replacement of punishment by these other kinds of practice that I have suggested would be morally objectionable. Such a society, or one where we found something similar to the institution of punishment but less carefully operated (perhaps they did not worry overmuch if penalties often fell on the innocent) would be a morally thinner place. Its members would have less responsibility for their own lives, less security in the future. This, then, is the sense in which my argument relates punishment to morality: the *institution* of punishment is morally more satisfactory than the alternatives. It does not of course follow from this that on any particular occasion punishment is automatically the morally appropriate response, that we are morally obliged invariably to punish offenders rather than, say, forgive them or remind them of the rules (and perhaps the reasons for the rules) that they have broken. This conclusion would require one of those more extreme theses, to the effect either that punishment is an important source of moral learning, or that retribution is good in itself, that I shall now examine.

I shall criticize first P.S. Wilson's attempts (1971 and 1974) to connect punishment with morality and with moral learning not because the case he makes out is an especially weak one but, on the contrary, because it is sophisticated and has proved influential. Wilson holds that we can properly speak of punishment only where breaches of specifically *moral* rules are in question. Where a person is made to pay simply for stepping outside limits laid down for the smooth running of an institution or society he is not, properly speaking, 'punished', Wilson believes, but penalized. Being penalized is just a matter of making a payment or suffering a disadvantage for breaking rules, while punishment is 'a matter of learning that breaking rules which one values *oneself* is not just something for which, if caught, one must pay, but something which, whether one is caught at it or not, is "wrong" and therefore, morally speaking, deserves to fail' (1971: p. 98). I penalize a pupil, then, for disrupting a lesson by talking at the back of the class, but I punish the child who wishes to learn my subject, agrees to do the homework but, through weakness of will perhaps, fails to do so. (These are my examples, not Wilson's.) Although probably few teachers make this distinction consciously I think that one of the conclusions Wilson draws will find an echo in many:

> Punishment, to me, is something educative. In it is revealed an entirely different dimension of value (namely, the moral dimension), from that which is bounded merely by fear of loss and hope of gain.
>
> (1971: p. 112)

Punishment, I have suggested, is part of our education. It helps to initiate us . . . into the moral dimension of life.

(*ibid.*: p. 117)

It is of some importance whether Wilson is right or not, for his argument seems to confer legitimacy on the view, widespread among teachers and others, that punishment may have a positively beneficial effect on the individual punished.

Wilson wants to ensure that punishment is something more than just a reflection of the will of the teacher, that it is not simply a device for making people do whatever the punisher happens to want them to do. So he ties punishment to specifically moral rules, which are independent of the will of particular persons. He also wants to argue that punishment brings about moral learning. There are two distinct claims here. One is a legitimate philosophical claim to the effect that it would make sense, or fit in with our best intuitions about the world, to regard punishment in the way Wilson describes. The other looks more like an empirical claim about what would as a matter of fact happen if we took this view of punishment. It will therefore require empirical evidence to support it, for it certainly is not guaranteed by a teacher's belief that he is punishing for the breach of a specifically moral rule that the pupil will come to see the rule in the same light. It is as always possible that he will interpret the teacher's action as mere revenge or simply injustice. Empirical evidence aside, however, we can still consider the coherence and plausibility of the second claim.

Reserving punishment for infringements of moral rules or for things that are 'wrong' rather than inconvenient would require us to be able to make a sufficiently clear distinction between moral rules and other ones, and between the action of punishing and that of penalizing. I have already cast doubt on the coherence of the distinction between punishments and penalties. It seems to me that there is a moral dimension to behaviour which Wilson would penalize rather than punish: parking on double yellow lines or running down the corridors are acts of selfishness or disregard for others. This begins to make the distinction look blurred. And what are the characteristics of a *punishment*, according to Wilson, by which a person may know he is being punished rather than merely penalized? We might expect a punishment, being for a breach of moral rules, to involve the offender being made to feel guilty or ashamed. That is exactly what we find in Wilson's clearest example of what a punishment looks like. A girl has failed to practise a piano piece adequately: at her next lesson her teacher rattles loose coins in his pocket, 'gets up and begins pacing up and down behind her back in a caged sort of way . . . looks out of the window, goes across to the bookcase, takes out a book and starts reading it; worst of all . . . throughout all this he heaves deep sighs from time to time' (1974: p. 107). This falls within the moral area, Wilson thinks, because the girl promised or agreed to practise the piano. So her teacher's behaviour communicates to her that she deserves as a moral agent to suffer the sort of displeasure with herself (pp. 126–7) that looks very much like guilt or shame, though Wilson does not use these words.

The trouble is that the range of actions for which we can and do make people feel guilty is vast. As I pointed out above, in this sense of punishment a great deal of 'punishing' goes on in human relationships. If someone close to me annoys me or has plans of their own which conflict with mine I can easily withdraw my love or approval and so cause them to feel rotten, guilty or obscurely displeased with themselves. There are some people who are quite capable of making one feel guilty for almost anything and everything, who radiate a kind of disapproval that suggests no one can quite come up to their exacting standards. A sensible scheme of things, I suggest, will make as sharp a distinction as possible between punishment and moral blackmail. Making people feel guilty is not a distinguishing mark of punishment. We can even turn wide areas of actions into *moral* failings by exacting solemn promises and then displaying shock at others' failure to keep them. In this way Wilson's music teacher appears to have turned what one might have thought was the morally insignificant business of not practising the piano into an occasion for hours of rumination and self-recrimination (*ibid.*: p. 107) by getting his pupil to make a promise. (No wonder the poor girl does not practise the piano: the adults around her are making it very clear that playing the piano is worth very little when compared with brooding on one's minor weaknesses of will.) My own memories of school are full of incidents of this sort: when teachers, leaving the classroom for a few minutes, would extract such solemn promises, or 'put us on our honour', to behave. Then they could later generate an atmosphere heavy with guilt and shame by lecturing us on how we had let ourselves down.

On the analysis of punishment that I favour it is of course perfectly possible for adults and teachers to punish children for absurd things. The rules we lay down can be trivial, self-contradictory or plain foolish. That is why it is so important that on this conception of punishment there are safeguards for offenders: they are at least to know the rules in advance and will have a pretty good idea of what they are likely to suffer from breaking them. Anyone disinclined to accept that some of the rules of his own society or institution may conceivably be foolish has only to look elsewhere, historically or geographically: rules forbidding the teaching of evolution in some parts of the USA until recently, forbidding mixed marriages in South Africa, forbidding freedom of speech in the Soviet Union. Where there is punishment, as I have defined it, for these offences at least it can be anticipated and avoided by those who want to. Furthermore, where you are punished, properly speaking, it is only your behaviour that is penalized: you can go on valuing what the state discounts and thinking what you like. Your mind is still free. Then too punishment comes to an end: the penalty is paid and the business is over. Where we set out to make people feel guilty, however, there is less possibility of anticipation. In fact, as I spell out below, if we think we are thus educating them morally we are likely to make them feel guilty for things they did not perceive as involving guilt and where therefore anticipation is impossible. To instil guilt is to colour the mind, not just to influence behaviour, and guilt has no limit or end in the way that punishment does. My point can be summed up by saying that it is true enough that we often punish people misguidedly and for the wrong things, but heaven forbid we move to a conception of punishment that we imagine justifies us in making people feel guilty. For when we cause people to feel guilty the damage we may do is much greater.

There is also a logical oddity in supposing that it is the business of punishment to bring about moral learning. This implies that the offender did not know that what he did was wrong. After all, it is in order to teach him the wrongness that, allegedly, he is being punished. But how can we punish someone who did not know he was doing wrong? At the very least it is strange to turn to punishment as a first resort in such cases: normally we would start with explanation and warning. In any case, we tend to think that motive and intention are of some importance in determining what offence, if any, has been committed, but a person who did not know he was doing wrong has not offended intentionally at all. On the other hand, if the offender knows he has done wrong, what (on this view of punishment) is the point of punishing him? Punishment only reveals the moral order if the offender is ready to see it as punishment, that is as something connected to morality rather than revenge, reprisal or what P.S. Wilson would call a 'penalty'. But if he sees it as a punishment he must already grasp the moral order and so the punishment appears superfluous. According to Wilson (1971: p. 118), 'the *force* of what we say or do in punishing hurts, while the *meaning* educates' (his italics). What is the connection between force and meaning here? If we are ready to perceive the meaning, what is the point of the force? It is gratuitous if the only aim of punishment is to educate morally.

Sometimes the slightly weaker claim is made that punishment *confirms* the moral order, reassuring the child that his growing intuitions about right and wrong are correct and conferring the security that comes from living in a morally regular world. If this means that punishments must clearly be fair, falling on the guilty rather than the innocent and being roughly in proportion to offences, I would not disagree. No doubt it is confusing and disturbing for a child to witness or suffer excessive punishment or victimization. Often, however, something more is meant: perhaps that a child who, say, copies another's work out of weakness of will, while appearing to know well enough that cheating is wrong, will have his knowledge ratified and his will strengthened by punishment. Or perhaps the idea is that when he sees another child punished for doing something that he was fairly sure was wrong his grasp of the moral issues is corroborated and becomes more certain. In both cases what is going on can either be interpreted as effectively deterrence or seen as a kind of teaching, but either way I think there are serious problems if punishment is linked specifically to infringements of the moral order.

For we need to consider rather more deeply what we mean by 'the moral order'. As I said at the beginning of this section, the moral dimension of our lives does not consist in a clear and unalterable list of injunctions and prohibitions. First, there is room for argument and disagreement about what is morally of most importance: cheating is to be deplored, but so is smugly turning a deaf ear to a friend's appeal for help. I happen to find it very objectionable (and I am prepared to justify calling this a moral matter) to stereotype people as typical feminists, socialists or whatever, yet I find some people whose opinion I generally respect place this very low in their list of moral priorities. Secondly, it is often very difficult to determine whether a particular action falls under a certain description even when you are clear that actions that do so fall are deplorable: bullying is deplorable, but what looks like bullying to me may strike you as teasing and some of the children involved may genuinely think they are just 'having a bit of fun'. Thirdly, to adopt a distinction of Hart's (1969: pp. 71 ff.), morality involves not just certain material values which may change with place and time, as our society generally now tolerates homosexuality, which at other times has been illegal, but also what he calls 'formal values', which are essential to having any kind of morality at all: impartiality, say, and a degree of readiness to take account of the values and preferences of others.

Morality, in short, is a complex and subtle area. The idea that punishment confirms or teaches the moral order or is an appropriate deterrent only where specifically moral wrongs are in question is plausible only with a drastically simplified view which reduces morality to a clear-cut set of rules. Punishment cannot teach the underlying principles. It cannot show just what it is in virtue of which we call this fruitful co-operation but that cheating, why this counts as teasing but that counts as bullying. Indeed if punishment in the name of moral education is likely to teach children anything it is that the spirit of concern for others or the passion for justice, which are at the root of much of our moral thinking, are of negligible importance beside the careful observance of the prevailing code. In the terms of P.S. Wilson's example, anxiety to keep to the letter of the moral law consigns to oblivion the love of music, without which the whole exercise loses its point.

Perhaps children, up to adolescence at least, prefer a morally rigid, codified environment and feel safer in it. But the real world is not like this: it is a place of moral conflicts, uncertainties and grey areas. An education in morality must acknowledge this complexity and not be satisfied with what can be most easily taught, what children will most readily accept or what is administratively most convenient. It is strange that on the one hand we like to think school rewards and punishments initiate children into the wider world of moral considerations while on the other schools' rules and values often seem part of nothing more than a bizarre, self-contained game. An extreme example: I was once with a senior teacher while he berated an adult-looking girl of about fifteen for failing to wear her uniform properly. She was, he told her, letting down both herself and the school. Clearly he felt there were moral issues at stake: 'You ought to be ashamed of yourself'. Later he confided to me that this was a difficult pupil, known to be working as a prostitute during weekends and with frequent truancies. It was hard not to see the girl's blank indifference to the fuss about uniform as a reasonable response to its true significance in her life as a whole.

If we wish to help children to a better understanding of the moral dimension, of why some things are right and others are wrong, to put it at its simplest, I suggest we have to take seriously the idea that in this area as in others the teacher has to explain and give reasons. Bringing home to somebody the wrongness of a course of action is not a causal process, a matter of making them feel guilty. We can make people feel guilty without their understanding why. This is hardly moral learning. Once we accept the importance of giving reasons here punishment begins to look an inadequate way to teach moral lessons, for it conveys no reasons or explanations. Not even the view that punishment exists to convey the brute fact *that* certain things are wrong entails that it is a particularly suitable way of doing so. As Hart (1969: p. 66) writes, 'The normal way in which moral condemnation is expressed is by *words*, and it is not clear, if denunciation is really what is required, why a solemn public statement of disapproval would not be the most "appropriate" or "emphatic" means of expressing this.'

This brings me to the last topic of this section, that of retribution, for there is a connection between retribution and the giving of reasons that I shall come to presently. First, however, it is necessary to make a distinction between retribution in distribution, as Hart puts it, and retribution as general justifying aim. To hold that punishment is or must be in its nature retributive may be no more than to insist that punishment may be inflicted only on offenders and not on the innocent. This is retribution in distribution, and in this sense most people's view of punishment is retributive. In fact it is possible to claim that this is part of the meaning of punishment and that measures which do not include at least this element of retribution really cannot be called punishment at all.

Some, however, go considerably further than this and maintain that where a person has done wrong and caused pain or suffering it is right and proper that suffering should be inflicted on him in return: 'Wicked conduct injuring others itself calls for punishment, and calls for it even if its infliction is not necessary in order to prevent repetition of that conduct by the offender or by others' (Hart 1968: p. 234). That is, they hold that punishment of the guilty is a kind of intrinsic good quite apart from any deterrent or even reformative effects it may happen to have. They may go so far as to insist that there is an obligation on us to punish offenders: an extreme version of this is expressed by Kant, who in an often-quoted passage in the *Philosophy of Law* (trans. Hastie, 1887) wrote that a society on the verge of dissolution (we might think of this as the brief space between warning of nuclear attack and annihilation) has the duty to execute the last murderer left in its gaols before the end. Perhaps this is just Kant's way of dramatizing his philosophical conviction that the moral value of punishment, as of other moral goods, does not consist in its having any beneficial *consequences*, for in the circumstances he describes there can of course be none. We should respect the difficulty that the retributivist of this sort finds himself in, for any reasons he gives for the good of punishment may suggest he in fact values punishment for something else, for what the reasons point to, and that is incompatible with punishment being an *intrinsic* good. Still, those of us who find the notion of the intrinsic goodness of punishment repugnant or baffling may fairly require the idea to be made clearer to us. For why should we take seriously a claim for which no justification is offered?

One line of defence is that it is unjust that a wrongdoer should prosper while his victims or others suffer – that the petty thief should enjoy the satisfaction of having eaten the sweets while those he has robbed are the poorer. Here retribution is closely related to two other ideas: those of compensation and of giving satisfaction to or assuaging the feelings of the aggrieved or injured. But we must distinguish reparation from retaliation. It is one thing, when a child deliberately spoils another's belongings, to make him exchange his own book for the one spoiled or pay for a replacement (no doubt with some indication that that was a mean or unkind thing to do). It is quite another for the teacher to spoil the child's own book in return. This may well appeal to a basic or primitive sense of justice, not least because the punishment seems so neatly to fit the offence, but it is precisely what weight we should give this desire for justice that is in question, especially in the face of the obvious fact that tit-for-tat adds to the sum of misery in the world. Not all our intuitions about the moral order, not even those which like the urge for justice appear unadulterated by non-moral considerations, are necessarily to be followed. In the balance against the kind of retribution I am discussing here stand not only factors which some would call non-moral, such as what *good* retribution does, but also other specifically moral motives such as mercy and patience. It seems unjust that the wrongdoer should prosper, but where there is no hope of compensation to the injured and where deterrence or teaching the wrongness of the offence are not at issue we must take seriously the possibility that simple retribution is more of an evil than a good.

In any case there is no question of compensation for many sorts of offence, especially in schools. For who is compensated when, for example, a pupil is put into detention for being late and missing morning assembly? As far as the teachers are concerned the punishment, like most school punishments, is a further inconvenience rather than a compensation. I must emphasize that my remarks here apply only to the justification of punishment on retributive grounds and not to punishment as a deterrent. It is the idea that punishment is all the more justified because the pupil 'must not be allowed to get away with it' that needs to be challenged. Do the feelings of the injured and the aggrieved deserve to be assuaged? These feelings are to the effect that the offender ought to suffer for what he has done, and are to be acted upon only if we can find independent grounds for thinking that he so ought. They do not in themselves give us a reason for retribution, any more than the offender's feeling that he should go scot-free is itself a reason for letting him go.

It is obvious enough that a teacher should not get into the habit of thinking that he is justified in punishing a pupil to the extent that it satisfies his feelings of resentment. When your lesson is disrupted or your instructions are ignored it is natural to be angry and the infringement of rule or routine may warrant a punishment for deterrent purposes, but the anger is not the reason for the punishment – it does not *justify* it – and had better not appear to be the reason. To take the line 'You've hurt me and now I'm going to hurt you' may conceivably bring a degree of satisfaction, varying from individual to individual, but is not thereby guaranteed as justice. Most of us have poweful intuitions about justice and injustice but our feelings are not an infallible guide to what is just in particular situations, especially when we are personally involved in the role of authority and our fragile self-esteem is at risk. What feels to me like justified resentment may to you look much more like a mixture of fear, insecurity and frustration. I part company entirely with those such as P.S. Wilson who believe it is beneficial for there to be a personal element in punishment on the grounds that this may repair the estrangement and alienation which, in schools, is likely to have been at the root of misbehaviour in the first place. There is such a wealth of evidence (such as Corrigan 1979) that pupils are only too ready to find personal elements in school punishments, regarding retribution for mischief as being motivated purely by the teacher's spite or desire for revenge. Where this happens a pupil may feel himself quite justified in further retaliation against the teacher, and the result is the familiar cycle of mutual recrimination. The better teachers I have known have not made their pupils feel that their misdemeanours consisted in their upsetting *them*, any more than they conveyed the message that the distinctive quality of good work was its bringing pleasure to the teacher. Their own sense of security, I think, was strong enough for them not to need to do that. Here is a further advantage of tying punishment to the breach of rules: it reduces the element of personal confrontation. If we wish to improve personal relationships between teachers and taught this is one way to begin, and there are better ways of continuing than through punishments.

Those writers impressed by the moral dimension of punishment have often leant towards a retributive view of the general justifying aim. In part this is because the way reasons enter into morality is far from simple. To give reasons for moral judgements can look suspiciously like appealing to non-moral considerations. This viewpoint owes much to Kant, who wrote that a 'good will', or specifically moral motive, 'is not good because of what it effects or accomplishes' (*Groundwork*, ed. Paton, 1976: para. 3): an action that had genuinely moral worth is not motivated by the thought that it is a means to some further end such as one's own or others' happiness, welfare or honour. That would mean the action was based on what Kant called 'empirical' principles, which 'are always unfitted to serve as a ground for moral laws' (*ibid.*: para. 90). Moral laws should hold for all human beings and not just those who happen to have various inclinations, towards maximizing others' well-being or anything else. It is easy to see how close this is to claiming that an action with moral worth is not done for any sort of *reason*. Thus in justifying punishment there has been a reluctance amongst some to talk in terms of deterrent or other effects which would constitute the *reason* for punishing, and a preference for claiming that the good of punishment simply consists in the plain fact that it inflicts suffering or inconvenience on the offender in return for the suffering or inconvenience he has caused. On similar grounds perhaps there has been a temptation to suppose that explanation is a flawed means of moral education: that giving children reasons why some things are right and others wrong comes perilously close to appealing to non-moral factors. Then it would be natural to look to the simple experience of punishment to bring about changes in moral thinking, and to hold, as John Wilson does (1983: p. 524), that 'Retribution is in effect partly an educational device, designed to achieve a particular kind of understanding.'

I have already tried to show how taking deterrent effects as the general justifying aim of punishment need not detract from punishment's having a specifically moral dimension which is not shared by certain alternative means of achieving order. I have also suggested that explaining can take many forms other than the explicit giving of reasons. We can appeal to the imagination of the child ('How would you like it if . . .?'), construct parables and allegories, use works of literature and films to enrich someone's conception of a quality such as pride or of a particular way of life. Thus we may be able to help children look quite deeply into why some ways of behaving are morally objectionable and others are to be emulated, more so than if we simply relied on retribution to teach them that doing harm to others is usually followed by comeuppance – the only lesson that retribution on its own can possibly teach. In any case what children need to learn about justice is not that it characteristically metes out measure for measure. Their vision of the world tends readily to encompass that idea of justice, as a few minutes observation of children at play is likely to confirm. What children (and not only children) are less quick to grasp is that justice may involve other, more subtle factors such as the evaluation of intention and that justice itself is only one element, albeit an important one, in the moral life. Emphasis on retribution will hardly help children to appreciate these factors and give them their proper weight: it may even hinder them.

There is one more argument in support of retribution that I want to consider finally because it raises both directly and in passing important educational issues. Some offenders, it is sometimes said, feel a positive need for punishment and may actually welcome it, in order to expiate their wrongdoing and 'wipe the slate clean'. The classic case of this, and one often cited in support of retributive doctrines, is that of Raskolnikov, in Dostoyevsky's novel *Crime and Punishment*. Raskolnikov murders an old woman, a miserly money-lender, not for the sake of personal gain but believing the world will be well rid of her and intending to distribute her money to the poor. After the murder he gradually has a change of heart. Eventually he admits his crime to the authorities and is sent to prison in Siberia, where he is followed by the devoted Sonia. There he first regards his situation with sullen indifference but after sometime he undergoes a transformation and comes to accept his imprisonment willingly: he feels sufficient remorse for his crime to want to atone for it by suffering punishment. There are still seven years of his sentence to run: 'What great suffering and what infinite joy till then! And he had come back to life, and he knew it, and felt it with every fibre in his renewed being' (Penguin translation, 1982: p. 558).

The first thing to notice is that Raskolnikov's case runs counter to many common ideas about retribution and punishment. For punishment does not cause him to feel remorse or repentance: on the contrary, it is his repentance that brings him to accept his imprisonment as proper punishment for what he has done. This may seem puzzling. What is the *good* to Raskolnikov of suffering retribution, since he already acknowledges the wrongfulness of his crime? Unless it quenches some masochistic thirst for humiliation, what satisfaction or benefit can legal punishment bring a man who fully accepts his guilt? It is hard to answer these questions explicitly. Yet Dostoyevsky's story has by many readers been felt to be not merely plausible but profoundly true. This is a second point of importance. Here we have an example of the way our moral understanding may be enriched, of how we may be morally educated, without having spelled out to us a series of clauses beginning 'because'. If *Crime and Punishment* is plausible we shall have to take more seriously the possibility that under certain circumstances retribution may be a good to the offender, even though it is difficult to give a clear account of the reasons why it is such a good. In this way novels, like plays and films and other works of art, can *show* truths that can hardly be stated explicitly. Novels, as one philosopher who has written about Raskolnikov's case puts it, enable us

> to imagine just what it would be like to be a particular individual in a particular moral crisis (however uncommon or extraordinary) and, through their power to bring alive these moral predicaments, exhibit the attractiveness or otherwise of particular moral solutions . . . when one reads depictions as vivid and detailed as those of Raskolnikov's acceptance of imprisonment, when his moral need for punishment is brought so compellingly before us, the notion of a right to punishment ceases to seem absurd and begins to become morally plausible.
>
> (Sophie Botros 1983)

Still, *Crime and Punishment*, however plausible, is not the last word on the subject. We might in the end decide that it was just 'part of Dostoyevsky's private world, described with such power that one momentarily took it to be how the real world is' (Glover 1970). However (and this is the third point of importance), to the extent that *Crime and Punishment* is convincing it suggests the limitations of accounts of punishment which emphasize the benefits for communities and institutions at the expense of what Sophie Botros (1983) calls the 'private conscience' or 'moral self' and its inner claims. Thus Dostoyevsky's novel is deeply anti-utilitarian in tendency and may appear a valuable corrective to theories of punishment in which deterrence is regarded as the general justifying aim, how ever carefully that position is qualified as I have tried to do with my own account. How far, then, can we accept Dostoyevsky's picture and generalize from it?

Obviously I am not attempting here to do full justice to the central theme of a complex novel: I confine myself to only a few remarks. I think it is essential to appreciate that Raskolnikov's is a special and unusual case. When he commits the crime he regards the old woman as 'vermin' and explicitly sees himself as a different species of person, one of a breed of extraordinary men who are above the law. For such a person, experiencing a change of heart will involve coming to think of himself as within the law once again, and repentance will naturally be accompanied by the need or desire to suffer legal punishment. For to repent of seeing yourself as above the law just is to accept the law's penalties where they are appropriate: repentance here cannot be separated from being subject to judicial punishment as it ordinarily can. In so far then as Raskolnikov is described as feeling a positive longing for punishment and standing to benefit by accepting suffering and being redeemed by it (the narrative can be interpreted differently), it is possible for us to find *Crime and Punishment* plausible without endorsing any kind of general thesis about the intrinsic good of retribution. Those who, like Raskolnikov, consciously and avowedly put themselves above the law are probably rare. They are seldom likely to include schoolchildren.

Certainly children sometimes misbehave so blatantly and repeatedly that we are tempted to conclude they really want to be punished. But we need to treat such cases cautiously. The child may be seeking the approval of its peers: perhaps showing contempt to authority and indifference to its punishments will bring prestige and a reputation for being tough. Or there are occasions when a person may seek punishment in order to rid himself of feelings of guilt and 'wipe the slate clean' with no better motive than to be able to re-offend with a clear conscience. Then too it is sometimes reasonable to regard blatant misbehaviour as a 'cry for attention' on the part of a child incoherently trying to communicate distress of some sort. Some teachers who pride themselves on hard-headed realism dismiss such ideas as 'liberal permissiveness' or like to reply grimly that if it is attention they want it is attention they are going to get. But there do exist such children as the pupil of mine whose father I discovered to have died after lengthy illness on the very morning I was contemplating how to punish the boy for his repeated interruptions and other infractions. It is not always at all easy to find which of the children laying claim to our attention in unacceptable ways have reasons, as in this case, with which we would sympathize. The possibility of making a cruel mistake should suggest a large degree of caution to even the most hard-headed. Perhaps any attention, even that of being punished, is welcome to a chronically unhappy or neglected child. Yet as we saw with moral education, so with attention: there are better ways of supplying it than through punishment.

I do not think we should be very impressed, then, by the claim that wrong-doers in general or even any very large class of them crave retribution and are positively benefited by it. Anyone still inclined to be so impressed ought certainly to read *Crime and Punishment* carefully and consider, among other matters, what role in Raskolnikov's slow change of heart is played by the patient unwavering love of his companion, Sonia. If Dostoyevsky has a lesson for us it is not about the ready benefits of brisk retribution.

References

Botros, S. (1983) 'Acceptance and morality', *Philosophy*, vol. 58, pp. 433–53.

Corrigan, P. (1979) *Schooling the Smash Street Kids* (London: Macmillan).

Dostoyevsky, F. (1982) *Crime and Punishment*, trans. D. Magarshack (Harmondsworth: Penguin).

Glover, J. (1970) *Responsibility* (London: Routledge & Kegan Paul).

Hart, H.L.A. (1968) *Punishment and Responsibility* (Oxford: Clarendon).

Hart, H.L.A. (1969) *Law, Liberty and Morality* (London: Oxford University Press).

Kant, I. (1887) *The Philosophy of Law*, trans. W. Hastie (Edinburgh: T. & T. Clark).

Kant, I. (1976) *Groundwork of the Metaphysic of Morals*, trans. H.J. Paton as *The Moral Law* (London: Hutchinson).

Rawls, J. (1972) *A Theory of Justice* (London: Oxford University Press).

Wilson, J. (1983) 'The purpose of retribution', *Philosophy*, vol. 58, pp. 521–7.

Wilson, P.S. (1971) *Interest and Discipline in Education* (London: Routledge & Kegan Paul).

Wilson, P.S. (1974) 'Perspectives on punishment', *Proceedings of the Philosophy of Education Society of Great Britain*, vol. 8, no. 1, pp. 103–34.

20

COERCION AND THE ETHICS
OF GRADING AND TESTING

Randall R. Curren

Two distinct but related issues in the ethics of grading and testing will concern me in this paper. The first of these is the charge, associated in the past two decades with libertarian educational theory, that the common practice of grading students' work is intrinsically coercive.[1] The second is the larger national debate about 'authentic' assessment, educational standards, and standardized measures of educational outcomes. With respect to the latter issue, my particular concern is the moral grounds that can be adduced in support of new measures of educational achievement or progress. There are important connections between these issues, and one I shall pursue here is that in developing an account of the ethics of grading rich enough to generate a satisfactory response to the charge of coercion, one also uncovers moral grounds for preferring some of the newer forms of standardized measures over the kind of multiple-choice examinations that have prevailed in recent decades. In essence, I will argue that there are morally preferable forms of measures, adaptable to both classroom and standardized uses, which constitute an acceptable middle way between a condemnation of all grading and testing and an acceptance of the status quo that has prevailed.

I will begin, in what follows, with the complaint that grading is intrinsically coercive, a complaint I shall refer to as the 'Coercion Argument'. I will then review some conventional answers to this argument, and will conclude that they suffice to show that the normal uses of testing and grading are not 'strongly coercive', that is, not wrongful *violations* of students' rights.[2] Yet I will also conclude that these answers are not wholly satisfactory, because even 'weak' intellectual coercion that involves an infringement justified by other interests of the child is a matter of serious concern. I will then present a response to this problem of 'weak' coercion, and in doing so will rely on the moral framework deployed by Allen Buchanan and Dan Brock in their book, *Deciding For Others*.[3] The object of their inquiry is responsible surrogate decision-making in a health care context, and I might well have chosen to offer an analysis similar to theirs

Source: *Educational Theory*, Fall 1995, Volume 45, Number 4.

without reference to anything beyond the educational domain; but the structural similarities between the two domains make their framework a convenient and illuminating one to use.

With the analysis developed in response to the problem of 'weak' coercion in hand, I will then consider the implications of this analysis for the kinds of measures of student progress we must develop and use if we are to respect properly students' rights of intellectual self-determination. Concluding that in the primary and secondary years the burden of respecting students' rights of intellectual self-determination is seldom met in practice, I will argue that measures of the sort I shall call 'process measures' are morally preferable to those most commonly used. In closing, I will outline the challenges involved in developing and making wider use of these 'process measures'.

The coercion argument and its libertarian origins

Libertarian views on children and education typically rely on some notion of equal rights for children and adults, and are opposed as much to compulsory schooling and curricula as to compulsory testing and evaluation.[4] They deny, in one way or another, that there are morally relevant differences between adults and children which could justify compelling children to attend school, study what no adult is compelled to study, or submit to examinations of how and what they think in order that others may more effectively change their minds. If it is wrong and obnoxious to judge, criticize, and compare adults (in the absence of special consensually based circumstances or understandings), then the logic of their position compels one to hold that the same is true in the case of children. Libertarians generally accept the legitimacy of freely negotiated contracts between adults, however, so they tend also to concede that evaluation may be acceptable on the basis of a freely negotiated contract encompassing the terms of attendance and instruction generally, or in instances in which the child's desire to be assisted in the pursuit of some autonomous intellectual pursuit is clear.[5] This is to hold, in effect, that a child may elect to solicit evaluations as an aid to her intellectual endeavors, but that in the absence of such an invitation the use of evaluations and grades would amount to wrongful and coercive impositions on the child's intellectual autonomy.

The picture we get here is that even in their central function as measures of achievement of course or unit objectives or measures of competence in some unit of an academic subject domain, good grades generally constitute rewards for intellectual conformity, and bad or mediocre grades constitute threatened and sometimes devastating penalties for nonconformity.[6] This assumes that many, if not all, children do care about what grades they get, or that they are at least vulnerable to the disapproval and the threat to their future interests implicit in bad grades.[7] The threats of disapproval and reduced life prospects are, on this picture, comparable to other threats that are wrongfully coercive inasmuch as they engender fear of an unjustified loss in order to produce compliance with some demand. To the extent that poor grades embody or signify unjustified penalties of these kinds, they would constitute, according to this view, coercion in a strong sense and hence a violation of the child's right of intellectual autonomy.

Conventional responses to the libertarian argument

One fairly obvious response to the Coercion Argument begins by separating the two forms of threats said to be at work in grades, the threat of disapproval and the threat of reduced life prospects, and holds that the latter is a spurious ground for finding grades coercive. Coercion involves the threat of an unjustified loss of something one has or will have a legitimate claim to, but it is hard to see how the difference that grades might make to a child's future prospects can qualify as such a loss. It might be that a given child's prospects would be better with good grades than with bad ones, *supposing some children continue to get worse grades*, but a child could have no just claim to a bright future secured through grades better than others' unless those superior grades were deserved.[8] Dropping the supposition that others will continue to get poor grades amounts to imagining a system in which all students always get good grades as a matter of policy, and that is a system scarcely distinguishable from one without any grades. So to ask what a child's prospects would be in the absence of the threats inherent in grades can only be to ask what those prospects would be in an educational, social, and economic system without any grades at all. There is no sure way to determine what a child's life would have been like in a world without academic grades. The idea that in getting bad grades a child's prospects are reduced from what they otherwise would have been, or from what they rightfully should be, is thus highly speculative at best.

To this, the defender of the Coercion Argument might respond that it is nevertheless true that in some cases there might be reasons to think that there is a clear loss of future prospects. The rejoinder to this would then be that even in those cases there remains the question of whether the child has any legitimate claim to the more promising future she might have had in a system without academic grades. The issue becomes at this point one of distributive justice, and to advance their position any further the defenders of the Coercion Argument would have to argue that, whatever benefits there may be to hiring on the basis of qualifications, and using grades as indicators of those qualifications, the distribution of goods that results is unjust. The commitments inherent in the general libertarian position make this a very difficult line of argument to pursue, however, so this leg of the libertarian argument appears quite unpromising.

This leaves us with the suggestion that it is the threat of disapproval inherent in grades that is intellectually coercive, and I will turn now to some of the standard arguments in the literature of grading and children's rights that provide responses to it.

One promising response may be found in James Terwilliger's 'Assigning Grades', though the defense of grading offered there is intended as a reply not to the Coercion Argument *per se*, but to what Terwilliger calls the 'humanistic' perspective on teaching and grading, a perspective sharing the libertarian concern with children's freedom.[9] Terwilliger's 'pragmatist' response to this 'humanistic' perspective is that students need to make practical choices about how much to study, what assistance with their studies they should obtain, and what courses of study to pursue; and that they are more, not less, free in being able to make those choices in light of the information provided by grades. This relies on the idea that in being able to make better choices one is *more free* and also on the idea that for children in school the better choices are the ones that will enable them to obtain a good education: to learn what they need and are expected to learn, and, where their school offers them choices, to pursue studies beyond the required core which are appropriate to their abilities and aspirations.

There is much good sense in this 'pragmatist' view, but there is a weakness inherent in its reliance on the idea that grades provide students with information that is useful in deciding how best to act in pursuit of their studies. Specifically, free and informed action is one thing, and freedom of thought quite another. For all that has been said, a loss of freedom of thought might be quite compatible with a gain in freedom of action. So even if this argument could establish that the student who is informed of her progress through grades is more free on balance, which it does not in its present form attempt to do, it would still not show that the student does not suffer a loss of freedom of thought. It might with proper amendment serve to justify the practice of grading, showing thereby that it cannot be coercive in a sense entailing a violation of freedom of thought, but as I will argue below that this would still leave us with a residual problem of whether children's intellectual freedom is being adequately respected.

Laura Purdy provides what is probably the best and most thorough refutation of the libertarian view of children's rights and education.[10] In the context of a discussion of the moral role of the school, she observes that

> Even quite thoughtful people sometimes talk as if there is something sacred about individuals' values so that it is wrong to attempt to persuade people to alter them. . . . It seems that what is taken to be vital about such beliefs is that they are taken to be *ours*. Underlying this view is some concept of 'pure', uninfluenced choice.[11]

Questioning the coherence of this idea of uninfluenced choice, and noting that even without schooling children will be bombarded by a nearly 'limitless array of ideas and positions', Purdy argues quite persuasively that the important question to be addressed is 'whether [children] *learn to make better judgments* if left entirely to their own devices or whether they should be exposed to teaching about important matters.'[12] Purdy relies here, much as Terwilliger does, on the idea that it is more important to children's interests that their choices be good, than that their choices be uninfluenced by the adults in their schools. Her argument goes well beyond his, however, in emphasizing the role of *judgment* in choice, and in identifying a class of judgments much broader than those implicit in the class of choices he has in mind, namely all those which may have practical significance, sooner or later, in the child's life. And what she argues is that the facts bear out the conclusion that 'teaching children how to test claims will do a great deal more for their welfare than abandoning them, unfortified by information and skills, to hard experience.'[13]

On this view, the development of skills in 'critical thinking' becomes a central task of education:

> The goal is to help individuals reason constructively. This task involves, among other things, stressing the importance of justifying beliefs and teaching what counts as justification. . . . Such teaching doesn't necessarily imply a single, clear standard for every knowledge claim, but rather a variety of strategies and tests that would enable one to judge the relative reliability of claims. It does imply that every significant claim to knowledge would be accompanied by discussion of the warrants for its belief.[14]

I am quite sympathetic to this general line of argument, and also to Purdy's insistence that 'respect for individuals is compatible with attempting to influence them [provided we use the right methods].'[15] Applied to the use of grades as measures of student progress in developing good judgment as a foundation for wise choices, it supports a reasonable justification of the use of grades to report students' progress to them.

Construed as an answer to the Coercion Argument, however, there are two problems with this line of argument. The first is a problem of insufficient scope. For though it is a reasonable defense of using grades in the way described, it is doubtful whether the entire standard curriculum, even imbued through and through with critical thinking, can be described as contributing to practical judgment in so substantial a way that the gain would justify the cost in intellectual regimentation. One cannot assume that skills and habits of 'test[ing] claims' will transfer easily from domains such as biology and geometry to the sphere of practical judgment in everyday living. Furthermore, even if one could make that assumption, it would still not be clear that expecting such critical thinking to transfer from all of the various parts of the standard curriculum would be an efficient way of cultivating good practical judgment.

The second problem is that this argument shares the same weakness as Terwilliger's argument, because they both assume that the improved quality of practical choices will justify efforts to shape children's minds. How ever much weight we assign to the child's interest in practical self-determination and the right corresponding to it, we are left, as before, with the question of whether the intellectual freedom of children is being sacrificed to competing interests. This residue of possible 'weak' coercion is a problem worth taking seriously, because an infringement of a right is something unfortunate and regrettable in itself, even if it occurs in the context of a course of action that is acceptable, all things considered. There are dilemmas in public and private life alike in which we are faced with no better choice than to sacrifice a lesser good to one that is greater. The appropriate moral attitude in such instances includes regret and remains vigilant to the prospect of avoiding the loss that occasions it, whenever possible. If it were true that we can only prepare children adequately for the demands of practical life at the cost of their intellectual freedom, we would be faced with such a dilemma, and I think that the course of action we would feel compelled to follow would be one we would seriously regret.

This dilemma is avoidable, however, and I will turn now to the elaboration of a moral framework that will make this clear.

The moral framework

Grading is a form of *substituted judgment*, or an act in which the judgment of one person is imposed on, and on behalf of, another person who is found to be unable to judge competently and decide some matter for herself. In practical contexts, the judgments imposed concern alternative courses of action and what it is best to do. The decisions are ones about what the person of impaired competence is to do, be assisted in doing, or what will be done on her behalf. In an academic context, such judgments and corresponding decisions concern what is true and what to assert, what strategy to adopt in pursuit of an answer or in assessing a claim, and so on. When students show that they are not yet able to make these judgments and decisions well on their own, teachers intervene by 'correcting' the judgments expressed in students' performances. Viewing a graded assignment as an intellectual performance, every correction amounts to a substitution of the teacher's judgment for the student's.[16]

Among the practical contexts in which substituted judgment is an issue, the domain of health care is noteworthy for the degree to which the standards governing substituted judgment have been thought through by ethicists. None have been more thorough or careful in this regard than Allen Buchanan and Dan Brock, and their account will prove helpful to us here, even though the health care and educational domains are different in some important ways. The two basic standards we will consider are the *substituted judgment standard* and the *best interest principle*,[17] and I will argue in what follows that they are both important to justifying evaluation and grading, and that they apply to different aspects of these educational practices.

At the foundation of Buchanan and Brock's account is the idea that the value and moral force of rights of self-determination vary with the competence of their possessor, in such a way that imposing substituted judgments may be justified when a lack of competence can be properly demonstrated. The capacities requisite to self-determination, when they are intact and reasonably well-developed, enable an agent to identify and satisfy her desires with enough success that a regard for her well-being and a respect for her claim to be self-determining converge, by and large. Regard for well-being and respect for claims of self-determination begin to pull in different directions, however, when the capacities required for competent self-determination are not fully present. These capacities are essentially those required for rational judgment and choice, and include abilities to perceive, comprehend, think things through, imagine and rationally project future courses of events, evaluate alternatives in light of a sound appreciation of one's own dominant interests and preferences, and so on.

Even though it is likely that every adult will at least occasionally lack the competence to make some *specific* complex decision that she will face, it is nevertheless true that adults can usually make decisions well enough that there is in their case no acceptable alternative to the policy of a general presumption of global decisional competence (in other words, competence to make all the decisions they face). As Buchanan and Brock point out, the alternatives are decidedly less attractive, those being 'a general presumption of incompetence . . . or . . . having no general presumption and so having to settle the competence of each instance of decision-making case by case.'[18] The substance of this presumption, as they say, is that

> it is presumed of any adult that he or she has sufficient decision-making capacities to make . . . decisions for him- or her-self and to warrant these decisions being respected by others . . . even if others view the decisions as less than optimal, foolish, or not the decisions those others would make in similar circumstances.[19]

This presumption may be overcome in particular cases when it can be demonstrated that the capacities needed for competent decision-making are substantially lacking, but in the absence of such a demonstration any attempt to impose a different choice would be morally intolerable. Their view is that the lack of the capacity for rational decision need only be *substantial* for intervention to be warranted, since even a partial lack of competence may undercut the value of making one's own decisions enough for that value to be outweighed in particular instances by the damage done to one's interests by poorly made decisions. It is also important to Buchanan and Brock's view that, when faced with an individual whom there is good reason (or 'probable cause') to regard as not globally competent, and whose competence to make specific decisions must therefore be determined, competence should be determined relative to the demands of the specific decisions to be made. They argue that this determination should take into account not only the cognitive demands imposed by the decision, but also the importance of the interests at stake, and the degree to which those interests are threatened. One of the most important interests that may be at stake is, of course, the interest in self-determination itself, since a person's choices can profoundly affect her interest in self-determination through the difference they make to the development or preservation of her capacity for competent judgment and choice.

Since competence is to be determined relative to the demands of the specific decisions to be made, a decision-relative standard of competence must be relied upon. A question of special importance for the present inquiry is what form this standard of competence should take. The alternatives that Buchanan and Brock consider are a *minimal competence standard*, an *outcome standard*, and a *process standard*, the process standard being the best choice of the three, since it affords the best protection of self-determination consistent with the patient's well-being.[20] Minimal standards, such as the condition that the patient 'merely be able to express a preference', are not really standards of *competence* at all, and so afford no protection to the patient's well-being. They are insufficiently sensitive to competence-based limitations on the scope of rights of self-determination, and would preclude beneficial intervention even when there would be no moral barrier to doing so. Outcome standards look only to the content or outcome of the patient's deliberations, and regard her as competent to make a decision only if that outcome is judged to be objectively reasonable. This kind of standard inevitably involves a judgment about the rationality of a decision with respect to aims and preferences that are presumed to be normal or objectively desirable; such a standard can therefore make little allowance for differences in judgment arising from legitimate differences of aim or preference. This kind of standard thus makes the opposite kind of error from the first, and accords no independent value to self-determination. By contrast with both of these, a process standard focuses on the quality of the understanding and processes of reasoning leading up to the patient's decision. In doing this, it makes room for the legitimate variability of human ends and preferences. Just as important, it can strike a reasonable balance between regard for well-being and regard for self-determination, and limit authorized substitutions of judgment to those compatible with the patient's rights of self-determination.

All of this pertains so far to the question of *when* it is appropriate for a duly authorized person to substitute her judgment for another's, and brings us now to the question of the standards that govern the judgments themselves when it *is* acceptable to make and impose them. The two standards to which I have already referred are the *substituted judgment standard* and the *best interests principle*.[21] The first of these takes priority in any case in which it is applicable, and holds that the authorized surrogate should choose 'as the incompetent individual would choose in the circumstances were he or she competent'.[22] In any case where differences of aim or preference might come into play, this requires a prior knowledge of the patient's aims and preferences, and so also a patient of enough maturity to *have* fairly stable aims and preferences. Where these requirements cannot be met, the principle that applies is the *best interests principle*, which directs the surrogate to choose the course of action 'with the greatest net benefit to the patient'.[23]

Turning now to children, what separates them from adults is that the capacities required for competent choice are generally not well enough developed to ensure that their well-being or future capacity for competent self-determination will be served by their choices. With respect to health care decisions, Buchanan and Brock take the developmental evidence to suggest that the capacities needed for competence have usually developed to adult-like levels by fourteen or fifteen years old. On the strength of that conclusion they recommend that the legally and socially recognized general presumption of incompetence for children be reversed for those fifteen or older, but that it be retained for those fourteen and below. For those between nine and fourteen they recommend the creation of suitable mechanisms through which this presumption of incompetence could be rebutted on a case-by-case, decision-by-decision basis. The more complex the decision, the greater the demonstrable decision-making capacity would have to be to overcome this presumption. The more serious the peril to the child's well-being, the higher the standard of evidence that would have to be met in establishing the presence of that capacity.

Buchanan and Brock identify two further and associated differences between adults and children. First, the well-being of children is more linked to developmental needs, and less to their relatively unstable expressed aims and preferences, than is the well-being of adults. Second, and similarly,

> an important part of children's and adolescent's interest in self-determination is not their interest *qua* children in making decisions for themselves, but their interest in developing the capacities to be self-determining adults.[24]

This would be true of anyone who lacked, but still had the potential to acquire, normal competence; no matter what a person values (short of wishing above all to be irrational), the value to a person of making decisions for herself is determined in part by how competently she can make those decisions. Accordingly, if the point of rights of self-determination is to protect personal interests in self-determination, then we must regard those who have the potential to acquire normal competence as owed a form of prospective, or forward-looking, respect. This is a form of respect assignable as an unqualified duty not to impede the development of the capacities that contribute to competent self-determination, together with a qualified duty to take positive steps to promote that development.[25] The latter duty falls most obviously on those with some responsibility for the bearer of the rights in question.

Regarding the content of that duty, the development of competence requires the exercise of the requisite emerging capacities, but also coaching, instruction, and sometimes intervention to prevent choices that could be expected to threaten substantially the continuation of that development. Such efforts in the cause of the child's developmental interests, and in the face of present incompetence to make choices consistent with those interests, would be no infringement of the interests in self-determination thereby promoted. Respect for the child's right of self-determination would *demand* such intervention by those with responsibility for the child, given the relative values to the child of making authoritative use of her present capacities, compared with acquiring the competence to judge and choose more wisely in the future.

Buchanan and Brock are concerned with practical self-determination, but there are no obvious grounds for supposing intellectual self-determination to be any less important, or significantly different in its logic from what they suggest. To the foregoing we need only add in connection with intellectual self-determination that promoting intellectual competence in those who lack it, in the right circumstances and in the right manner, would seem obligatory on the part of those charged with their care. Since it is obligatory it is surely permissible, and since it is justified not by extraneous interests, but by the interests in intellectual self-determination itself, it cannot be an infringement of the right of intellectual self-determination.

The legitimacy of evaluation

With this moral framework in hand, my suggestion is that the evaluation and grading of students is best regarded as combining in one process both a determination of competence and the imposition of substituted judgments in just those instances where the student's lack of competence to make the judgment in question is demonstrated. As we have seen, a process of this sort can be not only morally legitimate, but quite free of any infringement of the student's right of intellectual self-determination, if (1) it rests on either a legitimate presumption of incompetence or specific grounds for making an individual determination of competence; (2) it relies on an acceptable standard of competence; (3) the judgment that is substituted for the student's satisfies the appropriate standard; and (4) the student's prospective rights of intellectual self-determination are adequately respected. A final condition, discussed at length by Buchanan and Brock but so far unmentioned here, is that (5) the judgments of competence and substituted judgments must be made on proper authority and subject to appropriate institutional safeguards. In this section I shall develop the account of the ethics of evaluation and grading implied by this characterization, and show that these five conditions can be met. I will thus conclude that, with some adjustment of evaluation practices, the challenge to evaluation and grading posed by the Coercion Argument can be fully met.

The first point to be addressed in establishing the moral legitimacy of 'correcting' students' judgments through adverse assessments is the reliance on a general presumption of a lack of competence to make judgments of the kinds that those who have mastered an academic subject can make. It is reasonable to think that a presumption of subject-specific noncompetence for all students does need to be established, since they are routinely subjected to evaluations without any individualized showing of 'probable cause' to suspect that they lack the competence to make sound judgments in the subject-matter domains in question. In the absence of a showing of probable cause or of the legitimacy of an initial presumption of noncompetence one could reasonably regard the whole act of subjecting students to evaluations as unwarranted interference. So we must ask what the basis for an initial presumption of subject-specific noncompetence might be.

With regard to required courses of study, this presumption would have to be established on the strength of evidence about the general timing and patterns of cognitive development. One would need to be able to say on reasonable empirical evidence that people at the age of those required to undertake the various courses of study would generally not have prior competence to make the kinds of judgments at stake in those studies. It seems to me that we are already in a fairly good position to say this, but that efforts at curriculum development should probably be focused more on deficiencies of judgment and the development of good judgment in subject-domains, and less on what students do not and should know.

This leaves the matter of elective courses of study. In connection with these, one would have to regard a presumption of subject-matter specific incompetence as arising by contract or mutual understanding, subject to the proviso that curricula not be structured in such a way as to leave students only with optional courses of study in which they would generally already be competent. This proviso is not hard to satisfy, and so long as it is it would be quite reasonable to rely on students to sign up for studies in which they are not already expert. (Of course, if a student's prior mastery is known from the outset, she is best directed to an alternative course of study which would be more fruitful.) In these conditions, the student's act of signing up for the course could be understood to entail an admission of subject-specific and level-specific noncompetence, or an acceptance of a presumption of such noncompetence as a condition of instruction. This understanding can be regarded with some reason as implicit in current practice, and to the extent that it is this is morally unproblematic. It thus seems generally reasonable for teachers and examiners to rely on a rebuttable presumption that students are generally not competent to judge what is true and false, cogent and spurious, and so on, at their present level of study in the domains of study they undertake in school. That presumption provides a component of the moral grounds for evaluating students' progress toward full competence in those domains of study.

The second requirement for the moral soundness of evaluation and grading is that they rely on an acceptable standard for determining students' competence, and here problems with traditional practice do begin to emerge. As we have seen, Buchanan and Brock advocate the use of a process standard of competence in a health care setting; I believe this is also the most appropriate kind of standard to use in evaluation and grading, though for reasons that are only partly the same. Part of the argument for using a process standard in domains of practice is that it allows for legitimate variations in human aims and preferences that may make a difference to what choices are rational for a given person. The judgments at stake in evaluation and grading are not ones about what to do, however, but simply about what to believe, on what evidence to believe it, how to investigate what one does not know, and the like. The fundamental, universal interest at stake in all of this is the development of intellectual powers, good judgment, and an accurate appreciation of the nature of things. This is an interest that all agents, all human beings, share, whatever else they care about, even though children and many adults may give little thought to it. What concerns us, in other words, is epistemic rationality, and varitions in ends and preferences do not enter into it in the way they enter into practical rationality. So part of the argument for a process standard of competence does not apply in the academic context. Nevertheless, it is clearly the right standard to us, because it is a direct measure of the quality of reasoning and thought that constitute good judgment. An outcome measure, which detects nothing more than conclusory statements, cannot possibly provide an adequate measure of the competence of judgment. As a basis for making inferences about competence of judgment, any measure of this sort will inevitably be subject to both false positives and false negatives: the former in any instance in which an acceptable answer is produced without independent judgment (as for instance from simple memory), and the latter in any instance in which an unacceptable answer masks judgment that is largely competent but flawed or unanticipated. Evaluations of students typically do rely heavily on such outcome measures, measures that look simply at the correctness of conclusory statements, and little if any on the basis for making them. The analysis developed here suggests that this is morally problematic. Any time an outcome measure produces a false negative assessment of competence that a feasible process measure would have avoided, it would be reasonable to say that some form of interference with a student's interest in intellectual self-determination has occurred.

The third requirement is that the judgment that is substituted for the student's must satisfy the appropriate standard for substituted judgment. This is strongly linked in the present context to the determination of competence or its absence: the standards of rationality and good judgment that the process measures of competence rely on will be no different from the standards that guide the content of the substituted judgment. The appropriate standard here is the *substituted judgment standard*, because it takes priority over the best interests principle in any case in which it applies. It does apply here, even in the absence of any knowledge of individual student aims and preferences, since these have no pertinent bearing on epistemic rationality. Indeed, this principle may be applied even to children who still lack settled preferences, since it requires in this context simply that the teacher judge as the child would, were she, the child, competent to make the kinds of academic judgments at issue. The upshot of this is simply that the teacher or grader is warranted, first, in overturning any judgment that the student would not make were she competent in the forms of judgment belonging to the current level of study in the subject domain in question. Second, she is warranted in substituting the judgment the student would make if competent, or giving some indication of the range of judgments that would be competent. One implication of this is that if there is no uniquely competent judgment to be made, the teacher or grader should be sensitive to that. One possibility that may arise, though with what frequency it would be difficult to know, is that with respect to some forms of judgments, cultural differences might incline students toward different judgments from among those that are competent. Contingencies of this sort would demand a kind of sensitivity that requires not only an awareness of the different but reasonable premises that students may rely on, but also more attention and sensitivity to the quality of student inference, inquiry, and judgment than the training of many teachers may prepare them for.

The fourth condition for the moral soundness of evaluation and grading is the requirement that the student's prospective rights of intellectual self-determination be respected. The presumption underlying this condition is that children lack the competence to make many sorts of judgments that they need to be able to make in order to be intellectually autonomous or self-determining. The standard to be followed is the best interest principle, applied not with respect to the child's general interests, but rather with respect to her interest in intellectual development and autonomy.[26] This is not to say that the child's general interests will not be taken into account, for they should be in designing courses of study and many other aspects of schooling, but rather to add an additional requirement beyond respect for the child's general interests: to recognize the significance of the interest in intellectual self-determination as something distinct from an interest in being intellectually prepared to meet the practical challenges of life. Students only become intellectually self-determining by developing the capacities of thought and judgment this requires, so the development of such capacities must guide pedagogy, the curriculum, and evaluation itself, if the enterprise of evaluation and grading are to satisfy the moral requirements arising from students' rights of intellectual autonomy. This would require the adoption of a 'thinking' curriculum and the reform of evaluation practices to support more effectively efforts to promote development of competent thinking and judgment. With respect to the latter, process measures will again be preferable for their superior capacity to monitor and encourage quality of thought and judgment.

This provides us with an answer to the Coercion Argument that avoids the problem, noted in Purdy's response to the libertarians, of relying entirely on the idea of preparing students to make good practical judgments. For while it takes the development of good practical judgment to be an important goal of education, it assigns independent importance to intellectual freedom itself, and shows that freedom is not infringed, but rather promoted, by proper instruction and evaluation. The content and character of academic studies and evaluation must serve the student's developmental interests as they are related to her general future well-being, as Purdy insists, but they must also be designed to promote intellectual self-determination. It is only if they are that the restrictions of intellectual freedom they involve will be justified by the interest in intellectual freedom itself, which is what is required if we are to avoid infringing the right of intellectual self-determination.

393

This answer also avoids the other problem we saw in Purdy's account, which was that it seemed to apply to only that part of the curriculum that could be justified for its contribution to the development of practical judgment. The account I am suggesting here applies to any part of the curriculum to which the Coercion Argument might apply: any in which students are expected to make statements that might be challenged. My point is that all those parts of the curriculum that call upon students to say what is true are ones in which their intellectual self-determination can and should be served by promoting their capacity to think and judge for themselves.

The final requirement that I have identified calls upon teachers to be skilled in the forms of judgment they are teaching and monitoring, and calls upon schools and school districts, who authorize teachers to evaluate and grade students, to take reasonable measures to ensure that teachers have those skills. It also demands that some institutional safeguards exist, including mechanisms of appeal and oversight. Among the latter, one might include the use of standardized tests and assessments to provide models and accountability to a 'thinking' curriculum and system of evaluation.

Moreover, even if state and national standards and the measures through which they are maintained are not officially used as mechanisms of accountability, they will inevitably influence the goals and style of teaching and learning, shaping both the uses of classroom time and the character of classroom evaluations of students. It is thus quite important that they satisfy the moral demands enumerated here, even if (as seems likely) it would take a great deal more than the reform of standards and standardized measures to bring classroom practice into conformity with the requirements outlined here.

To summarize the results of this section, I have held that grading is a form of substituted judgment, which when carried out properly is a process of sorting the judgments that students produce into those that are competent and those that are not. It amounts to a procedure through which an initial presumption of subject- and level-specific incompetence can be rebutted on a decision-by-decision basis, and through which the epistemic decisions that can be competently made by the student (when they *are* competently made) are recognized and allowed to stand. It is thus, ideally, only judgments that a student is reasonably found not competent to make that are penalized or overridden. Provided the finding that competence is lacking is properly authorized and based on reasonable criteria, then, there is no infringement of the student's rights of intellectual self-determination. There is no infringement because the most reasonable view of these rights is that in the absence of intellectual competence the interest in acquiring that competence outweighs the interest in having the current judgments or choices of that incompletely developed capacity be authoritative.

It is important to emphasize that this analysis provides only part of a full investigation of the moral status of testing and grading practices. It does not answer every moral objection to testing and grading. Nor does it show that grades, as we know them, are the best vehicle for imparting the kinds of judgments defended here as necessary to promoting students' intellectual autonomy. For all I have said, a system of written evaluative comments might serve this purpose better, and be more desirable on other grounds as well.

The need for reform

To summarize: while a minimal *standard* of competence would require teachers to let incompetent academic judgments stand, an *outcome standard* would also be seriously defective in allowing teachers to focus only on the rightness or wrongness of conclusory statements and to ignore the processes of thought and judgment that yield those statements. Even when 'objective' test items have been successfully constructed in such a way as to eliminate all reasonable grounds for giving answers other than the designated right answer (which is less often than one might hope), an objectively incorrect answer may mask a quality of thought and judgment that should be acknowledged and cultivated.[27] Worse still, even correct outcomes may indicate little about the processes that yield them; and all too often they reveal nothing more than the ability to recall fragmentary facts.[28] Outcome measures are for this reason a poor vehicle for promoting epistemic competence and thereby respecting the student's interest in intellectual self-determination. A *process standard*, which provides the best guide for how to respect self-determination, would dictate continued reform of evaluation practices to focus less on recall of specific subject-matter content and more on processes of thought, the development of judgment, and deeper forms of understanding of the various domains of inquiry. This does not mean that all use of 'objective' test items is morally suspect, for the development of good judgment and mastery of different modes of inquiry does require, among other things, that one learn a great number of facts. There may yet be a place for well-crafted multiple-choice items that demand thinking rather than recall; but it means that the balance between process and content items should shift dramatically.[29]

The enactment of such reform will require efforts to develop techniques for designing prompts that elicit thinking and judgment, and related techniques for scoring responses so as to reveal the quality of thought and judgment elicited. The prompts will have to identify and elicit forms of response, whether written, oral, or performed, that will display thought in ways that make its quality observable, such as by demanding that an answer be justified or requesting an evaluation of an argument, a problem solution, or the design of an experiment or investigation. Explanatory thinking, which is as important to many domains of inquiry as their modes of inquiry and confirmation, should also be a focus of teaching and evaluation, and can be elicited and effectively assessed by prompts that call for multiple possible explanations of unfamiliar phenomena or critiques of proposed explanations.

It will take some work to identify the most productive forms of prompts suitable to each subject area at each grade level. This work, and the development of scoring guides and training for teachers and others who will set and score exams, must be grounded in an adequate conception of the nature of the thinking and judgments proper to each subject domain. Even the most progressive curriculum frameworks in use in the United States still lack this. They acknowledge the importance of observing, classifying, measuring, inferring, and the like (the so-called 'basic process skills'), but do not adequately identify and direct teachers' and examiners' efforts toward the larger structures of 'higher order' thinking. The past few years have seen some efforts in the right direction, however, at the National Assessment of Educational Progress, the Educational Testing Service, the New Standards Project, nationally, and in a number of states as well. In California, for example, a framework for the construction and scoring of essay items as process measures in standardized biology testing, based upon a division of biological thinking into explanatory, investigative, and confirmatory types, has proven successful in field trials, and might prove a useful point of departure for other subject domains as well.[30] The challenges entailed by this agenda are in any case quite substantial, and not unrelated to those involved in the design and implementation of the 'thinking curriculum' that evaluation of this sort would need to be linked to. If the foregoing analysis is correct, they are challenges that a proper moral regard for children's rights of intellectual self-determination compels us to accept.

Notes

1 Reports of grade inflation at the college level suggest that some university faculties have come to regard grading as coercive because they have lost their faith in reason. See John Leo, ' "A" for Effort: Or for Showing Up,' *U.S. News & World Report*, 18 October 1993, 22. I am not aware of any serious attempts to develop such an argument, however, and will confine my attention to the libertarian argument.

2 See Judith Jarvis Thomson, *Rights, Restitution and Risk* (Cambridge, Mass.: Harvard University Press, 1986), 40, 51–5, on the distinction between an 'infringement' of a right, which is justified by the overriding value or importance of competing interests, and a 'violation' of a right, which cannot be so justified and which is therefore wrongful, all things considered.

3 Allen Buchanan and Dan Brock, *Deciding for Others* (Cambridge: Cambridge University Press, 1989).

4 See for example, William Rickenbacker (ed.) *The Twelve Year Sentence: Radical Views of Compulsory Schooling* (La Salle, Ill.: Open Court Publishing, 1974); Beatrice Gross and Ronald Gross (eds) *The Children's Rights Movement: Overcoming the Oppression of Young People* (New York: Anchor/Doubleday, 1977); Ann Swidler, *Organization Without Authority: Dilemmas of Social Control in Free Schools* (Cambridge, Mass.: Harvard University Press, 1979); William Aiken and Hugh LaFollette (eds) *Whose Child?: Children's Rights, Parental Authority, and State Power* (Totowa, N.J.: Rowman and Littlefield, 1980); Howard Cohen, *Equal Rights For Children* (Totowa, N.J.: Littlefield, Adams, 1980); Michael Smith, *The Libertarians and Education* (London: George Allen & Unwin, 1983); and Geoffrey Scarre, *Children, Parents, and Politics* (Cambridge: Cambridge University Press, 1989).

5 See for example, Swidler, *Organization Without Authority*, ch. 1; Garth Boomer (ed.) *Negotiating the Curriculum* (Sydney: Ashton Scholastic, 1982); and Smith, *Libertarians and Education*, 83–97.

6 While recognizing that the character of the judgments expressed by grades is neither

this simple, nor uniform across all educational contexts (see R.J. Stiggins, 'Inside High School Grading Practices: Building a Research Agenda,' *Educational Measurement* 8 [1989]: 5–14), I will assume in what follows that we are concerned with grades as simple measures of achievement of course or unit objectives or competence in some part of an academic subject domain. To the extent that this is not how grades are used, they will require a different justification from the one I will propose. Some uses of grades may be more difficult or impossible to justify, but that is a topic best left for another occasion.

7 See Smith, *Libertarians and Education*, 64, 66–7.

8 A student who gained an advantage through undeserved superior grades would be, in economic or rational-choice theoretic terms, a 'free-rider', or one who enjoys goods (whatever they are) secured through the compliance of others with a cooperative scheme whose terms she herself defies.

9 James Terwilliger, 'Assigning Grades – Philosophical Issues and Practical Recommendations,' *Journal of Research and Development in Education* 10 (1977): 21–39, 24–7.

10 Laura Purdy, *In Their Best Interest? The Case Against Equal Rights For Children* (Ithaca, N.Y.: Cornell University Press, 1992).

11 *Ibid.*, 158.

12 *Ibid.*, 160, 159 (emphasis added). Rosemary Chamberlin makes a similar argument, in *Free Children and Democratic Schools* (New York: The Falmer Press, 1989), 100–2.

13 Purdy. *In Their Best Interest?* 162.

14 *Ibid.*, 165.

15 *Ibid.*, 158.

16 It is, of course, true that most corrections are supposed to be substitutions of right answers for wrong ones, but if this is the whole of the matter it is difficult to see how an adequate response to the Coercion Argument might be framed. One could argue that the possession of truth and knowledge is more conducive to intellectual autonomy than falsehood and ignorance, and that correcting students' work corrects their false beliefs and gives them knowledge, but this is not a wholly satisfactory answer. Unless corrections include or link up with evidence or justifications, it is doubtful that they do lead students to new knowledge. Even if they did, there are enough other dimensions of epistemic agency unaccounted for that one could scarcely judge whether the net result for the student is a gain in intellectual autonomy or a loss.

17 See Buchanan and Brock, *Deciding For Others*, 112 ff and 122 ff.

18 *Ibid.*, 21.

19 *Ibid.*

20 *Ibid.*, 48–51.

21 I should note here that there is a third – but for our purposes completely inapplicable – principle that takes the highest priority in Buchanan and Brock's hierarchy of standards. In general, their account is considerably more detailed and sophisticated than it is possible or necessary to make clear here.

22 Buchanan and Brock, *Deciding for Others*, 112.

23 *Ibid.*, 123.

24 *Ibid.*, 231.

25 The language and principles here are essentially Kantian, except that the two forms of duties are typically rendered in translation from the German as 'perfect' and 'imperfect' duties.

26 One could argue that this application of the *best interest standard* would necessarily coincide with a similar application of the *substituted judgment standard*, but the former captures better the character of the decision to be made. The point is not, as in grading itself, to suggest or impose the judgments that the student would make were she competent, but to make decisions that will promote the student's best interests.

27 I thus agree with Grant Wiggins when he insists, in 'A True Test: Toward More Authentic and Equitable Assessment,' *Phi Delta Kappan* 71 (1989): 708, that the reasons that test-takers have for their answers are not irrelevant, but on very different grounds from his. His suggestion, that there is inherent inequity in a test that 'is unable to encompass the inevitable idiosyncratic cases for which we ought always to make exceptions to the rule,' has significance only for those answers whose merits may be misjudged by the dominant kinds of measures, whereas the concern I have raised applies more pervasively.

28 Elliot Eisner offers grounds for concern about this lack of information about processes of thought and quality of reasoning when he notes that it leaves us in a poor position to further 'the development of problem-solving skills'; see Elliot W. Eisner, 'Reshaping Assessment in Education: Some Criteria in Search of Practice,' *Journal of Curriculum Studies* 25 (1993): 227. This is an important point, but different from the one I am making here. Problem-solving skills may play a role in thinking effectively and exercising independent and well-considered judgment, but they are not all there is to it, and the reasons for wanting students to be good problem-solvers might be quite different from the reasons for respecting their claims to self-determination.

29 One *can* evaluate content knowledge using process measures, such as essays that call for thinking and judgment but also require that the student rely upon an understanding of content knowledge, but this is not an efficient way to evaluate how completely a student has mastered the knowledge base of a subject domain.

30 This work, conducted by R. Darrell Bock, Randall Curren, Megan Martin, and Michele Zimowski, in cooperation with the Golden State Examinations Program of the California Assessment, is reported in R. Darrell Bock *et al.*, *Secondary School Science Assessment* (forthcoming).

Acknowledgement

I owe thanks to David Hoekema and Thomas Wren for their prepared responses to the version of this paper presented at a session of the Association for Philosophy of Education, held concurrently with the Eastern Divisional Meetings of the American Philosophical Association, in Atlanta, 29 December 1993. I would also like to thank R. Darrell Bock, Richard Feldman, David Hansen, Kenneth Strike, Tyll van Geel, and the editor and referees of *Educational Theory* for their valuable comments on earlier drafts.

21

IS THERE A COGENT PHILOSOPHICAL ARGUMENT AGAINST COMPETENCY STANDARDS?

Paul Hager

Currently in Australia there is debate occurring about the place, if any, of competency standards in the higher education system. This debate took some time to get started before being fuelled by the Finn Report (Australian Education Council Review Committee 1991) and the subsequent Mayer Committee (1992) discussion paper with their emphasis on key competencies which they recommended should be built into all levels of the Australian education and training system. This debate has now been fuelled further by the Higher Education Council discussion papers, *The quality of higher education* (1992). Major contributors to this debate have been the Australian Vice-Chancellors Committee (AVCC), which has repeatedly expressed the view that competency standards constitute a type of centralised control which is incompatible with the essential autonomy of university curricula. The National Training Board (NTB) has been seen by many as the focus of this alleged centralised control of curricula.

The main aim of this paper is to examine the arguments proposed by various philosophers about competency standards, dating back to the flurry of writing on this topic in the 1970s in the United States. These arguments will be related to the current situation in Australia.

General features of the competency debate in Australia

One remarkable feature of the discussions about the place, if any, of competency standards in the higher education system is that political allegiances seem to be no guide to a person's position on competency standards. Leonie Kramer thinks that they represent the end for the humanities, whereas Lauchlan Chipman sees

Source: *Australian Journal of Education*, Vol. 38, No. 1, 1994.

them injecting a welcome much-needed clarity into the way the humanities are taught and examined. Laurie Carmichael and others of the left see competency standards as the vehicle for achieving a range of desirable ends including workplace reform, overdue adequate recognition of women's skills, etc., although others see Carmichael and company as joining the new right. The vice-chancellor of one of Australia's more venerable universities has blamed Gramscian Marxism for the rise of competency standards (Penington 1992), whereas critics from a different university point to economic rationalism and corporate managerialism as the culprits (Porter Rizvi, Knight *et al.* 1992). All of this suggests that the debate, in order to advance, needs to get beyond assigning labels and take a much closer look at what competency standards have become, whatever their origins might be. After all, there is such a thing as the genetic fallacy – that is, the fallacy of arguing that, because something had certain characteristics at an earlier time, therefore it must have those characteristics now.

It is here that we run into a second remarkable feature of the current debate, namely the reluctance of most people in the higher education sector to take a dispassionate look at competency standards. There is, no doubt, a variety of reasons for this, but clearly a major one is that the influence of the vocational/ general dichotomy runs deep. The thinking of many people in the higher education sector is dominated by the traditional dichotomy between vocational education and 'genuine' education and all that this entails: body *vs.* mind, hand *vs.* head, manual *vs.* mental, skills *vs.* knowledge, applied *vs.* pure, knowing how *vs.* knowing that, practice *vs.* theory, particular *vs.* general, and training *vs.* education. Chipman (1992) is essentially correct in tracing the influence of these dichotomies on the thinking of many in the higher education sector back to Socrates. For those who think in terms of this series of contrasts, it is self-evident that competency standards are essentially concerned with the performance of particular and discrete vocational tasks which, how ever skilled they may be, involve a minimum of thought. As such, competency standards are clearly the proper concern of training, but have nothing to say to education. The seeming self-evidence of this line of thinking is presumably the reason why typical higher education opponents of competency standards show no signs of understanding what is actually in the competency standards developed so far by various professions in Australia.

That higher education opponents of competency standards do think in terms of the above dichotomies is clear from their writings, in particular in the contrasts drawn between the higher-level generic attributes (e.g. critical thinking, problem solving, etc.) fostered by universities, and the 'narrow' (this favourite epithet) outcomes which are seen as the concern of competency standards. (The contrast which results from thinking in terms of these dichotomies is shown in the first and second columns of the Appendix, which was compiled largely from claims made in the writings of a variety of higher education opponents of competency standards.)

There are several comments to make about the domninant influence in this

400

debate of the vocational/general and related dichotomies. First, there are some nice ironies in this situation. The theory/practice dichotomy and all the other dichotomies which it underpins support a particular kind of educational elitism which some of the higher education opponents of competency standards have elsewhere disowned in their writings. Likewise some of the higher education opponents of competency standards are people who have at other times attacked the theory/practice division as a false and misleading way of thinking. A further irony is that several of those who have been most trenchant in their rejection of the idea that vocational education might have any place in a university preside over institutions with many faculties that are clearly vocational in intent. In medical faculties, for instance, there has been a clear trend in the last decade for assessment in the final years to centre on assessment of clinical competence.

Secondly, there are a number of general reasons for maintaining that the vocational/general and related dichotomies are false ones (Australian Education Council 1991; Hager 1990). This is not the place to repeat the details of these arguments. Briefly there are economic, technological and educational reasons. From the economist's point of view, the vocational/general dichotomy is a false one, not only because graduates of supposedly general higher education courses end up in relatively well-paid jobs; the same result is found in all countries where schooling offers alternatives of general education or vocational education. In addition, underdeveloped countries which set out to achieve economic growth and development by deliberately making their education system specifically vocational have fared less well than those whose education system focused on basic general education. In both cases, the economist is left with the paradox that general education is more vocational than vocational education. The technological argument is that the major impact of microelectronic technology on work has been to create a demand for the broad skills that are the product of general education. The educational argument is complex, but it is essentially Whitehead's (1950), that 'the antithesis between a technical and a liberal education is fallacious' (p. 74). Whitehead's basic challenge is: 'Pedants sneer at an education which is useful. But if education is not useful, what is it?' (p. 3). Overall there are cogent reasons of various kinds for rejecting the vocational/general dichotomy.

Thirdly, and most importantly, there are serious epistemological reasons why the vocational/general and related dichotomies are false ones. For one thing, knowledge and competence are not as disparate as some commentators assume. Wolf (1989) argues for the position 'that there is no bifurcation between competence and education' (p. 39). She takes this to mean that competency-based education 'is perfectly compatible with the learning of higher-level skills, the acquisition of generalizable knowledge (and understanding), and with broad-based courses.' Wolf's reasons for supporting this position include:

- 'Competence is a construct, and not something that we can observe directly' (p. 40), but so too is knowledge. (We infer whether students' knowledge is adequate from their performance on various tests and assignments.)

- What we know of the structure of mind shows the importance of a variety of cognitive abilities. Knowledge recall is only the start. Far from involving practice without theory, as some higher education critics fear, what competence does is to take us beyond lower cognitive abilities, such as recall, to higher cognitive abilities, such as application and synthesis of knowledge.
- Not just that something is done, but why it is done is crucial, that is, '"knowing" something involves knowing when to access it, and being able to do so when appropriate – even if it is only in an examination room' (p. 42).

Drawing on Pearson's (1980, reprinted 1984) distinction between 'habitual skill knowledge' and 'intelligent skill knowledge', Elliott (1991: p. 122) suggests that Wolf may be still only admitting knowledge of a limited kind. According to Pearson (1984), knowledge is certainly necessary for competence because 'a person who is competent at something knows how to do something at more than a minimal level' (p. 37). However, this knowing how, which Pearson dubs 'skill knowledge', is claimed to be of two kinds. Habitual skill knowledge underpins 'those skills that a person can perform routinely without reflection', whereas intelligent skill knowledge underpins 'those skills whose performance requires insight, understanding and intelligence' (Pearson 1984: p. 37). Now Pearson and Elliott are correct in their conclusion that a narrow conception of competence, such as the one shown in the first column of the Appendix, requires only habitual skill knowledge. Equally convincing is their view that behaviourist approaches will seek to reduce all knowledge to habitual skill knowledge. Notwithstanding, and despite Elliott's claim to the contrary, I read Wolf's position to include both habitual skill knowledge and intelligent skill knowledge. In any case, later sections of this paper will outline a conception of competence that clearly incorporates both kinds of knowledge.

Incidentally Pearson's use of knowing how in the previous paragraph recalls Ryle's famous distinction between 'knowing how' and 'knowing that' (Ryle 1949). In fact, this distinction provides yet another epistemological reason for viewing the vocational/general education dichotomy as a false one. In specifying the distinction, Ryle was concerned originally to rebut the assumption that knowing how to do something is knowing the truth of certain principles and applying them to an activity. He pointed out that, although it is possible to theorise about, say, cooking, the principles of cooking are, logically speaking, a distillation from the practice of those who know how to cook. Knowing how to do things, being able to perform intelligently, is logically independent of any interior theorising. Though Ryle was seeking to elevate practice from its mistakenly subordinate role, the main effect of his drawing attention to the knowing how *vs.* knowing that distinction has been to entrench further the old dichotomies between practice and theory, doing and thinking, etc. Yet, as Edel (1973: pp. 43–51) has demonstrated, the knowing how *vs.* knowing that distinction applies only to a very restricted range of activities, which include the ones mentioned by Ryle. Ironically, complex work situations, of the kind that plausible professional competency standards would need to describe, are a prime example of the kind of activity that eludes classification as Rylean knowing how.

There are still other epistemological arguments against the vocational/general dichotomy. For instance, the Vice-Chancellor of the University of Leeds (Wilson 1992) has argued that, by shunning the vocational, universities risk inhibiting the growth of knowledge. His argument is that knowledge is a social product and so are the ways in which we package it. He discusses various sorts of boxes in which it might be packaged. He suggests an initial four-fold division: (1) enabling disciplines (philosophy, mathematics, computing, etc.); (2) disciplines concerned with the natural world (physics, chemistry, biology etc.); (3) disciplines concerned with the human world (the arts, the social sciences); and (4) disciplines concerned with practice in the human world (engineering, medicine, law, education, etc.). Wilson argues that all categories of the disciplines make valuable contributions to knowledge advance. Increasingly, significant advances require inter- and multi-disciplinary input. He suggests that disciplines concerned with practice in the human world offer unique skills (e.g. design, diagnosis, pattern recognition, etc.) and should not be neglected in favour of the first three categories. Eraut (1985) is another to claim that significant knowledge exists within professions that is typically not recognised by academics.

I have suggested some reasons why the debate in Australia about competency standards and their relation to higher education has taken the course that it has. In particular, I have suggested that the debate has been clouded by dubious assumptions about the nature of vocational education. These assumptions have, in turn, created confusion about the relation between competence and knowledge, and hence about the kinds of learning required to attain competence.

Arguments about the nature of competence

Higher education opponents of competency standards in Australia have virtually all agreed that narrow conceptions of competence are undesirable. On this view, competency standards are synonymous with lists of particular, discrete vocational tasks. Not surprisingly, the philosophers of education have been trenchant in their rejection of such conceptions of competence. A focus of their criticisms was competency- (or performance-)based teacher education (CBTE or PBTE), which had a brief flowering in the 1970s, particularly in the United States. (See Houston 1974 for a comprehensive discussion.) CBTE represented the attempt to apply theories of behaviourist psychology to the analysis of teaching. It was based on a very narrow conception of competence and was intended to revamp teacher education courses dramatically. According to Broudy (1984), the CBTE approach defines:

> competence in terms of prespecified performances stated as segments of overt behaviour; it argues that practising the performance directly is more efficient than achieving it indirectly through the conventional

courses . . . competence training . . . contrasts an overt performance with the conventional program's promise of performance.

(p. 3)

Broudy and others (e.g. Johnson 1975; Kaminsky 1975) had no difficulty in demolishing the theoretical foundations of this narrow approach to competence. Although their writings were focused on CBTE/PBTE, their criticisms are sufficiently general to apply to the conceptualisation of any occuaption in these terms. Some ramifications of this approach to competence are outlined in the first column of the Appendix.

Higher education critics of competency standards rightly reject such an approach, preferring instead to focus attention on generic attributes as the best indicators of future successful performance. Some ramifications of this second approach to competence are outlined in the middle column of the Appendix. The difficulty with this second approach is that the link between a generic attribute, such as analysis, and actual professional performance is doubly vague: first because the claim that graduates develop a capacity for analysis is typically not subjected to detailed scrutiny (see Chipman 1992), and secondly because what analysis typically means in the day-to-day practice of the profession is not considered.

However, that the above alternatives are not the only ways of conceptualising competence does not appear to be a welcome message in many quarters. The same critics who want to reject all narrow conceptions of competence typically do not look closely to see what the full range of alternatives might be. The preferred alternative has been that shown in the middle column of the Appendix (but often not called an approach to competency as such, thereby preserving the vocational/general dichotomy). There are some significant problems for this view.

To lead us on to a third model of competence, let us consider what some philosophers of education have suggested as alternatives to the first model. In an important paper, Noddings (1984) applied linguistic analysis to the problems of defining competence and of clarifying the relation between competence and human action. Her first main conclusion was that competence must be differentiated from performance. She arrived at this conclusion via a critique of Rylean behaviourism as an inadequate account of competence. The key argument here is that, if competence consists of a series of observable behaviours, then the same series of observable behaviours will be displayed by anyone competent in a given field. But it is evident that not everyone competent in a given field will display the same series of observable behaviours (think of competent teachers); hence competence is not the same thing as performance. Rather it is something that underlies performance. In addition, Noddings points out that the occurrence of observable behaviours associated with competence in a given field may be explicable by causes other than competence (think of actors playing the roles of, say, surgeons). She concluded:

404

If competence, as capacity, is to be retained as groundwork for performance, then the problem of identifying reliable indicators of competence arises and this, it seems to me, is a tough problem demanding sophisticated methods and extensive investigation.

(Noddings 1984: pp. 18–19)

She goes on to recommend an empirically based, comprehensive, naturalistic study of actual professionals indisputably held to be competent as the main source of a description of competence. From this, in relation to teaching, she suggests that it should be 'possible to construct theories that have some degree of the desired systematization . . . capable of producing categories that will aid us in describing competence and in evaluating it' (p. 21). Noddings states that she knows of no program of CBTE or PBTE that meets the considerations outlined in her paper. However, she commends earlier work by Kerr and Soltis (1974) as a promising extension of her ideas.

Kerr and Soltis attempted to provide 'a theoretical description of teaching which is at least adequate to the task of identifying teacher competencies' (p. 3). I will not consider in any detail those aspects of their paper that were specifically concerned with the nature of teaching (these ideas generated a significant debate, e.g. Johnson 1975; Noddings 1974a, 1974b). Rather I will outline some of their general points which are crucial to the third approach to competence, which is much to be preferred to the two other approaches already discussed.

Kerr and Soltis (1974) set out to develop 'a theoretical model of teaching that possesses descriptive adequacy' (p. 4). Following Green (1964), they propose an *action* description rather than a *behaviour* description:

One applies the adverb 'competently' only to those movements which a person *intends* as a *particular* type of activity. . . . Thus, while it is possible to describe teaching, or any other human activity, as either *action*, which necessarily involves intended activity and appeals to a person's reasons and goals to explain the activity, or as *behaviour*, which can be specified directly in terms of observable movement and appeals to causes for explanation, our interest in competency advises an action description.

(Kerr and Soltis 1974: pp. 4–5)

Kerr and Soltis recommend that professional competence be conceived in terms of a set of action categories that are necessary to carrying out the profession, with further elaboration and development reflecting the logic of this set of action categories. It is interesting that, though the Kerr–Soltis proposal was published and debated from 1974 onwards, Noddings in 1984 reported that, to her knowledge, nobody had attempted to apply it to the problem of teacher competence. Walker's (1992a) proposals on how to conceive of teacher competence are perhaps the next development of these ideas.

If Noddings and Kerr and Soltis provide a model of what linguistic analysis can contribute in this field, Price (1974) provides a model of what it cannot do. According to Price (in his presidential address to the 1974 Philosophy of Education Society meeting), there are four senses of the word 'performance'. The first applies to any action of a thing (e.g. the performance of a rock in its falling under gravity). The second applies to the action of any thing that accords with the design followed in that thing's production, and that leads to a specified concrete result (e.g. the action of a drill). The third applies to any action that has parts which a person makes answer to the parts of the work performed and connects in ways that correspond to relations of the parts of the work (e.g. performance of a Beethoven sonata). The fourth applies to any action that a person makes accord with a moral rule. After delineating and discussing each of these four senses, Price (1974) says: 'I can find no other senses of the word "performance"; I conclude that it is wrong, without the invention of some new sense, to describe teaching as a performance at all' (p. 326). Price's four senses are clearly not exhaustive. Can we not legitimately ask about Price's performance as President of the Philosophy of Education Society? What about job performance appraisal in general (e.g. David Hill's performance as general manager of the ABC)? It is clear, I think, that Price is arbitrarily ruling out an important sense of 'performance'.

The basic ideas on how professional competence might best be conceived, which I have identified in the work of Noddings and Kerr and Soltis, provide a good starting point for understanding the way in which professional competency standards have been developed in Australia under the aegis of the National Office of Overseas Skills Recognition (NOOSR). Although I will not describe the processes (see Ash, Gonczi and Hager 1992; Gonczi, Hager and Oliver 1990; Heywood, Gonczi and Hager 1992 for details), the focus is on applying a suitable combination of applied social science research methods to arrive at a logically structured set of action categories of the kind described by Kerr and Soltis. This approach to conceptualising professional competence has been called the 'integrated approach', because it brings together the 'tasks' (or, more accurately, 'key intentional actions') of the first approach and the attributes of the second approach.

According to the integrated conception, competence is conceptualised in terms of knowledge, abilities, skills and attitudes displayed in the context of a carefully chosen set of realistic professional tasks (intentional actions) which are of an appropriate level of generality. A feature of this integrated approach is that it avoids the problem of a myriad of tasks by selecting key tasks (intentional actions) which are central to the practice of the profession. The main attributes required for the competent performance of these key tasks (intentional actions) are then identified. Experience has shown that, when both of these are integrated to produce competency standards, the results do capture the holistic richness of professional practice.

It is worth highlighting some distinctive features of the professional competency standards that have been developed in Australia, since recently it has become evident that there is still a lot of misunderstanding of them (e.g. Dall'Alba and Sandberg 1992: p. 1, think that they are based on competences as individual attributes). One of the most overused terms in the debate about competency standards has been 'atomistic'. Authors seem to assume that, if an approach to conceptualising competence is labelled, usually by themselves, as 'atomistic', then it can be rejected without further argument. In chemistry, where atoms are discrete and independent units, they nevertheless combine to form molecules, which have quite different properties from those of their constituent atoms. Here atoms are a highly useful unit of analysis and are consistent with subsequent powerful synthesis. In reference to competency standards, 'atomistic' has no such clearcut meaning, nor does 'holistic'. Both are relative terms when applied to competency standards and their application needs to be justified by further argument. The fragmenting of a profession into a myriad of tasks, as the first approach to competence does, is overly atomistic precisely because actual practice is much richer than sequences of these isolated tasks, and the overall approach fails to provide any synthesis of the tasks. In that case, we are justified in concluding that the distinctive character of the profession has been destroyed by the analysis. However, the opposite mistake is adherence to a rigid, self-defeating monistic holism that rules out all analysis. In practice, some degree of atomism in approaches to competence will be acceptable, provided that it is accompanied by a suitable degree of holism. The above professional competency standards produced by the integrated approach are holistic in several important senses:

1   They are holistic in that competence is a construct that is inferred (as suggested by Noddings) from performance of relatively complex and demanding intentional actions (as suggested by Kerr and Soltis). The relative complexity of the actions can be gauged from the fact that a typical profession involves no more than 30 to 40 such key intentional actions.

2   The holistic character of such competency standards is reflected in the tasks (or intentional actions) not being discrete and independent. For example, actual professional practice will often simultaneously involve several of these intentional actions.

3   A further sense in which these kinds of competency standards are holistic is that the intentional actions involve what Walker (1992b, following Elliott 1991) calls 'situational understanding'; that is, the competency standards include the idea that the professional performer takes account of the varying contexts in which they are operating. A more general cognitive perspective is called on to frame a skilled intentional action appropriate to the context.

4   Yet another sense in which these kinds of competency standards are holistic is that, by integrating key tasks and attributes (i.e. integrating intentional actions with characteristics or qualities of individuals), competence is constituted by a relation between the professional and his/her work. (Contrary to Dall'Alba and Sandberg, 1992, this means that Sandberg's (1991) findings,

407

that occupational competence is best viewed as intentional achievement, actually provide strong support for the integrated approach to professional competency standards that has been used in Australia.)

By being holistic in the above senses, these competency standards are the opposite of any significantly atomistic approach, whether the atoms be tasks or attributes (once again, contrary to what Dall'Alba and Sandberg 1992: p. 2, claim). In this way, these professional competency standards strike a balance between the misguided extremes of fragmenting the profession to such a degree that its character is destroyed by the analysis and adhering to a rigid, monistic holism that rules out all analysis. That this balance is a reasonable one is indicated by the fact that these professional competency standards allow for professional discretion; that is, they do not prescribe that all professionals will necessarily act in the same way in a given situation. Nor do they require that all professionals will have identical overall conceptions of their work; that is, these professional competency standards are quite consistent with one practitioner having, say, a strong commitment to social justice, whereas another is just as strongly committed to excellence of practice.

The nature of these competency standards will obviously determine how they should best be assessed. Since they are based on the idea that competence is a construct that is not directly observable, but rather is inferred from successful performance, it is clear that performance will be vital for assessment. Equally vital will be the requirement that sufficient evidence be gathered to justify the inference. Although evidence from performance will be central to assessment, it may be supplemented by other kinds of evidence. This follows from the integrated nature of these competency standards in which attributes underpin performance. This means that the attributes often figure in the performance criteria. Thus, in some instances, evidence about possession of attributes, such as certain kinds of knowledge, might usefully supplement evidence of performance. (For a detailed treatment of these points see Gonczi, Hager and Athanasou 1993.)

Educational implications of the integrated approach

Finally this paper considers what integrated professional competency standards mean for higher education, though I believe that many of the same points are applicable to other providers of vocational education (e.g. TAFE). This discussion will be structured around the points in the third column of the Appendix. (The previous section dealt with the first two points: competence inferred from performance and the holistic nature of the competency standards. This discussion will start at the third point.)

Competency standards make no claim to exhaust all facets of a profession, just as traditional entry procedures for professionals do not claim to be totally comprehensive. A good set of competency standards provides a clear statement of what is considered to be important for competent performance in that profession. This is something which has been a long-felt need of registering authorities and the like, thereby pointing to weaknesses in the present arrangements. After all, it would be rather strange if people who are in the business of registering or educating professionals insisted that it was too hard to specify what it is that distinguishes professional from non-professional performance. This is essentially what competency standards do. To point out that professional work is complex is simply to require that valid standards will need to take account of this complexity. It is already evident in the professional competency standards which have been developed so far in Australia that it is possible to capture the complexity of professional work.

In regard to the fourth point, some people worry that competency standards will demand a uniformity in the way professionals practice which is totally inappropriate. There is more than one correct way to perform most professional tasks. The problem here is that 'standards' are taken to imply 'standardisation' of procedure. In fact, the standards are typically about outcomes, and leave it open as to how the outcomes are achieved. The professional competency standards which have been developed so far in Australia do allow for the diversity that is proper to the practice of a profession.

Another worry, which brings us to the fifth point, is that, as a result of establishing competency standards, the corresponding courses which prepare people for the profession will adopt competency-based training (see, e.g., Ashworth and Saxton 1990: pp. 18–19). Academics are correct in their rejection of professional courses becoming a series of practical modules, as the roles and tasks approach to analysing professional competence suggests. However, when competence is conceptualised via the integrated approach in terms of knowledge, abilities, skills and attitudes displayed in the context of realistic professional tasks (or intentional actions), these consequences no longer follow. Rather than recommending the adoption of competency-based training, the integrated approach, by also emphasising requisite knowledge, abilities, skills and attitudes, offers powerful guidance for improvement of traditional courses in respect of content, teaching strategies and asssment procedures. For example, testing graduates against the competency-based standards would effectively identify strengths and weaknesses of the course. Hence, though I uphold the integrated approach to conceptualising professional competence, I do not recommend the adoption of competency-based training for professional courses.

Competency standards offer educational and assessment benefits. The competency standards themselves are a powerful guide to providers of professional education. However, it needs to be emphasised that they are not a curriculum document. For example, entry-level competency standards specify what new graduates should be able to do, but say nothing about now this state is to be achieved. Hence, for providers, there is as much flexibility as ever to decide what to teach, how to teach it and how to assess it. However, assuming that there is room for improvement in most existing courses, a good set of competency standards will provide invaluable guidance on content changes as well as new methods of delivery and assessment. As always, there is more than one way to teach effectively.

Beyond entry level, competency standards offer considerable guidance for the longer-term development of the profession. Continuing professional education (CPE) has been criticised frequently for lack of direction and/or rationale. The clear specification of what a competent professional needs to be able to do will provide a much sharper focus for CPE. (See Hager and Gonczi 1991.) Similar considerations apply to refresher courses for people returning to the profession after an absence or people whose training is out of date. The value of competency standards for efficient and equitable recognition of overseas qualifications is also important.

A further worry, represented by the sixth point, holds that competency standards are developed and controlled by government bureaucrats (e.g. the National Training Board). In fact, the philosophy behind the development of competency standards in Australia is that the profession or industry owns and develops the standards. In many cases university staff are active members of the professional body; hence they have strong representation on the body which owns and develops the competency standards. In all cases, the professional body is a major stakeholder entitled to significant input into courses for the particular profession. Competency standards present a unique opportunity for professions in Australia to raise their community image by increasing their level of professionalism. The competency standards are an explicit public statement of what the profession does, something that has not previously been available publicly in most cases. One aspect of professions increasing their professionalism would be a mature and productive relationship between their professional body and the providers of the courses.

The above considerations give the lie to a related misconception about competency standards, that everything that takes place in a course is dictated centrally by faceless bureaucrats. In fact, given that the profession will own the competency standards, there will be no more central control than at present in, for example, accounting and engineering, where the professional bodies accredit the courses. (The Higher Education Council 1992, p. 6, notes and rejects the claim that a focus on outcomes will result in standardised or common courses.)

Since the competency standards are a powerful guide to providers of professional education without being a curriculum document, they furnish common ground for discussion between providers and the profession that does not exist at present. The lack of such common ground in the past has seen some providers fragment into a series of specialist departments which compete with one another for funds, staff, etc. and thereby lose sight of the totality of professional practice. The competency standards will enable the relative roles of the providers and profession to become clearer in a mutually co-operative environment.

A further concern, point seven, holds that assessment of competence involves ticking off a checklist of observable behaviours. Given the complexity of professional work, this is seen as a futile attempt to achieve objectivity at the cost of sacrificing validity (see, e.g., Ashworth and Saxton 1990: pp. 22–23). I accept this as a criticism of the behaviourist task approach to competency standards. However, when the integrated approach to competency standards is adopted, competence is not something that is directly observed. Rather competence is inferred from performance. This has the effect of placing assessment of competence in the same boat as other kinds of assessment in academic institutions in that procedures are available to maximise its validity and reliability (Gonczi, Hager and Athanasou 1993; Masters and McCurry 1990). If these procedures are followed, then assessment of competence is as 'objective' as any of the alternatives. Similar points apply to claims that competency standards are too vague for assessment purposes (see, e.g., Ashworth and Saxton 1990: pp. 21–2). A properly planned and executed competency analysis will yield standards as specific as the case requires. (See, e.g., Ash, Gonczi and Hager 1992.) The viability of validly assessing integrated competency standards of the kind described in this paper has received theoretical endorsement from the philosophers of education, Scriven (1978) and Siegel (1988). Siegel's endorsement is in the context of rejecting the possibility of validly assessing generic skills such as 'functional literacy' or 'life skill'.

Finally, point eight presents a criticism that is commonly put forward in relation to entry-level competency standards. It holds that, because they prescribe minimum standards, they therefore discourage excellence by reducing everything to the lowest common denominator. A variant on this is that they promote deskilling. (The Higher Education Council 1992, p. 6, notes and rejects the 'lowest common denominator' myth.) These charges are no more logical than making the same claims about traditional examinations on the ground that there is a minimum mark for gaining a pass. More specifically, this myth is based on a complete misunderstanding of the nature of the standards. For the charges to have any substance, the standards would have to relate to tasks that admit of no degrees of performance; that is, you can either do it or not. However, in professional work (and in most other kinds of work), such tasks are rare. Typically the standards relate to tasks which admit of many degrees of performance, as does the task of taking a traditional examination. In both cases, the existence of a minimum satisfactory level of performance is consistent with a full range of performances from excellent through to fail. (For a discussion of the kinds of standards, called 'described standards', appropriate for professional tasks, see Gonczi, Hager and Oliver 1990; Masters and McCurry 1990.)

In addition, entry-level competency standards are not a curriculum document. The expectation is that most graduates of professional courses will greatly exceed the performance levels specified by the entry-level competency standards, just as most entrants to the professional courses greatly exceed the entry requirements. (For further discussion, see Heywood, Gonczi and Hager 1992: Section 2.4.)

Conclusion

A series of arguments about competency standards by various writers has been considered. It has been found that a way of developing competency standards that conform with the general requirements and principles proposed by these arguments is possible. This way of developing competency standards appears to meet all of the theoretical objections that have been raised against competency standards. Those that have been developed so far in Australia for professions according to these principles also seem to be satisfactory. How well they work out in the long term remains to be seen.

These developments suggest that it is crucial that we be clear about our conception of competence and consider alternatives. The 'natural' way of conceiving competence (i.e. as a series of tasks) has fatal defects. Likewise the alternative of conceiving competence as consisting in attributes or generic skills has marked limitations. This paper has argued that a third conception of competence, which integrates tasks and attributes, offers many advantages and avoids the major limitations of the other two conceptions. One clear advantage is a better appreciation of the intimate relationship between vocational and general education and, within these, of the relationship between theory and practice. Another advantage is that integrated competency standards offer a corrective to the all too familiar mistake of education being centred on information absorption and recall. Instead, the structure of knowledge and its relationships and applications is highlighted, thereby promoting a more productive theory of learning.

The integrated approach to competence suggests some challenges for the implementation of the Finn/Mayer recommendations. If the schools and higher education institutions restrict themselves to teaching generic competencies, there will remain a problem about how these translate into life and occupational competencies. On the other hand, facing up to the challenge of integrating the generic and the specific promises a range of new and untried possibilities for teaching and assessment.

At the beginning of this paper, it was pointed out that critics have labelled competency standards with all kinds of (often incompatible) -isms. Here is another one. Elliott (1991) has suggested that the 'widespread emergence of *fundamentalism* in the late 20th century is not confined to religious traditions. It is evidenced in most of the "reforms" now sweeping our social institutions . . . The competency-based education and training movement is one example' (p. 119). Elliott further points out that fundamentalist movements generally possess four characteristics:

> First, they attempt to reduce social practices to a small number of essential elements, against which the practices as a whole can be judged. Their view of competence is an atomistic one. Competence is specified as a number of discrete, atomized abilities which are held to represent its essential elements. Second, the essentials are derived from what is held to be an indubitable foundation of knowledge, such as the Bible, or, in the case of the competency movement, a science of management concerned with the prediction and control of human behaviour. . . . Third, the essential elements of the fundamentalist's credo must refer to concrete tangible and measurable phenomena. Christ's resurrection and

412

virgin birth are considered by Christian fundamentalists to be concrete events in time and place. . . . Similarly 'competencies' were viewed . . . as concrete, tangible and measurable . . . Fourth, the essential elements are viewed as unchanging rather than culturally and socially relative.

(pp. 119–20)

All of these features applied to the failed conception of competence which flourished in the 1970s. This paper has argued that none of these limiting features need apply to the richer conception of competence which is currently being used in Australia.

Appendix

Three different conceptions of competence and their implications

Behaviourist or specific tasks approach	Attribute or generic skills approach	Integrated or task + attribute approach
1. Overt performance is competence	General attributes as predictors of future performance	Competence inferred from performance
2. Atomistic, reductive, trivial, mechanistic, standardised, routine, discrete tasks or skills	Abstract, remote from actual practice, problem of transfer – overall rationale often lacking	Holistic, richness of practice captured
3. Large number of specific competencies – list lengthens with complexity of work, e.g. professions	Small number of generic competencies	Manageable number of key competencies
4. Uniformity (1 right way)	Diversity (> 1 right way)	Diversity (> 1 right way)
5. 'Doing' curriculum Practical modules Jettison current curriculum	Conventional curriculum Fragmented into subjects	Powerful device for improving content delivery and assessment of current curriculum
6. Central control of curriculum	Provider autonomy in curriculum	Profession/provider joint control of curriculum
7. Checklist for ticking – invalid assessment	Traditional assessment – has its limitations	Competence demonstrated over time, portfolios, etc. Assessment needs careful planning
8. Minimum competence 'Lowest common denominator discourages excellence' 'Deskilling'	Encourages excellence that is remote from professional practice	Richness of quality professional performance is captured

References

Ash, S., Gonczi, A. and Hager, P. (1992) *Combining research methodologies to develop competency-based standards for dietitians: A case study for the professions* (National Office of Overseas Skills Recognition Research Paper No. 6). Canberra: AGPS.

Ashworth, P.D. and Saxton, J. (1990) 'On "competence"', *Journal of Further and Higher Education*, **4**, 3–25.

Australian Education Council Review Committee (Bruce Finn, Chair) (1991) *Young people's participation in post-compulsory education and training: Report*. Canberra: AGPS.

Broudy, H.S. (1984) 'The university and the preparation of teachers', in L. Katz and J. Rath (eds) *Advances in teacher education* (Vol. 1). Norwood, NJ: Ablex.

Chipman, L. (1992) 'The challenges of the competency movement', in L. Mineall (ed.) *The challenge of competencies in social welfare*: Proceedings of a National Conference held in Adelaide, July 9–10, 1992. Hawker, ACT: Australian Association of Social Workers Ltd.

Dall'Alba, G. and Sandberg, J. (1992) *A competency-based approach to education and training: Will it improve competence?* (Occasional Paper 92.4). Melbourne: Royal Melbourne Institute of Technology, Education Research and Development Unit.

Edel, A. (1973) 'Analytic philosophy of education at the crossroads', in J.F. Doyle (ed.) *Educational judgments*. London: Routledge & Kegan Paul. Reprinted as Volume I Paper 2.

Elliott, J. (1991) *Action research for educational change*. Milton Keynes: Open University Press.

Eraut, M. (1985) 'Knowledge creation and knowledge use in professional contexts', *Studies in Higher Education*. **10**, 117–33.

Gonczi, A., Hager, P. and Athanasou, J. (1993) *The development of competency-based assessment strategies for the professions* (National Office of Overseas Skills Recognition Research Paper, No. 8). Canberra: AGPS.

Gonczi, A., Hager, P. and Oliver, L. (1990) *Establishing competency-based standards in the professions* (National Office of Overseas Skills Recognition Research Paper No. 1). Canberra: AGPS.

Green, T.F. (1964) 'Teaching, acting and behaving,' *Harvard Educational Review*, **35**, 507–24.

Hager, P. (1990) 'Vocational education/general education – a false dichotomy?' *Studies in Continuing Education*, **12**, 13–23.

Hager, P. and Gonczi, A. (1991) 'Competency-based standards: A boon for continuing professional education?' *Studies in Continuing Education*, **13**, 24–40.

Heywood, L., Gonczi, A. and Hager, P. (1992) *A guide to development of competency standards for professions* (National Office of Overseas Skills Recognition Research Paper No. 7). Canberra: AGPS.

Higher Education Council (1992) *The quality of higher education* (National Board of Employment, Education and Training Discussion papers). Canberra: AGPS.

Houston, W.R. (ed.) (1974) *Exploring competency based education*. Berkeley, Calif.: McCutchan.

Johnson, H.C. (1975) 'Not one "unnecessary wriggle": Some questions about the presuppositions of C/PBTE', *Educational Theory*, **25**, 156–67.

Kaminsky, J.S. (1975) 'C/PBTE. An investigation in the philosophy of social science and competency/performance based teacher education', *Educational Theory*, **25**, 303–13.

Kerr, D.H. and Soltis, J.F. (1974) 'Locating teacher competency: An action description of teaching', *Educational Theory*, **24**, 3–16.

Masters, G. and McCurry, D. (1990) *Competency-based assessment in the professions* (National Office of Overseas Skills Recognition Research Paper No. 2). Canberra: AGPS.

Mayer Committee (Eric Mayer, Chair) (1992) *Employment-related key competencies for postcompul-*

sory education and training: A discussion paper. Melbourne: Australian Education Council/ Ministers of Vocational Education, Employment and Training.

Noddings, N. (1974a) 'Competence theories and the science of education', *Educational Theory*, **24**, 356–64.

Noddings, N. (1974b) 'Teacher competency: An extension of the Kerr–Soltis model', *Educational Theory*, **24**, 284–90.

Noddings, N. (1984) 'Competence in teaching: A linguistic analysis', in E.C. Short (ed.) *Competence: Inquiries into its meaning and acquisition in educational settings*. Lanham, Md: University Press of America.

Pearson, A.T. (1984) 'Competence: A normative analysis', in E.C. Short (ed.) *Competence: Inquiries into its meaning and acquisition in educational settings*. Lanham, Md: University of America.

Penington, D. (1992, November 19–25) [Speech to an Australian Council of Professions seminar.] *Australian Campus Review Weekly*, p. 7.

Porter, P., Rizvi, F., Knight, J. and Lingard, R. (1992) 'Competencies for a clever country: Building a house of cards?' *Unicorn*, **18**(3), 50–8.

Price, K. (1974) 'The sense of "performance" and its point', *Educational Theory*, **24**, 313–27.

Ryle, G. (1949) *The concept of mind*. New York: Barnes & Noble.

Sandberg, J. (1991) *Competence as intentional achievement: A phenomenographic study* (Occasional Paper 91.4). Melbourne: Royal Melbourne Institute of Technology, Education Research and Development Unit.

Scriven, M. (1978) 'How to anchor standards', *Journal of Educational Measurement*, **15**, 273–5.

Siegel, H. (1988) *Educating reason*. New York: Routledge.

Walker, J. (1992a) *A general rationale and conceptual approach to the application of competency based standards to teaching*. Paper prepared for the National Project on the Quality of Teaching and Learning. Canberra: University of Canberra.

Walker, J. (1992b) 'The value of competency based education', in J. Hattie (ed.) *The effects of competency based education on universities: Liberation or enslavement?* Perth: University of Western Australia.

Whitehead, A.N. (1950) *The aims of education and other essays*. London: Ernest Benn.

Wilson, A. (1992, May 1) 'New maps of old terrain', *Times Higher Education Supplement*, pp. 17–20.

Wolf, A. (1989) 'Can competence and knowledge Mix?' in J.W. Burke (ed.) *Competency based education and training*. London: Falmer Press.

Part III

CONTROVERSIAL ISSUES OF CURRICULUM DEVELOPMENT

22

CURRICULUM DESIGN

Robin Barrow

The style of curriculum design writing:
models, diagrams and vocabulary

Curriculum books and articles have a tendency to talk in terms of models. They are also prone to make use of diagrams, and to revert to a certain amount of quasi-technical jargon. Most of this dressing-up is irrelevant to the fundamental business of planning and justifying curricula, but it may serve to support a misleading impression of the nature of curriculum theory.

We are told that there are a number of models of curriculum dissemination (the social–interactive model, the centre–periphery model, the proliferation of centres model, the learning-systems network), as we are told that there are various models of teaching, models of classroom organisation, models of toilet-training, and so forth, as well as models of curriculum design.[1] Reference to a model carries with it connotations of the precise, mechanistic world of physics or engineering, the suggestion of distinct alternatives, each specific and inflexible in itself, though exchangeable for another model. Is there any justification for using such a term in situations where all that is being referred to are some few examples out of a multitude of subtly varied ways of proceeding? In fact, so-called models of curriculum design are often no such thing. They are not necessarily representations of the structure of an ideal or desirable curriculum plan, in the manner of an architect's drawing, or a three-dimensional model. When they come near to being true models, they are open to the objection that in this complex field it is inappropriate to reduce matters to a schematic and inflexible pattern of requirements or procedures. Models of classroom organisa-tion either illegitimately suggest that there is a limited number of precisely classifiable and distinct modes of organisation, or else they are not truly models. So-called models of curriculum dissemination are merely artificial attempts to fossilise in a series of rigid alternatives the perception that one might attempt to spread knowledge and information about a proposed curriculum in many various ways, ranging from attempts at autocratic imposition through to democratic

Source: Robin Barrow, *Giving Teaching Back to Teachers*, Wheatsheaf Books, 1984 Ch. 3.

participation, and that the effectiveness of these ways may vary, largely in ways and to degrees that we do not have much understanding or control of.

Perhaps it is not in itself a crime of major significance to talk of 'models', but it is misleading in that it implies clear distinctions and straightforward limited alternatives where they do not exist. Furthermore, this is merely one example of a more general tendency to create an aura of mechanistic and technical knowledge, implying precision and expertise, by using a language that is highly misleading. To think of the business of teaching in terms of even a dozen or so models is to distort and impoverish one's conception of teaching.[2] For teaching is not reducible to, or adequately characterised in terms of, some limited number of alternative, precisely specified packages of activity. Teaching may take one of a million forms so subtly distinguished and interrelated that it would be fruitless to clarify them, even if one had time, as a million models.

The too easy use of diagrams serves likewise to reinforce the idea that we are dealing with a relatively precise domain comparable to that of the natural sciences. Again there is nothing inherently wrong with a diagram, but, at least for most people, a diagram cannot convey more than can be conveyed in words, and is generally less subtle than verbal formulations. When a diagram is subtle, it is correspondingly incomprehensible to most people, simply because, as most people do their articulate thinking in words, in order to be understood it has to be explained. Diagrams, in short, in the context of education and other similarly complex areas, tend to be either pointless, because they merely present pictorially what is readily comprehensible, or misleading because they oversimplify or stand in need of verbal explanation before they can be understood. But the main objection to them in curriculum is that they may unwarrantably imply something of the certainty and precision of the natural sciences or technology, where they naturally find their home.

Diagrams have their place essentially in situations where they help us to visualise what is at rock-bottom a matter of seeing something that is there to be looked at – something that has a spatial dimension. A diagram of the water-pipes in a house usefully serves this function, as does the diagram of the interior of a house in a murder story. But now compare Figure 1, reproduced from a recent book on the art of the detective story. It is not immediately clear what it is telling us. When I explain that it represents the pattern of suspense engendered in a particular novel, and shows that 'the suspense builds gradually', it remains unclear what presenting it diagrammatically has added to the occasion.[3] Prior to the explanation it meant nothing; following it, it is scarcely necessary. Similarly, in the field of curriculum, straightforward accounts of the various factors that may effect a curriculum plan, and the interplay between them, are commonly represented in diagrammatic form, ranging from the banal to the visually incomprehensible. This diagram of Tyler's 'model' (Figure 2) adds nothing to what has been said in the text, while the diagram in Figure 3 is, as it stands, incomprehensible.[4] At best, even a simple diagram such as Tyler's can only be understood when the accompanying text is understood, for as yet the conventions

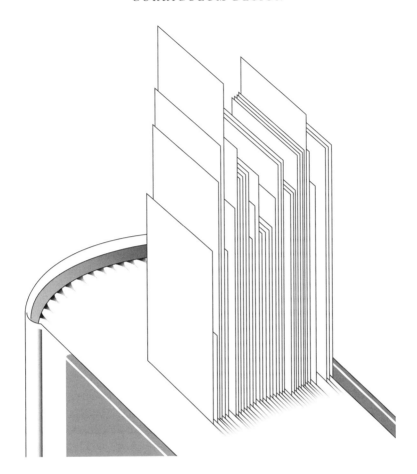

Figure 1

of diagrammatic language are not sophisticated enough to rule out misinterpretation even of something so simple. It is not, for example, *wrong* to interpret A→B→C as A follows B follows C, although experience suggests it is more likely to mean A leads to B leads to C, or perhaps A causes B causes C. But, at worst, diagrams may seriously mislead by wrongly suggesting that the interplay and connections they depict have some kind of mechanical inevitability. When a diagram is appropriate, for the wiring circuit of a hi-fi perhaps, for depicting human veins, or for an automobile engine, it offers a very accurate pictoral representation. To use a diagram to summarise one's interpretation of T.S. Eliot's *The Waste Land*, besides being almost certainly inadequate, is to suggest that a poem can profitably be treated like the cross-section of a motorbike engine.

Some of the vocabulary of curriculum development, indeed of education generally, is also a contributory factor to the impression that hard information is being conveyed when in reality we have only tentative or commonplace

421

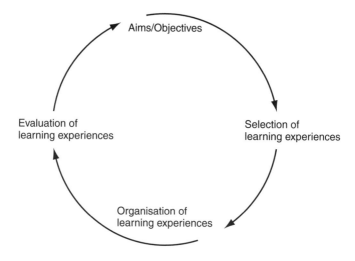

Figure 2 The Tyler model for curriculum planning

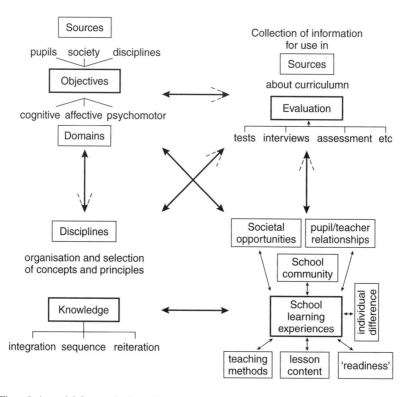

Figure 3 A model for curriculum theory

assumptions. A phrase such as 'teacher-input' may seem inoffensive enough, but its usage in the context of education being a metaphorical extension, it may carry over from its proper home potentially misleading connotations. 'Input' belongs to the world of electrical circuitry: teaching a child to understand something is not necessarily, if at all, like plugging in a current of power. Note, too, that the particular use of some words in *educanto*, as this educational jargon has been termed, reveals a basic ignorance: one may, of course, defend particular cases of extending or even changing the meaning of words, but one can hardly defend the practice of misusing the word 'parameter' as if it were a synonym of 'boundary', as many educationalists do, when it has a very precise and different meaning. Granted, language is flexible and does develop; but that can no more excuse the person who initiates misuse in ignorance by, for example, saying 'hopefully the plane will arrive on time' (which means, *per impossibile*, 'the plane will arrive full of hope on time') than such a plea could excuse calling a dog a cat.[5]

Much of the new vocabulary appears to have no further function than to enhance the mystique of curriculum theory. 'Brainstorming', for example, means no more than 'unstructured thinking',[6] though it misleadingly suggests that it is a skill, or particular kind of thinking. When we come across or devise a truly new concept (which is to say idea or thought), then it is important to mark it with a new and distinct name. But there is no obvious point in calling what the pupils learn 'learner-outcome', or referring to the various influences on curriculum as 'curriculum context', beyond that of giving the spurious impression that the study of curriculum involves specialist knowledge of various concepts peculiar to the subject. The truth is that very few worthwhile and original concepts have been thrown up by curriculum designers, and very few concepts are not familiar to most educated people, a point that the plethora of new phrases, or new uses for old phrases, in curriculum writing only serves to obscure. Why call the business of looking into potential difficulties before one sets about planning one's curriculum 'front-end analysis'? It has the merit of brevity certainly, as do many of the new coinages; but the value of brevity is lost when, being a new phrase, it needs to be explained. More serious an objection is the fact that this brief phrase, like 'brainstorming', misleadingly gives the impression that what it refers to is a skill, the province of experts, and a technical matter. The suggestion that curriculum planners should consider possible long-term consequences seems sensible enough, but in calling that activity 'engaging in impact analysis' we improperly suggest that there is a specialism akin, say, to psychonanalysis that some are trained to perform.

Some may feel that this issue of vocabulary, models and diagrams is a small one in itself. I doubt that: these are the 'clothes' that are disguising the Emperor's nakedness. Besides being aesthetically displeasing, inaccurate and unnecessary, such stylistic features are a sign that the world of curriculum design, perhaps like the world of fashion design, often has more pretension than precision, more scenery than science.

If we used plain English and resisted the tendency to hide behind models and diagrams, we would surely be less inclined to see educational issues in mechanical and technological terms, less inclined to think in terms of precise alternative procedures, and less inclined to reduce the matter to one of devising specific and rigid means to unquestioned ends. We are in fact in no position to treat education in this way and, in any case, to do so is to misrepresent fundamentally the nature of the educational enterprise. The phrase 'curriculum design' itself gives a wholly misleading impression of what arguing for, planning and outlining a curriculum involves. It suggests, particularly when it has recourse to models, diagrams and jargon, that we are dealing with an applied science. And that, I shall now suggest, is quite inappropriate.

Curriculum design as an applied science

If curriculum design is to be correctly categorised as an applied science, as Pratt and others explicitly want it to be, and others implicitly suggest, then there must be some science or sciences on which it draws substantially. There are unquestionably some scientific truths, even laws, that lie behind and relate to schooling. For example, research suggests (Seymour 1937) that dark writing on a light background is easier to read than a blackboard, and there are other specific, but limited, truths of like order of relevance to teaching of which we know. There are, besides, many more general laws of science that obviously have application in the sphere of schooling, as they do in most spheres of life. For example, a freezing temperature is not conducive to successful teaching, or many other things. But, beyond the level of commonplace, if far from inherently unimportant, scientific principles which naturally have to be taken account of by educationalists as by everyone else, the bulk of the science that lies behind curriculum theory comes not from the natural but from the social sciences.

It is a truth that the student of curriculum might be forgiven for forgetting, despite the fact that it is formally acknowledged by most curriculum theorists, including Pratt, and regardless of whether they would like to treat curriculum design as a scientific enterprise or not, that we do not know very much about the business of learning, or the particular effects of differing situations and various psychological and sociological factors on the effectiveness of teaching. Despite the impressive number of references to research to be encountered in any respectable curriculum book, nobody can point to any evidence that overwhelmingly establishes anything about the overall superiority of any method of teaching, ranging from standing before massed silent ranks and lecturing them to standing back and leaving students to proceed as they see fit. Nor do we have much in the way of sure information about the effects of particular practices in particular situations, or about the effects of such things as working with pre-specified objectives as opposed to working without them, about the effects of various evaluation techniques, about what will happen if we present curriculum in one way rather than another, or about most of the other issues involved in curriculum design. Well may Taylor and Richards (1979) quietly observe that as things are '"scientific" curriculum theory has little or no predictive power'.[7] The scientifically established data here are very limited. This being the case there is not very much that a curriculum design can legitimately specify about instruction, evaluation and so forth, even if it were agreed that that is what curriculum design should do.

But now we come to an even more important point. The view that curriculum design is an applied science can only be maintained if we not only exaggerate the number of scientifically attested facts that we have to draw on, but also ignore the crucial role of non-scientific problems in curricula, in particular the conceptual and evaluative issues that permeate the business. The natural sciences work with very precise and clear concepts and relatively unquestioned values and procedural assumptions; that is why they can proceed as they do. They are precise areas of inquiry, finely honed by time and tradition, working within agreed and sharply delineated boundaries. That is why they give rise to the sort of certainty we think of as 'scientific'. It is true that within the natural sciences, particularly in areas such as genetics and astronomy, some claims that we take to be true are not empirically attested and are by no means incontrovertibly established. It is a mistake to distinguish between the natural and the social sciences purely in terms of the former yielding unequivocally established truths and the latter merely poorly attested probabilities. However, it is the case that the natural sciences proceed without the degree of conceptual and procedural equivocation that plagues the social sciences in general, and their application to education in particular. Schooling is an area of discourse clogged with unclear and general concepts, and one that is marked by intense rivalry as to its ends, purposes and legitimate means, none of which is the case in, say, physics or chemistry. As was pointed out above, the very variety of analogies that curriculum designers have produced for their activity indicates that it cannot reasonably be asserted that it is clearly one particular kind of activity, let alone a specifically scientific one. To make the assumption that it is an applied science is comparable to assuming that marriage guidance is an applied science.

One could initiate courses in, and write books about, 'marriage design', meaning the business of writing out blueprints for married life, and one could treat the enterprise scientifically. But if you do, you miss rather a lot. You ignore the controversial issue of what marriage is supposed to be. You ignore questions such as whether it is the quality rather than the appearance of behaviours and responses that matters, and you unreasonably take it for granted that there is only one, or a limited number of ways, of setting about married life. Beyond that, your recommendations, being based on unproven claims about human psychology and social interaction, might be agonisingly poor. (Indeed it is arguable that many people's lives have been wrecked by taking too seriously the presumed scientifically established truths of marriage guidance experts.) The stark fact is that there are many things about marriage that we might in principle but do not as yet know, and there are other crucial things that by their very nature are not amenable to scientific research. But if one recognises that marriage cannot be

425

treated scientifically, then the notion of marriage design as a professional activity, the idea of expertise in setting out the format(s) for a good marriage, to be distinguished from the idea of particular individuals trying to understand and plan their particular marriages, becomes very suspect.

What is crucially missing from almost all curriculum designs is a recognition that the whole operation can only make sense, let alone be successfully carried out, in the light of a clear articulation of the central educational concepts. (There are exceptions to this. People such as Wiseman, Pidgeon and Wheeler do recognise the need to formulate aims, although their work is still imbued with the idea that everything has to be done in a certain order, and organised schematically and in detailed precision, so that we still end up with an invariant pattern of procedure for planning and writing up curriculum.) It can be seen in Pratt's approach, that he nowhere deals directly with the question of what we are doing is all for, or what it is all about. He does not ask what the curriculum is needed for in the first place, or explore the question of what our values and our ideas of education may be. He does recognise that there are questions to be raised about such things, but he is willing to comment on them only to the extent of pushing them aside to the philosophers' hinterland. In one page on curriculum rationale which contains all he has to say in 500-odd pages about the basic justification of the school curriculum, he is exclusively concerned not with what does justify a curriculum decision, but with how to present a rationale that will carry people with it. The rationale put forward should be 'eloquent and persuasive'; it 'should be written with a view to convincing everyone who will read the curriculum, but especially those who have the power to prevent or intervene in its implementation.' 'It will often be an advantage to adduce "extrinsic" arguments.'[8] Good Machiavellian stuff this, but not a word about what makes a rationale rationally defensible.

Pratt is concerned, as the title of one of his sections indicates, with aims *in* education, not with the aims *of* education. He sees the curriculum designer's job as being to organise learning experiences, *given* a set of values or desired ends. The designer takes the ultimate ends for granted and breaks them down for curriculum purposes into manageable aims. But he is not to trouble himself about the ends themselves. If they are not taken trustingly from wise philosophers, they may perhaps be taken from a consensus among the populace on the grounds that in a democracy aims and ideals should be decided by the people, while appropriate materials of instruction should be technical questions.[9]

But a curriculum designer cannot sensibly and legitimately take for granted fundamental questions about the purpose of the enterprise, as the bridge designer may reasonably take it for granted that his bridge should be able to stay up and take loads. There are indeed principles for designing bridges that cannot be ignored, whatever your personal values, so long as it is a bridge you want to build and not, say, a folly. But then all bridges, whatever their distinctive features, have certain clear, overriding purposes that are the same. Different curricula, by contrast, may have quite different purposes, and for that reason they may require quite different kinds of design. Furthermore, the aims of any curriculum are more contentious than the ends that bridges are designed to serve. Part of the problem is therefore that this divorce between ends and means, or purposes and techniques, so simple in the case of bridge-building, cannot easily be made in respect of schooling, where what are to count as the criteria of success is part of what the argument is about. We cannot begin to judge the efficacy of means so long as what constitute *successful* means remains obscure, as it must so long as the question of the purpose and nature of education is hived off and ignored. The notion that there are certain specific principles of curriculum design that can be formulated without explicit reference to particular educational ends simply does not make sense.

But now, assuming that we did reach agreement on our ends, is there any reason to suppose even then that any particular form of curriculum design would be more conducive to realising them than another, or that there are any principles of design that make a material difference to the successful teaching of curriculum in terms of attaining our ends? Pratt believes so and, in common with other curriculum theorists, refers to Soviet success in launching the first Sputnik satellite as an impetus towards redesigning curriculum in the United States, presumably on the grounds that the Soviet achievement was to be attributed to superior curriculum design.[10] But there is surely no secret or mystery about how the Soviets achieved their triumph. That leap forward in the space race was obviously *not* achieved because the Soviets had perfected better curricula in some technical sense, still less because they were in advance in curriculum design. It was achieved because they had been more committed to space exploration in terms of money and resolution, no doubt aided by some individual insights and luck. The idea that the Soviets had discovered a new science of instruction or better techniques of teaching, in the abstract, or that the Americans with better language programmes would have been more likely to read technical articles in the Soviet press, and hence to keep up with the competition, is faintly ridiculous. The difference was more likely one of conceptions of schooling than programmes of teaching. In just the same way, the Spartans in Classical Greece beat the Athenians in war not because they had a better methodology for teaching military training, but because they devoted themselves to military training. It was a political and evaluative decision that made the difference rather than a technical one.

It is still unclear, then, either why we should presume that general principles of curriculum design can be formulated and would lead to improved curriculum practice, or in the light of what aims such principles would be established.

Pratt, reasonably enough, goes on the offensive against the tendency of my argument by questioning the value of 'armchair' theorising.[11] 'Armchair theory', if it simply means one man's thoughts as he lounges in his chair and knocks back a whisky, is indeed no better than pseudo-science. But it is a mistake to confuse formality of procedure with objectivity in the sense of truth, duly determined by public procedures. An armchair theorist may hit upon the truth as readily as a questionnaire, or the systematic researcher. Furthermore, the relative value of armchair, questionnaire and observational research depends very much upon the questions being asked. How many people there are in Marks & Spencer in Granville Street on Monday 12 July at 2.00 pm is best researched by some observers armed with counting machines. What people in general feel about Marks & Spencer might best be left to questionnaires. But if we wish to inquire into the value of a store such as Marks & Spencer, then, in so far as we need opinions and observations to be collected at all, we need to hand the data we obtain over to the armchair theorist to *think* about. Even more obviously, questions such as how happy people are, how educated they are, what kinds of thing can be known in principle, and what the nature of moral upbringing is, are questions that will necessitate armchair theorising, and matters where it may be positively misleading to rely on observation.

It is true that the *test* of success in curriculum matters must lie in some kind of observation. The main value of tightly controlled empirical observation is to confirm or refute the hypotheses of armchair theory where possible. We may, for example, legitimately reject a curriculum design if we see that it consistently leads to results agreed to be disastrous. But even in an extreme case such as that, we should not be in a position from observation alone to know *why* the curriculum produces disastrous results, and we could not draw conclusions without agreement on what constitutes disaster. More to the point, there is very little either within particular curriculum designs or about the nature of curriculum design in general that ever has been put to the test.

We must, therefore, criticise any conception of design that fails to take account of the justification of schooling in general, and the evaluative and conceptual issues that arise in curriculum in particular, and that fails to see that without these everything else is necessarily merely an account of how to market and sell a package. Quite simply, we are in no position to treat curriculum design as an applied science.

Setting aside curriculum design

I have also tried to suggest that curriculum design is an otiose notion: we do not want curriculum designers in the sense of people adept at telling us formally how curricula should be set out, or laying down an invariant order of steps to be taken in formulating a curriculum. We want people to design particular curricula in intelligent ways. Much of the divergence between designers and between theories of curriculum design is essentially irrelevant, since it boils down to quibbling about how best to start tackling the problem, and how best to make an impact, rather than arguing about what a coherent curriculum proposal *should* involve. If it is said that that is so because curriculum design is a practical business, I reply that in this sense of 'practical business' it should not be. Maybe it is all right to sell soap, even life insurance, but it is not all right to sell education. Education should be thought about, explained and understood.

Furthermore, I suggest that the very determination to have a design is an impediment to clear thinking about schooling in general, for people trained to worry about the technicalities of design rather than the nature of the enterprise worry more about whether they can cut their cloth to the rules of their design, than about whether the cloth is worth designing.

The design bandwagon gains a lot of mileage from the idea that being a curriculum designer is a specific kind of job, like being an engineer. Thus Franklin Bobbitt wrote in 1918: 'It is more important that our profession agree upon a *method* of curriculum discovery than that we agree upon the details of curriculum content'; and Goodlad in 1958 called for 'a conceptual system to guide decision-making . . . in the field of curriculum'.[12] The time has come to say that this approach is entirely ill-founded. There is no 'method' of curriculum discovery, any more than there is a method of exploring the jungle or falling in love. There is just understanding something about jungles, love and school curricula, and the use of a motley collection of skills, disciplines of thought and ideas to make progress in them. There is no 'conceptual system' to guide decision-making. (At least, I do not think there is. I am not sure what a conceptual system to guide decision-making looks like. If Goodlad meant that we need some new ideas around which to organise our thinking, some new categorial concepts perhaps, it is far from evident that we do; if he meant that we need a new vocabulary, which is all he got in the event, he is mistaken.)

Planning a curriculum – and now I deliberately avoid the word 'design', which has connotations of precision, agreed procedures, and standards that are misleading and unwarranted in this context – is a complicated business, requiring primarily such tentative understanding of children as we can muster, both in general and particular, a well-thought-out and coherent view of human life in a social context, coupled with awareness of other competing views, such knowledge of what actions, beliefs and procedures produce or inhibit what results as may be possible, and, most important of all, understanding of the nature and purpose of schooling and all that that entails. There is no 'way' of doing it, no 'way' of designing curricula. Curricula are formulated and presented in a hundred ways, and may legitimately be so, provided that their authors understand the intricacies in the sphere in which they are operating.

Setting aside the idea of curriculum design on the grounds that it is a confused and unhelpful concept does not in any way militate against the importance of curriculum studies. Curriculum theory does not disappear, nor does the need for it diminish, because the idea of a proper manner of designing curricula disappears. (Nor incidentally does the good sense to be found in various curriculum designers' work disappear because of the weakness of the overall approach.) But rather than deploying various designs we should surely be addressing these fundamental questions: what kind of curriculum provision should we make for children, and what different kinds of question need to be raised in order to determine the answer? Beyond that we need to consider how best to approach and present particular curriculum proposals by reference to particular situations.

The emphasis in curriculum work should fall less on procedures or styles of operation, and more on establishing a sound theoretical base for such prescriptions as we feel we may legitimately make. What we must have is a coherent argument for our overall curriculum aims and a convincing case for particular curriculum recommendations, rather than strategies for devising, outlining and successfully implementing them. Once we have that, we can turn our attention to convincing people of the wisdom of our proposals. But there is no merit whatsoever in successful curriculum change unless the changes are inherently desirable in terms of schooling and education. Therefore we need, first, to consider what is desirable in the context of schools – not what people say they desire, but what is coherently defensible as desirable. That means that we must go back to theory, for inquiring into what is educationally worthwhile just is a theoretical pursuit.

A more flexible approach to curriculum is required than is suggested by the phrase curriculum design itself, simply because curriculum theory is necessarily a multidisciplinary exercise. We have to sort out not only and not primarily techniques and procedures of teaching and class organisation, but questions about our priorities and our ideas. We would be well-advised to approach this by thinking in terms of questions rather than strategies or taks. Perhaps we might go back to something like Tyler's approach, asking ourselves what educational purposes the school should seek to attain, how the learning experiences that are likely to be useful are best selected, how they can be organised, and how we can evaluate them. But this time we need to recognise that the first three questions are written out in their order of importance, that the second and third cannot be answered without reference to the first, and that the answers to the second and third are probably a great deal more open than some might anticipate.

More simply we want to deal thoroughly with these questions: What should we teach and why? How should we teach it? How should we organise it? What can we do to evaluate our progress and monitor and, if needs be, modify our practice? How, given that we have a good case, can we best see our curriculum implemented? What is required is not so much the misleading appearance of science in the form of diagrams, schemata, jargon and empirical procedures of inquiry, as a better idea of what is going on and what ought to be going on; a better idea is assessed not so much by the amount of information it purveys, or the manner of its acquisition, as by the quality of the thinking brought to bear on that information.

Those who are strongly wedded to the idea of curriculum design, especially if they also persist in seeing it as an applied science, may respond: 'That might give us a curriculum, but surely we need to present the curriculum to teachers in such a way that they will and can adopt it. Therefore we must have an account of how we should set it all out.' The reply to this is that we do indeed want teachers to be able and willing to adopt curricula that we have convincingly argued there is good reason to adopt. But there is a proper and honourable way to approach that, namely, to proceed in the same way with introducing proposals to teachers as we did in arriving at our curriculum proposals: by reason. Car salesmen need to sell cars, but it does not follow that they have to resort to the tricks they do, albeit they are very effective. If they had a good car to sell, the best way to sell it would be to educate people in the ways of automobile structure and performance. A good car then sells itself. In the same way, the best way to sell a curriculum, or to present it so that it is not misapplied, is to give teachers a clear idea of what they are being asked to do, why they are being asked to do it, and why they should be doing it. Teachers do not need books of rules or tips about curriculum design ('Remember to remember that the temperature of the room may affect concentration'; 'Remember not to forget the structure of knowledge.') They might reasonably feel somewhat offended that it is assumed they need to be reminded of the sorts of factor that may affect what is going on. What they do need, and may have to develop, is understanding of these factors, their significance, their implications, their interrelationships, and so forth, in respect of the nature and purposes of schooling and education. Teachers, like anybody else interested in education, should be given the opportunity not to memorise patterns of ways to draw up curriculum proposals, but to think about and increase their understanding of the justification for some curriculum proposals rather than others. In the final event they will, and they will only, successfully implement what they thoroughly understand.

Notes

1 See e.g. Taba (1962); Kerr (1968); Rubin (1977); Joyce (1979), Taylor and Richards (1979); and Pratt (1980). For a sensible comment on the situation see Jenkins and Shipman (1975).

2 See e.g. Joyce (1979).

3 Figure 1 from Keating (1982).

4 Figure 2 from Taylor and Richards (1979); Figure 3 from Kerr (1968).

5 The term 'educanto' was coined by James D. Koerner, *The Miseducation of American Teachers*. He sums up the knowledge gained by a graduate in educanto as follows: 'You will know that dynamically reinforced growth of your ideational and cross-fertilized learnings has occurred, hopefully through intravariable autorivalry, enriched need arousal, purposeful goal-orientated behavior, and persistent achievement motivations. Your self-actualization, together with your real-life readiness for situational and refractive testing against Yoakam's Readability Formula, will be concretioned', etc. As Koerner says, educanto, besides masking 'a lack of thought [that] in fact makes thought of any important kind extraordinarily difficult', can also 'reduce any mildly sensitive layman to a state of helpless fury in a matter of minutes.'

6 According to a standard dictionary. According to Pratt's (1980) glossary it means: 'the generation of ideas or solutions to problems involving free-flowing creative thought and spontaneous non-critical expression of ideas; often conducted in a group.' But what does that mean and how does one come by it?

7 Taylor and Richards (1979) p. 152.

8 Pratt (1980) p. 152.

9 This is not a quotation from Pratt, but from Rugg (1926) quoted by Pratt (1980) p. 32. I presume it represents the latter's view.

10 Pratt (1980), p. 35.

11 *Ibid.*, pp. 70, 71.
12 Goodlad (1958).

References

Bobbit, F. (1918) *The Curriculum*. Boston: Houghton Mifflin.

Goodlad, J.I. (1958) 'Toward a conceptual system for curriculum problems', *School Review*, 66, 391–401.

Jenkins, D. and Shipman, M. (1976) *Curriculum: An Introduction*. London: Open Books.

Joyce, B.R. and Weil, M. (1979) *Models of Teaching* (2nd edn). Englewood Cliffs, N.J.: Prentice-Hall.

Keating, H.R.F. (ed.) (1982) *Whodunit?* London: Windward.

Kerr, J. (ed.) (1968) *Changing the Curriculum*. London: University of London Press.

Pratt, D. (1980) *Curriculum: Design and Development*. New York: Harcourt Brace Jovanovich.

Rubin, L. (1977) *Curriculum Handbook: The Disciplines, Current Movements and Instructional Methodology*. Boston: Allyn & Bacon.

Seymour, W.D. (1937) 'An experiment showing the superiority of a light colored "blackboard"', *British Journal of Educational Psychology*, 7, 259–68.

Taba, H. (1962) *Curriculum Development: Theory and Practice*. New York: Harcourt Brace Jovanovich.

Taylor, P.H. and Richards, C. (1979) *An Introduction to Curriculum Studies*. Slough: NFER.

Tyler, R. (1949) *Basic Principles of Curriculum and Instruction*. Chicago: University of Chicago Press.

Wiseman, S. and Pidgeon, D. (1970) *Curriculum Evaluation*. Slough: NFER.

23

EDUCATIONAL PSYCHOLOGY AND TIMING IN THE CURRICULUM

Robin Barrow

In this paper I shall consider what we can learn from educational psychology that is useful for curriculum. It is likely that many readers will assume that psychology, particularly when it is conceived of as an empirical discipline, is one of the more practical and useful branches of educational theory. The prominence given to the subject in teacher preparation, particularly in North America, serves to reinforce this point of view. Without question, the problems to which psychology addresses itself are of educational interest. I shall argue, however, that there is very little of importance for educators that can be gained from the study of such things as learning theory and child development. I should make it clear at the outset that I do not need, and I therefore do not intend, to suggest that the study of psychology is in itself valueless. My argument is that we do not gain any significant knowledge of which practical use can be made in planning curriculum. Research into child psychology yields a startling number of disguised tautologies, unsubstantiated empirical claims and truisms, few of which in any case can be made use of when considering how to plan one's teaching, since they are at best generalisations that do not necessarily have, and cannot be known to have, application in particular situations.[1]

Learning theory

Maggie Inge (Lawton *et al.* 1978), while conceding that what one generally gets from learning theory or psychology of learning does not give much immediate guidance to teachers, none the less makes the more moderate claim that 'it is necessary to have some "theory" of how learning takes place and which conditions make for the most efficient learning.'[2] It is important, however, to stress the distinction between learning theory in the form it usually takes, and research into the conditions that make for efficient learning. It would indeed be useful to know

Source: Robin Barrow: *Giving Teaching Back to Teachers*, Wheatsheaf Books, 1984, Ch. 5.

about the latter, and in subsequent sections we shall consider what we do know about such things as the effects of anxiety, sequencing of material and motivation on learning. Learning theory, on the other hand, (or some types of learning theory) involves something rather different in kind from understanding of optimum learning conditions, and something which is not self-evidently an asset or a necessity for teachers. Learning theory describes what happens when learning takes place, rather than why or how it takes place. It seeks to offer an explanation of what goes on in the process of learning. Even on the admission of some of those who take it seriously it is 'a confused area' (Fontana 1981), and it is not at all clear that well-founded or 'intelligent teaching requires understanding of learning processes' (Tomlinson 1981) in this sense.[3] Intelligent musical composition does not necessarily require understanding of the creative mind; intelligent building does not necessarily require understanding of why bricks have solid substance; and human relationships are not necessarily improved by understanding of *why* we are as we are. It is often enough to know, for these purposes, *that* things are as they are. The same might well be true of teaching.

It is not clear that we know very much about learning anyway. The reason for this is not, as some philosophers claim, conceptual. It is not that there is ambiguity or incoherence in what 'learning' means, as there certainly is in the case of say, 'creativity', 'intelligence' and 'education'. It would be generally agreed that to learn is to acquire knowledge, not previously possessed, of propositions or skills. So far as the meaning of 'learning' goes it does not matter whether this acquisition of knowledge is accidental, deliberately imposed from without, or sought after. Nor does the length of time one retains the knowledge cause any serious problem, though one would hope that what is learned is retained for some time, and might quibble about the case of somebody who forgot as soon as he had 'learned'. There are no immediate problems in understanding this account of learning. Any conceptual problems that there may be arise indirectly from the fact that it involves reference to knowledge, where there are some problems, but again not overwhelming ones for the purpose of being understood. It is generally accepted that to 'know' means to believe something that is true, with sufficient evidence to support that belief; it follows that to learn something is to acquire evidence, which must be construed to include such things as appreciating reasoning, to support a true belief. There are problems about what may count as evidence and whether the evidence that people have acquired on particular occasions is sufficient, but these are not problems about the meaning of learning.[4]

This definition of learning is admittedly not couched in the sort of terms that learning theorists themselves tend to use. 'Most psychologists would agree that learning is a relatively persistent change in an individual's possible behaviour due to experience' (Fontana 1981).[5] But the differences are only superficial. It is characteristic of psychologists to use the broad term 'experience', and to emphasise change in behaviour. But in this instance what is meant by behaviour includes reference to verbal behaviour, so that the ability to recite some dates would count as a change in behaviour no less than the ability to tie one's shoelaces. Experience, likewise, is not narrowly conceived to cover only cases of learning through first-hand experimentation or discovery, but to cover also cases such as having information provided, or points explained. Reference to experience is designed to contrast with changes in behaviour that come about automatically through maturation and physical development. Consequently this formulation, though its phrasing might prove slightly misleading, does not essentially involve a different conception of learning.

We therefore return to the question of whether anything that is either useful or necessary for the practising teacher or the curriculum planner to know can be said about the process or the processes whereby people come to learn.

When spelt out in this way the first thing that strikes one is surely that the very phrase 'process of learning' may be suspect. Is there any such thing as a process of learning? Presumably we are not here concerned with the physiological level, for although there must be a tale to be told about the neurophysiological occurrences that take place when people perceive or come to understand things, this would parallel knowledge of physiological changes that take place when somebody is sick, or knowledge of the theoretical physics that explains what happens when an automobile engine functions efficiently. In either case it is neither necessary nor sufficient to have such knowledge in order to remain healthy or to maintain one's automobile in running order. Even a doctor or mechanic may successfully operate at the level of knowing what to do, while being ignorant of precisely what is happening. Indeed that is how, very often, we have to operate. To this day the medical profession is unable to give a clear account of how or why aspirin functions as it does, and many garages throughout the world are staffed by excellent mechanics who do not have a grasp of physics. There certainly seems no case for saying either that teachers need knowledge of the physiological transformations involved in learning or that, with it, they would necessarily be any better equipped for facilitating learning in their students.

But is there a process of learning, in any meaningful sense, at any other level? Certainly there is not a process as there is a process of mixing cement. For while it is true that there is a proper way in which to mix cement, such that radical departure from it will result in a failure to produce cement, there is not one way to proceed in order to learn. People may come to learn different things in a variety of different ways, and different people may learn the same things on different ways. Anything that is common to all instances of coming to learn something, such as perhaps that experience of something must always precede recognition of it, and that recognition must always precede analysis of what is perceived, seems to arise directly from the meaning of learning and anyway seems to be trivial in its practical importance. Naturally one cannot analyse or make sense of a proposition or an occurrence prior to recognising or focusing upon it in some way or other, for prior to recognition there is nothing there to analyse. Equally, one cannot recognise or focus upon something unless it is first presented to one's experience, since recognition logically presupposes experience in this broad sense.

This view is borne out by the fact that the theories of learning that have been produced have either been extremely implausible or a mere business of labelling with new terms steps that are not thereby any better understood. An example of the latter is provided by one part of Gagné's work on learning theory, which, despite being widely taught in colleges of education, is little more than a somewhat obscure account of what might be going on when people are learning, at a quasi-physiological and partly psychological level. Gagné depicts learning as an information-processing business, on the model of the workings of a computer (Gagné 1974). The central nervous system is posited to contain receptors, a short-term memory, a long-term memory, and a response generator. These of course are not actual identifiable parts of the nervous system, as the heart, the cerebellum and the liver are identifiable parts of the body. They are names given to fictional entities that represent certain things people do. People remember some things for a short time only, so a short-term memory bank is conceived to exist; people respond to external stimuli, so a response generator is posited. There is no reason to suppose, and Gagné is not committed to claiming, that there actually is an organ that generates all responses. He merely offers a rather mechanistic way of talking about some fairly obvious features of human behaviour. His procedure is comparable to talking about the weather in terms of the behaviour of the Greek gods: it thunders, so we say that Zeus is angry. A person forgets something, so we say his long-term memory is on the blink.

Gagné goes on to say that what happens when people learn is that information from the environment is coded by their receptors, and then that initial perception is transferred to the short-term memory. Things that make some impression, and are not more or less immediately to be forgotten, are then said to be transferred to the long-term memory. The response generator activates behaviour of some kind, aided by what are called the 'executive control' and 'expectancies', which refer respectively to such things as cognitive strategies and motivation.

To consider whether this account is true or nonsense is hardly to the point. It is a metaphorical way of talking about phenomena we are all perfectly well aware of. The important questions are whether it is a useful way of talking about them, and whether such talk has any practical interest for educators. As to the first point, I would suggest that it is not a useful way to talk, since it misleadingly oversimplifies and suggests a mechanistic chain of cause and effect that may be wildly misleading. It implies that we have some apparatus within us that autonomously processes stimuli from the environment, as the kidneys process liquid. As to the second point, it is difficult to see anything that follows from this account that is of relevance to teaching, curriculum planning, or indeed the business of learning itself.

It is true that Gagné has done a great deal more than posit this one learning model.[6] He has offered a classification of eight types of learning; he has filled out the contours of the basic model by suggesting eight elements in a typical act of learning; he has attempted to summarise external conditions that may affect the process of learning; and he has sought to draw on all of these to propose a theory of instruction that, by outlining important steps in a learning sequence, tells teachers something about how they should proceed. Unfortunately, in all of this work we do not appear to advance beyond statements of the obvious and unwarranted or artificial mechanistic descriptions and prescriptions that, when they are not logical necessities apparent to anyone who thinks about the terms involved, are backed by no reasonable empirical evidence.

The eight types of learning classified by Gagné (1970) are signal learning, stimulus response learning, chaining, verbal association, multiple discrimination, concept learning, rule learning and problem-solving. Although the broad nature of the various categories can be grasped readily enough, Gagné does not offer a very clear account of what he means by some of them. He tends to adopt the technique of explaining by means of example. But the distinctions are roughly as follows: signal learning refers to cases where the child makes a conditioned response of a non-specific type to a stimulus. Stimulus response refers to cases where a specific response is elicited by a stimulus. Chaining refers to the ability to join two or more stimulus response connections together. Verbal association involves chaining in respect of verbal response connections. Multiple discrimination is the name given to the business of identifying different stimuli that resemble each other. Concept learning refers to the ability to respond appropriately to a class of stimuli – for example, to treat all dogs as dogs. Rule learning refers to the type of learning involved in recognising that if A, then B. Problem-solving describes learning to combine the sort of principles learned in rule learning to form higher-order rules.

It is readily apparent that here again we are merely being presented with names for familiar phenomena. We are all aware that sometimes children (and adults) respond in a quasi-automatic way to stimuli (stimulus response learning), that sometimes they come to acquire concepts, which is to say learn to recognise particular instances of dogs as being dogs or grasp what is common to all dogs (concept learning), and that sometimes they may come to understand logical rules (rule learning), or combine rules and draw conclusions (problem-solving). We are not being given any insights into these various types of learning by this classification; we are not learning anything about them. And it is quite possible that some people will infer from the manner of classification that these eight types represent discrete forms of learning. If so, it is not clear that the inference is warranted, for it is not at all clear that verbal association and multiple discrimination, for example, might not be part and parcel of problem-solving.

Gagné himself believes that these types of learning are not merely distinct, but that they are also hierarchical. He is explicitly committed to the view both that the individual's learning must proceed through these stages in the order in which they have been presented, and that learning of particular subject matter must proceed through these stages. But what truth there is in these views seems to be a simple matter of logic. Of course problem-solving, as defined, presupposes rule learning, since it is defined in terms of combining rules, and, of course they both presuppose concept learning, since one could hardly understand a rule if one could not understand the concepts involved in the rule. But that is not the same thing as saying that these are separate steps through which one passes one at a time: a person who has learned to solve problems may still have many concepts to learn, and he may still sometimes operate on the level of stimulus response. A person learning something new may be involved in verbal association, chaining, multiple discrimination and rule learning at one and the same time.

More importantly, it therefore does not follow that particular subject matter has to be presented in a way that matches the eight types of learning in hierarchical order. Certainly, Gagné is correct to say that if the child is to 'learn rule IIc, "identify and draw the intersection of lines or parts of lines taken two at a time, as more than one point," he must know the rules that govern the construction of lines . . . and intersections of sets of points . . . and also the rules pertaining to various parts of lines.' But that is because, as Gagné says, 'the higher-order rule incorporates these other rules.'[7] What he does not appear to realise, as Phillips and Kelly (1975) have pointed out, is that to say that is to say that this is a logical and not an empirical point. There is no such logical necessity involved in a general prescription to the effect that when introducing new subject matter we should start by concentrating on signal learning and proceed through the other seven stages in order, or in Gagné's specific proposals for organising particular subjects such as the teaching of reading. And he does not produce any adequate empirical evidence for the advantages of adopting this approach. He has given us no good reason, therefore, to accept his contention that the teaching of reading should proceed by getting the child to master the art of distinguishing similar words, *then* to master nouns, verbs, prepositions and connectives, *then* to master the intricacies of word order, and *finally* to master the organisation of paragraphs and larger units. Quite apart from the fact that one might be teaching the child all these things at the same time, or switching between them as new concepts and rules arise, there is no obvious reason why one should not concentrate on these elements in a different order.

The eight elements in a typical act of learning listed by Gagné are motivation, apprehending or focusing, acquisition, retention, recall, generalisation or applying knowledge to new situations, performance or making use of knowledge, and feedback or obtaining knowledge of results. The external conditions or principles of procedure for enhancing learning that he lists include such things as the need for repeated practice when developing motor skills; the need to activate student attention by variation in the manner of presenting verbal information; the need to use a variety of contexts to promote transfer when developing intellectual skills; the need to pose novel problems when developing cognitive strategies; and the need to provide feedback in order to promote a positive attitude to learning.

It is rather difficult, when faced with this kind of theorising, to understand what Gagné thinks he is doing. Are the eight elements supposed to constitute a description of the events in a case of learning? If so, it seems a poor description, since motivation might be a cause of learning but is not part of learning – and one may learn something without putting it to use and without receiving any feedback. It seems more reasonable, therefore, to see both the list of elements within an act of learning and the list of external conditions as a prescription for enhancing learning. As such it is by no means to be dismissed out of hand, but it must be recognised that it is not saying very much that any thoughtful teacher would not think of (motivate, give practice, put the knowledge to use, vary one's approach, provide feedback), that some of the points are true by definition, that no evidence is being produced to support the claims that are not a matter of logic and, above all, that no guidance is given in respect of what the teacher should actually do. Advice of the order 'be varied' or 'pose novel problems' is not exactly useful.

And so we come to Gagné's specific proposals embodied in his theory of instruction. He claims that the teacher should follow five steps. First, he should inform the students of what is expected of them, and do so by presenting a list of his own objectives. Secondly, he should question students in such a way as to have them recall earlier aspects of learning which are necessary to the new task. Thirdly, he should present cues to the students that help them put together the current learning as a chain of concepts in the correct order. Fourthly, he should question the students in ways that allow them to display application of the new learning. And finally he should elicit from them statements of the rules learned.

It is not my intention to suggest that any of these are bad things to do. But what I hope is clear by now is (1) that these prescriptions are in no obvious way related to the initial theory of learning, which is therefore not shown to have any implications for teaching; (2) that some of them appear to be self-evident (who could fail to see that good teaching requires taking steps to help students make sense of what they are learning, which appears to be the meaning of the third step?); (3) that no adequate reasoning has been produced to suggest that any of these steps ought necessarily to be taken (why, for example, should a teacher necessarily spell out his objectives to students?); (4) that no case has been made for the necessity or even the desirability of always following all these steps; and (5) that, given the generality of the prescriptions, they offer no practical guidance to teachers. (It is made quite clear, for instance, that what are here referred to as 'questions' might take many forms, including such things as requiring project work or providing straightforward instruction.) It is not that what Gagné has to say about the steps in instruction is necessarily false or objectionable, so much as that at worst it is empty rhetoric and at best there is no obvious reason for us to be governed by it. It is difficult to avoid Sockett's (1976) conclusion that Gagné's account of the learning process, along with various other psychological accounts of the learning process, such 'as SR, the forming of gestalts, assimilation and accommodation . . . are largely metaphorical ways of describing this mysterious (and not worth searching for) process.'[8]

There are certainly learning theories that do have bite, in the sense of clear and specific implications for how we should teach, but they only seem capable of providing the bite at the cost of considerable implausibility. An example is provided by B.F. Skinner (1969), who takes the view that conditioning, in the sense of connecting a response to a particular stimulus, is the basic unit of learning. Starting from that premise he comes to the view that just as rats can be brought to press levers by reinforcing such behaviour with a food pellet so, in principle, proceeding one step at a time, human beings can be brought to learn items (whether of behaviour or propositional knowledge) by a process of reinforcement.

The basic problem here is that, regardless of how true it is that human beings can be conditioned, this simply ignores both the fact that humans have the capacity to do new things because they understand the reasons for doing them, and the evaluative assumption that education is concerned with our specifically human side, which is to say with providing something other than mere conditioning. Even if it were possible to get people to learn the causes of the Peloponnesian War or Euclidean geometry by means of operant conditioning (which despite what has been achieved by those of a Skinnerean persuasion seems extremely unlikely), and even if one chose to call conditioned acquisition of a coherent view 'learning' (which, because learning is conceptually tied to *appreciating* evidence, we should resist), it could still be said that this is not the kind of learning that we want to encourage in schools.

It may well be that all learning requires, or at any rate benefits from, reinforcement. Provided that 'behaviour' is understood as a very broad term that includes verbal, imaginative and cognitive behaviour, Skinner's view that all learning takes the form stimulus–behaviour–reinforcement could be said to be reasonable. But then it tells us nothing about the wide variety of stimuli to which we may be subject, ranging from merely being in certain situations to being deliberately acted upon by others; and it tells us nothing about the different kinds of reinforcement that might be appropriate for different kinds of behaviour. The truth is that learning not to wet the bed, learning the date of the Battle of Waterloo, learning the concept of time, learning a foreign language, and learning the causes of the Peloponnesian War are rather different in kind, and any account of learning designed to cover them all is necessarily going to be general to the point of emptiness. What we need to know is what kind of stimuli and what kind of reinforcements are most appropriate to enhance learning in each case. The danger, illustrated time and again in the work of those committed to operant conditioning, is that 'stimulus' and 'reinforcement' will in practice be interpreted very narrowly to exclude such factors as satisfaction in understanding, and that the part that may be played by the mind of the learner in perceiving and making sense of stimuli and in providing its own reinforcement will be ignored. When that is the case the theory ceases to be reasonable.

Gagné and Skinner may both be classified as adherents of a behaviourist theory of learning. By contrast Bruner (1966) adopts a cognitivist theory of learning. He emphasises the importance of activity of mind in learning and correctly stresses that a great deal of human behaviour is not simply reflex. Learning in many cases involves acquiring information, sorting it out or making sense of it, and testing it in various ways. One of the characteristics of human beings is the ability to ignore stimuli altogether. Bruner's view is that there are three systems or ways of making sense of incoming information. The enactive mode refers to learning by doing and is, typically, the type of learning involved in acquiring motor skills. The iconic mode involves the use of imagery, but not language, and refers to the type of learning involved in the ability to recognise instances of something without being able to give an account of the concept, or to picture things that one could not describe. The symbolic mode refers to learning through language.

Bruner's view seems rather more sensible than either Gagné's or Skinner's, but that may well be partly because it is very much less specific. Bruner himself is well aware of the fact that an individual may employ the iconic, the enactive or the symbolic mode of learning at any time (and, presumably, in conjunction with one another). This is not therefore a hierarchical model of learning such as Gagné offered. All that we are actually being told is that learning is not generally, if at all, just a matter of reflexive behaviour being reinforced by outside consequences. Rather, the agent's mind plays an important role, and there are some things that will be learned through constant repetition, some things that will be understood in pictorial terms, and some things of which the agent may learn to give some kind of account. This kind of theory of learning, therefore, although it is not obviously false, still does not tell us anything of practical significance for encouraging learning. The game is still one of providing labels for fairly self-evident phenomena. We are not being provided with any kind of reason for doing anything in particular when we wish to facilitate learning of various particular things.

The above may tempt us to adopt the view that thinking in terms of learning processes is preferable to thinking in terms of a learning process. That, I think, is true, provided that we do not repeat the mistakes inherent in the above accounts, and assume that it is merely a case of recognising a relatively small number of processes which we can set in motion at appropriate moments. For that is where the mistake lies. There are not, as far as we know, a number of ways of learning that people are capable of adopting and which may be tapped by the teacher, as there are a number of ways of pruning roses, arranging the furniture, or building a house, between which we may choose, or about the merits of which we may argue. Rather, people come to learn different things in different ways, partly as a result of difference in content, partly as a result of difference in context, and partly as a result of being different people, preferring or finding it easier to acquire understanding in different kinds of situation. If we wish to learn more about how children may come to learn, we need to acquire greater understanding of various particularities in the nature of what it is that is to be learned, and of what individuals most readily respond to out of a more or less limitless number of things we might do and situations we might engineer.

It is sufficient to assert the conclusion that learning theory, as it has been institutionalised, gives a spurious scientific respectability to what is at bottom an awesome mystery, and what, in more practical terms, requires far greater understanding of individual differences. As Peters (1974) says, 'the fact is that very little of learning theory is of much interest or relevance to the educator.'[9]

Developmental theory

Are developmental theories likely to prove any more helpful to the educator? In 1959 David P. Ausubel took the view that the study of growth and development could offer 'only a limited number of very crude generalisations and highly tentative suggestions.'[10] In my view that was a very fair summary of the situation, though it is important to distinguish here between insights and theories. Many of the perceptions of individual theorists are plausible and should be made familiar to practising teachers if they are not already familiar; reasonable generalisations, although of limited practical value, are important in so far as they oust false generalisations, and insights such as that young children do not normally operate at an abstract level, though they rapidly become commonplaces, do need to be recognised. What is to be avoided is either the assumption that these generalisations have been empirically validated, or the adoption of an exclusive monolithic theory of development that is treated as the pattern for planning all curricula or organising all teaching. Theories of development, as we shall see, even if they are regarded as beyond criticism in themselves, do not yield practical guidance for curriculum any more than learning theory does.

What, for instance, does Sigmund Freud have to offer educationalists, let alone curriculum planners, such that the study of Freud should be regarded in some institutions as crucial for the education of techers?[11] Freud made two decisive contributions to psychology: first, the method of free association (which might either be an instrument of research or an instrument of therapy in the right hands). He then evolved a theoretical position as a result of his experience and his conclusions using the technique of free association. The most famous elements in this theory are his terms the 'id', 'ego' and 'super-ego' to represent, roughly, appetite or instinctive needs, the executive will or spirited part of man, and the moral element.[12]

But the basis of Freud's theoretical position includes belief in causation for mental events. This is not to say he believed that mental events, such as love, fear, determination or anxiety, were determined in the sense of being unavoidable, but he did believe that they were explicable in terms of prior events, material or mental, rather than random moods, fancies or desires. He also believed that the causes of mental events were very often unconscious and, more specifically, the product of very early relationships. We should also add reference to his notion of the libido. Freud believed that sexual drive was far wider in scope than had previously been generally supposed; for example, he accepted homosexual activity, voyeurism and other taboo practices as straightforward manifestations of the sexual drive, and not as perversions of it. He also noted that many people can actively embrace more than one manifestation. His theory finally goes on to suggest that much of our behaviour is a transformation of early sexual drives into non-sexual activity.

Clearly one problem with making use of Freudian theory is that it is not necessarily correct. This is not because it is theory. Theory is not inherently more specious, uncertain or false than practice, and the polarity between theory and practice is greatly misconceived. But Freudian theory is at best to be treated tentatively, because it relates to an area in which it is very difficult to gain certain and total theoretical knowledge. Even many who classify themselves as neo-Freudian will often stress a lack of plausibility about some parts of the theory. Explaining all behaviour in terms of transformation of sexual instincts, for example, is not widely held to be very convincing. As J.A.C. Brown (1964) observes: 'experience suggests that for every stamp-collector who is satisfying his libidinous needs at the anal level, there are dozens who collect because it is profitable to do so, because their friends collect too, or simply because they were given a stamp album.'[13] This and other similar reservations about aspects of Freudian theory shade into what for our purposes is the more important point. Given that it is only a tentative theory, given that few, if any, embrace it wholeheartedly, and given that most people would see it as at best a possible explanation of some parts of some people's behaviour and personality, how helpful does it become in practice in our daily dealings with people? In particular, how useful is this theory of development to educationalists? How legitimate is it, given that no student can study everything, to devote part of the intending teacher's time to studying one such theory?

It is arguable that people concerned with the upbringing of very young children should be aware of the general claim about the importance of early relationships and practices, but only on condition that they do not imbibe it uncritically as a total explanation and a proven truth. One might also accept that teachers should be aware that some few individuals might benefit from psychoanalysis, provided we do not make too much of the point. As Morris (1958) remarks, although 'teaching is in some respects necessarily a therapeutic relationship . . . the therapy required is largely that of spontaneous intuitive understanding . . . not an extensive academic knowledge of the more intricate parts of dynamic psychology.'[14] But the practical value of awareness of these broad claims is necessarily very limited, since, even if the claims were true without qualification, we should still need to recognise in individual cases what significance what early experiences had had, and what we should therefore do about it, if we wished to take practical advantage of our theoretical insights. The famous Oedipus complex element in Freudian theory, if well-founded, warns us to appreciate that at about the age of four or five the individual comes to terms with his or her Oedipal stirrings. But the theory does not tell us how to recognise what is going on, how to interpret it, or what to do about it. Beyond the value of being aware of such very general points, it is difficult to see what relevance Freudian theory could have to practising teachers or curriculum planners, despite the fact that lectures on Freud play a part in many educational psychology courses.

Morrish (1967), a restrained and cautious commentator, suggests that a study of Freud leads us to seeing the need for teachers to have 'a fully realised personality' and to make 'good relationships', while more generally it leads to the view 'that really effective learning takes place only when a child's energies and drives are properly and fully employed.'[15] But the last remark is either a truism or untrue, depending upon interpretation, is not exclusively dependent on Freudian theory, and is not of much practical use. It is simply not true that people *cannot* learn effectively when frustrated or depressed, for example. So this knowledge does not lead directly to a general prescription along the lines that children should never be allowed to experience frustration or depression. If, on the other hand, it is claimed that necessarily learning would be more real if cheerfully engaged in, that becomes a definition of learning rather than an empirical observation. For granted that a person could learn something while depressed, the only way in which it can necessarily be true that it will not be real learning is if one arbitrarily defines true learning as 'learning cheerfully acquired'. But the main point remains that while no one would dispute the importance of recognising that learning may be inhibited by psychological problems which are sometimes the product of early experience, the questions of importance are what are the problems of particular children, what caused them (to which Freud offers one possible kind of answer, but still not a specific one) and how to deal with them in practice. Freudian theory does not offer an answer to such questions because it is not supposed to. Of course, if one were an uncritical, committed and simple-minded Freudian, there would be some kind of answers, and the immediate conclusion would be that teachers should become Freudian analysts. But that is quite unacceptable as a general prescription, given the extremely tentative and contentious nature of the theory.

Superficially more plausible than the idea that pure psychological theory is of especial value to those concerned with teaching is the idea that developmental theories, such as those of Piaget or Isaacs, and offshoots of these such as Kohlberg's theory of moral development, are of great importance for educational practice.

Susan Isaacs (1930) categorises stages of development into infancy (0–1 years), early childhood (1–5), later childhood (5–12), early adolescence (13–16) and later adolescence (16+). The differentiation between the stages is arrived at by reference to various alleged general truths of the order that the period of later childhood is marked by changes in emotions, a turning away from parents and towards other children, a move away from fantasy to the real world, an increase in linguistic skills and sociability, and an increase in the tendency to look for purposes. Devising such a theoretical structure is therefore a matter of assessing, and seeking to verify empirically, what seem to be particularly noteworthy age-spans in respect of the clear emergence of various itemised aspects of personality. The plausibility of any such theory has to be judged while bearing in mind that it consists of generalisations, and that their verification is not a simple matter of observation, since what counts as, say, an increasing interest in the real as opposed to fantasy is both difficult to conceptualise and, once conceptualised, difficult to discern. It is a matter of judgement as much as looking.

The value of any such theoretical account is less a question of truth than one of usefulness. For, provided that one's observations about the general tendency for children to develop certain characteristics at certain broad ages are not manifestly false, what matters, from the point of view of those debating how important the theory is, is whether the changes focused upon are of practical significance for some purpose or other. In addition, it is important to note that if anybody, such as a teacher, is to make use of the theory, it is not sufficient that he should merely learn the stages and what they involve by rote, as unfortunately too often happens in teacher education. He needs to know precisely what the originator of the theory means by all the itemised features of a stage, and he needs to be aware of the tentative nature of each generalisation, as well as that it is a generalisation. In this case Isaacs' divisions do not appear fanciful or absurd, and there is no reason to doubt the authenticity of the empirical studies backing up her theoretical account beyond reminding ourselves of the very grave general limitations inherent in any such research. The question is of what use this particular developmental framework is to us as educators.

Because the theoretical structure only claims to give us generalisations, we cannot apply the theory in any direct way when planning our curriculum or our teaching. We obviously cannot say: 'This is a class of ten-year-olds, so they must all be moving away from their parents and towards their peers.' (Nor can we say that they *should* be doing this, for the theory only purports to describe what normally happens; it would be quite illegitimate to deduce that this is the way things ought to be.) We have to look at each individual child in the class and make a judgement as to whether he does conform to the norm set up by the framework. This means that for practical purposes the art of recognising this and other elements of the items listed in the stage in question is more important than knowing the details of the stage. Learning the elements listed by Isaacs for the stage of late childhood may serve as a useful check-list of things to look out for, but it does not in itself help one to recognise them and, if it is treated as comprehensive, it will deflect one's attention from other features of particular children's stages of development. By contrast, the art of recognising what particular children are experiencing and what they are like is both necessary to taking any appropriate action, and sufficient, so far as anything that knowledge of any theoretical structure could add: if you recognise that John is growing away from his parents, increasingly interested in the real world, and so forth, you know what you need to know as a prerequisite for suitable action, and nothing would be gained by knowing in addition that John's state represents what Isaacs had chosen to term late childhood.

Secondly, it does not appear that the stages named by Isaacs introduce any new concepts, which is to say new ideas or, more colloquially still, things that nobody had previously thought of. The notion that a person might be more or less drawn to fantasy, for instance, is not one that was created by Isaacs. She has merely chosen to emphasise certain items (and sometimes introduced new names or descriptive phrases for them) with which many parents and teachers are already quite familiar, though perhaps under different names.

Thirdly, it is not at all obvious that the majority of the features of the various stages are of any great importance for educators. One should, no doubt, be aware that children do grow away from their parents, that they begin to develop an interest in the real world later than they do in fantasy, and that they gradually develop linguistic skills at the pre-puberty stage, because such knowledge may help to guide one's understanding, expectations and practice. But clearly one should not make too much of this. It is not going to make a very significant contribution to curriculum planning or teaching strategy, since it provides only rough guidelines to general points along the lines of 'one can usually afford to be more abstract with older children', or 'one can often gain a more positive response to facts about the world as children grow older.' But these general guiding principles are not exclusive to or dependent on particular theories of development; they are part and parcel of a general awareness that there is development in children.

The matter would be very different if, besides providing precisely articulated accounts of the various stages and pinpointing some rather more specific ones, we could tie them firmly to various ages. There are one or two people, such as Gesell (1928), who have tried to do this. But in no case has there been any adequate empirical backing for the claims, and indeed it seems clear to most of us, including developmental theorists, that it just is not true, for example, that the child *necessarily* walks holding on to furniture at nine months of age, stands alone well at eleven months and walks well at twelve months (Frankenburg and Dodds 1967). The best that we are able to do is put up a case for saying that the order of certain stages of development is invariable, as Kohlberg has argued for certain unchanging sequences in moral development, and that is not good enough for helping us in any significant way with curriculum planning or teaching.

Kohlberg's (1969) view is that any individual in any culture necessarily develops some way along a line of moral development through six stages, which must be passed through in this order: a stage of simple unreflective obedience, a stage of naive egoism, a good boy/girl orientation stage, a stage of deference to authority, a contractual stage in which moral behaviour is guided by a sense of honouring agreements, and a stage in which the individual is guided by his conscience. Kohlberg associates the first two 'pre-conventional' stages with the years 2–7, the next two 'conventional' stages with the years 2–1, and the final 'post-conventional' stages with 12 and beyond. But as the overlap between the ages given for the pre-conventional and the conventional stages mildly indicates,

446

he is not committed to a firm view about when these stages will occur, and in fact explicitly concedes that anybody might be at any stage.

Kohlberg claims that nobody could be at stage five without having previously passed through stages one, two, three and four, in that order. If somebody is at stage two, he will necessarily proceed to stage three, if he proceeds at all. This is not surprising, since the later stages are presumed logically to presuppose at least some of the earlier ones. How could anyone display deference to authority who did not already have a developed sense of obedience? How could an individual act autonomously in response to his own conscience if he had not previously acquired a conception of such things as the distinction between naive egoism, good-boy orientation and deference to authority? The main empirical claim is that progression from stage to stage is not brought about directly by the teaching of adults.

What precisely Kohlberg means by these claims, and whether he can convincingly maintain that he has demonstrated them, may be open to question, though I do not intend to challenge them here.[16] Our concern is with the practical value of such schemata for curriculum. What does the planner or teacher gain from this rather formalised theoretical account of moral development that is not encompassed by the common-sense observation that children slowly develop from being non-moral creatures, by means of a realisation of the value of cooperation, through to an abstract sense of justice? And how does knowledge of either help him to judge the state of the individual before him or lead him to the best way to teach that individual? Kohlberg's most significant claim would appear to be that the way to advance an individual from one stage to the next is to communicate with him in terms of the stage beyond his present one. But this again seems a matter of common sense; in order to advance learning or development in any sphere, it is clearly necessary to go beyond the individual's present state, and it is clearly foolish to communicate in terms far in advance of that state. We would gain more from Kohlberg if we had a clearer and more specific account of what is involved in the various stages, so that we had more guidance as to how we should actually proceed.

Just as relatively single-minded theories of learning are potentially more useful than general theories, but correspondingly more contentious, so relatively specific schemes of development, such as Piaget's, might conceivably prove more useful than a relatively plausible but open and general one such as Isaacs', but are also likely to be more debatable in their content.

Piaget's (1924) view is that how we handle concepts varies as we develop.[17] He has posited the following stages of development: the sensori-motor stage, which involves reflexive, non-thinking behaviour, generally associated with the years between birth and 2; the pre-operational stage, associated with the years 2–7, which may be broken down into the pre-conceptual stage (2–4), which involves recognition of particular signs and symbols, and the intuitive stage (4–7), which is characterised by thought centred on the self, thought centred on an isolated aspect of a situation, and irreversibility, by which is meant the lack of ability to work on an operation backwards. For example, the child can add 2 and 4 together to make 6, but not appreciate that 6 minus 4 equals 2. The next stage is that of concrete operations, which involves the ability to group and serialise objects, and is associated with the years 7–11. The final stage is that of formal operations, involving the ability to hypothesise and relate points to one another and associated with the age 12+.

There are a number of serious questions to be asked about, and grave problems in, this work. In the first place, has Piaget correctly understood and described what he observes? Many commentators think that he has often not done so. Isaacs, for example, challenges his view that what children are actually doing at the pre-operational stage is engaging in 'collective monologuism', and therefore rejects the characterisation of this stage as egocentric.[18] Hamlyn (1967, 1978) raises the more general point that some of his apparent findings may be due not to the developmental stage a child has reached, but to a misunderstanding between children and researchers. Thus the famous conservation experiment, designed to show that children at a certain stage cannot appreciate that volume is distinct from depth, could conceivably arise out of a conceptual difference between child and adult relating to the instructions given, rather than out of an inability to perceive or conceptualise volume. The children, when asked such questions as 'Is this the same amount of liquid?', may understand something different by that phrase than we do. It would not then be that they fail to appreciate that it is the same amount of liquid, as we would phrase it, but that they fail to understand what we mean by that phrase.[18a] If it be said that that is an implausible interpretation of what happens in the research, then it follows that our reasons for accepting Piaget's view that children do not have the concept of volume are not purely experimental, but are partly judgemental: we think it likely given what we observe and how we interpret it, that children cannot see that volume is distinct from depth. We may be correct, but we have not unequivocally demonstrated it.

Secondly, there is the question of how much of Piaget's theory is empirical and how much a matter of logic. (Piaget himself is equivocal on this point, merely acknowledging that his work is not simply empirical.) Is it, for instance, an empirical point that children cannot at first see the reverse implications of particular processes of thought they can engage in, or a matter of inevitability? If a child has not been introduced to the idea of subtraction, why should we expect him to see that since $2 + 4 = 6$, then $6 - 4$ must equal 2?

Thirdly, the previous example brings to the fore the question of the extent to which development through these stages is a matter of maturation and the extent to which it may be affected by teaching. Povey and Hill (1975) claim that children supposedly at the pre-conceptual stage can in fact handle concepts such as dog and food, in as much as they can correctly identify instances of them, provided that pictorial rather than verbal material is used. And Bryant and Trabasso (1971) claim that children at the same stage can be taught to appreciate reasoning of the form 'if A is bigger than B and B is bigger than C, then A is bigger than C', provided it is done carefully and firmly. If such claims are true, and they seem to be in accord with the experience of many people who deal with young children of their own, they suggest that some of the detailed elements in the various stages do not necessarily belong there as a matter of empirical fact, as well as that they are not a simple matter of maturation.

They also raise a fourth point. Given that the ages given are only contingently linked to the stages, and given that by taking certain steps we can bring children who might be expected to be at the pre-conceptual stage to operate in ways associated with the concrete and formal operational stages, how does one determine the stage which particular children have reached? Clearly it would be inadequate to reply 'by setting the child the sort of tasks that Piaget used in his research.' For the implication of the points raised by Isaacs, Hamlyn, Povery and Hill and Bryant and Trabasso, different as those points are, is that the Piagetian approach is not necessarily reading the situation correctly.

Such criticism at the theoretical level is obviously of great importance in itself, but again it should be recalled that from the point of view of curriculum the crucial question is not about how to interpret data and whether particular arguments are sound, but what their use may be. Developmental psychologists are, after all, concerned essentially with the *order* in which mental growth proceeds, not the actual ages at which things happen. In fact, the age ranges given as typical for particular stages of development in Piaget's work represent approximately 75 per cent of children tested. In other words, one in four children aged between 11 and 16 might be expected *not* to be at the stage of formal operations. This means once again that the teacher prepared with knowledge of Piaget's theoretical framework is not very well armed by that alone to deal with the individual children in his care. What he needs to know is which of his children can cope with abstractions, which of his children have developed what linguistic capacity, and so forth; and, of course, if one can recognise the particular, the generalities cease to be of importance. It must also be repeated that Piaget's primary interest is in the development of mind as it takes place without special intervention from people such as teachers. Unless this is clearly understood, studying Piaget can actually be very misleading. If it is understood, the value of the Piagetian framework to the teacher becomes less. Schooling is an activity based on the idea that by taking active steps and taking account of social factors that may alter expectations and possibilities envisaged within a psychological developmental framework, we can significantly hasten development.

Even if Piaget's claims were judged to be reasonable, they surely have far less practical pay-off for educators than the time usually devoted to them in courses for the preparation of teachers would suggest. It is true, as Stenhouse (1975) says, that developmental psychology in general helps us 'to set limits to readiness',[19] in the sense that it provides tentative hints as to what not to expect from children of various ages; but the limits set are for the most part fairly obvious (e.g. 'Don't expect elementary school children, as a rule, to be able to discuss democracy in abstract terms'), and, when faced with individuals, we still have to establish whether the generalisation applies.

It may perhaps be said that if the generalisations seem obvious they have become so thanks to developmental psychology. It seems possible to doubt that. Certainly several hundred years ago Plato had grasped the point that young children cannot usually handle abstractions, and it is difficult to think of any other generalisations from the corpus of developmental theory over the past fifty years that involve literally putting new ideas into our heads. But in any case the prime issue is not whether Piaget did or did not discover new truths, or whether his work has, as a matter of fact, led to wider currency for old truths. The issue is whether studying Piaget is a valuable activity for those who wish to teach or to plan curricula. Stenhouse may be correct to suggest that the value of developmental theory lies in a provision of norms for diagnostic and individual purposes, that is to say as a pointer to the sorts of consideration one might look for in order to explain the problems of particular individuals; but in that case what curriculum planners need is an awareness of general points, such as that children develop increasing powers of abstraction, that young children tend to be egocentric, and so forth, rather than a particular developmental framework, and what teachers need is experience at judging the problems of individuals. Given these observations (about the generality of such theories, their tentative nature, the need to make individual judgements, and the effects that social factors and the act of teaching itself may have on the generalisations) it cannot be right to plan a curriculum or teach a class by reference to a developmental theory, even if such theories had it in them to prescribe what we should do given a particular developmental stage (which they do not). The fact that John Stuart Mill could speak Greek and handle abstract concepts at the age of four better than some 44-year-olds does not 'disprove' Piaget; what it does is illustrate the practical limitations of such theory.[20]

Kieran Egan (1979) has recently argued strongly against the coherence and value of psychological developmental theories, and asserted instead the need for a truly educational development theory, such as, he contends, Plato and Whitehead tried to offer.[21] A minimal aspect of such a theory would be that it looked at development in the context of the school, precisely as Piaget did not. He himself offers the outline of such a theory, involving a mythic stage, associated with the years 4–7, characterised by the child's attempt to make sense of the outer world in terms of his own inner world and centred on the emotions; a romantic stage, associated with the years 8–14, in which the child sees the outside world as separate from himself and tends to identify with hero figures; a philosophic stage, between the years 14–19, characterised by enthusiasm and wholehearted commitment to causes and ideas; and finally, an ironic stage, which assimilates the previous stages but overlays them with an appreciation of the significance of mind.

While his emphasis on the question of what we can achieve, rather than what would happen if we did not try to achieve anything, is welcome, and while his educational development theory should in many respects prove more appealing to those interested in *education* than psychological developmental theories, his approach seems vulnerable to many of the criticisms we (and he) have directed at the latter. The status of his stages seems frankly prescriptive, with perhaps a small admixture of empirical support. But he offers no evidence that children are as he depicts them, and no strong case for saying that they ought to be so treated. Above all it is very difficult to see what specifically follows in terms of practical guidance for educators. Egan is working on the latter issue, but he does not yet appear to have produced any argument to support the adoption of his particular curriculum proposals, even supposing we were to accept his stages as a framework to be adopted.

Maggie Inge (Lawton *et al.* 1978) writes: 'Piaget may tell us that the concept of conservation is not reached until the stage of concrete operations; a theory of instruction should set out the best ways of promoting understanding of conservation. This involves not only psychological theory, but a sophisticated understanding of what is to be learned, of the structures of knowledge.'[22] Although she is correct about the need for the latter, we must conclude that a theory of instruction has no need at all of psychological theory, at least of this kind. A theory of instruction, if such is possible, should tell us simply how to teach conservation to those who apparently do not understand it. The question that begins to emerge is whether there can or should be such a thing as a theory of instruction.

Notes

1 An important book on this topic is Egan (1983).
2 Lawton (1978), p. 61.
3 Fontana (1981), p. 147; Tomlinson (1981).
4 On the meaning of know, see e.g. Hospers (1956).
5 Fontana (1981), p. 147.
6 See e.g. Gagné (1970).
7 *Ibid.*, p. 207.
8 Sockett (1976), p. 73.
9 Peters (1974), p. 203.
10 Ausubel (1959), p. 245.
11 See Freud (1901, 1938 and 1962).
12 The similarity between Freud's view and Plato's view of the three-part soul may be remarked.
13 Brown (1964), p. 12.
14 Morris (1958).
15 Morrish (1967), pp. 171–3.
16 For a good discussion of Kohlberg, see Peters (1974) chs 15, 16 and 17.
17 See also Piaget (1929 and 1947).
18 Isaacs (1930).
18a See also M. Cole (1975) 'An ethnographic psychology of cognition' in R.W. Brislin *et al.* (eds) *Cross Cultural Perspectives in Learning* (New York: Sage 1975) commenting on the fact that most Australian Aborigine adults fail Piagetian tests of conservation: 'are we to believe that Aborigine adults will store water in tall thin cans in order to "have more water"?'

19 Stenhouse (1975).
20 John Stuart Mill (1962). But see his autobiography in this connection.
21 A.N. Whitehead (1929). A classic text.
22 The logical points, if there are any to be made, will need to be discerned by clear thinking. See e.g. Claiborne (1983) on reading.

References

Ausubel, D.P. (1959) 'Viewpoints from related disciplines: Human growth and development,' *Teachers College Record*, 60, 245–54.

Brown, J.A.C. (1964) *Freud and the Post-Freudians*. Harmondsworth: Penguin Books.

Bruner, J. (1966) *Towards a Theory of Instruction*. Cambridge, Mass.: Harvard University Press.

Bryant, P.E. and Trabasso, T. (1971) 'Transitive inferences and memory in young children,' *Nature*, 232, 456–8.

Egan, K. (1979) *Educational Development*. New York: Oxford.

Fontana, D. (1981) *Psychology for Teachers*. London: Macmillan.

Frankenburg, W.K. and Dodds, J.B. (1967) 'The Denver developmental screening test,' *Journal of Pediatricians*, 71, 181–91.

Gagné, R.M. (1970) *Conditions of Learning*. London: Holt, Rinehart & Winston.

Gagné, R.M. (1974) *Essentials of Learning for Instruction*. Hinsdale, Ill.: Dryden Press.

Gesell, A. (1928) *Infancy and Human Growth*. New York: Macmillan.

Hamlyn, D. (1967) 'The logical and psychological aspects of learning,' in R.S. Peters (ed.) *The Concept of Education*. London: Allen & Unwin.

Isaacs, S. (1930) *Intellectual Growth in Young Children*. London: Routledge & Kegan Paul.

Kohlberg, L. (1969) 'Stage and sequence: The cognitive–developmental approach to socialization,' in D. Goslin (ed.) *Handbook of Socialization Theory*. Chicago: Rand McNally.

Lawton, D. *et al.* (1978) *Theory and Practice of Curriculum Studies*. London: Routledge & Kegan Paul.

Morris, B. (1958) 'Mental health in the classroom,' in *Studies in Education*, no. 7. London: Evans.

Morrish, I. (1967) *Disciplines of Education*. London: Allen & Unwin.

Mussen, P.A. *et al.* (1979) *Child Development and Personality* (5th edn). New York: Harper & Row.

Peters, R.S. (1974) *Psychology and Ethical Development*. London: Allen & Unwin.

Phillips, D.C. and Kelly, M.E. (1975) 'Hierarchical theories of development in education and psychology,' *Harvard Educational Review*, 45(3), 351–75.

Piaget, J. (1924) *Language and Thought of the Child*. London: Routledge & Kegan Paul.

Povey, R. and Hill, E. (1975) 'Can pre-school children form concepts?' *Educational Research*, 17, 180–92.

Skinner, B.F. (1969) *Contingencies of Reinforcement: A Theoretical Analysis*, New York: Appleton-Century-Crofts.

Sockett, H. (1976) *Designing the Curriculum*. London: Open Books.

Stenhouse, L. (1975) *An Introduction to Curriculum Research and Development*. London: Heinemann.

Tomlinson, P. (1981) *Understanding Teaching: Interactive Educational Psychology*. New York: McGraw-Hill.

24

WHAT SHOULD WE DO WITH A HIDDEN CURRICULUM WHEN WE FIND ONE?

Jane Roland Martin

At the end of very interesting article 'Hiding the Hidden Curriculum' (1973/74), Elizabeth Vallance raises the question of what to do with the hidden curriculum now that we have found it. We can embrace it wholeheartedly, she says, or we can attempt to expunge it altogether, or we can do something between these two extremes. Vallance leaves the question open and I have no intention of closing it here; indeed, I am not sure it is one that can or should be closed. I would, however, like to explore some of the things that can be done with a hidden curriculum once it is found and some of the pitfalls of doing those things. But first we need to be clearer than we now are on the nature of the beast.

1 Misleading labels

Most of the labels we use when talking about hidden curriculum are either singularly unilluminating or highly misleading. To call hidden curriculum 'covert' or 'latent', as people often do, does no harm, but neither does it promote our understanding. To call hidden curriculum 'what schooling does to people', 'by-products of schooling', or 'non-academic outcomes of schooling' would seem to promote our understanding but in fact lead us astray.[1] For these last three labels, and others, too, make it seem as if hidden curriculum is necessarily tied to schools and schooling when it is not. Much of our education – and I am talking now of formal education and not simply of the informal education which enters into all aspects of our lives – much of this education has always taken place outside of schools. In an earlier day, apprenticeships to craftsmen prevailed. Currently there are internships in hospitals, management training programs in industry, fieldwork placements in social agencies; there are private music lessons, group karate lessons, swimming programs at the Y; there are summer camps,

Source: *Curriculum Inquiry* 6: 2 (1976). The Ontario Institute for Studies in Education.

Cub Scouts, basic training in the armed forces. I see no reason whatsoever to suppose that schools have a hidden curriculum but that formal educational programs in non-school settings do not. Labels such as 'by-products of schooling' or 'what schooling does to people' do no harm if we realize that they refer to one particular class of hidden curricula, namely, the hidden curricula of schools. We must not, however, let them dominate our thinking lest they blind us to the hidden curricula lurking in other habitats.

These labels mislead in another way, too, for they give the impression that everything an educational setting does to people belongs to its hidden curriculum. But while hidden curriculum is not necessarily tied to schools and schooling, it is always and everywhere tied to learning. Both schools and nonschool educational settings do lots of things to people – they have all sorts of by-products. It needs to be stressed, therefore, that only *some* of the things done by a given educational setting constitute its hidden curriculum. Some hospitals because of their location create traffic jams, some swimming programs because of their pools cause ear aches, and some schools because of their expenditures produce rising tax rates, but these results or outcomes do not belong to the hidden curriculum of the educational setting in question. They do not because although they happen, they are not *learned*.

Implicit in hidden curriculum talk, moreover, is a contrast between hidden curriculum and what for want of a better name I will call *curriculum proper* – that thing, difficult as it is to define, about which philosophers and educational theorists have long debated and which curriculum specialists have long tried to plan and develop. The contrast is between what is openly intended that students learn and what, although not openly intended, they do, in fact, learn. Indeed, one important thrust of the critique of contemporary schooling mounted by those who have been called radical school reformers (see Gross 1969) is that curriculum proper is failing while hidden curriculum thrives: students do not learn to read, they do not learn math or science or any of the other subjects and skills endorsed by all parties to the educational enterprise; what they do learn is to be docile and obedient, to value competition over cooperation, to stifle their creative impulses, and to believe in what Ivan Illich calls the Myth of Unending Consumption (Illich 1971: p. 55). Thus, some results or outcomes of school or of non-school educational settings are not constituents of a hidden curriculum, because they are not states that individuals have attained through learning: what I will henceforth call *learning states*. Other results are not because they are openly intended learning states, hidden from neither teacher nor student. In a school which openly acknowledges the goal that students learn to speak French and provides courses to that end, the ability to speak French, if achieved, although a learning state, is not part of its hidden curriculum.

I do not mean to suggest that knowledge of French could never be part of a hidden curriculum. It is tempting to conceive of the contrast with curriculum proper implicit in hidden curriculum talk as one between academic and non-academic learning states in the manner of one of the labels listed above, but this is a mistake. Curriculum proper can and often does quite directly and openly aim at what is normally taken to be non-academic learning, be it of moral values, religious attitudes, political preferences, or vocational skills. We are so used to thinking of the academic dimension of curriculum proper that we forget this. And just as a curriculum proper can be non-academic, so a hidden curriculum can consist of what normally would be considered academic learning, be it learning of addition facts, scientific theories, or French. To be sure, the hidden curriculum of contemporary public schooling discovered to date is what most of us would call non-academic. But it does not follow from this dicovery that a hidden curriculum *could* not consist of academic learning states. A hidden curriculum, like a curriculum proper, has subject matter, but just as there is no particular subject matter which must be present in or absent from every curriculum proper, so there is none which must or cannot belong to every hidden curriculum.

In sum, a hidden curriculum consists of some of the outcomes or by-products of schools or of non-school settings, particularly those states which are learned yet are not openly intended. There is no special subject matter which always and everywhere characterizes hidden curriculum, although, of course, a hidden curriculum must have *some* subject matter. It should perhaps be stressed that this neutrality with respect to subject matter means not only that the learning states of a hidden curriculum can be academic as well as non-academic; it means that the subject matter can be significant as well as trivial, worthwhile as well as worthless.

Actually, when one speaks of learning states one is usually speaking of two things at once: some *state* a learner is in (for example, a state of knowing or believing or being interested or being cautious), and something which may be called the *object* of that state – provided 'object' is construed broadly enough to include not just physical objects but such things as the theory of relativity, *David Copperfield*, the free enterprise system, and love. Thus, a learning state is not $2 + 3 = 5$, but believing or remembering that $2 + 3 = 5$; it is not the free enterprise system as such, but being committed to or, perhaps, being adamantly opposed to the system.[2] When I said just now that there is no special subject matter necessarily associated with hidden curriculum, I meant that the learning states which consititute a hidden curriculum are not limited to one sort of object. But they are not limited to one sort of state either. The learning states of a hidden curriculum can be states which we think of as character trails – for example, docility or conformity. They can also be cognitive states such as believing or knowing, states of readiness or of skill, emotional states, attitudinal states, or some combination of those and other sorts of states.[3]

2　The hidden curriculum

Those who describe the hidden curriculum of contemporary schooling talk of the hidden curriculum as if there is and can be only one, as if hidden curriculum is everywhere the same. But of course it is not. A hidden curriculum is always *of* some setting, and there is no reason to suppose that different settings will have identical hidden curricula. Actually, a hidden curriculum is not only of some setting but is *at* some time; therefore, we cannot even assume that a single setting will have identical hidden curricula at different times. Settings change, and as they do some learning states may become extinct as new ones emerge.

It is sometimes said that learning states must occur systematically if they are to belong to a hidden curriculum.[4] I am not sure what this means. True, they must *be* results of the setting. However, the learning states of a hidden curriculum need not be systematic in the sense that they are mass products – learning states for all or even most learners in that setting. If John is the only one of his classmates who comes to appreciate good art as a result of the teacher's putting Picasso prints on the classroom walls – the teacher in this instance wanting to make the room more attractive and having no thought of learning states – this learning state of John's belongs to the hidden curriculum of his school, at least for him. A hidden curriculum, like a curriculum proper, is *of* some setting, *at* some time, and *for* some learner.

In view of this relativity to context, talk of *the* hidden curriculum is normally elliptical. Those who speak in this way usually have a particular setting in mind – often, but not always, public schooling in the United States – and they have a particular time, usually the present, in mind. From the standpoint of the learner, moreover, *the* hidden curriculum is an abstraction, for it is neither the set of learning states attained by anyone in particular nor the set attained by all the learners in a given setting. Idiosyncratic learning states are overlooked when a portrait of *the* hidden curriculum is painted, and rightly so, for *the* hidden curriculum of a setting consists not in all the learning states therein attained, but rather in the dominant ones. An account of *the* hidden curriculum of a setting, like an account of *the* history of an era, is selective. Attention is directed to common themes running through the learning states, presumably themes of some importance. Learning states which seem insignificant or which do not fit readily into the general pattern will be shunned, even though they are in fact produced by the setting.

The learning states of *the* hidden curriculum of a setting do, then, occur systematically in the sense that idiosyncratic states are ignored. But what is considered idiosyncratic will depend on one's interest. Learning states which are legitimately ignored when *the* hidden curriculum of some setting is the focus of attention may require attention when *the* hidden curriculum for some learner is at issue. Suppose, what is unlikely, namely that Mary is the only person in her school in the last twenty years who has come to believe as an unintended result of her schooling that women cannot be doctors. This idiosyncratic learning state is rightly ignored by those trying to determine *the* hidden curriculum *of Mary's school*. But those trying to discover *the* hidden curriculum of that school *for Mary* would remiss if they did not take it seriously, since it might well play a very significant role in Mary's life.

I want to emphasize here, because I think it too often forgotten, that our interest can be in hidden curricula for learners as well as of settings. And just as *the* hidden curriculum of a setting is an abstraction from the standpoint of learners, so *the* hidden curriculum for a learner is an abstraction from the standpoint of settings. *The* hidden curriculum for Mary 'cuts across' settings, so that to discover it we must look not simply at Mary's schooling, but at the other settings having hidden curricula in which Mary is a participant – or perhaps is simply an unwilling victim. Once again, *the* hidden curriculum is a selection from among the relevant learning states: it is a set of learning states thought to be dominant for Mary.

3 Finding a hidden curriculum

A hidden curriculum is not something one just finds; one must go hunting for it. Since a hidden curriculum is a set of learning states, ultimately one must find out what is learned as a result of the practices, procedures, rules, relationships, structures, and physical characterstics which constitute a given setting. But one can begin by spotting learning states and making sure they can be traced back to the setting, or by examining aspects of the setting and discovering what learning states they produce. Motivations for the search can, of course, vary. Some investigators may simply want to know what is learned in school, others will want to make their teaching methods more efficient, and still others will be intent on revealing connections between education and the larger social order. But whatever the motivation may be, a full-blown theory of curriculum cannot afford to neglect the hunt for hidden curricula, for the quarry plays a central role in the education of each one of us.

One consequence of the relativity of hidden curriculum to setting, time, and learner is that investigative work on it is never done. New settings with their own hidden curricula are forever being created and old ones are forever changing. Information gathered yesterday on the hidden curriculum of a given setting may not accurately portray that setting's hidden curriculum today. Thus, the scope of the search for hidden curricula needs to be extended beyond schools to non-school settings, and at the same time the searchers must continually retrace their steps.

Even if hidden curricula did not change over time, there would be reason to revisit the old haunts, for the information gathered at any time is never the whole story. Regardless of setting or time, what we find when we investigate hidden curricula is a function of what we look for and what we look at. The literature describing the hidden curriculum of public schooling in the United States published in the mid to late 1960s provides an interesting case in point. It draws our attention to learning states having class and racial overtones, but it overlooks those having sexist implications (e.g., Henry 1963; Herndon 1968; Kozol 1967). Yet no one who has seen the film 'High School' or read even a sampling of the articles in *And Jill Came Tumbling After* (Stacey *et al.* 1974) can

457

doubt that public schooling in the 1960s included a wide range of sexist practices and that its hidden curriculum included sexist beliefs, attitudes and values. If sexist learning states were not found it is not because they did not exist, but because they were not seen or – if they were seen – because they were not recognized for what they were.

A description of the hidden curriculum of public schooling of the 1960s, or for that matter of the 1970s, written today would most likely draw our attention to its sexist component. But who knows what other component it might overlook! Christian doctrine? Heterosexual bias? Speciesism? The search for hidden curricula needs to retrace its steps, then, because even if a hidden curriculum does not change over time, *we* change. Our interests shift, our knowledge of the world is enlarged, our consciousness is raised, and we therefore come to see and care about things in a hidden curriculum we did not care about, indeed perhaps could not see, before.

One way to determine if we have overlooked important parts of a hidden curriculum is to examine the different aspects or elements of the relevant setting or settings to see what learning states they produce. In other words, look beyond learning states to sources![5] Thanks to a variety of inquiries, many of which Vallance cites in her article, we have an idea of some of the sources of important elements of hidden curricula of schools. Vallance mentions, for example, the social structure of the classroom, the teacher's exercise of authority, the rules governing the relationship between teacher and student (1973/74: pp. 6-7). Standard learning activities are also sources. Who can forget Jules Henry's description of a classroom game of Spelling Baseball or John Holt's account of Twenty Questions (Henry 1963; Holt 1964). In a somewhat different vein, Joanne Bronars (1970) has drawn our attention to dissecting frogs and catching insects. Another source of hidden curricula is the teacher's use of language (Gayer 1970). And, of course, there are textbooks and audiovisual aids, furnishings and architecture, disciplinary measures, timetables, tracking systems, and curricular priorities.

The problem in looking to sources is that it is not clear that a list of sources of the learning states which constitute hidden curricula will have an end, for as new practices, procedures, environments and the like are introduced into educational settings, they become potential generators of hidden curricula. Can anyone doubt that the new classification of students as learning-disabled and the practices which accompany it are generating a hidden curriculum, or rather elements of one? As pocket calculators begin to be used in math and science classes, will they not generate hidden learning states? Just as there are no limits on the subject matter of the learning outcomes which can constitute a hidden curriculum, I think we must conclude that there are none on the elements or aspects of educational settings which can be sources of those states.

There is, of course, a good reason for looking to sources and for recognizing that when limits are placed on the sorts of things within a setting which can generate elements of hidden curricula, they are arbitrary. If our concern is not simply to discover hidden curricula but to do something about them, we must find out which elements or aspects of a given setting help bring about which components of that setting's hidden curriculum. For if we do not know the sources of the learning states belonging to a hidden curriculum, we must either let that hidden curriculum be or do away with the whole setting. But some hidden curricula or parts thereof quite clearly ought not to be left as they are; and on the other hand, if we do away with whole settings, we may be doing away with practices, procedures, physical environments and the like which on balance generate desirable learning outcomes.

Rational intervention requires that we know sources. It requires also that we return to the scene of our interventions to make sure we have not done more harm than good. There is no guarantee that, when we change an educational setting so as to do away with a portion of its hidden curriculum we find abhorrent, we will succeed; indeed, if we are not careful, the changes we make can generate the very learning states we are trying to banish or, for that matter, ones even more unsavory. The learning disabilities movement purports to be trying to end the practice of labeling students because of the hidden curriculum resulting from it, but one wonders if the movement is not in fact promoting the very learning states it claims to reject (see Schrag and Divoky 1975).

Once we recognize that any aspect of an educational setting can have learning states which are not openly intended, that changes in settings can produce such states, that the learning states produced be a setting may be different for every learner and that new learners constantly enter educational settings, then I think we must acknowledge that for any given setting hidden curricula cannot be avoided. We can get rid of a particular hidden curriculum of a setting, but in principle we cannot avoid some hidden curriculum or other unless we abolish the setting itself. I stress this point because educators often suppose that if their reforms are put into practice we will never again have to worry about hidden curricula. As the documentary film 'Infants School' unwittingly testifies, this is a terrible mistake, for the most enlightened practices can carry with them an undesirable hidden curriculum.[6] In many ways, the British infants school of the film is a model of school reform, yet if one looks closely one sees traditional sex roles and stereotypes being transmitted. Those of us concerned with educational settings cannot rest on our laurels. It is impossible to do away with all hidden curricula; hence, for any given setting, we must always be on our guard.

4 Two kinds of hiddenness

That *some* hidden curriculum or other for any given setting is inevitable ought not to be taken as grounds for maintaining the status quo in education.

To say that some hidden curriculum or other is inevitable for any given setting is not to say that a hidden curriculum consisting in learning states we take to be undesirable is inevitable. We need to guard against replacing an objectionable hidden curriculum with a worse one, but although there is always the possibility of our ending up with a worse one, there is no necessity at work here. And there is always the possibility that we will end up with a better one.

I realize that an important part of the message of Illich's *Deschooling Society* is that the hidden curriculum of contemporary public schooling cannot be changed – at least not for the better – by changes in the setting. Hence the need for deschooling. Illich has been attacked on this score by critics speaking from very different points on the educational spectrum. It is all too easy, however, to do less than justice to his claim. He is surely *not* saying that *none* of the hidden learning states produced by contemporary public schooling can be banished or that *no* changes for the better can be produced by changes in the setting. His view of *the* hidden curriculum of public schooling is highly selective, and his claim about the resistance of public schooling to reform that makes a real difference must be understood as holding only for the learning outcomes with which he is concerned. Exactly what these are and whether he is right about them is a topic for another occasion. But whether or not he is right, there is certainly nothing in his remarks which shows reform of hidden curricula to be *in general* impossible. His claim applies only to school settings, and he is the first to point out that non-school settings also have hidden curricula (1971: p. 48). Some of these latter might be as resistant to real reform as he says schools are, but there is no reason to suppose that all would be.

The inevitability thesis is not a counsel for inaction. Yet inaction is, in fact, one viable alternative when we find a hidden curriculum and wonder what we ought to do with it. I indicated above that we may be forced to let a hidden curriculum be when we find it because we do not know its exact sources. It should be clear, however, that even if we know its sources, we can nonetheless choose not to abolish or even alter them in any way. It may be wondered, however, if a hidden curriculum, once it is found, *can* be left as it is. Once we find a hidden curriculum does not it stop being hidden, hence being a hidden curriculum?

Our discussion has for too long avoided the question of the hiddenness of the learning states belonging to a hidden curriculum. Suppose a sociologist studies a school or school system and finds elements of its hidden curriculum. Is that hidden curriculum, simply by virtue of being known to the sociologist, no longer a *hidden* curriculum? Surely not. Being hidden, like being north of, is a relation: just as Boston is north of Miami but not north of Montreal, so something can be hidden from one person or group but not from another. When we speak of something as hidden, moreover, we usually have some context in mind in relation to which we make our judgments of hiddenness. In the game Hide and Seek, a player is hidden just so long as the one who is It has not found him or her; that others know where the player is has no bearing on the player's hiddenness from the standpoint of the game; and when the player is found, that others do not know where the player is also has no bearing on the player's hiddenness.

Education is no game, but nonetheless a hidden curriculum is in this respect like a hidden player in Hide and Seek. Once the learners in a setting are aware of the learning states they are acquiring or are supposed to acquire, these learning outcomes no longer belong to the hidden curriculum of that setting. Indeed, once learning states are openly acknowledged so that the learners can readily become aware of them even if they do not, the learning states can no longer be considered hidden. Until learning states are acknowledged or the learners are aware of them, however, they remain hidden if sociologists, bureaucrats, and teachers are all aware of them. Thus, a hidden curriculum can be found yet remain hidden, for finding is one thing and telling is another.

There are, in effect, two kinds of hiddenness, and an account of hidden curriculum needs to come to terms with both. Something can be hidden in the sense in which a cure for cancer is hidden or in the sense in which a penny in the game Hide the Penny is hidden. Both academics who investigate the hidden curriculum of public schooling today and radical school reformers who decry it vacillate on this issue. Some make it sound as if a hidden curriculum is hidden by someone or some group in the manner of the penny in the children's game. Others seem to assume that the learning states of a hidden curriculum have not been hidden by anyone: they just happen to be unknown to us, much as the cure for cancer is unknown to us at the present time.

Whether we are trying to explain why the hidden curriculum of a given setting is what it is or to change a hidden curriculum, we need to take into account this basic ambiguity in the notion of hidden curriculum. For any set of hidden learning states which interest us, we must try to settle the question of intent. It makes no sense to explain a hidden curriculum by mean of a conspiracy theory, as some of those writers who point out that the hidden curriculum of public schooling in the United States serves capitalism do, and at the same time describe its learning states as the unintended by-products of schooling. Nor does it make sense simply to tinker with school practices and procedures in order to do away with a given hidden curriculum if it is really the product of intent.

Some readers would doubtless prefer that I characterize hidden curriculum solely in terms of unintended learning states. To introduce intention muddies the waters, they will say. Yet I do not think we have any choice here. It is not only that those writers most concerned with hidden curricula move back and forth between the two kinds of hiddenness. The relevant research on intent has not all been done. We may assume that all the elements of the hidden curricula discovered to date are unintended, but we certainly do not know for sure that they are. A characterization which accommodates the descriptions of hidden curricula we now have is surely to be preferred over one which may require us when the evidence is in to reject some on the grounds that the learning states they describe were intended although we did not realize it.

Earlier I characterized hidden curriculum in terms of learning states which are not openly intended. The point of that negative formulation was to accommodate the two kinds of hiddenness. That characterization did not, however, take into account the learner's point of view. Although a learning state of a setting is not openly intended a learner can be aware of it, in which case it will not belong to the hidden curriculum of that setting for that learner. Thus, my earlier characterization must be amended. A hidden curriculum consists of those learning states of a setting which are either unintended or intended but not openly acknowledged to the learners in the setting unless the learners are aware of them.

5 Out of the frying pan

What then can we do with a hidden curriculum once we have found it? This depends, of course, on who 'we' are. Assuming we are the educators in a setting and have found both hidden curriculum and sources, there are a number of alternatives open to us.

1   We can do nothing: we can leave the setting alone rather than try to change it, in which case the relevant learning states become foreseen by us, whereas previously they were not, but they do not otherwise change; in particular, the hidden curriculum remains hidden. This may seem to be the alternative of despair but that is not necessarily the case, for there may be some hidden curricula, or elements thereof, with respect to which we are neutral – we do not positively value them but we do not consider them undesirable either. In relation to such learning states, doing nothing is a reasonable alternative.

2   We can change our practices, procedures, environments, rules and the like in an effort to root out those learning states we consider undesirable. The radical school reform movement known as open education has tried to do just this. It has opposed tracking, grading, and examinations, changed the physical environment of classrooms, introduced new learning activities and educational materials, and tried to alter both teacher–pupil and pupil–pupil relationships in order to avoid the hidden curriculum of contemporary public schooling. The free-school movement, while varying in its details from open education, can be understood in this same light.

3   Instead of changing a setting, we can simply abolish it. This, of course, is the alternative those in the deschooling movement recommend. I say 'simply' abolish, but for some educational settings, notably the public school systems of modern industrial societies, abolition is not a simple matter. Abolition of a setting does, however, guarantee abolition of that setting's hidden curriculum, but not of all hidden curricula like it.

4   It is always possible that we will want to embrace rather than abolish the hidden curriculum we find. There are many today who applaud the learning states of neatness and competitiveness, docility and obedience to authority attributed to the hidden curriculum of our public schools (e.g., Pursell 1976). They actually have two alternatives: (a) they can openly acknowledge these learning states, thereby shifting them from hidden curriculum to curriculum proper, or (b) they can intend these learning states but not openly, in which case they remain part of the hidden curriculum.[7]

What *should* we do with a hidden curriculum when we find it? The significance of the question is a function of the quality of the hidden curriculum we find. If a hidden curriculum is harmless, what we do with it will not matter very much. It is when the one we find is not harmless – when it instills beliefs, attitudes, values, or patterns of behaviour which are undesirable – that our question takes on urgency. And it becomes more urgent the more undesirable the learning states are. There can be no doubt that when the hidden curriculum we find contains harmful learning states, we must try to root them out. But this is sometimes easier said than done. A teacher can stop using the game of Spelling Baseball as a learning activity, but this will be but a small step toward rooting out learning states such as competitiveness, self-hatred, and hostility toward one's peers. Attitudes and traits such as these seldom have a single, easily isolated source; indeed, those which are most offensive, because very basic, are likely to be products of a complex set of interrelated and entrenched practices and struc- tures. To give up or modify one of these may well accomplish very little.

Large-scale changes, perhaps even total destruction, of a setting may be necessary if a hidden curriculum or some central part thereof is to be abolished. And this, of course, is what the radical school reform movement in all its variations has been about.[8] The hidden curriculum of contemporary public schooling in the United States has been held to be abhorrent – and rightly so. Drastic changes have been seen – again rightly in my view – as the only hope if its highly undesirable and very deep-seated learning outcomes are to be ban- ished. This is not the place to catalog or assess those proposals, although they need to be assessed in a way they have not yet been. I do, however, want to draw attention to a problem which confronts anyone who tries to change drastically or abolish altogether an educational setting in order to to do away with its hidden curriculum – a problem too many radical school reformers have ignored.

Some changes in educational settings involve the deliberate placing of the learners of that setting in other settings so as to break down the barriers between the setting and the 'real' world, meanwhile enhancing learning. Thus, for example, schools are encouraged to put students in non-school settings where they will learn through being apprenticed to master craftsmen and women, through working at a job, through helping others do their jobs or, perhaps, simply through watching and observing. Other changes in an educational setting involve restricting its function so as to reduce its power over its participants. It has been proposed, for example, that schools be limited to giving basic skills training (e.g, Bereiter 1973; Katz 1971). In this case, even if participants in the setting are not deliberately placed in other settings, the likelihood of their drifting into them is great. And of course there is the total abolition of a setting, in which case the participants may simply be abandoned to other settings. In all three sorts of reform, the risk is real that those on the receiving end of the offending learning states will be taken out of the frying pan only to be sent or allowed to leap into the fire.

It is not just formal educational settings which have hidden curricula. Any setting can have one and most do. When I argued initially that hidden curricula can exist in non-school settings, I limited the discussion to formal educational settings such as teaching hospitals, private piano lessons, and basic training in the armed services. But learning states occur in settings which are not usually considered educational at all. At IBM and Bell Telephone, at one's local gas station and City Hall, workers learn more than their jobs: attitudes, values, and patterns of behaviour are as much the product of these settings as of formal educational ones. It seems not only legitimate, therefore, but theoretically important that we recognize explicitly that hidden curricula can be found anywhere learning states are found. IBM and Bell Telephone are not exempt; neither are one's neighborhood streets, one's church, or the national book club one joins. And what is important to remember is that there is no good reason at all to suppose that the hidden curricula of these and kindred settings are significantly better than the one which is the target of school reforms.

Radical school reformers have been called romantics – this label, needless to say, having derogatory connotations. The source of their romanticism is seen as lying in their view of the child as by nature a happy, curious, creative, and good being who is ruined by school. Perhaps some radical school reformers do romanticize the child, but in general this is a caricature of their position. If the reformers are romantics it is not in their beliefs about human nature, but in their beliefs about the world outside schools. It is as if they bracket their critique of contemporary society when they begin to theorize about education. I am sure that they are as aware as anyone of the sorry state of the outside world. Indeed, they were probably aware of the sorry state of *it* long before they perceived the sorry state of schools. But they forget it in their excitement upon discovering the hidden curriculum of contemporary public schooling. Make the outside world, not schools, the dominant educational setting, they say, and all will be well – as if the world out there were a benign setting, one in which either there are no hidden curricula or only worthwhile ones thrive.[9]

A mistake we all tend to make – except perhaps when we are thinking of our own children – is to concentrate on the hidden curriculum *of* a given setting when what matters is the hidden curriculum *for* a given individual or group. To do away with the complex network of practices and structures which in a given setting produce highly undesirable learning outcomes – assuming this is possible, and to some extent I think it is – may leave the learning states *for someone* unchanged. This may be so because our very reforms send a person, or allow the person to drift, into settings having hidden curricula similar to the one we have been trying to abolish. Or it may be so because the learning states in question were all along the result of more than one setting. Settings can combine to produce learning states. And they surely do. The learning states of docility and conformity, competitiveness and unending consumption, which are said to belong to the hidden curriculum of publich schooling in the United States today, are certainly not the products of that schooling alone. Who can doubt that family, church, community organizations, place of work, and the media have all combined to produce them?

The problem I spoke of is really two problems, both hinging on the obvious point that different settings can but need not have significantly different hidden curricula. The one problem is that some educational reforms designed to rid us of undesirable hidden curricula can be self-defeating, because they substitute for the old setting new ones producing essentially the same learning states. The other problem is that the reform of a given educational setting may simply not be enough to do the job if other settings having the same old hidden curriculum survive. It has been pointed out that radical school reform can succeed only if it goes hand in hand with radical societal reform (e.g., by Graubard 1972). That this is so becomes especially clear once we shift our attention from the hidden curriculum of schooling to the hidden curriculum for those being schooled. For it is not just that wide-scale basic reform of public schooling – that is, reform of the whole system as opposed to small units within or alongside it – may not be possible without concomitant societal reform. Supposing it to be possible, it is not at all obvious that the hidden curriculum for those being schooled will be materially improved if the other dominant educational settings in their lives remain the same.

6 Knowledge can be power

I am not as optimistic as some about the prospects of radical societal reform. But whether one takes these prospects to be good or not, there are two courses of action open to us when we find a hidden curriculum we abhor which we still need to consider. One is part and parcel of many radical school reform programs. The other is not.

Radical school reformers do not all take learners out of the frying pan and, with no thought of the fire outside, send them to get burned. Both those who advocate open classrooms and those in the free-school movement try to provide their learners with insulation so that the fire, even if it singes, will not burn. They do this by advocating practices and structures which have a dual function: they are intended to do away with the hidden curriculum of public schooling and at the same time to substitute for the attitudes and values of that hidden curriculum ones considered to be admirable. Thus, competition is to be replaced by cooperation, while conformity is to be replaced by creativity and initiative. The attitudes and values espoused by radical school reformers are openly acknowledged by some and embraced not so openly by others. But be they part of the curriculum proper of radical school reform or of its hidden curriculum, they are expected to take hold not just while the learner is in school and until graduation, but in non-school settings too and for life. If any policy can successfully protect learners from the hidden curricula of the larger unreconstructed society, surely the policy of fostering learning states in conflict with those fostered by the larger society can.

465

It should be noted that some radical school reformers deplore this aspect of the reform movement. In their view, schools should get out of the business of forming attitudes and values altogether (see, e.g., Bereiter 1973; Katz 1971). It is not clear, however, that schools *can* get out of the business. Even schools whose functions are pared away and minimized through reform will have hidden curricula, hidden curricula which may or may not themselves be minimal so far as attitudes and values are concerned. I am afraid that those who condemn the hidden curriculum of public schooling today, yet want to preserve schools in some form or other without substituting better values and attitudes for the ones to be abolished, are being unrealistic. The question they should be asking of those who try to insulate learners from the fires outside is not whether the schools should do the insulating, but whether schools alone can do it. If the larger society remains as it is, will schools be allowed to foster values and attitudes counter to those of surrounding institutions? And if so, will these values and attitudes 'take'; will they really provide the needed protection?

I do not know the answer to these questions, but I am pessimistic enough to want to consider one more thing that can be done with a hidden curriculum when we find it, something which although independent of the course of action just described is compatible with it and indeed could be used to buttress it. When we find a hidden curriculum, we can show it to those destined to be its recipients: consciousness raising, if you will, with a view to counteracting the hidden curricula of settings we are not now in a position to change or abolish. Not that consciousness raising is any guarantee that a person will not succumb to a hidden curriculum. But still, one is in a better position to resist if one knows what is going on. Resistance to what one does not know is difficult, if not impossible.

The raising to consciousness of hidden curricula can proceed in many different ways. It can take place in informal rap sessions or formal seminars and can be aimed at those in a setting, those about to enter it, or those who once were in it. But whatever form it takes, it will consist in transforming the learning states of the hidden curriculum of a setting into the subject matter of a person's curriculum proper. I do not mean by this that the hidden curricula we find abhorrent are to be openly embraced. Quite the contrary. The point of raising a hidden curriculum to consciousness is not to *foster* but to *prevent* the acquisition of the learning states belonging to it. The method of prevention is to make these learning states themselves the objects of new and very different learning states.

Most of use never stop to think that the settings we enter have hidden curricula, let alone what those hidden curricula might be. A program of consciousness raising would aim at such simple yet not at all obvious learning states as realizing that a given setting has a hidden curriculum, knowing what that hidden curriculum is, knowing which practices of the setting are responsible for the various learning states of its hidden curriculum, and understanding the significance of these learning states for one's own life and for the larger society. It would aim not only at making the hidden curriculum of a setting an object of a cognitive state such as these, but of skill states, too – for example, being able to spot a hidden curriculum, being able to recognize heretofore undiscovered sources, and knowing how to avoid the learning outcomes one does not want to acquire.

Having knowledge and skill concerning hidden curricula can be a form of self-defense against the onslaught of unasked-for learning states. But consciousness raising, as I understand it, aims at the acquistion of attitudes and values too. Certainly consciousness raising in the women's movement is not thought to be successful if a woman in coming to know the facts about sexist practices in modern society also comes to approve of them. Knowledge of hidden curricula will not provide a defense against them if those subject to hidden curricula do not *want* to resist.

To do its job, consciousness raising with respect to hidden curricula must tend to attitudes and values and feelings while imparting knowledge and skill. In this respect it resembles the program of those who want to substitute cooperativeness for competitiveness and creativity for conformity. But if it, too, is in the business of forming attitudes and values there is a difference, for in consciousness raising the attitudes and values acquired are, or at least are supposed to be, the result of a direct confrontation between learner and hidden curriculum: to see it is to despise it, to want to resist it, perhaps even to want to go out in the world and try to change it. The attitudes and values honored by radical school reformers have perhaps been chosen by them because of their own confrontation with a hidden curriculum, but the students who are to acquire them do not do so as a result of such confrontation.

The consciousness raising I am suggesting would seem to require a knowledge of the hidden curricula of non-school settings which is not now available. Am I not then proposing a course of action for which we are not ready, one which would require an investment of funds and scholarly energy which is not likely to be forthcoming? Again, we must look to consciousness raising in the women's movement for our model. It has generated knowledge even while relying on it, for much if not all of the important research on women being done now is surely a direct result of it. I would expect the consciousness raising I am recommending to have a similar effect on our knowledge: that it would generate research into hidden curricula, research which in turn produced new subject matter for it. Thus, although knowledge of hidden curricula in non-school settings is surely needed, consciousness raising can begin with the little we have, in the expectation that we will soon have more.

Lest there be any doubt, we do have some with which to begin – if nothing else, our own experiences in these settings. We may, however, have more knowledge now than we realize. Our knowledge of the hidden curricula of schools comes primarily from two sources: from those who have worked in schools and those who have done research on schools. To discover the hidden curricula of other institutions we must turn to those who study them: to medical sociologists and to sociologists of family, church, science, sports, and business. We must turn also to those who have taken or given management training courses at Gulf and those who have worked the switchboard at the telephone company. Perceptive practitioners are not the monopoly of schools. Hospitals, businesses, even city halls have their James Herndons and John Holts who see and record hidden curricula for us.

Who should conduct this consciousness raising? Insofar as schools send their students into non-school settings to learn, one would hope that they would do their own consciousness raising: that medical schools would do it for prospective interns, social work schools for students doing fieldwork, education schools for practice teachers, and high schools for those sent out to learn on the job. One would also hope that schools trying to abolish their own hidden curriculum while keeping students within their walls would conduct consciousness-raising sessions about the hidden curricula in the larger society. Schools that did this would, in effect, become centers for the critique of social institutions. I believe strongly that schools should serve this function, but perhaps only an optimist would think they could or would serve it as long as they remain public and society remains the way it is. Schools are not the only possible forum for consciousness raising with respect to hidden curricula, however. Victims of a given hidden curriculum can do it for themselves as women have done and Blacks have done.

As I have said, there is no guarantee that consciousness raising will insulate us successfully against learning states we do not want and should not acquire. Certainly we must not view it as a substitute for institutional and societal reform. Yet, as the women's movement has shown, knowledge about what has happened or is happening to one can have powerful effects. I would not count on a single individual whose consciousness had been raised in private, so to speak, to with-stand the hidden curriculum of a setting in which he or she is put. But when knowledge is shared and there is strong peer support, consciousness raising may be the best weapon individuals who are subject to hidden curricula have.

Notes

1 I have taken these labels from Vallance (1973/74, p.6)
2 It is possible that some states of an individual have no object – for example, a generalized state of despair. Normally, however, the states that constitute learning states will have objects, albeit very complex ones at times. Thus, although the state of being competitive may seem to have no object, an individual will in fact be competitive with respect to certain situations or types of situations, and those would constitute the object of the state.
3 It will be noted that I have characterized hidden curriculum as what happens (and curriculum proper as what is intended to happen), rather than as statements about what happens (or is intended to happen). Should the reader prefer the linguistic level – that is, a characterization of hidden curriculum as a set of statements about learning states rather than as the learning states themselves – the present account can readily be translated into it.
4 Vallance suggests as much (1973/74, p.7).
5 As I have characterized hidden curriculum, the sources of the learning states of a

hidden curriculum do not themselves belong to that curriculum. Should the reader prefer a broader characterization, one that includes the practices that produce the relevant learning states, the necessary adjustments in the formulation of the problem of finding hidden curricula can readily be made.

6 'Infants School,' by Lillian Weber, is distributed by Education Development Center, Newton, Massachusetts.

7 It should be noted that learning outcomes unintended by us could all along have been intended by others, e.g., by those who hired us.

8 For purposes of this discussion I take the radical school reform movement to include not just open-classroom advocates, free-school proponents, and those wanting to decentralize the control of schools, but also deschoolers and those who advocate minimal schooling.

9 I do not mean to suggest that all radical school reformers romanticize the world outside the schools. Illich does not. Nor does Allen Graubard (1972).

References

Breiter, Carl. *Must we educate?* Englewood Cliffs, N.J.: Prentice-Hall, 1973.

Bronars, Joanne. 'Tampering with nature in elementary school science,' in *Readings in the philosophy of education: A study of curriculum*, edited by Jane R. Martin. Boston: Allyn & Bacon, 1970.

Gayer, Nancy. 'On making morality operational,' in *Readings in the philosophy of education: A study of curriculum*, edited by Jane R. Martin. Boston: Allyn & Bacon, 1970.

Graubard, Allen. *Free the children.* New York: Random House, 1972.

Gross, Beatrice and Gross, Ronald (eds). *Radical school reform.* New York: Simon & Schuster, 1969.

Henry, Jules. *Culture against man.* New York: Random House, 1963.

Herndon, James. *The way it spozed to be.* New York: Simon & Schuster, 1968.

Holt, John. *How children fail.* New York. Dell: 1964.

Illich, Ivan. *Deschooling society.* New York: Harper & Row, 1971.

Katz, Michael B. *Class, bureaucracy and schools: The illusion of educational change in America.* New York: Praeger, 1971.

Kozol, Jonathan. *Death at an early age.* Boston: Houghton Mifflin, 1967.

Pursell, William. *A conservative alternative school. The A+ school in Cupertino.* Bloomington, Ind.: Phi Delta Kappa, 1976.

Schrag, Peter and Divoky, Diane. *The myth of the hyperactive child.* New York: Pantheon Books, 1975.

Stacy, Judith. Bereaud, Susan and Daniels, Joan (eds). *And Jill came tumbling after: Sexism in American education.* New York: Dell, 1974.

Vallance, Elizabeth. 'Hiding the hidden curriculum: An interpretation of the languae of justification in nineteenth-century educational reform,' *Curriculum Theory Network* 4, no.1 (1973/74): 5-22.

25

POSTSTRUCTURALISM, PRAGMATISM, AND CURRICULUM

Cleo H. Cherryholmes

> There is no power that is exercised without a series of aims and objectives. But this does not mean that it results from the choice or decision of an individual subject; let us not look for the headquarters that presides over its rationality....It is often the case that no one is there to have invented them [the rationality of power and its tactics], and few who can be said to have formulated them: an implicit characteristic of the great anonymous, almost unspoken strategies which coordinate the loquacious tactics whose 'inventors' or decisionmakers are often without hypocrisy.
>
> (Foucault, 1980c: p. 95)

> With the linguistic resourcefulness and mobility accruing from an extreme language-scepticism, deconstruction had the capacity to come in under existing or emerging critical systems at their weakest point, the linguistic bad faith on which they were built.
>
> (Felperin, 1985: p. 110)

Curriculum is not derivative, as are many subfields of education, from other academic or applied disciplines. For example, educational psychology has roots in psychology; social foundations of education, in history and sociology; philosophy of education, in philosophy; the study of educational policy, in political science and the policy sciences; and educational administration, in the applied fields of business and public administration. Curriculum deals with problems that are uniquely educational in much the same way that instruction has its own special tasks. But instruction is confronted with the concrete situation of classrooms, students, content, and teachers. The tasks facing curriculum are less immediately demanding.

Such independence is rare. It is enviable, however, if one desires to chart one's

Source: *Power and Criticism: Poststructural Investigations in Education*, Cleo H. Cherryholmes, 1988, Teachers College Press, New York, Chapter 7.

course by picking and choosing among problems and orientations. But there are also costs. There is a sense of security, if not certainty, when it is possible to rely on an academic discipline to orient one's research, to help identify 'important' problems, and to outline accepted research techniques and methodologies. Given the disciplinary independence of curriculum, it is not surprising that its history is marked by repeated turmoil and conflict, because it is always possible to question its purposes, beliefs, values, assumptions, metaphors, and orientations that fix its purpose and meaning.

An array of metaphors related to death and illness have been used to describe the field: in 1969 Schwab used the work *moribund*, in 1975 Dwayne Huebner wrote about a *wake*, and in 1980 Philip Jackson questioned the *existence* of a field of curriculum. But there was plenty of counter-evidence that curriculum was alive and, if not well, at least kicking. There were heated exchanges between so-called reconceptualists, conceptual-empiricists, and traditionalists (Jackson 1980; Pinar 1980; Tanner and Tanner 1979). Additionally, remnants of old positivist debates (Eisner 1983; Phillips 1983) and discussions of phenomenology (Macdonald 1982; van Manen 1982), critical theory (Anyon 1981; Cherryholmes 1980, 1982; Giroux 1983a,b), and neo-Marxist criticism (Apple 1982; Popkewitz 1982) were explored in terms of curriculum. Curriculum, it is safe to conclude, is not dead. It is fair to ask, however, whether its conflicts and disagreements signify illness, moribundity, or death. These metaphors, I will argue, misconceptualize curriculum and its dynamics. Furthermore, its internal conflicts and turmoil are not anomalous but characterize all fields of study (for one argument along these lines, see Kuhn 1974). It just happens that the disciplinary and task independence of curriculum exacerbates this condition.

This paper proposes one argument to answer two questions: (1) Why has the study of curriculum been turbulent and full of conflict? (2) What is its central project? First, a definition of curriculum and then the 1960s movement to teach a structure of the disciplines will be described and given a poststructural reading. Then some implications of this for curriculum and education will be outlined.

One caveat before proceeding: any profession operates simultaneously at many levels. Some practitioners implement research findings and engage in the practices of the field on a day-to-day basis. Some researchers try to clarify and extend the knowledge of the field. Some trainers teach the literature, norms, and practices of the field to new entrants. Some developers work, in the case of curriculum, on new classroom materials and new approaches to school and classroom organization. Such different activities have distinct yet reinforcing discourses. They are concerned with different immediate tasks, while sharing larger goals and purposes. The substantive focus of this paper is with curriculum knowledge, purposes, and goals; how a particular movement proposed to organize the field; why it was persuasive at the time; and why it failed to live up to its promise. This analysis, I submit, clarifies the dynamics of the study of curriculum.

What is curriculum?

What is curriculum? Is it a program of studies? Course content? Planned learning experiences? Experiences 'had' under the auspices of the school? A structured series of intended learning outcomes? A 'written' plan for action? Or something more involved? This ground will not be covered in detail, since Mauritz Johnson (1967) and Robert Zais (1981), among others, have already analyzed and discarded many of these definitions.

Johnson defines curriculum as a structured series of intended learning outcomes. This is rejected for two reasons. First, Johnson's definition was selected in part because it distinguishes between curriculum and instruction, but this criterion is flawed because it presumes a categorical distinction between curriculum and instruction *before* curriculum is defined. Obviously, without a definition of curriculum it is not possible to know whether or not curriculum is distinct from instruction. Second, Johnson argues that curriculum cannot be defined *post hoc*; that is, it has to be defined before the act of instruction so that curriculum can guide instruction. Defining curriculum in this way has obvious instrumental and utilitarian appeal, but it places the study of curriculum, curriculum development, and so on at the service of immediate administrative and instructional demands. The functionalist nature of this definition is highlighted when one realizes that it would have administrative and instructional needs drive curriculum.

Zais, drawing on Hilda Taba's work, argues for a continuum between curriculum and instruction rather than a sharp distinction:

> The suggestion and central thrust of Taba's conception of curriculum, however, is that the broader (that is, the more general) aspects of purposes, content, and method belong in the realm of curriculum, while the more proximate and specific aspects are properly allocated to teaching and instruction.
>
> (1981: p. 40)

Gail McCutcheon captures Zais's meaning with more fruitful results:

> By curriculum I mean *what students have an opportunity to learn* in school, through both the hidden and overt curriculum, and what they do not have an opportunity to learn because certain matters were not included in the curriculum, referred to by Eisner (1979, p. 83) as the 'null curriculum.'
>
> (1982: p. 19; emphasis added)

What students have an opportunity to learn refers to legitimate and approved communications and actions. What students do not have an opportunity to learn are those things off-limits. This definition refers to the substance of what students

472

have an opportunity to learn and to the rules and procedures by which those opportunities are provided.

One might be tempted to criticize this definition because it includes everything: everything present and not present (*p* and *not p* in symbolic notation). This criticism both grasps and misses the point of the definition. It captures the point that when we have an opportunity to learn, our attention is directed toward an object and away from other objects. When students learn about the American Civil War, they are not learning about the French Revolution. Does this definition include everything and exclude nothing? No! The missed point is that what students have an opportunity to learn focuses attention on selecting an object of study and how it is presented to the exclusion of other objects. Students learn from excluded opportunites as well as from those overtly provided. But different things are learned, depending upon whether an object is present or absent. This distinction makes a difference. One task for the study of curriculum, in this view, is to discover how and why some opportunities are provided and others are bypassed. Curriculum, in part, is a study of what is valued and given priority and what is disvalued and excluded.

Curriculum defined as what students have an opportunity to learn has several advantages:

1 It acknowledges curriculum as a guideline for planning and evaluation, including intended learning outcomes.
2 It includes what students learn from school structure and organization; school administration is not *just* administration but is also part of the instructional system.
3 It includes what students learn from their peers, including what the Supreme Court discussed in *Brown v. Board of Education.*
4 It includes the fact that students learn from that which is excluded, from that which is not part of the discourse.
5 It avoids the error of distinguishing curriculum from instruction before defining curriculum.
6 It avoids making curriculum dependent on organizational needs of school administrators and teachers.

Structural analysis identifies categories and binary distinctions of an argument, myth, novel, poem, or, in the present case, curriculum theory, textbook content, curriculum guideline, or assessment test. Examples of binary distinctions that structure curriculum are achievement/failure, theory/practice, concept/fact, learner-centred/subject-centred, accountability/lack of accountability, terminal objective/intermediate objective, literate/illiterate, cognitive/affective, organization/disorganization, synthesis/knowledge of specifics, and sociocentric/egocentric. Several approaches to curriculum value the first over the second term in many of the preceding pairs, and which term is valued depends upon which transcendental signified is queen or king for a day. Some versions of humanistic education might be: learner-centred/subject-centred, practice/theory, lack of accountability/accountability, and affective/cognitive. Approaches to curriculum are topsy-turvy because these and other distinctions could be reversed and reversed again, depending upon the reigning transcendental signified. This is less likely to happen in other fields, such as educational administration or educational psychology, because their meaning is fixed, in part, by academic disciplines outside professional education, even if this dependence is unattributed. Privileged meanings that organize other fields also shift and change but often give the appearance of stability, or at least of slow evolution – not many Kuhnian revolutions having been reported recently. One point of Kuhn's (1974) analysis of scientific revolutions, although it is rarely read this way, is that a dominant paradigm functions as a transcendental signified until it is overthrown and replaced. A structural analysis of curriculum theory and practice offers insight into how the field is (or has been) conceptually organized, what the central tasks of the field are (or have been), and how curricularists are to go about their work (or have gone about their work). But structural assumptions contain elements that eventually undermine structural interpretations.

Poststructural analysis, in part, addresses questions about transcendental signifieds: Where do they come from? How were they produced? Why did they originate? What do they assert? Meaning is not centered or fixed, because it is caught in a play of references between words and definitions. This can be seen in written texts, which give the appearance of stability but have no center, no transcendental signified, no transcendental semantic meaning. In curriculum we have seen a succession of candidates, and many educators hope, no doubt, that one will come along to organize now and for all time the study of what students have an opportunity to learn. This seems to be what educators have in mind when yearnings are expressed for 'a' curriculum theory that will tell us what to do. But what would such a theory look like? How could it endure?

A poststructural analysis of the
structure of the disciplines

The succession of ideas put forward since World War II to serve as transcendental signifieds in curriculum attest to two things: (1) there has been a continuing search for a center to fix and ground thinking and arguments about curriculum; and (2) none has been found. In the early 1960s educators were urged to teach the structure of the academic disciplines. In many ways this was the high water mark of structuralism and positivism in American curricular thought. The discursive practice of leading educators of the early 1960s is my concern here, not classroom discourse (which from this vantage point would certainly be hard to document). It is not clear to what degree national curriculum development projects or teacher training institutes induced changes in classroom content or style. Textbooks published from the curriculum development projects of that period eventually were used in classrooms across the nation, but classroom practices may have remained largely unchanged. The immense size, complexity, and decentralized nature of American education militates against quickly instituted, enduring changes. Foucault's approach to discursive practices provides a likely character-ization of American education as an anonymous, powerful, slowly changing discourse that we inherit and over which we have little control.

It is always easy for politicians and lay people to kick the educational system around, but at the end of the 1950s American education was particularly vulnerable due to national embarrassment over Sputnik I. On 4 October 1957, the Soviet Union launched the first artificial Earth satellite. This was widely seen as a threat to the national security of the United States. It was important for the United States to compete technologically with and stay ahead of the Soviet Union. Therefore, for the sake of national security and in the name of patriotism, public education had to be upgraded.

How could schools be made better? One approach was 'back to the educa-tional basics'. But making everyone proficient in reading, writing, and arithmetic was not going to save the nation. Another approach was to make schools more academic. What students henceforth had an opportunity to learn could be academically advanced, reflecting the structure of the disciplines. This was, perhaps, best expressed by Jerome Bruner.

In September 1959 a group of distinguished scientists, scholars, and educators met at Woods Hole on Cape Cod. The task was to consider how science education in primary and secondary schools might be improved. In 1960 Bruner reported their deliberations and recommendations in a small but very influential book, *The Process of Education*. A central theme was that students should be given 'an understanding of the fundamental structure of whatever subjects we choose to teach' (p. 11). It was hypothesized that four outcomes would follow:

1 Understanding fundamentals makes a subject more comprehensible.

(p. 23)

2 Learning general or fundamental principles ensure(s) that memory loss will not mean total loss, that what remains will permit us to recon-struct the details when needed.

(p. 25)

3 To understand something as a specific instance of a more general case – which is what understanding a more fundamental principle or structure means – is to have learned not only a specific thing but also a model for understanding other things like it that one may encounter.

(p. 25)

4 By constantly reexamining material taught in elementary and second-ary schools for its fundamental character, one is able to narrow the gap between 'advanced' knowledge and 'elementary' knowledge.

(p. 26)

This was a persuasive argument, advocated by distinguished scholars. The advantages were obvious to anyone seriously interested in educational achievement. Teaching the structure of a subject, tapping the center of disciplinary knowledge, was economic, in terms of the number of ideas to be learned, and long-lasting in two ways, since there would be increased retention of what was learned and what was learned would become dated more slowly because of its fundamental character.

Two other discourses converged and contributed to the structure-of-the-disciplines movement. One was the explicit structural influence on education of Bloom et al.'s *Taxonomy of Educational Objectives* (1956). It was clearly stated by highly respected authorities that concepts were superior to facts; comprehension, to knowledge of specifics; application, to comprehension; analysis, to application; synthesis, to analysis; and evaluation, to synthesis. The valued and disvalued categories in discourse about educational objectives could not have been set forth more clearly. It was codified and certified. Not only was there a structure to the disciplines; there was also a structure to educational objectives. Conversely, the taxonomy assumed that subject matter had a structure conducive to such arrangement.

A third contributing discourse was Tyler's (1949) well-known rationale. Ten years before the Woods Hole Conference, Tyler applied principles of scientific management to education, which showed educators how to think systematically: decide upon objectives, list learning experiences, organize learning experiences, and evaluate outcomes. Tyler's argument is a classic application of structuralism to education. Learning objectives by themselves mean little; but in a structure of organized learning experiences and evaluation, learning objectives contribute to systematic instruction. Likewise, by itself a measurement instrument used for evaluation has little significance; but in a structure of objectives and learning experiences, it can be given an interpretation straight off. By itself each stage of the Tyler rationale means little; the meaning of each stage depends upon differences from and relations to other parts of the process.

Structured interpretations were given to disciplinary knowledge, learning objectives, and curriculum. What had happened was remarkable: the disciplines had fundamental structures, which, if taught, had powerful and long-lasting benefits; learning objectives had been organized hierarchically; and systematic steps of scientific management had been applied to education. The interpretation of the Bloom et al. taxonomy and the Tyler rationale in support of teaching disciplinary structure was difficult to resist, to the degree resistance was considered. It all fitted. Everything, from a curricular point of view, had seemingly fallen into place.

At this point a Foucauldian analyst might ask: how could it have turned out differently? Powerful discourses were operative. They reinforced each other: Bruner drew from positivist and logical–empiricist epistemology; Bloom et al., from educational psychology (also influenced by logical empiricism); and Tyler, from scientific (and efficient) management. Given the political imperatives of an internationally threatening situation, the discourse was set, limited, and legitimated. For a variety of reasons, each powerful and persuasive in its own way, teaching the structure of the disciplines had become for the time being the transcendental signified for the field of curriculum. It *centered* the system and it *fixed* meanings in education. Working from disciplinary structure, everything could be figured out, from objectives to evaluation. In retrospect, however, the idea of disciplinary structure was largely based on a positivist view of knowledge whose philosophical underpinnings had by then eroded.

The structure-of-the-disciplines argument seems to have presumed the following:

1   The structure of disciplinary knowledge was logically coherent and complete.
2   Disciplinary knowledge was logically valid and truth-preserving, from first principles to testable hypotheses.
3   Disciplinary knowledge was factual and explanatory, not evaluative.
4   Scientific language was value-neutral and passive in describing and explaining phenomena.

The first and second points assume a distinction between analytic and synthetic statements; the third, between fact and values; and the fourth, a view of language as passive and descriptive, not active or evaluative. An important consequence of the analytic/synthetic distinction is that a conclusion in a logically valid argument *necessarily* follows from the premises of the argument. Thus if a theory or explanation is stated in a valid deductive manner and its first principles are true, then its conclusion must also be true. It is easy to understand why this assumption is central to a structural approach to disciplinary knowledge. The latter two assumptions conceptualized knowledge and science somehow as separate from the world being described and explained.

Developments in modern logic by Quine (1953) and philosophy of language by Austin (1968) and Wittgenstein (1953) cut the ground from beneath these assumptions. Quine argued that it was not possible to account for truth-preserving natural-language arguments. (This depended on the notion of analyticity, which defied, then and now, clear characterization. See Quine (1953) for the original argument.) Therefore it could not be shown that disciplinary knowledge was logically complete or truth-preserving. Austin and Wittgenstein, in different ways, showed that speech is action, not just description (which Austin called the descriptivist fallacy), and that value and institutional commitments infiltrate language and what is said. Disciplinary knowledge then, did not consist of passive, unambiguously truth-preserving factual arguments that excluded evaluation. A new account of disciplinary structure was in order. It was not forthcoming.

Not to be put off, many promoted curricula based on disciplinary structures that presumably were truth-preserving, objective, and cumulative, even though the precise nature of these structures, for good reason, was never spelled out. At Woods Hole there were six mathematicians, nine psychologists, four physicists, five biologists, and eight who represented history, classics, medicine, and cinematography. The issues discussed were philosophical to the core, but no philosophers participated. Elsewhere wars had been fought whose outcomes were important to a structural approach to the disciplines, but no one was there to report on battles, casualties, or outcomes.

These events illustrate Foucault's argument that power makes truth possible. The arguments of Quine, Wittgenstein, and Austin did not, nor would other contrary educational positions have been expected to, curb the structure-of-the-disciplines movement. The driving force was grounded in political exigencies internal as well as external to professional education, not in the substantive merits of the arguments.

Foucauldian analysis points to a continual movement from discourse (for example, Bruner's argument for a structural approach to curriculum) to history (for example, contemporary events within education and national and international political developments). That disciplinary structure became a transcendental signified for curriculum was an accident of history with no single author. Once it was in place, it determined who could speak and what could be said. Curricularists were not in control of their discourse; quite the reverse, dominant discursive practices dictated who was a curricularist. The discursive practice had shifted, and those who formerly had spoken with authority on curriculum were on the outside and those who had previously been on the outside of curriculum, for example, academic specialists, were now on the inside. And no one asked: why not teach about racism, sexism, labor history, minority history, social inequality, or injustice. The configuration of power from several discourses, practices, and situations conferred upon the arguments of Bruner, Bloom *et al.*, and Tyler the effects of truth. Power as well as truth had spoken, because power preceded and produced statements that were received as truth.

A deconstructive analysis in the manner of Derrida focuses less on the historical setting and more on the argument. One question is: what binary distinctions does a structure-of-the-disciplines approach advance and do they deconstruct? Disciplinary structure assumes the existence of a cumulative and hierarchical body of knowledge. It was assumed that academic scholars should set the educational agenda, and their assumptions about disciplinary structure led to a set of valued/disvalued categories. Some of these categorical distinctions were theory/practice, concept/fact, subject-centered learning/learner-centered learning, and cognitive/affective, with the first terms valued over the second. These distinctions separate what is central from what is marginal.

Are these distinctions stable? Of the theory/practice opposition, Michael Ryan (1984) writes, 'All theory is either a theory of a past practice which it describes, or of a future practice toward which it aims, in addition to being itself a practice. Pure practice . . . is always itself a certain theory of practice' (p. 14: see chapter 5 in Cherryholmes 1988 for an argument deconstructing the theory/practice distinction).

As for the hypothesized superiority of concepts to facts, it is well known that scientific concepts are not empirical unless they point to the possibility of factual observations. Conversely, factual observations are only possible given a conceptual background. Concepts and facts point to things in the world and depend upon each other. If concepts and facts are mutually constitutive, one is led to ask why educators would value scientific concepts over facts. When disciplinary concepts are valued over facts, the world as conceptualized by academics is privileged over alternative conceptualizations, such as artistic, humanistic, aesthetic, and political ones, and facts highlighted by such alternative orientations are slighted.

As for subject-centered learning and learner-centered learning, learners do not exist without subjects and a subject to learn does not exist without previous learners. When subjects are valued over learners, the interests of learners who constituted the subjects (experts) are valued over the interests of other learners (students). It is simply the case that the subject-centered/learner-centered distinction privileges learners who are subject-matter experts.

Finally, let us address the cognitive/affective distinction. Presumably a cognitive emphasis values 'objective' knowledge and an affective emphasis deals with values, feelings, attitudes, and opinions. But a cognitive orientation cannot exist without prior value judgments that single out some cognitions as more important or worthwhile than others. What is cognitive can be neither produced nor taught without reference to prior evaluations. The cognitive/affective distinction operates to hide prior value judgments. Those hidden commitments turn out to be the ones held by authorities and experts.

By 1970 a number of developments illuminated the shortcomings of a structure-of-the-disciplines approach to curriculum. It deconstructed, although this term was not used, when it became widely recognized that the rhetorical claims of Bruner exceeded the logic of his argument. First, as noted earlier, logical positivism and its successor, logical empiricism, each of which had contributed to the epistemological foundation for teaching disciplinary structure, could no longer sustain claims made on their behalf. No alternative interpretation of disciplinary structure had surfaced; given Kuhn's influential 1962 book on *The Structure of Scientific Revolutions*, coming as it did two years after Bruner's, one was sorely needed. Second, academics who sought in the early 1960s to map the structure of their respective disciplines were less than successful in doing so (Bruner 1971). Third, the international political situation *vis-à-vis* the Soviet Union had changed. Fourth, domestic politics in the United States was now dominated by the civil rights movement, the war on poverty, and rising controversy over United States military involvement in Vietnam. Disciplinary structure no longer drove curriculum efforts. By the 1970s there were voices, including Bruner's (1973), asking why we were not teaching about racism, sexism, and social inequality and injustice. By the 1980s these demands, in turn, had almost been silenced as the cry shifted to educational 'excellence'. Forces external to professional education were making different demands from those voiced ten years earlier. Power was speaking again and this time telling a different story. What is considered true and authoritative often shifts as power moves, settles, and is relocated. That is what happened in curriculum.

Critical pragmatism and curriculum

Teaching the structure of the disciplines is one proposal among many that have been promoted to center, organize, fix the meaning of, and bring coherence to curriculum. The history of curriculum theory and practice can be read as a series of repeated invasions of organizing ideas that command attention for a while before they are turned out by the next invasion. Each new invader was beyond the control of any individual educator, reflected political events external as well as internal to education, represented prominent contemporary ideologies, and could be deconstructd. Proposed transcendental signifieds, such as teaching disciplinary structure, recede for at least two reasons: (1) the material, external events that push for their adoption disappear or become less demanding and/or new developments disrupt the discourse and its related practices, a Foucauldian hypothesis; and (2) the organizing persuasiveness of the idea is subsequently shown to be suspect, due either to direct criticism or indirect analysis, a Derridean hypothesis. The argument from Foucault tends toward a synthetic, empirical claim, whereas the Derridean is more analytic.

The study and practice of curriculum determines where and on what grounds opportunities to learn are provided and at what point the deconstruction of those opportunities will stop. Construction and deconstruction circle around a central question: why do we provide an opportunity to learn about something in the first place? Curricula can help students gain insight into their discourse, into how knowledge and power create and recreate each other, or it can focus on accepting existing discourses along with their unique opportunities, constraints, and oppressiveness. Curricular constructions and deconstructive criticisms allow judgments to be made about objectives, learning experiences, the organizaition of learning experiences, and their evaluation – all of which are necessary in some fashion some of the time but should not be mistaken as transcendental. If poststructural criticism teaches nothing else, it teaches us to be suspicious of argumentative, knowledge, and policy claims based on appeals to precision, certainty, clarity, and rigor.

This argument may seem a bit curious, unsettling, and unfamiliar, because academic and professional arguments are expected to begin with a question and end with an answer. Academic and theoretical arguments push toward certainty and promise identity, by identifying – if nothing else – what it is we are studying, if not truth. For example, it would seem that curriculum theory should tell us what curriculum is and authoritatively tell us what to do when it comes to developing, implementing, and evaluating curriculum. The poststructural lesson is to be suspicious of such authority. Much of the unfamiliarity and strangeness of poststructuralism recedes when applied to everyday life. Work, relationships, beliefs, skills, and we ourselves are not identical from one day, or even one moment, to the next or from one place to another. There are always differences. Theories and organizing principles put forward as transcendental signifieds are products of human activity; therefore they are necessarily marked by the uncertainties and transience of human efforts.

480

Think of social practice and theory allegorically. Social practice, in this case curriculum and education, may be compared to humanity after the Fall. What we do in everyday life is negotiated, compromised, contingent, subect to mis-calculation, and flawed. Theories and first principles promise redemption. There is hope, an expectation, that theory will tell us what is good and what is true, how to make correct calculations and avoid errors. Because theory is produced by humanity in its fallen state, it should not be surprising, then, that it is also characterized by incompleteness, ambiguity, error, and contradiction.

How to proceed? Both constructors and deconstructors are needed. Some people are better at constructing, others at deconstructing. Constructors must realize that what is built is temporal, fallible, limited, compromised, negotiated, and incomplete or contradictory. Each construction will eventually be replaced. And deconstructive arguments must be shaped so that construction will be encour-aged and followed. The field of curriculum has unwittingly experienced cycles of construction and deconstruction. These have been interpreted as illness, mori-bundity, and a foreshadowing of the death of the field. The hope of finding a purpose or cause that grounds work in curriculum and education and fixes its meaning once and for all, however, is misplaced. It appears to be fictional. But the continuing search for meaning and purpose and the subsequent deconstruction of the candidates that turn up need not cause despair. The realization that this is the nature of history, politics, and texts brings with it important changes in thinking about curriculum and education. If the structure, of curriculum and how it moves continues to be unrecognized, however, elation is likely to be followed by despon-dency by elation by . . ., with no basis for sustained insight or dialogue.

If discourse in the field is accepted as fragmented, pushed and pulled, contra-dictory and incomplete, responding to professional and political forces beyond our control, subject to deconstruction, and we consciously choose to constitute a dialectic of construction–deconstruction, then the nature of curricular discourse will change. Instead of talking about taxonomies of objectives, structures of disciplines, learning objectives, and what 'a' curriculm theory would be like, the conversation will turn to what kind of society and schools we want, knowing full well that they constitute each other. Our concerns will be pragmatic and focus, as Rorty puts it, 'about what self-image our society should have of itself' (1985: p. 11). For example, do we want to provide opportunities to learn a structure of the disciplines at the expense of teaching about the causes and consequences of racism, sexism, and social inequality and injustice? If the argu-ment Bruner made in 1960 is compared with that he came back with in 1971 and 1973 – that social issues should be moved closer to center stage in curriculum – we see the ebb and flow. Each argument was persuasive when it was made, but *the discursive practices and social structures that made each argument persuasive were never addressed.* How to get behind the discourse? How to get at what structures what we say? Why do we choose the words and make the statements we do?

Even though poststructural criticism is relatively new to discussions of social practice, even though it promises no final, transcendent meaning, it is still possible to outline what curriculum and education might look like when criticism feeds into pragmatic choices. Curriculum is what students have an opportunity to learn. What students have an opportunity to learn depends upon what they do not have an opportunity to learn. Power distributes opportunities and non-opportunities. And curriculum is intimately linked to educational administration and instruction, because each set of activities produces opportunities and constrains what can be learned. Curriculum is not more isolated than any other field of education. They are all part of a larger society and are moved to and fro by the same rhythms that shape our politics, music, business, technology, and so forth. Complaints about the illness, death, or moribundity of curriculum resulted from a failure to grasp these connections in combination with monumental expectations made of the field. It was as though curricularists were expected to tell educators what to do. But the acceptability of what was uttered would have reflected the contemporary interests of those in power, and there is little reason to think the rhetoric of the answer would have matched its logic. The study of curriculum is the process of rolling over one answer onto the next when asked what students should have an opportunity to learn. To expect curricularists to give a definitive answer to what students should have an opportunity learn is to display an ignorance of the question and the field. Given this, what curricular strategies seem promising?

Curricular work takes place in a wide variety of settings with different scope and generality: there are the United States Department of Education, publishing companies that market textbooks nationwide, state departments of education, teaching-methods classes, school district curriculum committees, and individual classrooms. What is constructed at each level is shaped by what is inherited from previous social, organizational, or professional generations. Saussure states this general point very clearly, and here structural and poststructural thought converge and then separate:

> The word, though to all appearances freely chosen with respect to the idea that it represents, is fixed, not free, with respect to the linguistic community that uses it. . . . No individual, even if he willed it, could modify in any way at all the choice that has been made; and what is more, the community itself cannot control so much as a single word; *it is bound to the existing language.*
>
> (1916/1966, p. 71; emphasis added)

Inherited discourses come into contact with each other, sometimes reinforcing, sometimes conflicting. A first step in a poststructural, critical, pragmatic strategy is to describe relationships between historical developments and political practices and curriculum theory and practice. For example, what were the historical and political conditions that made the Tyler rationale, the Bloom *et al. Taxonomy of Educational Objectives*, and Schwab's 'Practical 4' persuasive? This should not be approached, however, in a simplistic and overdeterministic manner. Politics does not create curriculum out of whole cloth. Instead, power transforms discourses such that a category, like disciplinary structure, is given more salience and importance than others. International tensions did not create the notion of structure, but they did, however, assign an educational value it did not have before to disciplinary structure. Power creates opportunities for speech and discourse but does not create each category in the discourse. How does power shape curricular discourse and why are certain subjects privileged over others?

A second poststructural strategy follows from the point that power precedes curriculum discourse. Who, individually, or what goup is rewarded and indulged and, conversely, who are those sanctioned and deprived? Who benefits under a curriculum organized in terms of disciplinary structure is easy to identify. Students from groups that did well in school would be expected to do well with an academic curriculum. Students from backgrounds that did not emphasize academic achievement would not be expected to do well. Academic specialists would be financially rewarded. Curricularists who argue humanistic or social-issue positions would be, for the time being, professionally marginalized.

A third poststructual move gives curricular discourse a close reading and analysis: Who listens? Who is excluded? What metaphors and arguments are deployed? Fourth, what are the dominant and valued categories? Since dominant categories cannot ground the logic of the system, it is only prudent to inquire into the values and ideologies that led to the choice of the organizing principles. Fifth, alternative interpretations of what students have an opportunity to learn should be generated, because it is a reasonable inference that subtexts tell stories different from those on the surface. Sixth, curriculum proposals, demands, and so forth should be examined in light of changes and developments in other disciplines, because their placement in a broader setting may provide insights into curricular discourses–practices, for example, that structural approaches to knowledge are not entirely defensible.

Structural approaches lend themselves to checklists; poststructural criticism defies the compilation of an enduring checklist. There are, to be sure, things to keep in mind in pursuing either Foucauldian or Derridean criticism, but it may be more productive to think of curriculum construction, the geneology of the construction, and its deconstruction more metaphorically. Poststructural criticism argues that linearity in text, organization, rationale, and argument is deceptive. Here are three metaphors offering contrasting yet dependent images useful in thinking about these things: normal and revolutionary science, normal and abnormal discourse, and canny and uncanny thinking. Although Kuhn in *The Structure of Scientific Revolutions* (1974) did not couch his account in poststructural terms, it roughly parallels the Derridean account. Scientific activity moves between normal science, whch is governed by a paradigm that 'stands for the entire constellation of beliefs, values, techniques, and so on shared by the members of a given community' or 'denotes one sort of element in that constellation, the concrete puzzle-solutions . . . employed as models or examples' (1974: p. 175), and revolutionary science, which rejects and replaces paradigms. Normal science is, more or less, a hypothesis-testing activity wherein theories are elaborated and filled in. Occasionally the paradigm, the transcendental signified, breaks down. Scientific activity then takes on revolutionary overtones, and the search is on for a new set of governing principles and guiding puzzle-solutions, a new paradigm. Science, in this view, is movement between normal and rule-governed activity and a revolutionary search for new rules.

Normal and abnormal discourse is discussed by Rorty in *Philosophy and the Mirror of Nature* (1980). After recounting repeated failed attempts by twentieth-century philosophers to provide a foundation for knowledge, he notes that Wittgenstein, Dewey, and Heidegger came around to a common historicist message:

> Each of the three reminds us that investigations of the foundations of knowledge or morality or language or society may be simply apologetics, attempts to eternalize a certain contemporary language-game, social practice, or self image.
>
> (pp. 9–10)

This passes quite well as a general description of what was claimed for disciplinary structure in curriculum. In curriculum terms the search for 'a' curriculum theory, 'a' first principle, 'an' organizing scheme, 'an' evaluation procedure is an attempt to eternalize a particular social practice that is an accident of time and space. It represents an effort to deny our humanity by denying differences and movement.

Rorty devotes a fair amount of attention in his last chapter to education and edification where *edification* stands for 'finding new, better, more interesting, more fruitful ways of speaking' (p. 360). Edification begins with normal discourse dominated by 'descriptions of the world offered by our culture (e.g., by learning the results of the natural sciences)' (p. 365). The move, then, is to abnormal discourse, which is always parasitic on normal discourse. On his final point he is worth quoting at length:

> The point of edifying philosophy is to keep the conversation going rather than to find objective truth. Such truth, in the view I am advocating, is the normal result of normal discourse. Edifing philosopy is not only abnormal but reactive. . . . The danger which edifying discourse tries to avert is that some given vocabulary, some way in which people might come to think of themselves, will deceive them into thinking that from now on all discourse could be, or should be, normal discourse. The resulting freezing-over of culture would be, in the eyes of edifying philosophers, the dehumanization of human beings.
>
> (p. 377)

Edifying discourse moves in and out from construction to deconstruction, from structure to its criticism, from normal to abnormal conversation and argumentation, always suspicious of certainty and precision.

Another way to think about structural and poststructural criticism is described by Culler in *On Deconstruction: Theory and Criticism After Structuralism* (1984). Building on work of J. Hillis Miller, he writes about canny and uncanny criticism about literature. The canny critic brings 'literature out into the sunlight in a "happy positivism"' (p. 23, quoting Miller). The uncanny critic pursues logical analysis into regions that are alogical and absurd, thus suggesting deeper meanings: 'Uncanny post-structuralism arrives to waken canny structuralism from the dogmatic slumbers into which it was lulled by its "unshakable faith" in thought and "the promise of a rational ordering"' (p. 24). Being canny, shrewd, and clever about the world as it appears entraps, dehumanizes, and deludes us. Curriculum needs to be uncanny as well as canny.

It is time to bring the argument full circle and explain why historically the study of curriculum has appeared so turbulent. This has variously been interpreted as signifying illness, death, or moribundity, whereas other fields of education have seemingly displayed more stability. It is arguable that the disciplines from which educational psychology, social foundations of education, philosophy of education, educational policy analysis, and educational administration are, in part, derivative contribute to their apparent stability. Teacher education or instruction, as you will, attends to concrete situations. But curriculum is neither historically situated in the tradition of an academic discipline nor constrained by a concrete situation. The complexity of the demands thrust upon the study and practice of curriculum contribute to its looseness, its thrashing about, its contradictions, and its lack of a center, grounding, and foundation.

But the apparent stability of other fields in education and the lack of stability in curriculum are both illusory. Academic disciplines and the knowledge they produce are not stable, as Kuhn (1974) has peruasively demonstrated. But following a 'scientific revolution', disciplines still have traditions and legacies. Questions shift and puzzle-solutions are discarded, but there is still some sense of what a field is about, whether it is philosophy or economics or political science. Transcendental signifieds for academic desciplines are in the long run fictional; but in the short run, say the length of an average professional career, they are stable. The life expectancy of foundational ideas may be longer in an academic discipline than in the field or curriculum for several reasons:

1   Academic disciplines are more loosely coupled to political events and exigencies, such as the surprise launching of an artificial Earth satellite by the Soviet Union, than is the field of curriculum.
2   Research problems and tasks of disciplines are more closely framed and policed than the holistic tasks facing curriculum; for example, Kuhn argues that paradigms are often shared by communties of fewer than 100 members (1974: p. 178).
3   Disciplines do not have to respond to specific, immediate, and changing demands for excellence and performance as does professional education; for example, scholars can quietly admit within their community that they cannot solve a problem, as did political scientists who spent 20 years trying to solve a problem known as Arrow's impossibility theorem. It turned out to be impossible to solve.

485

4   Whereas disciplines may reflect ideological orientations and problems of the larger society, such as a fixation on rational choice theories in microeconomics, psychology, and political science, they are not continually confronted, as is curriculum, by the contradictions, frustrations, ambiguities, and, in some cases, helplessness of society.

The traditions, orientations, commitments, obligations, and, not least of all, focus of disciplinary and professional activity external to education give the appearance of stability to many fields in education. Curriculum does not have such a reserve.

Solid, immutable foundations do not exist for any of these endeavors. The absence of foundations is simply more noticeable in curriculum than in academic disciplines and other areas of professional education. The norm for curriculum, then, is not consensus, stability, and agreement but conflict, instability, and disagreement, because the process is one of construction followed by deconstruction by construction . . . of what students have an opportunity to learn. By explicitly adopting a poststructural attitude, educators will avoid the false hope of structural certainty and be in a stronger position to deal with, anticipate, and sometimes, perhaps, predict the fate of the latest proposal to guide curriculum. If the field of curriculum moves to a poststructural era along with its uncertainties, ambiguities, and criticisms, there is the promise of understanding more fully how we and others around us have become who we are. The possiblility of such understanding brings with it the promise of increased freedom and power, increased freedom from exisitng social structures, and more power to create our societies and schools rather than the other way around.

References

Anyon, Jean. 'Ideology and United States History Textbooks.' *Harvard Educational Review*, 49 (August 1979), 361–86.

Anyon, Jean. 'Social Class and School Knowledge.' *Curriculum Inquiry*, 11 (Spring 1981), 3–42.

Apple, Michael. *Education and Power*. London: Routledge and Kegan Paul, 1982.

Apple, Michael. *Teachers and Texts: A Political Economy of Class & Gender Relations in Education*. New York: Routledge and Kegan Paul, 1986.

Austin, J.L. *How To Do Things with Words*, New York: Oxford University Press, 1968.

Bloom, Benjamin S., *et al*. *Taxonomy of Educational Objectives: Cognitive Domain*. New York: David McKay, 1956.

Bruner, Jerome. *The Processs of Education*. Cambridge, Mass.: Harvard University Press, 1960.

Bruner, Jerome. 'The Process of Education Revisited.' *Phi Delta Kappan*, 52 (1971), 18–21.

Bruner, Jerome. *The Relevance of Education*. New York: Norton, 1973.

Cherryholmes, Cleo H. 'Social Knowledge and Citizenship Education: Two Views of Truth and Criticism.' *Curriculum Inquiry*, 10 (June 1980), 115–41.

Cherryholmes, Cleo H. 'Discourse and Criticism in the Social Studies Classroom.' *Theory and Research in Social Education*, 9 (Winter 1982), 57–73.

Cherryholmes, Cleo H. 'An Exploration of Meaning and the Dialogue Between Textbooks and Teaching.' *Journal of Curriculum Studies* 20 (January–March 1988), 1–21.

Cherryholmes, Cleo H. *Power and Criticism: Poststructural Investigations in Education*. New York: Teachers College Press, 1988.

Culler, Jonathan. *On Deconstruction: Theory and Criticism Afer Structuralism*. Ithaca, NY: Cornell University Press, 1984.

Eisner, Eliot. *The Educational Imagination*. New York: Macmillan, 1979.

Eisner, Eliot. 'Anastasia Might Still be Alive, but the Monarchy is Dead.' *Educational Researcher*, 12 (1983), 13–24.

Felperin, Howard. *Beyond Deconstruction: The Uses and Abuses of Literary Theory*. Oxford, England: Clarendon Press, 1985.

Foucault, Michel. *The History of Sexuality*. Vol. 1. New York: Pantheon, 1980c.

Giroux, Henry A. *Theory and Resistance in Education*. Boston: Bergin and Garvey Publishers, 1983a.

Giroux, Henry A. 'Theories of Reproduction and Resistance in the New Sociology of Education.' *Harvard Educational Review*, 53 (1983b), 257–93.

Jackson, Philip W. 'Curriculum and its Discontents.' *Curriculum Inquiry*, 10 (1980), 28–43.

Johnson, Mauritz. 'Definitions and Models in Curriculum Theory.' *Educational Theory*, 17 (Spring 1967), 127–40.

Kuhn, Thomas S. *The Structure of Scientific Revolutions*, 2nd edn. Chicago: The University of Chicago Press, 1974.

Macdonald, James B. 'How Literal is Curriculum Theory?' *Theory Into Practice*, XXI (Winter 1982), 55–61.

McCutcheon, Gail. 'What in the World is Curriculum Theory.' *Theory Into Practice*, XXI (Winter 1982), 18–22.

Phillips, D.C. 'After the Wake: Post-Positivistic Educational Thought.' *Educational Researcher*, 12 (May 1983), 4–12.

Pinar, William. 'A Reply to My Critics.' *Curriculum Inquiry*, 10 (Summer 1980), 199–205.

Popkewitz, Thomas. *Paradigm and Ideology in Education*. New York: The Falmer Press, 1984.

Popkewitz, Thomas. 'Teaching and Teacher Education Reforms: Reconstituting a State Bureaucratic Apparatus and Forming a Political Discourse.' Madison, Wis.: College of Education of the University of Wisconsin at Madison, 1988.

Quine, W.V.O. *From a Logical Point of View*. Cambridge, Mass.: Harvard University Press, 1953.

Rorty, Richard. *Philosophy and the Mirror of Nature*. Princeton, NJ: Princeton University Press, 1980.

Rorty, Richard. 'Solidarity or Objectivity?' In John Rajchman and Cornel West (eds) *Post-Analytic Philosophy*, 3–19. New York: Columbia University Press, 1985.

Saussure, Ferdinand de. *Course in General Linguistics*. New York: McGraw-Hill, 1966. Originally published 1916.

Schwab, Joseph. 'The Practical 4: Something for Curriculum Professors To Do.' *Curriculum Inquiry*, 13 (Fall 1983), 239–66.

Tanner, Daniel and Tanner, Laurel N. 'Emancipation from Research: The Reconceptualist Prescription.' *Educational Researcher*, 8 (June 1979), 8–12.

Tyler, Ralph W. *Basic Principles of Curriculum and Instruction*. Chicago: The University of Chicago Press, 1949.

van Manen, Max. "Edifying Theory: Serving the Good.' *Theory Into Practice*, XXI (Winter 1982), 44–49.

Wittgenstein, Ludwig. *Philosophical Investigations*. Oxford, England: Basil Blackwell, 1953.

Zais, Robert S. 'Conceptions of Curriculum and the Curriculum Field.' In Giroux, Penna, and Pinar (eds) *Curriculum and Instruction*, 31–49. Berkeley, Calif.: McCutchan, 1981.